Jeep
Wrangler
Automotive
Repair
Manual

by Mike Stubblefield
and John H Haynes
Member of the Guild of Motoring Writers

Models covered:
All Jeep Wrangler gasoline models
1987 through 2017
Does not include information specific to diesel engine models

(50030 - 11W35)   ABCD

3

Haynes Publishing Group
Sparkford Nr Yeovil
Somerset BA22 7JJ England

Haynes North America, Inc
859 Lawrence Drive
Newbury Park
California 91320 USA
www.haynes.com

Acknowledgements

We are grateful to the Chrysler Corporation for assistance with technical information and certain illustrations. Technical writers who contributed to this project include Tim Imhoff, Larry Warren, Robert Maddox, Doug Nelson, Ed Scott, Jeff Killingsworth, Demian Hurst and Scott "Gonzo" Weaver.

A book in the Haynes Automotive Repair Manual Series

Printed in Malaysia

ISBN-13: 978-1-62092-284-2
ISBN-10: 1-62092-284-3

Library of Congress Control Number: 2017955809

Contents

Haynes photographer, writer and mechanic with a Jeep Wrangler "S" model

About this manual

Its purpose

The purpose of this manual is to help you get the best value from your vehicle. It can do so in several ways. It can help you decide what work must be done, even if you choose to have it done by a dealer service department or a repair shop; it provides information and procedures for routine maintenance and servicing; and it offers diagnostic and repair procedures to follow when trouble occurs.

We hope you use the manual to tackle the work yourself. For many simpler jobs, doing it yourself may be quicker than arranging an appointment to get the vehicle into a shop and making the trips to leave it and pick it up. More importantly, a lot of money can be saved by avoiding the expense the shop must pass on to you to cover its labor and overhead costs. An added benefit is the sense of satisfaction and accomplishment that you feel after doing the job yourself.

Using the manual

The manual is divided into Chapters. Each Chapter is divided into numbered Sections, which are headed in bold type between horizontal lines. Each Section consists of consecutively numbered paragraphs.

The reference numbers used in illustration captions pinpoint the pertinent Section and the Step within that Section. That is, illustration 3.2 means the illustration refers to Section 3 and Step (or paragraph) 2 within that Section.

Procedures, once described in the text, are not normally repeated. When it's necessary to refer to another Chapter, the reference will be given as Chapter and Section number. Cross references given without use of the word "Chapter" apply to Sections and/or paragraphs in the same Chapter. For example, "see Section 8" means in the same Chapter.

References to the left or right side of the vehicle assume you are sitting in the driver's seat, facing forward.

Even though we have prepared this manual with extreme care, neither the publisher nor the author can accept responsibility for any errors in, or omissions from, the information given.

NOTE

A **Note** provides information necessary to properly complete a procedure or information which will make the procedure easier to understand.

CAUTION

A **Caution** provides a special procedure or special steps which must be taken while completing the procedure where the Caution is found. Not heeding a Caution can result in damage to the assembly being worked on.

WARNING

A **Warning** provides a special procedure or special steps which must be taken while completing the procedure where the Warning is found. Not heeding a Warning can result in personal injury.

Introduction

Jeep Wrangler models are all equipped with a roll bar and a removable hard top or soft top. The body style varies slightly with the different models.

The 2.4L and 2.5L four cylinder and the 4.0L and 4.2L six-cylinder engines used in these vehicles through 2006 are equipped with a carburetor or fuel injection system, depending on the model. The engine drives the rear wheels through either a four- or five-speed manual or three- or four-speed automatic transmission via a driveshaft and solid rear axle. A transfer case and driveshaft are used to drive the front axle when the vehicle is switched into 4WD. 2007 through 2011 models are equipped with a 3.8L V6 engine and either a six-speed manual transmission or a four- or five-speed automatic transmission. 2012 and later models are equipped with a 3.6L V6 engine and either a six-speed manual transmission or five-speed automatic transmission.

The suspension features solid axles at the front and rear. On 19985 and earlier models, the front axle is suspended by leaf springs and shock absorbers and is located by a track bar. The rear axle is suspended by leaf springs and shock absorbers. 1997 and later models have coil springs at all four corners. All models have a front stabilizer bar to reduce body roll.

The steering box is mounted to the left of the engine and is connected to the steering arms through a series of rods which incorporates a damper. Power assist is optional on most models.

The brakes are disc at the front and either disc or drum at the rear, with power assist standard.

Vehicle identification numbers

1   Modifications are a continuing and unpublicized process in vehicle manufacturing. Since spare parts manuals and lists are compiled on a numerical basis, the individual vehicle numbers are essential to correctly identify the component required.

Vehicle Identification Number (VIN)

2   This very important identification number is stamped on a plate attached to the dashboard inside the windshield on the driver's side of the vehicle. It can also be found on the certification label located on the driver's side door post. The VIN also appears on the Vehicle Certificate of Title and Registration. It contains information such as where and when the vehicle was manufactured, the model year and the body style.

3   On the models covered by this manual the model year codes* are:

    F   1985
    G   1986
    H   1987
    J   1988
    K   1989
    L   1990
    M   1991
    N   1992
    P   1993
    R   1994
    S   1995
    T   1996
    V   1997
    W   1998
    X   1999
    Y   2000
    1   2001
    2   2002
    3   2003
    4   2004
    5   2005
    6   2006
    7   2007
    8   2008
    9   2009
    A   2010
    B   2011
    C   2012
    D   2013
    E   2014
    F   2015
    G   2016
    H   2017

Note:* *The model year code is the tenth character in the VIN.*

Vehicle Identification/Body Code Plate

4   This plate is located on the radiator support on the driver's side on 1987 through 1989 models and on the left (driver's) side of the engine compartment on the dash panel on 1990 and later models. On some later models the plate is attached to the floor pan under the driver's seat. It contains information on the vehicle model, emission certification, engine and transmission type as well as the paint code (see illustration).

Safety Certification label

5   The Safety Certification label is affixed to the left front door pillar. The plate contains the name of the manufacturer, the month and year of production, the Gross Vehicle Weight Rating (GVWR) and the certification statement.

Engine identification number

6   The engine ID number on 2.5L four-cylinder engines is located on a machined surface on the right side of the block between the number three and four cylinders (see illustration). On the 2.4L four-cylinder engine, the identification number is located on the left rear of the engine block. On inline six-cylinder engines, the ID number is located on a machined surface on the right side of the block between number two and three cylinders (see illustration). On V6 engines, the ID number is on the rear of the block, below the left cylinder head.

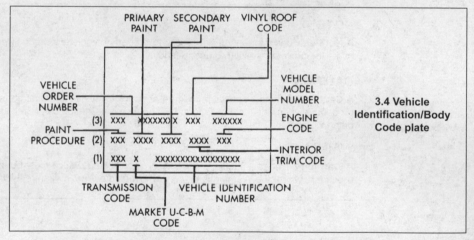

3.4 Vehicle Identification/Body Code plate

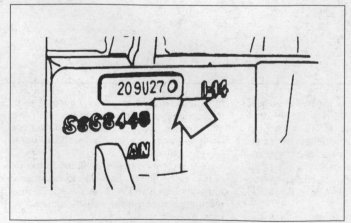

3.6a Four-cylinder engine ID number location

3.6b Inline six cylinder engine ID location; on V6 engines it's located on the rear of the block near the left cylinder head

Transmission identification number

7   On AX 4/5 manual transmissions, there are two identification codes: a model/code shipping date stamped on the shift tower and an eight digit code stamped on the bottom surface of the case (see illustration) On the BA 10/5 manual transmission, the ID plate is attached to the left side of the front case (see illustration). On three-speed automatic transmissions the ID numbers are stamped on the left edge of the case (see illustration). The ID plate on four-speed automatic transmissions is located on the right rear of the case (see illustration).

Transfer case identification number

8   On most models the transfer case identification plate is located on the left rear side of the case (see illustration).

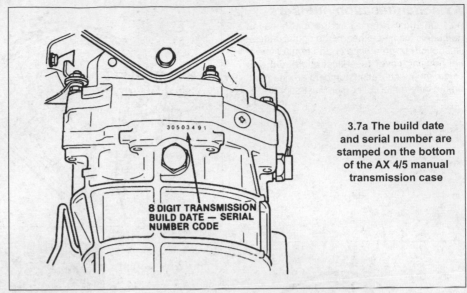

3.7a The build date and serial number are stamped on the bottom of the AX 4/5 manual transmission case

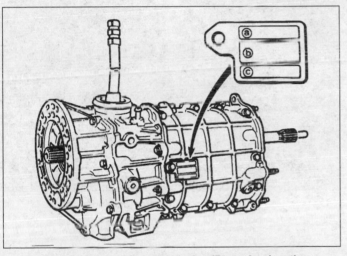

3.7b BA 10/5 manual transmission ID number location

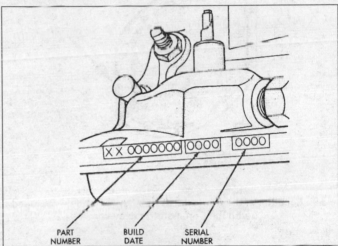

3.7c The three-speed automatic transmission numbers are stamped on the edge of the left side of the case

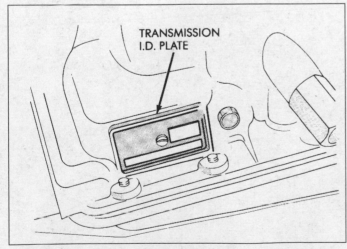

3.7d The four-speed automatic transmission ID plate is on the right side of the case. On five-speed transmissions it's located on the left side

3.8 Typical transfer case ID tag

Axle identification numbers

9   On most front axles the identification number is located either on the right side (see illustration) or on a plate on the front differential housing cover (see illustration). On rear axles, the identification numbers are stamped on the differential cover (see illustration).

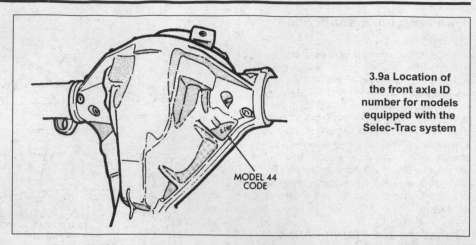

3.9a Location of the front axle ID number for models equipped with the Selec-Trac system

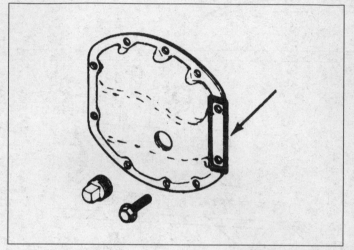

3.9b Location of the front axle ID number for models equipped with the Command-Trac system

3.9c Rear axle number location

Buying parts

Replacement parts are available from many sources, which generally fall into one of two categories - authorized dealer parts departments and independent retail auto parts stores. Our advice concerning these parts is as follows:

Retail auto parts stores: Good auto parts stores will stock frequently needed components which wear out relatively fast, such as clutch components, exhaust systems, brake parts, tune-up parts, etc. These stores often supply new or reconditioned parts on an exchange basis, which can save a considerable amount of money. Discount auto parts stores are often very good places to buy materials and parts needed for general vehicle maintenance such as oil, grease, filters, spark plugs, belts, touch-up paint, bulbs, etc. They also usually sell tools and general accessories, have convenient hours, charge lower prices and can often be found not far from home.

Authorized dealer parts department: This is the best source for parts which are unique to the vehicle and not generally available elsewhere (such as major engine parts, transmission parts, trim pieces, etc.).

Warranty information: If the vehicle is still covered under warranty, be sure that any replacement parts purchased - regardless of the source - do not invalidate the warranty!

To be sure of obtaining the correct parts, have engine and chassis numbers available and, if possible, take the old parts along for positive identification.

Maintenance techniques, tools and working facilities

Maintenance techniques

There are a number of techniques involved in maintenance and repair that will be referred to throughout this manual. Application of these techniques will enable the home mechanic to be more efficient, better organized and capable of performing the various tasks properly, which will ensure that the repair job is thorough and complete.

Fasteners

Fasteners are nuts, bolts, studs and screws used to hold two or more parts together. There are a few things to keep in mind when working with fasteners. Almost all of them use a locking device of some type, either a lockwasher, locknut, locking tab or thread adhesive. All threaded fasteners should be clean and straight, with undamaged threads and undamaged corners on the hex head where the wrench fits. Develop the habit of replacing all damaged nuts and bolts with new ones. Special locknuts with nylon or fiber inserts can only be used once. If they are removed, they lose their locking ability and must be replaced with new ones.

Rusted nuts and bolts should be treated with a penetrating fluid to ease removal and prevent breakage. Some mechanics use turpentine in a spout-type oil can, which works quite well. After applying the rust penetrant, let it work for a few minutes before trying to loosen the nut or bolt. Badly rusted fasteners may have to be chiseled or sawed off or removed with a special nut breaker, available at tool stores.

If a bolt or stud breaks off in an assembly, it can be drilled and removed with a special tool commonly available for this purpose. Most automotive machine shops can perform this task, as well as other repair procedures, such as the repair of threaded holes that have been stripped out.

Flat washers and lockwashers, when removed from an assembly, should always be replaced exactly as removed. Replace any damaged washers with new ones. Never use a lockwasher on any soft metal surface (such as aluminum), thin sheet metal or plastic.

Fastener sizes

For a number of reasons, automobile manufacturers are making wider and wider use of metric fasteners. Therefore, it is important to be able to tell the difference between standard (sometimes called U.S. or SAE) and metric hardware, since they cannot be interchanged.

All bolts, whether standard or metric, are sized according to diameter, thread pitch and length. For example, a standard 1/2 - 13 x 1 bolt is 1/2 inch in diameter, has 13 threads per inch and is 1 inch long. An M12 - 1.75 x 25 metric bolt is 12 mm in diameter, has a thread pitch of 1.75 mm (the distance between threads) and is 25 mm long. The two bolts are nearly identical, and easily confused, but they are not interchangeable.

In addition to the differences in diameter, thread pitch and length, metric and standard bolts can also be distinguished by examining the bolt heads. To begin with, the distance across the flats on a standard bolt head is measured in inches, while the same dimension on a metric bolt is sized in millimeters (the same is true for nuts). As a result, a standard wrench should not be used on a metric bolt and a metric wrench should not be used on a standard bolt. Also, most standard bolts have slashes radiating out from the center of the head to denote the grade or strength of the bolt, which is an indication of the amount of torque that can be applied to it. The greater the number of slashes, the greater the strength of the bolt. Grades 0 through 5 are commonly used on automobiles. Metric bolts have a property class (grade) number, rather than a slash, molded into their heads to indicate bolt strength. In this case, the higher the number, the stronger the bolt. Property class numbers 8.8, 9.8 and 10.9 are commonly used on automobiles.

Strength markings can also be used to distinguish standard hex nuts from metric hex nuts. Many standard nuts have dots stamped into one side, while metric nuts are marked with a number. The greater the number of

dots, or the higher the number, the greater the strength of the nut.

Metric studs are also marked on their ends according to property class (grade). Larger studs are numbered (the same as metric bolts), while smaller studs carry a geometric code to denote grade.

It should be noted that many fasteners, especially Grades 0 through 2, have no distinguishing marks on them. When such is the case, the only way to determine whether it is standard or metric is to measure the thread pitch or compare it to a known fastener of the same size.

Standard fasteners are often referred to as SAE, as opposed to metric. However, it should be noted that SAE technically refers to a non-metric fine thread fastener only. Coarse thread non-metric fasteners are referred to as USS sizes.

Since fasteners of the same size (both standard and metric) may have different

strength ratings, be sure to reinstall any bolts, studs or nuts removed from your vehicle in their original locations. Also, when replacing a fastener with a new one, make sure that the new one has a strength rating equal to or greater than the original.

Tightening sequences and procedures

Most threaded fasteners should be tightened to a specific torque value (torque is the twisting force applied to a threaded component such as a nut or bolt). Overtightening the fastener can weaken it and cause it to break, while undertightening can cause it to eventually come loose. Bolts, screws and studs, depending on the material they are made of and their thread diameters, have specific torque values, many of which are noted in the Specifications at the beginning of each Chapter. Be sure to follow the torque recommen-

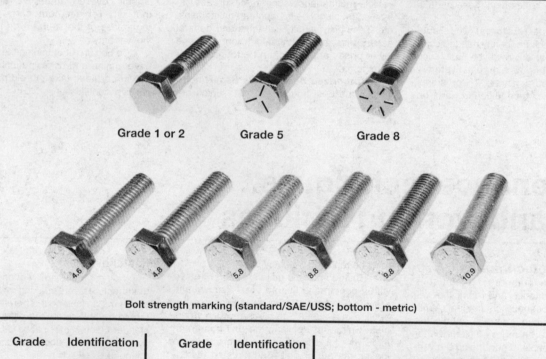

Grade 1 or 2   Grade 5   Grade 8

Bolt strength marking (standard/SAE/USS; bottom - metric)

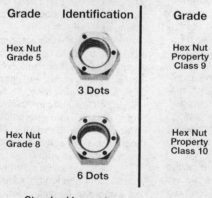

Grade   Identification

Hex Nut Grade 5   3 Dots

Hex Nut Grade 8   6 Dots

Standard hex nut strength markings

Grade   Identification

Hex Nut Property Class 9   Arabic 9

Hex Nut Property Class 10   Arabic 10

Metric hex nut strength markings

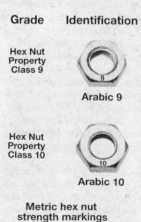

Class 10.9   Class 9.8   Class 8.8

Metric stud strength markings

dations closely. For fasteners not assigned a specific torque, a general torque value chart is presented here as a guide. These torque values are for dry (unlubricated) fasteners threaded into steel or cast iron (not aluminum). As was previously mentioned, the size and grade of a fastener determine the amount of torque that can safely be applied to it. The figures listed here are approximate for Grade 2 and Grade 3 fasteners. Higher grades can tolerate higher torque values.

Fasteners laid out in a pattern, such as cylinder head bolts, oil pan bolts, differential cover bolts, etc., must be loosened or tightened in sequence to avoid warping the component. This sequence will normally be shown in the appropriate Chapter. If a specific pattern is not given, the following procedures can be used to prevent warping.

Initially, the bolts or nuts should be assembled finger-tight only. Next, they should be tightened one full turn each, in a crisscross or diagonal pattern. After each one has been tightened one full turn, return to the first one and tighten them all one-half turn, following the same pattern. Finally, tighten each of them one-quarter turn at a time until each fastener has been tightened to the proper torque. To loosen and remove the fasteners, the procedure would be reversed.

Metric thread sizes	Ft-lbs	Nm
M-6	6 to 9	9 to 12
M-8	14 to 21	19 to 28
M-10	28 to 40	38 to 54
M-12	50 to 71	68 to 96
M-14	80 to 140	109 to 154

Pipe thread sizes		
1/8	5 to 8	7 to 10
1/4	12 to 18	17 to 24
3/8	22 to 33	30 to 44
1/2	25 to 35	34 to 47

U.S. thread sizes		
1/4 - 20	6 to 9	9 to 12
5/16 - 18	12 to 18	17 to 24
5/16 - 24	14 to 20	19 to 27
3/8 - 16	22 to 32	30 to 43
3/8 - 24	27 to 38	37 to 51
7/16 - 14	40 to 55	55 to 74
7/16 - 20	40 to 60	55 to 81
1/2 - 13	55 to 80	75 to 108

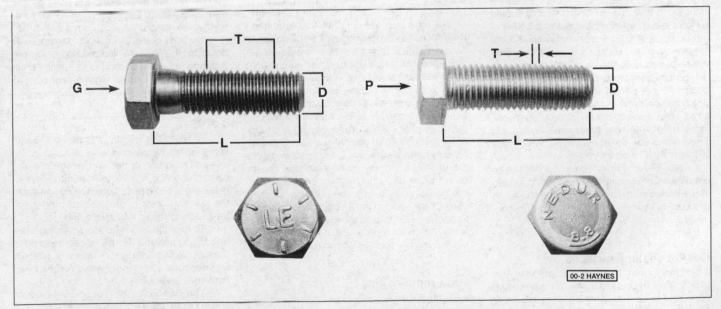

Standard (SAE and USS) bolt dimensions/grade marks

G   Grade marks (bolt strength)
L   Length (in inches)
T   Thread pitch (number of threads per inch)
D   Nominal diameter (in inches)

Metric bolt dimensions/grade marks

P   Property class (bolt strength)
L   Length (in millimeters)
T   Thread pitch (distance between threads in millimeters)
D   Diameter

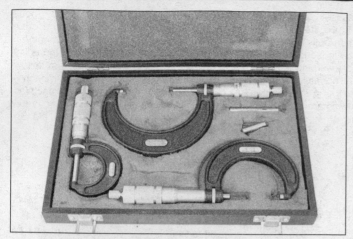

Micrometer set

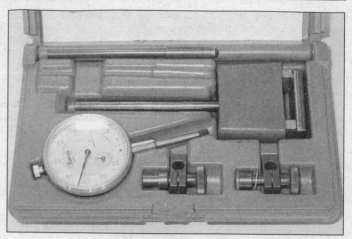

Dial indicator set

Component disassembly

Component disassembly should be done with care and purpose to help ensure that the parts go back together properly. Always keep track of the sequence in which parts are removed. Make note of special characteristics or marks on parts that can be installed more than one way, such as a grooved thrust washer on a shaft. It is a good idea to lay the disassembled parts out on a clean surface in the order that they were removed. It may also be helpful to make sketches or take instant photos of components before removal.

When removing fasteners from a component, keep track of their locations. Sometimes threading a bolt back in a part, or putting the washers and nut back on a stud, can prevent mix-ups later. If nuts and bolts cannot be returned to their original locations, they should be kept in a compartmented box or a series of small boxes. A cupcake or muffin tin is ideal for this purpose, since each cavity can hold the bolts and nuts from a particular area (i.e. oil pan bolts, valve cover bolts, engine mount bolts, etc.). A pan of this type is especially helpful when working on assemblies with very small parts, such as the carburetor, alternator, valve train or interior dash and trim pieces. The cavities can be marked with paint or tape to identify the contents.

Whenever wiring looms, harnesses or connectors are separated, it is a good idea to identify the two halves with numbered pieces of masking tape so they can be easily reconnected.

Gasket sealing surfaces

Throughout any vehicle, gaskets are used to seal the mating surfaces between two parts and keep lubricants, fluids, vacuum or pressure contained in an assembly.

Many times these gaskets are coated with a liquid or paste-type gasket sealing compound before assembly. Age, heat and pressure can sometimes cause the two parts to stick together so tightly that they are very difficult to separate. Often, the assembly can

be loosened by striking it with a soft-face hammer near the mating surfaces. A regular hammer can be used if a block of wood is placed between the hammer and the part. Do not hammer on cast parts or parts that could be easily damaged. With any particularly stubborn part, always recheck to make sure that every fastener has been removed.

Avoid using a screwdriver or bar to pry apart an assembly, as they can easily mar the gasket sealing surfaces of the parts, which must remain smooth. If prying is absolutely necessary, use an old broom handle, but keep in mind that extra clean up will be necessary if the wood splinters.

After the parts are separated, the old gasket must be carefully scraped off and the gasket surfaces cleaned. Stubborn gasket material can be soaked with rust penetrant or treated with a special chemical to soften it so it can be easily scraped off. **Caution:** *Never use gasket removal solutions or caustic chemicals on plastic or other composite components.* A scraper can be fashioned from a piece of copper tubing by flattening and sharpening one end. Copper is recommended because it is usually softer than the surfaces to be scraped, which reduces the chance of gouging the part. Some gaskets can be removed with a wire brush, but regardless of the method used, the mating surfaces must be left clean and smooth. If for some reason the gasket surface is gouged, then a gasket sealer thick enough to fill scratches will have to be used during reassembly of the components. For most applications, a non-drying (or semi-drying) gasket sealer should be used.

Hose removal tips

Warning: *If the vehicle is equipped with air conditioning, do not disconnect any of the A/C hoses without first having the system depressurized by a dealer service department or a service station.*

Hose removal precautions closely parallel gasket removal precautions. Avoid scratching or gouging the surface that the

hose mates against or the connection may leak. This is especially true for radiator hoses. Because of various chemical reactions, the rubber in hoses can bond itself to the metal spigot that the hose fits over. To remove a hose, first loosen the hose clamps that secure it to the spigot. Then, with slip-joint pliers, grab the hose at the clamp and rotate it around the spigot. Work it back and forth until it is completely free, then pull it off. Silicone or other lubricants will ease removal if they can be applied between the hose and the outside of the spigot. Apply the same lubricant to the inside of the hose and the outside of the spigot to simplify installation.

As a last resort (and if the hose is to be replaced with a new one anyway), the rubber can be slit with a knife and the hose peeled from the spigot. If this must be done, be careful that the metal connection is not damaged.

If a hose clamp is broken or damaged, do not reuse it. Wire-type clamps usually weaken with age, so it is a good idea to replace them with screw-type clamps whenever a hose is removed.

Tools

A selection of good tools is a basic requirement for anyone who plans to maintain and repair his or her own vehicle. For the owner who has few tools, the initial investment might seem high, but when compared to the spiraling costs of professional auto maintenance and repair, it is a wise one.

To help the owner decide which tools are needed to perform the tasks detailed in this manual, the following tool lists are offered: *Maintenance and minor repair, Repair/overhaul* and *Special.*

The newcomer to practical mechanics should start off with the *maintenance and minor repair* tool kit, which is adequate for the simpler jobs performed on a vehicle. Then, as confidence and experience grow, the owner can tackle more difficult tasks, buying additional tools as they are needed. Eventually the basic kit will be expanded into the *repair and overhaul* tool set. Over a period of time, the

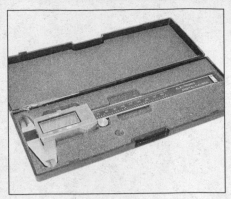

Dial caliper

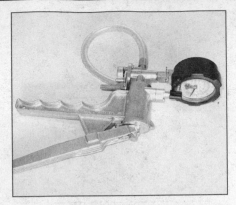

Hand-operated vacuum pump

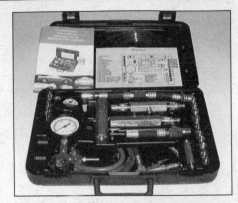

Fuel pressure gauge set

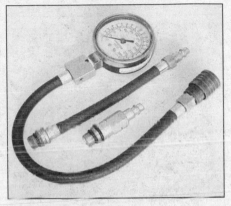

Compression gauge with spark plug hole adapter

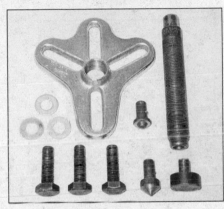

Damper/steering wheel puller

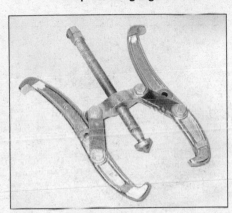

General purpose puller

Hydraulic lifter removal tool

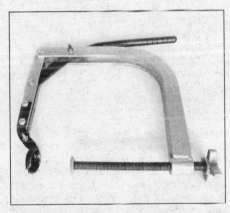

Valve spring compressor

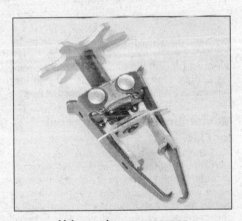

Valve spring compressor

Ridge reamer

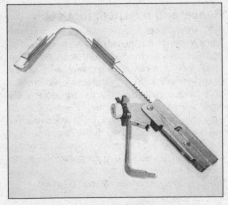

Piston ring groove cleaning tool

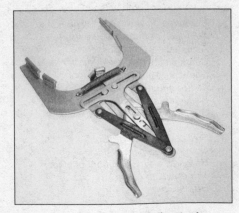

Ring removal/installation tool

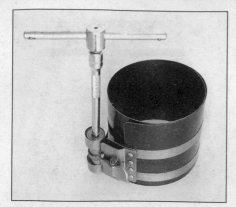

Ring compressor

Cylinder hone

Brake hold-down spring tool

Torque angle gauge

Clutch plate alignment tool

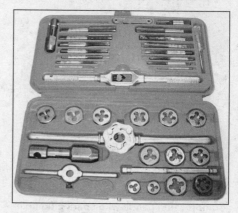

Tap and die set

experienced do-it-yourselfer will assemble a tool set complete enough for most repair and overhaul procedures and will add tools from the special category when it is felt that the expense is justified by the frequency of use.

Maintenance and minor repair tool kit

The tools in this list should be considered the minimum required for performance of routine maintenance, servicing and minor repair work. We recommend the purchase of combination wrenches (box-end and open-end combined in one wrench). While more expensive than open end wrenches, they offer the advantages of both types of wrench.

Combination wrench set (1/4-inch to 1 inch or 6 mm to 19 mm)
Adjustable wrench, 8 inch
Spark plug wrench with rubber insert
Spark plug gap adjusting tool
Feeler gauge set
Brake bleeder wrench
Standard screwdriver (5/16-inch x 6 inch)
Phillips screwdriver (No. 2 x 6 inch)
Combination pliers - 6 inch
Hacksaw and assortment of blades
Tire pressure gauge
Grease gun
Oil can
Fine emery cloth

Wire brush
Battery post and cable cleaning tool
Oil filter wrench
Funnel (medium size)
Safety goggles
Jackstands (2)
Drain pan

Note: *If basic tune-ups are going to be part of routine maintenance, it will be necessary to purchase a good quality stroboscopic timing light and combination tachometer/dwell meter. Although they are included in the list of special tools, it is mentioned here because they are absolutely necessary for tuning most vehicles properly.*

Repair and overhaul tool set

These tools are essential for anyone who plans to perform major repairs and are in addition to those in the maintenance and minor repair tool kit. Included is a comprehensive set of sockets which, though expensive, are invaluable because of their versatility, especially when various extensions and drives are available. We recommend the 1/2-inch drive over the 3/8-inch drive. Although the larger drive is bulky and more expensive, it has the capacity of accepting a very wide range of large sockets. Ideally, however, the mechanic should have a 3/8-inch drive set and a 1/2-inch drive set.

Socket set(s)
Reversible ratchet

Extension - 10 inch
Universal joint
Torque wrench (same size drive as sockets)
Ball peen hammer - 8 ounce
Soft-face hammer (plastic/rubber)
Standard screwdriver (1/4-inch x 6 inch)
Standard screwdriver (stubby - 5/16-inch)
Phillips screwdriver (No. 3 x 8 inch)
Phillips screwdriver (stubby - No. 2)
Pliers - vise grip
Pliers - lineman's
Pliers - needle nose
Pliers - snap-ring (internal and external)
Cold chisel - 1/2-inch
Scribe
Scraper (made from flattened copper tubing)
Centerpunch
Pin punches (1/16, 1/8, 3/16-inch)
Steel rule/straightedge - 12 inch
Allen wrench set (1/8 to 3/8-inch or 4 mm to 10 mm)
A selection of files
Wire brush (large)
Jackstands (second set)
Jack (scissor or hydraulic type)

Note: *Another tool which is often useful is an electric drill with a chuck capacity of 3/8-inch and a set of good quality drill bits.*

Special tools

The tools in this list include those which are not used regularly, are expensive to buy, or which need to be used in accordance with their manufacturer's instructions. Unless these tools will be used frequently, it is not very economical to purchase many of them. A consideration would be to split the cost and use between yourself and a friend or friends. In addition, most of these tools can be obtained from a tool rental shop on a temporary basis.

This list primarily contains only those tools and instruments widely available to the public, and not those special tools produced by the vehicle manufacturer for distribution to dealer service departments. Occasionally, references to the manufacturer's special tools are included in the text of this manual. Generally, an alternative method of doing the job without the special tool is offered. However, sometimes there is no alternative to their use. Where this is the case, and the tool cannot be purchased or borrowed, the work should be turned over to the dealer service department or an automotive repair shop.

> Valve spring compressor
> Piston ring groove cleaning tool
> Piston ring compressor
> Piston ring installation tool
> Cylinder compression gauge
> Cylinder ridge reamer
> Cylinder surfacing hone
> Cylinder bore gauge
> Micrometers and/or dial calipers
> Hydraulic lifter removal tool
> Balljoint separator
> Universal-type puller
> Impact screwdriver
> Dial indicator set
> Stroboscopic timing light (inductive
>   pick-up)
> Hand operated vacuum/pressure pump
> Tachometer/dwell meter
> Universal electrical multimeter
> Cable hoist
> Brake spring removal and installation
>   tools
> Floor jack

Buying tools

For the do-it-yourselfer who is just starting to get involved in vehicle maintenance and repair, there are a number of options available when purchasing tools. If maintenance and minor repair is the extent of the work to be done, the purchase of individual tools is satisfactory. If, on the other hand, extensive work is planned, it would be a good idea to purchase a modest tool set from one of the large retail chain stores. A set can usually be bought at a substantial savings over the individual tool prices, and they often come with a tool box. As additional tools are needed, add-on sets, individual tools and a larger tool box can be purchased to expand the tool selection. Building a tool set gradually allows the cost of the tools to be spread over a longer period of time and gives the mechanic the freedom to choose only those tools that will actually be used.

Tool stores will often be the only source of some of the special tools that are needed, but regardless of where tools are bought, try to avoid cheap ones, especially when buying screwdrivers and sockets, because they won't last very long. The expense involved in replacing cheap tools will eventually be greater than the initial cost of quality tools.

Care and maintenance of tools

Good tools are expensive, so it makes sense to treat them with respect. Keep them clean and in usable condition and store them properly when not in use. Always wipe off any dirt, grease or metal chips before putting them away. Never leave tools lying around in the work area. Upon completion of a job, always check closely under the hood for tools that may have been left there so they won't get lost during a test drive.

Some tools, such as screwdrivers, pliers, wrenches and sockets, can be hung on a panel mounted on the garage or workshop wall, while others should be kept in a tool box or tray. Measuring instruments, gauges, meters, etc. must be carefully stored where they cannot be damaged by weather or impact from other tools.

When tools are used with care and stored properly, they will last a very long time. Even with the best of care, though, tools will wear out if used frequently. When a tool is damaged or worn out, replace it. Subsequent jobs will be safer and more enjoyable if you do.

How to repair damaged threads

Sometimes, the internal threads of a nut or bolt hole can become stripped, usually from overtightening. Stripping threads is an all-too-common occurrence, especially when working with aluminum parts, because aluminum is so soft that it easily strips out.

Usually, external or internal threads are only partially stripped. After they've been cleaned up with a tap or die, they'll still work. Sometimes, however, threads are badly damaged. When this happens, you've got three choices:

1) *Drill and tap the hole to the next suitable oversize and install a larger diameter bolt, screw or stud.*
2) *Drill and tap the hole to accept a threaded plug, then drill and tap the plug to the original screw size. You can also buy a plug already threaded to the original size. Then you simply drill a hole to the specified size, then run the threaded plug into the hole with a bolt and jam nut. Once the plug is fully seated, remove the jam nut and bolt.*
3) *The third method uses a patented thread repair kit like Heli-Coil or Slimsert. These easy-to-use kits are designed to repair damaged threads in straight-through holes and blind holes. Both are available as kits which can handle a variety of sizes and thread patterns. Drill the hole, then tap it with the special included tap. Install the Heli-Coil and the hole is back to its original diameter and thread pitch.*

Regardless of which method you use, be sure to proceed calmly and carefully. A little impatience or carelessness during one of these relatively simple procedures can ruin your whole day's work and cost you a bundle if you wreck an expensive part.

Working facilities

Not to be overlooked when discussing tools is the workshop. If anything more than routine maintenance is to be carried out, some sort of suitable work area is essential.

It is understood, and appreciated, that many home mechanics do not have a good workshop or garage available, and end up removing an engine or doing major repairs outside. It is recommended, however, that the overhaul or repair be completed under the cover of a roof.

A clean, flat workbench or table of comfortable working height is an absolute necessity. The workbench should be equipped with a vise that has a jaw opening of at least four inches.

As mentioned previously, some clean, dry storage space is also required for tools, as well as the lubricants, fluids, cleaning solvents, etc. which soon become necessary.

Sometimes waste oil and fluids, drained from the engine or cooling system during normal maintenance or repairs, present a disposal problem. To avoid pouring them on the ground or into a sewage system, pour the used fluids into large containers, seal them with caps and take them to an authorized disposal site or recycling center. Plastic jugs, such as old antifreeze containers, are ideal for this purpose.

Always keep a supply of old newspapers and clean rags available. Old towels are excellent for mopping up spills. Many mechanics use rolls of paper towels for most work because they are readily available and disposable. To help keep the area under the vehicle clean, a large cardboard box can be cut open and flattened to protect the garage or shop floor.

Whenever working over a painted surface, such as when leaning over a fender to service something under the hood, always cover it with an old blanket or bedspread to protect the finish. Vinyl covered pads, made especially for this purpose, are available at auto parts stores.

Jacking and towing

Jacking

1   The jack supplied with the vehicle should only be used for raising the vehicle when changing a tire or placing jackstands under the frame.

Warning: *Never work under the vehicle or start the engine while this jack is being used as the only means of support.*

2   The vehicle should be on level ground with the hazard flashers on, the wheels blocked, the parking brake applied and the transmission in Park (automatic) or Reverse (manual). If a tire is being changed, loosen the lug nuts one-half turn and leave them in place until the wheel is raised off the ground.

3   Place the jack under the vehicle suspension in the indicated position (see illustration). Operate the jack with a slow, smooth motion until the wheel is raised off the ground. Remove the lug nuts, pull off the wheel, install the spare and thread the lug nuts back on with the beveled sides facing in. Tighten them snugly, but wait until the vehicle is lowered to tighten them completely. Note that some spare tires are designed for temporary use only - don't exceed the recommended speed, mileage or other restrictions accompanying the spare.

4   Lower the vehicle, remove the jack and tighten the lug nuts (if loosened or removed) in a criss-cross pattern.

Towing

5   These vehicles can be towed with all four wheels on the ground. If towing a 2WD model, the transmission must be in Neutral, whether it's a manual or automatic. If towing a 4WD model, the transmission must be in Neutral (automatic) or in gear (manual) and the transfer case must be in Neutral. When attaching a 4WD model to a tow vehicle, observe the following:

a) *Shift the transfer case into 2H and make sure the 4WD light goes off*
b) *Drive ten feet backwards and ten feet forwards to make sure the front axle is disengaged, then turn the engine off (key in the OFF position, not LOCK)*
c) *Shift the transfer case into Neutral, then place the shift lever in Park (automatic) or in gear (manual)*
d) *Set the parking brake*
e) *Once the towing equipment is secure, place the transmission in Neutral (automatic); on models with a manual transmission, leave the transmission in gear.*
f) *Release the parking brake*

6   Equipment specifically designed for towing should be used and should be attached to the main structural members of the vehicle, not the bumper or brackets. Tow hooks are attached to the frame at both ends of the vehicle. However, they are for emergency use only and should not be used for highway towing. Stand clear of vehicles when using the tow hooks - tow straps, cables or chains may break, causing serious injury.

7   Safety is a major consideration when towing and all applicable state and local laws must be obeyed. A safety chain must be used for all towing (in addition to the tow bar).

Caution: *While towing, the steering must be unlocked (ignition switch in the Off position).*

Caution: *Do not tow the vehicle with one end of the vehicle on a dolly - damage to the drivetrain will result.*

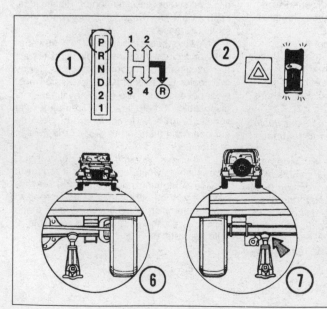

6.3 Jacking pointers and procedures

1 Place the transmission in Park (automatic) or Reverse (manual)
2 Turn on the hazard flushers
3 Apply the parking brake
4 Block the wheel diagonally opposite the one being changed
5 Use the jack to raise the vehicle
6 Rear jacking point
7 Front jacking point

Booster battery (jump) starting

1   Observe these precautions when using a booster battery to start a vehicle:
   a) *Before connecting the booster battery, make sure the ignition switch is in the Off position.*
   b) *Turn off the lights, heater and other electrical loads.*
   c) *Your eyes should be shielded. Safety goggles are a good idea.*
   d) *Make sure the booster battery is the same voltage as the dead one in the vehicle.*
   e) *The two vehicles MUST NOT TOUCH each other!*
   f) *Make sure the transaxle is in Neutral (manual) or Park (automatic).*
   g) *If the booster battery is not a maintenance-free type, remove the vent caps and lay a cloth over the vent holes.*

2   Connect the red jumper cable to the positive (+) terminals of each battery (see illustration).

3   Connect one end of the black jumper cable to the negative (-) terminal of the booster battery. The other end of this cable should be connected to a good ground on the vehicle to be started, such as a bolt or bracket on the body.

4   Start the engine using the booster battery, then, with the engine running at idle speed, disconnect the jumper cables in the reverse order of connection.

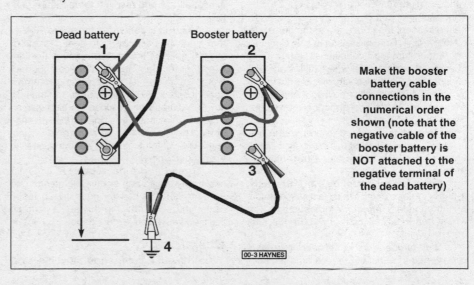

Make the booster battery cable connections in the numerical order shown (note that the negative cable of the booster battery is NOT attached to the negative terminal of the dead battery)

Automotive chemicals and lubricants

A number of automotive chemicals and lubricants are available for use during vehicle maintenance and repair. They include a wide variety of products ranging from cleaning solvents and degreasers to lubricants and protective sprays for rubber, plastic and vinyl.

Cleaners

Carburetor cleaner and choke cleaner is a strong solvent for gum, varnish and carbon. Most carburetor cleaners leave a dry-type lubricant film which will not harden or gum up. Because of this film it is not recommended for use on electrical components.

Brake system cleaner is used to remove brake dust, grease and brake fluid from the brake system, where clean surfaces are absolutely necessary. It leaves no residue and often eliminates brake squeal caused by contaminants.

Electrical cleaner removes oxidation, corrosion and carbon deposits from electrical contacts, restoring full current flow. It can also be used to clean spark plugs, carburetor jets, voltage regulators and other parts where an oil-free surface is desired.

Demoisturants remove water and moisture from electrical components such as alternators, voltage regulators, electrical connectors and fuse blocks. They are non-conductive and non-corrosive.

Degreasers are heavy-duty solvents used to remove grease from the outside of the engine and from chassis components. They can be sprayed or brushed on and, depending on the type, are rinsed off either with water or solvent.

Lubricants

Motor oil is the lubricant formulated for use in engines. It normally contains a wide variety of additives to prevent corrosion and reduce foaming and wear. Motor oil comes in various weights (viscosity ratings) from 0 to 50. The recommended weight of the oil depends on the season, temperature and the demands on the engine. Light oil is used in cold climates and under light load conditions. Heavy oil is used in hot climates and where high loads are encountered. Multi-viscosity oils are designed to have characteristics of both light and heavy oils and are available in a number of weights from 0W-20 to 20W-50.

Gear oil is designed to be used in differentials, manual transmissions and other areas where high-temperature lubrication is required.

Chassis and wheel bearing grease is a heavy grease used where increased loads and friction are encountered, such as for wheel bearings, balljoints, tie-rod ends and universal joints.

High-temperature wheel bearing grease is designed to withstand the extreme temperatures encountered by wheel bearings in disc brake equipped vehicles. It usually contains molybdenum disulfide (moly), which is a dry-type lubricant.

White grease is a heavy grease for metal-to-metal applications where water is a problem. White grease stays soft under both low and high temperatures (usually from -100 to +190-degrees F), and will not wash off or dilute in the presence of water.

Assembly lube is a special extreme pressure lubricant, usually containing moly, used to lubricate high-load parts (such as main and rod bearings and cam lobes) for initial start-up of a new engine. The assembly lube lubricates the parts without being squeezed out or washed away until the engine oiling system begins to function.

Silicone lubricants are used to protect rubber, plastic, vinyl and nylon parts.

Graphite lubricants are used where oils cannot be used due to contamination problems, such as in locks. The dry graphite will lubricate metal parts while remaining uncontaminated by dirt, water, oil or acids. It is electrically conductive and will not foul electrical contacts in locks such as the ignition switch.

Moly penetrants loosen and lubricate frozen, rusted and corroded fasteners and prevent future rusting or freezing.

Heat-sink grease is a special electrically non-conductive grease that is used for mounting electronic ignition modules where it is essential that heat is transferred away from the module.

Sealants

RTV sealant is one of the most widely used gasket compounds. Made from silicone, RTV is air curing, it seals, bonds, waterproofs, fills surface irregularities, remains flexible, doesn't shrink, is relatively easy to remove, and is used as a supplementary sealer with almost all low and medium temperature gaskets.

Anaerobic sealant is much like RTV in that it can be used either to seal gaskets or to form gaskets by itself. It remains flexible, is solvent resistant and fills surface imperfections. The difference between an anaerobic sealant and an RTV-type sealant is in the curing. RTV cures when exposed to air, while an anaerobic sealant cures only in the absence of air. This means that an anaerobic sealant cures only after the assembly of parts, sealing them together.

Thread and pipe sealant is used for sealing hydraulic and pneumatic fittings and vacuum lines. It is usually made from a Teflon compound, and comes in a spray, a paint-on liquid and as a wrap-around tape.

Chemicals

Anti-seize compound prevents seiz-ing, galling, cold welding, rust and corrosion in fasteners. High-temperature ant-seize, usually made with copper and graphite lubricants, is used for exhaust system and exhaust manifold bolts.

Anaerobic locking compounds are used to keep fasteners from vibrating or working loose and cure only after installation, in the absence of air. Medium strength locking compound is used for small nuts, bolts and screws that may be removed later. High-strength locking compound is for large nuts, bolts and studs which aren't removed on a regular basis.

Oil additives range from viscosity index improvers to chemical treatments that claim to reduce internal engine friction. It should be noted that most oil manufacturers caution against using additives with their oils.

Gas additives perform several functions, depending on their chemical makeup. They usually contain solvents that help dissolve gum and varnish that build up on carburetor, fuel injection and intake parts. They also serve to break down carbon deposits that form on the inside surfaces of the combustion chambers. Some additives contain upper cylinder lubricants for valves and piston rings, and others contain chemicals to remove condensation from the gas tank.

Miscellaneous

Brake fluid is specially formulated hydraulic fluid that can withstand the heat and pressure encountered in brake systems. Care must be taken so this fluid does not come in contact with painted surfaces or plastics. An opened container should always be resealed to prevent contamination by water or dirt.

Weatherstrip adhesive is used to bond weatherstripping around doors, windows and trunk lids. It is sometimes used to attach trim pieces.

Undercoating is a petroleum-based, tar-like substance that is designed to protect metal surfaces on the underside of the vehicle from corrosion. It also acts as a sound-deadening agent by insulating the bottom of the vehicle.

Waxes and polishes are used to help protect painted and plated surfaces from the weather. Different types of paint may require the use of different types of wax and polish. Some polishes utilize a chemical or abrasive cleaner to help remove the top layer of oxidized (dull) paint on older vehicles. In recent years many non-wax polishes that contain a wide variety of chemicals such as polymers and silicones have been introduced. These non-wax polishes are usually easier to apply and last longer than conventional waxes and polishes.

Conversion factors

Length (distance)

Inches (in)	X	25.4	= Millimeters (mm)	X 0.0394	= Inches (in)
Feet (ft)	X	0.305	= Meters (m)	X 3.281	= Feet (ft)
Miles	X	1.609	= Kilometers (km)	X 0.621	= Miles

Volume (capacity)

Cubic inches (cu in; in³)	X	16.387	= Cubic centimeters (cc; cm³)	X 0.061	= Cubic inches (cu in; in³)
Imperial pints (Imp pt)	X	0.568	= Liters (l)	X 1.76	= Imperial pints (Imp pt)
Imperial quarts (Imp qt)	X	1.137	= Liters (l)	X 0.88	= Imperial quarts (Imp qt)
Imperial quarts (Imp qt)	X	1.201	= US quarts (US qt)	X 0.833	= Imperial quarts (Imp qt)
US quarts (US qt)	X	0.946	= Liters (l)	X 1.057	= US quarts (US qt)
Imperial gallons (Imp gal)	X	4.546	= Liters (l)	X 0.22	= Imperial gallons (Imp gal)
Imperial gallons (Imp gal)	X	1.201	= US gallons (US gal)	X 0.833	= Imperial gallons (Imp gal)
US gallons (US gal)	X	3.785	= Liters (l)	X 0.264	= US gallons (US gal)

Mass (weight)

Ounces (oz)	X	28.35	= Grams (g)	X 0.035	= Ounces (oz)
Pounds (lb)	X	0.454	= Kilograms (kg)	X 2.205	= Pounds (lb)

Force

Ounces-force (ozf; oz)	X	0.278	= Newtons (N)	X 3.6	= Ounces-force (ozf; oz)
Pounds-force (lbf; lb)	X	4.448	= Newtons (N)	X 0.225	= Pounds-force (lbf; lb)
Newtons (N)	X	0.1	= Kilograms-force (kgf; kg)	X 9.81	= Newtons (N)

Pressure

Pounds-force per square inch (psi; lbf/in²; lb/in²)	X	0.070	= Kilograms-force per square centimeter (kgf/cm²; kg/cm²)	X 14.223	= Pounds-force per square inch (psi; lbf/in²; lb/in²)
Pounds-force per square inch (psi; lbf/in²; lb/in²)	X	0.068	= Atmospheres (atm)	X 14.696	= Pounds-force per square inch (psi; lbf/in²; lb/in²)
Pounds-force per square inch (psi; lbf/in²; lb/in²)	X	0.069	= Bars	X 14.5	= Pounds-force per square inch (psi; lbf/in²; lb/in²)
Pounds-force per square inch (psi; lbf/in²; lb/in²)	X	6.895	= Kilopascals (kPa)	X 0.145	= Pounds-force per square inch (psi; lbf/in²; lb/in²)
Kilopascals (kPa)	X	0.01	= Kilograms-force per square centimeter (kgf/cm²; kg/cm²)	X 98.1	= Kilopascals (kPa)

Torque (moment of force)

Pounds-force inches (lbf in; lb in)	X	1.152	= Kilograms-force centimeter (kgf cm; kg cm)	X 0.868	= Pounds-force inches (lbf in; lb in)
Pounds-force inches (lbf in; lb in)	X	0.113	= Newton meters (Nm)	X 8.85	= Pounds-force inches (lbf in; lb in)
Pounds-force inches (lbf in; lb in)	X	0.083	= Pounds-force feet (lbf ft; lb ft)	X 12	= Pounds-force inches (lbf in; lb in)
Pounds-force feet (lbf ft; lb ft)	X	0.138	= Kilograms-force meters (kgf m; kg m)	X 7.233	= Pounds-force feet (lbf ft; lb ft)
Pounds-force feet (lbf ft; lb ft)	X	1.356	= Newton meters (Nm)	X 0.738	= Pounds-force feet (lbf ft; lb ft)
Newton meters (Nm)	X	0.102	= Kilograms-force meters (kgf m; kg m)	X 9.804	= Newton meters (Nm)

Vacuum

Inches mercury (in. Hg)	X	3.377	= Kilopascals (kPa)	X 0.2961	= Inches mercury
Inches mercury (in. Hg)	X	25.4	= Millimeters mercury (mm Hg)	X 0.0394	= Inches mercury

Power

Horsepower (hp)	X	745.7	= Watts (W)	X 0.0013	= Horsepower (hp)

Velocity (speed)

Miles per hour (miles/hr; mph)	X	1.609	= Kilometers per hour (km/hr; kph)	X 0.621	= Miles per hour (miles/hr; mph)

Fuel consumption*

Miles per gallon, Imperial (mpg)	X	0.354	= Kilometers per liter (km/l)	X 2.825	= Miles per gallon, Imperial (mpg)
Miles per gallon, US (mpg)	X	0.425	= Kilometers per liter (km/l)	X 2.352	= Miles per gallon, US (mpg)

Temperature

Degrees Fahrenheit = (°C x 1.8) + 32

Degrees Celsius (Degrees Centigrade; °C) = (°F - 32) x 0.56

*It is common practice to convert from miles per gallon (mpg) to liters/100 kilometers (l/100km), where mpg (Imperial) x l/100 km = 282 and mpg (US) x l/100 km = 235

DECIMALS to MILLIMETERS

Decimal	mm	Decimal	mm
0.001	0.0254	0.500	12.7000
0.002	0.0508	0.510	12.9540
0.003	0.0762	0.520	13.2080
0.004	0.1016	0.530	13.4620
0.005	0.1270	0.540	13.7160
0.006	0.1524	0.550	13.9700
0.007	0.1778	0.560	14.2240
0.008	0.2032	0.570	14.4780
0.009	0.2286	0.580	14.7320
		0.590	14.9860
0.010	0.2540		
0.020	0.5080		
0.030	0.7620		
0.040	1.0160	0.600	15.2400
0.050	1.2700	0.610	15.4940
0.060	1.5240	0.620	15.7480
0.070	1.7780	0.630	16.0020
0.080	2.0320	0.640	16.2560
0.090	2.2860	0.650	16.5100
		0.660	16.7640
0.100	2.5400	0.670	17.0180
0.110	2.7940	0.680	17.2720
0.120	3.0480	0.690	17.5260
0.130	3.3020		
0.140	3.5560		
0.150	3.8100		
0.160	4.0640	0.700	17.7800
0.170	4.3180	0.710	18.0340
0.180	4.5720	0.720	18.2880
0.190	4.8260	0.730	18.5420
		0.740	18.7960
0.200	5.0800	0.750	19.0500
0.210	5.3340	0.760	19.3040
0.220	5.5880	0.770	19.5580
0.230	5.8420	0.780	19.8120
0.240	6.0960	0.790	20.0660
0.250	6.3500		
0.260	6.6040		
0.270	6.8580	0.800	20.3200
0.280	7.1120	0.810	20.5740
0.290	7.3660	0.820	21.8280
		0.830	21.0820
0.300	7.6200	0.840	21.3360
0.310	7.8740	0.850	21.5900
0.320	8.1280	0.860	21.8440
0.330	8.3820	0.870	22.0980
0.340	8.6360	0.880	22.3520
0.350	8.8900	0.890	22.6060
0.360	9.1440		
0.370	9.3980		
0.380	9.6520		
0.390	9.9060		
		0.900	22.8600
0.400	10.1600	0.910	23.1140
0.410	10.4140	0.920	23.3680
0.420	10.6680	0.930	23.6220
0.430	10.9220	0.940	23.8760
0.440	11.1760	0.950	24.1300
0.450	11.4300	0.960	24.3840
0.460	11.6840	0.970	24.6380
0.470	11.9380	0.980	24.8920
0.480	12.1920	0.990	25.1460
0.490	12.4460	1.000	25.4000

FRACTIONS to DECIMALS to MILLIMETERS

Fraction	Decimal	mm	Fraction	Decimal	mm
1/64	0.0156	0.3969	33/64	0.5156	13.0969
1/32	0.0312	0.7938	17/32	0.5312	13.4938
3/64	0.0469	1.1906	35/64	0.5469	13.8906
1/16	0.0625	1.5875	9/16	0.5625	14.2875
5/64	0.0781	1.9844	37/64	0.5781	14.6844
3/32	0.0938	2.3812	19/32	0.5938	15.0812
7/64	0.1094	2.7781	39/64	0.6094	15.4781
1/8	0.1250	3.1750	5/8	0.6250	15.8750
9/64	0.1406	3.5719	41/64	0.6406	16.2719
5/32	0.1562	3.9688	21/32	0.6562	16.6688
11/64	0.1719	4.3656	43/64	0.6719	17.0656
3/16	0.1875	4.7625	11/16	0.6875	17.4625
13/64	0.2031	5.1594	45/64	0.7031	17.8594
7/32	0.2188	5.5562	23/32	0.7188	18.2562
15/64	0.2344	5.9531	47/64	0.7344	18.6531
1/4	0.2500	6.3500	3/4	0.7500	19.0500
17/64	0.2656	6.7469	49/64	0.7656	19.4469
9/32	0.2812	7.1438	25/32	0.7812	19.8438
19/64	0.2969	7.5406	51/64	0.7969	20.2406
5/16	0.3125	7.9375	13/16	0.8125	20.6375
21/64	0.3281	8.3344	53/64	0.8281	21.0344
11/32	0.3438	8.7312	27/32	0.8438	21.4312
23/64	0.3594	9.1281	55/64	0.8594	21.8281
3/8	0.3750	9.5250	7/8	0.8750	22.2250
25/64	0.3906	9.9219	57/64	0.8906	22.6219
13/32	0.4062	10.3188	29/32	0.9062	23.0188
27/64	0.4219	10.7156	59/64	0.9219	23.4156
7/16	0.4375	11.1125	15/16	0.9375	23.8125
29/64	0.4531	11.5094	61/64	0.9531	24.2094
15/32	0.4688	11.9062	31/32	0.9688	24.6062
31/64	0.4844	12.3031	63/64	0.9844	25.0031
1/2	0.5000	12.7000	1	1.0000	25.4000

Safety first!

Regardless of how enthusiastic you may be about getting on with the job at hand, take the time to ensure that your safety is not jeopardized. A moment's lack of attention can result in an accident, as can failure to observe certain simple safety precautions. The possibility of an accident will always exist, and the following points should not be considered a comprehensive list of all dangers. Rather, they are intended to make you aware of the risks and to encourage a safety conscious approach to all work you carry out on your vehicle.

Essential DOs and DON'Ts

DON'T rely on a jack when working under the vehicle. Always use approved jackstands to support the weight of the vehicle and place them under the recommended lift or support points.

DON'T attempt to loosen extremely tight fasteners (i.e. wheel lug nuts) while the vehicle is on a jack - it may fall.

DON'T start the engine without first making sure that the transmission is in Neutral (or Park where applicable) and the parking brake is set.

DON'T remove the radiator cap from a hot cooling system - let it cool or cover it with a cloth and release the pressure gradually.

DON'T attempt to drain the engine oil until you are sure it has cooled to the point that it will not burn you.

DON'T touch any part of the engine or exhaust system until it has cooled sufficiently to avoid burns.

DON'T siphon toxic liquids such as gasoline, antifreeze and brake fluid by mouth, or allow them to remain on your skin.

DON'T inhale brake lining dust - it is potentially hazardous (see *Asbestos* below).

DON'T allow spilled oil or grease to remain on the floor - wipe it up before someone slips on it.

DON'T use loose fitting wrenches or other tools which may slip and cause injury.

DON'T push on wrenches when loosening or tightening nuts or bolts. Always try to pull the wrench toward you. If the situation calls for pushing the wrench away, push with an open hand to avoid scraped knuckles if the wrench should slip.

DON'T attempt to lift a heavy component alone - get someone to help you.

DON'T rush or take unsafe shortcuts to finish a job.

DON'T allow children or animals in or around the vehicle while you are working on it.

DO wear eye protection when using power tools such as a drill, sander, bench grinder, etc. and when working under a vehicle.

DO keep loose clothing and long hair well out of the way of moving parts.

DO make sure that any hoist used has a safe working load rating adequate for the job.

DO get someone to check on you periodically when working alone on a vehicle.

DO carry out work in a logical sequence and make sure that everything is correctly assembled and tightened.

DO keep chemicals and fluids tightly capped and out of the reach of children and pets.

DO remember that your vehicle's safety affects that of yourself and others. If in doubt on any point, get professional advice.

Steering, suspension and brakes

These systems are essential to driving safety, so make sure you have a qualified shop or individual check your work. Also, compressed suspension springs can cause injury if released suddenly - be sure to use a spring compressor.

Airbags

Airbags are explosive devices that can **CAUSE** injury if they deploy while you're working on the vehicle. Follow the manufacturer's instructions to disable the airbag whenever you're working in the vicinity of airbag components.

Asbestos

Certain friction, insulating, sealing, and other products - such as brake linings, brake bands, clutch linings, torque converters, gaskets, etc. - may contain asbestos or other hazardous friction material. Extreme care must be taken to avoid inhalation of dust from such products, since it is hazardous to health. If in doubt, assume that they do contain asbestos.

Fire

Remember at all times that gasoline is highly flammable. Never smoke or have any kind of open flame around when working on a vehicle. But the risk does not end there. A spark caused by an electrical short circuit, by two metal surfaces contacting each other, or even by static electricity built up in your body under certain conditions, can ignite gasoline vapors, which in a confined space are highly explosive. Do not, under any circumstances, use gasoline for cleaning parts. Use an approved safety solvent.

Always disconnect the battery ground (-) cable at the battery before working on any part of the fuel system or electrical system. Never risk spilling fuel on a hot engine or exhaust component. It is strongly recommended that a fire extinguisher suitable for use on fuel and electrical fires be kept handy in the garage or workshop at all times. Never try to extinguish a fuel or electrical fire with water.

Fumes

Certain fumes are highly toxic and can quickly cause unconsciousness and even death if inhaled to any extent. Gasoline vapor falls into this category, as do the vapors from some cleaning solvents. Any draining or pouring of such volatile fluids should be done in a well ventilated area.

When using cleaning fluids and solvents, read the instructions on the container carefully. Never use materials from unmarked containers.

Never run the engine in an enclosed space, such as a garage. Exhaust fumes contain carbon monoxide, which is extremely poisonous. If you need to run the engine, always do so in the open air, or at least have the rear of the vehicle outside the work area.

The battery

Never create a spark or allow a bare light bulb near a battery. They normally give off a certain amount of hydrogen gas, which is highly explosive.

Always disconnect the battery ground (-) cable at the battery before working on the fuel or electrical systems.

If possible, loosen the filler caps or cover when charging the battery from an external source (this does not apply to sealed or maintenance-free batteries). Do not charge at an excessive rate or the battery may burst.

Take care when adding water to a non maintenance-free battery and when carrying a battery. The electrolyte, even when diluted, is very corrosive and should not be allowed to contact clothing or skin.

Always wear eye protection when cleaning the battery to prevent the caustic deposits from entering your eyes.

Household current

When using an electric power tool, inspection light, etc., which operates on household current, always make sure that the tool is correctly connected to its plug and that, where necessary, it is properly grounded. Do not use such items in damp conditions and, again, do not create a spark or apply excessive heat in the vicinity of fuel or fuel vapor.

Secondary ignition system voltage

A severe electric shock can result from touching certain parts of the ignition system (such as the spark plug wires) when the engine is running or being cranked, particularly if components are damp or the insulation is defective. In the case of an electronic ignition system, the secondary system voltage is much higher and could prove fatal.

Hydrofluoric acid

This extremely corrosive acid is formed when certain types of synthetic rubber, found in some O-rings, oil seals, fuel hoses, etc. are exposed to temperatures above 750-degrees F (400-degrees C). The rubber changes into a charred or sticky substance containing the acid. *Once formed, the acid remains dangerous for years. If it gets onto the skin, it may be necessary to amputate the limb concerned.*

When dealing with a vehicle which has suffered a fire, or with components salvaged from such a vehicle, wear protective gloves and discard them after use.

Troubleshooting

Contents

This section provides an easy reference guide to the more common problems which may occur during the operation of your vehicle. These problems and their possible causes are grouped under headings denoting various components or systems, such as Engine, Cooling system, etc. They also refer you to the chapter and/or section which deals with the problem.

Remember that successful troubleshooting is not a mysterious black art practiced only by professional mechanics. It is simply the result of the right knowledge combined with an intelligent, systematic approach to the problem. Always work by a process of elimination, starting with the simplest solution and working through to the most complex - and never overlook the obvious. Anyone can run the gas tank dry or leave the lights on overnight, so don't assume that you are exempt from such oversights.

Finally, always establish a clear idea of why a problem has occurred and take steps to ensure that it doesn't happen again. If the electrical system fails because of a poor connection, check the other connections in the system to make sure that they don't fail as well. If a particular fuse continues to blow, find out why - don't just replace one fuse after another. Remember, failure of a small component can often be indicative of potential failure or incorrect functioning of a more important component or system.

Engine and performance

1 Engine will not rotate when attempting to start

1   Battery terminal connections loose or corroded. Check the cable terminals at the battery; tighten cable clamp and/or clean off corrosion as necessary (see Chapter 1).
2   Battery discharged or faulty. If the cable ends are clean and tight on the battery posts, turn the key to the On position and switch on the headlights or windshield wipers. If they won't run, the battery is discharged.
3   Automatic transmission not engaged in park (P) or Neutral (N).
4   Broken, loose or disconnected wires in the starting circuit. Inspect all wires and connectors at the battery, starter solenoid and ignition switch (on steering column).
5   Starter motor pinion jammed in flywheel ring gear. If manual transmission, place transmission in gear and rock the vehicle to manually turn the engine. Remove starter (Chapter 5) and inspect pinion and flywheel.
6   Starter solenoid faulty (Chapter 5).
7   Starter motor faulty (Chapter 5).
8   Ignition switch faulty (Chapter 12).
9   Engine seized. Try to turn the crankshaft with a large socket and breaker bar on the pulley bolt.

2 Engine rotates but will not start

1   Fuel tank empty.
2   Battery discharged (engine rotates slowly). Check the operation of electrical components as described in previous Section.
3   Battery terminal connections loose or corroded. See previous Section.
4   Fuel not reaching carburetor or fuel injector. Check for clogged fuel filter or lines and defective fuel pump. Also make sure the tank vent lines aren't clogged (Chapter 4).
5   Choke not operating properly (Chapter 4).
6   Faulty distributor components. Check the cap and rotor (Chapter 1).
7   Low cylinder compression. Check as described in Chapter 2F.
8   Water in fuel. Drain tank and fill with new fuel.
9   Defective ignition coil (Chapter 5).

10   Dirty or clogged carburetor jets or fuel injector. Carburetor out of adjustment. Check the float level (Chapter 4). Check the needle valve and its seat Chapter 4).
11   Wet or damaged ignition components (Chapter 1 and Chapter 5).
12   Worn, faulty or incorrectly gapped spark plugs (Chapter 1).
13   Broken, loose or disconnected wires in the starting circuit (see previous Section).
14   Loose distributor (changing ignition timing). Turn the distributor body as necessary to start the engine, then adjust the ignition timing as soon as possible (Chapter 1).
15   Broken, loose or disconnected wires at the ignition coil or faulty coil (Chapter 1).
16   Timing chain failure or wear affecting valve timing Chapter 2B, Chapter 2C, Chapter 2D, or Chapter 2E).

3 Starter motor operates without turning engine

1   Starter pinion sticking. Remove the starter (Chapter 5) and inspect.
2   Starter pinion or flywheel/driveplate teeth worn or broken. Remove the inspection cover and inspect.

4 Engine hard to start when cold

1   Battery discharged or low. Check as described in Chapter 1.
2   Fuel not reaching the carburetor or fuel injectors. Check the fuel filter, lines and fuel pump (Chapter 1 and Chapter 4).
3   Choke inoperative (Chapter 1 and Chapter 4).
4   Defective spark plugs (Chapter 1).

5 Engine hard to start when hot

1   Air filter dirty (Chapter 1).
2   Fuel not reaching carburetor or fuel injectors (see Chapter 4). On carbureted models, check for a vapor lock situation, brought about by clogged fuel tank vent lines.
3   Bad engine ground connection.
4   Choke sticking (Chapter 1).
5   Defective pick-up coil in distributor (Chapter 5).
6   Float level too high.

7   Defective crankshaft position sensor (Chapter 6).

6 Starter motor noisy or engages roughly

1   Pinion or flywheel/driveplate teeth worn or broken. Remove the inspection cover on the left side of the engine and inspect.
2   Starter motor mounting bolts loose or missing.

7 Engine starts but stops immediately

1   Loose or damaged wire harness connections at distributor, coil or alternator.
2   Intake manifold vacuum leaks. Make sure all mounting bolts/nuts are tight and all vacuum hoses connected to the manifold are attached properly and in good condition.
3   Insufficient fuel flow (see Chapter 4).

8 Engine "lopes" while idling or idles erratically

1   Vacuum leaks. Check mounting bolts at the intake manifold for tightness. Make sure that all vacuum hoses are connected and in good condition. Use a stethoscope or a length of fuel hose held against your ear to listen for vacuum leaks while the engine is running. A hissing sound will be heard. A soapy water solution will also detect leaks. Check the intake manifold gasket surfaces.
2   Leaking EGR valve or plugged PCV valve (see Chapter 1 and Chapter 6).
3   Air filter clogged (Chapter 1).
4   Fuel pump not delivering sufficient fuel (Chapter 4).
5   Leaking head gasket. Perform a cylinder compression check (Chapter 2F).
6   Timing chain worn (Chapter 2B, Chapter 2C, Chapter 2D, or Chapter 2E).
7   Camshaft lobes worn (Chapter 2A, Chapter 2B, Chapter 2C, Chapter 2D, or Chapter 2E).
8   Valves burned or otherwise leaking.
9   Ignition timing out of adjustment (Chapter 5).
10   Ignition system not operating properly (Chapter 1 and Chapter 5).

11 Thermostatic air cleaner not operating properly (Chapter 4).
12 Choke not operating properly (Chapter 1 and Chapter 4).
13 Dirty or clogged injectors. Carburetor dirty, clogged or out of adjustment. Check the float level (Chapter 4).
14 Idle speed out of adjustment (Chapter 1).

9 Engine misses at idle speed

1 Spark plugs faulty or not gapped properly (Chapter 1).
2 Faulty spark plug wires (Chapter 1).
3 Wet or damaged distributor components (Chapter 5).
4 Faulty connections in ignition, coil or spark plug wires (Chapter 1).
5 Faulty emissions systems (Chapter 6).
6 Clogged fuel filter and/or foreign matter in fuel. Remove the fuel filter (Chapter 1) and inspect.
7 Vacuum leaks at intake manifold or hose connections.
8 Incorrect idle speed (Chapter 1) or idle mixture (Chapter 1).
9 Incorrect ignition timing (Chapter 1).
10 Low or uneven cylinder compression. Check as described in Chapter 2F.
11 Choke not operating properly (Chapter 1).
12 Clogged or dirty fuel injectors (Chapter 4).

10 Excessively high idle speed

1 Sticking throttle linkage (Chapter 1).
2 Choke opened excessively at idle (Chapter 1).
3 Idle speed incorrectly adjusted (Chapter 1).

11 Battery will not hold a charge

1 Alternator drivebelt defective or not adjusted properly (Chapter 1).
2 Battery cables loose or corroded (Chapter 1 and Chapter 5).
3 Alternator not charging properly (Chapter 5).
4 Loose, broken or faulty wires in the charging circuit.
5 Short circuit causing a continuous drain on the battery.
6 Battery defective internally.

12 Alternator light stays on

1 Fault in alternator or charging circuit (Chapter 5).
2 Alternator drivebelt defective or not properly adjusted (Chapter 1).

13 Alternator light fails to come on when key is turned on

1 Faulty bulb (Chapter 12).
2 Defective alternator (Chapter 5).
3 Fault in the instrument cluster, dash wiring or bulb holder (Chapter 12).

14 Engine misses throughout driving speed range

1 Fuel filter clogged and/or impurities in the fuel system. Check fuel filter (Chapter 1) or clean system.
2 Faulty or incorrectly gapped spark plugs (Chapter 1).
3 Incorrect ignition timing (Chapter 1).
4 Cracked distributor cap, disconnected distributor wires or damaged distributor components (Chapter 1 and Chapter 5).
5 Defective spark plug wires (Chapter 1).
6 Emissions system components faulty (Chapter 6).
7 Low or uneven cylinder compression pressures. Check as described in Chapter 2F.
8 Weak or faulty ignition coil (Chapter 5).
9 Weak or faulty ignition system (Chapter 5).
10 Vacuum leaks at intake manifold or vacuum hoses.
11 Dirty or clogged carburetor or fuel injector (Chapter 4).
12 Leaky EGR valve (Chapter 6).
13 Carburetor out of adjustment (Chapter 4).
14 Idle speed out of adjustment (Chapter 1).

15 Hesitation or stumble during acceleration

1 Ignition timing incorrect (Chapter 1).
2 Ignition system not operating properly (Chapter 5).
3 Dirty or clogged carburetor or fuel injector (Chapter 4).
4 Low fuel pressure. Check for proper operation of the fuel pump and for restrictions in the fuel filter and lines (Chapter 1).
5 Carburetor out of adjustment (Chapter 1).

16 Engine stalls

1 Idle speed incorrect (Chapter 1).
2 Fuel filter clogged and/or water and impurities in the fuel system (Chapter 1).
3 Choke not operating properly (Chapter 1).
4 Damaged or wet distributor cap and wires (Chapter 1 and Chapter 5).
5 Emissions system components faulty (Chapter 6).
6 Faulty or incorrectly gapped spark plugs. Also check the spark plug wires (Chapter 1).
7 Vacuum leak at the carburetor, intake manifold or vacuum hoses.

17 Engine lacks power

1 Incorrect ignition timing (Chapter 1).
2 Excessive play in distributor shaft. At the same time check for faulty distributor cap, wires, etc. (Chapter 5).
3 Faulty or incorrectly gapped spark plugs (Chapter 1).
4 Air filter dirty (Chapter 1).
5 Faulty ignition coil (Chapter 5).
6 Brakes caliper(s) seized (Chapter 9).
7 Automatic transmission fluid level incorrect, causing slippage (Chapter 1).
8 Clutch slipping (Chapter 8).
9 Fuel filter clogged and/or impurities in the fuel system (Chapter 1 and Chapter 4).
10 EGR system not functioning properly (Chapter 6).
11 Use of sub-standard fuel. Fill tank with proper octane fuel.
12 Low or uneven cylinder compression pressures. Check as described in Chapter 2F.
13 Vacuum leak at carburetor or intake manifold.
14 Dirty or clogged carburetor jets or malfunctioning choke (Chapter 1 and Chapter 4).
15 Restricted exhaust system or catalytic converter (Chapter 4 or Chapter 6).

18 Engine backfires

1 EGR system not functioning properly (Chapter 6).
2 Ignition timing incorrect (Chapter 1).
3 Thermostatic air cleaner system not operating properly (Chapter 6).
4 Vacuum leak (Chapter 2F).
5 Damaged valve springs or sticking valves.
6 Intake air leak.
7 Carburetor float level out of adjustment (Chapter 4).

19 Engine surges while holding accelerator steady

1 Intake air/vacuum leak.
2 Fuel pump not working properly (Chapter 4).

20 Pinging or knocking engine sounds when engine is under load

1 Incorrect grade of fuel. Fill tank with fuel of the proper octane rating.
2 Ignition timing incorrect (Chapter 1).
3 Carbon build-up in combustion chambers. Remove cylinder head(s) and clean combustion chambers.
4 Incorrect spark plugs (Chapter 1).
5 EGR system not functioning properly (Chapter 6).

21 Engine diesels (continues to run) after being turned off

1   Idle speed too high (Chapter 1).
2   Ignition timing incorrect (Chapter 1).
3   Incorrect spark plug heat range (Chapter 1).
4   Intake air/vacuum leak (see Chapter 2F).
5   Carbon build-up in combustion chambers. Remove the cylinder head(s) and clean the combustion chambers.
6   EGR system not operating properly (Chapter 6).
7   Check for causes of overheating (Chapter 3).

22 Low oil pressure

1   Improper grade of oil.
2   Oil pump worn or damaged (Chapter 2A, Chapter 2B, Chapter 2C, Chapter 2D, or Chapter 2E).
3   Engine overheating (Chapter 3).
4   Clogged oil filter (Chapter 1).
5   Clogged oil strainer (Chapter 2A, Chapter 2B, Chapter 2C, Chapter 2D, or Chapter 2E).
6   Oil pressure gauge not working properly.

23 Excessive oil consumption

1   Oil leak, check oil pan, timing chain cover, crankshaft oil seals, valve cover (Chapter 2A, Chapter 2B, Chapter 2C, Chapter 2D, or Chapter 2E).
2   Loose oil filter (Chapter 1).
3   Loose or damaged oil pressure switch (Chapter 2F).
4   Pistons and cylinders excessively worn (Chapter 2F).
5   Piston rings not installed correctly on pistons (Chapter 2F).
6   Worn or damaged piston rings (Chapter 2F).
7   Intake and/or exhaust valve oil seals worn or damaged (Chapter 2A, Chapter 2B, Chapter 2C, Chapter 2D, or Chapter 2E).
8   Worn valve stems.
9   Worn or damaged valves/guides.

24 Excessive fuel consumption

1   Dirty or clogged air filter element (Chapter 1).
2   Incorrect ignition timing (Chapter 1).
3   Incorrect idle speed (Chapter 1).
4   Low tire pressures (Chapter 1).
5   Fuel leakage. Check all connections, lines and components in the fuel system (Chapter 4).
6   Choke not operating properly (Chapter 1).
7   Dirty or clogged carburetor jets or fuel injectors (Chapter 4).

26 Fuel odor

1   Fuel leakage. Check all connections, lines and components in the fuel system (Chapter 4).
2   Fuel tank overfilled. Fill only to automatic shut-off.
3   Charcoal canister filter in Evaporative Emissions Control system clogged (Chapter 1).
4   Vapor leaks from Evaporative Emissions Control system lines (Chapter 6).

27 Miscellaneous engine noises

1   A strong dull noise that becomes more rapid as the engine accelerates indicates worn or damaged crankshaft bearings or an unevenly worn crankshaft. To pinpoint the trouble spot, remove the spark plug wire from one plug at a time and crank the engine over. If the noise stops, the cylinder with the removed plug wire indicates the problem area. Replace the bearing and/or service or replace the crankshaft (Chapter 2F).
2   A similar (yet slightly higher pitched) noise to the crankshaft knocking described in the previous paragraph, that becomes more rapid as the engine accelerates, indicates worn or damaged connecting rod bearings (Chapter 2F). The procedure for locating the problem cylinder is the same as described in Paragraph 1.
3   An overlapping metallic noise that increases in intensity as the engine speed increases, yet diminishes as the engine warms up indicates abnormal piston and cylinder wear (Chapter 2F). To locate the problem cylinder, use the procedure described in Paragraph 1.
4   A rapid clicking noise that becomes faster as the engine accelerates indicates a worn piston pin or piston pin hole. This sound will happen each time the piston hits the highest and lowest points in the stroke (Chapter 2F). The procedure for locating the problem piston is described in Paragraph 1.
5   A metallic clicking noise coming from the water pump indicates worn or damaged water pump bearings or pump. Replace the water pump with a new one (Chapter 3)..
6   A rapid tapping sound or clicking sound that becomes faster as the engine speed increases indicates "valve tapping". This can be identified by holding one end of a section of hose to your ear and placing the other end at different spots along the valve cover. The point where the sound is loudest indicates the problem valve. If the problem persists, you likely have a collapsed valve lifter or other damaged valve train component. Changing the engine oil and adding a high viscosity oil treatment will sometimes cure a stuck lifter problem. If the problem still persists, the lifters, pushrods and rocker arms must be removed for inspection (see Chapter 2B, Chapter 2C, or Chapter 2D).
7   A steady metallic rattling or rapping sound coming from the area of the timing chain cover indicates a worn, damaged or out-of-adjustment timing chain. Service or replace the chain and related components (Chapter 2B, Chapter 2C, Chapter 2D, or Chapter 2E).

Cooling system

27 Overheating

1   Insufficient coolant in system (Chapter 1).
2   Drivebelt defective or not adjusted properly (Chapter 1).
3   Radiator core blocked or radiator grille dirty and restricted (Chapter 3).
4   Thermostat faulty (Chapter 3).
5   Fan not functioning properly (Chapter 3).
6   Radiator cap not maintaining proper pressure. Have cap pressure tested by gas station or repair shop.
7   Ignition timing incorrect (Chapter 3).
8   Defective water pump (Chapter 3).
9   Improper grade of engine oil.
10 Inaccurate temperature gauge.

28 Overcooling

1   Thermostat faulty (Chapter 3).
2   Inaccurate temperature gauge.

29 External coolant leakage

1   Deteriorated or damaged hoses. Loose clamps at hose connections.
2   Water pump seals defective. If this is the case, water will drip from the weep hole in the water pump body (Chapter 3).
3   Leakage from radiator core or header tank. This will require the radiator to be replaced or professionally repaired (see Chapter 3).
4   Engine drain plugs or water jacket freeze plugs leaking.
5   Leak from coolant temperature switch (Chapter 3).
6   Leak from damaged gaskets or small cracks.
7   Damaged head gasket. This can be verified by checking the condition of the engine oil as noted in Chapter 1.

30 Internal coolant leakage

Note: *Internal coolant leaks can usually be detected by examining the oil. Check the dipstick and inside the valve cover for water deposits and an oil consistency like that of a milkshake.*

8   Leaking cylinder head gasket. Have the system pressure tested or remove the cylinder head and inspect (Chapter 2A, Chapter 2B, Chapter 2C, Chapter 2D, or Chapter 2E).

9   Cracked cylinder bore or cylinder head. Dismantle engine and inspect (Chapter 2F).

31   Abnormal coolant loss

1   Overfilling system (Chapter 1).
2   Coolant boiling away due to overheating (Chapter 3).
3   Internal or external leakage (see Sections 29 and 30).
4   Faulty radiator cap. Have the cap pressure tested.
5   Cooling system being pressurized by engine compression. This could be due to a cracked head or block or leaking head gasket(s).

32   Poor coolant circulation

1   Inoperative water pump. A quick test is to pinch the top radiator hose closed with your hand while the engine is idling, then release it. You should feel a surge of coolant if the pump is working properly.
2   Restriction in cooling system. Drain, flush and refill the system (Chapter 1). If necessary, remove the radiator (Chapter 3) and have it reverse flushed or professionally cleaned.
3   Loose drivebelt (Chapter 1).
4   Thermostat sticking (Chapter 3).
5   Insufficient coolant (Chapter 1).

33   Corrosion

1   Excessive impurities in the water. Soft, clean water is recommended. Distilled or rainwater is satisfactory.
2   Insufficient antifreeze solution (refer to Chapter 1 for the proper ratio of water to antifreeze).
3   Infrequent flushing and draining of system. Regular flushing of the cooling system should be carried out at the specified intervals as described in Chapter 1.

Clutch

34   Fails to release (pedal pressed to the floor - shift lever does not move freely in and out of Reverse)

1   Clutch contaminated with oil. Remove clutch plate and inspect.
2   Clutch plate warped, distorted or otherwise damaged.
3   Diaphragm spring fatigued. Remove clutch cover/pressure plate assembly and inspect.
4   Leakage of fluid from clutch hydraulic system. Inspect master cylinder, operating cylinder and connecting lines.

5   Air in clutch hydraulic system. Bleed the system.
6   Insufficient pedal stroke. Check and adjust as necessary.
7   Piston seal in operating cylinder deformed or damaged.
8   Lack of grease on pilot bushing.

35   Clutch slips (engine speed increases with no increase in vehicle speed)

1   Worn or oil soaked clutch plate.
2   Clutch plate not broken in. It may take 30 or 40 normal starts for a new clutch to seat.
3   Diaphragm spring weak or damaged. Remove clutch cover/pressure plate assembly and inspect.
4   Flywheel warped.
5   Debris in master cylinder preventing the piston from returning to its normal position.
6   Clutch hydraulic line damaged.

36   Grabbing (chattering) as clutch is engaged

1   Oil on clutch plate. Remove and inspect. Repair any leaks.
2   Worn or loose engine or transmission mounts. They may move slightly when clutch is released. Inspect mounts and bolts.
3   Worn splines on transmission input shaft. Remove clutch components and inspect.
4   Warped pressure plate or flywheel. Remove clutch components and inspect.
5   Diaphragm spring fatigued. Remove clutch cover/pressure plate assembly and inspect.
6   Clutch linings hardened or warped.
7   Clutch lining rivets loose.

37   Squeal or rumble with clutch engaged (pedal released)

1   Improper pedal adjustment. Adjust pedal free play.
2   Release bearing binding on transmission shaft. Remove clutch components and check bearing. Remove any burrs or nicks, clean and relubricate before reinstallation.
3   Pilot bushing worn or damaged.
4   Clutch rivets loose.
5   Clutch plate cracked.
6   Fatigued clutch plate torsion springs. Replace clutch plate.

38   Squeal or rumble with clutch disengaged (pedal depressed)

1   Worn or damaged release bearing.
2   Worn or broken pressure plate diaphragm fingers.

39   Clutch pedal stays on floor when disengaged

Binding linkage or release bearing. Inspect linkage or remove clutch components as necessary.

Manual transmission

40   Noisy in Neutral with engine running

1   Input shaft bearing worn.
2   Damaged main drive gear bearing.
3   Insufficient transmission lubricant (Chapter 1).
4   Transmission oil in poor condition. Drain and fill with proper grade oil (Chapter 1). Check old oil for water and debris.
5   Noise can be caused by variations in engine torque. Change the idle speed and see if noise disappears.

41   Noisy in all gears

1   Any of the above causes, and/or:
2   Worn or damaged output gear bearings or shaft.

42   Noisy in one particular gear

1   Worn, damaged or chipped gear teeth.
2   Worn or damaged synchronizer.

43   Slips out of gear

1   Transmission loose on clutch housing.
2   Stiff shift lever seal.
3   Shift linkage binding.
4   Broken or loose input gear bearing retainer.
5   Dirt between clutch lever and engine housing.
6   Worn linkage.
7   Damaged or worn check balls, fork rod ball grooves or check springs.
8   Worn mainshaft or countershaft bearings.
9   Loose engine mounts (Chapter 2A, Chapter 2B, Chapter 2C, Chapter 2D, or Chapter 2E).
10   Excessive gear endplay.
11   Worn synchronizers.

44   Oil leaks

1   Excessive amount of lubricant in transmission (Chapter 1). Drain lubricant as required.
2   Rear oil seal or speedometer oil seal damaged.

3   To pinpoint a leak, first remove all built-up dirt and grime from the transmission. Degreasing agents and/or steam cleaning will achieve this. With the underside clean, drive the vehicle at low speeds so the air flow will not blow the leak far from its source. Raise the vehicle and determine where the leak is located.

45 Difficulty engaging gears

1   Clutch not releasing completely.
2   Loose or damaged shift linkage. Make a thorough inspection, replacing parts as necessary.
3   Insufficient transmission lubricant (Chapter 1).
4   Transmission oil in poor condition. Drain and fill with proper grade oil (Chapter 1) Check oil for water and debris.
5   Worn or damaged striking rod.
6   Sticking or jamming gears.

46 Noise occurs while shifting gears

1   Check for proper operation of the clutch (Chapter 8).
2   Faulty synchronizer assemblies. Measure baulk ring-to-gear clearance. Also, check for wear or damage to baulk rings or any parts of the synchromesh assemblies.

Automatic transmission

47 Fluid leakage

1   Automatic transmission fluid is a deep red color, and fluid leaks should not be confused with engine oil which can easily be blown by air flow to the transmission.
2   To pinpoint a leak, first remove all built-up dirt and grime from the transmission. Degreasing agents and/or steam cleaning will achieve this. With the underside clean, drive the vehicle at low speeds so the air flow will not blow the leak far from its source. Raise the vehicle and determine where the leak is located. Common areas of leakage are:

a) **Pan:** *Tighten the mounting bolts and/ or replace the pan gasket as necessary (Chapter 1).*
b) **Filler pipe:** *Replace the rubber seal where the pipe enters the transmission case.*
c) **Transmission oil lines:** *Tighten the connectors where the lines enter the transmission case and/or replace the lines.*
d) **Vent pipe:** *Transmission overfilled and/ or water in fluid (see checking procedures in Chapter 1).*

e) **Speedometer connector:** *Replace the O-ring where the speedometer sensor enters the transmission case (Chapter 12).*

48 General shift mechanism problems

1   Chapter 7B deals with checking and adjusting the shift linkage on automatic transmissions. Common problems which may be caused by out of adjustment linkage are:

a) *Engine starting in gears other than P (park) or N (Neutral).*
b) *Indicator pointing to a gear other than the one actually engaged.*
c) *Vehicle moves with transmission in P (Park) position.*

49 Transmission will not downshift with the accelerator pedal pressed to the floor

Chapter 7B deals with adjusting the TV linkage to enable the transmission to downshift properly.

50 Engine will start in gears other than Park or Neutral

Chapter 7B deals with adjusting the Neutral start switch installed on automatic transmissions.

51 Transmission slips, shifts rough, is noisy or has no drive in forward or reverse gears

1   There are many probable causes for the above problems, but the home mechanic should concern himself only with one possibility; fluid level.
2   Before taking the vehicle to a shop, check the fluid level and condition as described in Chapter 1. Add fluid, if necessary, or change the fluid and filter if needed. If problems persist, have a professional diagnose the transmission.

Driveshaft

52 Leaks at front of driveshaft

Defective transmission rear seal. See Chapter 7B or Chapter 7C for replacement procedure. As this is done, check the splined yoke for burrs or roughness that could damage the

new seal. Remove burrs with a fine file or whetstone.

53 Knock or clunk when transmission is under initial load (just after transmission is put into gear)

1   Loose or disconnected rear suspension components. Check all mounting bolts and bushings (Chapter 10).
2   Loose driveshaft bolts. Inspect all bolts and nuts and tighten them securely.
3   Worn or damaged universal joint bearings. Replace driveshaft.
4   Worn sleeve yoke and mainshaft spline.

54 Metallic grating sound consistent with vehicle speed

Pronounced wear in the universal joint bearings. Replace U-joints or driveshafts, as necessary.

55 Vibration

Note: *Before blaming the driveshaft, make sure the tires are perfectly balanced and perform the following test.*
1   Install a tachometer inside the vehicle to monitor engine speed as the vehicle is driven. Drive the vehicle and note the engine speed at which the vibration (roughness) is most pronounced. Now shift the transmission to a different gear and bring the engine speed to the same point.
2   If the vibration occurs at the same engine speed (rpm) regardless of which gear the transmission is in, the driveshaft is NOT at fault since the driveshaft speed varies.
3   If the vibration decreases or is eliminated when the transmission is in a different gear at the same engine speed, refer to the following probable causes.
4   Bent or dented driveshaft. Inspect and replace as necessary.
5   Undercoating or built-up dirt, etc. on the driveshaft. Clean the shaft thoroughly.
6   Worn universal joint bearings. Replace the U-joints or driveshaft as necessary.
7   Driveshaft and/or companion flange out of balance. Check for missing weights on the shaft. Remove driveshaft and reinstall 180-degrees from original position, then recheck. Have the driveshaft balanced if problem persists.
8   Loose driveshaft mounting bolts/nuts.
9   Defective center bearing, if so equipped.
10   Worn transmission rear bushing.

56 Scraping noise

Make sure the dust cover on the sleeve yoke isn't rubbing on the transmission extension housing.

57 Whining or whistling noise

Defective center bearing, if so equipped.

Axle and differential

58 Noise - same when in drive as when vehicle is coasting

1   Road noise. No corrective action available.
2   Tire noise. Inspect tires and check tire pressures (Chapter 1).
3   Front wheel bearings loose, worn or damaged (Chapter 8).
4   Insufficient differential lubricant (Chapter 1).
5   Defective differential.

59 Knocking sound when starting or shifting gears

Defective or incorrectly adjusted differential.

60 Noise when turning

Defective differential.

61 Vibration

See probable causes under Driveshaft. Proceed under the guidelines listed for the driveshaft. If the problem persists, check the rear wheel bearings by raising the rear of the vehicle and spinning the wheels by hand. Listen for evidence of rough (noisy) bearings. Remove and inspect (Chapter 8).

62 Oil leaks

1   Pinion oil seal damaged.
2   Axleshaft oil seals damaged.
3   Differential cover leaking. Tighten mounting bolts or replace the gasket as required (Chapter 1).
4   Loose filler or drain plug on differential.
5   Clogged or damaged breather on differential.

Transfer case

63 Gear jumping out of mesh

1   Incorrect control lever free play.
2   Interference between the control lever and the console.
3   Play or fatigue in the transfer case mounts.
4   Internal wear or incorrect adjustments.

64 Difficult shifting

1   Lack of oil.
2   Internal wear, damage or incorrect adjustment.

65 Noise

1   Lack of oil in transfer case.
2   Noise in 4H and 4L, but not in 2H indicates cause is in the front differential or front axle.
3   Noise in 2H, 4H and 4L indicates cause is in rear differential or rear axle.
4   Noise in 2H and 4H but not in 4L, or in 4L only, indicates internal wear or damage in transfer case.

Brakes

66 Vehicle pulls to one side during braking

1   Defective, damaged or oil contaminated brake pad on one side. Inspect as described in Chapter 1. Refer to Chapter 9 if replacement is required.
2   Excessive wear of brake pad material or disc on one side. Inspect and repair as necessary.
3   Loose or disconnected front suspension components. Inspect and tighten all bolts securely (Chapter 10).
4   Defective caliper assembly. Remove caliper and inspect for stuck piston or damage.
5   Brake pad to rotor adjustment needed. Inspect automatic adjusting mechanism for proper operation.
6   Scored or out of round rotor.
7   Loose caliper mounting bolts.
8   Incorrect wheel bearing adjustment (Chapter 8).

67 Noise (high-pitched squeal)

1   Front brake pads worn out. This noise comes from the wear sensor rubbing against the disc. Replace pads with new ones immediately!

2   Glazed or contaminated pads.
3   Dirty or scored rotor.
4   Bent support plate.

68 Excessive brake pedal travel

1   Partial brake system failure. Inspect entire system and correct as required.
2   Insufficient fluid in master cylinder. Check (Chapter 1) and add fluid - bleed system if necessary.
3   Air in system. Bleed system.
4   Excessive lateral rotor play.
5   Brakes out of adjustment. Check the operation of the automatic adjusters.
6   Defective proportioning valve. Replace valve and bleed system.

69 Brake pedal feels spongy when depressed

1   Air in brake lines. Bleed the brake system.
2   Deteriorated rubber brake hoses. Inspect all system hoses and lines. Replace parts as necessary.
3   Master cylinder mounting nuts loose. Inspect master cylinder bolts (nuts) and tighten them securely.
4   Master cylinder faulty.
5   Incorrect shoe or pad clearance.
6   Defective check valve. Replace valve and bleed system.
7   Clogged reservoir cap vent hole.
8   Deformed rubber brake lines.
9   Soft or swollen caliper seals.
10 Poor quality brake fluid. Bleed entire system and fill with new approved fluid.

70 Excessive effort required to stop vehicle

1   Power brake booster not operating properly.
2   Excessively worn linings or pads. Check and replace if necessary.
3   One or more caliper pistons seized or sticking. Inspect and rebuild as required.
4   Brake pads or linings contaminated with oil or grease. Inspect and replace as required.
5   New pads or linings installed and not yet seated. It'll take a while for the new material to seat against the rotor or drum.
6   Worn or damaged master cylinder or caliper assemblies. Check particularly for frozen pistons.

71 Pedal travels to the floor with little resistance

Little or no fluid in the master cylinder reservoir caused by leaking caliper piston(s) or loose, damaged or disconnected brake lines. Inspect entire system and repair as necessary.

72 Brake pedal pulsates during brake application

1 Wheel bearings damaged, worn or out of adjustment (Chapter 8).
2 Caliper not sliding properly due to improper installation or obstructions. Remove and inspect.
3 Rotor not within specifications. Remove the rotor and check for excessive lateral runout and parallelism. Have the rotors resurfaced or replace them with new ones. Also make sure that all rotors are the same thickness.
4 Out of round rear brake drums. Remove the drums and have them turned or replace them with new ones.

73 Brakes drag (indicated by sluggish engine performance or wheels being very hot after driving)

1 Output rod adjustment incorrect at the brake pedal.
2 Obstructed master cylinder compensator. Disassemble master cylinder and clean.
3 Master cylinder piston seized in bore. Overhaul master cylinder.
4 Caliper assembly in need of overhaul.
5 Brake pads or shoes worn out.
6 Piston cups in master cylinder or caliper assembly deformed. Overhaul master cylinder.
7 Disc not within specifications.
8 Parking brake assembly will not release.
9 Clogged brake lines.
10 Brake pedal height improperly adjusted.
11 Wheel cylinder piston frozen.
12 Improper shoe to drum clearance. Adjust as necessary.

74 Rear brakes lock up under light brake application

1 Tire pressures too high.
2 Tires excessively worn.

75 Rear brakes lock up under heavy brake application

1 Tire pressures too high.
2 Tires excessively worn.
3 Front brake pads contaminated with oil, mud or water. Clean or replace the pads.

4 Front brake pads excessively worn.
5 Defective master cylinder or caliper assembly.

Suspension and steering

76 Vehicle pulls to one side

1 Tire pressures uneven (Chapter 1).
2 Defective tire.
3 Excessive wear in suspension or steering components.
4 Front end alignment incorrect.
5 Front brakes dragging.
6 Wheel bearings improperly adjusted (Chapter 8).
7 Wheel lug nuts loose.

77 Shimmy, shake or vibration

1 Tire or wheel out of balance or out of round. Have them balanced on the vehicle.
2 Loose, worn or out of adjustment wheel bearings (Chapter 8).
3 Shock absorbers and/or suspension components worn or damaged.
4 Wheel lug nuts loose.
5 Incorrect tire pressures.
6 Excessively worn or damaged tire.
7 Loosely mounted steering gear housing.
8 Steering gear improperly adjusted.
9 Loose, worn or damaged steering components.
10 Damaged idler arm.
11 Worn balljoint.

78 Excessive pitching and/or rolling around corners or during braking

1 Defective shock absorbers. Replace as a set.
2 Broken or weak leaf springs and/or suspension components.
3 Worn or damaged stabilizer bar or bushings.

79 Wandering or general instability

1 Improper tire pressures.
2 Worn or out of adjustment wheel bearings (Chapter 8).
3 Incorrect front end alignment.
4 Worn or damaged steering linkage or suspension components.
5 Improperly adjusted steering gear.
6 Out of balance wheels.
7 Loose wheel lug nuts.
8 Worn rear shock absorbers.
9 Fatigued or damaged rear leaf springs.

80 Excessively stiff steering

1 Lack of lubricant in power steering fluid reservoir (Chapter 1).
2 Incorrect tire pressures (Chapter 1).
3 Lack of lubrication at balljoints (Chapter 1).
4 Front end out of alignment.
5 Steering gear out of adjustment or lacking lubrication.
6 Improperly adjusted wheel bearings.
7 Worn or damaged steering gear.
8 Interference of steering column with turn signal switch.
9 Low tire pressures.
10 Worn or damaged balljoints.
11 Worn or damaged steering linkage.

81 Excessive play in steering

1 Loose wheel bearings (Chapter 8).
2 Excessive wear in suspension bushings.
3 Steering gear improperly adjusted.
4 Incorrect front end alignment.
5 Steering gear mounting bolts loose.
6 Worn steering linkage.

82 Lack of power assistance

1 Steering pump drivebelt faulty or not adjusted properly (Chapter 1).
2 Fluid level low (Chapter 1).
3 Hoses or pipes restricting the flow. Inspect and replace parts as necessary.
4 Air in power steering system. Bleed system.
5 Defective power steering pump.

83 Steering wheel fails to return to straight-ahead position

1 Incorrect front end alignment.
2 Tire pressures low.
3 Steering gears improperly engaged.
4 Steering column out of alignment.
5 Worn or damaged balljoint.
6 Worn or damaged steering linkage.
7 Improperly lubricated idler arm.
8 Insufficient oil in steering gear.
9 Lack of fluid in power steering pump.

84 Steering effort not the same in both directions (power system)

1 Leaks in steering gear.
2 Clogged fluid passage in steering gear.

85 Noisy power steering pump

1 Insufficient oil in pump.
2 Clogged hoses or oil filter in pump.
3 Loose pulley.
4 Improperly adjusted drivebelt (Chapter 1).
5 Defective pump.

86 Miscellaneous noises

1 Improper tire pressures.
2 Insufficiently lubricated balljoint or steering linkage.
3 Loose or worn steering gear, steering linkage or suspension components.
4 Defective shock absorber.
5 Defective wheel bearing.
6 Worn or damaged suspension bushings.
7 Damaged leaf spring.
8 Loose wheel lug nuts.
9 Worn or damaged rear axleshaft spline.
10 Worn or damaged rear shock absorber mounting bushing.
11 Incorrect rear axle endplay.
12 See also causes of noises at the rear axle and driveshaft.

87 Excessive tire wear (not specific to one area)

1 Incorrect tire pressures.
2 Tires out of balance. Have them balanced on the vehicle.
3 Wheels damaged. Inspect and replace as necessary.
4 Suspension or steering components worn.

88 Excessive tire wear on outside edge

1 Incorrect tire pressure.
2 Excessive speed in turns.
3 Front end alignment incorrect (excessive toe-in).

89 Excessive tire wear on inside edge

1 Incorrect tire pressure.
2 Front end alignment incorrect (toe-out).
3 Loose or damaged steering components.

90 Tire tread worn in one place

1 Tires out of balance. Have them balanced on the vehicle.
2 Damaged or buckled wheel. Inspect and replace if necessary.
3 Defective tire.

Chapter 1
Tune-up and routine maintenance

Contents

Specifications

Recommended lubricants and fluids

Note: *Listed here are manufacturer recommendations at the time this manual was written. Manufacturers occasionally upgrade their fluid and lubricant specifications, so check with your local auto parts store for current recommendations.*

Engine oil
  Type .... API grade "certified for gasoline engines"
  Viscosity

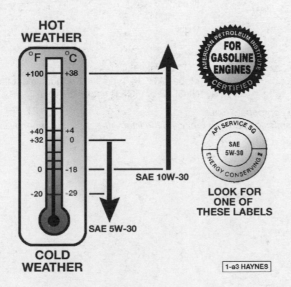

ENGINE OIL VISCOSITY

For best fuel economy and cold starting, select the lowest SAE viscosity grade oil for the expected temperature range

1-a3 HAYNES

Recommended lubricants and fluids (continued)

Four-cylinder engines and 4.2L inline six cylinder engines	
Below 32-degrees F	SAE 5W-30
Above 32-degrees F	SAE 10W-30
4.0L inline six-cylinder engines	SAE 10W-30
3.6L V6 engine	SAE 5W-30
3.8L V6 engine	SAE 5W-20
Capacity (with new oil filter)*	
Four-cylinder engines	4 qts
Six-cylinder engines	6 qts
Manual transmission lubricant	
Type	
AX-4, AX-5, AX-15	
1997 and earlier models	SAE 75/90W GL-5 gear lubricant
1998 and later models	SAE 75/90W GL-3 gear lubricant
NV1500	Mopar, manual transmission lubricant
NV3550 and NSG370 six-speed	Mopar, manual transmission lubricant
Capacity*	
AX-4/5 and AX-15	3.5 qts
NV1500	4.8 pts
NV3550 and NSG370 six-speed	4.2 pts
Automatic transmission fluid	
Type	
2000 and earlier models	Mopar ATF Plus +3 type 7126 or equivalent fluid
2001 and later models	Mopar ATF Plus +4 type 9602 or equivalent fluid
Capacity (drain and refill**)	4 qts
Transfer case lubricant	
Type	Mopar, ATF Plus+4, type 9602 or equivalent fluid
Capacity (approximate)*	
NP 207	4.5 pints
NP 231	3 pints
NP 241	4 pints
NP242	
2006 and earlier models	3 pints
2007 and later models	
Model 30	2.1 pints
Model 44	2.7 pints
Differential lubricant type	
Normal operation	SAE 75W-90 API GL-5 gear lubricant
Trailer towing or severe service	SAE 75W-140 synthetic gear lubricant
Limited-slip differential	Include 4 oz. (188 ml) of Mopar, Friction Modifier additive
Coolant	
Type	
2000 and earlier models	50-percent distilled or deionized water and 50-percent ethylene glycol-based antifreeze
2001 and later models	50-percent distilled or deionized water and 50-percent Mopar, 100,000 mile Antifreeze/coolant with Hybrid Organic technology (HOAT) additives
Capacity*	
Four-cylinder engines	9 qts
Six-cylinder engines	10.5 qts
3.8L V6 engines, 2007 and later	13 quarts
Brake fluid type	DOT 3 brake fluid
Power steering fluid	Mopar, ATF +4 Type 9602 or equivalent fluid
Chassis grease type	NLGI LB or GC-LB chassis grease

All capacities approximate. Add as necessary to bring to appropriate level.

** This is the approximate capacity when draining the transmission pan and replacing the filter. After overhaul, when filling the transmission from "dry," the capacity will be much higher.

Tune-up information

Spark plug type and gap
  2.5L four-cylinder engine
    Type
      1987 through 1998 .... Champion RC12YLC or equivalent
      1999 through 2002 .... Champion RE12ECC pr equivalent
    Gap .... 0.035 inch
  2.4L four-cylinder engine
    Type
      2003 and 2004 .... Champion RE14MCC5 or equivalent
      2005 and 2006 .... Champion RE16MC or equivalent
    Gap
      2003 and 2004 .... 0.048 to 0.053 inch
      2005 and 2006 .... 0.037 to 0.042 inch
  4.2L inline six-cylinder engine
    Type .... Champion RFN14LY or equivalent
    Gap .... 0.035 inch
  4.0L inline six-cylinder engine
    1991 through 1998
      Type .... Champion RC12LYC or equivalent
      Gap .... 0.035 inch
    1999 through 2002
      Type .... Champion RE12ECC or equivalent
      Gap .... 0.035 inch
    2003 through 2006
      Type .... NGK ZFR5N or equivalent
      Gap .... 0.040 inch
  3.8L V6 engine
    Type .... Champion RF14PLP5 or equivalent
    Gap .... 0.048 to 0.053 inch
  3.6L V6 engine
    Type .... Champion RER8ZYCB4 or equivalent
    Gap .... 0.043 inch
Firing order
  Four-cylinder engines 1-3-4-2
  Inline six-cylinder engines 1-5-3-6-2-4
  V6 engines 1-2-3-4-5-6
Cylinder numbers .... See accompanying illustrations
Ignition timing (carbureted models only)* .... 9 to 11-degrees BTDC
Engine idle speed (carbureted models only)*
  Manual transmission .... 680 plus or minus 70 rpm
  Automatic transmission .... 600 plus or minus 70 rpm
*The Vehicle Emission Control Information label in the engine compartment, if different, supersedes this information.

Brakes

Disc brake pad lining thickness (minimum) 1/8-inch
Drum brake shoe lining thickness (minimum)
  Bonded shoes 1/16-inch
  Riveted shoes (thickness above rivets).................... 1/32-inch

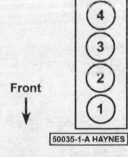

2.4L four-cylinder engine

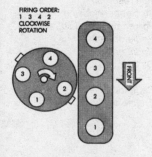

2.5L four-cylinder engine

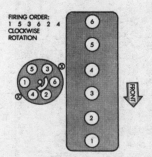

Inline six-cylinder engines

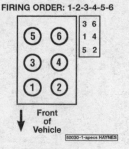

3.8L V6 engine

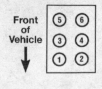

3.6L V6 engine

Torque specifications

Ft-lbs (unless otherwise indicated)

Note: *One foot-pound (ft-lb) of torque is equivalent to 12 inch-pounds (in-lbs) of torque. Torque values below approximately 15 foot-pounds are expressed in inch-pounds, because most foot-pound torque wrenches are not accurate at these smaller values.*

Oil filter housing cap (3.6L V6 engine)	103 in-lbs
Automatic transmission	
Filter screws	
30RH and 32RH	35 in-lbs
42RLE	45 in-lbs
Pan bolts	14
Carburetor/throttle body mounting nuts/bolts	14
Rear differential cover bolts...	30
Front differential cover bolts...	30
Differential drain plug...	25
Transfer case fill/drain plug..	20
Manual transmission fill/drain plug	
AX-4/5	32.5
AX-1500	25
NV3550	14 to 20
Spark plugs	
2.4L four-cylinder engine..	132 in-lbs
2.5L four-cylinder engine	
1990 and earlier models	20
1991 through 2002 models	27
4.2L inline six cylinder engine	30
4.0L inline six-cylinder engine	27
3.6L and 3.8L V6 engines	156 in-lbs
Engine oil drain plug	
All except V6 engines..	25
3.6L and 3.8L V6 engines	20
Oxygen sensor	22
Wheel lug nuts	
2008 and earlier models..	80 to 110
2009 through 2011 models...	92 to 132
2012 and later models...	95

2.1a Engine compartment component checking points (2.5L four-cylinder engine shown)

1   *Distributor cap and wires*
2   *PVC valve*
3   *Brake fluid reservoir*
4   *Clutch fluid reservoir*
5   *Coolant reservoir*
6   *Windshield washer fluid reservoir*
7   *Air cleaner housing*
8   *Power steering fluid reservoir*
9   *Radiator cap*
10 *Radiator*
11 *Oil filler cap*
12 *Drivebelt*
13 *Radiator hose*
14 *Engine oil dipstick*
15 *Battery*

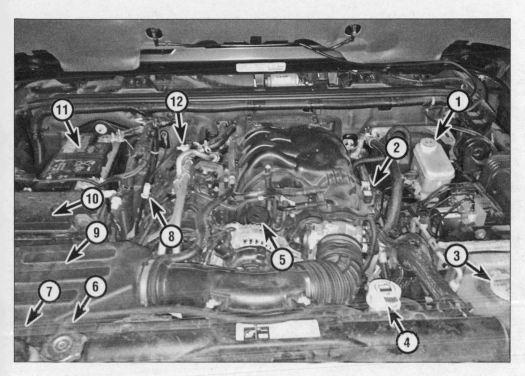

2.1b Engine compartment checking points (2012 and later 3.6L V6 engine)

1　Brake fluid reservoir
2　Oil filler cap
3　Windshield washer fluid reservoir
4　Coolant reservoir
5　Oil filter housing
6　Radiator cap
7　Power steering fluid reservoir
8　Engine oil dipstick
9　Air filter housing
10　Engine compartment fuse/relay box (Totally Integrated Power Module - TIPM)
11　Battery
12　Automatic transmission fluid dipstick

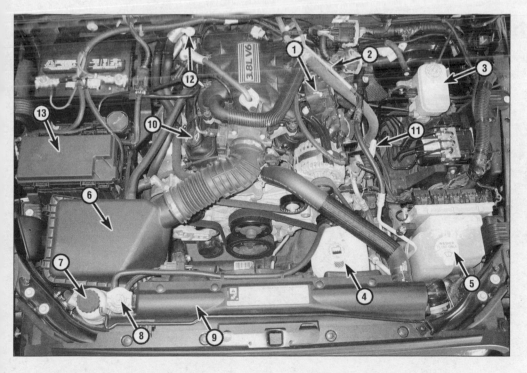

2.1c Engine compartment checking points (2007 through 2011 3.8L V6 engine)

1　Ignition coil-pack
2　PCV valve (rear of coil)
3　Brake fluid reservoir
4　Coolant reservoir
5　Windshield washer fluid reservoir
6　Air filter housing
7　Power steering fluid reservoir
8　Radiator cap
9　Radiator
10　Oil filler cap
11　Engine oil dipstick
12　Automatic transmission fluid dipstick
13　Engine compartment fuse/relay box

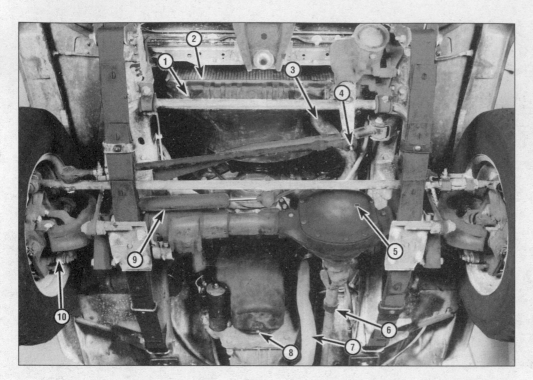

2.1d Typical engine compartment underside components (1987 through 1996 models)

1 Radiator drain fitting
2 Radiator
3 Radiator hose
4 Steering grease fitting
5 Differential check plug
6 Front driveshaft grease fitting
7 Exhaust pipe
8 Engine oil drain plug
9 Steering damper
10 Disc brake caliper

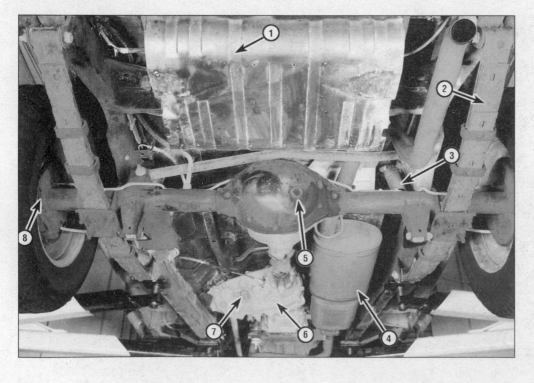

2.1e Typical rear underside vehicle components (1987 through 1996 models)

1 Fuel tank skid plate
2 Leaf spring
3 Shock absorber
4 Exhaust system
5 Differential check plug
6 Transfer case
7 Transfer case check plug
8 Drum brake

2.1f Typical engine compartment underside component locations (1997 and later models)

1 Steering damper
2 Steering grease fitting
3 Differential check/fill plug
4 Driveaxle boot (4WD models)
5 Driveshaft grease fitting (4WD models)
6 Automatic transmission fluid pan
7 Engine oil pan
8 Exhaust system
9 Brake caliper

2.1g Typical rear underside component locations (1997 and later models)

1 Brake caliper
2 Differential check/fill plug
3 Rear shock absorber
4 Exhaust system
5 Driveshaft universal joint

1 Jeep Wrangler Maintenance schedule

1   The following maintenance intervals are based on the assumption that the vehicle owner will be doing the maintenance or service work, as opposed to having a dealer service department do the work. Although the time/mileage intervals are loosely based on factory recommendations, most have been shortened to ensure, for example, that such items as lubricants and fluids are checked/changed at intervals that promote maximum engine/driveline service life. Also, subject to the preference of the individual owner interested in keeping his or her vehicle in peak condition at all times, and with the vehicle's ultimate resale in mind, many of the maintenance procedures may be performed more often than recommended in the following schedule. We encourage such owner initiative.

2   When the vehicle is new it should be serviced initially by a factory authorized dealer service department to protect the factory warranty. In many cases the initial maintenance check is done at no cost to the owner (check with your dealer service department for more information).

Every 250 miles or weekly, whichever comes first

Check the engine oil level (Section 4)
Check the engine coolant level (Section 4)
Check the windshield washer fluid level (Section 4)
Check the brake and clutch fluid levels (Section 4)
Check the tires and tire pressures (Section 5)

Every 3000 miles or 3 months, whichever comes first

Check the automatic transmission fluid level (Section 6)
Check the power steering fluid level (Section 7)
Check and service the battery (Section 8)
Check the cooling system (Section 9)
Inspect and replace, if necessary, all underhood hoses (Section 10)
Inspect and replace, if necessary, the windshield wiper blades (Section 11)

Every 7500 miles or 12 months, whichever comes first

Change the engine oil and filter (Section 12)*
Lubricate the chassis components (Section 13)
Inspect the suspension and steering components (Section 14)*
Inspect the exhaust system (Section 15)*
Check the manual transmission lubricant level (Section 16)*
Check the differential lubricant level (Section 17)*
Check the transfer case lubricant level (Section 17)
Rotate the tires (Section 19)
Check the brakes (Section 20)*
Inspect the fuel system (Section 21)
Check the carburetor choke operation (Section 22)
Check the carburetor/throttle body mounting nut torque (Section 23)
Check the throttle linkage (Section 24)
Check the thermostatically-controlled air cleaner (Section 25)
Check the engine drivebelts (Section 26)
Check the seatbelts (Section 27)
Check the starter safety switch (Section 28)
Check the spare tire and jack (Section 29)

Every 30,000 miles or 24 months, whichever comes first

Check and adjust, if necessary, the engine idle speed (Section 30)
Replace the fuel filter (1987 through 1995 models only) (Section 31)
Replace the air and PCV filters (Section 32)
Check and adjust, if necessary, the ignition timing (Section 33)
Change the automatic transmission fluid (Section 34)**
Change the manual transmission lubricant (Section 35)
Change the differential lubricant (Section 36)
Change the transfer case lubricant (Section 37)
Service the cooling system (drain, flush and refill) (Section 38)
Inspect and replace, if necessary, the PCV valve (Section 39)
Inspect the evaporative emissions control system (Section 40)
Replace the spark plugs (Section 41)
Inspect the spark plug wires, distributor cap and rotor (2003 and earlier models) (Section 42)

Every 82,500 miles or 82 months, whichever comes first

Replace the oxygen sensor and emissions timer (49-state models) (Section 43)
Inspect and replace, if necessary, all underhood hoses

* This item is affected by "severe" operating conditions as described below. If your vehicle is operated under severe conditions, perform all maintenance indicated with an asterisk (*) at 3000 miles/3 month intervals.

a) In dusty areas
b) Off road use
c) Towing a trailer
d) Idling for extended periods an/or low speed operation
e) When outside temperatures remain below freezing and most trips are less than four miles

** If operated under one or more of the following conditions, change the automatic transmission fluid every 12,000 miles:

a) In heavy city traffic where the outside temperature regularly reaches 90-degrees F (32-degrees C) or higher
b) In hilly or mountainous terrain
c) Frequent trailer pulling
d) Frequent off road use

2   Introduction

1   This Chapter is designed to help the home mechanic maintain the Jeep Wrangler with the goals of maximum performance, economy, safety and reliability in mind. Included is a master maintenance schedule (see the previous page) followed by procedures dealing specifically with each item on the schedule. Visual checks, adjustments, component replacement and other helpful items are included. Refer to the accompanying illustrations of the engine compartment and the underside of the vehicle for the locations of various components.

2   Servicing your vehicle in accordance with the mileage/time maintenance schedule and the step-by-step procedures will result in a planned maintenance program that should produce a long and reliable service life. Keep in mind that it is a comprehensive plan, so maintaining some items but not others at the specified intervals will not produce the same results.

3   As you service your vehicle, you will discover that many of the procedures can - and should - be grouped together because of the nature of the particular procedure you're performing or because of the close proximity of two otherwise unrelated components to one another.

4   For example, if the vehicle is raised for chassis lubrication, you should inspect the exhaust, suspension, steering and fuel systems while you're under the vehicle. When you're rotating the tires, it makes good sense to check the brakes since the wheels are already removed. Finally, let's suppose you have to borrow or rent a torque wrench. Even if you only need it to tighten the spark plugs, you might as well check the torque of as many critical fasteners as time allows.

5   The first step in this maintenance program is to prepare yourself before the actual work begins. Read through all the procedures you're planning to do, then gather up all the parts and tools needed. If it looks like you might run into problems during a particular job, seek advice from a mechanic or an experienced do-it-yourselfer.

3   Tune-up general information

1   The term tune-up is used in this manual to represent a combination of individual operations rather than one specific procedure.

2   If, from the time the vehicle is new, the routine maintenance schedule is followed closely and frequent checks are made of fluid levels and high wear items, as suggested throughout this manual, the engine will be kept in relatively good running condition and the need for additional work will be minimized.

3   More likely than not, however, there will be times when the engine is running poorly due to lack of regular maintenance. This is even more likely if a used vehicle, which has not received regular and frequent maintenance checks, is purchased. In such cases, an engine tune-up will be needed outside of the regular routine maintenance intervals.

4   The first step in any tune-up or diagnostic procedure to help correct a poor running engine is a cylinder compression check. A compression check (see Chapter 2F) will help determine the condition of internal engine components and should be used as a guide for tune-up and repair procedures. If, for instance, a compression check indicates serious internal engine wear, a conventional tune-up will not improve the performance of the engine and would be a waste of time and money. Because of its importance, the compression check should be done by someone with the right equipment and the knowledge to use it properly.

5   The following procedures are those most often needed to bring a generally poor running engine back into a proper state of tune.

Minor tune-up

6   Check all engine related fluids (Section 4)
7   Clean, inspect and test the battery (Section 8)
8   Check and adjust the drivebelts (Section 26)
9   Replace the spark plugs (Section 41)
10   Inspect the distributor cap and rotor (2003 and earlier models) (Section 42)
11   Inspect the spark plug and coil wires (Section 42)
12   Check and adjust the ignition timing (Section 33)
13   Check the PCV valve (Section 39)
14   Check the air and PCV filters (Section 39)
15   Check the cooling system (Section 38)
16   Check all underhood hoses (Section 10)

Major tune-up

17   Check the ignition system (Chapter 5)
18   Check the charging system (Chapter 5)
19   Check the fuel system (Section 21)
20   Replace the air and PCV filters (Section 32)
21   Replace the distributor cap and rotor (2003 and earlier models) (Section 42)
22   Replace the spark plug wires (Section 42)

4   Fluid level checks

Note: *The following are fluid level checks to be done on a 250 mile or weekly basis. Additional fluid level checks can be found in specific maintenance procedures which follow. Regardless of intervals, be alert to fluid leaks under the vehicle which would indicate a fault to be corrected immediately.*

1   Fluids are an essential part of the lubrication, cooling, brake, clutch and windshield washer systems. Because the fluids gradually become depleted and/or contaminated during normal operation of the vehicle, they must be periodically replenished. See *Recommended lubricants and fluids* at the beginning of this Chapter before adding fluid to any of the following components.

Note: *The vehicle must be on level ground when fluid levels are checked.*

Engine oil

2   The engine oil level is checked with a dipstick that extends through a tube and into the oil pan at the bottom of the engine.

3   The oil level should be checked before the vehicle has been driven, or about 5 minutes after the engine has been shut off. If the oil is checked immediately after driving the vehicle, some of the oil will remain in the upper engine components, resulting in an inaccurate reading on the dipstick.

4   Pull the dipstick from the tube and wipe all the oil from the end with a clean rag or paper towel. Insert the clean dipstick all the way back into the tube, then pull it out again. Note the oil at the end of the dipstick. Add oil as necessary to keep the level between the ADD mark and the FULL mark on the dipstick (see illustration).

5   Do not overfill the engine by adding too much oil since this may result in oil fouled spark plugs, oil leaks or oil seal failures.

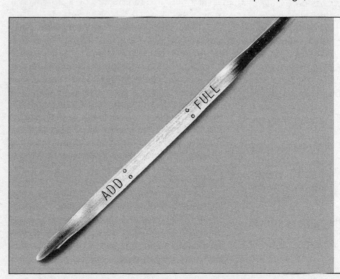

4.4 The oil level should be at or near the FULL mark on the dipstick - if it isn't, add enough oil to bring the level to or near the FULL mark (it takes about one quart to raise the level from ADD to FULL)

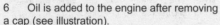

4.6 The twist-off oil filler cap is located on the valve cover - always makes sure the area around this opening is clean before unscrewing the cap to prevent dirt from contaminating the engine

4.8 The coolant reservoir allows for contraction and expansion of the coolant - it can be checked visually with the engine hot or cold

4.14 The windshield washer fluid reservoir is located on the driver's side of the engine compartment - keep the level at or near the FULL line; fluid can be added after flipping up the cap

6   Oil is added to the engine after removing a cap (see illustration).

7   Checking the oil level is an important preventive maintenance step. A consistently low oil level indicates oil leakage through damaged seals, defective gaskets or past worn rings or valve guides. If the oil looks milky in color or has water droplets in it, the cylinder head gasket(s) may be blown or the head(s) or block may be cracked. The engine should be checked immediately. The condition of the oil should also be checked. Whenever you check the oil level, slide your thumb and index finger up the dipstick before wiping off the oil. If you see small dirt or metal particles clinging to the dipstick, the oil should be changed (see Section 12).

Engine coolant

Warning: *Do not allow antifreeze to come in contact with your skin or painted surfaces of the vehicle. Rinse off spills immediately with plenty of water. Antifreeze is highly toxic if ingested. Never leave antifreeze lying around in open containers or in puddles on the floor; children and pets are attracted by its sweet smell and may drink it. Check with local authorities about disposing of used antifreeze. Many communities have collection centers which will see that antifreeze is disposed of safely.*

8   All vehicles covered by this manual are equipped with a pressurized coolant recovery system. A white plastic coolant reserve or pressure bottle located on the driver's side of the engine compartment is connected by a hose to the radiator or radiator filler neck (see illustration). If the engine overheats, coolant escapes through a valve in the radiator cap and travels through the hose into the reservoir. As the engine cools, the coolant is automatically drawn back into the cooling system to maintain the correct level.

9   The coolant level in the reservoir should be checked regularly.

Warning: *Do not remove the radiator cap to check the coolant level when the engine is warm. The coolant level in the reservoir should be kept between the FULL and ADD marks on the side of the reservoir. If it is necessary to add coolant, allow the engine to cool, then remove the cap from the reservoir and add a 50/50 mixture of ethylene glycol-based antifreeze and water.*

10   Drive the vehicle and recheck the coolant level. If only a small amount of coolant is required to bring the system up to the proper level, water can be used. However, repeated additions of water will dilute the antifreeze and water solution. In order to maintain the proper ratio of antifreeze and water, always top up the coolant level with the correct mixture. An empty plastic milk jug or bleach bottle makes an excellent container for mixing coolant. Do not use rust inhibitors or additives.

11   If the coolant level drops consistently, there may be a leak in the system. Inspect the radiator, hoses, filler cap, drain plugs and water pump. If no leaks are noted, have the radiator cap pressure tested by a service station.

12   If you have to remove the radiator cap, wait until the engine has cooled, then wrap a thick cloth around the cap and turn it to the first stop. If coolant or steam escapes, let the engine cool down longer, then remove the cap.

13   Check the condition of the coolant as well. It should be relatively clear. If it's brown or rust colored, the system should be drained, flushed and refilled. Even if the coolant appears to be normal, the corrosion inhibitors wear out, so it must be replaced at the specified intervals.

Windshield washer fluid

14   Fluid for the windshield washer system is located in a plastic reservoir in the engine compartment (see illustration).

15   In milder climates, plain water can be

used in the reservoir, but it should be kept no more than 2/3 full to allow for expansion if the water freezes. In colder climates, use windshield washer system antifreeze, available at any auto parts store, to lower the freezing point of the fluid. Mix the antifreeze with water in accordance with the manufacturer's directions on the container.

Caution: *Don't use cooling system antifreeze - it will damage the vehicle's paint.*

16   To help prevent icing in cold weather, warm the windshield with the defroster before using the washer.

Battery electrolyte

17   All vehicles with which this manual is concerned are equipped with a battery which is permanently sealed (except for vent holes) and has no filler caps. Water doesn't have to be added to these batteries at any time. If a maintenance-type battery is installed, the caps on the top of the battery should be removed periodically to check for a low water level. This check is most critical during the warm summer months.

Brake and clutch fluid

18   The brake master cylinder is mounted on the front of the power booster unit in the engine compartment. The clutch master cylinder used on manual transmissions is mounted adjacent to it on the firewall (see illustration). The reservoir is translucent plastic so the fluid level can be checked visually. To add fluid, you'll have to loosen the nuts and swing the radiator grille support rod out of the way (see illustrations). Be sure to tighten the bolt and nuts securely when you are finished.

19   On early models, use a screwdriver to pry the brake fluid reservoir clip free; then remove the cover (see illustrations). Be sure to wipe the top of the reservoir caps or cover with a clean rag to prevent contamination of the brake and/or clutch system before removing the caps or cover.

4.18a The clutch master cylinder is located next to the brake booster - maintain the fluid level between the MAX and MIN marks; you'll have to move the grille support rod to add fluid by first loosening the bolt...

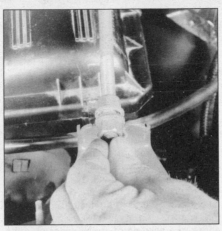

4.18b ... then these nuts and swing the radiator grille support rod out of the way...

4.18c ... so you can remove the cap and add fluid to the clutch reservoir - be sure to tighten everything securely afterward

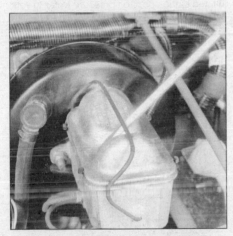

4.19a Pry the clip off the brake master cylinder cover with a screwdriver (non-ABS models)

4.19b The brake fluid level should be kept 1/4-inch below the top edge of the reservoir

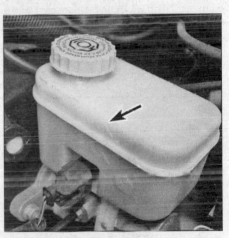

4.21 Brake fluid level, indicated on the translucent white plastic brake fluid reservoir, should be kept at the upper (MAX) mark

20   On early ABS-equipped models and all later models, a plastic brake fluid reservoir is located on top of the brake master cylinder on the driver's side of the engine compartment near the firewall.

21   On models with a plastic fluid reservoir, the fluid level should be maintained at the upper (FULL or MAX) mark on reservoir (see illustration).

22   When adding fluid, remove the cap(s) and pour it carefully into the reservoir to avoid spilling it onto surrounding painted surfaces. Be sure the specified fluid is used, since mixing different types of brake fluid can cause damage to the system. See *Recommended lubricants and fluids* at the front of this Chapter or your owner's manual.

Warning: *Brake fluid can harm your eyes and damage painted surfaces, so use extreme caution when handling or pouring it. Do not use brake fluid that has been standing open*

or is more than one year old. Brake fluid absorbs moisture from the air. Excess moisture can cause a dangerous loss of braking effectiveness.

23   At this time the fluid and master cylinder can be inspected for contamination. The system should be drained and refilled if deposits, dirt particles or water droplets are seen in the fluid.

24   After filling the reservoir to the proper level, make sure the cover or cap is on tight to prevent fluid leakage. Push the rubber gasket on the brake fluid cover up before reinstalling it so it doesn't hang down and cause the fluid to gush out.

25   The brake fluid level in the brake master cylinder will drop slightly as the pads and the brake shoes at each wheel wear down during normal operation. If the master cylinder requires repeated additions to keep it at the proper level, it's an indication of leakage in

the brake system, which should be corrected immediately. Check all brake lines and connections (see Section 20 for more information).

26   If, upon checking the master cylinder fluid level, you discover one or both reservoirs empty or nearly empty, the brake system should be bled (see Chapter 9).

5   Tire and tire pressure checks

1   Periodic inspection of the tires may spare you the inconvenience of being stranded with a flat tire. It can also provide you with vital information regarding possible problems in the steering and suspension systems before major damage occurs.

2   The original tires on this vehicle are equipped with 1/2-inch wide bands that will appear when tread depth reaches 1/16-inch,

5.2 Use a tire tread depth indicator to monitor tire wear - they are available at auto parts stores and service stations and cost very little

at which point the tires can be considered worn out. Tread wear can be monitored with a simple, inexpensive device known as a tread depth indicator (see illustration).

3   Note any abnormal tread wear (see illustration). Tread pattern irregularities such as cupping, flat spots and more wear on one side than the other are indications of front end alignment and/or balance problems. If any of these conditions are noted, take the vehicle to a tire shop or service station to correct the problem.

4   Look closely for cuts, punctures and embedded nails or tacks. Sometimes a tire will hold air pressure for a short time or leak down very slowly after a nail has embedded itself in the tread. If a slow leak persists, check the valve stem core to make sure it's tight (see illustration). Examine the tread for an object that may have embedded itself in the tire or for a "plug" that may have begun to leak (radial tire punctures are repaired with a plug that's installed in a puncture). If a puncture is suspected, it can be easily verified by spraying a solution of soapy water onto the puncture area (see illustration). The soapy solution will bubble if there's a leak. Unless the puncture is unusually large, a tire shop or service station can usually repair the tire.

5   Carefully inspect the inner sidewall of each tire for evidence of brake fluid leakage. If you see any, inspect the brakes immediately.

6   Correct air pressure adds miles to the lifespan of the tires, improves mileage and enhances overall ride quality. Tire pressure cannot be accurately estimated by looking at a tire, especially if it's a radial. The correct tire pressures are located on a label on the inside of the glove box door. A tire pressure gauge is essential. Keep an accurate gauge in the vehicle. The pressure gauges attached to the nozzles of air hoses at gas stations are often inaccurate.

7   Always check tire pressure when the tires are cold. Cold, in this case, means the vehicle has not been driven over a mile in the three hours preceding a tire pressure check. A pressure rise of four to eight pounds is not uncommon once the tires are warm.

8   Unscrew the valve cap protruding from the wheel or hubcap and push the gauge firmly onto the valve stem (see illustration). Note the reading on the gauge and compare the figure to the recommended tire pressure shown on the placard on the driver's side door pillar. Be sure to reinstall the valve cap to keep dirt and moisture out of the valve stem mechanism. Check all four tires and, if necessary, add enough air to bring them up to the recommended pressure.

9   Don't forget to keep the spare tire inflated to the specified pressure (refer to your owner's manual or the tire sidewall). Note that the pressure recommended for the compact spare is higher than for the tires on the vehicle.

UNDERINFLATION

CUPPING

Cupping may be caused by:
- Underinflation and/or mechanical irregularities such as out-of-balance condition of wheel and/or tire, and bent or damaged wheel.
- Loose or worn steering tie-rod or steering idler arm.
- Loose, damaged or worn front suspension parts.

OVERINFLATION

INCORRECT TOE-IN OR EXTREME CAMBER

FEATHERING DUE TO MISALIGNMENT

5.3 This chart will help you determine the condition of the tires, the probable cause(s) of abnormal wear and the corrective action necessary

5.4a If a tire loses air on a steady basis, check the valve core first to make sure it's snug (special inexpensive wrenches are commonly available at auto parts stores)

5.4b If the valve core is tight, raise the corner of the vehicle with the low tire and spray a soapy solution onto the tread as the tire is turned slowly - leaks will cause small bubbles to appear

5.8 To extend the life of the tires, check the air pressure at least once a week with an accurate gauge (don't forget the spare!)

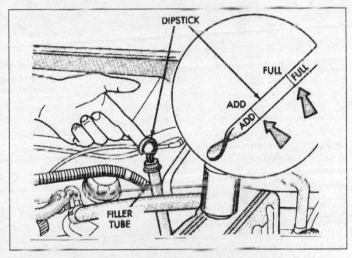

6.6 The automatic transmission dipstick is located in the long tube at the rear of the engine compartment on the passenger's side

6 Automatic transmission fluid level check

1   The automatic transmission fluid level should be carefully maintained. Low fluid level can lead to slipping or loss of drive, while overfilling can cause foaming and loss of fluid.

2   Warm the transmission by driving the vehicle at least 15 miles. With the parking brake set, start the engine, then move the shift lever through all the gear ranges, ending in Neutral. The fluid level must be checked with the vehicle level and the engine running at idle.

2011 and earlier models

3   With the transmission at normal operating temperature, remove the dipstick from the filler tube. The dipstick is located at the rear of the engine compartment, near the firewall on the passenger's side.

4   Wipe the fluid from the dipstick with a clean rag and push it back into the filler tube until the cap seats.

5   Pull the dipstick out again and note the fluid level.

6   The level should be between the ADD and FULL marks (see illustration). If additional fluid is required, add it directly into the tube using a funnel. It takes about one pint to raise the level from the ADD mark to the FULL mark with a warm transmission, so add the fluid a little at a time and keep checking the level until it's correct.

7   The condition of the fluid should also be checked along with the level. If the fluid at the end of the dipstick is a dark reddish-brown color, or if it smells burned, it should be changed. If you are in doubt about the condition of the fluid, purchase some new fluid and compare the two for color and smell.

2012 and later models

Note: *These models require the use of a scan tool to check transmission fluid temperature and special tool #9336A to measure the fluid level. If you do not have both tools to make the proper temperature-to-fluid level comparisons, we do not recommend attempting this procedure.*

8   Make sure the vehicle is parked on a level area.

Warning: *Be sure to set the parking brake and block the front wheels to prevent the vehicle from moving when the engine is running.*

9   Apply the parking brake, start the engine and allow it to idle for a minute, then move the shift lever through each gear position, ending in Park or Neutral.

10   Allow the transmission to warm up, waiting at least two minutes, then remove the dipstick tube cap.

11   Insert the tool into the dipstick tube until

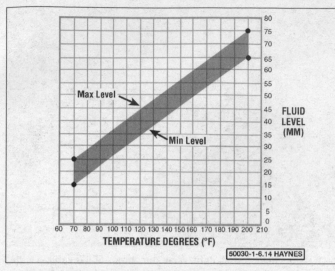

6.14 Transmission fluid level-to-temperature indexing chart

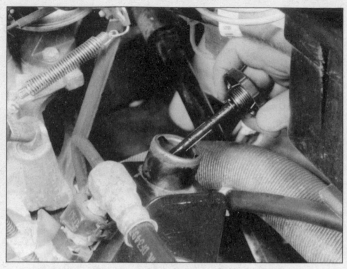

7.5 Twist the cap counterclockwise and lift it out of the reservoir - 3.6L model shown

the tip of the tool contacts the oil pan then pull it out. It may be necessary to repeat this several times to get an accurate reading.

12   With the engine warmed up and running, depress the brake pedal, place the shift lever into Drive, then check transmission fluid temperature with a scan tool.

Note: *The shift lever must be placed in Drive in order to obtain an accurate fluid temperature reading.*

13   Compare the reading on the dipstick tool with the transmission fluid temperature reading on the scan tool.

14   Match the two readings with the transmission fluid level chart (see illustration) to make sure the fluid level is correct

15   Add or remove fluid as necessary, then recheck the fluid level and install the dipstick tube cap.

7   Power steering fluid level check

1   Unlike manual steering, the power steering system relies on fluid which may, over a period of time, require replenishing.

2006 and earlier models

2   The fluid reservoir for the power steering pump is located on the pump body at the front of the engine.

3   For the check, the front wheels should be pointed straight ahead and the engine should be off.

4   Use a clean rag to wipe off the reservoir cap and the area around the cap. This will help prevent any foreign matter from entering the reservoir during the check.

5   Twist off the cap and check the temperature of the fluid at the end of the dipstick with your finger (see illustration).

6   Wipe off the fluid with a clean rag, reinsert the dipstick, then withdraw it and read the fluid level. The level should be at the FULL HOT mark if the fluid was hot to the touch (see illustration). It should be at the FULL COLD mark if the fluid was cool to the touch. Never allow the fluid level to drop below the ADD mark.

7   If additional fluid is required, pour the specified type directly into the reservoir, using a funnel to prevent spills.

8   If the reservoir requires frequent fluid additions, all power steering hoses, hose connections and the power steering pump should be carefully checked for leaks.

2006 and later models

Caution: *DO NOT hold the steering wheel against either stop (extreme left or right turn) for more than five seconds. If you do, the power steering pump could be damaged.*

9   The power steering reservoir is located at the right-front corner of the engine compartment (see illustration).

10   For the check, the front wheels should be pointed straight ahead and the engine should be off.

11   The reservoir has MIN and MAX fluid level marks on the side. The fluid level can be seen without removing the reservoir cap.

12   If additional fluid is required, pour the specified type directly into the reservoir, using a funnel to prevent spills.

13   If the reservoir requires frequent fluid additions, all power steering hoses, hose connections, steering gear and the power steering pump should be carefully checked for leaks.

7.6 The power steering fluid dipstick is marked on both sides so the level can be checked with the fluid hot or cold

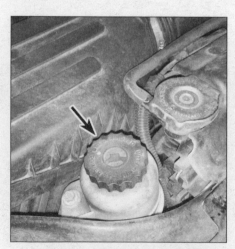

7.9 Location of the power steering fluid reservoir (2007 and later models)

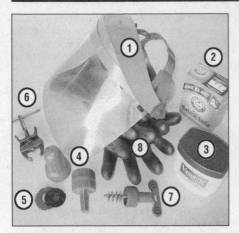

8.1 Tools and materials required for battery maintenance

1   **Face shield/safety goggles** - *When removing corrosion with a brush, the acidic particles can easily fly up into your eyes*
2   **Baking soda** - *A solution of baking soda and water can be used to neutralize corrosion*
3   **Petroleum jelly** - *A layer of this on the battery posts will help prevent corrosion*
4   **Battery post/cable cleaner** - *This wire brush cleaning tool will remove all traces of corrosion from the battery posts and cable clamps*
5   **Treated felt washers** - *Placing one of these on each post, directly under the cable clamps, will help prevent corrosion*
6   **Puller** - *Sometimes the cable clamps are very difficult to pull off the posts, even after the nut/bolt has been completely loosened. This tool pulls the clamp straight up and off the post without damage*
7   **Battery post/cable cleaner** - *Here is another cleaning tool which is a slightly different version of Number 4 above, but it does the same thing*
8   **Rubber gloves** - *Another safety item to consider when servicing the battery; remember that's acid inside the battery!*

8   Battery check, maintenance and charging

Warning: *Certain precautions must be followed when checking and servicing the battery. Hydrogen gas, which is highly flammable, is always present in the battery cells, so keep lighted tobacco and all other open flames and sparks away from the battery. The electrolyte in the battery cells is actually dilute sulfuric acid, which will cause injury if splashed on your skin or in your eyes. It will also ruin clothes and painted surfaces. When removing the battery cables, always detach the negative*

8.8a Battery terminal corrosion usually appears as light fluffy powder

8.8c When cleaning the cable clamps, all corrosion must be removed (the inside of the clamp is tapered to match the taper on the post, so don't remove too much material)

cable first and hook it up last!
1   Battery maintenance is an important procedure which will help ensure that you're not stranded because of a dead battery. Several tools are required for this procedure (see illustration).
2   Before servicing the battery, always turn the engine and all accessories off and disconnect the cable from the negative terminal.
3   A sealed (sometimes called maintenance-free) battery is standard equipment on these vehicles. The cell caps cannot be removed, no electrolyte checks are required and water cannot be added to the cells. However, if an aftermarket battery that requires regular maintenance has been installed, the following procedure can be used.
4   Check the electrolyte level in each of the battery cells. It must be above the plates. There's usually a split-ring indicator in each cell to indicate the correct level. If the level is low, add distilled water only, then install the cell caps.
Caution: *Overfilling the cells may cause electrolyte to spill over during periods of heavy*

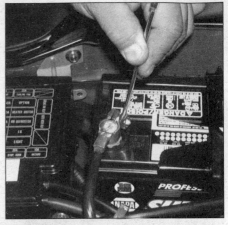

8.8b Removing the cable from a battery post with a wrench - sometimes special battery pliers are required for this procedure if corrosion has caused deterioration of the hex nut (always remove the negative cable first and hook it up last!)

8.8d Regardless of the type of tool used on the battery posts, a clean, shiny surface should be the result

charging, causing corrosion and damage to nearby components.
5   If the positive terminal and cable clamp on your vehicle's battery is equipped with a rubber protector, make sure that it's not torn or damaged. It should completely cover the terminal.
6   The external condition of the battery should be checked periodically. Look for damage such as a cracked case.
7   Check the tightness of the battery cable clamps to ensure good electrical connections and inspect the entire length of each cable, looking for cracked or abraded insulation and frayed conductors.
8   If corrosion (visible as white, fluffy deposits) is evident, remove the cables from the terminals, clean them with a battery brush and reinstall them (see illustrations). Corrosion can be kept to a minimum by installing specially treated washers available at auto parts stores or by applying a layer of petroleum jelly or grease to the terminals and cable clamps after they are assembled.
9   Make sure that the battery carrier is in

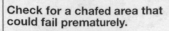

Check for a chafed area that could fail prematurely.

Check for a soft area indicating the hose has deteriorated inside.

Overtightening the clamp on a hardened hose will damage the hose and cause a leak.

Check each hose for swelling and oil-soaked ends. Cracks and breaks can be located by squeezing the hose.

9.4 Hoses, like drivebelts, have a habit of failing at the worst possible time - to prevent the inconvenience of a blown radiator or heater hose, inspect them carefully as shown here

good condition and that the hold-down clamp bolt is tight. If the battery is removed (see Chapter 5 for the removal and installation procedure), make sure that no parts remain in the bottom of the carrier when it's reinstalled. When reinstalling the hold-down clamp, don't overtighten the bolt.

10   Corrosion on the carrier, battery case and surrounding areas can be removed with a solution of water and baking soda. Apply the mixture with a small brush, let it work, then rinse it off with plenty of clean water.

11   Any metal parts of the vehicle damaged by corrosion should be coated with a zinc-based primer, then painted.

Charging

12   Remove all of the cell caps (if equipped) and cover the holes with a clean cloth to prevent spattering electrolyte. Disconnect the

negative battery cable and hook the battery charger leads to the battery posts (positive to positive, negative to negative), then plug in the charger. Make sure it is set at 12 volts if it has a selector switch.

13   If you're using a charger with a rate higher than two amps, check the battery regularly during charging to make sure it doesn't overheat. If you're using a trickle charger, you can safely let the battery charge overnight after you've checked it regularly for the first couple of hours.

14   If the battery has removable cell caps, measure the specific gravity with a hydrometer every hour during the last few hours of the charging cycle. Hydrometers are available inexpensively from auto parts stores - follow the instructions that come with the hydrometer. Consider the battery charged when there's no change in the specific gravity reading for two hours and the electrolyte in the cells is gassing (bubbling) freely. The specific gravity reading from each cell should be very close to the others. If not, the battery probably has a bad cell(s).

15   Some batteries with sealed tops have built-in hydrometers on the top that indicate the state of charge by the color displayed in the hydrometer window. Normally, a bright-colored hydrometer indicates a full charge and a dark hydrometer indicates the battery still needs charging. Check the battery manufacturer's instructions to be sure you know what the colors mean.

16   If the battery has a sealed top and no built-in hydrometer, you can hook up a digital voltmeter across the battery terminals to check the charge. A fully charged battery should read 12.6 volts or higher.

17   Further information on the battery and jump starting can be found in Chapter 5 and at the front of this manual.

9   Cooling system check

1   Many major engine failures can be attributed to a faulty cooling system. If the vehicle is equipped with an automatic transmission, the cooling system also cools the transmission fluid and thus plays an important role in prolonging transmission life.

2   The cooling system should be checked with the engine cold. Do this before the vehicle is driven for the day or after it has been shut off for at least three hours.

3   Remove the radiator cap by turning it to the left until it reaches a stop. If you hear a hissing sound (indicating there is still pressure in the system), wait until this stops. Now press down on the cap with the palm of your hand and continue turning to the left until the cap can be pulled off. Thoroughly clean the cap, inside and out, with clean water. Also clean the filler neck on the radiator. All traces of corrosion should be removed. On inline six-cylinder engines, unscrew the cap on the coolant pressure bottle and clean the cap. The coolant inside the radiator or pressure bottle

should be relatively transparent. If it is rust colored, the system should be drained and refilled (see Section 38). If the coolant level is not up to the top, add additional antifreeze/coolant mixture (see Section 4).

4   Carefully check the large upper and lower radiator hoses along with the smaller diameter heater hoses which run from the engine to the firewall. On some models the heater return hose runs directly to the radiator. Inspect each hose along its entire length, replacing any hose which is cracked, swollen or shows signs of deterioration. Cracks may become more apparent if the hose is squeezed (see illustration). Regardless of condition, it's a good idea to replace hoses with new ones every two years.

5   Make sure that all hose connections are tight. A leak in the cooling system will usually show up as white or rust colored deposits on the areas adjoining the leak. If wire-type clamps are used at the ends of the hoses, it may be a good idea to replace them with more secure screw-type clamps.

6   Use compressed air or a soft brush to remove bugs, leaves, etc., from the front of the radiator or air conditioning condenser. Be careful not to damage the delicate cooling fins or cut yourself on them.

7   Every other inspection, or at the first indication of cooling system problems, have the cap and system pressure tested. If you don't have a pressure tester, most gas stations and repair shops will do this for a minimal charge.

10   Underhood hose check and replacement

General

Caution: *Replacement of air conditioning hoses must be left to a dealer service department or air conditioning shop that has the equipment to depressurize the system safely. Never remove air conditioning components or hoses until the system has been depressurized.*

1   High temperatures in the engine compartment can cause the deterioration of the rubber and plastic hoses used for engine, accessory and emission systems operation. Periodic inspection should be made for cracks, loose clamps, material hardening and leaks. Information specific to the cooling system hoses can be found in Section 9.

2   Some, but not all, hoses are secured to the fittings with clamps. Where clamps are used, check to be sure they haven't lost their tension, allowing the hose to leak. If clamps aren't used, make sure the hose has not expanded and/or hardened where it slips over the fitting, allowing it to leak.

Vacuum hoses

3   It's quite common for vacuum hoses, especially those in the emissions system, to be color coded or identified by colored stripes molded into them. Various systems require hoses with different wall thicknesses, collapse

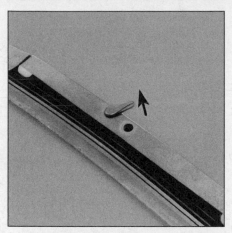

11.6a Lift the release lever up and slide the wiper off the stud on the arm

11.6b To release the blade holder, push the release lever…

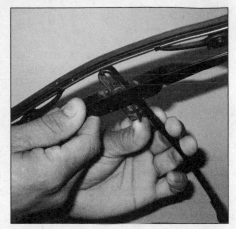

11.6c … and pull the wiper blade in the direction of the arrow to separate it from the arm (later models)

resistance and temperature resistance. When replacing hoses, be sure the new ones are made of the same material

4   Often the only effective way to check a hose is to remove it completely from the vehicle. If more than one hose is removed, be sure to label the hoses and fittings to ensure correct installation.

5   When checking vacuum hoses, be sure to include any plastic T-fittings in the check. Inspect the fittings for cracks and the hose where it fits over the fitting for distortion, which could cause leakage.

6   A small piece of vacuum hose (1/4-inch inside diameter) can be used as a stethoscope to detect vacuum leaks. Hold one end of the hose to your ear and probe around vacuum hoses and fittings, listening for the "hissing" sound characteristic of a vacuum leak. **Warning:** *When probing with the vacuum hose stethoscope, be very careful not to come into contact with moving engine components such as the drivebelt, cooling fan, etc.*

Fuel hoses

Warning: *There are certain precautions which must be taken when inspecting or servicing fuel system components. Work in a well ventilated area and do not allow open flames (cigarettes, appliance pilot lights, etc.) or bare light bulbs near the work area. Mop up any spills immediately and do not store fuel soaked rags where they could ignite. On vehicles equipped with fuel injection, the fuel system is under pressure, so if any fuel lines are to be disconnected, the pressure in the system must be relieved first (see Chapter 4 for more information).*

7   Check all rubber fuel lines for deterioration and chafing. Check especially for cracks in areas where the hose bends and just before fittings, such as where a hose attaches to the fuel filter.

8   High quality fuel line, usually identified by the word Fluroelastomer printed on the hose, should be used for fuel line replacement. Never, under any circumstances, use unreinforced vacuum line, clear plastic tubing

or water hose for fuel lines.

9   Spring-type clamps are commonly used on fuel lines. These clamps often lose their tension over a period of time, and can be "sprung" during removal. Replace all spring-type clamps with screw clamps whenever a hose is replaced.

Metal lines

10   Sections of metal line are often used for fuel line between the fuel pump and carburetor or fuel injection unit. Check carefully to be sure the line has not been bent or crimped and that cracks have not started in the line.

11   If a section of metal fuel line must be replaced, only seamless steel tubing should be used, since copper and aluminum tubing don't have the strength necessary to withstand normal engine vibration.

12   Check the metal brake lines where they enter the master cylinder and brake proportioning unit (if used) for cracks in the lines or loose fittings. Any sign of brake fluid leakage calls for an immediate thorough inspection of the brake system.

---

11   Wiper blade inspection and replacement

1   The windshield wiper and blade assembly should be inspected periodically for damage, loose components and cracked or worn blade elements.

2   Road film can build up on the wiper blades and affect their efficiency, so they should be washed regularly with a mild detergent solution.

3   The action of the wiping mechanism can loosen the bolts, nuts and fasteners, so they should be checked and tightened, as necessary, at the same time the wiper blades are checked.

4   If the wiper blade elements (sometimes called inserts) are cracked, worn or warped, the blade assemblies should be replaced with new ones.

5   Pull the wiper blade/arm assembly away from the glass

Front wiper blades

6   To remove the wiper blades:

a) *On early models, lift the release lever and slide the blade assembly off the wiper arm and over the retaining stud (see illustration). The blade/element assembly must be replaced as a unit.*

b) *On later models, lift the wiper arm assembly away from the glass for clearance, press the release lever then slide the wiper-blade assembly out of the hook at the end of the arm (see illustrations).*

Rear wiper blades

7   To remove the wiper blades:

a) *On early models, follow the procedure in Step 6a. The blade/element assembly must be replaced as a unit.*

b) *On later models, lift the wiper arm assembly away from the glass for clearance, swing the wiper blade (arm side) away from the wiper arm to its fullest travel. Press the blade (arm side) against its stop on the wiper arm to unsnap the wiper blade pivot pin from the latch on the underside of the wiper arm.*

All wiper blades

8   Compare the new blade assembly to the old one for length, design, etc.

9   Reinstall the blade assembly on the arm, wet the windshield and check for proper operation.

---

12   Engine oil and filter change

1   Frequent oil changes are the most important preventive maintenance procedures that can be done by the home mechanic. As engine oil ages, it becomes diluted and contaminated, which leads to premature engine wear.

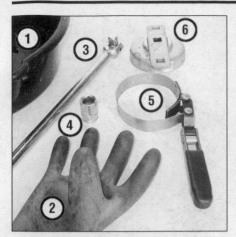

12.3 These tools are required when changing the engine oil and filter

1   *Drain pan - It should be fairly shallow in depth, but wide to prevent spills*
2   *Rubber gloves - When removing the drain plug and filter, you will get oil on your hands (the gloves will prevent burns)*
3   *Breaker bar - Sometimes the oil drain plug is tight, and a long breaker bar is needed to loosen it*
4   *Socket – To be used with the breaker bar or a ratchet (must be the correct size to fit the drain plug - six-point preferred)*
5   *Filter wrench - This is a metal band-type wrench, which requires clearance around the filter to be effective*
6   *Filter wrench - This type fits on the bottom of the filter and can be turned with a ratchet or breaker bar (different-size wrenches are available for different types of filters)*

12.9 Use the correct size box-end wrench or six-point socket to avoid rounding off the drain plug when removing or installing it

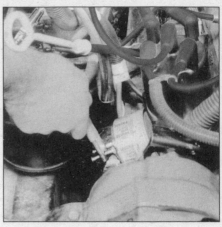

12.14 The oil filter is on very tight and will require a special wrench for removal - DO NOT use the wrench to tighten the new filter

12.16 Some inline six-cylinder engines use a metric 20 mm filter - if the old filter is so marked, make sure the new one is too

2   Although some sources recommend oil filter changes every other oil change, we feel that the minimal cost of an oil filter and the relative ease with which it is installed dictate that a new filter be installed every time the oil is changed.
3   Gather together all necessary tools and materials before beginning this procedure (see illustration).
4   You should have plenty of clean rags and newspapers handy to mop up any spills. Access to the underside of the vehicle is greatly improved if the vehicle can be lifted on a hoist, driven onto ramps or supported by jackstands. **Warning:** *Do not work under a vehicle which is supported only by a bumper, hydraulic or scissors-type jack.*
5   If this is your first oil change, get under the vehicle and familiarize yourself with the locations of the oil drain plug and the oil filter. The engine and exhaust components will be warm during the actual work, so note how they are situated to avoid touching them when working under the vehicle.
6   Warm the engine to normal operating

temperature. If the new oil or any tools are needed, use this warm-up time to gather everything necessary for the job. The correct type of oil for your application can be found in *Recommended lubricants and fluids* at the beginning of this Chapter.
7   With the engine oil warm (warm engine oil will drain better and more built-up sludge will be removed with it), raise and support the vehicle. Make sure it's safely supported!
8   Move all necessary tools, rags and newspapers under the vehicle. Set the drain pan under the drain plug. Keep in mind that the oil will initially flow from the pan with some force; position the pan accordingly.
9   Being careful not to touch any of the hot exhaust components, use a wrench to remove the drain plug near the bottom of the oil pan (see illustration). Depending on how hot the oil is, you may want to wear gloves while unscrewing the plug the final few turns. **Caution:** *When performing an engine oil change on the 3.6L V6, the oil filter cap must be removed. Removing the oil filter cap releases oil held within the oil filter cavity and allows it to drain into the oil pan. If the cap is not removed prior to installation of the oil drain plug, some old oil will not completely drain*

from the engine.
10   Allow the old oil to drain into the pan. It may be necessary to move the pan as the oil flow slows to a trickle.
11   After all the oil has drained, wipe off the drain plug with a clean rag. Small metal particles may cling to the plug and would immediately contaminate the new oil.
12   Clean the area around the drain plug opening and reinstall the plug. Tighten the plug securely with the wrench. If a torque wrench is available, use it to tighten the plug.
13   Move the drain pan into position under the oil filter.

All except 3.6L V6 engines
14   Use the filter wrench to loosen the oil filter (see illustration). Chain or metal band filter wrenches may distort the filter canister, but it doesn't matter since the filter will be discarded anyway.
15   Completely unscrew the old filter. Be careful; it's full of oil. Empty the oil inside the filter into the drain pan.
16   Compare the old filter with the new one to make sure they're the same type (see illustration).
17   Use a clean rag to remove all oil, dirt

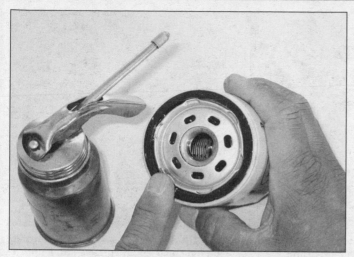

12.18 Lubricate the oil filter gasket with clean engine oil before installing the filter on the engine

12.21 Using a box end wrench or socket, turn the filter cap counterclockwise to remove it (3.6L engine)

and sludge from the area where the oil filter mounts to the engine. Check the old filter to make sure the rubber gasket isn't stuck to the engine. If the gasket is stuck to the engine (use a flashlight if necessary), remove it.

18 Apply a light coat of clean oil to the rubber gasket on the new oil filter (see illustration)

19 Attach the new filter to the engine, following the tightening directions printed on the filter canister or packing box. Most filter manufacturers recommend against using a filter wrench due to the possibility of overtightening and damage to the seal.

3.6L engines

20 Lift up on the outer edges of the engine cover to disengage the rubber mounts from the ballstuds, and remove the engine cover.

21 Place a rag at the base of the filter housing, then loosen the filter cap by turning it counterclockwise (see illustration).

22 Remove the cap and filter from the engine, then pull the filter out of the cap.

23 Remove and discard the O-ring from the filter cap.

24 Insert a new filter into the cap, making sure the filter clips lock into the cap (see illustration).

25 Install a new O-ring onto the cap and apply a light amount of engine oil to the O-ring.

26 Place the filter assembly into the filter housing and carefully thread the cap into the housing. Tighten the cap to the torque listed in this Chapter's Specifications.

All models

27 Remove all tools, rags, etc., from under the vehicle, being careful not to spill the oil in the drain pan, then lower the vehicle.

28 Move to the engine compartment and locate the oil filler cap.

29 If an oil can spout is used, push the spout into the top of the oil can and pour the fresh oil through the filler opening. A funnel may also be used.

12.24 Oil filter details (3.6L engine)

1 Filter element
2 Filter clips
3 Filter cap
4 O-ring

30 On four-cylinder engines, pour four quarts of fresh oil into the engine. On inline six-cylinder engines, pour in five quarts. Wait a few minutes to allow the oil to drain into the pan, then check the level on the oil dipstick (see Section 4 if necessary). If the oil level is above the ADD mark, start the engine and allow the new oil to circulate.

31 Run the engine for only about a minute checking the pressure gauge or indicator light to make sure normal oil pressure is achieved. Shut off the engine. Immediately look under the vehicle and check for leaks at the oil pan drain plug and around the oil filter. If either is leaking, tighten with a bit more force.

32 With the new oil circulated and the filter now completely full, recheck the level on the dipstick and add more oil as necessary.

33 During the first few trips after an oil change, make it a point to check frequently for leaks and proper oil level.

34 The old oil drained from the engine cannot be reused in its present state and should be disposed of. Oil reclamation centers, and some recycling centers will accept the oil, which can be refined and used again. After the oil has cooled it can be drained into a suit-

able container (capped plastic jugs, topped bottles, milk cartons, etc.) for transport to one of these disposal sites.

Oil change indicator resetting

Note: *It is possible that, driving under the best possible conditions, the oil life monitoring system may not indicate the oil needs to be changed. The manufacturer states that the oil and filter must be changed at least once every year and the oil life monitor reset.*

Note: *If the "Oil Change Required" message comes on when the vehicle is immediately restarted, the oil life monitor was not reset and the reset procedure must be done again.*

Note: *If the message is not reset, it will continue to show up each time you turn the ignition switch On or start the vehicle. It is possible to temporarily turn off the message by pressing and releasing the "Menu" button.*

35 Turn the ignition key to the "ON" position but DO NOT start the engine.

36 Slowly depress the accelerator pedal all the way to the floor, three times within 10 seconds.

37 Turn the ignition key to the "OFF" or "LOCK" position, then start the vehicle.

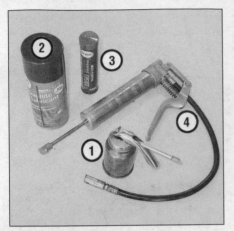

13.1 Materials required for chassis and body lubrication

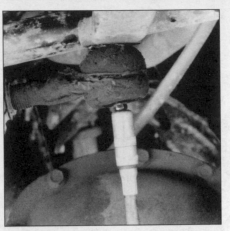

13.6 Pump grease into the steering end fittings until the boot is firm

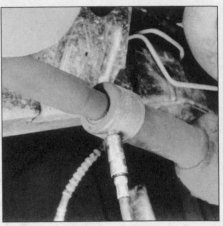

13.9 The slip joint grease fitting is located on the collar - pump grease into it until it comes out the collar

1   *Engine oil* - Light engine oil in a can like this can be used for door and hood hinges
2   *Graphite spray* - Used to lubricate lock cylinders
3   *Grease* - Grease, in a variety of types and weights, is available for use in a grease gun. Check the Specifications for your requirements
4   *Grease gun* - A common grease gun, shown here with a detachable hose and nozzle, is needed for chassis lubrication. After use, clean it thoroughly!

13   Chassis lubrication

1   Refer to *Recommended lubricants and fluids* at the front of this Chapter to obtain the necessary grease, etc. You will also need a grease gun (see illustration). Occasionally plugs will be installed rather than grease fittings. If so, grease fittings will have to be purchased and installed.
2   Look under the vehicle for grease fittings or plugs on the steering, suspension, and driveline components. They are normally found on the balljoints, tie-rod ends and universal joints. If there are plugs, remove them and buy grease fittings, which will thread into the component. A dealer or auto parts store will be able to supply the correct fittings. Straight, as well as angled, fittings are available.
3   For easier access under the vehicle, raise it with a jack and place jackstands under the frame. Make sure it is safely supported by the stands. If the wheels are to be removed at this interval for tire rotation or brake inspection, loosen the lug nuts slightly while the vehicle is still on the ground.
4   Before beginning, force a little grease out of the nozzle to remove any dirt from the end of the gun. Wipe the nozzle clean with a rag.
5   With the grease gun and plenty of clean rags, crawl under the vehicle and begin lubri-

cating the components.
6   Wipe the balljoint grease fitting nipple clean and push the nozzle firmly over it. Squeeze the trigger on the grease gun to force grease into the component. The balljoints should be lubricated until the rubber seal is firm to the touch. Do not pump too much grease into the fittings as it could rupture the seal. For all other suspension and steering components, continue pumping grease into the fitting until it oozes out of the joint between the two components (see illustration). If it escapes around the grease gun nozzle, the nipple is clogged or the nozzle is not completely seated on the fitting. Resecure the gun nozzle to the fitting and try again. If necessary, replace the fitting with a new one.
7   Wipe the excess grease from the components and the grease fitting. Repeat the procedure for the remaining fittings.
8   Lubricate the transfer case shift mechanism contact surfaces with clean engine oil.
9   Lubricate the driveshaft slip joint by pumping grease into the fitting until it can be seen coming out of the slip joint seal (see illustration)
10 Lubricate conventional universal joints

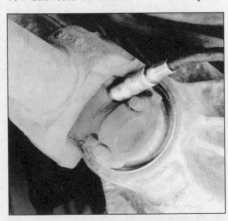

13.10 You may have to rotate the driveshaft for access to the universal joint grease fitting - pump grease into it until grease can be seen coming out of the contact surfaces

until grease can be seen coming out of the contact points (see illustration).
11 While you are under the vehicle, clean and lubricate the parking brake cable along with the cable guides and levers. This can be done by smearing some chassis grease onto the cable and its related parts with your fingers.
12 The manual steering gear seldom requires the addition of lubricant, but if there is obvious leakage of grease at the seals, remove the plug or cover and check the lubricant level. If the level is low, add the specified lubricant.
13 Lubricate the contact points on the steering knuckle and adjustment bolt.
14 Open the hood and smear a little chassis grease on the hood latch mechanism. Have an assistant pull the hood release lever from inside the vehicle as you lubricate the cable at the latch.
15 Lubricate all the hinges (door, hood, etc.) with engine oil to keep them in proper working order.
16 The key lock cylinders can be lubricated with spray-on graphite or silicone lubricant, which is available at auto parts stores.
17 Lubricate the door weatherstripping with silicone spray. This will reduce chafing and retard wear.

14   Suspension and steering check

1   Indications of a fault in these systems are excessive play in the steering wheel before the front wheels react, excessive sway around corners, body movement over rough roads, noise from the axle or wheel areas or binding at some point as the steering wheel is turned.
2   Raise the front of the vehicle periodically and visually check the suspension and steering components for wear. Because of the work to be done, make sure the vehicle cannot fall from the stands.
3   Check the wheel bearings. Do this by spinning the front wheels. Listen for any

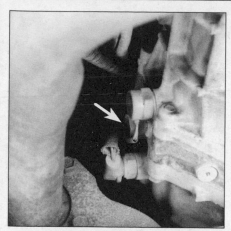

16.1 The manual transmission fill plug is mounted high on the passenger's side of the case - you'll need a hand pump to add oil

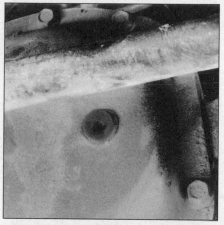

17.2a Some differentials use a screw-in check/fill plug - use a 3/8 inch drive ratchet and extension to remove it

17.2b The check/fill plug on some differentials is rubber; pry it out with a screwdriver

abnormal noises and watch to make sure the wheel spins true (doesn't wobble). Grab the top and bottom of the tire and pull in and out on it. Notice any movement which would indicate a loose wheel bearing assembly. If the bearings are suspect, refer to Chapter 10 for more information.

4   From under the vehicle, check for loose bolts, broken or disconnected parts and deteriorated rubber bushings on all suspension and steering components. Look for grease or fluid leaking from the steering assembly. Check the power steering hoses and connections for leaks.

5   Have an assistant turn the steering wheel from side-to-side and check the steering components for free movement, chafing and binding. If the steering doesn't react simultaneously with the movement of the steering wheel, try to determine where the slack is located.

15   Exhaust system check

1   With the engine cold (at least three hours after the vehicle has been driven), check the complete exhaust system from the manifold to the end of the tailpipe. Be careful around the catalytic converter, which may be hot even after three hours. The inspection should be done with the vehicle on a hoist to permit unrestricted access. If a hoist isn't available, raise the vehicle and support it securely on jackstands.

2   Check the exhaust pipes and connections for signs of leakage and/or corrosion indicating a potential failure. Make sure that all brackets and hangers are in good condition and tight.

3   Inspect the underside of the body for holes, corrosion, open seams, etc., which may allow exhaust gases to enter the passenger compartment. Seal all body openings with silicone or body putty.

4   Rattles and other noises can often be traced to the exhaust system, especially the

hangers, mounts and heat shields. Try to move the pipes, mufflers and catalytic converter. If the components can come in contact with the body or suspension parts, secure the exhaust system with new brackets and hangers.

16   Manual transmission lubricant level check

1   The manual transmission has a fill plug which must be removed to check the lubricant level (see illustration). If the vehicle is raised to gain access to the plug, be sure to support it safely on jackstands - DO NOT crawl under a vehicle which is supported only by a jack!

2   Remove the fill plug from the transmission and use your little finger to reach inside the housing to feel the oil level. The level should be at or near the bottom of the plug hole.

3   If it isn't, add the recommended oil through the plug hole with a fluid pump or squeeze bottle.

4   Install and tighten the plug and check for leaks after the first few miles of driving.

17   Differential lubricant level check

Note: *4WD vehicles have two differentials - one in the center of each axle. Be sure to check the lubricant level in both differentials.*

1   The differential has a check/fill plug which must be removed to check the lubricant level. If the vehicle must be raised to gain access to the plug, be sure to support it safely on jackstands - DO NOT crawl under the vehicle when it's supported only by the jack.

2   Remove the oil check/fill plug from the back of the rear differential or the front of the front differential (see illustrations).

3   The oil level should be at the bottom of the plug opening. If it isn't, use a fluid pump or squeeze bottle to add the specified lubricant

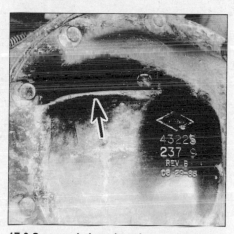

17.3 Some axle housings have a tag which contains information on the differential

until it just starts to run out of the opening. On some models a tag is located in the area of the plug which gives information regarding lubricant type, particularly on models equipped with a limited slip differential (see illustration).

4   Install the plug and tighten it securely.

18   Transfer case lubricant level check

1   The transfer case lubricant level is checked by removing the upper plug located in the side of the case (see illustration).

2   After removing the plug, reach inside the hole. The lubricant level should be just at the bottom of the hole. If not, add the appropriate lubricant through the opening.

19   Tire rotation

1   The tires should be rotated at the specified intervals and whenever uneven wear is noticed.

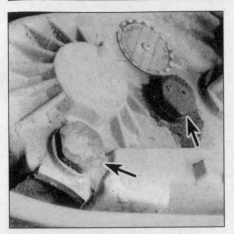

18.1 The transfer case drain and fill plugs are located on the front face of the housing - the upper one is the check/fill plug and the lower one is the drain plug

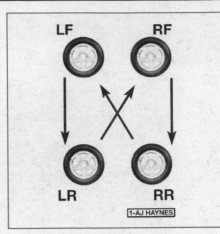

19.2 The recommended tire rotation pattern for these vehicles

20.6 You will find an inspection hole like this in each caliper - placing a steel ruler across the window should enable you to determine the thickness of remaining pad materials for both the inner and outer pads (arrows)

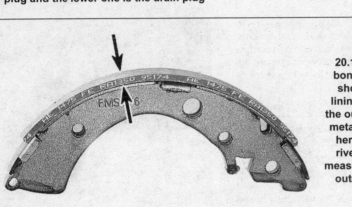

20.12 If the lining is bonded to the brake shoe, measure the lining thickness from the outer surface to the metal shoe, as shown here; if the lining is riveted to the shoe, measure from the lining outer surface to the rivet head

2   Refer to the accompanying illustration for the preferred tire rotation pattern (see illustration).

3   Refer to the information in *Jacking and towing* at the front of this manual for the proper procedures to follow when raising the vehicle and changing a tire. If the brakes are to be checked, don't apply the parking brake as stated. Make sure the tires are blocked to prevent the vehicle from rolling as it's raised.

4   Preferably, the entire vehicle should be raised at the same time. This can be done on a hoist or by jacking up each corner and then lowering the vehicle onto jackstands placed under the frame rails. Always use four jackstands and make sure the vehicle is safely supported.

5   After rotation, check and adjust the tire pressures as necessary and be sure to check the lug nut tightness.

6   For additional information on the wheels and tires, refer to Chapter 10.

20   Brake check

Note: *For detailed photographs of the brake system, refer to Chapter 9.*
Warning: *Brake system dust is hazardous to your health. DO NOT blow it out with com-*

pressed air and DO NOT inhale it. DO NOT use gasoline or solvents to remove the dust. Use brake system cleaner or denatured alcohol only.

1   In addition to the specified intervals, the brakes should be inspected every time the wheels are removed or whenever a defect is suspected.

2   To check the brakes, raise the vehicle and place it securely on jackstands. Remove the wheels (see *Jacking and towing* at the front of the manual, if necessary).

Disc brakes

3   Disc brakes are used on the front wheels. Extensive rotor damage can occur if the pads are not replaced when needed.

4   These vehicles are equipped with a wear sensor attached to the inner pad. This is a small, bent piece of metal which is visible from the inner side of the brake caliper. When the pad wears to the specified limit, the metal sensor rubs against the rotor and makes a squealing sound.

5   The disc brake calipers, which contain the pads, are visible with the wheels removed. There is an outer pad and an inner pad in each caliper. All pads should be inspected.

6   Each caliper has an inspection hole to inspect the pads. Check the thickness of the

pad lining by looking into the caliper at each end and down through the inspection hole at the top of the housing (see illustration). If the wear sensor is very close to the rotor or the pad material has worn to about 1/8-inch or less, the pads should be replaced.

7   If you're unsure about the exact thickness of the remaining lining material, remove the pads for further inspection or replacement (refer to Chapter 9).

8   Before installing the wheels, check for leakage and/or damage (cracks, splitting, etc.) around the brake hose connections. Replace the hose or fittings as necessary, referring to Chapter 9.

9   Check the condition of the disc. Look for score marks, deep scratches and burned spots. If any of these conditions exist, the hub/disc assembly should be removed for servicing (see Chapter 10).

Drum brakes

10   On rear brakes, remove the drum by pulling it off the axle and brake assembly (see Chapter 9).

11   With the drum removed, do not touch any brake dust (see the Warning at the beginning of this Section).

12   Note the thickness of the lining material on both the front and rear brake shoes. If the material has worn away to within 1/16-inch of the recessed rivets or metal backing, the shoes should be replaced (see illustration). The shoes should also be replaced if they're cracked, glazed (shiny surface) or contaminated with brake fluid.

13   Make sure that all the brake assembly springs are connected and in good condition.

14   Check the brake components for any signs of fluid leakage. With your finger or a small screwdriver, carefully pry back the rubber cups on the wheel cylinders located at the top of the brake shoes (see illustration). Any leakage is an indication that the wheel cyl-

20.14 Peel the wheel cylinder boot back carefully and check for leaking fluid - any leakage indicates the cylinder must be replaced

inders should be replaced immediately (see Chapter 9). Also check brake hoses and connections for signs of leakage.

15   Wipe the inside of the drum with a clean rag and brake cleaner or denatured alcohol. Again, be careful not to breathe the dangerous asbestos dust.

16   Check the inside of the drum for cracks, score marks, deep scratches and hard spots, which will appear as small discolorations. If these imperfections cannot be removed with fine emery cloth, the drum must be taken to a machine shop equipped to turn the drums.

17   If after the inspection process all parts are in good working condition, reinstall the brake drum (see Chapter 9).

18   Install the wheels and lower the vehicle.

Parking brake

19   The parking brake operates from a foot pedal and locks the rear brake system. The easiest, and perhaps most obvious method of periodically checking the operation of the parking brake assembly is to park the vehicle on a steep hill with the parking brake set and the transmission in Neutral. If the parking brake cannot prevent the vehicle from rolling, it's in need of adjustment (see Chapter 9).

21   Fuel system check

Warning: *Take certain precautions when inspecting or servicing the fuel system components. Work in a well ventilated area and don't allow open flames (cigarettes, appliance pilot lights, etc.) in the work area. Mop up spills immediately and don't store fuel soaked rags where they could ignite. On fuel-injected models the fuel system is under pressure. No components should be disconnected until the pressure has been relieved (see Chapter 4).*

1   On all models, the fuel tank is located under the rear of the vehicle, covered by a shield.

2   The fuel system is most easily checked with the vehicle raised on a hoist so the components underneath the vehicle are readily visible and accessible.

3   If the smell of gasoline is noticed while driving or after the vehicle has been in the sun, the system should be thoroughly inspected immediately.

4   Remove the gas tank cap and check it for damage, corrosion and an unbroken sealing imprint on the gasket. Replace the cap with a new one if necessary.

5   With the vehicle raised, check the gas tank and filler neck for punctures, cracks and other damage. The connection between the filler neck and the tank is especially critical. Sometimes a rubber filler neck will leak due to loose clamps or deteriorated rubber; these are problems a home mechanic can usually rectify.

Warning: *Do not, under any circumstances, try to repair a fuel tank yourself (except rubber components). A welding torch or any open flame can easily cause the fuel vapors to explode if the proper precautions are not taken!*

6   Carefully check all rubber hoses and metal lines attached to the fuel tank. Look for loose connections, deteriorated hoses, crimped lines and other damage. Follow the lines to the front of the vehicle, carefully inspecting them all the way. Repair or replace damaged sections as necessary.

7   If a fuel odor is still evident after the inspection, refer to Section 40.

22   Carburetor choke check

1   The choke operates only when the engine is cold, so this check should be performed before the engine has been started for the day.

2   Remove the top plate of the air cleaner assembly. It's usually held in place by a wing nut at the center. If any vacuum hoses must be disconnected, make sure you tag the hoses for reinstallation in their original positions. Place the top plate and wing nut aside, out of the way of moving engine components.

3   Look at the center of the air cleaner housing. You will notice a flat plate at the carburetor opening. This is the choke plate.

4   Press the accelerator pedal to the floor. The plate should close completely. Start the engine while you watch the choke plate. Don't position your face near the carburetor, as the engine could backfire, causing serious burns. When the engine starts, the choke plate should open slightly.

5   Allow the engine to continue running at an idle speed. As the engine warms up to operating temperature, the plate should slowly open, allowing more air to enter through the top of the carburetor.

6   After a few minutes, the choke plate should be fully open to the vertical position. Tap the accelerator to make sure the fast idle cam disengages.

7   You'll notice that the engine speed cor-

responds to the plate opening. With the plate fully closed, the engine should run at a fast idle speed. As the plate opens and the throttle is moved to disengage the fast idle cam, the engine speed will decrease.

8   Refer to Chapter 4 for specific information on adjusting and servicing the choke components.

23   Carburetor/throttle body mounting nut torque check

1   The carburetor, Throttle Body Injection (TBI) unit or throttle body on multi-port fuel injected models is attached to the intake manifold by four bolts or nuts. These fasteners can sometimes work loose from vibration and temperature changes during normal engine operation and cause a vacuum leak.

2   If you suspect that a vacuum leak exists at the bottom of the carburetor or throttle body, obtain a length of hose. Start the engine and place one end of the hose next to your ear as you probe around the base with the other end. You will hear a hissing sound if a leak exists (be careful of hot or moving engine components when performing this check).

3   Remove the air cleaner assembly, tagging each hose to be disconnected with a piece of numbered tape to make reassembly easier.

4   Locate the mounting nuts or bolts at the base of the carburetor or throttle body. Decide what special tools or adapters will be necessary, if any, to tighten the fasteners.

5   Tighten the nuts to the specified torque. Don't overtighten them, as the threads could strip.

6   If, after the nuts or bolts are properly tightened, a vacuum leak still exists, the carburetor or throttle body must be removed and a new gasket installed. See Chapter 4 for more information.

7   After tightening the fasteners, reinstall the air cleaner and return all hoses to their original positions.

24   Throttle linkage inspection

1   Inspect the throttle linkage for damage and missing parts and for binding and interference when the accelerator pedal is depressed.

2   Lubricate the various linkage pivot points with engine oil.

25   Thermostatic air cleaner check

1   Some older engines are equipped with a thermostatically controlled air cleaner which draws air to the carburetor from different locations, depending on engine temperature.

2   This is a visual check. If access is limited, a small mirror may have to be used.

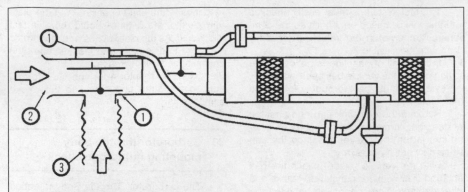

25.3 Thermostatic air cleaner operation (air valve shown open) - when the engine is cold, the air valve (1) should close off the snorkel end (2) allowing warm air to flow through the flexible duct (3), which is attached to the exhaust manifold and heat stove passage - when the engine is at normal operating temperature, the air valve should be open, allowing cool air to flow through the snorkel end (2)

3   Locate the air valve inside the air cleaner assembly. It's inside the snorkel of the air cleaner housing (see illustration).

4   If there is a flexible air duct attached to the end of the snorkel, leading to an area behind the grille, disconnect it at the snorkel.

This will enable you to look through the end of the snorkel and see the air valve inside.

5   The check should be done when the engine is cold. Start the engine and look through the snorkel at the air valve, which should move to a closed position. With the valve closed, air cannot enter through the end of the snorkel, but instead enters the air cleaner through the flexible duct attached to the exhaust manifold and the heat stove passage.

6   As the engine warms up to operating temperature, the air valve should open to allow air through the snorkel end. Depending on outside temperature, this may take 10-to-15 minutes. To speed up this check, you can reconnect the snorkel air duct, drive the vehicle until it reaches normal operating temperature, then check to see if the air valve is

completely open.

7   If the thermostatically controlled air cleaner isn't operating properly, see Chapter 6 for more information.

26   Drivebelt check, adjustment and replacement

1   The drivebelts, or V-belts as they are often called, are located at the front of the engine and play an important role in the overall operation of the engine and accessories. Due to their function and material makeup, the belts are prone to failure after a period of time and should be inspected and adjusted periodically to prevent major engine damage.

2   The number of belts used on a particular vehicle depends on the accessories installed. Drivebelts are used to turn the alternator, power steering pump, water pump and air conditioning compressor. Depending on the pulley arrangement, more than one of these components may be driven by a single belt. Six-cylinder and later four-cylinder models are equipped with one serpentine drivebelt that runs all engine accessories.

3   With the engine off, locate the drivebelts at the front of the engine. Using your fingers (and a flashlight, if necessary), move along the belts checking for cracks and separation of the belt plies. Also check for fraying and glazing, which gives the belt a shiny appearance (see illustrations). Both sides of each belt should be inspected, which means you will have to twist the belt to check the underside. Check the pulleys for nicks, cracks, distortion and corrosion.

4   The tension of each V-belt is checked by pushing on it at a distance halfway between

STREAKED SIDEWALL

FRAYING

CRACKS

SEPARATION

GLAZING

OIL SOAKED

TENSILE BREAK

26.3a Here are some of the more common problems associated with early type V-belts (check the belts very carefully to prevent an untimely breakdown)

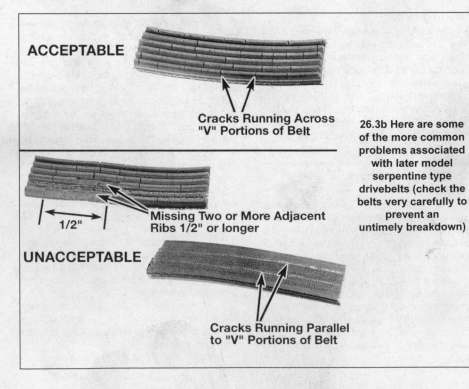

ACCEPTABLE

Cracks Running Across "V" Portions of Belt

1/2"

Missing Two or More Adjacent Ribs 1/2" or longer

UNACCEPTABLE

Cracks Running Parallel to "V" Portions of Belt

26.3b Here are some of the more common problems associated with later model serpentine type drivebelts (check the belts very carefully to prevent an untimely breakdown)

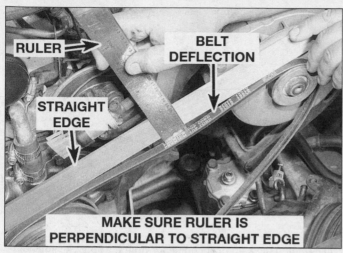

26.4a Measuring drivebelt deflection with a straightedge and ruler

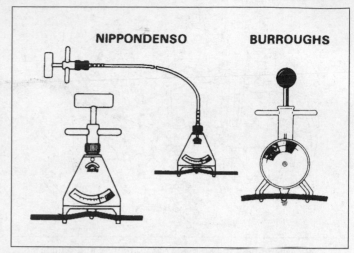

26.4b If you are able to borrow either a Nippondenso or Burroughs belt tension gauge, this is how it's installed on the belt - compare the reading on the scale with the specified drivebelt tension

26.6 Insert the half-inch drive into the square hole (A), then slip the belt from the water pump pulley (B) (3.8L V6 shown)

26.7 Loosen the adjusting bolt, then move the alternator in-or-out to adjust the drivebelt tension

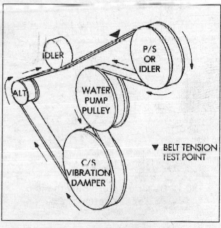

26.12 Typical serpentine drivebelt routing

the pulleys. Push firmly and see how much the belt moves (deflects) (see illustration). A rule of thumb is that if the distance from pulley center-to-pulley center is between 7 and 11-inches, the belt should deflect 1/4-inch. If the belt travels between pulleys spaced 12-to-16 inches apart, the belt should deflect 1/2-inch. The tension on serpentine belts can only be checked using a belt tension gauge, available at auto parts stores (see illustration).

5   If adjustment is needed, either to make the belt tighter or looser, it's done by moving the belt-driven accessory on the bracket.

6   For each component there will be an adjusting bolt and a pivot bolt. Both bolts must be loosened slightly to enable you to move the component. On later models, the belt tension is maintained automatically by a tensioner (see illustration). To remove the drivebelt, use the square lug on a half-inch breaker bar to

rotate the tensioner clockwise, while slipping the belt off the water pump pulley.
Note: *On 3.6L V6 models, the alternator lower mounting bracket bolts and bracket must be removed to replace the drivebelt.*

7   After the bolts have been loosened, move the component away from the engine to tighten the belt or toward the engine to loosen the belt. Hold the accessory in position and check the belt tension (see illustration). If it's correct, tighten the bolts until just snug, then recheck the tension. If the tension is all right, tighten the bolts.

8   On models without a serpentine belt, it will often be necessary to use some sort of pry bar to move the accessory while the belt is adjusted. If this must be done to gain the proper leverage, be very careful not to damage the component being moved or the part being pried against.

9   To replace a belt, follow the above proce-

dures for drivebelt adjustment, but slip the belt off the pulleys and remove it. Since belts tend to wear out more or less at the same time, it's a good idea to replace all of them at the same time. Mark each belt and the corresponding pulley grooves so the replacement belts can be installed properly.

10   Take the old belts with you when purchasing new ones in order to make a direct comparison for length, width and design.

11   Adjust the belts as described earlier in this Section.

12   When replacing a serpentine drivebelt (used on later models), make sure the new belt is routed correctly or the water pump could turn backwards, causing overheating (see illustration). A belt routing diagram is usually located in the engine compartment. Also, the belt must completely engage the grooves in the pulleys.

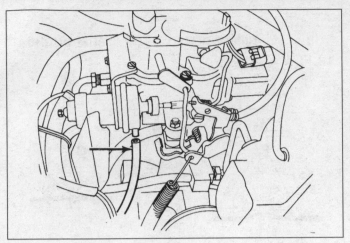

30.7 Disconnect the sole-vac vacuum hose and plug it

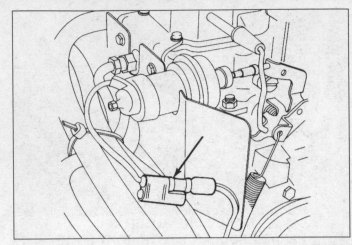

30.8 Unplug the electrical connector from the sole-vac solenoid

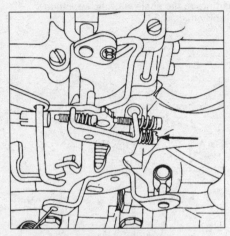

30.12 Be sure to turn only the idle speed screw

27 Seatbelt check

1   Check the seatbelts, buckles, latch plates and guide loops for any obvious damage or signs of wear.

2   Make sure the seatbelt reminder light comes on when the key is turned on.

3   The seatbelts are designed to lock up during a sudden stop or impact, yet allow free movement during normal driving. The retractors should hold the belt against your chest while driving and rewind the belt when the buckle is unlatched.

4   If any of the above checks reveal problems with the seatbelt system, replace parts as necessary.

28 Neutral start switch check

Warning: *During the following checks there is a chance that the vehicle could lunge forward, possibly causing damage or injuries. Allow plenty of room around the vehicle, apply the* parking brake firmly and hold down the regular brake pedal during the checks.

1   Automatic transmission equipped models have a Neutral start switch which prevents the engine from starting unless the shift lever is in Neutral or Park.

2   Try to start the vehicle in each gear. The engine should crank only in Park or Neutral.

3   Make sure the steering column lock allows the key to go into the Lock position only when the shift lever is in Park.

4   The ignition key should come out only in the Lock position.

5   Refer to Chapter 7B for further information on the Neutral start switch.

29 Spare tire and jack check

1   Check the spare tire to make sure it's securely fastened so it cannot come loose when the vehicle is in motion.

2   Make sure the jack and components are secured in place.

30 Idle speed check and adjustment (1987 and 1988 carbureted models only)

Note: *Idle speed check and adjustment are not routine maintenance procedures on vehicles other than those identified in the heading above.*

1   Engine idle speed is the speed at which the engine operates when no throttle pedal pressure is applied. The idle speed is critical to the performance of the engine itself, as well as many engine sub-systems.

2   A hand-held tachometer must be used when adjusting idle speed to get an accurate reading. The exact hook-up for these meters varies with the manufacturer, so follow the particular directions included.

3   Set the parking brake and block the wheels. Be sure the transmission is in Neu-tral (manual transmission) or Park (automatic transmission).

4   Turn off the air conditioner (if equipped), the headlights and any other accessories during this procedure.

5   Start the engine and allow it to reach normal operating temperature.

6   Shut off the engine.

7   Disconnect and plug the vacuum hose on the sole-vac vacuum actuator (see illustration).

8   Unplug the sole-vac holding solenoid electrical connector (see illustration).

9   On automatic transmission equipped vehicles, have an assistant shift to Drive while keeping the brake pedal firmly depressed. Place the manual transmission equipped vehicles in Neutral.

10   Increase the engine speed to 1200 rpm for three to five seconds, then let it return to idle.

11   Check the engine idle speed reading on the tachometer and compare it to the value listed in this Chapter's Specifications. If your vehicle has a VECI label located in the engine compartment refer instead to the idle speed there.

12   If the idle speed is not correct, turn the idle speed adjusting screw until the idle speed is correct (see illustration).

13   After adjustment, reconnect the sole-vac hose, shift the automatic transmission into Park and turn the engine off.

31 Fuel filter replacement (1987 through 1995 models)

Note: *Only 1987 through 1995 models use a replaceable in-line fuel filter. The manufacturer does not suggest periodic fuel filter replacement on 1997 and later models. Since the fuel filter is part of the fuel pump assembly inside the fuel tank on 1997 and later models, refer to Chapter 4 if fuel contamination makes it necessary to replace the fuel filter.*

1   1995 and earlier models employ an in-

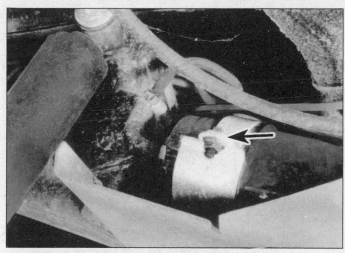

31.3 Remove the shield, then unscrew the fuel hose clamps, pull off the hoses and remove the securing strap bolt (arrow)

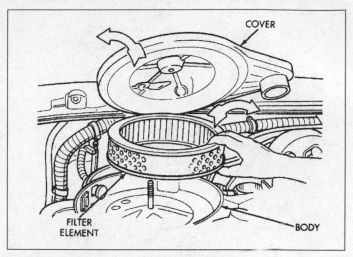

32.2a On carbureted models, remove the air cleaner wing nut, disconnect the clips, lift the cover off and remove the filter element

32.2b On fuel-injected models, clips on the sides hold the cover on the air cleaner housing - they can be pried loose with a screwdriver

32.4 Hold the cover up out of the way and lift the filter element out of the housing (fuel-injected model shown)

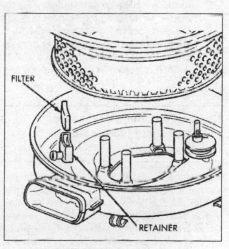

32.6 The PCV filter used on some carbureted models

line fuel filter. The filter is located on the left side frame rail, near the fuel tank. On port fuel Injected engines, the system is under pressure even when the engine is off.
Warning: *On port fuel injected engines, the system must be depressurized (see Chapter 4) before any work is performed.*

2   With the engine cold, place a container, newspapers or rags under the fuel filter.

3   Remove the metal shield, disconnect the fuel hoses and detach the filter from the frame (see illustration).

4   Install the new filter by reversing the removal procedure. Make sure the arrow or the word "OUT" on the filter points toward the engine, not the fuel tank. Tighten the screw clamps securely, but not to the point where the rubber hose is badly distorted.

32   Air filter and PCV filter replacement

1   At the specified intervals, the air filter and (if equipped) PCV filter should be replaced with new ones. The engine air cleaner also supplies filtered air to the PCV system.

2   The filter on carburetor-equipped models is located on top of the carburetor and is replaced by unscrewing the wing nut from the top of the filter housing body, disconnecting the clips and lifting off the cover (see illustration). On most fuel-injected models, the filter is located in a housing in the engine compartment. It can be replaced after disengaging the clips holding the top plate in place (see illustrations).

3   While the top plate is off, be careful not to drop anything into the carburetor or air cleaner assembly.

4   Lift the air filter element out (see illustration) and wipe out the inside of the air cleaner housing with a clean rag.

5   Place the new filter in the air cleaner housing. Make sure it seats properly in the bottom of the housing.

6   The PCV filter is also located inside the air cleaner housing on some models (see illustration). Remove the cover and air filter as previously described, then locate the PCV filter on the inside of the housing.

7   Remove the old filter.

8   Install the new PCV filter and the new air filter.

9   Install the cover and any hoses which were disconnected.

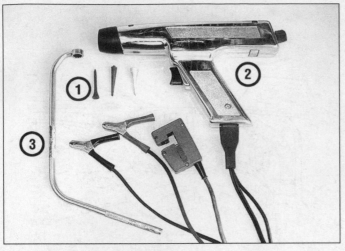

33.2 Tools needed to check and adjust the ignition timing

1 **Vacuum plugs** - *Vacuum hoses will, in most cases, have to be disconnected and plugged. Molded plugs in various shapes and sizes are available for this*
2 **Inductive pick-up timing light** - *Flashes a bright concentrated beam of light when the number one spark plug fires. Connect the leads according to the instructions supplied with the light*
3 **Distributor wrench** - *On some models, the hold-down bolt for the distributor is difficult to reach and turn with a conventional wrench or socket. A special wrench like this must be used*

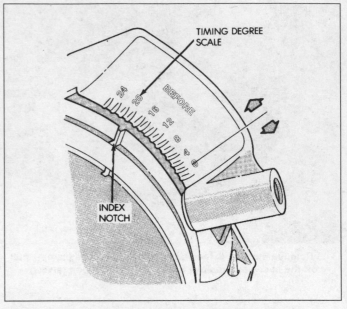

33.5 The ignition timing marks are located at the front of the engine

33 Ignition timing check and adjustment (carbureted models only)

Note: *Ignition timing check and adjustment are not required on vehicles other than those identified in the heading above. If the information in this Section differs from the Vehicle Emission Control Information label (located in the engine compartment of your vehicle), the label should be considered correct.*

1   The engine must be at normal operating temperature and the air conditioner must be Off. Make sure the idle speed is correct (see Section 30).
2   Some special tools will be required for this procedure (see illustration).
3   Apply the parking brake and block the wheels to prevent movement of the vehicle. The transmission must be in Park (automatic) or Neutral (manual).
4   Disconnect and plug the hose connected to the vacuum advance unit on the distributor and unplug the electrical connector from the CEC system switch assembly on top of the valve cover.
5   Locate the timing marks at the front of the engine (they should be visible from above after the hood is opened) (see illustration). The crankshaft pulley or vibration damper has a groove in it and a scale with notches and numbers is either molded into or attached to the engine's timing cover. Clean the scale with solvent so the numbers are visible.
6   Use chalk or white paint to mark the groove in the pulley/vibration damper.

7   Highlight the notch or point on the scale that corresponds to the ignition timing specification on the Vehicle Emission Control Information label.
8   Hook up the timing light, following the manufacturer's instructions (an inductive pick-up timing light is preferred). Generally, the power leads are attached to the battery terminals and the pick-up lead is attached to the number one spark plug wire. The number one spark plug is the very front one.
Caution: *If an inductive pick-up timing light isn't available, don't puncture the spark plug wire to attach the timing light pick-up lead. Instead, use an adapter between the spark plug and plug wire. If the insulation on the plug wire is damaged, the secondary voltage will jump to ground at the damaged point and the engine will misfire.*
9   Connect a tachometer, following the manufacturer's instructions.
10   Make sure the timing light and tachometer wires are routed away from the drivebelts and fan, then start the engine.
11   Allow the idle speed to stabilize, then point the flashing timing light at the timing marks - be very careful of moving engine components!
12   Increase the engine speed to 1600 rpm. The mark on the pulley/vibration damper will appear stationary. If it's aligned with the specified point on the scale, the ignition timing is correct.
13   If the marks aren't aligned, adjustment is required. Loosen the distributor hold-down bolt and turn the distributor very slowly until the marks are aligned. Since access to the

bolt is tight, a special distributor wrench may be needed.
14   Tighten the bolt and recheck the timing.
15   Turn off the engine and remove the timing light (and adapter, if used).
16   Reconnect any components which were disconnected.

34 Automatic transmission fluid and filter change

1   At the specified time intervals, the transmission fluid should be drained and replaced. Since the fluid will remain hot long after driving, perform this procedure only after the engine has cooled down completely.
2   Before beginning work, purchase the specified transmission fluid (see *Recommended lubricants and fluids* at the front of this Chapter) and a new filter.
3   Other tools necessary for this job include jackstands to support the vehicle in a raised position, a drain pan capable of holding at least eight pints, newspapers and clean rags.
4   Raise the vehicle and support it securely on jackstands.
5   With a drain pan in place, remove the front and side pan mounting bolts.
Note: *2007 through 2011 models have one bolt that is coated with adhesive sealant.*
6   Loosen the rear pan bolts approximately one turn.
7   If the pan does not loosen and fluid does not begin to drain, carefully pry the transmission pan loose with a putty knife.
8   Remove the remaining bolts, pan and

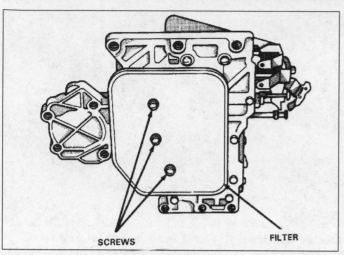

34.10 The automatic transmission fluid filter on some models is held in place by three screws. On other models the filter pulls straight out of the valve body

SCREWS   FILTER

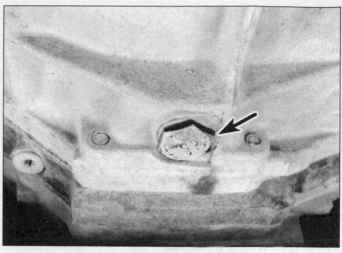

35.3 The transmission drain plug is located at the bottom of the case

gasket. Carefully clean the gasket surface of the transmission to remove all traces of the old gasket and sealant.

9   Drain the fluid from the transmission pan, clean it with solvent and dry it with compressed air.

10   Remove the filter from the transmission valve body (see illustration). With the vehicle raised and the pan off, this is a good time to adjust the transmission bands (see Chapter 7B).

11   Install a new filter and O-ring (on models so equipped).

12   Make sure the gasket surface on the transmission pan is clean, then install a new gasket. Put the pan in place against the transmission and, working around the pan, tighten each bolt a little at a time until the final torque figure is reached. On 2007 through 2011 models, clean the adhesive-coated bolt and apply new adhesive sealant.

13   Lower the vehicle and add the specified amount of automatic transmission fluid through the filler tube (see Section 6).

14   With the transmission in Park and the parking brake set, run the engine at a fast idle, but don't race it.

15   Move the gear selector through each range and back to Neutral. Check the fluid level (see Section 6).

16   Check under the vehicle for leaks during the first few trips.

35   Manual transmission lubricant change

1   Raise the vehicle and support it securely on jackstands.

2   Move a drain pan, rags, newspapers and wrenches under the transmission.

3   Remove the transmission drain plug at the bottom of the case (see illustration) and

36.4a Remove the bolts from the lower edge of the cover…

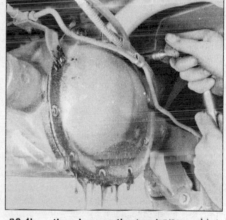

36.4b … then loosen the top bolts and let the lubricant drain out

allow the oil to drain into the pan.

4   After the oil has drained completely, reinstall the plug and tighten it securely.

5   Remove the fill plug from the side of the transmission case (see Section 16). Using a hand pump or squeeze bottle, fill the transmission with the correct amount of the specified lubricant. Reinstall the plug and tighten it securely.

6   Lower the vehicle.

7   Drive the vehicle for a short distance then check the drain and fill plugs for leakage.

36   Differential lubricant change

1   2011 and earlier models don't have a drain plug so a hand suction pump is used to remove the differential lubricant through the filler hole. If the cover plate is leaking and/or a suction pump isn't available, the lubri-

cant can be drained by removing the cover plate, so be sure to obtain a tube of gasket sealant when the lubricant is purchased. On models equipped with a limited slip differential (denoted by a tag attached to the differential cover), a packet of special additive will be required (Section 17). 2012 and later models have a drain plug on the side of the housing and a fill plug installed on the differential cover.

2   Raise the vehicle and support it securely on jackstands. Move a drain pan, rags, newspapers and wrenches under the vehicle.

3   If a suction pump is being used, insert the flexible hose. Work the hose down to the bottom of the differential housing and pump the lubricant out.

4   If the differential is being drained by removing the cover, remove the bolts on the lower half of the cover (see illustration). Loosen the bolts on the upper half and use them to keep the cover loosely attached (see illustration). Allow the lubricant to drain into

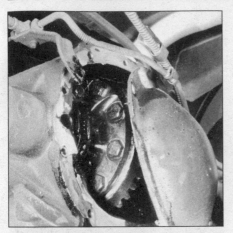

36.4c After the lubricant has completely drained, remove the cover

36.6 Carefully scrape the old sealant material off to ensure a clean surface

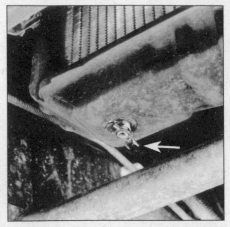

38.3 The drain plug is located at the bottom of the radiator - you might need a pair of pliers to turn it

the pan, then completely remove the cover (see illustration).

5   Using a lint-free rag, clean the inside of the cover and the accessible areas of the differential housing. As this is done, check for chipped gears and metal particles in the lubricant, indicating that the differential should be more thoroughly inspected and/or repaired.

6   Thoroughly clean the gasket mating surfaces of the differential housing and the cover plate. Use a gasket scraper or putty knife to remove all traces of the old sealant (see illustration).

7   Apply a thin layer of sealant to the cover flange, then place the cover on the differential housing and install the bolts. Tighten the bolts securely.

8   On all models, use a hand pump, syringe or funnel to fill the differential housing with the specified lubricant until it's level with the bottom of the plug hole. On limited slip-equipped differentials, add the packet of additive first, before filling the housing.

9   Install the filler plug and tighten it securely.

10   On limited slip differential-equipped models, drive the vehicle slowly in a figure-8 pattern seven or eight times to work the lubricant into the clutch packs.

37   Transfer case lubricant change

1   Drive the vehicle for at least 15 minutes in stop and go traffic to warm the lubricant in the case. Perform this warm-up procedure in 4WD. Use all gears, including Reverse, to ensure the lubricant is sufficiently warm to drain completely.

2   Raise the vehicle and support it securely on jackstands.

3   Remove the filler plug from the case (see Section 18).

4   Remove the drain plug from the lower part of the case and allow the old lubricant to drain completely.

5   Carefully clean and install the drain plug

after the case is completely drained. Tighten the plug to the torque listed in this Chapter's Specifications.

6   Fill the case with the specified lubricant until it is level with the lower edge of the filler hole.

7   Install the filler plug and tighten it securely.

8   Drive the vehicle for a short distance and recheck the lubricant level. In some instances a small amount of additional lubricant will have to be added.

38   Cooling system servicing (draining, flushing and refilling)

Warning: *Wait until the engine is completely cool before beginning this procedure.*

Warning: *Do not allow antifreeze to come in contact with your skin or painted surfaces of the vehicle. Rinse off spills immediately with plenty of water. Antifreeze is highly toxic if ingested. Never leave antifreeze lying around in an open container or in puddles on the floor; children and pets are attracted by its sweet smell and may drink it. Check with local authorities about disposing of used antifreeze. Many communities have collection centers which will see that antifreeze is disposed of safely.*

1   Periodically, the cooling system should be drained, flushed and refilled to replenish the antifreeze mixture and prevent formation of rust and corrosion, which can impair the performance of the cooling system and cause engine damage. When the cooling system is serviced, all hoses and the radiator cap should be checked and replaced if necessary.

Draining

2   Apply the parking brake and block the wheels. If the vehicle has just been driven, wait several hours to allow the engine to cool down before beginning this procedure.

3   Move a large container under the radiator drain fitting to catch the coolant. Once the

engine is completely cool, open the drain fitting (a pair of pliers may be required to turn it) (see illustration).

4   Remove the radiator cap.

5   After the coolant stops flowing out of the radiator, move the container under the engine block drain plug(s) on the engine (see illustrations). On four-cylinder engines, the drain plug is located at the left rear side of the block. Inline six-cylinder engines have two drain plugs located on the left side of the block (on some models there may be a coolant temperature sensor). V6 engines have a drain plug on each side of the engine block. Loosen the plug(s) and allow the coolant in the block to drain.

6   While the coolant is draining, check the condition of the radiator hoses, heater hoses and clamps (refer to Section 10 if necessary).

7   Replace any damaged clamps or hoses (refer to Chapter 3 for detailed replacement procedures).

Flushing

8   Once the system is completely drained, flush the radiator with fresh water from a garden hose until water runs clear at the drain. The flushing action of the water will remove sediments from the radiator but will not remove rust and scale from the engine and cooling tube surfaces.

9   These deposits can be removed by the chemical action of a cleaner. Follow the procedure outlined in the manufacturer's instructions. If the radiator is severely corroded, damaged or leaking, it should be removed (see Chapter 3) and taken to a radiator repair shop, or replaced.

Refilling

10   Close and tighten the radiator drain. Install and tighten the block drain plug(s).

11   Place the heater temperature control in the maximum heat position.

12   Slowly add new coolant (a 50/50 mixture of water and antifreeze) to the radiator until it's full. Add coolant to the reservoir bottle until

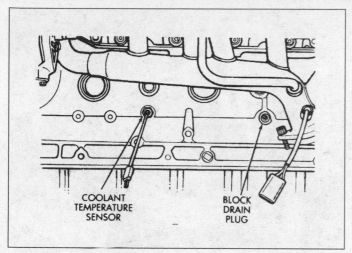

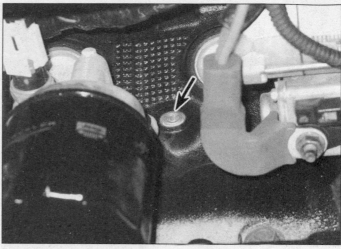

38.5a The block drain plug holes are located on the driver's side of the engine block (some, like this inline six-cylinder, may have coolant temperature sensors screwed into the plug hole)

38.5b The block drain plugs on V6 engines are located about one or two inches above the oil pan - there is one on each side of the engine block (3.6L V6 shown)

the level is at the upper mark.

13   Leave the radiator cap off and run the engine in a well-ventilated area until the thermostat opens (coolant will begin flowing through the radiator and the upper radiator hose will become hot).

14   Turn the engine off and let it cool. Add more coolant mixture to bring the level back up to the lip on the radiator filler neck.

15   Squeeze the upper radiator hose to expel air, then add more coolant mixture if necessary. Replace the radiator cap.

16   Start the engine, allow it to reach normal operating temperature and check for leaks.

39 Positive Crankcase Ventilation (PCV) valve or Crankcase Ventilation (CCV) hose - valve replacement/orifice cleaning

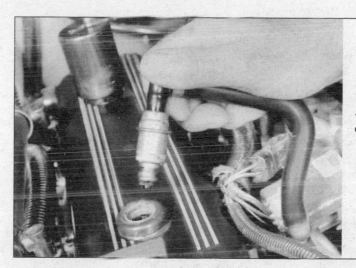

39.2a Pull the PCV valve from the valve cover, then detach it from the hose (inline engines)

PCV valve replacement

1   The PCV valve is located in the top of the valve cover on inline engines. On the 3.8L V6 engine it is located in the left-side valve cover. On the 3.6L V6 engine it's located at the rear of the right-side valve cover.

2   Inline engines and 3.8L V6 engine: Pull the valve from its grommet in the valve cover, then pull it from the end of the hose, noting its installed position and direction (see illustrations).

3   3.6L V6 engine: Squeeze the hose clamp and slide it back on the hose, then remove the two screws and pull the valve from the rear of the right valve cover (see illustration).

4   Push the valve into the end of the hose until it's seated.

5   Inspect the rubber grommet or O-ring for damage and replace it with a new one if necessary.

6   Push the PCV valve and hose securely into position. On 3.6L V6 engines, tighten the screws securely

39.2b On the 3.8L engine, the PCV valve is located in the left-side valve cover, near the ignition coil pack

39.3 On 3.6L V6 engines, the PCV valve is secured to the rear of the right valve cover with two screws

39.8 A paper clip can be used to clean the CCV system orifice

40.2a On 2002 and earlier models, the evaporative emissions canister is located on the passenger's side firewall - check the housing and hoses for damage

40.2b EVAP canister location - 2007 and later models

CCV hose and orifice cleaning

7   Later inline six-cylinder models are equipped with a CCV system which performs the same function as the PCV system but uses a rubber fitting with a molded-in orifice which is pressed into a hole in the valve cover. The fitting is connected to the intake manifold by a plastic hose.

8   If there is no vacuum at the end of the hose (Step 3), turn off the engine, remove the fitting and clean the hose with solvent. Clean the fitting orifice (see illustration) if it's plugged. If the fitting or hose are cracked or deteriorated, replace them with new ones.

9   Install the fitting and hose securely in the valve cover.

40   Evaporative emissions control system check

1   The function of the evaporative emissions control system is to draw fuel vapors

from the gas tank and fuel system, store them in a charcoal canister and route them to the intake manifold during normal engine operation.

2   The most common symptom of a fault in the evaporative emissions system is a strong fuel odor in the engine compartment (2002 and earlier models) or from the rear of the vehicle (2003 and later models). If a fuel odor is detected, inspect the charcoal canister, located in the right rear corner of the engine compartment (see illustration). On 2002 and earlier models, the vapor canister is located in the engine compartment. On 2003 through 2006 models, the EVAP canister is located to the rear of the right-rear wheel, under the inner fender splash shield. On 2007 and later models, it is located under the vehicle, near the driveshaft (see illustration). Check the canister and all hoses for damage and deterioration.

3   The evaporative emissions control system is explained in more detail in Chapter 6.

41   Spark plug replacement

Note: *On models with 2.4L engines, remove the throttle body for access to the spark plugs for cylinders 2 and 3 (see Chapter 4).*
Note: *On 2000 through 2006 models with a 4.0L six-cylinder engine, remove the coil rail for access to the spark plugs (see Chapter 5).*
Note: *On 2012 and later models with 3.6L engines, remove the ignition coils (see Chapter 5). To access the ignition coils and spark plugs for cylinders 2, 4 and 6, the upper intake manifold must be removed (see Chapter 2E).*

1   Open the hood.

2   In most cases, the tools necessary for spark plug replacement include a spark plug socket which fits onto a ratchet (spark plug sockets are padded inside to prevent damage to the porcelain insulators on the new plugs), various extensions and a gap gauge to check and adjust the gaps on the new plugs (see illustration). A special plug wire removal tool is available for separating the wire boots from the spark plugs, but it isn't absolutely necessary. A torque wrench should be used to tighten the new plugs.

3   The best approach when replacing the spark plugs is to purchase the new ones in advance, adjust them to the proper gap and replace them one at a time. When buying the new spark plugs, be sure to obtain the correct plug type for your particular engine. This information can be found in the Specifications Section at the beginning of this Chapter, or in the vehicle owner's manual.

4   Allow the engine to cool completely before attempting to remove any of the plugs. While you're waiting for the engine to cool, check the new plugs for defects and adjust the gaps.

5   The gap is checked by inserting the proper thickness gauge between the electrodes at the tip of the plug (see illustration).

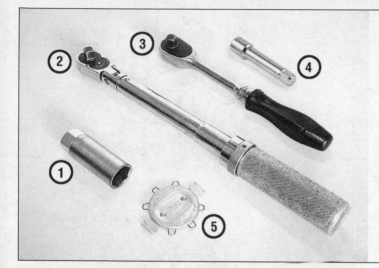

41.2 Tools required for changing spark plugs

1   **Spark plug socket** - This will have special padding inside to protect the spark plug's porcelain insulator
2   **Torque wrench** - Although not mandatory, using this tool is the best way to ensure the plugs are tightened properly
3   **Ratchet** - Standard hand tool to fit the spark plug socket
4   **Extension** - Depending on model and accessories, you may need special extensions and universal joints to reach one or more of the plugs
5   **Spark plug gap gauge** - This gauge for checking the gap comes in a variety of styles. Make sure the gap for your engine is included

41.5a Spark plug manufacturers recommend using a wire type gauge when checking the gap - if the wire does not slide between the electrodes with a slight drag, adjustment is required

41.5b To change the gap, bend the side electrode only, as indicated by the arrows, and be very careful not to crack or chip the porcelain insulator surrounding the center electrodes

The gap between the electrodes should be the same as the one specified. The wire should just slide between the electrodes with a slight amount of drag. If the gap is incorrect, use the adjuster on the gauge body to bend the curved side electrode slightly until the proper gap is obtained (see illustration). If the side electrode is not exactly over the center electrode, bend it with the adjuster until it is. Check for cracks in the porcelain insulator (if any are found, the plug should not be used).

6   With the engine cool, remove the spark plug wire or ignition coil from one spark plug. On plug wires pull only on the boot at the end of the wire - do not pull on the wire. A plug wire removal tool should be used if available (see illustration).

7   If compressed air is available, use it to blow any dirt or foreign material away from the spark plug hole to eliminate the possibility of debris falling into the cylinder as the spark plug is removed.

8   Place the spark plug socket over the plug and remove it from the engine by turning it in a counterclockwise direction (see illustration).

41.6 Grasp the spark plug wire boot and use a twisting/pulling motion - it's a good idea to use a tool such as the one shown here to get a good grip

41.8 A socket with an extension makes it easier to remove the spark plug

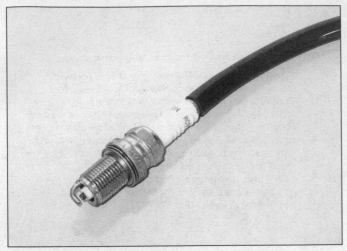

41.10 A length of snug-fitting rubber hose will save time and prevent damaged threads when installing the spark plug

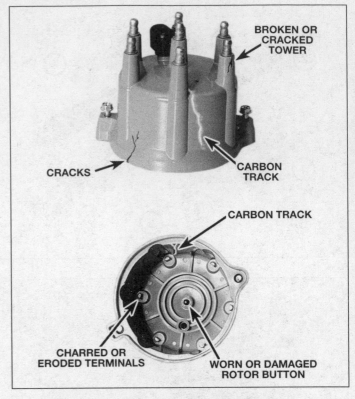

42.11 Shown here are some of the common defects to look for when inspecting the distributor cap (if in doubt about its condition, install a new one)

9   Compare each old spark plug to those shown on the inside of the back cover to get an indication of the general running condition of the engine.

10   Thread one of the new plugs into the hole until you can no longer turn it with your fingers, then tighten it with a torque wrench (if available) or the ratchet. It is a good idea to slip a short length of rubber hose over the end of the plug to use as a tool to thread it into place (see illustration). The hose will grip the plug well enough to turn it, but will start to slip if the plug begins to cross-thread in the hole - this will prevent damaged threads and the accompanying repair costs.

11   Before pushing the spark plug wire onto the end of the plug, inspect it following the procedures outlined in Section 42.

12   Attach the plug wire to the new spark plug, again using a twisting motion on the boot until it's seated on the spark plug.

13   Repeat the procedure for the remaining spark plugs, replacing them one at a time to prevent mixing up the spark plug wires.

42   Spark plug wire, distributor cap and rotor check and replacement

Note: *2003 through 2011 models do not have a distributor or rotor. The spark plug wires connect the ignition coil pack directly to the spark plugs. 2012 and later models use coil-over plug type ignition and do not have spark plug wires.*

1   The spark plug wires should be checked whenever new spark plugs are installed.

2   Begin this procedure by making a visual check of the spark plug wires while the engine is running. In a darkened garage (make sure there is ventilation) start the engine and observe each plug wire. Be careful not to come into contact with any moving engine parts. If there is a break in the wire, you will see arcing or a small spark at the damaged area. If arcing is noticed, make a note to obtain new wires, then allow the engine to cool and check the distributor cap and rotor.

3   The spark plug wires should be inspected one at a time to prevent mixing up the order, which is essential for proper engine operation. Each original plug wire should be numbered to help identify its location. If the number is illegible, a piece of tape can be marked with the correct number and wrapped around the plug wire.

4   Disconnect the plug wire from the spark plug. A removal tool can be used for this purpose or you can grasp the rubber boot, twist the boot half a turn and pull the boot free. Do not pull on the wire itself.

5   Check inside the boot for corrosion, which will look like a white crusty powder.

6   Push the wire and boot back onto the end of the spark plug. It should fit tightly onto the end of the plug. If it doesn't, remove the wire and use pliers to carefully crimp the metal connector inside the wire boot until the fit is snug.

7   Using a clean rag, wipe the entire length of the wire to remove built-up dirt and grease. Once the wire is clean, check for burns, cracks and other damage. Do not bend the wire sharply, because the conductor might break.

8   Disconnect the wire from the distributor. Again, pull only on the rubber boot. Check for corrosion and a tight fit. Replace the wire in the distributor.

9   Inspect the remaining spark plug wires, making sure that each one is securely fastened at the distributor and spark plug when the check is complete.

10   If new spark plug wires are required, purchase a set for your specific engine model. Pre-cut wire sets with the boots already installed are available. Remove and replace the wires one at a time to avoid mix-ups in the firing order.

11   Detach the distributor cap by removing the two cap retaining bolts. Look inside it for cracks, carbon tracks and worn, burned or loose contacts (see illustration).

12   Pull the rotor off the distributor shaft and examine it for cracks and carbon tracks (see illustration). Replace the cap and rotor if any damage or defects are noted.

13   It is common practice to install a new cap and rotor whenever new spark plug wires are installed, but if you wish to continue using the old cap, check the resistance between the spark plug wires and the cap first. If the indicated resistance is more than the speci-

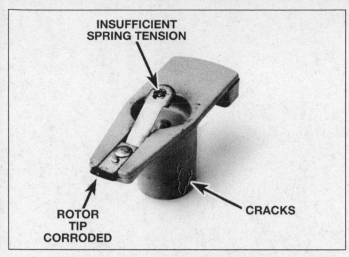

42.12 The ignition rotor should be checked for wear and corrosion as indicated here (if in doubt about its condition, buy a new one)

INSUFFICIENT
SPRING TENSION

ROTOR
TIP
CORRODED

CRACKS

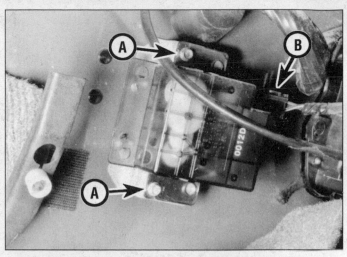

43.3 The emissions timer details (1990 and earlier models)

A   *Retaining screws*   B   *Electrical connectors*

fied maximum value, replace the cap and/or wires.

14   When installing a new cap, remove the wires from the old cap one at a time and attach them to the new cap in the exact same location - do not simultaneously remove all the wires from the old cap or firing order mix-ups may occur.

43   Oxygen sensor(s) and emission maintenance timer replacement

Oxygen sensor(s)

1   See Chapter 6 for the oxygen sensor replacement procedure.

Emissions maintenance timer

2   On 1990 and earlier models an emission maintenance timer (mounted under the right side of the dashboard) activates the emissions maintenance indicator light on the instrument panel when the oxygen sensor is

scheduled for replacement (approximately 82,500 miles). The timer cannot be reset and must be replaced or disconnected to turn out the indicator light.

3   The timer is located under the instrument panel, to the right of the steering column (see illustration). Unplug the electrical connector, remove the screws and lower the timer from the instrument panel. Installation is the reverse of removal.

4   On 1991 and later models, the emissions maintenance indicator light can only be reset with a special tool available at most auto parts stores. After replacing the oxygen sensor take the vehicle to a dealer service department or other properly equipped repair facility and have the light reset.

44   Cabin air filter(s) replacement

Warning: *The models covered by this manual are equipped with a Supplemental Restraint System (SRS), more commonly known as*

airbags. Always disable the airbag system before working in the vicinity of any airbag system component to avoid the possibility of accidental deployment of the airbag, which could cause personal injury (see Chapter 12).

1   Disengage the clips on each side of the glove box, then pull the sides inwards until the stops are clear and lower the glove box.

2   Disengage the two retaining tabs at the front edge of each cover and open the covers.

Note: *On some models with two filters, the right side cover door may be obstructed by the speaker housing. If so, remove the left filter then slide the right cabin air filter to the left and remove it.*

3   Remove the filters from the housing.

4   Install the filter, making sure the arrow on the filter is pointing towards the floor.

Note: *The cabin air filter(s) is labeled with an arrow and the word "Airflow" on it. The filter should be installed with the arrow pointing towards the floor.*

5   Installation is the reverse of the removal procedure.

Notes

Chapter 2 Part A
2.4L four-cylinder engine

Contents

Specifications

General

Bore	3.445 inches (87.5 mm)
Stroke	3.976 inches (101 mm)
Compression ratio	9.5 . 1
Displacement	2.4 liters (148 cubic inches)
Firing order	1-3-4-2

Camshaft

Bearing bore diameter	1.024 to 1.025 inches (26.020 to 26.041 mm)
Bearing journal diameter	1.021 to 1.022 inches (25.951 to 25.970 mm)
Bearing clearance	0.0027 to 0.003 inch (0.0691 to 0.071 mm)
Endplay	0.0019 to 0.0066 inch (0.05 to 0.17 mm)
Lobe lift	
Intake	0.324 inch (8.25 mm)
Exhaust	0.259 inch (6.60 mm)

Cylinder head

Head gasket surface warpage limit	0.004 inch maximum (0.1 mm)
Intake and exhaust manifold mounting surface warpage limit	0.006 inch per foot maximum (0.15 mm per 300 mm)

Intake and exhaust manifolds

Warpage limit	0.006 inch per foot maximum (0.15 mm per 300 mm)

Oil pump

Cover warpage limit	0.001 inch (0.025 mm)
Inner rotor thickness (minimum)	0.370 inch (9.40 mm)
Outer rotor thickness (minimum)	0.370 inch (9.40 mm)
Outer rotor diameter (minimum)	3.148 inch (79.95 mm)
Rotor-to-pump cover clearance (maximum)	0.004 inch (0.10 mm)
Outer rotor-to-housing clearance (maximum)	0.015 inch (0.039 mm)
Inner rotor-to-outer rotor lobe clearance (maximum)	0.008 inch (0.20 mm)
Pressure relief spring free length	2.39 inches (approximate)

Front

50035-1-A HAYNES

Cylinder locations (2.4L four-cylinder)

Torque specifications*   Ft-lbs (unless otherwise indicated)

Note: *One foot-pound (ft-lb) of torque is equivalent to 12 inch-pounds (in-lbs) of torque. Torque values below approximately 15 foot-pounds are expressed in inch-pounds, because most foot-pound torque wrenches are not accurate at these smaller values.*

Camshaft bearing cap bolts (see illustration 11.5 for bolt tightening sequence)	
M6 bolts	105 in-lbs
M8 bolts	21
Camshaft timing belt sprocket bolt	75
Crankshaft damper bolt	100
Cylinder head bolts (in sequence - see illustration 15.18)	
Step 1	25
Step 2	50
Step 3	50
Step 4	Tighten an additional 1/4-turn (90-degrees)
Driveplate-to-crankshaft bolts	70
Exhaust manifold-to-cylinder head bolts	17
Exhaust manifold-to-exhaust pipe bolts	21
Intake manifold bolts	21
Oil pan bolts	105 in-lbs
Oil pump	
Attaching bolts	21
Cover screws	105 in-lbs
Pick-up tube bolt	20
Relief valve cap bolt	30
Timing belt	
Cover bolts	105 in-lbs
Idler pulley bolt	45
Tensioner assembly	
Tensioner pulley bolt	22
Tensioner assembly mounting bolt	45
Valve cover bolts	
Step 1	40 in-lbs
Step 2	80 in-lbs
Step 3	105 in-lbs

Refer to Chapter 2F for additional torque specifications

1 General Information

1   This Part of Chapter 2 is devoted to in-vehicle engine repair procedures for the 2.4L four-cylinder engine. Information concerning engine removal and installation and overhaul can be found in Chapter 2F.

2   The following repair procedures are based on the assumption that the engine is installed in the vehicle. If the engine has been removed from the vehicle and mounted on a stand, many of the steps outlined in this Part of Chapter 2 will not apply.

3   The Specifications included in this Part of Chapter 2 apply only to the procedures contained in this Part.

2 Repair operations possible with the engine in the vehicle

1   Many major repair operations can be accomplished without removing the engine from the vehicle.

2   Clean the engine compartment and the exterior of the engine with some type of degreaser before any work is done. It will make the job easier and help keep dirt out of the internal areas of the engine.

3   Depending on the components involved, it may be helpful to remove the hood to improve access to the engine as repairs are performed (refer to Chapter 2F if necessary). Cover the fenders to prevent damage to the paint. Special pads are available, but an old bedspread or blanket will also work.

4   If vacuum, exhaust, oil or coolant leaks develop, indicating a need for gasket or seal replacement, the repairs can generally be made with the engine in the vehicle. The intake and exhaust manifold gaskets, oil pan gasket, camshaft and crankshaft oil seals and cylinder head gasket are all accessible with the engine in place.

5   Exterior engine components, such as the intake and exhaust manifolds, the oil pan, the oil pump, the water pump, the starter motor, the alternator, the distributor and the fuel system components can be removed for repair with the engine in place.

6   Since the camshafts and cylinder head can be removed without pulling the engine, valve component servicing can also be accomplished with the engine in the vehicle. Replacement of the timing belt and sprockets is also possible with the engine in the vehicle.

7   In extreme cases caused by a lack of necessary equipment, repair or replacement of piston rings, pistons, connecting rods and rod bearings is possible with the engine in the vehicle. However, this practice is not recommended because of the cleaning and preparation work that must be done to the components involved.

3 Top Dead Center (TDC) for number one piston - locating

1   Top Dead Center (TDC) is the highest point in the cylinder that each piston reaches as it travels up-and-down when the crankshaft turns. Each piston reaches TDC on the compression stroke and again on the exhaust stroke, but TDC generally refers to piston position on the compression stroke. The cast-in timing mark arrow on the crankshaft timing belt pulley (installed on the front of the crankshaft) refers to the number one piston at TDC - when the arrow is straight up, or at "12 o'clock," and aligned with the cast-in timing mark arrow on the oil pump housing (see Section 17).

2   Positioning a specific piston at TDC is an essential part of many procedures such as camshaft(s) removal, rocker arm removal, timing belt and sprocket replacement.

3   In order to bring any piston to TDC, the crankshaft must be turned using one of the methods outlined below. When looking at the front of the engine, normal crankshaft rotation is clockwise.

Warning: *Before beginning this procedure, be sure to set the parking brake, place the transmission in Park or Neutral and disable the ignition system by disconnecting the primary electrical connector from the ignition coil pack.*

   a) *The preferred method is to turn the crankshaft with a large socket and breaker bar attached to the crankshaft balancer hub bolt that is threaded into the front of the crankshaft.*

   b) *A remote starter switch, which may save some time, can also be used. Attach the switch leads to the S (switch) and B (battery) terminals on the starter solenoid. Once the piston is close to TDC, discontinue with the remote switch and use a socket and breaker bar as described in the previous paragraph.*

   c) *If an assistant is available to turn the ignition switch to the Start position in short bursts, you can get the piston close to TDC without a remote starter switch. Use a socket and breaker bar as described in Paragraph a) to complete the procedure.*

4   Remove all of the spark plugs as this will make it easier to rotate the engine by hand.

5   Insert a compression gauge (screw-in type with a hose) in the number 1 spark plug hole. Place the gauge dial where you can see it while turning the crankshaft pulley hub bolt.

Note: *The number one cylinder is located at the front of the engine.*

6   Turn the crankshaft clockwise until you see compression building up on the gauge - you are on the compression stroke for that cylinder. If you did not see compression build up, continue with one more complete revolution to achieve TDC for the number one cylinder.

7   Remove the compression gauge.

Through the number one cylinder spark plug hole insert a length of wooden dowel or plastic rod and slowly push it down until it reaches the top of the piston.

Caution: *Don't insert a metal or sharp object into the spark plug hole as the piston crown may be damaged.*

8   With the dowel or rod in place on top of the piston crown, slowly rotate the crankshaft clockwise until the dowel or rod is pushed upward, stops, and then starts to move back down. At this point, rotate the crankshaft slightly counterclockwise until the dowel or rod has reached its uppermost travel. At this point the number one piston is at the TDC position.

9   Remove the upper timing belt cover (see Section 7). Then check the alignment of the camshaft timing marks (see illustration 7.11). At this point, the camshaft's timing marks should be aligned. If not repeat this procedure until alignment is correct.

10   After the number one piston has been positioned at TDC on the compression stroke, TDC for any of the remaining cylinders can be located by turning the crankshaft 180-degrees (1/2-turn) at a time and following the firing order (refer to this Chapter's Specifications).

4 Valve cover - removal and installation

Removal

1   Disconnect the cable from the negative terminal of the battery (see Chapter 5).

2   Remove the upper intake manifold (see Section 5).

3   Remove the ignition coil pack from the valve cover (see Chapter 5).

4   Clearly label and detach any electrical wiring harnesses which connect to or cross over the valve cover.

5   Disconnect the PCV valve hose and breather hose from the valve cover.

6   Remove the valve cover bolts in the reverse order of the tightening sequence (see illustration 4.9), then lift off the cover. If the cover sticks to the cylinder head, tap on it with a soft-face hammer or place a wood block against the cover and tap on the wood with a hammer.

Caution: *If you have to pry between the valve cover and the cylinder head, be extremely careful not to gouge or nick the gasket surfaces of either part - which could cause a leak to develop after reassembly.*

7   Remove the valve gaskets and spark plug well seals. Thoroughly clean the valve cover and remove all traces of old gasket material. Gasket removal solvents are available from auto parts stores and may prove helpful. After cleaning the surfaces, degrease them with a rag soaked in brake system cleaner.

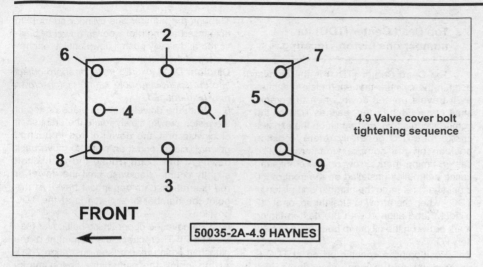

4.9 Valve cover bolt tightening sequence

FRONT

50035-2A-4.9 HAYNES

Installation

8   Install a new gasket and spark plug well seals on the cover, using RTV sealant to hold them in place. Apply RTV sealant to the camshaft cap corners and the top edges of the half-round seal. Place the cover on the engine and install the cover bolts.
Note: *Make sure the two bolts with the sealing washers are in their proper locations.*
9   Tighten the valve cover bolts in three stages in the proper sequence to the torque listed in this Chapter's Specifications (see illustration).
10   The remaining steps are the reverse of removal. When finished, run the engine and check for oil leaks.

5   Intake manifold - removal and installation

Removal

1   The intake manifold is a two-piece aluminum design.
Note: *If you are removing the intake manifold simply to access the spark plugs or valve cover, it's not necessary to remove the entire intake manifold unit - only remove the upper intake manifold. Otherwise, the intake manifold can be removed as a complete unit (upper and lower plenum sections bolted together).*
2   If removing the complete intake manifold, relieve the fuel system pressure (see Chapter 4). If only removing the upper intake manifold, this step may be skipped.
3   Disconnect the cable from the negative terminal of the battery (see Chapter 5).
4   Disconnect the electrical connector at the Intake Air Temperature (IAT) sensor and remove the air intake tube and air filter upper housing.
5   Disconnect the electrical connectors at the Idle Air Control (IAC) motor, Throttle Position Sensor (TPS) and Manifold Absolute Pressure (MAP) sensor.
6   Disconnect the vacuum hoses at the intake manifold from the PCV valve, Leak Detection Pump (LDP), evaporative system

purge solenoid, EGR transducer, power brake booster and, if equipped, the cruise control vacuum reservoir.
7   Disconnect the accelerator cable from its bracket and lever and, if equipped, remove the cruise control and transmission control cables.
8   Remove the EGR pipe bolts at the EGR valve and at the intake manifold, then remove the EGR pipe.
9   Remove the oil dipstick.
Note: *If the upper and lower intake manifolds are being removed as a unit, skip to step 11. If only the upper intake manifold is being removed, proceed as follows:*

a) *Remove the bolt from the manifold support bracket at the front of the upper intake manifold.*
b) *Remove the upper intake manifold attaching bolts and lift the upper manifold off.*
c) *Refer to Step 17 for the inspection procedure.*
d) *Use a new manifold gasket and install the upper intake manifold and tighten the upper intake manifold bolts gradually and evenly, starting with the center bolts and working outward, to the torque listed in this Chapter's Specifications.*
e) *The remainder of installation is the reverse of removal.*

10   If you are removing the complete intake manifold unit, remove the electrical connector at the Coolant Temperature Sensor (CTS) and proceed with the remaining steps.
11   Remove the fuel injector harness connectors.
12   Remove the fuel rail, fuel pressure regulator and fuel injectors as a single assembly (see Chapter 4).
13   If you're planning to replace or service the intake manifold plenum, remove the throttle body (see Chapter 4). If you're simply removing the intake manifold plenum to remove or service the cylinder head, it's not necessary to remove the throttle body from the intake manifold plenum.
14   Remove the bolts from the intake manifold support bracket.

15   Remove the intake manifold bolts and washers, then remove the intake manifold and the manifold gasket.

Inspection

16   Using a straightedge and feeler gauge, check the intake manifold mating surface for warpage.
17   Check the intake manifold surface on the cylinder head also.
18   If the warpage on either surface exceeds the limit listed in this Chapter's Specifications, the intake manifold and/or the cylinder head must be resurfaced at an automotive machine shop or, if the warpage is too excessive for resurfacing, it should be replaced.

Installation

19   Using a new manifold gasket, install the intake manifold and tighten the intake manifold-to-cylinder head bolts gradually and evenly, starting with the inner bolts and working outward, to the torque listed in this Chapter's Specifications.
20   The remainder of installation is the reverse of removal.

6   Exhaust manifold - removal and installation

Warning: *Allow the engine to cool completely before beginning this procedure.*

Removal

1   Raise the front of the vehicle and place it securely on jackstands.
2   Disconnect the exhaust pipe from the exhaust manifold and lower the vehicle.
3   Remove the air filter housing and bracket (see Chapter 4).
4   Remove the exhaust manifold heat shield.
5   Unplug the electrical connector for the oxygen sensor, then remove the oxygen sensor from the exhaust manifold (see Chapter 6).
6   Unscrew the mounting bolts and remove the exhaust manifold and the old manifold gasket.

Inspection

7   Inspect the exhaust manifold for cracks and any other obvious damage. If the manifold is cracked or damaged in any way, replace it.
8   Using a wire brush, clean up the threads of the exhaust manifold bolts and inspect the threads for damage. Replace any bolts that have thread damage.
9   Using a scraper, remove all traces of gasket material from the mating surfaces and inspect them for wear and cracks.
Caution: *When removing gasket material from any surface, especially aluminum, be very careful not to scratch or gouge the gasket surface. Any damage to the surface may result in a leak after reassembly. Gasket removal solvents are available from auto parts stores and may prove helpful.*

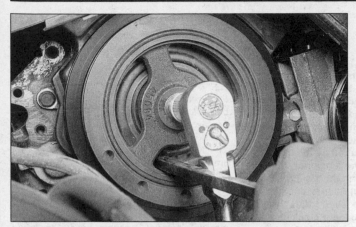

7.7 Insert a large screwdriver or bar through the opening in the pulley and wedge it against the engine block, then loosen the bolt with a socket and breaker bar

7.8 Install a 3-jaw puller onto the damper pulley, position the center post of the puller on the crankshaft end (use the proper insert to keep from damaging the crankshaft threads), tighten the puller and remove the pulley from the crankshaft

10   Using a straightedge and feeler gauge, inspect the exhaust manifold mating surface for warpage. Check the exhaust manifold surface on the cylinder head also. If the warpage on any surface exceeds the limits listed in this Chapter's Specifications, the exhaust manifold and/or cylinder head must be replaced or resurfaced at an automotive machine shop.

Installation

11   Using a new exhaust manifold gasket, install the exhaust manifold and hand-tighten the mounting bolts.
12   Raise the front of the vehicle and place it securely on jackstands.
13   Hand-tighten the exhaust pipe bolts.
14   Starting in the center and working your way outward, tighten the exhaust manifold mounting bolts to the torque listed in this Chapter's Specifications.
15   Tighten the exhaust pipe bolts to the torque listed in this Chapter's Specifications.
16   The remainder of installation is the reverse of removal.

7   Timing belt - removal, inspection and installation

Caution: *Do not try to turn the crankshaft with a camshaft sprocket bolt and do not rotate the crankshaft counterclockwise.*
Caution: *Do not turn the camshafts after the timing belt has been removed. Doing so will damage the valves from contact with other valves and/or the piston(s).*

Removal

Caution: *The timing system is complex. Severe engine damage will occur if you make any mistakes. Do not attempt this procedure unless you are highly experienced with this type of repair. If you are at all unsure of your abilities, consult an expert. Double-check all your work and be sure everything is correct before you attempt to start the engine.*

1   Position the number one piston at Top Dead Center (see Section 3).
2   Disconnect the cable from the negative terminal of the battery (see Chapter 5).
3   Remove the air filter housing and tube (see Chapter 4).
4   Remove the drivebelt (see Chapter 1).
5   Set the parking brake and block the rear wheels. Raise the front of the vehicle and support it securely on jackstands.
6   Remove the drivebelt splash shield from underneath the vehicle.
7   Loosen the large bolt in the center of the crankshaft damper pulley. It might be very tight; to break it loose, insert a large screwdriver or bar through the opening in the pulley to keep the pulley stationary and loosen the bolt with a socket and breaker bar (see illustration).
8   Install a 3-jaw puller onto the damper pulley and remove the pulley from the crankshaft (see illustration). Use the proper insert to keep the puller from damaging the crank-

shaft bolt threads. If the pulley is difficult to remove, tap the center bolt of the puller with a brass mallet to break it loose. Reinstall the bolt with a spacer so you can rotate the crankshaft later.
9   Remove the drivebelt tensioner and pulley assembly (right below the alternator).
10   Remove the lower timing belt cover bolts and remove the cover. Remove the upper timing belt cover bolts and remove the cover.
Note: *Lower the vehicle, if necessary.*
11   Before removing the timing belt, make sure that the camshaft timing marks are aligned and that the TDC mark on the crankshaft timing belt sprocket is aligned with the stationary index mark on the oil pump housing (see illustration). Note that the crankshaft sprocket TDC mark is located on the trailing edge of the sprocket tooth. If you don't align the trailing edge of the sprocket tooth with the TDC mark on the oil pump housing, the camshaft timing marks won't be aligned.

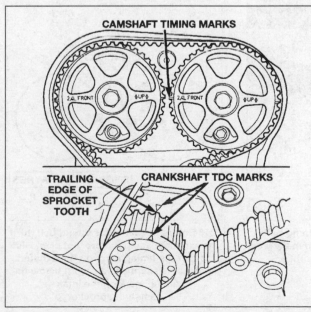

7.11 Before removing the timing belt, make sure the camshaft timing marks are aligned and the TDC mark on the crankshaft timing belt sprocket is aligned with the stationary mark on the oil pump housing (note that the crankshaft timing belt sprocket TDC mark is located on the trailing edge of the sprocket tooth)

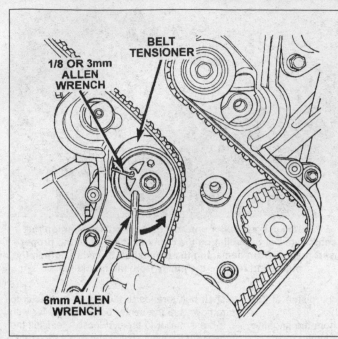

7.12 Insert a 1/4-inch (6 mm) Allen wrench into the belt tensioner and insert the long end of a 1/8 inch (3 mm) Allen wrench into the small hole located on the front of the tensioner; then using the 1/4-inch (6 mm) Allen wrench as the lever, rotate the tensioner clockwise and simultaneously and lightly, push in the 1/8 inch (3 mm) Allen wrench until it slides into the hole in the tensioner

12   Release tension on the timing belt. Insert a 1/4-inch (6 mm) Allen wrench into the belt tensioner and insert the long end of a 1/8-inch (3 mm) Allen wrench into the small hole located on the front of the tensioner (see illustration). Then, using the 1/4-inch (6 mm) Allen wrench as a lever, rotate the tensioner COUNTERCLOCKWISE and simultaneously and lightly push in the 1/8-inch (3 mm) Allen wrench until it slides into the locking hole in the tensioner.

13   Carefully slip the timing belt off the sprockets and set it aside. If you plan to reuse the timing belt, place it in a plastic bag - do not allow the belt to come in contact with any type of oil or water as this will greatly shorten belt life.

Inspection

14   Rotate the tensioner pulley and idler pulley by hand and move them side-to-side to detect roughness and excess play. Replace parts as necessary (see Section 8). Visually inspect the sprockets for any signs of damage and wear.

15   Inspect the timing belt for cracks, separation, wear, missing teeth and oil contamination. Replace the belt if it's in questionable condition (see illustration). If the timing belt is excessively worn or damaged on one side, it might be due to incorrect tracking (misalignment). If the belt looks like it was misaligned, be sure to replace the belt tensioner assembly.

16   Check the automatic tensioner for leaks or any obvious damage to the body.

Installation

Caution: *Before starting the engine, carefully rotate the crankshaft by hand through at least two full revolutions (use a socket and breaker bar on the crankshaft pulley center bolt). If you feel any resistance, STOP! There is something wrong - most likely, valves are contacting the pistons. You must find the problem before proceeding. Check your work and see if any updated repair information is available.*

17   Make sure that the TDC mark on the crankshaft timing belt sprocket is still aligned with the stationary index mark on the oil pump housing (see illustration 7.11).

18   Turn the exhaust camshaft sprocket clockwise so that the timing mark on the exhaust sprocket is slightly below the timing mark on the intake camshaft sprocket (see illustration).

19   Install the timing belt as follows: Start at the crankshaft sprocket, then thread the belt onto the water pump sprocket, the idler pulley, the camshaft sprockets and then finally the tensioner (see illustration). Now take up tension by moving the exhaust camshaft sprocket counterclockwise until the timing marks on the two cam sprockets are realigned.

20   Insert a 6 mm Allen wrench into the hexagon opening located on the top plate

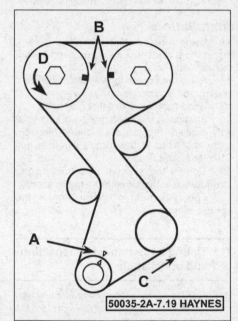

7.19 When installing the belt, start at the crankshaft sprocket and thread the belt around the water pump sprocket, the idler pulley, the cam sprockets and the tensioner pulley

A   Crankshaft TDC marks aligned
B   Exhaust camshaft mark 1/2-notch below the intake camshaft mark
C   Install the belt in a counterclockwise direction (looking at the front of the engine)
D   Rotate the exhaust camshaft counterclockwise to remove the timing belt slack

7.15 Carefully inspect the timing belt; bending it backwards will often make wear or damage more apparent

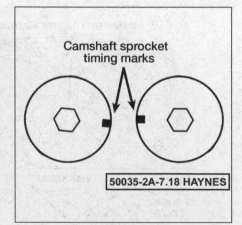

7.18 Before installing the timing belt, turn the exhaust camshaft sprocket clockwise so that the timing mark on the exhaust sprocket is slightly (1/2-notch) below the timing mark on the intake camshaft sprocket

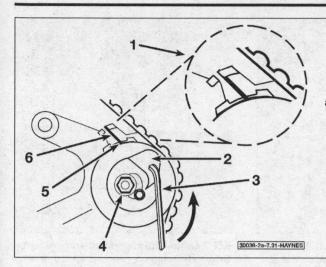

7.20 Rotate the tensioner until the setting notch aligns with the spring tang

1 Setting notch and spring tang alignment details
2 Top plate
3 6 mm Allen wrench
4 Lock nut
5 Setting notch
6 Spring tang

8.9 When installing a camshaft sprocket, make sure the pin in the camshaft is aligned with the hole in the sprocket

of the belt tensioner pulley. Then, using the 6 mm Allen wrench as a lever, rotate the belt tensioner COUNTERCLOCKWISE until there is tension on the timing belt. Continue to rotate the tension until the setting notch is aligned with the spring tang (see illustration). Grip the Allen wrench to prevent the tensioner from rotating, and torque the tensioner bolt to this Chapter's Specifications. Recheck the alignment marks. If they are incorrect, loosen the bolt and repeat the procedure.
Note: *Be sure to unlock the tensioner by removing the 3 mm Allen wrench from the locking hole.*
21 Rotate the crankshaft 720-degrees (two complete revolutions) and verify that the TDC marks on the crankshaft sprocket and the oil pump housing are still aligned and that the timing marks on the camshaft sprockets are still aligned. If they're not, stop right here, go back to Step 17 and install the belt again.
22 Install the upper and lower timing belt covers and tighten the fasteners to the torque listed in this Chapter's Specifications.
23 Install the drivebelt idler pulley and tighten the idler pulley bolt to the torque listed in this Chapter's Specifications.
24 Install the crankshaft vibration damper, the washer and pulley bolt. Tighten the pulley bolt to the torque listed in this Chapter's Specifications.
25 The remainder of installation is the reverse of removal.

8 Timing belt tensioner and pulley - removal and installation

Removal

1 Remove the timing belt (see Section 7).
2 Remove the timing belt idler pulley bolt, then remove the timing belt idler pulley.
3 Using a suitable holding tool, remove the camshaft sprocket bolts.
Caution: *Don't allow the camshafts to turn as the bolts are loosened. Then, using two large screwdrivers, lever the sprockets off the camshafts.*

4 Remove the bolts for the rear timing belt cover and then remove the rear cover.
5 Remove the lower timing belt tensioner bolt and remove the tensioner assembly.

Installation

6 Place the timing belt tensioner in position on the front of the engine and then install the lower mounting bolt to hold it in place, but don't tighten the lower bolt yet. Install an engine bracket mounting bolt (M10) in the upper tensioner bolt hole and then screw it in five to seven turns. Tighten the lower tensioner bolt to the torque listed in this Chapter's Specifications and then remove the upper bolt.
7 Install the rear timing belt cover and tighten the cover fasteners securely.
8 Install the timing belt idler pulley and tighten the bolt to the torque listed in this Chapter's Specifications.
9 Install each camshaft sprocket, aligning the pin in the camshaft with the hole in the sprocket (see illustration). Use an appropriate tool to hold the camshaft sprocket while tightening the bolt to the torque listed in this Chapter's Specifications.
10 Install the timing belt (see Section 7).

9 Crankshaft front oil seal - replacement

Caution: *Do not rotate the camshafts when the timing belt is removed or damage to the engine may occur.*
1 Remove the timing belt and timing belt covers (see Section 7 and Section 8).
Caution: *When installing the crankshaft sprocket, it must be positioned in its original position to ensure proper timing belt alignment. Before removing the sprocket, measure the distance between the end of the crankshaft and the sprocket and record this distance. When installing the sprocket, be sure to return it to the same position on the crankshaft.*
2 Pull the crankshaft sprocket from the crankshaft with a bolt-type gear puller (see illustration). Remove the Woodruff key.
Caution: *Because the nose of the crankshaft is recessed, an adapter may be needed between the puller bolt and the crankshaft (to prevent damage to the bore and threads in the end of the crankshaft).*

9.2 Attach a bolt-type gear puller to the crankshaft sprocket and remove the sprocket from the crankshaft

9.3 Carefully pry the seal out of its bore

9.5a Lubricate the new seal with engine oil and drive the seal into place with a hammer and seal driver or a socket

9.5b Position the crankshaft sprocket with the mark facing out, and install it onto the crankshaft in its original position

3   Use a screwdriver or seal removal tool to pry the seal out of its bore (see illustration). Take care to prevent damaging the oil pump assembly, the crankshaft and the seal bore.

4   Thoroughly clean and inspect the seal bore and sealing surface on the crankshaft. Minor imperfections can be removed with emery cloth. If there is a groove worn in the crankshaft sealing surface (from contact with the seal), installing a new seal will probably not stop the leak.

5   Lubricate the new seal with engine oil and drive the seal into place with a hammer and an appropriate size socket (see illustration).
Caution: *Position the crankshaft sprocket with the arrow mark or "FRONT" facing out and in its original position on the crankshaft (as discussed in Step 2)(see illustration). Use a hammer and socket to install the sprocket.*

6   The remaining steps are the reverse of removal. Reinstall the timing belt (see Section 7).

7   Run the engine and check for oil leaks.

10   Camshaft oil seal - replacement

Caution: *Do not rotate the camshafts when the timing belt is removed or damage to the engine may occur.*

1   Remove the timing belt (see Section 7)

2   Remove the camshaft sprockets and rear timing belt cover (see Section 8). Remove the exhaust camshaft target ring and sensor.

3   Note how far the seal is seated in the bore, then carefully pry it out with a small screwdriver (see illustration). Don't scratch the bore or damage the camshaft in the process (if the camshaft is damaged, the new seal will end up leaking).

4   Clean the bore and coat the outer edge of the new seal with engine oil or multi-purpose grease. Also lubricate the seal lip.

5   Using a socket with an outside diameter slightly smaller than the outside diameter of the seal (see illustration), carefully drive the new seal into place with a hammer. Make sure it's installed squarely and driven in to

the same depth as the original. If a socket isn't available, a short section of pipe will also work.

6   Install the rear timing belt cover part and camshaft sprockets (see Section 8).

7   Install the timing belt (see Section 7).

8   Run the engine and check for oil leaks at the camshaft seal.

11   Camshafts - removal, inspection and installation

Removal

1   Remove the valve cover (see Section 4).

2   Remove the Camshaft Position Sensor (CMP) (see Chapter 6) and the camshaft target magnet.

3   Remove the timing belt (see Section 7).

4   Remove the camshaft sprockets and the rear timing belt cover (see Section 8).

5   The camshaft bearing caps are identified with their numbered location in the cylinder

10.3 Carefully pry the camshaft seal out of the bore - DO NOT nick or scratch the camshaft or seal bore

10.5 Gently tap the new seal into place with the spring side toward the engine

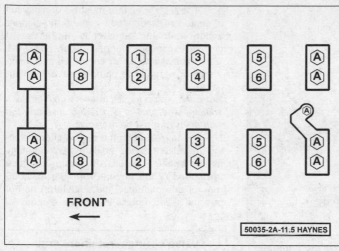

11.5 First, remove the outside bearing caps (A), then loosen the remaining camshaft bearing cap bolts a little at a time in the sequence shown

11.9 Measure the camshaft bearing journal diameters with a micrometer

head. They must be returned to their original locations. Remove the front and rear bearing caps at each end of the camshafts. Remove the remaining camshaft bearing caps. Loosen the bolts a little at a time to prevent distorting the camshafts, in the sequence shown (see illustration). When the bearing caps have all been loosened enough for removal, they may still be difficult to remove. Use the bearing cap bolts for leverage and move the cap back and forth to loosen the cap from the cylinder head. If they are still difficult to remove you can tap them gently with a soft face mallet until they can be lifted off.

Caution: *Store the caps in order so they can be returned to their original locations, with the same side facing forward.*

6   Carefully lift the camshafts out of the cylinder head. Mark the camshafts INTAKE and EXHAUST. They cannot be interchanged.

7   Remove the front seal from each camshaft.

Note: *It would be a good idea to inspect the rocker arms and lash adjusters at this time (see Section 12 and Section 13).*

Inspection

8   Clean the camshaft(s) and the gasket surface. Inspect the camshaft for wear and/or damage to the lobe surfaces, bearing journals, and seal contact surfaces. Inspect the camshaft bearing surfaces in the cylinder head and bearing caps for scoring and other damage.

9   Measure the camshaft bearing journal diameters (see illustration). Measure the inside diameter of the camshaft bearing surfaces in the cylinder head, using a telescoping gauge (temporarily install the bearing caps). Subtract the journal measurement from the bearing measurement to obtain the camshaft bearing oil clearance. Compare this clearance with the value listed this Chapter's Specifications. Replace worn components as required.

10   Replace the camshaft if it fails any of the

above inspections. The cylinder head may need to be replaced, if the camshaft bearing surfaces in the head are damaged or excessively worn.

Note: *If the lobes are worn, replace the rocker arms and lash adjusters along with the camshaft.*

11   Clean and inspect the cylinder head (see Section 15).

Camshaft endplay measurement

12   Lubricate the camshaft(s) and cylinder head bearing journals with clean engine oil.

13   Place the camshaft in its original location in the cylinder head.

Note: *Do not install the rocker arms for this check. Install the rear bearing cap and tighten the bolts to the torque listed in this Chapter's Specifications.*

14   Install a dial indicator on the cylinder head and place the indicator tip on the camshaft at the sprocket end.

15   Use a screwdriver to carefully pry the camshaft fully to the rear until it stops. Zero the dial indicator and pry the camshaft fully to

the front. The amount of indicator travel is the camshaft endplay. Compare the endplay with the tolerance given in this Chapter's Specifications. If the endplay is excessive, check the camshaft and cylinder head bearing journals for wear. Replace as necessary.

Installation

16   Install the valve lash adjusters and rocker arms (see Sections 12 and 13).

17   Clean the camshaft and bearing journals and caps. Liberally coat the journals, lobes, and thrust portions of the camshaft with assembly lube or engine oil (see illustration).

18   Carefully install the camshafts in the cylinder head in their original location. Temporarily install the camshaft sprockets and rotate the camshafts so that their timing marks align (see illustration 7.11). Make sure the crankshaft is positioned with the crankshaft sprocket timing mark at three teeth BTDC.

Caution: *If the pistons are at TDC when tightening the camshaft bearing caps, damage to the engine may occur.*

19   Install the bearing caps, except for the No. 1 and No. 6 (left side) end caps. Tighten

11.17 Prior to installing each camshaft, lubricate the bearing journals, thrust surfaces and lobes with assembly lube or clean engine oil

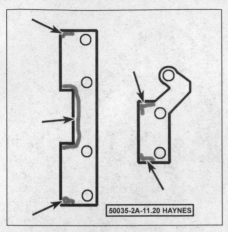

11.20 Apply a bead of anaerobic sealant to the indicated areas on the No. 1 and No. 6 bearing caps, then install these bearing caps

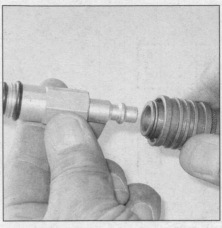

14.4 Thread the air hose adapter into the spark plug hole - adapters are generally available from auto parts stores

14.7 Use needle-nose pliers (shown) or a small magnet to remove the valve spring keepers - be careful not to drop them down into the engine!

the bolts in several steps, in the proper sequence (see illustration 11.5) to the torque listed in this Chapter's Specifications.

20   Apply a small bead of anaerobic sealant (approximately 1/8-inch) to the No. 1 and No. 6 (left side) bearing caps (see illustration). Install the bearing caps and tighten the bolts to the torque listed in this Chapter's Specifications.

21   Install new camshaft oil seals (see Section 10).

22   Install the timing belt, covers, and related components (see Sections 7 and 8).

23   Install the valve cover (see Section 4).

12   Rocker arms - removal, inspection and installation

Removal

1   Remove the valve cover (see Section 4).

2   Remove both camshafts (see Section 11).

3   Once the camshafts have been removed,

the rocker arms can be lifted off. The lash adjusters can remain in the head at this time, unless they are being replaced (see Section 13).

Caution: *Each rocker arm must be placed back in the same location it was removed from, so mark each rocker arm or place them in a container (such as an egg carton) so they won't get mixed up.*

Inspection

4   Inspect the rocker arm tip, roller and lash adjuster pocket for wear. Replace them if evidence of wear or damage is found.

5   Carefully inspect each lash adjuster for signs of wear and damage, particularly on the ball tip that contacts the rocker arm. The lash adjusters become clogged as they age, so it's a good idea to replace them if you're concerned about their condition or if the engine is making valve "tapping" noises.

Installation

6   Installation is the reverse of removal. When reinstalling the rocker arms, make sure that you install them at the same locations from which they were removed.

13   Valve lash adjusters - removal, inspection and installation

1   Remove the rocker arms (see Section 12).

2   If the lash adjusters aren't already removed from the head, lift them out now.

Caution: *Be sure to keep the adjusters in order so they can be placed back in the same location in the cylinder head it was removed from.*

3   Inspect each adjuster carefully for signs of wear and damage, particularly on the ball tip that contacts the rocker arm. Since the lash adjusters can become clogged, we recommend replacing them if you're concerned about their condition or if the engine is exhibiting valve "tapping" noises.

4   The lash adjusters must be partially full of engine oil - indicated by little or no plunger action when the adjuster is depressed. If there's excessive plunger travel, place the lash adjuster into clean engine oil and pump the plunger until the plunger travel is eliminated.

Note: *If the plunger still travels within the lash adjuster when full of oil it's defective and the lash adjuster must be replaced.*

5   When re-starting the engine after replacing the adjusters, the adjusters will normally make "tapping" noises. After warm-up, raise the speed of the engine from idle to 3,000 rpm for one minute. If the adjuster(s) do not become silent, replace the defective ones.

14   Valve springs, retainers and seals - replacement

Note: *Broken valve springs and defective valve stem seals can be replaced without removing the cylinder heads. Two special tools and a compressed air source are normally required to perform this operation, so read through this Section carefully and rent or buy the tools before beginning the job.*

1   Remove the rocker arms (see Section 12).

2   Remove the spark plug from the cylinder that has the defective component. If all of the valve stem seals are being replaced, all of the spark plugs should be removed.

3   Turn the crankshaft until the piston in the affected cylinder is at top dead center on the compression stroke (refer to Section 3). If you're replacing all of the valve stem seals, begin with cylinder number one and work on the valves for one cylinder at a time. Move from cylinder-to-cylinder following the firing order sequence (see this Chapter's Specifications).

4   Thread an adapter into the spark plug hole (see illustration) and connect an air hose from a compressed air source to it. Most auto parts stores can supply the air hose adapter.

Note: *Many cylinder compression gauges utilize a screw-in fitting that may work with your air hose quick-disconnect fitting.*

5   Remove the camshaft(s) and the rocker arm(s) (see Section 11 and Section 12).

6   Apply compressed air to the cylinder.

Warning: *The piston may be forced down by compressed air, causing the crankshaft to turn suddenly. If the wrench used when positioning the number one piston at TDC is still attached to the bolt in the crankshaft nose, remove it as it could cause damage or injury when the crankshaft moves.*

7   Stuff clean shop rags into the various oil-drain holes in the cylinder head, to prevent parts and tools from falling into the engine. Use a valve spring compressor to compress the spring. Remove the keepers with small needle-nose pliers or a magnet (see illustration).

8   Remove the spring retainer and valve spring, then remove the valve guide seal/

spring seat assembly (see illustration).

Caution: *If air pressure fails to hold the valve in the closed position during this operation, the valve face and/or seat is probably damaged. If so, the cylinder head will have to be removed for additional repair operations.*

9 Wrap a rubber band or tape around the top of the valve stem so the valve won't fall into the combustion chamber, then release the air pressure.

10 Inspect the valve stem for damage. Rotate the valve in the guide and check the end for eccentric movement, which would indicate that the valve is bent.

11 Move the valve up-and-down in the guide and make sure it doesn't bind. If the valve stem binds, either the valve is bent or the guide is damaged. In either case, the head will have to be removed for repair.

12 Pull up on the valve stem to close the valve, reapply air pressure to the cylinder to retain the valve in the closed position, then remove the tape or rubber band from the valve stem.

13 Lubricate the valve stem with engine oil and install a new valve guide seal/spring seat assembly. Tap into place with a deep socket (see illustration).

14 Install the spring in position over the valve.

15 Install the valve spring retainer. Compress the valve spring and carefully position the keepers in the groove. Apply a small dab of grease to the inside of each keeper to hold it in place if necessary (see illustration).

16 Remove the pressure from the spring tool and make sure the keepers are seated.

17 Disconnect the air hose and remove the adapter from the spark plug hole.

18 The remainder of the installation is the reverse of removal.

19 Start and run the engine, then check for oil leaks and unusual sounds coming from the valve cover area.

15 Cylinder head - removal and installation

Warning: *Allow the engine to cool completely before beginning this procedure.*

Removal

1 Position the number one piston at Top Dead Center (see Section 3).

2 Disconnect the cable from the negative terminal of the battery (see Chapter 5).

3 Drain the cooling system (see Chapter 1).

4 Remove the intake manifold (see Section 5). Cover the intake ports with duct tape to keep out debris (see illustration).

5 Remove the spark plug wires, spark plugs and ignition coil (see Chapter 1).

6 Remove the upper radiator and heater hoses (see Chapter 3). Remove the heater tube support bracket.

7 Detach the power steering pump bolts from the engine (leaving the hoses attached) and set the pump aside (see Chapter 10). Remove the accessory bracket(s).

14.8 Remove the valve guide seal with a pair of pliers

14.13 Gently tap the new seal into place with a hammer and a deep socket

14.15 Apply a small dab of grease to each keeper before installation to hold it in place on the valve stem until the spring is released

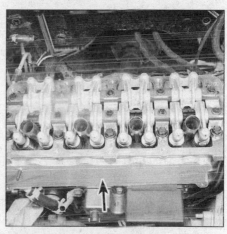

15.4 Cover the intake ports with duct tape to keep out debris before removing the cylinder head (typical)

8 Raise the front of the vehicle and place it securely on jackstands. Disconnect the exhaust pipe from the exhaust manifold (see Chapter 4) and lower the vehicle.

9 Remove the timing belt (see Section 7).

10 Remove the valve cover, camshafts and rocker arms (see Section 4, Section 11, Section 12).

11 Loosen the cylinder head bolts 1/4-turn at a time, in the reverse of the tightening sequence (see illustration 15.18) until they can be removed by hand.

Note: *Write down the location of the different length bolts so they will be reinstalled in the correct location.*

12 Carefully lift the cylinder head straight up and place the head on wood blocks to prevent damage to the sealing surfaces. If the head sticks to the engine block, dislodge it by placing a wood block against the head casting and tapping the wood with a hammer or by prying the head with a prybar placed carefully on a casting protrusion (see illustration).

Caution: *The cylinder head is aluminum, so you must be very careful not to gouge the sealing surfaces.*

15.12 If the head sticks to the engine block, dislodge it by placing a wood block against the head casting and tapping the wood with a hammer or by prying the head with a prybar placed carefully on a casting protrusion (typical)

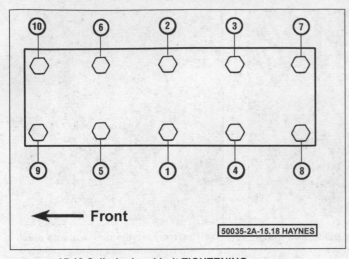

15.18 Cylinder head bolt TIGHTENING sequence

16.11a Using a criss-cross pattern, loosen and remove the oil pan bolts (typical)…

Inspection

13   Special gasket removal solvents that soften gaskets and make removal much easier are available at auto parts stores. Remove all traces of old gasket material from the block and head. Do not allow anything to fall into the engine.

14   Using a straightedge and feeler gauge, check the gasket mating surfaces for warpage. If the warpage on either surface exceeds the limit listed in this Chapter's Specifications, the cylinder head must be resurfaced at an automotive machine shop. The machine shop can also clean and inspect the cylinder head components.

15   Clean and inspect all threaded bolts and be sure the threaded holes in the block are clean and dry. Inspect the threads on the cylinder head bolts with a straightedge. If any of the threads don't touch the straight edge, the bolts are stretched, and should be replaced.

Installation

16   Place a new gasket and the cylinder head in position on the engine block.

17   Apply clean engine oil to the cylinder head bolt threads prior to installation. The four short bolts (4.33 inch long) are to be installed in each corner of the cylinder head.

18   Tighten the cylinder head bolts in several stages in the recommended sequence (see illustration) to the torque listed in this Chapter's Specifications.

19   Reinstall the timing belt (see Section 7).

20   Reinstall the remaining parts in the reverse order of removal.

21   Refill the cooling system and change the engine oil and filter (see Chapter 1). Rotate the crankshaft clockwise slowly by hand through six complete revolutions. Recheck the camshaft timing marks (see Section 7).

22   Start the engine and run it until normal operating temperature is reached. Check for leaks and proper operation.

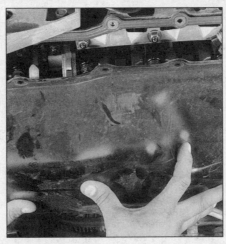

16.11b … then lower the pan carefully (there might still be some residual oil in the pan) (typical)

16   Oil pan - removal and installation

Removal

1   Disconnect the cable from the negative terminal of the battery (see Chapter 5).

2   Remove the air filter housing (see Chapter 4).

3   Raise the vehicle and support it securely on jackstands.

4   Drain the engine oil (see Chapter 1).

5   Disconnect the exhaust pipe at the exhaust manifold (see Chapter 4).

6   Remove the structural collar.

7   On 4WD models, support the front axle assembly with a floor jack, remove the front axle assembly mounting bolts (see Chapter 8), then lower the axle housing as much as possible.

8   Remove nuts from the engine mounts.

9   Support the engine from above with an

16.11c If the pan is stuck, tap it with a soft-face hammer or place a wood block against the pan and tap the wood block with a hammer (typical)

engine hoist (but not on the intake manifold), take the weight off the engine mounts with the hoist and remove the engine mount throughbolts (see Section 20).

10   Raise the engine sufficiently to allow access for oil pan removal.

11   Remove the mounting bolts and lower the oil pan from the vehicle (see illustrations). If the pan is stuck, tap it with a soft-face hammer (see illustration) or place a wood block against the pan and tap the wood block with a hammer.

Caution: *If you're wedging something between the oil pan and the engine block to separate the two, be extremely careful not to gouge or nick the gasket surface of either part; an oil leak could result.*

12   Remove the oil pump pickup tube and screen assembly (see illustration) and clean both the tube and screen thoroughly. Install the pick-up tube and screen with a new seal (see illustration).

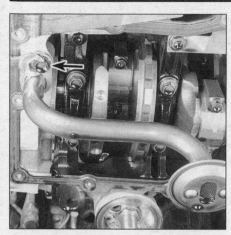

16.12a Remove the bolt and remove the oil
pump pick-up tube and screen assembly -
clean both the tube and screen thoroughly
before reassembly

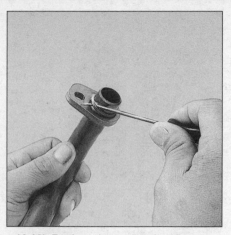

16.12b Replace the seal at the oil pump
pick-up tube mounting flange with a
new one

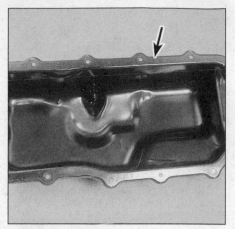

16.13 Thoroughly clean the oil pan and
sealing surfaces on the engine block and
oil pan (arrow) with a scraper to remove
all traces of old gasket material (typical)

17.3a Remove the oil pump assembly mounting bolts and remove
the assembly (typical)

17.3b If the pump doesn't come off by hand, tap it gently with a
soft-faced hammer or pry gently on a casting protrusion (typical)

13   Thoroughly clean the oil pan and sealing surfaces on the block and pan (see illustration). Use a scraper to remove all traces of old gasket material. Gasket removal solvents are available at auto parts stores and may prove helpful. Check the oil pan sealing surface for distortion. Straighten or replace as necessary. After cleaning and straightening (if necessary), wipe the gasket surfaces of the pan and block clean with a rag soaked in lacquer thinner or acetone.

Installation

14   Apply a 1/8-inch bead of RTV sealant at the cylinder block-to-oil pump assembly joint at the oil pan flange. Install a new oil pan gasket.
15   Place the oil pan into position and install the bolts finger-tight. Working side-to-side

from the center out, tighten the bolts to the torque listed in this Chapter's Specifications.
16   Lower the engine and install the through-bolts in the engine mounts (see Section 20). Tighten them securely.
17   Install the structural collar as follows:
  a) *Place the collar in position between the transmission and the oil pan and then hand-start the collar-to-transmission bolts.*
  b) *Install and then hand-tighten the collar-to-oil pan bolts.*
  c) *Tighten the collar-to-transmission bolts.*
  d) *Tighten the collar-to-oil pan bolts.*
18   The remainder of installation is the reverse of removal.
19   Refill the crankcase with the correct quantity and grade of oil, run the engine and check for leaks.

20   Road test the vehicle and check for leaks again.

17   Oil pump - removal, inspection and installation

Removal

1   Remove the timing belt, timing belt covers and the crankshaft front seal (see Section 7, Section 8 and Section 9).
2   Remove the oil pan and pick-up tube/screen assembly (see Section 16).
3   Remove the bolts and detach the oil pump assembly from the engine (see illustration). If the pump doesn't come off by hand, tap it gently with a soft-faced hammer or pry on a casting boss (see illustration).

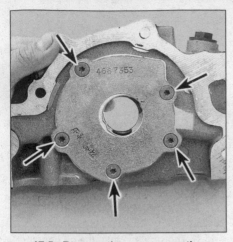

17.5a Remove the cover mounting screws (typical)…

17.5b … and the cover (typical)

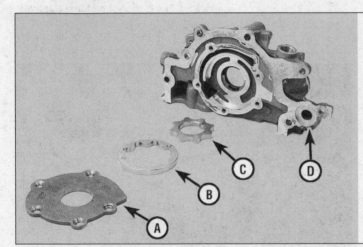

17.5c Arrangement of oil pump components (typical)

A   Cover
B   Outer rotor
C   Inner rotor
D   Oil pump body

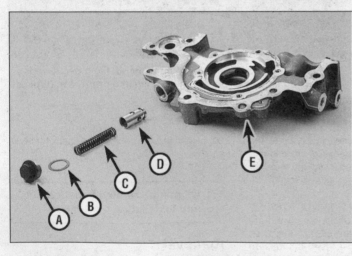

17.7 Oil pressure relief valve components (typical)

A   Cap
B   Gasket
C   Spring
D   Relief valve
E   Oil pump body

7   To disassemble the relief valve, remove the cap bolt, washer, spring and relief valve (see illustration). Check the oil pressure relief valve piston sliding surface and valve spring. If either the spring or the valve is damaged, they must be replaced as a set. If no damage is found reassemble the relief valve parts. Coat the parts with oil and reinstall them in the oil pump body. Tighten the cap bolt to this Chapter's Specifications.

Caution: *Be sure to install the relief valve into the pump body with the grooved end going in first - otherwise engine damage may occur.*

8   Check the clearance of the oil pump components with a micrometer and a feeler gauge (see illustrations) and compare the results to this Chapter's Specifications.

Installation

9   Lubricate the housing and the inner and outer rotors with clean engine oil and install both rotors in the body. Prime the oil pump by filling the rotor cavities with clean engine oil. Install the cover and tighten the cover screws to the torque listed in this Chapter's Specifications.

Caution: *When installing the inner rotor, the chamfer faces the pump cover.*

10   Install a new O-ring in the oil discharge passage (see illustration). Apply sealant to the oil pump body (see illustration), and raise the pump assembly to the block. Align the flat parts of the rotor with the flat parts of the crankshaft. Tighten the bolts to the torque listed in this Chapter's Specifications.

11   Install the crankshaft seal (see Section 9).

12   Install the pick-up tube/strainer assembly and oil pan (see Section 16).

13   Install the crankshaft sprocket (see Section 9)

14   Install the rear timing belt cover (see Section 8).

15   Install the timing belt (see Section 7).

16   Install a new oil filter and engine oil (see Chapter 1).

17   Start the engine and check for oil pressure and leaks.

18   Recheck the engine oil level.

18   Flywheel/driveplate - removal and installation

Removal

1   Raise the vehicle and support it securely on jackstands.

2   Remove the transmission assembly (see Chapter 7A or Chapter 7B).

3   If the vehicle has a manual transmission, remove the pressure plate and clutch disc (see Chapter 8). Now is a good time to check/replace the clutch components.

4   To ensure correct alignment during reinstallation, mark the position of the flywheel/driveplate to the crankshaft before removal.

5   Remove the bolts that secure the flywheel/driveplate to the crankshaft (see illus-

4   Remove the crankshaft oil seal from the oil pump, by prying it out with a screwdriver wrapped in a rag.

Caution: *To prevent an oil leak after the new seal is installed, be very careful not to scratch or otherwise damage the seal-bore in the pump body.*

5   Remove the mounting screws and remove the cover (see illustration). Remove the inner and outer rotor from the body (see illustrations).

Caution: *Be very careful with these parts. Close tolerances are critical in creating the correct oil pressure. Any nicks or other damage will require replacement of the complete pump assembly.*

Inspection

6   Clean all components including the block surfaces with solvent, then inspect all surfaces for excessive wear and/or damage.

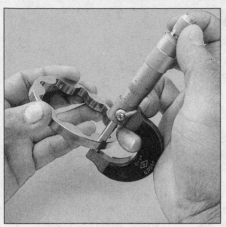

17.8a Measure the outer rotor thickness

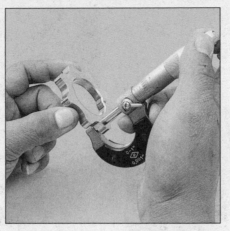

17.8b Measure the inner rotor thickness

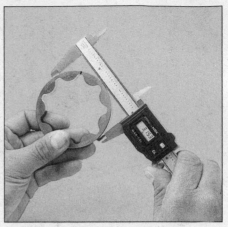

17.8c Use a caliper and measure the outer diameter of the outer rotor

17.8d Use a feeler gauge and measure the outer rotor-to-case clearance

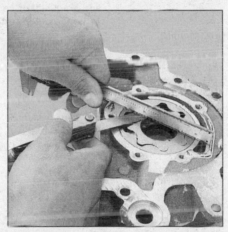

17.8e Place a precision straightedge over the rotors and measure the clearance between the rotors and the cover

17.10a Replace the O-ring seal in the oil pump body - apply clean engine oil to the seal

tration). A tool is available at most auto parts stores to hold the flywheel/driveplate while loosening the bolts. If the tool is not available, wedge a screwdriver in the ring gear teeth to jam the flywheel.

6   Remove the flywheel/driveplate from the crankshaft. Since the flywheel is fairly heavy, be sure to support it while removing the last bolt.

7   Clean the flywheel to remove grease and oil. Inspect the flywheel (see Chapter 7B).

8   Clean and inspect the mating surfaces of the flywheel/driveplate and the crankshaft. If the crankshaft rear main seal is leaking, replace it before reinstalling the flywheel/driveplate (see Section 19).

Installation

9   Position the flywheel/driveplate against the crankshaft. Align the previously applied match marks. Before installing the bolts, apply thread locking compound to the threads.

17.10b Apply a bead of anaerobic sealant to the housing sealing surface as shown

18.5 Mark the relative position of the flywheel or driveplate to the crankshaft and, using an appropriate tool to hold the flywheel, remove the bolts (typical)

19.5 Carefully pry the crankshaft seal out of the bore - DO NOT nick or scratch the crankshaft or seal bore

19.7 Position the new seal with the words THIS SIDE OUT facing out, toward the rear of the engine. If the seal is not marked, the seal lip (that seals against the crankshaft) must face in. Gently and gradually drive the seal into the cylinder block until it is flush with the outer surface of the block. Do not drive it past flush or there will be an oil leak - the seal must be flush

10   Hold the flywheel/driveplate with the holding tool, or wedge a screwdriver in the ring gear teeth to keep the flywheel/driveplate from turning as you tighten the bolts to the torque listed in this Chapter's Specifications.

11   The remainder of installation is the reverse of the removal procedure.

19   Rear main oil seal - replacement

1   The one-piece rear main oil seal is pressed into a bore machined into the rear main bearing cap and engine block.

2   Remove the transmission (see Chapter 7A or 7B).

3   If equipped, remove the clutch components (see Chapter 8).

4   Remove the flywheel or driveplate (see Section 18).

5   Using the chamfered edge on the crankshaft, pry out the old seal with a 3/16-inch flat blade screwdriver (see illustration).

Caution: *To prevent an oil leak after the new seal is installed, be very careful not to scratch or otherwise damage the crankshaft sealing surface or the bore in the engine block.*

6   Clean the crankshaft and seal bore in the block thoroughly and de-grease these areas by wiping them with a rag soaked in lacquer thinner or acetone. If there is a burr or scratch on the crankshaft chamfer edge, sand it with 400-grit sandpaper. Do not lubricate the lip or outer diameter of the new seal - it must be installed as it comes from the manufacturer.

7   Position the new seal onto the crankshaft. Using an appropriate size driver and pilot tool, gently and gradually drive the seal into the cylinder block until it is flush with the

outer surface of the block (see illustration).

Caution: *If the seal is driven-in past the flush-position, there will be an oil leak.*

Note: *When installing the new seal, the words THIS SIDE OUT on the seal must face out, toward the rear of the vehicle. If the seal is not marked, the seal lip (that seals against the crankshaft) must face in.*

8   The remainder of installation is the reverse of removal.

20   Engine mounts - check and replacement

1   Engine mounts seldom require attention, but broken or deteriorated mounts should be replaced immediately or the added strain placed on the driveline components may cause damage or wear.

Check

2   During the check, the engine must be raised slightly to remove the weight from the mounts.

3   Raise the vehicle and support it securely on jackstands, then position a jack under the engine oil pan. Place a large wood block between the jack head and the oil pan to prevent oil pan damage, then carefully raise the engine just enough to take the weight off the mounts.

Warning: *DO NOT place any part of your body under the engine when only a jack supports it.*

4   Check the mounts to see if the rubber is cracked, hardened or separated from the metal backing. Sometimes the rubber will split

right down the center.

5   Check for relative movement between the mount plates and the engine or frame (use a large screwdriver or pry bar to attempt to move the mounts). If movement is noted, lower the engine and tighten the mount fasteners.

6   Rubber preservative may be applied to the mounts to slow deterioration.

Replacement

7   Disconnect the cable from the negative terminal of the battery, then raise the vehicle and support it securely on jackstands (if not already done).

8   Place a floor jack under the engine (with a wood block between the jack head and oil pan) and raise the engine slightly to relieve the weight from the mounts.

9   Remove the through-bolt from the engine mount.

10   Remove the engine mount from the side of the engine block.

Note: *Do not disconnect more than one mount at a time, except during engine removal.*

11   Install the new engine mount assembly to the engine block and tighten the bolts securely.

12   Slowly lower the engine, while watching for proper mount-to-frame alignment, and then install the through-bolt. Hand-tighten the nut on the through-bolt.

13   Completely lower the engine and tighten the through-bolt securely.

14   If necessary, repeat the process for the motor mount on the other side of the engine.

15   The remainder of installation is the reverse of removal.

Chapter 2 Part B
2.5L four-cylinder engine

Contents

Specifications

General

Displacement	150 cu. in. (2.5 liters)
Cylinder numbers (front-to-rear)	1-2-3-4
Firing order	1-3-4-2

Camshaft

Lobe lift (intake and exhaust)	0.265 in
End-play	None
Journal-to-bearing (oil) clearance	0.001 to 0.003 in
Journal out-of-round limit	0.002 in
Fuel pump eccentric diameter	1.615 to 1.625 in
Journal diameter (journals numbered from front-to-rear of engine)	
No. 1	2.029 to 2.030 in
No. 2	2.019 to 2.020 in
No. 3	2.009 to 2.010 in
No. 4	1.999 to 2.000 in

FIRING ORDER:
1 3 4 2
CLOCKWISE
ROTATION

Cylinder location and distributor rotation

Torque specifications   Ft-lbs (unless otherwise indicated)

Note: *One foot-pound (ft-lb) of torque is equivalent to 12 inch-pounds (in-lbs) of torque. Torque values below approximately 15 foot-pounds are expressed in inch-pounds, because most foot-pound torque wrenches are not accurate at these smaller values.*

Camshaft sprocket bolt	80
Crankshaft pulley-to-vibration damper bolts	20
Cylinder head bolts (see illustration 8.15a and 8.15b for tightening sequence)	
1987 and 1988	
Bolts 1 through 7 and 9, 10	85
Bolt 8 only	75
1989	
Bolts 1 through 7 and 9, 10	110
Bolt 8 only	100
1990 and later	
Step 1, Bolts 1 through 10	22
Step 2, Bolts 1 through 10	45
Step 3, All bolts	45
Step 4	
Bolts 1 through 6	110
Bolt 7	100
Bolts 8 through 10	110
Driveplate-to-crankshaft bolts	
First step	40
Second step	60 degrees additional turn
Exhaust manifold nuts	23
Flywheel-to-crankshaft bolts	
First step	50
Second step	60 degrees additional turn
Intake manifold-to-cylinder head bolts	23
Oil pan mounting bolts	
1/4 x 20	84 in-lbs
5/16 x 18	132 in-lbs
Oil pump bolts	
Short	120 in-lbs
Long	17
Rocker arm capscrews	19
Valve cover-to-cylinder head bolts	
With RTV	55 in-lbs
With pre-cured permanent gasket	44 in-lbs
Timing chain tensioner-to-block bolt	168 in-lbs
Timing chain cover-to-block	
Bolts	60 in-lbs
Nuts	16
Vibration damper bolt (lubricated)	80

1 General Information

1   This Part of Chapter 2 is devoted to in-vehicle repair procedures for the 2.5 liter four-cylinder engine. Information concerning engine removal and installation, as well as engine overhaul, is in Chapter 2F.

2   The following repair procedures are based on the assumption that the engine is installed in the vehicle. If the engine has been removed from the vehicle and mounted on a stand, many of the steps included in this Part of Chapter 2 will not apply.

3   The Specifications included in this Part of Chapter 2 apply only to the engine and procedures in this Part. The Specifications necessary for rebuilding the block and cylinder head are found in Chapter 2F.

2 Repair operations possible with the engine in the vehicle

1   Many major repair operations can be accomplished without removing the engine from the vehicle.

2   Clean the engine compartment and the exterior of the engine with some type of pressure washer before any work is done. A clean engine will make the job easier and will help keep dirt out of the internal areas of the engine.

3   If vacuum, exhaust, oil or coolant leaks develop, indicating a need for gasket or seal replacement, the repairs can generally be made with the engine in the vehicle. The intake and exhaust manifold gaskets, oil pan gasket and cylinder head gasket are all accessible with the engine in place.

4   Exterior engine components such as the intake and exhaust manifolds, the oil pan (and the oil pump), the water pump, the starter motor, the alternator, the distributor and the carburetor or fuel injection components can be removed for repair with the engine in place.

5   Since the cylinder head can be removed without pulling the engine, valve component servicing can also be accomplished with the engine in the vehicle.

6   In extreme cases caused by a lack of necessary equipment, repair or replacement of piston rings, pistons, connecting rods and rod bearings is possible with the engine in the vehicle. However, this practice is not recommended because of the cleaning and preparation work that must be done to the components involved.

3 Top Dead Center (TDC) for number one piston - locating

Note: *The following procedure is based on the assumption that the distributor is correctly installed. If you are trying to locate TDC to install the distributor correctly, piston position must be determined by feeling for compression at the number one spark plug hole, then aligning the ignition timing marks as described in Step 8.*

1   Top Dead Center (TDC) is the highest point in the cylinder that each piston reaches as it travels up-and-down when the crankshaft turns. Each piston reaches TDC on the compression stroke and again on the exhaust stroke, but TDC generally refers to piston position on the compression stroke.

2   Positioning the piston(s) at TDC is an essential part of many procedures such as rocker arm removal, camshaft and timing chain/sprocket removal and distributor removal.

3   Before beginning this procedure, be sure to place the transmission in Neutral and apply the parking brake or block the rear wheels. Also, remove the spark plugs (see Chapter 1) and disable the ignition system. Detach the coil wire from the center terminal of the distributor cap and ground it on the block with a jumper wire.

4   In order to bring any piston to TDC, the crankshaft must be turned using one of the methods outlined below. When looking at the front of the engine, normal crankshaft rotation is clockwise.

a)   *The preferred method is to turn the crankshaft with a socket and ratchet attached to the bolt threaded into the front of the crankshaft.*

b)   *A remote starter switch, which may save some time, can also be used. Follow the instructions included with the switch. Once the piston is close to TDC, use a socket and ratchet, as described in the previous paragraph.*

c)   *If an assistant is available to turn the ignition switch to the Start position in short bursts, you can get the piston close to TDC without a remote starter switch. Make sure your assistant is out of the vehicle, away from the ignition switch, then use a socket and ratchet (as described in Paragraph a) to complete the procedure.*

5   Note the position of the terminal for the number one spark plug wire on the distributor cap. If the terminal isn't marked, follow the plug wire from the number one cylinder spark plug to the cap.

6   Use a felt-tip pen or chalk to make a mark on the distributor body directly under the terminal (see illustration).

7   Detach the cap from the distributor and set it aside (see Chapter 1 if necessary).

8   Turn the crankshaft (see Paragraph 3 above) until the notch in the crankshaft pulley is aligned with the 0 on the timing plate (located at the front of the engine) (see illustration).

9   Look at the distributor rotor - it should be pointing directly at the mark you made on the distributor body. If it is, go to Step 12.

10   If the rotor is 180 degrees off, the number one piston is at TDC on the exhaust stroke.

3.6 Make a mark on the aluminum distributor body directly below the number one spark plug wire terminal on the distributor cap (arrow)

3.8 Turn the crankshaft clockwise until the notch aligns with the 0

Go to Step 11.

11   To get the piston to TDC on the compression stroke, turn the crankshaft one complete turn (360 degrees) clockwise. The rotor should now be pointing at the mark on the distributor. When the rotor is pointing at the number one spark plug wire terminal in the distributor cap and the ignition timing marks are aligned, the number one piston is at TDC on the compression stroke.

12   After the number one piston has been positioned at TDC on the compression stroke, TDC for any of the remaining pistons can be located by turning the crankshaft and following the firing order. Mark the remaining spark plug wire terminal locations on the distributor body just like you did for the number one terminal, then number the marks to correspond with the cylinder numbers. As you turn the crankshaft, the rotor will also turn. When it's pointing directly at one of the marks on the distributor, the piston for that particular cylinder is at TDC on the compression stroke.

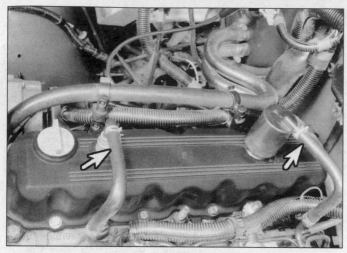

4.3a Typical valve cover - before removing, disconnect the vacuum and crankcase ventilating hoses (arrows)

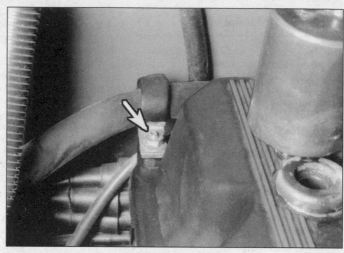

4.3b Remove the nut (arrow) and clamp from the valve cover and place the heater hose toward the rear of the engine compartment

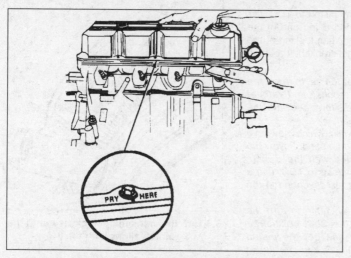

4.4 If the valve cover is specifically marked, carefully pry the cover loose after breaking the seal with a putty knife or razor blade

4.5a Remove the old sealant from the valve cover flange and the cylinder head with a gasket scraper, then clean the mating surfaces with lacquer thinner or acetone

4.5b On engines equipped with plastic valve covers, pry the rubber gasket from the groove along the perimeter

4   Valve cover - removal and installation

1   Disconnect the negative cable from the battery (see Chapter 5).

2   Remove the air cleaner (see Chapter 4).

3   Label and then remove all hoses and/or wires necessary to provide clearance for valve cover removal (see illustrations).

4   Remove the valve cover retaining bolts and lift off the cover. The cover may stick. Detach the cover by breaking the seal with a putty knife or razor blade. Locations for prying have been provided (see illustration).

Caution: *To avoid damaging the cover, do not pry up until the seal has been broken.*

5   Prior to installation, remove all traces of dirt, oil and old gasket material from the cover and cylinder head with a scraper (see illustra-tions). Clean the mating surfaces with lacquer thinner or acetone and a clean rag.

6   Inspect the mating surface on the cover for damage and warpage. Correct or replace as necessary.

7   On models which use RTV, apply a con-tinuous 1/8-inch (3mm) bead of sealant (Jeep Gasket-In-a-Tube or equivalent) to the cover flange. Be sure the sealant is applied to the inside of the bolt holes (see illustration). On models with plastic valve covers (see illustra-tion), RTV or a gasket may be used. Check with an automotive parts department. On models equipped with an aluminum valve cover, RTV must be used. Later models use a pre-cured reusable gasket - install these with-out sealant.

8   Place the valve cover on the cylinder head while the sealant (if used) is still wet and install the mounting bolts. Tighten the bolts

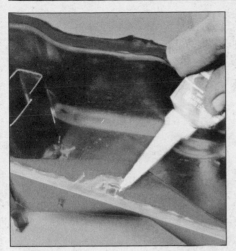

4.7a Make sure the sealant is applied to the INSIDE of the bolt holes or oil will leak out around the bolt threads

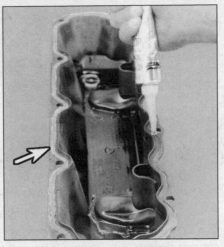

4.7b On engines equipped with plastic valve covers, the rubber gasket may not be available for replacement. Instead, apply a continuous 3/16-inch diameter bead of the sealant (arrow) to the valve cover flange

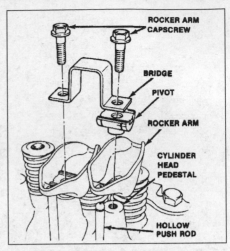

5.3 Rocker arm mounts - exploded view

a little at a time until the torque listed in this Chapter's Specifications is reached.
9   Complete the installation procedure by reversing the removal procedure.
10   Start the engine and check for oil leaks.

5   Rocker arms and pushrods - removal, inspection and installation

Removal

1   Detach the valve cover from the cylinder head, referring to Section 4.
2   Beginning at the front of the cylinder head, loosen the rocker arm bolts.
3   Remove the capscrews, bridges, pivots and rocker arms (see illustration). Store them in marked containers (they must be reinstalled in their original locations).
4   Remove the pushrods and store them separately to make sure they don't get mixed up during installation (see illustration).

Inspection

5   Check each rocker arm for wear, cracks and other damage, especially where the pushrods and valve stems contact the rocker arm faces.
6   Make sure the hole at the pushrod end of each rocker arm is open.
7   Check each rocker arm pivot area for wear, cracks and galling. If the rocker arms are worn or damaged, replace them with new ones and use new pivots as well.
8   Inspect the pushrods for cracks and excessive wear at the ends. Roll each pushrod across a piece of plate glass to see if it's bent (if it wobbles, it's bent).

5.4 If more than one pushrod is being removed, store them in a perforated cardboard box to prevent mix-ups during installation - note the label indicating the front of the engine

Installation

9   Lubricate the lower ends of the pushrods with clean engine oil or moly-base grease and install them in their original locations. Make sure each pushrod seats completely in the lifter socket.
10   Apply moly-base grease to the ends of the valve stems and the upper ends of the pushrods before positioning the rocker arms and installing the capscrews.
11   Set the rocker arms in place, then install the pivots, bridges and capscrews. Apply moly-base grease to the pivots to prevent damage to the mating surfaces before engine oil pressure builds up. Tighten the bolts to the torque listed in this Chapter's Specifications.
12   Reinstall the valve cover and run the engine. Check for oil leaks and unusual valve train noises.

6   Valve springs, retainers and seals - replacement

Note: *Broken valve springs and defective valve stem seals can be replaced without removing the cylinder heads. Two special tools and a compressed air source are normally required to perform this operation, so read through this Section carefully and rent or buy the tools before beginning the job. If compressed air isn't available, a length of nylon rope can be used to keep the valves from falling into the cylinder during this procedure.*
1   Remove the valve cover referring to Section 4.
2   Remove the spark plug from the cylinder which has the defective component. If all of the valve stem seals are being replaced, all of the spark plugs should be removed.

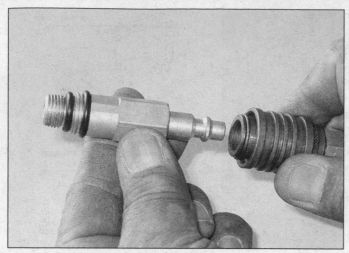

6.4 Thread the air hose adapter into the spark plug - adapters are commonly available from auto parts stores

6.9 Once the spring is depressed, the keepers can be removed with a small magnet or needle-nose pliers (a magnet is preferred to prevent dropping the keepers)

6.17 Apply a small dab of grease to the keepers before installation - it will hold them in place on the valve stem as the spring is released

3   Turn the crankshaft until the piston in the affected cylinder is at top dead center (TDC) on the compression stroke (see Section 3 for instructions). If you're replacing all of the valve stem seals, begin with cylinder number one and work on the valves for one cylinder at a time. Move from cylinder-to-cylinder following the firing order sequence listed in this Chapter's Specifications.

4   Thread an adapter into the spark plug hole (see illustration) and connect an air hose from a compressed air source to it. Most auto parts stores can supply the air hose adapter. **Note:** *Many cylinder compression gauges utilize a screw-in fitting that may work with your air hose quick-disconnect fitting.*

5   Remove the rocker arm and pivot for the valve with the defective part and pull out the pushrod. If all of the valve stem seals are being replaced, all of the rocker arms and pushrods should be removed (see Section 5).

6   Apply compressed air to the cylinder.

Warning: *The piston may be forced down by compressed air, causing the crankshaft to turn suddenly. If the wrench used when positioning the number one piston at TDC is still attached to the bolt in the crankshaft nose, it could cause damage or injury when the crankshaft moves.*

7   The valves should be held in place by the air pressure. If the valve faces or seats are in poor condition, leaks may prevent air pressure from retaining the valves - refer to the alternative procedure below.

8   If you don't have access to compressed air, an alternative method can be used. Position the piston at a point just before TDC on the compression stroke, then feed a long piece of nylon rope through the spark plug hole until it fills the combustion chamber. Be sure to leave the end of the rope hanging out of the engine so it can be removed easily. Use a large ratchet and socket to rotate the crankshaft in the normal direction of rotation until slight resistance is felt.

9   Stuff shop rags into the cylinder head holes above and below the valves to prevent parts and tools from falling into the engine, then use a valve spring compressor to compress the spring. Remove the keepers with small needle-nose pliers or a magnet (see illustration). **Note:** *A couple of different types of tools are available for compressing the valve springs with the head in place. One type grips the lower spring coils and presses on the retainer as the knob is turned, while the other type, shown here, utilizes the rocker arm capscrews for leverage. Both types work very well, although the lever type is usually less expensive.*

10   Remove the spring retainer, oil shield and valve spring, then remove the guide seal. **Note:** *If air pressure fails to hold the valve in the closed position during this operation, the valve face and/or seat is probably damaged. If so, the cylinder head will have to be removed for additional repair operations.*

11   Wrap a rubber band or tape around the

top of the valve stem so the valve won't fall into the combustion chamber, then release the air pressure. **Note:** *If a rope was used instead of air pressure, turn the crankshaft slightly in the direction opposite normal rotation.*

12   Inspect the valve stem for damage. Rotate the valve in the guide and check the end for eccentric movement, which would indicate that the valve is bent.

13   Move the valve up-and-down in the guide and make sure it doesn't bind. If the valve stem binds, either the valve is bent or the guide is damaged. In either case, the head will have to be removed for repair.

14   Reapply air pressure to the cylinder to retain the valve in the closed position, then remove the tape or rubber band from the valve stem. If a rope was used instead of air pressure, rotate the crankshaft in the normal direction of rotation until slight resistance is felt.

15   Lubricate the valve stem with engine oil and install a new guide seal.

16   Install the spring and shield in position over the valve.

17   Install the valve spring retainer. Compress the valve spring and carefully position the keepers in the groove. Apply a small dab of grease to the inside of each keeper to hold it in place (see illustration).

18   Remove the pressure from the spring tool and make sure the keepers are seated.

19   Disconnect the air hose and remove the adapter from the spark plug hole. If a rope was used in place of air pressure, pull it out of the cylinder.

20   Refer to Section 5 and install the rocker arm(s) and pushrod(s).

21   Install the spark plug(s) and hook up the wire(s).

22   Refer to Section 6 and install the valve cover.

23   Start and run the engine, then check for oil leaks and unusual sounds coming from the valve cover area.

7.2 Disconnect any coolant lines from the intake manifold

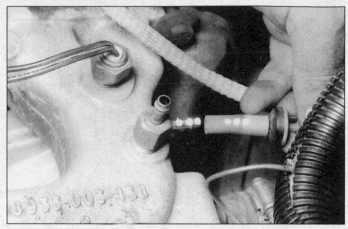

7.4 Use paint or masking tape to mark each hose for proper Installation

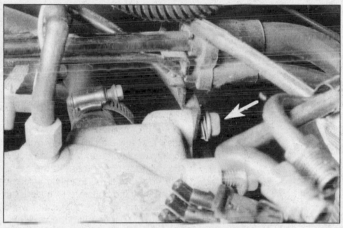

7.5 Remove the bolt (arrow) that retains the vacuum assembly to the intake manifold

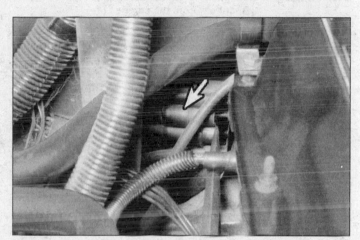

7.6 Disconnect the multiple vacuum connector (arrow) from the main assembly

7 Intake and exhaust manifold - removal and installation

Intake manifold

Warning: *Allow the engine to cool to room temperature before following this procedure.*

1   Disconnect the negative cable from the battery (see Chapter 5).

2   Drain the cooling system (see Chapter 1). Disconnect any coolant hoses that connect to the intake manifold (see illustration).

3   Remove the throttle body (see Chapter 4).

4   Label and then disconnect any wiring, hoses (see illustration) and control cables still connected to the intake manifold.

5   Disconnect the bolt (see illustration) that retains the vacuum tubing bracket to the intake manifold.

6   Reach around the back of the cylinder head and disconnect the multiple vacuum connector (see illustration).

7   Carefully lift the vacuum tube assembly from the engine compartment (see illustration).

7.7 Lift the vacuum assembly off the engine

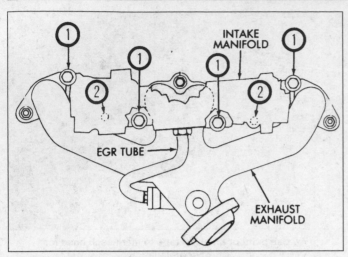

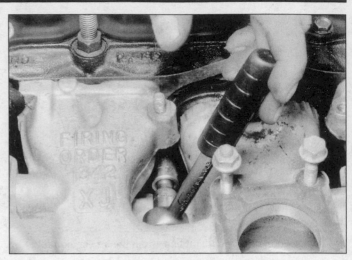

7.11a Remove the bolts (1), pull the manifold away from the engine slightly to disengage it from the dowel pins (2), then lift the manifold from the engine

7.11b Use an extension to reach the two lower bolts on the intake manifold

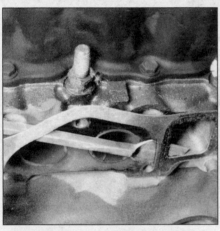

7.12a Remove the old intake manifold gasket with a scraper - don't leave any material on the mating surfaces

7.12b The intake manifold gasket can be removed without removing the exhaust manifold on the later engines

8   Unbolt the power steering pump (if equipped), and set it aside without disconnecting the hoses (see Chapter 10).

9   Disconnect the throttle valve (TV) linkage, if equipped with an automatic transmission (see Chapter 7B).

10   Disconnect the EGR tube from the intake manifold (see Chapter 6).

11   Remove the intake manifold bolts (see illustrations). Pull the manifold away from the engine slightly to disengage it from the dowel pins in the cylinder head, then lift the manifold from the engine. If the manifold sticks to the engine after all the bolts are removed, tap it with a softface hammer or a block of wood and a hammer while supporting the manifold.

12   Thoroughly clean the mating surfaces, removing all traces of gasket material (see illustration). Some early engines are equipped with a gasket that covers both the intake and exhaust manifold surfaces while later engines are equipped with an intake manifold gasket only (see illustration). On the early type, it is necessary to remove the exhaust manifold in order to replace the gasket properly (see Steps 18 through 26).

13   If the manifold is being replaced, transfer all fittings to the new one.

14   Position the replacement gasket on the cylinder head and install the manifold.

15   Install the intake manifold bolts and tighten them (along with the exhaust manifold nuts and EGR tube nut and bolts) in several stages, following the sequence shown to the torque listed in this Chapter's Specifications (see illustration).

16   Reinstall the remaining parts in the reverse order of removal.

17   Run the engine and check for vacuum leaks and proper operation.

Exhaust manifold

Warning: *Allow the engine to cool to room temperature before following this procedure.*

18   Remove the intake manifold (see Steps 1 through 11).

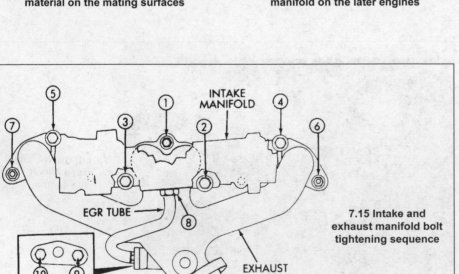

7.15 Intake and exhaust manifold bolt tightening sequence

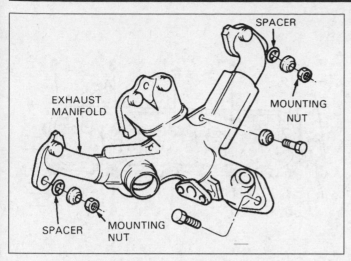

7.22 Exhaust manifold mounting details

8.8 If necessary, use a prybar to separate the cylinder head from the block. Be sure not to damage any gasket surfaces while applying pressure on the tool

19   Disconnect the EGR tube (see Chapter 6).

20   Remove the two nuts and bolts that secure the exhaust pipe to the exhaust manifold. It may be necessary to apply penetrating oil to the threads.

21   Unplug the oxygen sensor wire connector (see Chapter 6, if necessary).

22   Remove the mounting nuts and spacers (see illustration) and detach the exhaust manifold from the engine.

23   Clean the mating surfaces and, if the manifold is being replaced, transfer the oxygen sensor to the new manifold.

24   Reinstall the exhaust manifold and finger-tighten the nuts on the end studs.

25   Reinstall the intake manifold (see Steps 12 through 16) and tighten all mounting fasteners to the torque listed in this Chapter's Specifications, following the sequence shown in illustration 7.15. Reinstall the remaining components in the reverse order of removal.

26   Run the engine and check for exhaust leaks.

8   Cylinder head - removal and installation

Warning: *Allow the engine to cool to room temperature before following this procedure.*

1   Remove the rocker arms and pushrods (see Section 5).

2   Remove the intake and exhaust manifolds (see Section 7).

3   Remove the drivebelt(s) as described in Chapter 1.

4   Unbolt the power steering pump (if equipped) and set it aside without disconnecting the hoses.

5   On air conditioned models, remove the bolt that secures the air conditioning compressor/alternator bracket to the cylinder head, then unbolt the compressor/alternator bracket from the engine. Set the compressor

8.9 A die should be used to remove sealant and corrosion from the head bolt threads

aside without disconnecting the hoses.

6   Label, then disconnect the wire from the coolant temperature sending unit on the cylinder head.

7   Label the spark plug wires and remove the spark plugs.

8   Remove the ten bolts that secure the cylinder head and lift it off the engine (see illustration). If the head is stuck to the engine block, it may be necessary to tap it with a soft-face hammer or a block of wood and a hammer to break the seal.

9   Stuff clean shop towels into the cylinders. Thoroughly clean the gasket surfaces, removing all traces of gasket material. Run an appropriate sized tap into the bolt holes in the cylinder head and run a die over the bolt threads (see illustration). Ensure all bolt holes are clean and dry.

10   Inspect the cylinder head for cracks and check it for warpage. Refer to Chapter 2F for cylinder head servicing procedures.

11   1987 and 1988 four-cylinder engines use different head gaskets than 1989 and later models. The two types of gaskets are NOT interchangeable and require different tightening torques.

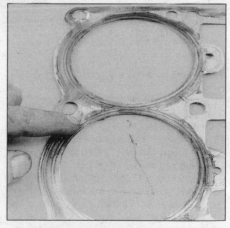

8.12 Use a sealant appropriate for steel gaskets on the surface of the metal head gasket.

12   1987 and 1988 models use stamped steel gaskets. Apply an even coat of gasket sealing compound suitable for steel gaskets, available at most auto parts stores, to both sides of the new gasket (see illustration).

13   1989 and later models use a composi-

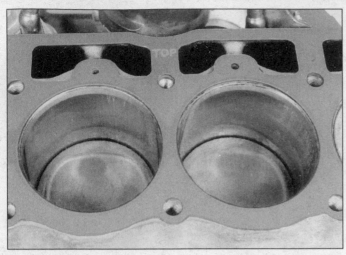

8.14 Be sure the designation on the head gasket (Top) faces up

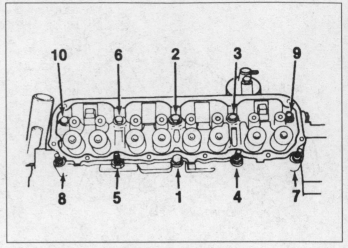

8.15a Cylinder head bolt/nut tightening sequence (1987 through 1989)

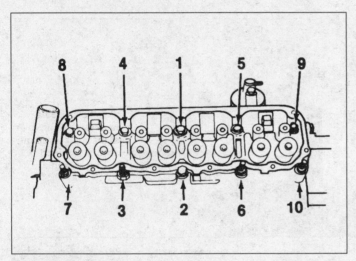

8.15b Cylinder head bolt/nut tightening sequence (1990 and later)

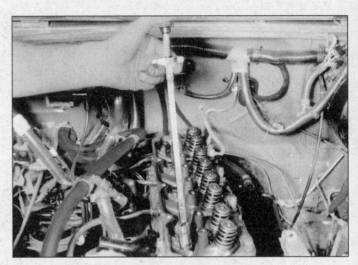

9.5 Removing lifters with the special tool

tion gasket. Install it dry (without any sealing compound).

14   Install the new gasket with the word TOP (see illustration) on the cylinder head side. Place the cylinder head on the engine.

15   Coat the threads of the stud bolt (no. 8 [1987 through 1989] or 7 [1990 and later] in the tightening sequence) with Loctite Pipe Sealant with Teflon no. 592 (or equivalent). Install the bolts and tighten them in the sequence shown (see illustrations). Tighten them in the steps and to the torque listed in this Chapter's Specifications.

Caution: *During the final tightening step, bolt no. 8 is tightened to a lower torque than the other bolts.*

16   Install the remaining components in the reverse order of removal.

17   Change the oil and filter (see Chapter 1).

18   Refill the cooling system and run the engine, checking for leaks and proper operation.

9   Hydraulic lifters - removal, inspection and installation

Removal

1   A noisy valve lifter can be isolated when the engine is idling. Place a length of hose or tubing on the valve cover near the position of each valve while listening at the other end. Or remove the valve cover and, with the engine idling, place a finger on each of the valve spring retainers, one at a time. If a valve lifter is defective, it'll be evident from the shock felt at the retainer as the valve opens.

2   The most likely cause of a noisy valve lifter is a piece of dirt trapped between the plunger and the lifter body.

3   Remove the valve cover (see Section 4).

4   Remove both rocker arms and both pushrods at the cylinder with the noisy lifter (see Section 5).

5   Remove the lifters through the push-

rod openings in the cylinder head. A special removal tool is available (see illustration), but isn't always necessary. On newer engines without a lot of varnish buildup, lifters can often be removed with a magnet attached to a long handle.

6   Store the lifters in a clearly labeled box to insure their reinstallation in the same lifter bores (see illustration).

Inspection

7   Clean the lifters with solvent and dry them thoroughly. Do this one lifter at a time to avoid mixing them up.

8   Check each lifter wall, pushrod seat and foot for scuffing, score marks and uneven wear. Each lifter foot (the surface that rides on the cam lobe) must be slightly convex, although this can be difficult to determine by eye. If the base of the lifter is concave or rough (see illustrations), the lifters and camshaft must be replaced. If the lifter walls are

9.6 If you're removing more than one lifter, keep them in order in a clearly labeled box

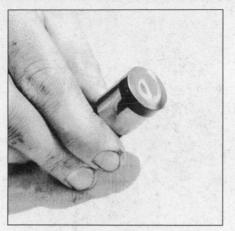

9.8a If the bottom (foot) of any lifter is worn concave (shown here), scratched or galled, replace the entire set with new lifters

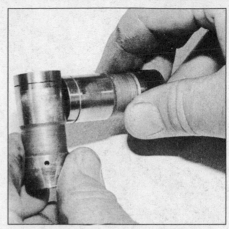

9.8b The foot of each lifter should be slightly convex - the side of another lifter can be used as a straightedge to check it; if it appears flat, it's worn and must not be used

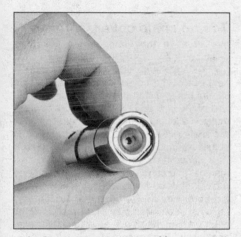

9.8c Check the pushrod seal in the top of each lifter for wear

9.8d If the lifters are pitted or rough, they shouldn't be reused

10.6 To remove the vibration damper, use a puller that bolts to the hub

damaged or worn (which isn't very likely), inspect the lifter bores in the engine block as well. If the pushrod seats (see illustration) are worn, check the pushrod ends.

9   If new lifters are being installed, a new camshaft must also be installed. If a new camshaft is installed, then use new lifters as well. Never install used lifters unless the original camshaft is used and the lifters can be installed in their original locations!

Installation

10   The used lifters must be installed in their original bores. Coat them with moly-base grease or engine assembly lube.
11   Lubricate the bearing surfaces of the lifter bores with engine oil.
12   Install the lifter(s) in the lifter bore(s).
13   Install the pushrods and rocker arms (see Section 5).
Caution: *Make sure that each pair of lifters is on the base circle of the camshaft; that is, with both valves closed, before tightening the rocker arm bolts.*

14   Tighten the rocker arm capscrews to the torque listed in this Chapter's Specifications.
15   Install the valve cover (see Section 4).

---

10   Vibration damper - removal and installation

---

1   Disconnect the cable from the negative terminal of the battery (see Chapter 5).
2   Remove the drivebelts (see Chapter 1). Tag each belt as it's removed to simplify reinstallation. If the vehicle is equipped with a fan shroud, unscrew the mounting bolts and position the shroud out of the way.
3   Raise the vehicle and support it securely on jackstands.
4   If the vehicle is equipped with a manual transmission, apply the parking brake and put the transmission in gear to prevent the crankshaft from turning, then remove the crankshaft pulley bolts. If your vehicle is equipped with an automatic transmission, it may be necessary to remove the starter motor (see Chapter 5) and

immobilize the starter ring gear with a large screwdriver while an assistant loosens the pulley bolts.
Note: *On vehicles with serpentine bolts, the pulley and vibration damper are combined as one piece - there are no pulley bolts to remove.*
5   To loosen the vibration damper retaining bolt, install a bolt in one of the pulley bolt holes. Attach a breaker bar, extension and socket to the vibration damper retaining bolt and immobilize the crankshaft by wedging a large screwdriver between the bolt and the socket. Remove the retaining bolt.
6   Remove the vibration damper. Use a puller if necessary (see illustration).
Caution: *Because the nose of the crankshaft is recessed, an adapter may be needed between the puller bolt and the crankshaft (to prevent damage to the bore and threads in the end of the crankshaft).*
7   Refer to Section 11 for the front oil seal replacement procedure.
8   Apply a thin layer of multi-purpose grease to the seal contact surface of the

11.2 The front crankshaft seal can be removed with a seal removal tool or a large screwdriver

11.6 Once the timing chain cover is removed, place it on a flat surface and gently pry the old seal out with a large screwdriver

11.8a Clean the bore, then apply a small amount of oil to the outer edge of the new seal and drive it squarely into the opening with a large socket...

11.8b ... or a block of wood and a hammer - don't damage the seal in the process!

vibration damper.

9   Slide the vibration damper onto the crankshaft. Note that the slot in the hub must be aligned with the Woodruff key in the end of the crankshaft. Once the key is aligned with the slot, tap the damper onto the crankshaft with a soft-face hammer. The retaining bolt can also be used to press the damper into position.

10   Tighten the vibration damper-to-crankshaft bolt to the torque listed in this Chapter's Specifications.

11   Install the crankshaft pulley (if equipped) on the hub and tighten the bolts to the specified torque. Use Locktite on the bolt threads.

12   Install the drivebelt(s) (see Chapter 1) and replace the fan shroud (if equipped).

---

11   Crankshaft front oil seal - replacement

Note: *The crankshaft front oil seal can be replaced with the timing chain cover in place. However, due to the limited amount of room available, you may conclude that the procedure would be easier if the cover were removed from the engine first. If so, refer to Section 12 for the cover removal and installation procedure.*

Timing chain cover in place

1   Disconnect the negative battery cable from the battery (see Chapter 5), then remove the vibration damper (see Section 10).

2   Note how the seal is installed - the new one must face the same direction! Carefully pry the oil seal out of the cover with a seal puller or a large screwdriver (see illustration). Be very careful not to distort the cover or scratch the crankshaft!

3   Apply clean engine oil or multi-purpose grease to the outer edge of the new seal, then install it in the cover with the lip (open end) facing in. Drive the seal into place with a seal driver or large socket and a hammer (if a large socket isn't available, a piece of pipe will also work). Make sure the seal enters the bore squarely and stop when the front face is flush with the cover.

4   Install the vibration damper (see Section 10).

Timing chain cover removed

5   Remove the timing chain cover as described in Section 12.

6   Using a large screwdriver, pry the old seal out of the cover (see illustration). Be careful not to distort the cover or scratch the wall of the seal bore. If the engine has accumulated a lot of miles, apply penetrating oil to the seal-to-cover joint and allow it to soak in before attempting to remove the seal.

7   Clean the bore to remove any old seal material and corrosion. Support the cover on a block of wood and position the new seal in the bore with the lip (open end) of the seal facing in. A small amount of oil applied to the outer edge of the new seal will make installation easier - don't overdo it!

8   Drive the seal into the bore with a large socket and hammer until it's completely seated (see illustration). Select a socket that's the same outside diameter as the seal. A section of pipe or even a block of wood can be used if a socket isn't available (see illustration).

9   Reinstall the timing chain cover.

---

12   Timing chain cover - removal and installation

1   Remove the vibration damper (see Section 10).

2   Remove the fan and hub assembly (see Chapter 3).

3   Remove the air conditioning compressor (if equipped) and the alternator bracket assembly from the cylinder head and set aside.

4   Remove the oil pan-to-timing chain cover bolts and the timing chain cover-to-block bolts and stud nuts. Mark the locations of the studs to ensure correct reassembly (see illustration 12.13).

5   Separate the timing chain cover from the engine. Avoid damaging the sealing surfaces;

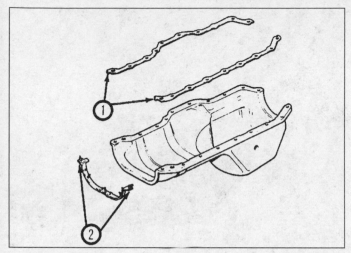

12.6 Cut the end tabs (1) flush with the block and trim the end seal tabs (2)

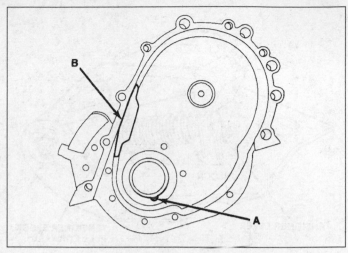

12.7 Inside view of timing chain cover

A   *Cutout for driving out oil seal*
B   *Timing chain guide*

do not force tools between the cover and block.

6   Cut off the oil pan gasket end tabs flush with the front face of the cylinder block and trim off the end seal tabs (see illustration).

7   Thoroughly clean the cover and all sealing surfaces, removing any traces of gasket material. Drive the old oil seal out from the rear of the timing chain cover and replace it with a new one (see Section 11). Also replace the chain guide, if necessary (see illustration).

8   Apply sealing compound (Perfect Seal or equivalent) to both sides of the new timing cover gasket and position the gasket on the engine block.

9   Trim the end tabs off the new oil pan gaskets to correspond with those cut off the original gasket. Attach the new end tabs to the oil pan with cement.

10   Coat the timing chain cover-to-oil pan seal tab recesses generously with RTV sealant (Jeep Gasket-In-A-Tube or equivalent) and position the seal onto the timing chain cover. Then apply a film of oil to the seal-to-oil pan contact surface.

11   Position the timing chain cover on the engine block.

12   Install the vibration damper to center the timing chain cover.

13   Install the cover-to-block nuts and bolts and the oil pan-to-cover bolts and tighten them to the torque listed in this Chapter's Specifications (see illustration).

14   Reinstall the remaining parts in the reverse order of removal.

15   Run the engine and check for oil leaks.

13   Timing chain and sprockets - removal, inspection and installation

Caution: *The timing system is complex. Severe engine damage will occur if you make*

any mistakes. Do not attempt this procedure unless you are at all highly experienced with this type of repair. If you are at all unsure of your abilities, consult an expert. Double-check all your work and be sure everything is correct before you attempt to start the engine.

1   Set the number one piston at Top Dead Center (TDC) (see Section 3).

2   Remove the timing chain cover (see Section 12).

3   Reinstall the vibration damper bolt and rotate the crankshaft until the zero timing mark on the crankshaft sprocket is lined up with the timing mark on the camshaft sprocket (see illustration).

4   Slide the oil slinger off the crankshaft.

12.13 Use paint to mark the locations of the studs in the timing cover

13.3 The timing marks on the sprockets (arrows) should be lined up as shown

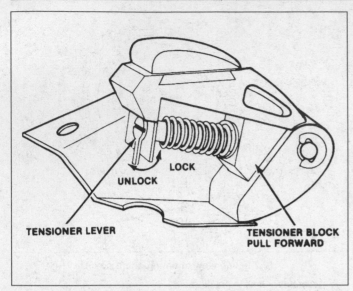

13.5a The timing chain tensioner is locked or unlocked with the tensioner lever

13.5b While compressing the tensioner with one screwdriver, lock the mechanism with the other screwdriver

13.6 Use a small screwdriver to remove the clip from the tensioner mount

13.7 The timing chain and sprockets are removed and installed as an assembly

5   Turn the tensioner lever to the unlock position. Pull the tensioner block toward the tensioner lever to compress the spring. Hold the block and turn the tensioner lever to the lock position (see illustrations).

6   If necessary, use a small screwdriver to remove the retaining clip (see illustration) and remove the tensioner from the block.

7   Remove the camshaft retaining bolt and slip both sprockets and the chain off as an assembly (see illustration).

8   Clean the components and inspect for wear and damage. Excessive chain slack and teeth that are deformed, chipped, pitted or discolored call for replacement. Always replace the sprockets and chain as a set. Inspect the tensioner for excessive wear and replace it, if necessary.

9   Install the tensioner, crankshaft camshaft sprockets and timing chain. Ensure the marks on the sprockets are still properly aligned (see illustration 13.3).

10   Install the camshaft sprocket retaining bolt and washer and tighten to the torque listed in this Chapter's Specifications.

11   On 1996 and earlier models, verify correct installation of the timing chain by turning the crankshaft to place the camshaft sprocket timing mark at approximately the one o'clock position. This positions the crankshaft timing mark where the adjacent tooth meshes with the chain at the three o'clock position. Count the number of chain pins between the timing marks of both sprockets. There must be 20 pins (see illustration).

12   Release the tensioner by turning the lever to the unlock position. Be sure the tensioner is released before installing the timing cover.

13   Install the oil slinger and the remaining parts in the reverse order of removal. Refer to

13.11 On 1996 and earlier models, with the camshaft sprocket timing mark at one o'clock, count the chain pins between the two timing marks - there must be 20 pins

14.3 When checking the camshaft lobe lift, the dial indicator plunger must be positioned directly above the pushrod

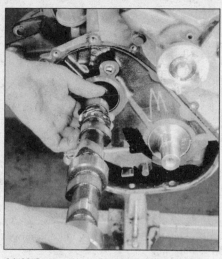

14.19 Support the camshaft near the block

14.21 The camshaft bearing journal diameters are checked to pinpoint excessive wear and out-of-round conditions

the appropriate sections for instructions.
Caution: *Before starting the engine, carefully rotate the crankshaft by hand through at least two full revolutions (use a socket and breaker bar on the crankshaft pulley center bolt). If you feel any resistance, STOP! There is something wrong - most likely, valves are contacting the pistons. You must find the problem before proceeding.*

14 Camshaft and bearings - removal, inspection and installation

Camshaft lobe lift check

1   To determine the extent of cam lobe wear, the lobe lift should be checked prior to camshaft removal. Refer to Section 4 and remove the valve cover.
2   Position the number one piston at TDC on the compression stroke (see Section 3).
3   Beginning with the number one cylinder valves, mount a dial indicator on the engine and position the plunger against the top surface of the first rocker arm. The plunger should be directly above and in line with the pushrod (see illustration).
4   Zero the dial indicator, then very slowly turn the crankshaft in the normal direction of rotation until the indicator needle stops and begins to move in the opposite direction. The point at which it stops indicates maximum cam lobe lift.
5   Record this figure for future reference, then reposition the piston at TDC on the compression stroke.
6   Move the dial indicator to the remaining number one cylinder rocker arm and repeat the check. Be sure to record the results for each valve.
7   Repeat the check for the remaining

valves. Since each piston must be at TDC on the compression stroke for this procedure, work from cylinder-to-cylinder following the firing order sequence.
8   After the check is complete, compare the results to the specifications. If camshaft lobe lift is less than specified, cam lobe wear has occurred and a new camshaft should be installed.

Removal

0   Set the number one piston at Top Dead Center (see Section 3).
10   Disconnect the negative cable from the battery (see Chapter 5).
11   Remove the radiator (see Chapter 3).
12   On models equipped with air conditioning, unbolt the air conditioning compressor and set it aside without disconnecting the refrigerant lines.
13   On carburetor equipped models, remove the fuel pump (see Chapter 4).
14   Remove the distributor (see Chapter 5).
15   If not removed already, detach the valve cover (see Section 4).
16   Remove the rocker arms and pushrods (see Section 5).
17   Remove the hydraulic lifters (see Section 9).
18   Remove the timing chain and sprockets (see Section 13).
Note: *If the camshaft appears to have been rubbing against the timing chain cover, examine the oil pressure relief holes in the rear cam journal and ensure they are free of debris.*
19   Install a bolt in the end of the camshaft to use as a handle. Carefully slide the camshaft out of the block. To avoid damage to the camshaft bearings as the lobes pass over them, support the camshaft near the block as it is withdrawn (see illustration).

Inspection

20   After the camshaft has been removed from the engine, cleaned with solvent and dried, inspect the bearing journals for uneven wear, pitting and evidence of seizure. If the journals are damaged, the bearing inserts in the block are probably damaged also. Both the camshaft and bearings will have to be replaced.
21   If the bearing journals are in good condition, measure them with a micrometer and record the measurements (see illustration). Measure each journal at several locations around its circumference. If you get different measurements at different locations, the journal is out of round.
22   Check the inside diameter of each camshaft bearing with a telescoping gauge and measure the gauge with a micrometer. Subtract each cam journal diameter from the corresponding camshaft bearing inside diameter to obtain the bearing oil clearance.
23   Compare the clearance for each bearing to the specifications. If it is excessive, for any of the bearings, have new bearings installed by an automotive machine shop.
24   Inspect the distributor drive gear for wear. Replace the camshaft if the gear is worn.
25   Inspect the camshaft lobes (including the fuel pump lobe on carburetor equipped models) for heat discoloration, score marks, chipped areas, pitting and uneven wear. If the lobes are in good condition and if the lobe lift measurements are as specified, the camshaft can be reused.

Bearing replacement

26   Camshaft bearing replacement requires special tools and expertise that place it outside the scope of the home mechanic. Take the engine block (see Part F of this Chapter) to an automotive machine shop to ensure the job is done correctly.

14.27 Be sure to apply moly-base grease or engine assembly lube to the cam lobes and bearing journals before installing the camshaft

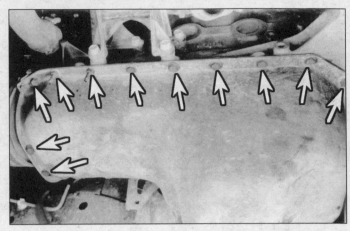

15.6 Remove the bolts from the perimeter of the oil pan

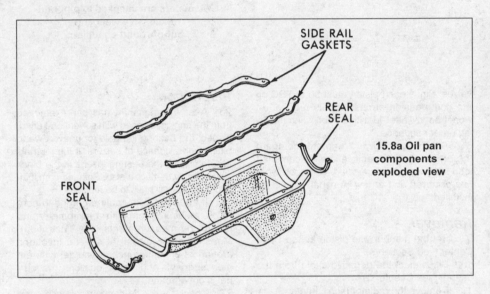

15.8a Oil pan components - exploded view

SIDE RAIL GASKETS

REAR SEAL

FRONT SEAL

15.8b Be sure to apply RTV sealant to the corners of the gasket over the rear main bearing cap...

15.8c ... and in the corners and seams over the timing cover

Installation

27   Lubricate the camshaft bearing journals and lobes with moly-base grease or engine assembly lube (see illustration).

28   Slide the camshaft into the engine. Support the cam near the block and be careful not to scrape or nick the bearings.

29   Temporarily place the camshaft sprocket onto the camshaft and turn the camshaft until the timing mark is aligned with the centerline of the crankshaft (see Section 13). Remove the sprocket.

30   Install the timing chain and sprockets and the remaining components in the reverse order of removal. Refer to the appropriate Sections for installation instructions.

Note: *If the original cam and lifters are being reinstalled, be sure to install the lifters in their original locations. If a new camshaft was installed, be sure to install new lifters also.*

31   Add coolant and change the oil and filter (see Chapter 1).

32   Start the engine and check the ignition timing. Check for leaks and unusual noises.

---

15   Oil pan - removal and installation

1   Disconnect the cable from the negative battery terminal.

2   Raise the vehicle and support it securely on jackstands.

3   Drain the engine oil and remove the oil filter (Chapter 1).

4   Disconnect the exhaust pipe at the manifold (see Section 7) and hangers and tie the system aside.

5   Remove the starter (see Chapter 5) and the bellhousing dust cover.

6   Remove the bolts (see illustration) and detach the oil pan. Don't pry between the block and pan or damage to the sealing surfaces may result and oil leaks could develop. If the pan is stuck, dislodge it with a soft-face hammer or a block of wood and a hammer.

7   Use a scraper to remove all traces of sealant from the pan and block, then clean the mating surfaces with lacquer thinner or acetone.

8   Using gasket adhesive, position new oil pan seals and gaskets on the engine (see illustrations).

9   Install the oil pan and tighten the mounting bolts to the torque listed in this Chapter's Specifications. Note that the 1/4-inch diameter and 5/16-inch diameter bolts have different torques. Start at the center of the pan and work out toward the ends in a spiral pattern.

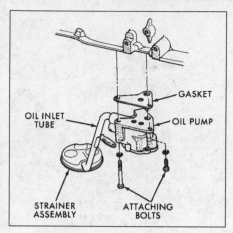

16.2 Oil pump and components

17.3 Before removing the flywheel, index it to the crankshaft (arrow)

17.4 To prevent the flywheel from turning, hold a pry bar against two bolts or wedge a large screwdriver into the flywheel ring gear

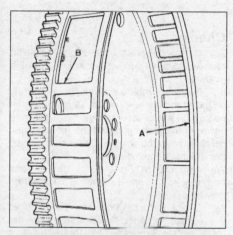

17.8 The driveplate on a four-cylinder engine with an automatic transmission has a trigger wheel - check the inner surface (A) for excessive runout with a dial indicator - inspect the timing slot separators (B) for dents, distortion and cracks

10   Install the bellhousing dust cover and the starter, then reconnect the exhaust pipe to the manifold and hanger brackets.
11   Lower the vehicle.
12   Install a new filter and add oil to the engine.
13   Reconnect the negative battery cable.
14   Start the engine and check for leaks.

16   Oil pump - removal and installation

1   Remove the oil pan (see Section 15).
2   Remove the two oil pump attaching bolts from the engine block (see illustration).
3   Detach the oil pump and strainer assembly from the block.
4   If the pump is defective, replace it with a new one. If the engine is being completely overhauled, install a new oil pump - don't

reuse the original or attempt to rebuild it.
5   On four-cylinder engines, to install the oil pump, turn the shaft so the gear tang mates with the slot on the lower end of the distributor shaft. The oil pump should slide easily into place. If it doesn't, pull it off and turn the tang until it's aligned with the lower end of the shaft.
6   On six-cylinder engines, to install the oil pump, turn the shaft so the gear tang mates with the slot on the lower end of the distributor shaft on 1987 through 1999 models, or the camshaft position sensor drive shaft on 2000 models. The oil pump should slide easily into place. If it doesn't, pull it off and turn the tang until it's aligned with the lower end of the shaft.
7   Install the pump attaching bolts. Tighten them to the torque listed in this Chapter's Specifications.
8   Reinstall the oil pan (see Section 15).
9   Add oil, run the engine and check for leaks.

17   Flywheel/driveplate - removal and installation

1   Raise the vehicle and support it securely on jackstands, then refer to Chapter 7A or Chapter 7B and remove the transmission. If it's leaking, now would be a very good time to replace the front pump seal/O-ring (automatic transmission only).
2   Remove the pressure plate and clutch disc (see Chapter 8) (manual transmission equipped vehicles). Now is a good time to check/replace the clutch components and pilot bearing.
3   Use paint or a center-punch to make alignment marks on the flywheel/driveplate and crankshaft to ensure correct alignment during reinstallation (see illustration).
4   Remove the bolts that secure the flywheel/driveplate to the crankshaft (see illustration). If the crankshaft turns, hold the flywheel with a pry bar or wedge a screwdriver into the ring gear teeth to jam the flywheel.

5   Remove the flywheel/driveplate from the crankshaft. Since the flywheel is fairly heavy, be sure to support it while removing the last bolt.
6   Clean the flywheel to remove grease and oil. Inspect the surface for cracks, rivet grooves, burned areas and score marks. Light scoring can be removed with emery cloth. Check for cracked and broken ring gear teeth or a loose ring gear. Lay the flywheel on a flat surface and use a straightedge to check for warpage.
7   Clean and inspect the mating surfaces of the flywheel/driveplate and the crankshaft. If the crankshaft rear seal is leaking, replace it before reinstalling the flywheel/driveplate.
8   On certain models equipped with a four-cylinder engine and an automatic transmission, the trigger wheel portion of the driveplate assembly provides the timing signal for the fuel and ignition systems. If the trigger wheel becomes damaged when removing/installing the engine, transmission or torque converter, ignition performance will be affected. The general result is either rough engine operation and backfire, or a no-start condition. Check for suspected trigger wheel damage as follows:

a)   Check the trigger wheel radial runout on the inner surface (A) with a dial indicator (see illustration). Replace the driveplate assembly if runout is excessive.
b)   Inspect the timing slot separators (B) in the trigger wheel. Replace the driveplate assembly if the separators are dented, distorted, or cracked. Do not attempt to repair the wheel as the results are usually not satisfactory.

9   Position the flywheel/driveplate against the crankshaft. Be sure to align the marks made during removal. Note that some engines have an alignment dowel or staggered bolt holes to ensure correct installation. Before installing the bolts, apply thread locking compound to the threads.
10   Wedge a screwdriver into the ring gear teeth to keep the flywheel/driveplate from turning as you tighten the bolts to the torque

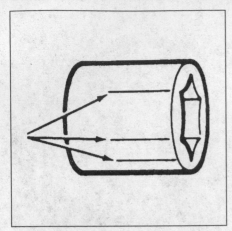

17.10 Make marks every 60 degrees on the socket to indicate how much you have turned the bolt

18.5 Carefully pry the oil seal out with a removal tool or a screwdriver - don't nick or scratch the crankshaft or the new seal will be damaged and leaks will develop

18.8 If the socket isn't available, tap around the outer edge of the new seal with a hammer and punch to seat it squarely in the bore

19.8 Remove the through-bolt and nut (A) and mount bolt (B), then remove the mount nut (not visible in this photo) from beneath the frame bracket

listed in this Chapter's Specifications. After the initial torque has been reached, turn each bolt an additional 60 degrees as outlined in the specifications. A 3/4-inch socket should be marked every 60 degrees on the outside (see illustration). After reaching the specified torque, make a reference mark below one of the marks on the socket. Turn the bolt until the next 60 degrees mark is reached.
11   The remainder of installation is the reverse of the removal procedure.

18   Rear main oil seal - replacement

1   The rear main bearing oil seal can be replaced without removing the oil pan or crankshaft.

2   Remove the transmission (see Chapter 7A or Chapter 7B).
3   If equipped with a manual transmission, remove the pressure plate and clutch disc (see Chapter 8).
4   Remove the flywheel or driveplate (see Section 17).
5   Using a seal removal tool or a large screwdriver, carefully pry the seal out of the block (see illustration). Don't scratch or nick the crankshaft in the process.
6   Clean the bore in the block and the seal contact surface on the crankshaft. Check the crankshaft surface for scratches and nicks that could damage the new seal lip and cause oil leaks. If the crankshaft is damaged, the only alternative is a new or different crankshaft.
7   Apply a light coat of engine oil or multi-purpose grease to the outer edge of the new seal. Lubricate the seal lip with multi-purpose grease.
8   Carefully work the seal lip over the end of the crankshaft, then tap the new seal into place with a hammer and a large socket (if available) or a rounded punch (see illustration). The seal lip must face toward the front of the engine.
9   Install the flywheel or driveplate.
10   If equipped with a manual transmission, reinstall the clutch disc and pressure plate.
11   Reinstall the transmission as described in Chapter 7A or Chapter 7B.

19   Engine mounts - check and replacement

1   Engine mounts seldom require attention, but broken or deteriorated mounts should be replaced immediately or the added strain placed on the driveline components may cause damage or wear.

Check

2   During the check, the engine must be raised slightly to remove the weight from the mounts.
3   Raise the vehicle and support it securely on jackstands, then position a jack under the engine oil pan. Place a large block of wood between the jack head and the oil pan, then carefully raise the engine just enough to take the weight off the mounts.
Warning: *DO NOT place any part of your body under the engine when it's supported only by a jack!*
4   Check the mounts to see if the rubber is cracked, hardened or separated from the metal plates. Sometimes the rubber will split right down the center.
5   Check for relative movement between the mount plates and the engine or frame (use a large screwdriver or prybar to attempt to move the mounts). If movement is noted, lower the engine and tighten the mount fasteners.
6   Rubber preservative should be applied to the mounts to slow deterioration.

Replacement

7   Disconnect the negative battery cable from the battery, then raise the vehicle and support it securely on jackstands (if not already done).
8   Loosen the nut on the through bolt and remove the bolt and nut that secure the mount to the frame bracket (see illustration).
9   Raise the engine slightly with a jack or hoist (make sure the fan doesn't hit the radiator or shroud). Remove the through-bolt and nut and detach the mount.
10   Installation is the reverse of removal. Use thread locking compound on the mount bolts and be sure to tighten them securely.

Chapter 2 Part C
4.0L and 4.2L six-cylinder engines

Contents

Specifications

General

Displacement
4.0L engine	243 cubic inches
4.2L engine	258 cubic inches
Cylinder numbers (front-to-rear)	1-2-3-4-5-6
Firing order	1-5-3-6-2-4

Camshaft

Lobe lift (intake and exhaust)	0.253 inch
Endplay	None

Journal diameter
No. 1	2.029 to 2.030 inches
No. 2	2.019 to 2.020 inches
No. 3	2.009 to 2.010 inches
No. 4	1.999 to 2.000 inches
Journal-to-bearing (oil) clearance	0.001 to 0.003 inch

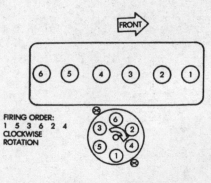

FIRING ORDER:
1 5 3 6 2 4
CLOCKWISE
ROTATION

Cylinder location and distributor rotation

Torque specifications   Ft-lbs (unless otherwise indicated)

Note: *One foot-pound (ft-lb) of torque is equivalent to 12 inch-pounds (in-lbs) of torque. Torque values below approximately 15 foot-pounds are expressed in inch-pounds, because most foot-pound torque wrenches are not accurate at these smaller values.*

Camshaft sprocket bolt	50
Crankshaft pulley-to-vibration damper bolts	20
Cylinder head bolts (see illustration 9.21 for tightening sequence)	
4.2L engine	85
4.0L engine	
Step A	22
Step B	45
Step C	45
Step D	
Bolt no. 11	100
All other bolts	110
Flywheel/driveplate bolts	105
Intake and exhaust manifold retaining bolts and nuts (all except 1989 models)	
Nos. 1 through 5 and 8 through 11	23
Nos. 6 and 7	17
1989 models	
Nos. 1 and 2	30
Nos. 3 through 12	23
Oil pan mounting bolts	
1/4 x 20	84 in-lbs
5/16 x 18	132 in-lbs
Oil pump mounting bolt	
Short	120 in-lbs
Long	17
Rear main bearing cap bolts	80
Rocker arm bolts	19
Tensioner bracket-to-block bolts	168 in-lbs
Timing chain cover-to-block	
Bolts	60 in-lbs
Studs	16
Valve cover-to-cylinder head bolts	
With RTV	28 in-lbs
With permanent gasket	55 in-lbs
Vibration damper center bolt (lubricated)	80

1   General Information

1   This Part of Chapter 2 is devoted to in-vehicle repair procedures for the inline six-cylinder engine. Information concerning engine removal and installation and engine overhaul can be found in Chapter 2F.

2   The following repair procedures are based on the assumption that the engine is installed in the vehicle. If the engine has been removed from the vehicle and mounted on a stand, many of the steps outlined in this Part of Chapter 2 will not apply.

3   The Specifications included in this Part of Chapter 2 apply only to the procedures contained in this Part. Chapter 2F contains the Specifications necessary for cylinder head and engine block rebuilding.

2   Repair operations possible with the engine in the vehicle

1   Many major repair operations can be accomplished without removing the engine from the vehicle.

2   Clean the engine compartment and the exterior of the engine with some type of pressure washer before any work is done. It will make the job easier and help keep dirt out of the internal areas of the engine.

3   Remove the hood, if necessary, to improve access to the engine as repairs are performed (refer to Chapter 11 if necessary).

4   If vacuum, exhaust, oil or coolant leaks develop, indicating a need for gasket or seal replacement, the repairs can generally be made with the engine in the vehicle. The intake and exhaust manifold gaskets, timing cover gasket, oil pan gasket, crankshaft oil

seals and cylinder head gaskets are all accessible with the engine in place.

5   Exterior engine components, such as the intake and exhaust manifolds, the oil pan (and the oil pump), the water pump, the starter motor, the alternator, the distributor and the fuel system components can be removed for repair with the engine in place.

6   Since the cylinder heads can be removed without pulling the engine, valve component servicing can also be accomplished with the engine in the vehicle. Replacement of the camshaft and timing chain and sprockets is also possible with the engine in the vehicle.

7   In extreme cases caused by a lack of necessary equipment, repair or replacement of piston rings, pistons, connecting rods and rod bearings is possible with the engine in the vehicle. However, this practice is not recommended because of the cleaning and preparation work that must be done to the components involved.

3   Top Dead Center (TDC) for number one piston - locating

1   See Chapter 2A, Section 3, for this procedure, but refer to the illustrations included in this Section (see illustrations).

4   Valve cover - removal and installation

1   Pull the crankcase breather tube and hose off the valve cover (see illustration).

2   Remove the cruise control servo, if equipped.

3   Remove the wire harness clips (see illustration), noting the locations of their studs for reinstallation.

4   Remove the valve cover retaining bolts and lift the cover off. If the cover is stuck, tap

3.1a Align the notch on the vibration damper with the "0" on the timing cover

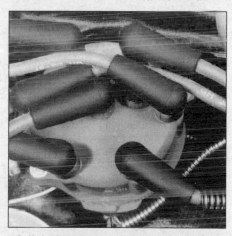

3.1b Locate the number one spark plug terminal on the distributor cap; make a mark on the distributor housing, directly under the number one plug terminal...

3.1c ... then remove the distributor cap and verify that the rotor is pointing at the mark

4.1 View from above shows the locations of the crankcase breather tube and hose (arrows)

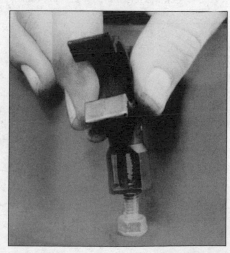

4.3 Pull off the wire harness clips

on it gently with a soft-face mallet (see illustration). Do not pry on the gasket flange.
Note: *These covers have a reusable pre-cured gasket that is attached to the cover.*

5   Clean the sealing surfaces, removing any traces of oil with brake system cleaner and a clean rag.

6   Small cracks in the pre-cured gasket are allowable and can be repaired by applying RTV sealant to the cracked area before the cover is installed.

7   Install the cover and bolts. Tighten the bolts to the torque listed in this Chapter's Specifications.

8   Reinstall the crankcase breather hoses and cruise control servo, if equipped.

9   Run the engine and check for oil leaks.

---

5   Rocker arms and pushrods - removal, inspection and installation

Removal

1   Remove the valve cover (see Section 4).

2   Beginning at the front of the cylinder head, loosen and remove the rocker arm mounting bolts in pairs (see illustration).

3   Remove the rocker arms, bridges and fulcrums (see illustration) and store them with their respective mounting bolts. Store each set of rocker arm components separately in a marked plastic bag to ensure they are reinstalled in their original locations. The bridges may be reinstalled in any location.

4   Remove the pushrods and store them separately to make sure they don't get mixed up during installation (see illustration).

Inspection

5   Check each rocker arm for wear, cracks and other damage, especially where the pushrods and valve stems contact the rocker arm faces. Check the fulcrum seat in each rocker

arm and the fulcrum faces. Look for galling, stress cracks and unusual wear patterns. If the rocker arms are worn or damaged, replace them with new ones and install new fulcrums as well.

6   Make sure the oil hole at the pushrod end of each rocker arm is open.

7   Inspect the pushrods for cracks and excessive wear at the ends. Roll each pushrod across a piece of plate glass to see if it's bent (if it wobbles, it's bent).

Installation

8   Lubricate the lower end of each pushrod with clean engine oil or moly-base grease and install it in its original location. Make sure each pushrod seats completely in the lifter socket.

9   Bring the number one piston to Top Dead Center (TDC) on the compression stroke (see Section 3).

10   Apply moly-base grease to the ends of the valve stems and the upper ends of the pushrods before placing the rocker arms in position.

11   Apply moly-base grease to the fulcrums to prevent damage to the mating surfaces before engine oil pressure builds up. Install the rocker arms, fulcrums, bridges and bolts in their original locations. Tighten the bolts to the torque listed in this Chapter's Specifications.

12   Install the valve cover (see Section 4).

13   Start the engine, listen for unusual valvetrain noises and check for oil leaks at the valve cover joint.

---

6   Valve springs, retainers and seals - replacement

1   See Chapter 2B, Section 6 for this procedure, but be sure to follow the valve cover and rocker arm/pushrod procedures outlined in this Part.

4.4 Use a soft-face mallet to break the cover loose - DO NOT pry between the cover and head

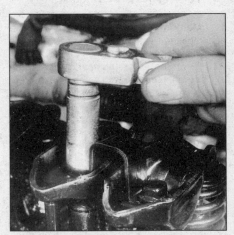

5.2 Go back and forth between the intake and exhaust rocker arms, loosening each bolt 1/4-turn at a time

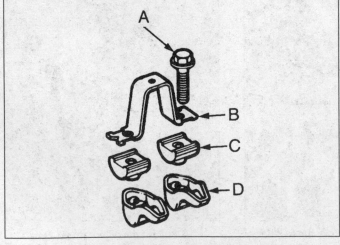

5.3 Rocker arm components - exploded view

A   Bolt   C   Fulcrum
B   Bridge   D   Rocker arm

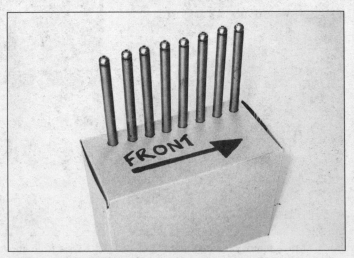

5.4 Store the pushrods in a box like this to ensure reinstallation in the same location

7 Intake manifold - removal and installation

Warning: *Allow the engine to cool completely before following this procedure.*

Note: *Since the intake and exhaust manifolds share a common gasket, they must be removed and replaced at the same time.*

Note: *If you are working on a carbureted model (4.2L engine), simply ignore all references to the fuel injection system.*

1   Disconnect the negative cable from the battery (see Chapter 5).

2   Remove the air filter housing and the accelerator cable (see Chapter 4).

3   On automatic transmission equipped models, disconnect the transmission line pressure (TV) cable (see Chapter 7B).

4   Detach the cruise control cable, if equipped.

5   Disconnect the vacuum connector on the intake manifold by lifting the connector assembly up and out of the bracket and then pulling it apart (see illustration).

6   Label and disconnect all vacuum and electrical connectors on the intake manifold (see illustration).

7   Relieve the fuel pressure and then disconnect the fuel supply and return lines from the fuel rail assembly (see Chapter 4). Cap the open ends.

8   Loosen the serpentine drivebelt (see Chapter 1).

9   Remove the power steering pump and bracket from the intake manifold and set it aside without disconnecting the hoses. Be sure to leave the pump in an upright position so fluid won't spill.

10   Remove the fuel rail and injectors (see Chapter 4).

11   Remove the intake manifold heat shield (see illustration).

12   Unscrew the intake manifold bolts (see illustration).

13   Remove the EGR tube from the intake manifold (see Chapter 6). Pull the manifold away from the engine slightly to disengage it from the locating dowels in the cylinder head, then lift the manifold out of the engine compartment.

14   Remove the exhaust manifold (see Section 8). This is necessary because the intake and exhaust manifolds share a common gasket.

15   Thoroughly clean the gasket mating surfaces, removing all traces of old gasket material.

16   If the manifold is being replaced, make sure all the fittings, etc., are transferred to the replacement manifold.

17   Position a new gasket on the cylinder head, using the locating dowels to hold it in

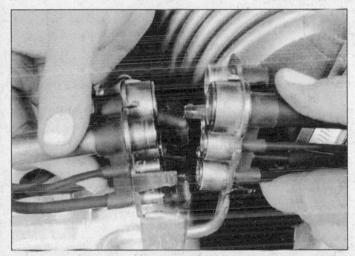

7.5 Lift the vacuum connector from its bracket and pull it apart

7.6 Label the connections before detaching them

7.11 Remove the bolts (arrows) and lift the heat shield off

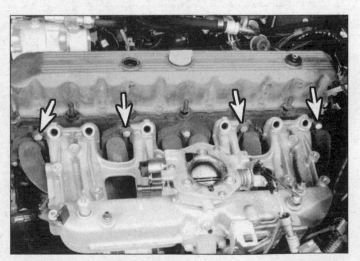

7.12 Four of the intake manifold mounting bolts (arrows) can be accessed from the top - you must reach below the manifold to remove the remaining four, which are visible in illustration 7.20 (1987 through 1999 shown)

place. Install the exhaust manifold and hand-tighten the nuts.

18 Position the intake manifold loosely on the cylinder head.

19 Install the EGR tube between the manifolds.

20 Install the manifold retaining bolts and tighten all fasteners in sequence (see illustrations) to the torque listed in this Chapter's Specifications.

21 Reinstall the remaining parts in the reverse order of removal.

Caution: *Before connecting the fuel lines to the fuel rail, replace the O-rings in the quick-connect fuel line couplings (see Chapter 4).*

22 Run the engine and check for leaks.

---

8 Exhaust manifold - removal and installation

Warning: *Allow the engine to cool completely before following this procedure.*

1 Remove the intake manifold (see Section 7).

2 Apply penetrating oil to the threads of the exhaust manifold attaching studs and the exhaust pipe-to-manifold attaching bolts.

3 On 1987 through 1999 models, remove the nuts that secure the exhaust pipe to the exhaust manifold and detach the pipe from the manifold. On models since 2000, remove the nuts that secure the exhaust pipe assembly to the exhaust manifolds.

4 On 1987 through 1999 models, remove the three nuts that secure the exhaust manifold to the cylinder head and pull the manifold off the engine. On 2000 models, remove the remaining nuts that secure the exhaust manifolds to the cylinder head and pull both manifolds off the engine.

5 Remove all traces of old gasket material from the mating surfaces.

6 If the manifold gasket was blown out, have the manifold checked for warpage by an automotive machine shop and repaired as necessary.

7 Position a new gasket on the locating dowels and slide the manifold over the studs.

8 Install the attaching nuts on the studs finger-tight.

9 Reinstall the intake manifold (see Section 7) and tighten all fasteners, in the sequence shown in illustration 7.20, to the torque listed in this Chapter's Specifications.

10 Reconnect the exhaust pipe, run the engine and check for leaks.

---

9 Cylinder head - removal and installation

Warning: *Allow the engine to cool completely before following this procedure.*

Removal

1 Disconnect the negative cable from the battery (see Chapter 5).

2 Drain the cooling system (see Chapter 1).

3 Remove the air cleaner assembly (see Chapter 4).

4 Detach the fuel pipe and vacuum advance hose.

5 Remove the valve cover (see Section 4).

6 Remove the rocker arms and pushrods (see Section 5).

7 Unbolt the power steering pump bracket (if equipped) and set the pump aside without disconnecting the hoses. Leave the pump upright so fluid doesn't spill.

8 Remove the intake and exhaust manifolds (see Section 7 and 8).

Air-conditioned models

9 Remove the bracket on the cylinder head that supports the idler pulley for the air conditioning compressor drivebelt (see Chapter 3).

10 Loosen the alternator drivebelt and remove the alternator bracket-to-cylinder head mounting bolt.

11 Unplug the wiring and unbolt the air conditioning compressor (see Chapter 3) without disconnecting the refrigerant hoses. Set the compressor aside and remove the upper two bolts from the bracket (see illustration).

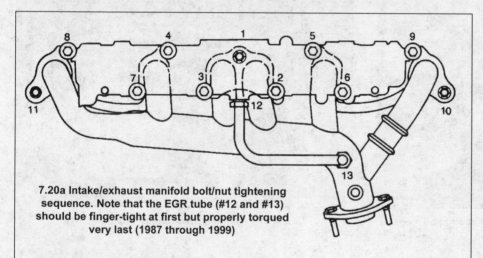

7.20a Intake/exhaust manifold bolt/nut tightening sequence. Note that the EGR tube (#12 and #13) should be finger-tight at first but properly torqued very last (1987 through 1999)

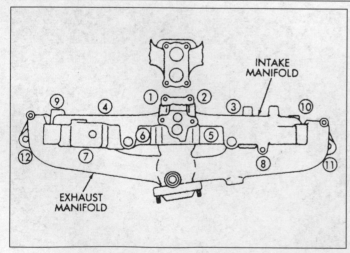

7.20b Intake/exhaust manifold bolt/nut tightening sequence 1989 models only

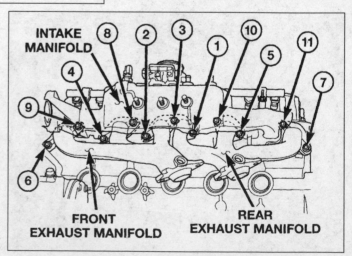

7.20c Intake and exhaust manifold bolt/nut tightening sequence (2000 4.0L)

All models

12 Label the spark plug wires and remove the distributor cap with the wires attached to it. Remove the spark plugs as described in Chapter 1.

13 Disconnect the wire from the temperature sending unit, which is on the top left rear corner of the cylinder head. Also disconnect the battery ground cable, which is on the right side of the engine.

14 Remove the ignition coil and bracket assembly (see Chapter 5).

15 Remove the heater hose bracket, if equipped (see illustration).

16 Remove the cylinder head bolts and lift the head off the engine.

Note: *Bolt number 14 (see illustration 9.21) cannot be removed until the cylinder head is moved forward enabling the bolt to clear the firewall.*

Note: *If the head sticks to the engine, insert a prybar into an exhaust port and pry gently to break the seal.*

17 Thoroughly clean the gasket mating surfaces, removing all traces of old gasket material. Stuff shop towels into each cylinder so scraped material doesn't fall in.

18 Inspect the head for cracks and warpage. See Chapter 2F, for cylinder head servicing information. If you are replacing the cylinder head, be sure to transfer all fittings, etc., to the new head.

Installation

19 On models equipped with the 4.2L engine, apply an even coat of Perfect Seal sealing compound (or equivalent) to both sides of the replacement head gasket (metal type). On models equipped with the 4.0L engine, it is not necessary to use any type of sealant on the head gasket (composition type). Position the new head gasket on the engine block with the word TOP facing up (see illustration).

20 Install the cylinder head on the engine block.

21 Coat the threads of bolt number 11 (see illustration) with Loctite 592 sealant (or equivalent) and install the head bolts hand-tight.

Note: *Clean each bolt and mark it with a dab of paint. Replace any bolts which were painted and reused during an earlier servicing operation.*

22 Tighten the cylinder head bolts in sequence (see illustration 9.21) to the torque values listed in this Chapter's Specifications.

23 Reinstall the remaining components in the reverse order of removal.

24 Add coolant and run the engine, checking for proper operation and coolant and oil leaks.

9.11 Set the compressor aside with the refrigerant lines still attached - then remove the upper bracket bolts

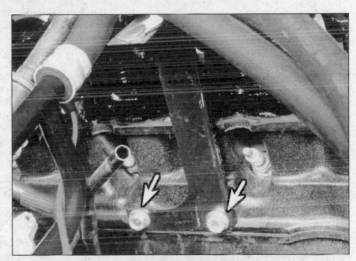

9.15 Remove the two bolts (arrows) to disconnect the heater hose bracket

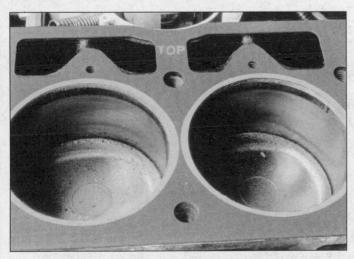

9.19 Install the head gasket with the TOP mark facing up

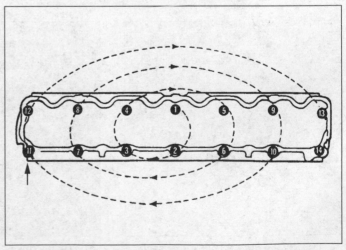

9.21 Cylinder head bolt tightening sequence - be sure to coat the threads of bolt no. 11 (arrow) with Loctite 592 sealant (or equivalent)

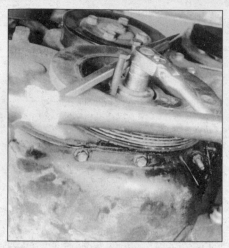

10.6 Install two bolts in the damper and use them to keep the crankshaft from rotating

10.7 Use a puller that bolts to the hub of the damper - do not use a gear puller with jaws; it will damage the damper

10   Vibration damper - removal and installation

1   Disconnect the negative cable from the battery (see Chapter 5).
2   Raise the front of the vehicle and support it securely on jackstands.
3   Remove the splash pan which is mounted below the front of the engine.
4   Remove the drivebelts (see Chapter 1).
5   Remove the radiator and cooling fan(s) as described in Chapter 3.
6   Remove the vibration damper retaining bolt and washer. To prevent the crankshaft from rotating, place two 5/16 x 1-1/2-inch long bolts into the damper holes and hold a prybar between them (see illustration), then rotate the crankshaft until the bar contacts the frame.
7   Using a puller, pull the damper off the crankshaft (see illustration).
Caution: *Because the nose of the crankshaft is recessed, an adapter may be needed between the puller bolt and the crankshaft (to prevent damage to the bore and threads in the end of the crankshaft).*
8   Clean and inspect the area on the center hub of the damper where the front oil seal contacts it. Minor imperfections can be cleaned up with fine emery cloth. If there is a groove worn in the hub, replace the vibration damper or have a special sleeve installed on the hub to restore the contact surface.
9   Apply clean engine oil to the seal contact surface of the damper hub.
10   Align the key slot of the vibration damper hub with the crankshaft key and tap the damper onto the crankshaft with a soft-face mallet.
11   Install the vibration damper bolt and tighten it to the torque listed in this Chapter's Specifications.
12   Reinstall the remaining parts in the reverse order of removal.

11   Crankshaft front oil seal - replacement

1   Remove the vibration damper (see Section 10).
2   Carefully pry the oil seal out of the timing chain cover with a seal removal tool or screwdriver (see illustration). Don't scratch the cover bore or damage the crankshaft in the process (if the crankshaft is damaged the new seal will end up leaking).
3   Clean the bore in the cover and coat the outer edge of the new seal with engine oil or multi-purpose grease. Using a socket with an outside diameter slightly smaller than the outside diameter of the seal, carefully drive the new seal into place with a hammer (see illustration). If a socket isn't available, a short section of large diameter pipe will work. Check the seal after installation to be sure that the spring didn't pop out of place.
4   Reinstall the vibration damper.
5   The parts removed to gain access to the damper can now be reinstalled.
6   Run the engine and check for leaks.

12   Timing chain cover - removal and installation

Removal
1   Disconnect the negative cable from the battery.
2   Remove the fan, fan shroud, radiator and water pump pulley (see Chapter 3).
3   Remove the vibration damper (see Section 10).
4   Unbolt the alternator and bracket assembly (see illustration).
5   Remove the oil pan-to-timing chain cover bolts and timing chain cover-to-engine block bolts.
6   Separate the timing chain cover from the

11.2 Pry the old seal out with a seal removal tool (shown here) or a screwdriver

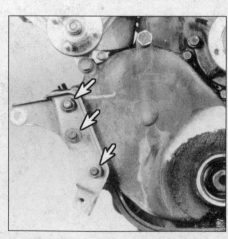

11.3 Gently drive the new seal into place with a hammer and large socket

12.4 Once the alternator has been removed, remove the bracket retaining nuts (arrows), then unbolt the timing chain cover

engine. If necessary, tap on it gently with a soft-face mallet to break the seal. Temporarily stuff a rag into the oil pan opening to prevent entry of debris.

7   Cut off the oil pan side gasket end tabs flush with the front face of the engine block (see illustration). Save the cut off gasket tabs for reference later.

8   Clean the mating surfaces of the timing chain cover, oil pan and engine block, removing all traces of oil and old gasket material.

Installation

9   Apply RTV sealant to both sides of the new timing chain cover-to-engine block gasket and position the gasket on the engine.

10   Using the end tabs you cut off as guides, trim the replacement oil pan side gasket ends to the appropriate sizes. Apply RTV sealant to the gasket ends and install them on the exposed portions of the oil pan side rails.

11   Using RTV sealant, generously coat the timing chain cover end tab recesses of the new timing chain cover-to-oil pan seal. Position the seal on the timing chain cover. Apply engine oil to the seal-to-oil pan contact surface.

12   Position the timing chain cover on the engine block.

13   Use the vibration damper to center the timing chain cover (see illustration). Be sure the old oil seal (not the new one) is in place, as it may be damaged.

14   Install the timing chain cover-to-block and oil pan-to-cover bolts and tighten them to the torque listed in this Chapter's Specifications.

15   Replace the crankshaft front oil seal (see Section 11).

16   With the key inserted in the crankshaft, install the vibration damper as described in Section 10.

17   Reinstall the remaining components in the reverse order of removal.

18   Run the engine and check for oil leaks.

13   Timing chain and sprockets - inspection, removal and installation

1   Set the number one piston at Top Dead Center (see Section 3).

2   Remove the timing chain cover (see Section 12).

Inspection

3   Slip the oil slinger off the crankshaft (see illustration) and reinstall the vibration damper bolt. Using this bolt, rotate the crankshaft clockwise just enough to take up the slack on one side of the chain.

4   Count the pins on the timing chain. The correct timing chain has 48 pins. A chain with more pins will cause excessive slack

5   Establish a reference point on the block. Move the slack side of the chain from side-to-side with your fingers and measure the movement. The difference between the two measurements is the deflection.

6   If the deflection exceeds 1/2 inch, replace the timing chain and sprockets.

Removal

7   Align the sprocket timing marks (see illustration).

8   Remove the camshaft thrust pin and spring and the sprocket retaining bolt and washer (see illustration).

12.7 Cut off the end tabs at both sides where the oil pan and engine block meet

12.13 Use the vibration damper to center the timing chain cover during installation

13.3 Slip the oil slinger off the crankshaft, noting that the cupped side faces away from the engine

13.7 Install the timing chain with the sprocket index dots directly opposite each other

13.8 Remove the thrust pin and spring (arrow), then remove the bolt in the center of the camshaft sprocket - put a large screwdriver through one of the holes in the sprocket to keep it from turning

9   Pull the crankshaft sprocket, camshaft sprocket and timing chain off as an assembly (see illustration).

Caution: *Do not turn the crankshaft or camshaft while the timing chain is removed.*

Installation

10   Be sure the crankshaft key is still pointing up. Note the locations of the locating dowel on the camshaft and the corresponding hole in the cam sprocket (see illustrations).

11   Pre-assemble the timing chain, crankshaft sprocket and camshaft sprocket with the timing marks aligned and facing out. Slip the assembly onto the engine in such a way that a line drawn through the timing marks will also pass through the centers of the sprockets.

12   Install the camshaft sprocket bolt and tighten it to the torque listed in this Chapter's Specifications. Reinstall the thrust pin and spring.

13   To verify the correct installation of the timing chain, turn the crankshaft clockwise until the camshaft sprocket timing mark is at the one o'clock position. This positions the crankshaft sprocket timing mark where the

adjacent tooth meshes with the chain at the three o'clock position. There must be 15 chain pins between the sprocket timing marks.

Note: *New replacement chains and gears no longer require pins to be counted. Line up the timing marks on the gears dot to dot and install the gears and chain.*

14   Install the crankshaft oil slinger on the crankshaft with the cupped side facing out.

15   Install the timing chain cover and vibration damper as described in (see Sections 10 and 12).

16   Reinstall the remaining parts in the reverse order of removal.

17   Run the engine and check for oil leaks and proper operation.

---

14   Camshaft, bearings and lifters - removal, inspection and installation

---

1   The extent of camshaft wear can be determined by measuring the lobe lift. This procedure does not involve removing the camshaft. Refer to Chapter 2B, Section 14 for

the lobe lift measuring procedure, but use the specifications provided in this this Chapter's Specifications.

2   To remove the lifters only, follow steps 7 through 9, 12, 16 and 17 of this procedure.

3   Remove the radiator, fan and fan shroud (see Chapter 3).

4   On air-conditioned models, unbolt the condenser assembly (see Chapter 3) WITHOUT disconnecting the refrigerant lines. Set the condenser aside. It may be necessary to remove the battery case (see Chapter 5).

5   Remove the distributor (see Chapter 5).

6   Remove the front bumper and/or grille as necessary for the camshaft to be slid out the front of the engine (see Chapter 11).

7   Label and remove the spark plug wires from the spark plugs.

8   Remove the cylinder head (see Section 9).

9   Remove the valve lifters (see illustration) and store them separately so they can be reinstalled in the same bores.

10   Remove the timing chain and sprockets (see Section 13).

11   Carefully pull the camshaft out. Temporarily install the sprocket bolt, if necessary, to use as a handle. Support the cam so the lobes don't nick or gouge the bearings as it's withdrawn (see illustration).

12   See Chapter 2B, Section 9 for the lifter inspection procedure. Camshaft and bearing inspection are covered in Chapter 2B, Section 14. Be sure to use the specifications provided in this Chapter's Specifications.

13   Camshaft bearing replacement requires special tools and expertise that place it outside the scope of the home mechanic. Remove the engine and take the block to an automotive machine shop to ensure the job is done correctly.

Note: *If the camshaft appears to have been rubbing hard against the timing chain cover, first check the camshaft thrust pin and spring and then examine the oil pressure relief holes in the rear cam journal to make sure they are open.*

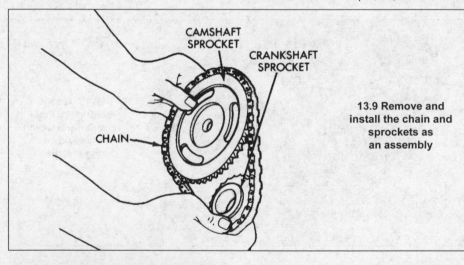

13.9 Remove and install the chain and sprockets as an assembly

13.10a Note that the engine side of the camshaft sprocket has a hole . . .

13.10b . . . for the camshaft locating dowel - be sure they are aligned properly during installation

14.9 Remove the lifters with a magnetic pick-up tool (shown here) or a special lifter removal tool

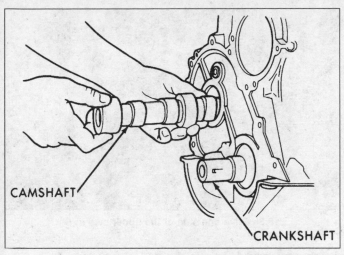

14.11 Support the camshaft as you slowly withdraw it from the block

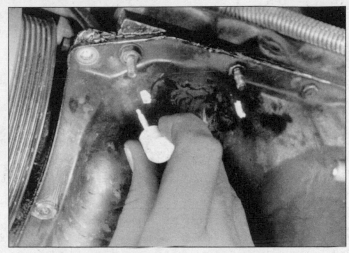

15.10 Mark the location of the studs with paint to ensure proper reassembly

14   Lubricate the camshaft journals and lobes with moly-base grease or engine assembly lube.
15   Slide the camshaft into the engine. Support the cam near the block and be careful not to scrape or nick the bearings.
16   The rest of the installation procedure is the reverse of removal.
17   Before starting and running the engine, change the oil and filter (see Chapter 1).

15   Oil pan - removal and installation

Removal

1   Disconnect the negative cable from the battery (see Chapter 5).

2   Raise the vehicle and support it securely on jackstands.
3   Remove the belly pan from under the front of the engine.
4   Drain the oil and replace the oil filter (see Chapter 1).
5   Remove the starter motor (see Chapter 5).
6   Remove the bellhousing inspection cover from the front of the transmission.
7   Detach the steering damper from the center steering link (see Chapter 10).
8   Support the front axle with a jack and remove the lower shock absorber bolts.
9   Lower the jack and allow the axle to hang free.
10   Mark the locations of the oil pan mounting studs (see illustration).

11   Remove the oil pan mounting bolts/studs and carefully separate the pan from the engine block. If the pan sticks to the block, tap the side of the pan gently with a soft-face mallet.
12   If necessary, set the oil pan on the axle and remove the oil pump and pick-up tube (see illustration).
13   Remove the oil pan by sliding it out to the rear (see illustration).
14   Thoroughly clean the mating surfaces, removing all traces of oil and old gasket material.

Installation

15   Check the oil pan flange for distortion and warpage. Straighten the flange by placing the distorted area on a block of wood and

15.12 The oil pick-up tube interferes with pan removal - remove the two attaching bolts and detach the oil pump...

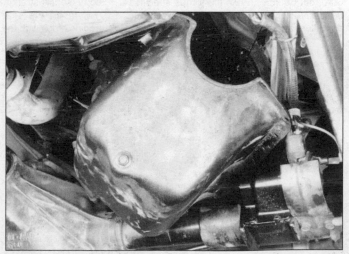

15.13 ... then remove the oil pan from the rear by sliding it out between the axle and bellhousing

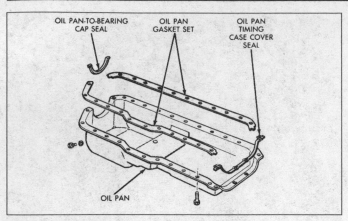

15.16 Oil pan gaskets - exploded view

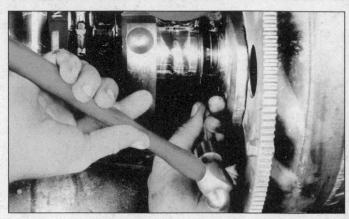

18.3a Drive one side of the upper seal in...

pounding it flat with a hammer.

16   Position new gaskets (see illustration) on the pan with Jeep Spray-a-Gasket (or equivalent). Apply a generous amount of RTV sealant at the corners where the gaskets join. Coat the inside curved surface of the replacement rear gasket section (where it contacts the bearing cap) with soap.

17   Slide the oil pan up under the engine and reinstall the oil pump and pick-up tube, tightening the oil pump mounting bolts to the torque listed in this Chapter's Specifications. Install the oil pan and tighten the bolts to the specified torque, working from the center out in several steps.

18   Reinstall the remaining parts in the reverse order of removal.

19   Check that the drain plug is tight and then add the amount of oil specified in Chapter 1.

20   Run the engine and check for oil leaks.

16   Oil pump - removal and installation

1   See Chapter 2B, Section 16 this procedure, but be sure to use the torque specifications listed in this Chapter's Specifications and (illustration 15.12).

17   Flywheel/driveplate - removal and installation

1   Refer to Chapter 2B for this procedure, but be sure to use the torque specifications listed in this Chapter's Specifications.

18   Rear main oil seal - replacement

1   Remove the oil pan (see Section 15).

2   Remove the rear main bearing cap and pry the old seal half out of the bearing cap with a small screwdriver.

3   Carefully drive the old upper main seal out with a small brass punch and a hammer until it protrudes sufficiently from the engine block to be gripped with needle-nose pliers and removed (see illustrations). Use great care to avoid damaging the crankshaft.

4   Thoroughly clean the main bearing cap and the rear of the block/crankshaft, removing all traces of oil and old sealant.

5   Coat the lip of the new upper seal with engine oil. Coat the outside surface with liquid soap (see illustration).

6   Insert the seal into the groove in the engine block with the lip facing forward.

7   Coat both sides of the lower seal ends with RTV sealant and put liquid soap on the outside of the seal (see illustration 18.5). Do not apply RTV or soap to the seal lip. Press the seal into place in the cap and apply a film of engine oil to the seal lip. Doing this would alter the bearing-to-journal clearance.

Caution: *Do not apply sealant to the cylinder block mating surfaces of the rear main bearing cap.*

8   Apply RTV sealant to the chamfered edges of the rear main bearing cap (see illustration 18.5) and install the cap. Tighten the bolts to the torque listed in this Chapter's Specifications.

9   Reinstall the remaining components in the reverse order of removal.

10   Add the amount of oil specified in Chapter 1, run the engine and check for oil leaks.

19   Engine mounts - check and replacement

1   Refer to Chapter 2B. The inline six-cylinder engine mounts are slightly different, but this doesn't affect the check and replacement procedures.

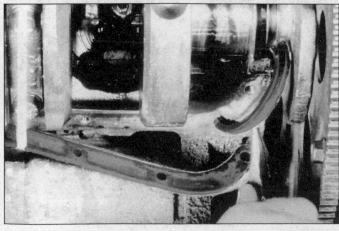

18.3b ... until the other side protrudes far enough to grasp it with needle-nose pliers and pull it out

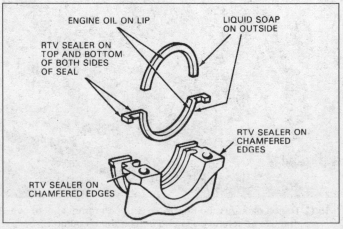

18.5 Rear main seal components - exploded view

Chapter 2 Part D
3.8L V6 engine

Contents

Specifications

General

Displacement	231 cubic inches
Bore	3.779 inches
Stroke	3.425 inches
Compression ratio	9.6: 1
Cylinder numbers (drivebelt end-to-transmission end)	
Right bank	1-3-5
Left bank	2-4-6
Firing order	1-2-3-4-5-6
Oil pressure	
At idle speed	5 psi (minimum)
At 3,000 rpm	30 to 80 psi

Oil pump

Cover warpage limit	0.001 inch
Outer rotor thickness (minimum)	0.301 inch
Inner rotor thickness (minimum)	0.301 inch
Rotor-to-pump cover clearance	0.004 inch
Outer rotor-to-housing clearance	0.015 inch
Inner rotor-to-outer rotor lobe clearance	0.008 inch

FIRING ORDER: 1-2-3-4-5-6

Front of Vehicle

| 1 | 3 | 5 |
| 2 | 4 | 6 |

| 5 | 1 | 3 |
| 2 | 4 | 6 |

50030-1-specs HAYNES

Cylinder and coil terminal locations

Camshaft

Camshaft journal diameter
    Journal no. 1 .... 1.997 to 1.999 inch
    Journal no. 2 .... 1.9809 to 1.9829 inch
    Journal no. 3 .... 1.9659 to 1.9679 inch
    Journal no. 4 .... 1.9499 to 1.9520 inch
Camshaft bearing inside diameter
    Journal no. 1 .... 1.999 to 2.0009 inch
    Journal no. 2 .... 1.9839 to 1.9849 inch
    Journal no. 3 .... 1.9690 to 1.9699 inch
    Journal no. 4 .... 1.9529 to 1.9540 inch
Bearing clearance
    Standard.. 0.001 to 0.004 inch
    Maximum.. 0.005 inch
Camshaft endplay.. 0.010 to 0.020 inch

Torque specifications   Ft-lbs (unless otherwise indicated)

Note: *One foot-pound (ft-lb) of torque is equivalent to 12 inch-pounds (in-lbs) of torque. Torque values below approximately 15 foot-pounds are expressed in inch-pounds, because most foot-pound torque wrenches are not accurate at these smaller values.*

Camshaft sprocket bolt.. 40
Camshaft thrust plate bolts.. 105 in-lbs
Crankshaft pulley bolt.. 40
Cylinder head bolts (in sequence - see illustration 12.18)
    Step 1 45
    Step 2 65
    Step 3 65
    Step 4 .... Tighten an additional 90-degrees (1/4 turn)
Drivebelt idler sprocket bolt 24
Driveplate-to-crankshaft bolts 65
Engine mount bracket bolts
    M8 21
    M10 40
Exhaust manifold-to-cylinder head bolts.................................. 17
Exhaust manifold heat shield nut.. 105 in-lbs
Flywheel-to-crankshaft bolts.. 60
Hydraulic lifter retaining bolts .... 105 in-lbs
Intake manifold (upper) retaining bolts*................................... 105 in-lbs
Intake manifold (lower)-to-block bolts...................................... 17
Oil cooler fitting.. 20
Oil pan drain plug 20
Oil pan bolts... 105 in-lbs
Oil pump pick-up tube mounting bolts 21
Oil pump cover (plate) screws .... 105 in-lbs
Rear main oil seal retainer bolts .... 105 in-lbs
Rocker arm shaft bolts.. 17
Timing chain cover bolts (see illustration 10.13)
    M8 20
    M10 40
Timing chain sprocket-to-camshaft bolt................................... 40
Valve cover-to-cylinder head bolts... 105 in-lbs
Water pump bolts .... See Chapter 3

Apply a non-hardening thread-locking compound to the bolt threads before installation

1 General Information

1 This Chapter is devoted to in-vehicle repair procedures for the 2007 and later 3.8L V6 engines. These engines utilize a cast-iron engine block with six cylinders arranged in a "V" shape with a 60-degree angle between the two banks. The aluminum cylinder heads are equipped with replaceable valve guides and seats. An in-block camshaft is chain-driven from the crankshaft, and hydraulic roller lifters actuate the valves through tubular pushrods.

2 Information concerning engine removal and installation and camshaft removal and installation can be found in Chapter 2F. The following repair procedures are based on the assumption that the engine is installed in the vehicle. If the engine has been removed from the vehicle and mounted on a stand, many of the steps outlined in this Chapter do not apply.

2 Repair operations possible with the engine in the vehicle

1 Many major repair operations can be done without removing the engine from the vehicle.

2 Clean the engine compartment and the exterior of the engine with degreaser before any work is done. It'll make the job easier and help keep dirt out of internal parts of the engine.

3 It may be helpful to remove the hood to improve engine access when repairs are performed (see Chapter 11). Cover the fenders to prevent damage to the paint. Special pads are available, but an old bedspread or blanket will also work.

4 If vacuum, exhaust, oil, or coolant leaks develop, indicating a need for gasket or seal replacement, the repairs can generally be done with the engine in the vehicle. The intake and exhaust manifold gaskets, timing chain cover gasket, oil pan gasket, crankshaft oil seals, and cylinder head gaskets are all accessible with the engine in the vehicle.

5 Exterior engine components, such as the intake and exhaust manifolds, the oil pan, the oil pump, the timing chain cover, the water pump, the starter motor, the alternator, and fuel system components can be removed for repair with the engine in the vehicle.

6 Cylinder heads can be removed without pulling the engine. Valve component servicing can also be done with the engine in the vehicle. Replacement of the timing chain and sprockets is also possible with the engine in the vehicle, but the camshaft cannot be removed with the engine in the vehicle. Refer to Chapter 2F for camshaft removal and installation.

7 Repair or replacement of piston rings, pistons, connecting rods, and rod bearings is possible with the engine in the vehicle, however, this practice is not recommended because of the cleaning and preparation work that must be done to the components.

3 Top Dead Center (TDC) for number one piston - locating

1 Top Dead Center (TDC) is the highest point in the cylinder that each piston reaches as it travels up the cylinder bore. Each piston reaches TDC on the compression stroke and again on the exhaust stroke, but TDC generally refers to piston position on the compression stroke.

2 Positioning the piston(s) at TDC is an essential part of certain procedures such as camshaft and timing chain/sprocket removal.

3 Before beginning this procedure, be sure to place the transmission in Neutral and apply the parking brake or block the rear wheels. Disable the ignition system by disconnecting the primary electrical connector at the ignition coil pack and remove the spark plugs (see Chapter 1). Also disable the fuel pump (see Chapter 4, Section 2).

4 In order to bring any piston to TDC, the crankshaft must be turned using one of the methods outlined below. When looking at the front of the engine, normal crankshaft rotation is clockwise.

a) *The preferred method is to turn the crankshaft with a socket and ratchet attached to the bolt threaded into the front of the crankshaft. Turn the bolt in a clockwise direction only. Never turn the bolt counterclockwise.*

b) *A remote starter switch, which may save some time, can also be used. Follow the instructions included with the switch. Once the piston is close to TDC, use a socket and ratchet as described in the previous paragraph.*

c) *If an assistant is available to turn the ignition switch to the Start position in short bursts, you can get the piston close to TDC without a remote starter switch. Make sure your assistant is out of the vehicle, away from the ignition switch, then use a socket and ratchet as described in Paragraph (a) to complete the procedure.*

5 Install a compression pressure gauge in the number one spark plug hole (see Chapter 2F). It should be a gauge with a screw-in fitting and a hose at least six inches long.

6 Rotate the crankshaft using one of the methods described above while observing for pressure on the compression gauge. The moment the gauge shows pressure, indicates that the number one cylinder has begun the compression stroke.

7 Once the compression stroke has begun, TDC for the compression stroke is reached by bringing the piston to the top of the cylinder.

8 If there was no compression, the piston was on the exhaust stroke. Continue rotating the crankshaft 360-degrees (1-turn).

Note: *If a compression gauge is not available, you can simply place a blunt object over the spark plug hole and listen for compression as the engine is rotated. Once compression at the No.1 spark plug hole is noted, the remain-*

der of the Step is the same.

9 These engines are not equipped with external components (crankshaft pulley, flywheel, timing hole, etc.) that are marked to identify the position of number 1 TDC. Therefore, the only method to double-check the location of TDC number 1 is to remove the timing chain cover to access the timing gears and alignment marks (see Section 10) or with the use of a degree wheel and a positive stop timing device threaded into the spark plug hole for cylinder number 1. This procedure is described in detail in the *Haynes Chrysler Engine Overhaul Manual*.

10 After the number one piston has been positioned at TDC on the compression stroke, TDC for any of the remaining cylinders can be located by turning the crankshaft 120-degrees and following the firing order (see the this Chapter's Specifications). For example on V6 engines, rotating the engine 120-degrees past TDC number 1 will put the engine at TDC compression for cylinder number 2.

4 Valve covers - removal and installation

Removal

1 Disconnect the cable from the negative terminal of the battery (see Chapter 5, Section 3).

Right valve cover

2 Remove the spark plug wires from the spark plugs (see Chapter 1). Label each wire before removal to ensure correct reinstallation.

3 Remove the crankcase vent hose from the valve cover.

4 Remove the valve cover bolts.

5 Remove the valve cover.

Note: *If the valve cover sticks to the cylinder head, slide a putty knife under the edge to dislodge it.*

Left valve cover

6 Remove the spark plug wires from the spark plugs (see Chapter 1). Label each wire before removal to ensure correct reinstallation.

7 Remove the ignition coil pack (see Chapter 5).

8 Remove the breather hose from the PCV valve.

9 Remove the alternator brace (see Chapter 5).

10 Remove the valve cover bolts.

11 Detach the valve cover.

Note: *If the valve cover sticks to the cylinder head, slide a putty knife under the edge to dislodge it.*

Installation

12 The mating surfaces of the cylinder heads and valve covers must be perfectly clean when the valve covers are installed. If there's sealant or oil on the mating surfaces

5.2 Remove the rocker arm shaft bolts from the cylinder head - be sure to start with the outer ones first

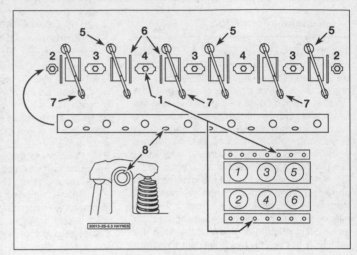

5.3 Rocker arm, washers, shaft retainer/spacer and shaft assembly details

1   *Rocker arm shaft oil feed bolt (longer length)*
2   *Shaft retainer/spacer (0.84 inch)*
3   *Shaft retainer/spacer (1.47 inches)*
4   *Shaft retainer/spacer (1.61 inches)*
5   *Rocker arm - exhaust*
6   *Washer*
7   *Rocker arm - intake (larger offset)*
8   *Rocker arm lubrication feed hole*
     (position upward and toward the feed hole)

when the valve cover is installed, oil leaks may develop. Be extra careful not to nick or gouge the mating surfaces while cleaning.

13   Clean the mounting bolt threads with a die, if necessary, to remove corrosion and restore damaged threads. Use a tap to clean the threaded holes in the cylinder heads.

14   Place the valve cover and new gasket in position, then install the bolts. Tighten the bolts in several steps to the torque listed in this Chapter's Specifications.

15   Installation of the remaining components is the reverse of removal.

16   Start the engine and check carefully for oil leaks.

5   Rocker arms and pushrods - removal, inspection and installation

Removal

1   Remove the valve covers (see Section 4).

2   Loosen each rocker arm shaft bolt a little at a time, until they are all loose enough to be removed by hand (see illustration).
Note: *The bolts are captive on the rocker shaft.*

3   Remove the rocker arm and shaft assembly. If the rocker arms, washers and shaft retainer/spacers are going to be removed

from the shaft, be sure to note how they are positioned (see illustration). To remove the bolts and retainer/spacers, use pliers and grip the edges of the retainer/spacers and pull them straight up off the shaft.

4   Remove the pushrods and store them in order to make sure they don't get mixed up during installation (see illustration).

Inspection

5   Check each rocker arm for wear, cracks and other damage (see illustration), especially where the pushrods and valve stems contact the rocker arm.

6   Check the pivot seat in each rocker arm and the pivot faces. Look for galling, stress cracks and unusual wear patterns. If the rocker arms are worn or damaged, replace them with new ones and install new pivots or shafts as well.
Note: *Keep in mind that there is no valve adjustment on these engines, so excessive wear or damage in the valve train can easily result in excessive valve clearance, which in turn will cause valve noise when the engine is running.*

7   On shaft mounted rocker arms, inspect the shafts for galling and excessive wear. Inspect the oil holes for plugging.

8   Inspect the pushrods for cracks and excessive wear at the ends. Roll each pushrod across a piece of plate glass to see if it's bent (if it wobbles, it's bent).

Installation

Caution: *Be sure that the one rocker shaft bolt that is longer than the other bolts is installed*

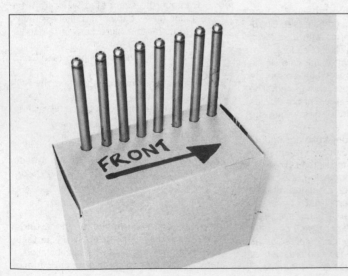

5.4 Be sure to store the pushrods in an organized manner to make sure they're reinstalled in their original locations

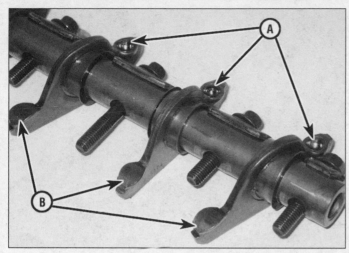

5.5 Check each rocker arm at the ball socket pivots (A) for chipping and wear and at the tips (B) for scuffing, wear and other damage

6.12 Here, shop towels have been installed in the manifold runners to prevent any objects falling into the lower intake manifold

into the correct position (see illustration 5.3).
Caution: *The rocker shafts should be tightened down slowly starting with the center bolts and working toward the outer bolts. Allow at least 20 minutes bleed-down time after installing both rocker arm shafts before operating the engine.*

9 Lubricate the lower end of each pushrod with clean engine oil or moly-base grease and install them in their original locations. Make sure each pushrod seats completely in the lifter socket.

10 Apply moly-base grease to the ends of the valve stems and the upper ends of the pushrods.

11 Apply moly-base grease to the rocker arm shaft. If removed, install the rocker arms, washers, shaft retainer/spacers and bolts in the correct order. Install the rocker arm assembly onto the cylinder head. Tighten the bolts, a little at a time (working from the center out), to the torque listed in this Chapter's Specifications. As the bolts are tightened, make sure the pushrods engage properly in the rocker arms.

Caution: *Allow the engine to set for 20 minutes before starting.*

12 Install the valve covers.

6.19 Pry on the intake manifold only in the areas where the gasket mating surface will not get damaged

6 Intake manifold - removal and installation

Warning: *Wait until the engine is completely cool before beginning this procedure.*

Removal

1 Relieve the fuel system pressure (see Chapter 4).

2 Disconnect the cable from the negative terminal of the battery (see Chapter 5, Section 1).

3 Drain the cooling system (see Chapter 3).

Upper intake manifold

4 Disconnect the IAT electrical connector and remove the air filter housing and the air intake duct (see Chapter 4).

5 Disconnect the large ETC connector at the throttle body.

6 Disconnect the Automatic Idle Speed (AIS) motor, the Throttle Position Sensor (TPS) and Manifold Absolute Pressure (MAP) sensor connectors (see Chapter 6).

7 Disconnect the vapor purge vacuum hose (see Chapter 6).

8 Disconnect the Positive Crankcase Ventilation (PCV) hose (see Chapter 6).

9 Tag and disconnect the power brake booster (see Chapter 9) and Leak Detection Pump (LDP) or Natural Vacuum Leak Detection (NVLD) system vacuum hoses from the manifold (see Chapter 6).

10 Remove the two bolts securing the EGR pipe to the intake manifold.

11 Remove the EGR pipe from the manifold (see Chapter 6).

12 Remove the upper intake manifold bolts (see illustration 6.29). Separate the assembly from the lower intake manifold. Be sure to cover the intake manifold runners to prevent any objects from falling into the lower intake manifold while the upper manifold is off (see illustration).

Lower intake manifold

13 Remove the upper intake manifold (see Steps 1 through 12).

14 Disconnect the fuel hose fitting. Remove the fuel line (see Chapter 6).

15 Remove the ignition coil pack and bracket (see Chapter 5).

16 Disconnect the heater supply hose (see Chapter 3) and the engine coolant temperature sensor (ECT) (see Chapter 6).

17 Remove the fuel rail and injector assembly (see Chapter 4).

18 Disconnect the upper radiator hose (see Chapter 3).

19 Remove the bolts and the lower intake manifold and separate the lower intake manifold from the engine (see illustration 6.26). If the lower intake manifold is stuck, carefully pry on a casting protrusion (see illustration) - don't pry between the lower intake manifold, and the cylinder heads, as damage to the gasket sealing surfaces may result. If you're installing a new lower intake manifold, transfer all fittings and sensors to the new lower intake manifold.

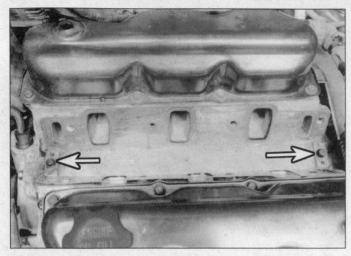

6.20 Remove the intake manifold gasket retainer fasteners

6.23 Apply RTV sealant to the corners of the cylinder head and engine block

6.26 Lower intake manifold bolt tightening sequence

6.27 Be sure to replace the upper intake manifold seals with new ones if they are damaged

20 Remove the lower intake manifold gasket retaining fasteners and remove the gasket from the cylinder block (see illustration).

Installation

Lower intake manifold

Note: *The mating surfaces of the cylinder heads, cylinder block, and the intake manifold must be perfectly clean when the lower intake manifold is installed. Gasket removal solvents are available at most auto parts stores and may be helpful when removing old gasket material that's stuck to the cylinder heads, cylinder block and lower intake manifold (the lower intake manifold is made of aluminum - aggressive scrapping can cause damage). Be sure to follow the instructions printed on the solvent container.*

21 Use a gasket scraper to remove all traces of sealant and old gasket material, then clean the mating surfaces with lacquer thinner or acetone. If there's old sealant or oil on the mating surfaces when the lower intake manifold is installed, oil or vacuum leaks may develop. Use a vacuum cleaner to remove gasket material that falls into the intake ports or the lifter valley.

22 Use a tap of the correct size to chase the threads in the bolt holes, then use compressed air (if available) to remove debris from the holes.

Warning: *Wear safety glasses or a face shield to protect your eyes when using compressed air!*

23 Apply a 1/4-inch bead of RTV sealant or equivalent to the cylinder heads-to-engine block junctions (see illustration).

24 Install the lower intake gasket and tighten the retainer fasteners.

25 Carefully lower the lower intake mani-

fold into place and install the mounting bolts finger-tight.

26 Tighten the mounting bolts in three steps, following the recommended tightening sequence (see illustration), to the torque listed in this Chapter's Specifications.

Upper intake manifold

27 Check the condition of the rubber seals that are installed into each intake runner on the upper intake manifold (see illustration). If they are damaged, replace the seals in the upper intake manifold.

28 Install the upper intake manifold onto the lower intake manifold. Clean the manifold bolts of old sealant and apply "medium" thread-locking compound to them. Install the special screws into the composite material and turn slowly to prevent damage to the upper intake manifold.

6.29 Upper intake manifold bolt tightening sequence

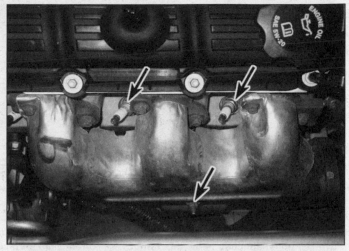

7.7 Left side exhaust manifold fasteners securing the heat shield

29   Tighten the mounting screws following the correct sequence (see illustration) to the torque listed in this Chapter's Specifications.
30   Installation of the remaining components is the reverse of removal.
31   Refill the cooling system (see Chapter 1), start the engine and check for leaks and proper operation.

7   Exhaust manifolds - removal and installation

Removal

1   Disconnect the cable from the negative terminal of the battery (see Chapter 5, Section 1).
2   Disconnect the spark plug wires.
3   Disconnect the IAT electrical connector and remove the air filter housing and the air intake duct (see Chapter 4).
4   Disconnect and remove the upstream and downstream oxygen sensor connectors (see Chapter 4).
5   Remove the bolts and disconnect the catalytic converter from the exhaust manifold (see Chapter 6).
6   Disconnect the Automatic Idle Speed (AIS) motor, the Throttle Position Sensor (TPS), and the vapor purge vacuum hose (see Chapter 6).
7   If you're working on the left side exhaust manifold, remove the fasteners securing the heat shield (see illustration).
8   Remove the bolts attaching the left side exhaust manifold to the cylinder head, and remove the exhaust manifold.
9   Remove the bolts attaching the right side exhaust manifold to the cylinder head, and remove the front exhaust manifold.

Installation

10   Clean the mating surfaces to remove all traces of old gasket material, then inspect the

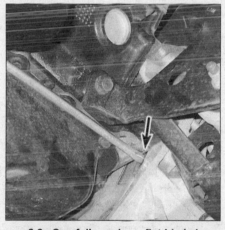

8.3a Carefully wedge a flat-bladed screwdriver between the driveplate teeth and the engine block at the transaxle bellhousing to lock the crankshaft in place

exhaust manifolds for distortion and cracks. Check for warpage with a precision straight edge held against the mating surface. If a feeler gauge thicker than 0.030-inch can be inserted between the straightedge and the mating surface, take the exhaust manifold(s) to an automotive machine shop for resurfacing.
11   Place the exhaust manifold in position with a new gasket and install the mounting bolts finger-tight.
Note: Be sure to identify the exhaust manifold gasket by the correct cylinder designation and the position of the exhaust ports on the gasket.
12   Starting in the middle and working out toward the ends, tighten the bolts to the torque listed in this Chapter's Specifications.
13   Installation of the remaining components is the reverse of removal.
14   Start the engine and check for exhaust leaks between the exhaust manifolds and

8.3b Remove the crankshaft pulley bolt with a breaker bar and a socket

the cylinder heads and between the exhaust manifolds, crossover pipe and catalytic converter.

8   Crankshaft pulley - removal and installation

Removal

1   Disconnect the cable from the negative terminal of the battery (see Chapter 5, Section 1).
2   Remove the serpentine drivebelt (see Chapter 1).
3   Remove the driveplate cover and position a large screwdriver in the ring gear teeth to keep the crankshaft from turning (see illustration) while a helper removes the crankshaft pulley-to-crankshaft bolt (see illustration).

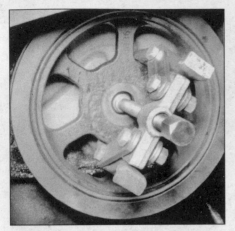

8.4 Remove the crankshaft pulley with a two-jaw puller attached to the inner hub - DO NOT pull on the outer edge of the pulley or damage may result!

9.2 Be very careful not to damage the crankshaft surface when removing the front seal

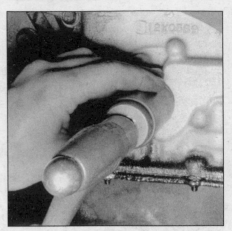

9.3 Use a seal driver or a large deep socket and gently tap the seal into place

4   Pull the crankshaft pulley off the crankshaft with a two-jaw puller attached to the inner hub (see illustration).
Caution: *Do not attach the puller to the outer edge of the pulley or damage to the pulley may result.*
Caution: *Because the nose of the crankshaft is recessed, an adapter may be needed between the puller bolt and the crankshaft (to prevent damage to the bore and threads in the end of the crankshaft).*

Installation

5   Install the crankshaft pulley with a special installation tool that threads to the crankshaft in place of the crankshaft pulley bolt (available at most automotive parts stores). Be sure to apply clean engine oil or multi-purpose grease to the seal contact surface of the damper hub (if it isn't lubricated, the seal lip could be damaged and oil leakage would result). If the tool isn't available, the crankshaft pulley bolt and several washers used as spacers, may be used as long as the crankshaft pulley bolt torque is not exceeded.
6   Remove the tool and install the crankshaft pulley bolt and tighten it to the torque

listed in this Chapter's Specifications.
7   Installation of the remaining components is the reverse of removal.

---

9   Crankshaft front oil seal - replacement

1   Remove the crankshaft pulley (see Section 8).
2   Note how the seal is installed - the new one must be installed to the same depth and face the same way. Carefully pry the oil seal out of the cover with a seal puller or a large screwdriver (see illustration). Be very careful not to distort the cover or scratch the crankshaft! Wrap tape around the tip of the screwdriver to avoid damage to the crankshaft.
3   Apply clean engine oil or multi-purpose grease to the outer edge of the new seal, then install it in the cover with the lip (spring side) facing IN. Drive the seal into place (see illustration) with a seal driver or a large socket and a hammer. Make sure the seal enters the bore squarely. Stop when the front face is at the proper depth.
4   Reinstall the crankshaft pulley.

---

10   Timing chain and sprockets - removal, inspection and installation

Warning: *Wait until the engine is completely cool before beginning this procedure.*

Removal

1   Disconnect the cable from the negative terminal of the battery (see Chapter 5, Section 1).
2   Drain the coolant (see Chapter 1).
3   Raise the vehicle and support it securely on jackstands. Drain the engine oil (see Chapter 1).
4   Remove the drivebelt and tensioner (see Chapter 1).
5   Remove the oil pan (see Section 13) and the oil pump pick-up tube.
6   Unbolt and set aside the alternator (see Chapter 5).
7   Unbolt the air conditioning compressor from its bracket and set it off to one side. Use mechanics wire to tie the assembly to the fender to keep it away from the work area (see Chapter 3).
Warning: *The refrigerant hoses are under pressure - don't disconnect them.*
8   Remove the crankshaft pulley (see Section 8).
9   Remove the radiator lower hose (see Chapter 3). Remove the heater hose from the timing chain cover housing, or water pump inlet (oil cooler equipped models).
10   Remove the camshaft sensor from the timing chain cover (see Chapter 6).
11   Remove the water pump (see Chapter 3).
12   Unbolt the power steering pump and set it aside (see Chapter 10).
13   Remove the timing chain cover-to engine block bolts (see illustration).
14   Temporarily install the crankshaft pulley bolt and turn the crankshaft with the bolt to align the timing marks on the crankshaft and camshaft sprockets. The crankshaft arrow

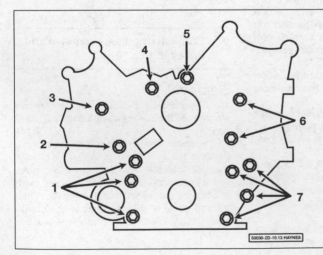

10.13 Timing chain cover bolt locations

1   M8 1.25 X 80
2   M10 1.5 X 85
3   M8 1.25 X 80
4   M10 1.5 X 85
5   M8 1.25 X 80
6   M10 1.5 x 85
7   M8 1.25 X 80

50030-2D-10.13 HAYNES

10.14 Timing chain and sprocket alignment details

A   Crankshaft sprocket alignment mark
B   Camshaft sprocket alignment mark
C   Camshaft sprocket bolt

10.23 Be sure the timing chain colored reference links align with marks on the sprockets

should be at the top (12 o'clock position) and the camshaft sprocket arrow should be in the 6 o'clock position (see illustration).

15   Remove the camshaft sprocket bolt. Do not turn the camshaft in the process (if you do, realign the timing marks before the sprocket is removed).

16   Use two large screwdrivers to carefully pry the camshaft sprocket off the camshaft dowel pin.

17   Timing chains and sprockets should be replaced in sets. If you intend to install a new timing chain, remove the crankshaft sprocket with a puller and install a new one. Be sure to align the key in the crankshaft with the keyway in the sprocket during installation.

Inspection

18   Inspect the timing chain dampener (guide) for cracks and wear and replace it, if necessary.

19   Clean the timing chain and sprockets with solvent and dry them with compressed air (if available).

Warning: *Wear eye protection when using compressed air.*

20   Inspect the components for wear and damage. Look for teeth that are deformed, chipped, pitted, and cracked.

21   The timing chain and sprockets should be replaced with a new one if the engine has high mileage, the chain has visible damage, or total freeplay midway between the sprockets exceeds one inch. Failure to replace a worn timing chain and sprockets may result in erratic engine performance, loss of power, and decreased fuel mileage. Loose chains can jump timing. In the worst case, chain jumping or breakage will result in severe engine damage.

Installation

22   Use a gasket scraper to remove all traces of old gasket material and sealant from the cover and engine block. The cover is made of aluminum, so be careful not to nick or gouge it. Clean the gasket sealing surfaces with lacquer thinner or acetone.

23   Turn the camshaft to position the dowel pin at 6 o'clock (see illustration 10.14). Mesh the timing chain with the camshaft sprocket, then engage it with the crankshaft sprocket. The timing marks should be aligned (see illustration 10.14).

Note: *If the crankshaft has moved, turn it until the arrow stamped on the crankshaft sprocket is exactly at the top. If the camshaft was turned, install the sprocket temporarily and turn the camshaft until the sprocket timing mark is at the bottom, opposite the mark on the crankshaft sprocket. The arrows should point to each other. The timing chain colored reference links should align with the camshaft and crankshaft timing marks that are in the 3 o'clock position (see illustration). If you are using replacement parts, check this alignment.*

24   Install the camshaft sprocket bolt and tighten it to the torque listed in this Chapter's Specifications.

25   Lubricate the chain and sprocket with clean engine oil.

26   Stick the new gasket to the cover, making sure the bottom edge of the gasket is flush with the bottom of the cover. Attach the cover to the engine block, making sure the flats of the oil pump gear are aligned with the flats on the crankshaft. Install the bolts and tighten them in a criss-cross pattern, in three steps, to the torque listed in this Chapter's Specifications.

27   Installation of the remaining components

is the reverse of removal.

28   Add oil and coolant (see Chapter 1), start the engine and check for leaks.

11   Camshaft and lifters - removal, inspection and installation

Warning: *Wait until the engine is completely cool before beginning this procedure.*

1   Drain the cooling system (see Chapter 1).

Lifters

2   A noisy valve lifter can be isolated when the engine is idling. Hold a mechanic's stethoscope or a length of hose near each valve while listening at the other end. Another method is to remove the valve cover and, with the engine idling, touch each of the valve spring retainers, one at a time. If a valve lifter is defective, it'll be evident from the shock felt at the retainer each time the valve seats. The most likely causes of noisy valve lifters are dirt trapped inside the lifter and lack of oil flow, viscosity, or pressure. Before condemning the lifters, check the oil for fuel contamination, correct level, cleanliness, and correct viscosity.

Removal

3   Remove the intake manifold (see Section 6) and valve covers (see Section 4).

4   Remove the rocker arms and pushrods (see Section 5).

5   Remove the cylinder heads (see Section 12).

6   Remove the retaining plate bolts (see illustration) and lift the plate to gain access to the hydraulic roller lifters.

11.6 Remove the bolts that attach the lifter retaining plate

11.7 Lift off the alignment yokes

11.8 On engines with low mileage, the roller lifters can be removed by hand - if the lifters are coated with varnish, a special lifter removal tool may be required

11.9 Store the lifters in a box so each one will be reinstalled in its original bore

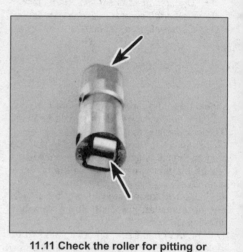

11.11 Check the roller for pitting or excessive looseness and the lifter surfaces for gouges, scoring, wear or damage

7   Each pair of lifters is retained with an alignment yoke. Lift the yoke from the lifters (see illustration).

8   There are several ways to extract the lifters from the bores. A special tool designed to grip and remove lifters is manufactured by many tool companies and is available at most automotive parts stores, but it may not be required in every case. On newer engines without a lot of varnish buildup, the lifters can often be removed with a small magnet or even with your fingers (see illustration). A machinist's scribe with a bent end can be used to pull the lifters out by positioning the point under the retainer ring in the top of each lifter. **Caution:** *Don't use pliers to remove the lifters unless you intend to replace them with new ones. The pliers may damage the precision machined and hardened lifters, rendering them useless.*

9   Store the lifters in a box clearly labeled to ensure they're reinstalled in their original locations (see illustration).

Inspection

10   Clean the lifters with solvent and dry them thoroughly. Do not mix them up.

11   Check each lifter wall and pushrod seat for scuffing, score marks, and uneven wear (see illustration). If the lifter walls are damaged or worn, inspect the lifter bores in the engine block.

12   Check the roller of each lifter for freedom of movement, excessive looseness, flat spots, or pitting. The camshaft must also be inspected for signs of abnormal wear. **Note:** *Used roller lifters can be reinstalled with a new camshaft or the original camshaft can be used if new roller lifters are installed, provided the used components are in good condition.*

Installation

13   When installing used lifters, make sure they're replaced in their original bores. Position the valve lifter with the lubrication hole facing upward toward the middle of the engine

block. Soak the lifters in oil to remove trapped air. Coat the lifters with moly-based grease or engine assembly lube prior to installation.

14   Installation of the remaining components is the reverse of removal.

15   Tighten the retaining plate bolts to the torque listed in this Chapter's Specifications.

16   Change the engine oil and filter, and refill the cooling system (see Chapter 1).

Camshaft

Removal

17   Remove the engine cooling fans and the radiator (see Chapter 3).

18   Remove the timing chain and sprockets (see Section 10) and the lifters (see Steps 1 through 9).

19   Remove the bolts and the camshaft thrust plate from the engine block.

20   Use a long bolt in the camshaft sprocket bolt hole as a handle when removing the camshaft from the block.

21   Carefully pull the camshaft out. Support

11.23 Check the diameter of each camshaft bearing journal to pinpoint excessive wear and out-of-round conditions

11.24 Measure the camshaft lobe height (greatest dimension) with a micrometer

11.25 Check the cam lobes for pitting, excessive wear and scoring. If scoring is excessive, as shown here, replace the camshaft

the cam in the block so the lobes don't nick or gouge the bearings as the cam is pulled out.

Inspection

22   After the camshaft has been removed from the engine, cleaned with solvent and dried, inspect the bearing journals for uneven wear, pitting and evidence of seizure. If the journals are damaged, the bearings in the block are probably damaged as well. Both the camshaft and bearings will have to be replaced.

Note: *Camshaft bearing replacement requires special tools and expertise that place it beyond the scope of the average home mechanic. The tools for bearing removal and installation are available at stores that carry automotive tools, possibly even found at a tool rental business. It is advisable though, if bearings are bad and the procedure is beyond your ability, remove the engine block and take it to an automotive machine shop to ensure that the job is done correctly.*

23   Measure the bearing journals with a micrometer to determine if they are excessively worn or out-of-round (see illustration).

24   Measure the lobe height of each cam lobe on the intake camshaft and record your measurements (see illustration). Compare the measurements for excessive variations. If the lobe heights vary more than 0.005 inch (0.125 mm), replace the camshaft. Compare the lobe height measurements on the exhaust camshaft and follow the same procedure. Do not compare intake camshaft lobe heights with exhaust camshaft lobe heights as they are different. Only compare intake lobes with intake lobes and exhaust lobes with other exhaust lobes.

25   Check the camshaft lobes for heat discoloration, score marks, chipped areas, pitting and uneven wear (see illustration). If the lobes are in good condition and if the lobe lift variation measurements recorded earlier are within the limits, the camshaft can be reused.

26   The inside diameter of each bearing can be determined with a bore gauge and outside

11.30 Be sure to apply camshaft assembly lube to the cam lobes and bearing journals before installing the camshaft

micrometer, or an inside micrometer. Subtract the camshaft bearing journal diameters from the corresponding bearing inside diameters to determine the bearing oil clearance. If it's excessive, new bearings will be required regardless of the condition of the originals. Check this Chapter's Specifications.

27   Clean the lifters with solvent and dry them thoroughly without mixing them up.

28   Check each lifter wall, pushrod seat and foot for scuffing, score marks and uneven wear. If the lifter walls are damaged or worn (which is not very likely), inspect the lifter bores in the engine block as well. If the pushrod seats are worn, check the pushrod ends.

29   Check the rollers carefully for wear and damage and make sure they turn freely without excessive play.

Installation

30   Lubricate the camshaft bearing journals and cam lobes with moly-base grease or engine assembly lube (see illustration).

31   Slide the camshaft into the engine. Support the cam near the block and be careful not to scrape or nick the bearings.

32   Install the thrust plate and bolts. Tighten the bolts to the torque listed in this Chapter's Specifications.

33   The remainder of installation is the reverse of removal.

34   Change the engine oil and filter, and refill the cooling system (see Chapter 1).

12   Cylinder heads - removal and installation

Warning: *The engine must be completely cool before beginning this procedure.*

Removal

1   Disconnect the cable from the negative terminal of the battery (see Chapter 5).

2   Remove the intake manifold (see Section 6). If removing the left cylinder head, remove the oil dipstick and the dipstick tube.

3   Disconnect all wires and vacuum hoses from the cylinder heads. Label them to simplify reinstallation.

4   Disconnect the spark plug wires and

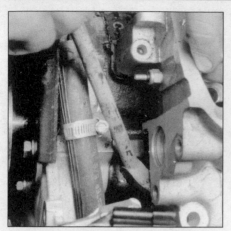

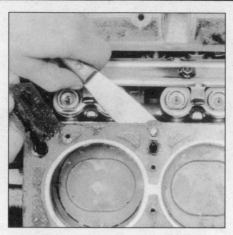

12.9 Do not pry on the cylinder head near the gasket mating surface - use the corners under the casting protrusions

12.12 Use a putty knife or gasket scraper to remove the gasket from the cylinder head

12.15 Be sure the stamped designations are facing up and forward

remove the spark plugs (see Chapter 1). Label the wires to simplify reinstallation.

5   Remove the exhaust manifolds (see Section 7).

6   Remove the valve covers (see Section 4).

7   Remove the rocker arms and pushrods (see Section 5).

8   Using the new cylinder head gasket, outline the cylinders and bolt pattern on a piece of cardboard. Be sure to indicate the front (timing chain end) of the engine for reference. Punch holes at the bolt locations. Loosen each of the cylinder head mounting bolts, 1/4-turn at a time, until they can be removed by hand - work from bolt-to-bolt in a pattern that's the reverse of the tightening sequence (see illustration 12.18). Store the bolts in the cardboard holder as they're removed - this will ensure they are reinstalled in their original locations, which is absolutely essential.

9   Lift the cylinder heads from the engine. If resistance is felt, don't pry between the cylinder head and engine block, damage to the mating surfaces will result. Recheck for cylinder head bolts that may have been overlooked, then use a hammer and wood block

to tap up on the cylinder head and break the gasket seal (see illustration). Be careful because there are locating dowels in the engine block to position each cylinder head. As a last resort, pry each cylinder head up at the rear corner only and be careful not to damage anything. After removal, place the cylinder head on wood blocks to prevent damage to the gasket surfaces.

10   Have the cylinder head inspected and serviced by a qualified automotive machine shop.

Installation

11   The mating surfaces of each cylinder head and the engine block must be perfectly clean when the cylinder head is installed.

12   Use a gasket scraper to remove all traces of carbon and old gasket material (see illustration), then clean the mating surfaces with lacquer thinner or acetone. If there's oil on the mating surfaces when the cylinder head is installed, the gasket may not seal correctly and leaks may develop. When working on the engine block, it's a good idea to cover the lifter valley with shop rags to keep debris out of the engine. Use a shop rag or vacuum

cleaner to remove any debris that falls into the cylinders.

13   Check the engine block and cylinder head mating surfaces for nicks, deep scratches, and other damage. If damage is slight, it can be removed with a file; if it's excessive, machining may be the only alternative.

14   Use a tap of the correct size to chase the threads in the cylinder head bolt holes. Dirt, corrosion, sealant, and damaged threads will affect torque readings.

15   Position the new gasket over the dowel pins in the engine block. Some gaskets are marked TOP or FRONT to ensure correct installation (see illustration). The left gasket should be marked with an "L" near the front of the gasket, and the right gasket should be marked with an "R" near the rear of the gasket.

16   Carefully position the cylinder head on the engine block without disturbing the gasket.

17   With a straight-edge, check each cylinder head bolt for necking-down or stretching. If all of the threads do not contact the straight-edge, replace the bolt.

18   Install the head bolts and tighten them in the recommended sequence to the torque listed in this Chapter's Specifications (Step 1) (see illustration). Next, tighten them following the recommended sequence to the Step 2 torque listed in this Chapter's Specifications. Tighten the bolts again to the same torque as a double check (Step 3). Finally, tighten each bolt an additional 90-degrees (1/4-turn) following the recommended sequence (Step 4). Do not use a torque wrench for this step; apply a paint mark to the bolt head or use a torque-angle gauge (available at most automotive parts stores) and a socket and breaker bar.

19   Installation of the remaining components is the reverse of removal.

20   Change the oil and filter (see Chapter 1).

21   Refill the cooling system (see Chapter 1). Start the engine and check for leaks and proper operation.

12.18 Cylinder head bolt TIGHTENING sequence

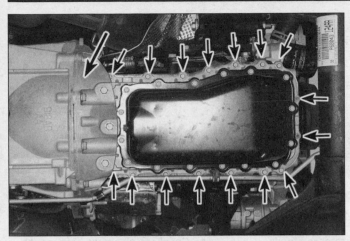

13.6a Remove the structural cover (large arrow), then remove the upper pan-to-engine bolts

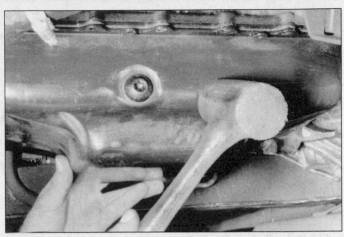

13.6b Use a soft face hammer to loosen the oil pan - be careful not to dent the pan

13 Oil pan - removal and installation

Removal

1 Disconnect the cable from the negative terminal of the battery (see Chapter 5).

2 Raise the front of the vehicle and support it securely on jackstands. Apply the parking brake and block the rear wheels to keep it from rolling off the stands.

3 Drain the engine oil and remove the oil filter (see Chapter 1). Remove the oil dipstick and the dipstick tube.

4 Remove the 7 bolts and the lower driveplate structural cover.

5 Remove the starter (see Chapter 5).

6 Remove the upper oil pan bolts and nuts, then carefully separate the upper oil pan from the engine block (see illustration).

Note: *Do not remove the lower oil pan bolts. Don't pry between the engine block and the upper pan or damage to the sealing surfaces could occur and oil leaks may develop. Tap the pan with a soft-face hammer to break the gasket seal (see illustration). If it still sticks, slip a putty knife between the engine block* and oil pan to break the bond (but be careful not to scratch the surfaces).

Installation

7 Clean the pan with solvent and remove all old sealant and gasket material from the engine block and pan mating surfaces. Clean the mating surfaces with lacquer thinner or acetone and make sure the bolt holes in the engine block are clear. Check the oil pan flange for distortion, particularly around the bolt holes.

8 Apply a bead of RTV sealant to the bottom surface of the timing chain cover and to the bottom of the rear main oil seal retainer, where they mate with the block. Install a new gasket on the oil pan flange.

9 Place the oil pan in position on the engine block and install the nuts/bolts.

10 Tighten the bolts to the torque listed in this Chapter's Specifications. Starting at the center, follow a criss-cross pattern and work up to the final torque in three steps.

11 Installation of the remaining components is the reverse of removal.

12 Install a new oil filter and refill the engine with oil (see Chapter 1), run it until normal operating temperature is reached, and check for leaks.

14 Oil pump - removal, Inspection and Installation

Removal

1 Remove the oil pan (see Section 13).

2 Remove the timing chain cover (see Section 10). Remove the oil pump cover (plate) from the timing chain cover (see illustration).

Inspection

3 Clean all parts thoroughly in solvent and carefully inspect the rotors, pump cover, and timing chain cover for nicks, scratches, or burrs. Replace the assembly if it is damaged.

4 Use a straightedge and a feeler gauge to measure the oil pump cover for warpage (see illustration). If it's warped more than the limit listed in this Chapter's Specifications, the pump should be replaced.

5 Measure the thickness of the outer rotor

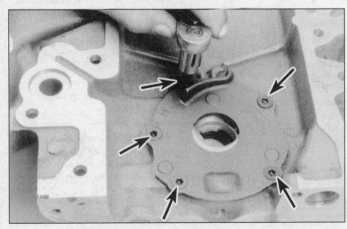

14.2 Remove the oil pump cover screws

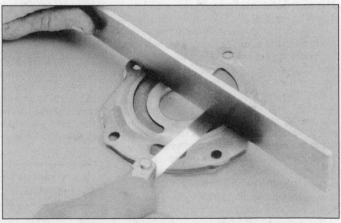

14.4 Place a straightedge across the oil pump cover and check it for warpage with a feeler gauge

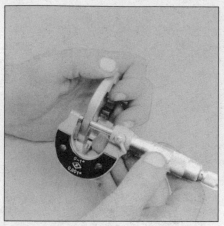

14.5 Use a micrometer to measure the thickness of the outer rotor

14.7 Check the outer rotor-to-housing clearance with a feeler gauge

14.8 Check the clearance between the lobes of the inner and outer rotors

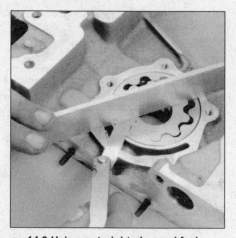

14.9 Using a straightedge and feeler gauge, check the clearance between the surface of the oil pump cover and the rotors

17.1a Location of the right engine mount through-bolt (A) and mount-to-engine bolts (B)

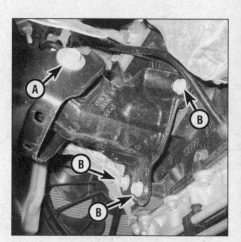

17.1b Location of the left engine mount through-bolt (A) and mount-to-engine bolts (B)

(see illustration). If the thickness is less than the value listed in this Chapter's Specifications, the pump should be replaced.

6   Measure the thickness of the inner rotor. If the thickness is less than the value listed in this Chapter's Specifications, the pump should be replaced.

7   Insert the outer rotor into the timing chain cover/oil pump housing and measure the clearance between the rotor and housing (see illustration). If the measurement is more than the maximum allowable clearance listed in this Chapter's Specifications, the pump should be replaced.

8   Install the inner rotor in the oil pump assembly (with the chamfer on the inner rotor facing the iron pump cover) and measure the clearance between the lobes on the inner and outer rotors (see illustration). If the clearance is more than the value listed in this Chapter's Specifications, the pump should be replaced. **Note:** *Install the inner rotor with the mark facing up.*

9   Place a straightedge across the face of the oil pump assembly (see illustration). If

the clearance between the pump surface and the rotors is greater than the limit listed in this Chapter's Specifications, the pump should be replaced.

Installation

10   Install the pump cover and tighten the bolts to the torque listed in this Chapter's Specifications.

11   Install the timing chain cover (see Section 10) and tighten the bolts to the torque listed in this Chapter's Specifications.

12   Installation of the remaining components is the reverse of removal.

13   Refill the engine with oil and change the oil filter (see Chapter 1).

15   Driveplate - removal and installation

1   This procedure is essentially the same for all engines. Refer to Chapter 2A, Section 18, and follow the procedure outlined there,

but use the torque listed in this Chapter's Specifications.

16   Rear main oil seal - replacement

1   This procedure is essentially the same for all engines. Refer to Chapter 2F, Section 14, and follow the procedure outlined there.

17   Engine mounts - check and replacement

1   This procedure is essentially the same for all engines. Refer to Chapter 2A, Section 20, and follow the procedure outlined there, but refer to the illustrations shown here.

Chapter 2 Part E
3.6L V6 engine

Contents

Specifications

General

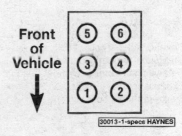

Front of Vehicle

5   6
3   4
1   2

30013-1-specs HAYNES

Cylinder locations

Displacement	220 cubic inches
Bore	3.779 inches
Stroke	3.268 inches
Compression ratio	10.2:1
Cylinder numbers (front-to-rear)	
Left (driver's side) bank	2-4-6
Right bank	1-3-5
Firing order	1-2-3-4-5-6
Oil pressure	
At idle speed	5 psi (minimum)
At 1,200 to 3000 rpm	30 (warm) to 139 (cold) psi

Camshaft

Bore diameter	
Cam tower 1	1.2606 to 1.2615 inches
Cam tower 2, 3, and 4	0.9457 to 0.9465 inch
Bearing journal diameter	
No. 1	1.2589 to 1.2596 inches
No. 2, 3, and 4	0.9440 to 0.9447 inch
Bearing clearance	
No. 1	0.0001 to 0.0026 inch
No. 2, 3, and 4	0.0009 to 0.0025 inch
End play	0.003 to 0.01 inch

Crankshaft main bearing

Main journal diameter	2.8345 ± 0.0035 inches
Clearance	0.0009 to 0.002 (limit) inch
End play	0.002 to 0.0114 (limit) inch

Cylinder head

Gasket thickness (compressed)	0.019 to 0.024 inch
Valve seat width	
Intake	0.04 to 0.05 inch
Exhaust	0.055 to 0.063 inch
Valve seat runout (maximum)	0.002 inch

Valves

Stem-to-guide clearance
  Intake
    Standard .... 0.0009 to 0.0024 inch
    Maximum .... 0.011 inch
  Exhaust
    Standard .... 0.0012 to 0.0027 inch
    Maximum .... 0.0146 inch

Torque specifications   Ft-lbs (unless otherwise indicated)

Note: *One foot-pound (ft-lb) of torque is equivalent to 12 inch-pounds (in-lbs) of torque. Torque values below approximately 15 ft-lbs are expressed in inch-pounds, since most foot-pound torque wrenches are not accurate at these smaller values.*

Crankshaft balancer bolt
  Step 1 30
  Step 2 .... Tighten an additional 105-degrees
Cylinder head bolts* (in sequence - see illustrations 10.30a and 10.30b)
  2014 and earlier models...
    Step 1 22
    Step 2 33
    Step 3 .... Tighten an additional 75-degrees
    Step 4 .... Tighten an additional 50-degrees
    Step 5 .... Loosen all in reverse of tightening sequence
    Step 6 22
    Step 7 33
    Step 8 .... Tighten an additional 70-degrees
    Step 9 .... Tighten an additional 70-degrees
  2015 and later models**
    Step 1 22
    Step 2 33
    Step 3 33
    Step 4 .... Tighten an additional 125 degrees
    Step 5 .... Loosen all in reverse of tightening sequence
    Step 6 22
    Step 7 33
    Step 8 33
    Step 9 .... Tighten an additional 130 degrees
Drivebelt idler sprocket bolt 18
Driveplate-to-crankshaft bolts.. 70
Catalytic converter to cylinder head fasteners........................... 27
Exhaust crossover bolts 21
Intake manifold bolts
  Upper .... 71 in-lbs
  Lower .... 71 in-lbs
Oil cooler
  Bolts .... 35 in-lbs
  Screws .... 106 in-lbs
Oil pan drain plug 20
Oil pan
  Lower pan-to-upper pan nut/bolts .... 97 in-lbs
  Upper pan-to-rear main seal housing (M6 bolts)..................... 108 in-lbs
  Upper pan-to-cylinder block (M8 bolts) 18
  Upper pan-to-transaxle bolts 41
Oil pump pick-up tube mounting bolts .... 106 in-lbs
Oil pump cover (plate) screws .... 105 in-lbs
Oil pump-to-engine block fasteners... 106 in-lbs
Rear main oil seal retainer bolts .... 105 in-lbs
Timing chain cover bolts
  M6 bolts.. 106 in-lbs
  M8 bolts.. 18
  M10 bolts.. 41
Timing gear splash shield bolts .... 35 in-lbs
Camshaft oil control valves.. 110
Oil pump timing chain sprocket (T45) 18
Valve cover-to-cylinder head bolts... 106 in-lbs
Water pump bolts .... See Chapter 3

* Use new bolts
** If using a new engine block, follow all nine Steps. If using the existing block, follow Steps 6 to 9.

1 General information

1 This chapter is devoted to in-vehicle repair procedures for the 3.6L VVT V6 engine.

2 The 3.6 liter engine utilizes Variable Valve Timing (VVT), Dual Overhead Camshafts (DOHC), four timing chains, an aluminum cylinder block, steel cylinder sleeves or liners with six cylinders arranged in a "V"-shape, with 60-degrees between the two banks. The engine has a chain-driven oil pump with a multi-stage pressure regulator to increase fuel economy. The exhaust manifolds are integral with the cylinder heads to make the engine lighter.

Caution: *This engine is not of a freewheeling design and severe engine damage will occur if the timing chain breaks.*

3 Information concerning engine removal and installation can be found in Chapter 2F. The following repair procedures are based on the assumption that the engine is installed in the vehicle. If the engine has been removed from the vehicle and mounted on a stand, many of the steps outlined in this Chapter do not apply.

2 Repair operations possible with the engine in the vehicle

1 Many major repair operations can be done without removing the engine from the vehicle.

2 Clean the engine compartment and the exterior of the engine with degreaser before any work is done. It'll make the job easier and help keep dirt out of internal parts of the engine.

3 It may be helpful to remove the hood to improve engine access when repairs are performed (see Chapter 11). Cover the fenders to prevent damage to the paint. Special pads are available, but an old bedspread or blanket will also work.

4 If vacuum, exhaust, oil, or coolant leaks develop, indicating a need for gasket or seal replacement, the repairs can generally be done with the engine in the vehicle. The intake and exhaust manifold gaskets, timing chain cover gasket, oil pan gasket, crankshaft oil seals, and cylinder head gaskets are all accessible with the engine in the vehicle.

5 Exterior engine components, such as the intake and exhaust manifolds, the oil pan, the oil pump, the timing chain cover, the water pump, the starter motor, the alternator, and fuel system components can be removed for repair with the engine in the vehicle.

6 Cylinder heads can be removed without pulling the engine. Valve component servicing can also be done with the engine in the vehicle. Replacement of the timing chain and sprockets is also possible with the engine in the vehicle, as is camshaft and valvetrain removal and installation.

7 Repair or replacement of piston rings,

4.4 Lift the insulator up and off of the retaining posts then remove it from the front valve cover

pistons, connecting rods, and rod bearings is possible with the engine in the vehicle, however, this practice is not recommended because of the cleaning and preparation work that must be done to the components.

3 Top Dead Center (TDC) for number one piston - locating

1 Top Dead Center (TDC) is the highest point in the cylinder that each piston reaches as it travels up the cylinder bore. Each piston reaches TDC on the compression stroke and again on the exhaust stroke, but TDC generally refers to piston position on the compression stroke.

2 Positioning the piston(s) at TDC is an essential part of certain procedures such as camshaft and timing chain/sprocket removal.

3 Before beginning this procedure, be sure to place the transmission in Neutral and apply the parking brake or block the rear wheels. Disconnect the cable from the negative terminal of the battery (see Chapter 5). Remove the ignition coils (see Chapter 5) and the spark plugs (see Chapter 1).

4 Install a compression pressure gauge in the number one spark plug hole (refer to Chapter 2F). It should be a gauge with a screw-in fitting and a hose at least six inches long.

5 Rotate the crankshaft using a socket and breaker bar on the crankshaft pulley bolt while observing for pressure on the compression gauge. The moment the gauge shows pressure, indicates that the number one cylinder has begun the compression stroke.

6 Once the compression stroke has begun, TDC for the compression stroke is reached by bringing the piston to the top of the cylinder.

7 These engines are not equipped with external components (crankshaft pulley, flywheel, timing hole, etc.) that are marked to identify the position of number 1 TDC. Therefore, the only method to double-check the location of TDC number 1 is to remove the valve cover to access the camshaft sprockets and alignment marks (see Section 4) and

note the rocker arm position, or use a degree wheel and a positive stop timing device threaded into the spark plug hole for cylinder number 1.

8 After the number one piston has been positioned at TDC on the compression stroke, TDC for any of the remaining cylinders can be located by turning the crankshaft 120-degrees and following the firing order (refer to the Specifications). For example, rotating the engine 120-degrees past TDC number 1 will put the engine at TDC compression for cylinder number 2.

4 Valve covers - removal and installation

Removal

1 Disconnect the cable from the negative terminal of the battery (see Chapter 5).

2 Remove the engine cover.

3 Remove the upper intake manifold (see Section 5).

Note: *Cover open ports on the intake to prevent debris from entering the engine.*

Caution: *Once the valve covers are removed, the magnetic timing wheels are exposed(see illustration 9.9). The magnetic timing wheels on the camshafts must not come in contact with any type of magnet or magnetic field. If contact is made, the timing wheels will need to be replaced.*

4 Remove insulator from the left valve cover, if equipped (see illustration).

5 Before removing the variable valve timing solenoid connectors from the front of each valve cover, mark them appropriately so they can be reinstalled in their original locations.

6 Disconnect the wiring harness retainers from the valve cover and move the harnesses out of the way.

7 Remove the ignition coils (see Chapter 5).

8 Mark the Camshaft Position (CMP) sensors to each valve cover so they can be reinstalled in their original locations, then remove the sensor(s) (see Chapter 6).

9 Remove the PCV valve from the right-side cover (see Chapter 6).

4.10 Left valve cover mounting bolts

5.3 Lift the cover up from both sides to release the cover from the ballstuds

10   Remove the valve cover fasteners (see illustration) and remove the cover(s).

Caution: *If the cover is stuck to the cylinder head, tap one end with a block of wood and a hammer to jar it loose. If that doesn't work, slip a flexible putty knife between the cylinder head and cover to break the gasket seal. Don't pry at the cover-to-cylinder head joint or damage to the sealing surfaces may occur (leading to future oil leaks).*

11   Remove the valve cover gasket, then remove the spark plug tube seals.

Note: *The cover gaskets can be reused if they are not damaged.*

Installation

12   The mating surfaces of each cylinder head and valve cover must be perfectly clean when the covers are installed. Use a gasket scraper to remove all traces of sealant and old gasket material, then clean the mating surfaces with brake system cleaner. If there's sealant or oil on the mating surfaces when the

cover is installed, oil leaks may develop.

13   Inspect spark plug tube seals; if damaged, carefully remove the seals using an appropriate pry tool. Position the new seal with the part number facing the valve cover, then use a socket that contacts the outer edge to drive the seal in place.

14   Apply a dab of RTV sealant at the joints where the engine front cover meets the cylinder head.

15   Install the valve cover and bolts, then tighten the bolts to the torque listed in this Chapter's Specifications.

16   The remainder of installation is the reverse of removal.

---

5   Intake manifolds - removal and installation

Warning: *Wait until the engine is completely cool before beginning this procedure.*

Removal

1   If you will be removing the lower intake manifold, relieve the fuel system pressure (see Chapter 4).

2   Disconnect the cable from the negative terminal of the battery (see Chapter 5).

3   If equipped, remove the engine cover (see illustration).

Upper intake manifold

4   Disconnect the wiring harness from the MAP sensor and the throttle body (see illustration).

5   Loosen the clamp and detach the intake duct from the throttle body.

6   Disconnect the PCV valve hose (see Chapter 6), vapor purge hose and brake booster hoses.

7   Disconnect the wiring harness retainers from the upper intake support bracket and the retainer from the stud bolt (see illustration).

8   Remove the nuts and stud bolt, then remove the upper intake manifold bracket (see illustration).

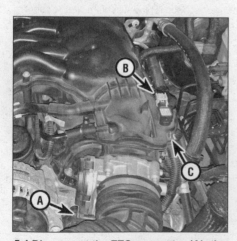

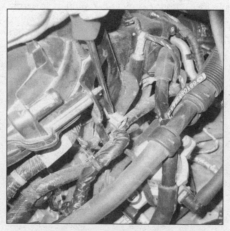

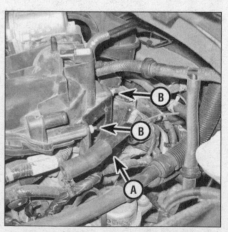

5.4 Disconnect the ETC connector (A), the MAP sensor (B) and the electrical harness (C) retainer

5.7 Pry the wiring harness retainer off of the bracket stud

5.8 Remove the stud bolt (A) and bracket nuts (B), and remove the bracket

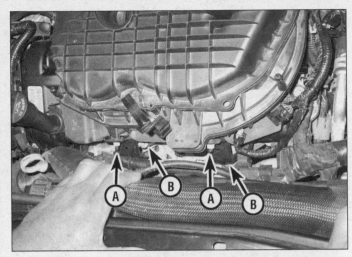

5.10 Remove the support bracket upper nuts (A), loosen the lower nuts (B) and remove the brackets from the upper intake manifold

5.11 Upper intake manifold bolts

9   Remove the nut from the bracket on the heater core return tube.

10   Remove the support bracket-to-upper manifold nuts (see illustration).

11   Loosen, but do not remove, the bolts on the manifold, and remove the upper intake manifold (see illustration).

12   Discard the six upper-to-lower intake manifold seals, and cover the open intake ports to prevent debris from entering the engine.

13   If required, remove the insulator from the left valve cover (see illustration 4.4).

Lower intake manifold

14   Remove the upper intake manifold (see Steps 4 through 13).

15   Remove the fuel injectors and fuel rail (see Chapter 4).

Note: *The lower intake manifold can be removed with the injectors and fuel rail in place. Be careful not to damage the fuel injectors once the manifold is removed.*

16   Pry the wiring harness retainer from the end of the manifold and move the harness out of the way.

17   Remove the lower intake manifold bolts (see illustration), and remove the manifold from the cylinder heads.

18   Discard the six manifold-to-cylinder head seals.

Installation

Lower Intake manifold

Note: *The mating surfaces of the cylinder heads, cylinder block, and the intake manifold must be perfectly clean when the lower intake*

manifold is installed.

19   Use a gasket scraper to remove all traces of sealant and old gasket material, then clean the mating surfaces with brake system cleaner. If there's old sealant or oil on the mating surfaces when the lower intake manifold is installed, oil or vacuum leaks may develop. Use a vacuum cleaner to remove any debris that falls into the intake ports or the valley between the cylinder banks.

20   Install the fuel injectors and the fuel rail (see Chapter 4).

21   Install new intake manifold seals to the manifold.

Note: *Remove any rags placed in the cylinder head ports.*

22   Carefully lower the lower intake manifold into place (see illustration) and install the mounting bolts finger-tight.

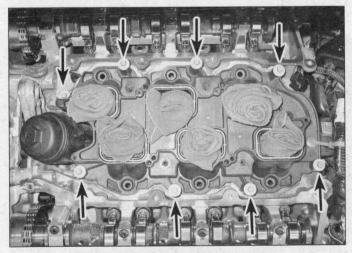

5.17 Lower intake manifold bolt locations

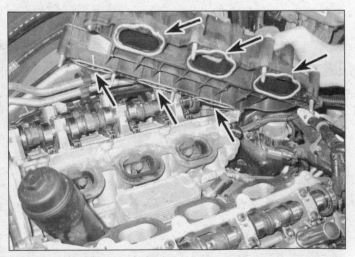

5.22 Install the manifold making sure the intake seals do not fall out of the manifold

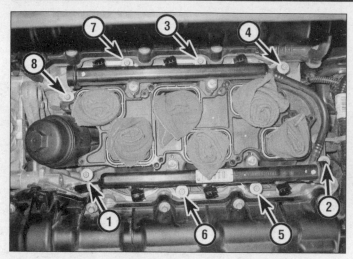

5.23 Lower intake manifold bolt tightening sequence

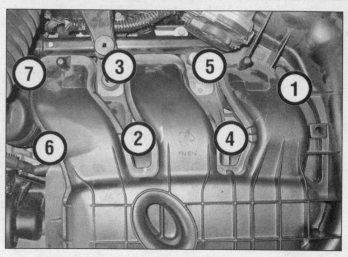

5.28 Upper intake manifold bolt tightening sequence

23   Tighten the mounting bolts in steps, following the tightening sequence (see illustration), to the torque listed in this Chapter's Specifications.
24   Install the upper intake manifold.

Upper intake manifold

25   Check the condition of the rubber seals that are installed into each intake runner on the upper intake manifold. If they are damaged, replace the seals in the upper intake manifold.
26   Place the insulator on the mounting pins (see illustration 5.4), if removed.
27   Install the upper intake manifold onto the lower intake manifold while pulling the bolts up.
28   Tighten the mounting bolts in sequence (see illustration) to the torque listed in this Chapter's Specifications.
29   Installation of the remaining components is the reverse of removal.
30   Start the engine and check for leaks and proper operation.

6   Crankshaft balancer - removal and installation

Removal

1   Disconnect the cable from the negative terminal of the battery (see Chapter 5).
2   Raise the vehicle and support it securely on jackstands.
3   Remove the drivebelt (see Chapter 1).
4   The crankshaft balancer bolt is incredibly tight; using a breaker bar, socket and special tool #10198 or equivalent (see illustration), hold the balancer from turning while loosening the bolt.
5   Pull the crankshaft balancer off the crankshaft (see illustration).

Installation

6   Apply clean engine oil or multi-purpose grease to the seal contact surface of the balancer hub (if it isn't lubricated, the seal lip could be damaged and oil leakage would result).

7   Install the crankshaft balancer, aligning the keyway on the crankshaft with the slot in the balancer. Install the bolt and tighten it by hand.
8   Prevent the engine from rotating (see Step 5) then tighten the bolt to the torque listed in this Chapter's Specifications.
9   Installation of the remaining components is the reverse of removal.

7   Crankshaft front oil seal - replacement

1   Remove the crankshaft balancer (see Section 6).
2   Use a screwdriver or hook tool to carefully pry out the seal (see illustration).
Note: *Be careful not to damage the oil pump cover bore where the seal is seated, or the nose and sealing surface of the crankshaft.*
3   Another procedure for removing the seal is to drill a small hole on each side of the seal and place a self-tapping screw in each

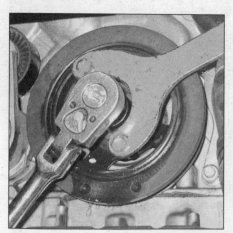

6.4 Using a special holding tool to prevent the crankshaft from turning, loosen, then remove the bolt

6.5 Slide the pulley from the end of the crankshaft; a puller shouldn't be required

7.2 Use a hook tool and pry the seal from the timing cover

hole (see illustration). Use these screws as a means of pulling the seal out without having to pry on it.

4   If the seal is being replaced when the timing chain cover is removed, support the cover on top of two blocks of wood and drive the seal out from the backside with a hammer and punch.

Caution: *Be careful not to scratch, gouge or distort the area that the seal fits into or a leak will develop.*

5   Apply clean engine oil or multi-purpose grease to the outer edge of the new seal, then install it in the cover with the lip (spring side) facing IN. Drive the seal into place with a seal driver or a large socket and a hammer (see illustration). Make sure the seal enters the bore squarely and stop when the front face is at the proper depth.

Note: *If a large socket isn't available, a piece of pipe will also work.*

6   Check the surface on the balancer hub that the oil seal rides on. If the surface has been grooved from long-time contact with the seal, the balancer will need to be replaced.

7   Lubricate the balancer hub with clean engine oil and install the crankshaft balancer (see Section 6).

8   The remainder of installation is the reverse of the removal.

8   Timing chain cover, chain and sprockets - removal, inspection and installation

Warning: *Wait until the engine is completely cool before beginning this procedure.*

Caution: *The timing system is complex, and severe engine damage will occur if you make any mistakes. Do not attempt this procedure unless you are highly experienced with this type of repair. If you are at all unsure of your abilities, be sure to consult an expert. Double-check all your work and be sure everything is correct before you attempt to start the engine.*

Caution: *Do not rotate the crankshaft or cam-shafts separately during this procedure (with the timing chains removed), as damage to the valves may occur.*

Note: *Several special tools are required to complete these procedures, so read through the entire Section and obtain the special tools before beginning work.*

Removal

Timing chain cover

1   Disconnect the cable from the negative terminal of the battery (see Chapter 5).

2   Drain the engine coolant (see Chapter 1).

3   Raise the vehicle and support it securely on jackstands. Drain the engine oil (see Chapter 1).

4   Remove the drivebelt, drivebelt tensioner and idler pulley (see Chapter 1).

5   Remove the thermostat housing, upper radiator hose and disconnect the heater hose

7.3 Another way of removing an old oil seal is to screw a self-tapping screw partially into the seal, then use pliers as a lever to pull it from the engine

from the water pump (see Chapter 3).

6   Remove the heater core supply pipe fasteners from the right-side cylinder head and move the pipes out of the way.

7   Remove the power steering pump and tie it out of the way with wire (see Chapter 10).

8   Remove the crankshaft balancer (see Section 6).

9   Remove the valve covers (see Section 4).

Caution: *Once the valve covers are removed, the magnetic timing wheels at the front and rear of the camshafts are exposed (see illustration 9.9). The magnetic timing wheels on the camshafts must not come in contact with any type of magnet or magnetic field. If contact is made, the timing wheels will need to be replaced.*

10   Remove the lower and upper oil pans (see Section 11).

11   Remove the timing chain cover mount-

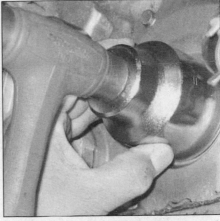

7.5 Drive the seal squarely into the cover using a socket and hammer

ing bolts (see illustration). There are seven indented prying points, one on top and three on each side; carefully pry the cover free of the engine block and cylinder heads. If it still sticks, slip a putty knife between the engine block and cover to break the bond (but be careful not to scratch the surfaces).

12   Once the cover is removed, discard the coolant housing and water pump gaskets from the back side of the timing chain cover.

Timing chain

Warning: *When the timing chains are removed, do not rotate the camshafts or crankshaft; the valves and pistons can be damaged if contact is made.*

13   Temporarily install the crankshaft pulley bolt. Turn the crankshaft with the bolt to TDC number 1, on the exhaust stroke to align the timing marks on the crankshaft and camshaft sprockets. Rotate the engine clockwise only, until the mark on the crankshaft aligns with the line made where the engine block and

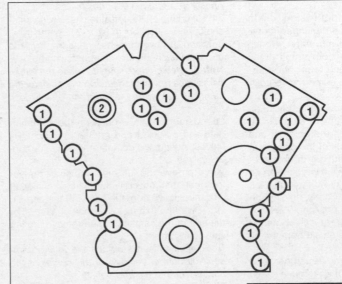

8.11 Timing chain cover bolt size and locations:

1   *M6 size bolts locations*
2   *M8 size bolt location*

30014-2B-10.63 HAYNES

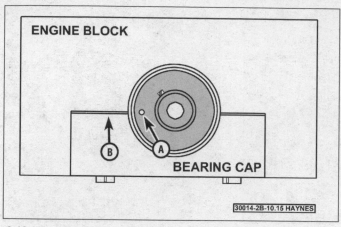

8.13 Align the dimple (A) on the crankshaft with the line (B) made where the engine block and bearing cap meet

8.15 Verity that there are 12 pins between the mark on each phaser

bearing cap meet (see illustration).

14   On the left (driver's side) camshaft phasers, the machined scribe lines should be facing away from each other, and the arrows should be pointing towards each other in a parallel line with the gasket surface of the cylinder head. On the right side camshaft phaser, the arrows should be facing away from each other and the machined scribe lines should be pointing towards each other in a parallel line with the gasket surface of the cylinder head (see illustrations 9.10a and 9.10b). If, when you align the crankshaft mark with the bearing cap parting line, the camshaft marks are not in alignment as shown in illustration 8.57, rotate the engine one full revolution, realign the crankshaft mark, and verify that the camshaft marks are in proper alignment.

15   Verify the phaser marks are aligned with the plated links; if the plated links cannot be distinguished make sure there are 12 pins between the two marks (see illustration).

Note: *Use paint or a permanent marker to mark the direction of rotation on all chains before removing them so they can be installed in the same direction.*

16   Starting with the right side chain tensioner, press the tensioner plunger in until special tool #8514 or a 3 mm Allen wrench can be inserted through both small holes in the top and bottom of the tensioner body, holding the plunger in the compressed position.

17   Working on the left side chain tensioner, locate the access hole on the side of the tensioner. Working through the hole, lift and hold the pawl off of the rack of the plunger in the tensioner. Press the plunger in until special tool #8514 or a 3 mm Allen wrench can be inserted through both small holes in the top and bottom of the tensioner body, holding the plunger in the compressed position.

18   Remove the timing gear splash shield fasteners, then remove the shield from the oil pump housing.

19   Remove the oil pump tensioner and sprocket (see Section 12), then remove the oil pump chain from the crankshaft gear.

Note: *The oil pump chain and sprocket do not have to be timed, but the chain should be marked to make sure it is installed in the same direction of rotation.*

20   Starting with the right side chain, slide camshaft phaser lock tool #10202-1 from the front, between the two camshaft phasers, towards the chain (with the tool number facing up).

Note: *It may be necessary to rotate the intake camshaft a few degrees using a wrench on the camshaft flat when installing the phaser lock tool.*

21   Using a large wrench on the camshaft flats and a socket and ratchet on the oil control valves, loosen, but do not remove, the oil control valves.

22   Remove the right side camshaft phaser lock tool, then unscrew the intake camshaft oil control valve from the center of the phaser.

23   Slide the intake camshaft phaser off of the end of the camshaft, then remove the right side timing chain.

Note: *If necessary, remove the exhaust camshaft oil control valve from the center of the phaser and remove the phaser.*

24   Working on the left side chain, slide camshaft phaser lock tool #10202-2 from the front, between the two camshaft phasers, towards the chain (with the tool number facing up).

Note: *It may be necessary to rotate the intake camshaft a few degrees using a wrench on the camshaft flat when installing the phaser lock tool.*

25   Using a large wrench on the camshaft flats and a socket and ratchet on oil control valves, loosen, but do not remove, the oil control valves.

26   Remove the left side camshaft phaser lock tool, then unscrew the exhaust camshaft oil control valve from the center of the phaser.

27   Slide the exhaust camshaft phaser off of the end of the camshaft, then remove the left side timing chain.

Note: *If necessary, remove the intake camshaft oil control valve from the center of the phaser and remove the phaser.*

28   Locate the primary chain tensioner to

the side of the crankshaft chain and press the tensioner plunger in until special tool #8514 or a 3 mm Allen wrench can be inserted through the small hole in the side of the tensioner body, holding the plunger in the compressed position.

29   With the tensioner in the compressed position, remove the TORX (T30) mounting fasteners and the tensioner.

30   Remove the primary chain guide TORX (T30) mounting fasteners and the guide.

31   Remove the idler sprocket TORX (T45) mounting fastener and washer, then remove the idler sprocket, primary chain and crankshaft sprocket.

Note: *The chain should be marked to make sure it is installed in the same direction of rotation.*

32   If necessary, remove the chain tensioner (T30) fasteners and remove the tensioner(s), keeping the tensioners in the compressed position.

33   If necessary, remove the chain guide fasteners and guides for both chains.

Inspection

34   Inspect the timing chain dampener (guide) for cracks and wear and replace it, if necessary.

35   Clean the timing chain and sprockets with solvent and dry them with compressed air (if available).

Warning: *Wear eye protection when using compressed air.*

36   Inspect the components for wear and damage. Look for teeth that are deformed, chipped, pitted, and cracked.

37   The timing chain and sprockets should be replaced with new ones if the engine has high mileage, the chain has visible damage, or total freeplay midway between the sprockets exceeds one inch. Failure to replace a worn timing chain and sprockets may result in erratic engine performance, loss of power, and decreased fuel mileage. Loose chains can jump timing. In the worst case, chain jumping or breakage will result in severe engine damage.

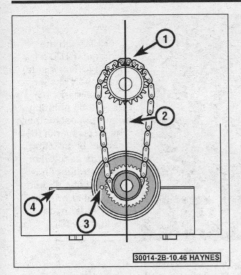

8.44 Primary chain alignment details;

1   Primary chain plated link
2   12 o'clock position
3   Crankshaft dimple
4   Line formed where engine block
    and bearing cap meet

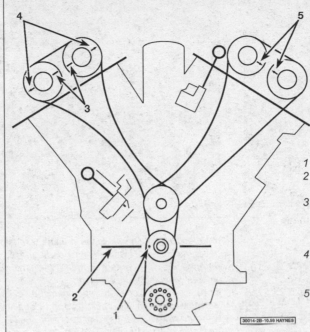

8.57 Timing mark alignment details

1   Dimple on crankshaft
2   Junction of main bearing
    cap and cylinder block
3   Lines on right side cam
    phasers - must be pointing
    toward each other and
    parallel with cylinder head
4   Arrows on right side cam
    phasers - must be pointing
    away from each other
5   Arrows on left side cam
    phasers - must be pointing
    toward each other

Installation

Caution: *Before starting the engine, carefully rotate the crankshaft by hand through at least two full revolutions (use a socket and breaker bar on the crankshaft pulley center bolt). If you feel any resistance, STOP! There is something wrong - most likely, valves are contacting the pistons. You must find the problem before proceeding.*

38   Use a plastic gasket scraper to remove all traces of old gasket material and sealant from the cover, engine block and cylinder heads. The cover is made of aluminum, so be careful not to nick or gouge it. Only clean the gasket sealing surfaces with rubbing alcohol (isopropyl) or brake system cleaner - do not use any oil based fluids.

39   If removed, install the chain guides and tensioners (still in the compressed position).

40   Make sure the keyway is installed on the crankshaft and the dimple on the crankshaft is aligned with the line made where the engine block and bearing cap meets (see illustration 8.13).

41   Verify the camshafts are at TDC, with the alignment holes pointing up (see illustration 9.29).

42   Place the primary chain on the crankshaft sprocket, with the plated link of the primary chain aligned with the arrow on the bottom of the sprocket. Insert the idler sprocket into the chain, aligning the other plated link with the machined mark of the idler sprocket.

43   Using clean engine oil, coat the sprockets and chain. Install the assembly while keeping the marks aligned, then install the idler sprocket mounting fastener finger-tight.

44   Check the alignment of the marks; the plated link on the idler sprocket should be on top (12 o'clock) and the machined mark on

the crankshaft should be aligned with the line made where the engine block and bearing cap meet (see illustration). If the marks are all aligned, tighten the idler sprocket fastener to the torque listed in this Chapter's Specifications.

45   Install the primary chain guide and tensioner, then tighten the fasteners to the torque listed in this Chapter's Specifications. Remove the special tool from the tensioner plunger.

46   Starting with the left side chain, install the intake camshaft phaser and oil control valve, then tighten the valve finger-tight, if removed.

47   Place the left side chain over the intake phaser and around the inside cogs of the idler sprocket so that the plate link of the chain is aligned with the machined arrow on the sprocket.

48   With the chain aligned at the idler sprocket, install the exhaust camshaft phaser so that the arrows are pointing towards each other and in a parallel line with the cylinder head gasket surface (see illustration 9.10a), then install the oil control valve finger tight.

49   Slide camshaft phaser lock tool # 10202-2 from the front, between the two camshaft phasers towards the chain with the tool number facing up.

50   Using a large wrench on the camshaft flats and a socket and ratchet on the oil control valves, tighten both valves to the torque listed in this Chapter's Specifications.

51   Working on the right (passenger's side) chain, install the exhaust camshaft phaser and oil control valve, tightening the valve finger tight, if removed.

52   Place the right side chain over the intake phaser and around the outside cogs of the idler sprocket so that the plate link of the

chain is aligned with the machined circle on the sprocket.

53   With the chain aligned at the idler sprocket, install the intake camshaft phaser so that the machined lines are pointing towards each other and in a parallel line with the gasket surface of the cylinder head (see illustration 9.10b), then install the oil control valve finger-tight.

54   Slide camshaft phaser lock tool # 10202-1 from the front, between the two camshaft phasers, towards the chain (with the tool number facing up).

55   Using a large wrench on the camshaft flats and a socket and ratchet on the oil control valves, tighten both valves to the torque listed in this Chapter's Specifications.

56   Install the oil pump timing chain, tensioner, sprocket and splash shield (see Section 12).

Note: *There are no timing or timing marks on the oil pump chain or sprocket.*

57   Verify all the marks are aligned (see illustration), then remove the special tool or Allen wrenches from the primary and secondary tensioners. Also remove the camshaft phaser lock tools.

58   Rotate the engine two complete turns using the machined mark on the crankshaft with the line made where the engine block and bearing caps meet as the reference. Verify all the marks are aligned and there are 12 pins between the phaser marks (see illustration 8.15); if the marks are off, rotate the engine two more complete turns and check again.

59   Once the timing marks are correct, install the new coolant housing and water pump housing gaskets into the grooves on the back side of the timing cover

60   Apply a 1/8-inch wide by 1/16-inch high,

9.9 Location of the magnetic timing wheels

9.10a With the engine at TDC #1, the left (driver's side) camshaft phaser scribe marks (A) should be pointing away from each other, the arrow marks (B) should be pointing towards each other in a straight line and that line should be parallel with the cylinder head surface (C)...

9.10b ... and the right-side phaser scribe marks should be pointing towards each other in a straight line (and that line should be parallel with the cylinder head surface)

bead of RTV sealant to the sealing surface of the cover, then install the cover on the alignment dowels.

61   Install the cover bolts (see illustration 8.11) and tighten them in a criss-cross pattern, in three steps, to the torque listed in this Chapter's Specifications.

62   Installation of the remaining components is the reverse of removal.

63   Add oil and coolant (see Chapter 1), start the engine and check for leaks.

9   Camshaft(s) – removal, inspection and installation

Caution: *The timing system is complex, and severe engine damage will occur if you make any mistakes. Do not attempt this procedure unless you are highly experienced with this type of repair. If you are at all unsure of your abilities, be sure to consult an expert. Double-check all your work and be sure everything is correct before you attempt to start the engine.*
Caution: *Once the valve covers are removed, the magnetic timing wheels are exposed. The*

magnetic timing wheels on the camshafts must not come in contact with any type of magnet or magnetic field. If contact is made, the timing wheels will need to be replaced.
Note: *The timing chain for each camshaft can be removed from the camshafts individually, without removing all the timing chains, using the tools outlined in this Section. If the tools are not available, the timing chain cover and all chains will need to be removed before the camshafts can be removed (see Section 8).*

Removal

1   Disconnect the cable from the negative terminal of the battery (see Chapter 5).
2   Drain the engine oil and coolant (see Chapter 1).
3   Remove the drivebelt (see Chapter 1).
4   Remove the air filter housing (see Chapter 4) and resonator.
5   Remove the intake manifolds (see Section 5) and unbolt the exhaust from the cylinder head(s).
6   Disconnect all wires and vacuum hoses from the cylinder heads. Label them to simplify reinstallation.
7   Disconnect the ignition coils and remove the spark plugs (see Chapter 1). Label the ignition coils to simplify installation.
8   Remove the valve covers (see Section 4).
9   Once the valve covers are removed, the magnetic timing wheels are exposed (see illustration). The magnetic timing wheels on the camshafts must not come in contact with any type of magnet or magnetic field. If contact is made, the timing wheels will need to be replaced.
10   Rotate the crankshaft clockwise and place the #1 piston at TDC on the exhaust stroke. On the left (driver's side) camshaft phaser, the machined scribe lines should be facing away from each other, and the arrows should be pointing towards each other in a parallel line with the gasket surface of the cylinder head. On the right side camshaft phaser, the arrows should be facing away from each other, and the machined scribe lines should be pointing towards each other in a parallel line with the gasket's surface of the cylinder

head (see illustrations).
11   Using a permanent marker or paint, mark the camshaft phasers to the timing chains for reinstallation.
12   Working from the top of the timing chain cover, insert special tool #10200-3 down the side of the tensioner to the access hole on the side of the tensioner. Working through the small hole in the side of the tensioner, lift and hold the pawl off of the rack of the plunger in the tensioner. Slide the chain holding tool #10200-1 between the cylinder head and the back side of the chain against the chain guide forcing the rack and plunger back into the tensioner body.
Caution: *The chain holding tool must remain in place while the phasers are removed or the timing chain will fall off into the timing cover.*
13   Slide camshaft phaser lock tool # 10202-1 (right side) or 10202-2 (left side), from the front, between the two camshaft phasers, towards the chain.
Note: *It may be necessary to rotate the intake camshaft a few degrees using a wrench on the camshaft flat when installing the phaser lock tool.*
14   Using a large wrench on the camshaft flats and a socket and ratchet on the oil control valves, loosen, then remove each of the oil control valves from the phaser end of the camshaft.
15   At the same time, carefully slide both the intake and exhaust phaser (with the phaser lock securely between them) forward until they are off the end of the camshafts.
Caution: *Do not remove the phaser lock or try to disassemble the phasers.*
16   Using the alignment holes in the camshaft as a reference point, slowly rotate both camshafts counterclockwise approximately 30-degrees Before Top-Dead-Center (BTDC). In this position the camshafts are in a neutral or no load position.
Note: *The camshaft bearing caps are marked with a number and letter code; " 1I " is for the number one Intake camshaft bearing cap. The notch on the caps should always be installed towards the front.*
17   Loosen the camshaft bearing cap bolts in the reverse order of the tightening sequence (see illustration 9.29).

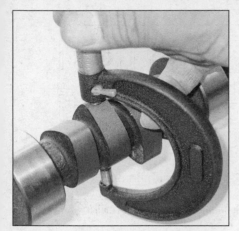

9.22 Use a micrometer to measure cam lobe height

9.28 Camshaft bearing cap tightening sequence 3.6L engines – left (front) side shown, right side is identical

18 Remove the camshaft bearing caps and carefully lift the camshafts from the cylinder head.
19 With the camshafts removed, mark the rocker arms so they can be installed in the same locations; then remove the rocker arms.
20 Mark the hydraulic lash adjusters so they can be installed in the same locations, then remove them from the cylinder head.

Inspection

21 Check the camshaft bearing surfaces for pitting, score marks, galling, and abnormal wear. If the bearing surfaces are damaged, the cylinder head will have to be replaced.
22 Compare the camshaft lobe height by measuring each lobe with a micrometer (see illustration). Measure each of the intake lobes and record the measurements and relative positions. Then measure each of the exhaust lobes and record the measurements and relative positions. This will let you compare all of the intake lobes to one another and all of the exhaust lobes to one another. If the difference between the lobes exceeds 0.005 inch, the camshaft should be replaced. Do not compare intake lobe heights to exhaust lobe heights as lobe lift may be different. Only compare intake lobes to intake lobes and exhaust lobes to exhaust lobes for this comparison.
23 Check the rocker arms and shafts for abnormal wear, pits, galling, score marks, and rough spots. Don't attempt to restore rocker arms by grinding the pad surfaces. Replace defective parts.

Installation

Caution: *Before starting the engine, carefully rotate the crankshaft by hand through at least two full revolutions (use a socket and breaker bar on the crankshaft pulley center bolt). If you feel any resistance, STOP! There is something wrong - most likely, valves are contacting the pistons. You must find the problem before proceeding. Check your work and see if any updated repair information is available.*

24 Dip the hydraulic lash adjusters in clean engine oil and install them into their original locations.
25 Apply moly-base grease or engine assembly lube to the rocker arm contact points and rollers and install them into their original locations.
26 Lubricate the camshaft bearing journals and lobes with moly-base grease or engine assembly lube, then install them carefully in the cylinder head about 30-degrees before (counterclockwise of) TDC. Don't scratch the bearing surfaces with the cam lobes!
Caution: *Do not rotate the camshafts more than a few degrees to prevent the valves from contacting the pistons.*
27 Install the camshaft bearing caps, then install the mounting bolts and finger-tighten them.
28 Tighten the bearing caps in sequence (see illustration) to the torque listed in this Chapter's Specifications.
29 Rotate the camshafts clockwise 30-degrees, verify the alignment holes in the camshafts are at 12 o'clock (pointing straight up) or neutral position (see illustration).

9.29 Locate the alignment holes on the camshafts and make sure they are in the neutral position (pointing straight up) – right side shown, left side is identical

30 Carefully slide both the intake and exhaust phaser (with the phaser lock tool securely between them) onto the camshafts and verify the marks are aligned.
31 Install the oil control valves onto the camshaft phasers and install the bolts, then tighten the bolts to the torque listed in this Chapter's Specifications. Remove the chain holding tool and release the tensioner plunger.
Caution: *Make sure to prevent the camshafts from turning by holding the camshaft with a large wrench on the camshaft flats.*
32 Slowly rotate the engine two complete turns (360-degrees) and verify the alignment marks are correct (see illustrations 9.10a and 9.10b).
33 The remainder of installation is the reverse of removal.

10 Cylinder heads - removal and installation

Warning: *Wait until the engine is completely cool before beginning this procedure.*

Removal

1 Disconnect the cable from the negative terminal of the battery (see Chapter 5).
2 Drain the engine oil and coolant (see Chapter 1).
3 Remove the drivebelt (see Chapter 1).
4 Remove the air filter housing and resonator (see Chapter 4).
5 Disconnect all wires and vacuum hoses from the intake manifolds and cylinder heads. Label them to simplify reinstallation.
6 Remove the intake manifolds (see Section 5).
7 Disconnect the ignition coils and remove the spark plugs (see Chapter 1).
8 Remove the catalytic converter(s) (see Chapter 6).
9 Remove the valve covers (see Section 4).
10 Remove the crankshaft balancer (see Section 6).
11 Remove the oil pans (see Section 11).
12 Remove the alternator (see Chapter 5).

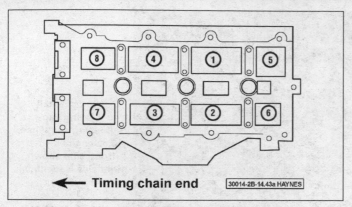

10.30a Left side cylinder head bolt TIGHTENING sequence

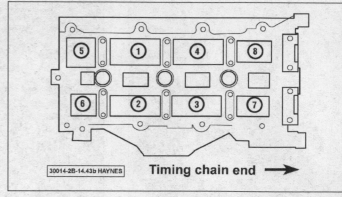

10.30b Right side cylinder head bolt TIGHTENING sequence

13   If you're working on the left cylinder head:

a) *Remove the air conditioning compressor (see Chapter 3), without disconnecting the refrigerant lines.*

b) *Disconnect the main engine harness connectors at the rear of the cylinder and move the harness and retainers out of the way.*

c) *Remove upper intake support bracket nuts and and bracket.*

14   If you're working on the right cylinder head:

a) *Remove the power steering pump (see Chapter 10).*

b) *Remove the heater core tube fasteners and move the tube away from the cylinder head.*

c) *Remove the battery and battery tray (see Chapter 5).*

d) *Remove the oil dipstick tube fastener and remove the tube from the oil pan.*

15   Remove the timing chain cover (see Section 8).

16   Rotate the crankshaft clockwise and place the #1 piston at TDC on the exhaust stroke. When the crankshaft is at TDC, the dimple on the crankshaft will be in line with the line made where the bearing cap meets the engine block. The front cylinder bank cam phaser arrows should be pointing toward each other and be parallel with where the cylinder head and valve cover meets. The rear side cam phaser arrows should point away from each other and the lines on the phasers should be pointing towards each other (see illustration 8.57).

17   Remove the timing chain for the cylinder head or, if both cylinder heads are being removed, remove both chains (see Section 8).

18   Remove the oil control valves from the cam phasers (sprockets) (see Section 9).

19   Remove the timing chain tensioner and chain guides (see Section 8).

20   Remove the camshafts, rocker arms and lash adjusters (see Section 9).

Caution: *Once the valve covers are removed the magnetic timing wheels are exposed. The magnetic timing wheels on the camshafts must*

not come in contact with any type of magnet or magnetic field. If contact is made the timing wheels will need to be replaced (see Section 9).
Note: *Keep the rocker arms and lash adjusters in order so that they can be installed in their original locations.*

21   Loosen the cylinder head bolts in the reverse order of the tightening sequence (see illustrations 10.30a and 10.30b).

22   Lift the cylinder head off the block. If resistance is felt, dislodge the cylinder head by striking it with a wood block and hammer. If prying is required, pry only on a casting protrusion - be very careful not to damage the cylinder head or block!

Caution: *Do not set the cylinder head on its gasket side; the sealing surface can be easily damaged.*

23   Have the cylinder head inspected and serviced by a qualified automotive machine shop.

Installation

24   The mating surfaces of each cylinder head and the engine block must be perfectly clean when the cylinder head is installed.

25   Carefully use a gasket scraper to remove all traces of carbon and old gasket material, then clean the mating surfaces with brake system cleaner. If there's oil on the mating surfaces when the cylinder head is installed, the gasket may not seal correctly and leaks may develop.

26   When working on the engine block, it's a good idea to cover the lifter valley with shop rags to keep debris out of the engine. Use a shop rag or vacuum cleaner to remove any debris that falls into the cylinders.

27   Check the engine block and cylinder head mating surfaces for nicks, deep scratches, and other damage. If damage is slight, it can be removed with a file; if it's excessive, machining may be the only alternative.

28   Position the new gasket over the dowel pins in the engine block. Some gaskets are marked TOP or FRONT to ensure correct installation.

29   Carefully position the cylinder head on the engine block without disturbing the gasket.

30   Install NEW cylinder head bolts and tighten them in the recommended sequence (see illustrations) to the torque steps listed in

this Chapter's Specifications.
Note: *Do not apply additional oil to the bolt threads.*
Caution: *Do not use a torque wrench for steps requiring additional rotation or turns; apply a paint mark to the bolt head or use a torque-angle gauge (available at most automotive parts stores) and a socket and breaker bar.*

31   Installation of the remaining components is the reverse of removal.

32   Change the engine oil and filter (see Chapter 1).

33   Refill the cooling system (see Chapter 1). Start the engine and check for leaks and proper operation.

11   Oil pan - removal and installation

Removal

1   Disconnect the cable from the negative terminal of the battery (see Chapter 5).

2   Raise the front of the vehicle and support it securely on jackstands. Apply the parking brake and block the rear wheels to keep it from rolling off the stands.

3   Drain the engine oil (see Chapter 1).

4   Remove the lower splash shield fasteners and remove the splash shield.

Lower oil pan

5   Remove the bolts, nuts and studs, then carefully separate the lower oil pan from the upper oil pan. Don't pry between the upper pan and the lower pan or damage to the sealing surfaces could occur and oil leaks may develop. Tap the pan with a soft-face hammer to break the gasket seal. If it still sticks, slip a putty knife between the upper pan and lower pan to break the bond (but be careful not to scratch the surfaces).

Upper oil pan

6   Remove the dipstick tube bracket mounting bolt. Using a twisting motion, pull the dipstick tube out of the upper oil pan.

7   Remove the lower oil pan, if desired (see Step 5).
Note: *The upper oil pan can be removed without removing the lower oil pan.*

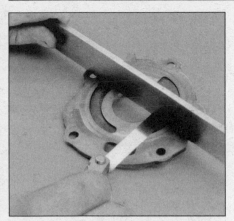

12.16 Place a straightedge across the oil pump cover and check it for warpage with a feeler gauge

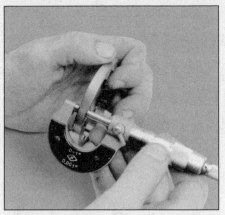

12.17 Use a micrometer to measure the thickness of the outer rotor

12.19 Check the outer rotor-to-housing clearance with a feeler gauge

8   Unbolt the exhaust hanger bracket.
9   Remove the four transmission-to-oil pan mounting bolts.
10   Remove the rubber plugs from the bottom of the bellhousing.
11   Remove the two upper pan-to-rear main seal housing bolts (M6 size).
Caution: *The oil pan-to-rear main seal bolts are hard to see and can easily be missed. If they are not removed, the rear main seal housing will be severely damaged when the pan is lowered.*
12   Remove the nineteen upper oil pan bolts (M8 size) around the perimeter of the pan, then carefully separate the oil pan from the engine block. Use the two indented prying points on each side of the oil pan to carefully pry the pan free of the engine block. If it still sticks, slip a putty knife between the engine block and oil pan to break the bond (but be careful not to scratch the surfaces).

Installation

13   Clean the pan(s) with solvent and remove all old sealant and gasket material from the engine block and pan mating surfaces. Clean the mating surfaces with brake system cleaner and make sure the bolt holes in the engine block are clear. Check the oil pan flange(s) for distortion, particularly around the bolt holes. If necessary, place the pan(s) on a wood block and use a hammer to flatten and restore the gasket surface.

Upper oil pan

14   Apply a 1/8-inch wide by 1/16-inch high bead of RTV sealant to the sealing surface of the pan. Install the upper pan and the bolts, then tighten the bolts finger-tight.
15   Tighten the upper pan-to-transaxle bolts first to the torque listed in this Chapter's Specifications.
16   Tighten the remaining bolts in a circular pattern, starting from the middle working your way outwards, to the torque listed in this Chapter's Specifications.
17   Installation of the remaining components is the reverse of removal.

18   Refill the engine with oil (see Chapter 1), Start and run the engine until normal operating temperature is reached, then check for leaks.

Lower oil pan

19   Apply a 1/8-inch wide by 1/16-inch high bead of RTV sealant to the sealing surface of the pan. Install the lower pan to the upper pan and the bolts. Then tighten the bolts in a circular pattern, starting from the middle working your way outwards, to the torque listed in this Chapter's Specifications.
20   Installation of the remaining components is the reverse of removal.
21   Refill the engine with oil (see Chapter 1). Start and run the engine until normal operating temperature is reached, then check for leaks.

12   Oil pump - removal, inspection and installation

Removal

1   Disconnect the cable from the negative terminal of the battery (see Chapter 1).
2   Raise the front of the vehicle and support it securely on jackstands. Apply the parking brake and block the rear wheels to keep it from rolling off the stands.
3   Drain the engine oil (see Chapter 1).
4   Remove the lower splash shield fasteners and remove the splash shield.
5   Remove the lower and upper oil pans (see Section 11).
6   Remove the oil pump pick-up tube fastener, and remove the tube from the pump. Discard the pick-up tube O-ring.
7   Disconnect the oil pump solenoid electrical connector from the side of the engine then remove the connector retaining clip.
8   Working from the side of the block, depress the oil pump solenoid electrical connector locking tab and push the connector into the block.
Note: *The connector will have to be rotated slightly clockwise and maneuvered around the tensioner mounting bolt.*

9   Remove the oil pump timing gear splash shield bolts and remove the splash shield.
10   Press the oil pump chain tensioner away from the chain until a 3 mm Allen wrench can be inserted into the housing to hold the tensioner back.
11   Using a permanent marker or paint, make reference marks on the chain and oil pump gear.
12   Hold the oil pump gear from moving, then remove the T45 Torx mounting bolt and the oil pump gear.
13   Hold the tensioner and remove the Allen wrench, allowing the tensioner to release. Remove the spring from the dowel pin and slide the tensioner from the oil pump.
14   Remove the oil pump mounting bolts and remove the pump.

Inspection

Note: *The oil pump is not serviceable; if there is a problem, the pump must be replaced as an assembly.*
15   Clean all parts thoroughly in solvent and carefully inspect the rotors, pump cover, and timing chain cover for nicks, scratches, or burrs. Replace the assembly if it is damaged.
16   Use a straightedge and a feeler gauge to measure the oil pump cover for warpage (see illustration). If it's warped more than the limit listed in this Chapter's Specifications, the pump must be replaced.
17   Measure the thickness of the outer rotor (see illustration). If the thickness is less than the value listed in this Chapter's Specifications, the pump must be replaced.
18   Measure the thickness of the inner rotor. If the thickness is less than the value listed in this Chapter's Specifications, the pump must be replaced.
19   Insert the outer rotor into the oil pump housing and measure the clearance between the rotor and housing (see illustration). If the measurement is more than the maximum allowable clearance listed in this Chapter's Specifications, the pump must be replaced.

12.20 Check the clearance between the lobes of the inner and outer rotors

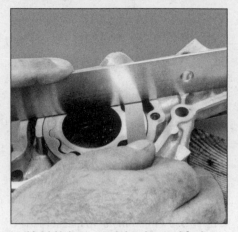

12.21 Using a straightedge and feeler gauge, check the clearance between the surface of the oil pump cover and the rotors

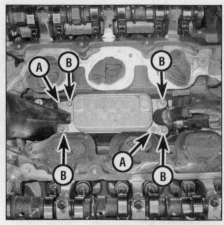

13.4 Remove the oil cooler mounting screws (A) then remove the mounting bolts (B) and cooler

20   Install the inner rotor in the oil pump assembly and measure the clearance between the lobes on the inner and outer rotors (see illustration). If the clearance is more than the value listed in this Chapter's Specifications, the pump must be replaced.

21   Place a straightedge across the face of the oil pump assembly (see illustration). If the clearance between the pump surface and the rotors is greater than the limit listed in this Chapter's Specifications, the pump must be replaced.

Installation

22   Place the oil pump onto the engine block using the aligning dowels. Install the mounting bolts and tighten them to the torque listed in this Chapter's Specifications.

23   Slide the oil pump chain tensioner onto the pivot, then push the tensioner back against the spring. Insert a 3 mm Allen wrench into the tensioner to hold it in place.

24   Place the oil pump timing chain gear into the chain, center it onto the oil pump shaft and install the T45 mounting bolt. Tighten the bolt to the torque listed in this Chapter's Specifications.

Note: *Make sure the gear is facing the same way as when it was removed (see Step 11). There are no timing marks on the pump gear or chain, and no timing is necessary.*

25   Maneuver the oil pump solenoid into position and insert it through the block opening until it snaps in place.

26   Install the timing gear splash shield and bolts, then tighten the bolts to the torque listed in this Chapter's Specifications.

27   Installation of the remaining components is the reverse of removal.

28   Refill the engine with oil and change the oil filter (see Chapter 1).

13   Oil cooler - removal and installation

Warning: *Wait until the engine is completely cool before beginning this procedure.*

Removal

Note: *The oil cooler cannot be serviced separately from the oil filter housing and must be replaced as an assembly.*

1   Disconnect the cable from the negative terminal of the battery (see Chapter 5).

2   Drain the coolant (see Chapter 1).

3   Remove the lower intake manifold (see Section 5).

4   Remove the oil cooler mounting fasteners (see illustration).

5   Remove the oil cooler and discard the seals.

Installation

6   Install new seals to the oil cooler.

7   Place the oil cooler onto the block and install the two mounting screws.

8   Install the mounting bolts and tighten the

screws and bolts to the torque listed in this Chapter's Specifications.

9   Installation of the remaining components is the reverse of removal.

10   Refill the cooling system (see Chapter 1). Run the engine until normal operating temperature is reached, and check for leaks.

14   Flywheel/driveplate - removal and installation

1   This procedure is essentially the same for all engines. Refer to Chapter 2A, Section 18 and follow the procedure outlined there, but use the torque listed in this Chapter's Specifications.

15   Rear main oil seal - replacement

1   This procedure is essentially the same for all engines. Refer to Chapter 2F, Section 14, and follow the procedure outlined there.

16   Engine mounts - check and replacement

1   This procedure is essentially the same as for the 3.8L engine. Refer to Chapter 2D, Section 17 and follow the procedure outlined there.

Chapter 2 Part F
General engine overhaul procedures

Contents

Specifications

2.4L four-cylinder engine
General
Displacement	2.4 liters (148 cubic inches)
Bore and Stroke	3.445 x 3.976 inches (87.5 x 101.0 mm)
Cylinder compression pressure (minimum)	100 psi (690 kPa)
Maximum variation between cylinders	25 percent
Oil pressure (engine warmed-up)	
At idle	4 psi* (25 kPa)
At 3000 rpm	25 to 80 psi (170 to 550 kPa)

If the oil pressure at idle is less than the specified minimum, don't run the engine at 3000 rpm.

Torque specifications   Ft-lbs (unless otherwise indicated)

Note: *One foot-pound (ft-lb) of torque is equivalent to 12 inch-pounds (in-lbs) of torque. Torque values below approximately 15 foot-pounds are expressed in inch-pounds, because most foot-pound torque wrenches are not accurate at these smaller values.*

Balance shaft assembly	
Chain cover	105 in-lbs
Carrier-to-block bolts	40
Gear cover bolt/stud	105 in-lbs
Sprocket bolt	250 in-lbs
Tensioner bolts	105 in-lbs
Connecting rod cap bolts	
Step 1	20
Step 2	Tighten an additional 1/4-turn
Main bearing/bedplate bolts	
Step one	
Tighten bolts 11, 17 and 20	Hand-tighten until bedplate contacts block mating surface
Step two	
Tighten bolts 1 through 10	30
Step three	
Tighten bolts 1 through 10	Tighten an additional 1/4-turn
Step four	
Tighten bolts 11 through 20	20

* Refer to Part A for additional torque specifications.

2.5L four-cylinder engine

General

Cylinder compression pressure	155 to 185 psi
Maximum allowable variation between cylinders	30 psi
Oil pressure	
At idle	25 to 35 psi
Above 1600 rpm	37 to 75 psi

Engine block

Cylinder bore diameter (standard)	3.8751 to 3.8775 inches
Maximum allowable taper and out-of-round	0.001 inch
Warpage limit	0.002 inch per 6 inches
Valve lifter bore diameter	0.9055 to 0.9065 inch

Cylinder head and valves

Cylinder head warpage limit	0.002 inch per 6 inches (0.006 inch overall)
Minimum valve margin	1/32-inch
Valve stem diameter	0.311 to 0.312 inch
Valve stem-to-guide clearance	0.001 to 0.003 inch
Valve spring pressure	
Valve closed	80 to 90 lbs at 1.64 inch
Valve open	200 lbs at 1.216 inch
Valve spring free length	1.967 inch
Valve spring installed height	Not available
Valve lifter	
Diameter	0.904 to 0.9045 inch
Lifter-to-bore clearance	0.001 to 0.0025 inch

Crankshaft and connecting rods

Connecting rod journal	
Diameter	02.0934 to 2.0955 inches
Bearing oil clearance	
Desired	0.0015 to 0.0020 inch
Allowable	0.001 to 0.0025 inch
Connecting rod side clearance (endplay)	0.0010 to 0.0019 inch
Main bearing journal	
Diameter	2.4996 to 2.5001 inches
Bearing oil clearance	
Desired	0.002 inch
Allowable	0.001 to 0.0025 inch
Crankshaft endplay	0.0015 to 0.0065 inch
Maximum taper and out-of-round (all journals)	0.0005 inch

Pistons and rings
Piston-to-bore clearance .... 0.0013 to 0.0021 inch
Piston ring end gap
    Compression rings .... 0.0010 to 0.020 inch
    Oil control ring (steel rail) .... 0.015 to 0.055 inch
Piston ring side clearance
    Compression rings .... 0.001 to 0.0032 inch
    Oil control ring .... 0.001 to 0.0085 inch

Torque specifications *   **Ft-lbs**
Connecting rod cap nuts.. 33
Main bearing cap bolts 80

Refer to Part B for additional torque specifications.

4.0L and 4.2L six-cylinder engines

General
Cylinder compression pressure .... 120 to 150 psi
Maximum variation between cylinders... 30 psi
Oil pressure
    At idle (600 rpm).. 13 psi
    Above 1600 rpm... 37 to 75 psi

Cylinder head and valves
    Warpage limit .... 0.002 inch per 6 Inches
    Minimum valve margin 1/32-inch
Valve stem diameter
    4.2L engine .... 0.372 inch
    4.0L engine .... 0.312 inch
    Valve stem-to-guide clearance... 0.001 to 0.003 inch
Valve spring pressure
    Valve open .... 205 to 220 lbs at 1.2 inch
    Valve closed .... 64 to 74 lbs at 1.625 inch
Valve lifter
    Diameter... 0.904 to 0.9045 inch
    Lifter-to-bore clearance .... 0.001 to 0.0025 inch

Crankshaft and connecting rods
Connecting rod journal
    Diameter.. 2.0934 to 2.0955 inches
    Bearing oil clearance
        Desired .... 0.0015 to 0.002 inch
        Allowable .... 0.001 to 0.003 inch
Connecting rod side clearance (endplay)................................... 0.010 to 0.019 inch
Main bearing
    Journal diameter .... 2.4996 to 2.5001 inches
    Bearing oil clearance
        Desired .... 0.002 inch
        Allowable .... 0.001 to 0.0025 inch
Crankshaft endplay (at thrust bearing) .... 0.0015 to 0.0065 inch
Maximum taper and out-of-round (all journals)........................... 0.0005 inch

Pistons and rings
Piston-to-bore clearance
    4.2L engine
        Desired .... 0.0012 to 0.0013 inch
        Allowable .... 0.0009 to 0.0017 inch
    4.0L engine
        Desired .... 0.0013 to 0.0021 inch
        Allowable .... 0.0013 to 0.0015 inch
Piston ring end gap
    Compression rings .... 0.010 to 0.020 inch
    Oil control ring (steel rails) .... 0.010 to 0.025 inch

Pistons and rings (continued)

Piston ring side clearance
    4.2L engine
        Compression rings
            Desired .... 0.0017 inch
            Allowable .... 0.0017 to 0.0032 inch
        Oil control ring
            Desired .... 0.003 inch
            Allowable .... 0.001 to 0.008 inch
    4.0L engine
        Compression rings
            Desired .... 0.001 inch
            Allowable .... 0.001 to 0.0032 inch
        Oil control ring
            Desired .... 0.003 inch
            Allowable .... 0.001 to 0.0095 inch

Engine block

Maximum warpage .... 0.002 inch per 6 inches (0.008 inch overall)
Cylinder bore diameter (standard)
    4.0L engine .... 3.8751 to 3.8775 inches
    4.2L engine .... 3.7501 to 3.7533 inches
Maximum taper and out-of-round .... 0.001 inch

Torque specifications*   Ft-lbs

Main bearing cap bolts 80
Connecting rod cap nuts.. 33

Refer to Part C for additional torque specifications.

3.8L V6 engine

General

Displacement.. 230 cubic inches
Cylinder compression pressure
    Minimum... 100 psi
    Maximum variation between cylinders .... 25 percent
Oil pressure
    At curb idle (600 rpm)... 5 psi or more
    At 3000 rpm... 30 to 80 psi

Cylinder head and valves

Warpage limit... 0.002 inch per six inches
Valve head margin
    Intake .... 0.032 to 0.038 inch
    Exhaust .... 0.061 to 0.067 inch
Valve stem diameter (intake and exhaust) .... 0.2718 to 0.2725 inch
Stem-to-guide clearance
    Intake .... 0.0001 to 0.00025 inch
    Exhaust .... 0.0020 to 0.0037 inch
Valve spring pressure
    Valve open .... 199 to 221 lbs at 1.22 inches
    Valve closed .... 84.6 to 95.4 lbs at 1.65 inches
Valve lifter
    Diameter
        Mid-2008 and earlier models .... 0.903 to 0.904 inch
        Mid-2008 and later models .... 0.842 to 0.843 inch
Crankshaft and connecting rods
Connecting rod
    Journal diameter .... 2.2829 to 2.2837 inches
    Bearing oil clearance (allowable) .... 0.0007 to 0.0026 inch
    Connecting rod side clearance.............................. 0.005 to 0.016 inch
Main bearing
    Journal diameter .... 2.5192 to 2.5202 inches
    Bearing clearance (allowable) .... 0.0005 to 0.0022 inch
Crankshaft end play.. 0.0036 to 0.0095 inch
Maximum taper and out-of-round .... 0.0001 to 0.0002 inch

Pistons and rings

Piston-to-bore clearance .... 0.0002 to 0.0015 inch
Piston ring end gap
    Top ring .... 0.008 to 0.014 inch
    Second ring .... 0.012 to 0.023 inch
    Oil control ring .... 0.010 to 0.030 inch
Piston ring side clearance
    Top ring .... 0.0012 to 0.0027 inch
    Second ring .... 0.0016 to 0.0033 inch
    Oil control ring .... 0.0006 to 0.0089 inch

Engine block

Maximum deck warpage.. 0.002 inch per 6 inches
Cylinder bore diameter (standard)... 3.7792 to 3.780 inches
Maximum taper and out-of-round .... 0.001 inch

Torque specifications*
                        Ft-lbs (unless otherwise indicated)

Note: *One foot-pound (ft-lb) of torque is equivalent to 12 inch-pounds (in-lbs) of torque. Torque values below approximately 15 ft-lbs are expressed in inch-pounds, since most foot-pound torque wrenches are not accurate at these smaller values.*

Main bearing cap bolts
    Step 1 30
    Step 2 .... Tighten an additional 1/4-turn (90 degrees)
Main bearing cap cross-bolts... 45
Connecting rod cap nuts
    Rods with nuts
        Step 1 40
        Step 2 .... Tighten an additional 1/4-turn (90 degrees)
    Rods with bolts
        Step 1 .... 60 in-lbs
        Step 2 15
        Step 3 .... Tighten an additional 1/4-turn (90 degrees)

* Refer to Part D for additional torque specifications.

3.6L V6 engine

General

Displacement.. 220 cubic inches
Cylinder compression pressure
    Minimum.. 100 psi
    Maximum variation between cylinders .... 25 percent
Oil pressure
    At curb idle (600 rpm).. 5 psi or more
    At 3000 rpm
        Cold .... 128 psi
        Warm .... 30 psi

Cylinder head and valves

Warpage limit.. 0.0035 inch per six inches
Valve head margin
    Intake .... 0.032 to 0.038 inch
    Exhaust .... 0.061 to 0.067 inch
Valve stem diameter
    Intake .... 0.2350 +/- 0.0004 inch
    Exhaust .... 0.2347 +/- 0.0004 inch
Stem-to-guide clearance
    Standard
        Intake .... 0.0009 to 0.0024 inch
        Exhaust.. 0.0012 to 0.0027 inch
    Maximum (rocking method)
        Intake .... 0.011 inch
        Exhaust.. 0.015 inch
Valve spring pressure
    Valve open .... 199 to 221 lbs at 1.22 inches
    Intake .... 148 to 162 lbs at 0.4055 inch
    Exhaust.. 146 to 158 lbs at 0.3937 inch
    Valve closed .... 63 to 69 lbs at 1.57 inches

Crankshaft and connecting rods

Connecting rod
    Journal diameter .... 2.3193 to 2.3263 inches
    Bearing oil clearance (allowable) .... 0.0009 to 0.0025 inch
    Connecting rod side clearance.. 0.005 to 0.016 inch
Main bearing
    Journal diameter .... 2.8310 to 2.8485 inches
    Bearing clearance (allowable)... 0.0009 to 0.0020 inch
Crankshaft end play... 0.0020 to 0.0114 inch
Maximum taper and out-of-round .... 0.0002 inch

Pistons and rings

Piston-to-bore clearance .... 0.0004 to 0.0012 inch
Piston ring end gap
    Top ring .... 0.010 to 0.016 inch
    Second ring... 0.012 to 0.018 inch
    Oil control ring .... 0.006 to 0.026 inch
Piston ring side clearance
    Top ring .... 0.0010 to 0.0033 inch
    Second ring... 0.0012 to 0.0031 inch
    Oil control ring .... 0.0003 to 0.0068 inch

Engine block

Maximum deck warpage... 0.002 inch per 6 inches
Cylinder bore diameter (standard).. 3.7791 to 3.7795 inches
Maximum taper.. 0.0002 inch
Maximum out-of-round .... 0.00035 inch

Torque specifications*

Ft-lbs (unless otherwise indicated)

Note: *One foot-pound (ft-lb) of torque is equivalent to 12 inch-pounds (in-lbs) of torque. Torque values below approximately 15 ft-lbs are expressed in inch-pounds, since most foot-pound torque wrenches are not accurate at these smaller values.*

Main bearing cap bolts
    Step 1 (inner bolts, M11)... 15
    Step 2 (inner bolts, M11) .... Tighten an additional 1/4-turn (90 degrees)
    Step 3 (outer bolts and windage tray, M8) 16
    Step 4 (outer bolts and windage tray, M8) .... Tighten an additional 1/4-turn (90 degrees)
    Step 5 (side bolts, M8) 21
Connecting rod cap bolts
    Step 1 15
    Step 2 .... Tighten an additional 1/4-turn (90 degrees)

  * Refer to Part E for additional torque specifications.

1.9a An engine block being bored. An engine rebuilder will use special machinery to recondition the cylinder bores

1.9b If the cylinders are bored, the machine shop will normally hone the engine on a machine like this

1 Engine overhaul - general information

1   Included in this portion of Chapter 2 are general information and diagnostic testing procedures for determining the overall mechanical condition of your engine.

2   The information ranges from advice concerning preparation for an overhaul and the purchase of replacement parts and/or components to detailed, step-by-step procedures covering removal and installation.

3   The following Sections have been written to help you determine whether your engine needs to be overhauled and how to remove and install it once you've determined it needs to be rebuilt. For information concerning in-vehicle engine repair, see Chapter 2A, 2B, 2C, 2D or 2E.

4   It's not always easy to determine when, or if, an engine should be completely overhauled, because a number of factors must be considered.

5   High mileage is not necessarily an indication that an overhaul is needed, while low mileage doesn't preclude the need for an overhaul. Frequency of servicing is probably the most important consideration. An engine that's had regular and frequent oil and filter changes, as well as other required maintenance, will most likely give many thousands of miles of reliable service. Conversely, a neglected engine may require an overhaul very early in its service life.

6   Excessive oil consumption is an indication that piston rings, valve seals and/or valve guides are in need of attention. Make sure that oil leaks aren't responsible before deciding that the rings and/or guides are bad. Perform a cylinder compression check to determine the extent of the work required (see Section 3). Also check the vacuum readings under various conditions (see Section 4).

7   Check the oil pressure with a gauge installed in place of the oil pressure sending unit and compare it to this Chapter's Specifications (see Section 2). If it's extremely low,

the bearings and/or oil pump are probably worn out.

8   Loss of power, rough running, knocking or metallic engine noises, excessive valve train noise and high fuel consumption rates may also point to the need for an overhaul, especially if they're all present at the same time. If a complete tune-up doesn't remedy the situation, major mechanical work is the only solution.

9   An engine overhaul involves restoring the internal parts to the specifications of a new engine. During an overhaul, the piston rings are replaced and the cylinder walls are reconditioned (rebored and/or honed) (see illustrations 1.9a and 1.9b). If a rebore is done by an automotive machine shop, new oversize pistons will also be installed. The main bearings, connecting rod bearings and camshaft bearings are generally replaced with new ones and, if necessary, the crankshaft may be reground to restore the journals (see illustration 1.9c). Generally, the valves are serviced as well, since they're usually in less-than-perfect condition at this point. While the engine is being overhauled, other components, such as the starter and alternator, can be rebuilt as

well. The end result should be similar to a new engine that will give many trouble free miles.

Note: *Critical cooling system components such as the hoses, drivebelts, thermostat and water pump should be replaced with new parts when an engine is overhauled. The radiator should be checked carefully to ensure that it isn't clogged or leaking (see). If you purchase a rebuilt engine or short block, some rebuilders will not warranty their engines unless the radiator has been professionally flushed. Also, we don't recommend overhauling the oil pump - always install a new one when an engine is rebuilt.*

10   Overhauling the internal components on today's engines is a difficult and time consuming task which requires a significant amount of specialty tools and is best left to a professional engine rebuilder (see illustrations 1.10a, 1.10b and 1.10c). A competent engine rebuilder will handle the inspection of your old parts and offer advice concerning the reconditioning or replacement of the original engine. Never purchase parts or have machine work done on other components until the block has been thoroughly inspected by a professional machine shop. As a general rule, time is the primary

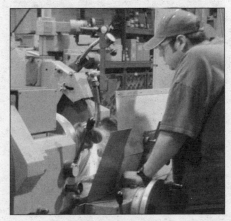

1.9c A crankshaft having a main bearing journal ground

1.10a A machinist checks for a bent connecting rod, using specialized equipment

1.10b A bore gauge being used to check a cylinder bore

1.10c Uneven piston wear like this indicates a bent connecting rod

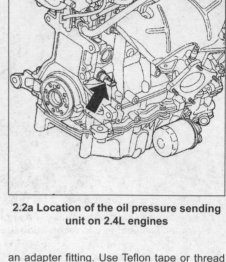

2.2a Location of the oil pressure sending unit on 2.4L engines

cost of an overhaul, especially since the vehicle may be tied up for a minimum of two weeks or more. Be aware that some engine builders only have the capability to rebuild the engine you bring them while other rebuilders have a large inventory of rebuilt exchange engines in stock. Also be aware that many machine shops could take as much as two weeks time to completely rebuild your engine depending on shop workload. Sometimes it makes more sense to simply exchange your engine for another engine that's already rebuilt to save time.

2   Oil pressure check

1   Low engine oil pressure can be a sign of an engine in need of rebuilding. A low oil pressure indicator (often called an idiot light) is not a test of the oiling system. Such indicators only come on when the oil pressure is dangerously low. Even a factory oil pressure gauge in the instrument panel is only a relative indication, although much better for driver information than a warning light. A better test is with a mechanical (not electrical) oil pressure gauge.

2   Locate the oil pressure indicator sending unit:

a) *On 2.4L engines, the oil pressure sending unit is located at the right rear (passenger's side) of the engine block (see illustration).*

b) *On 3.6L V6 engines, the oil pressure sending unit is located on the oil cooler/filter adapter below the intake manifolds (see illustration). Refer to Chapter 2E for removal and installation of the manifolds.*

c) *On 3.8L V6 engines, the oil pressure sending unit is located directly above the oil filter at the right front of the engine (see illustration).*

d) *On 2.5L four-cylinder and 4.0L and 4.2L inline six-cylinder engines, the oil pressure sending unit is located near the distributor and oil filter (see illustration).*

Note: *On 3.6L engines, the manifolds must be removed and installed with the hose for the pressure gauge in place to perform the test.*

3   Unscrew and remove the oil pressure sending unit and then screw in the hose for your oil pressure gauge. If necessary, install

an adapter fitting. Use Teflon tape or thread sealant on the threads of the adapter and/or the fitting on the end of your gauge's hose.

4   Connect an accurate tachometer to the engine, according to the tachometer manufacturer's instructions.

5   Check the oil pressure with the engine running (normal operating temperature) at the specified engine speed, and compare it to this Chapter's Specifications. If it's extremely low, the bearings and/or oil pump are probably worn out.

3   Cylinder compression check

1   A compression check will tell you what mechanical condition the upper end (pistons, rings, valves, head gaskets) of your engine is in. Specifically, it can tell you if the compression is down due to leakage caused by worn piston rings, defective valves and seats or a blown head gasket.

Note: *The engine must be at normal operating temperature and the battery must be fully charged for this check. Also, if the engine is*

2.2b Location of the oil pressure sending unit on 3.6L engines

2.2c Location of the oil pressure sending unit on 3.8L V6 engines

2.2d Location of the oil pressure sending unit on inline four- and six-cylinder engines

3.6 A compression gauge with a threaded fitting for the spark plug hole is preferred over the type that requires hand pressure to maintain the seal

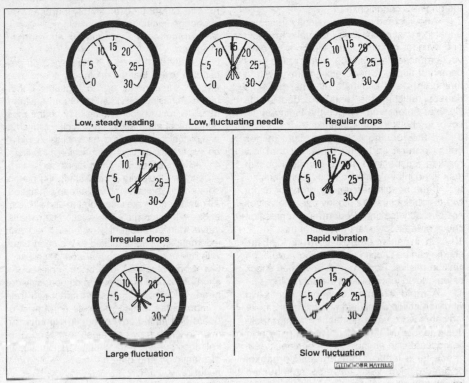

4.6 Typical vacuum gauge readings

equipped with a carburetor, the choke valve must be all the way open to get an accurate compression reading (if the engine's warm, the choke should be open).

2   Begin by cleaning the area around the spark plugs before you remove them (compressed air should be used, if available, otherwise a small brush or even a bicycle tire pump will work). The idea is to prevent dirt from getting into the cylinders as the compression check is being done.

3   Remove all of the spark plugs from the engine (see Chapter 1).

4   On models with distributor ignition, detach the coil wire from the center of the distributor cap and ground it on the engine block. Use a jumper wire with alligator clips on each end to ensure a good ground. On fuel-injected models, the fuel pump circuit should also be disabled (see Chapter 4, Section 2).

5   On models with a coil pack, detach the primary (low-voltage control wires) wiring harness from the coil pack. On models with a coil rail (2000 to 2006 inline six cylinder models), detach the electrical connector from the coil rail. On models with coil-over ignition, the ignition system will already be disabled because the coils were removed for access to the spark plugs.

6   Install the compression gauge in the number one spark plug hole (see illustration).

7   Have an assistant depress the accelerator pedal to the floor and crank the engine over at least seven compression strokes while you watch the gauge. The compression should build up quickly in a healthy engine. Low compression on the first stroke, followed by gradually increasing pressure on successive strokes, indicates worn piston rings. A low compression reading on the first stroke, which doesn't build up during successive strokes, indicates leaking valves or a blown head gasket (a cracked head could also be the cause). Deposits on the undersides of the valve heads can also cause low compression. Record the highest gauge reading obtained.

8   Repeat the procedure for the remaining cylinders and compare the results in this Chapter's Specifications.

9   Add some engine oil (about three squirts

from a plunger-type oil can) to each cylinder, through the spark plug hole, and repeat the test.

10   If the compression increases after the oil is added, the piston rings are definitely worn. If the compression doesn't increase significantly, the leakage is occurring at the valves or head gasket. Leakage past the valves may be caused by burned valve seats and/or faces or warped, cracked or bent valves.

11   If two adjacent cylinders have equally low compression, there's a strong possibility that the head gasket between them is blown. The appearance of coolant in the combustion chambers or the crankcase would verify this condition.

12   If one cylinder is about 20-percent lower than the others, and the engine has a slightly rough idle, a worn exhaust lobe on the camshaft could be the cause.

13   If the compression is unusually high, the combustion chambers are probably coated with carbon deposits. If that's the case, the cylinder head should be removed and decarbonized.

14   If compression is way down or varies greatly between cylinders, it would be a good idea to have a leak-down test performed by an automotive repair shop. This test will pinpoint exactly where the leakage is occurring and how severe it is.

4   Vacuum gauge diagnostic checks

1   A vacuum gauge provides inexpensive but valuable information about what is going

on in the engine. You can check for worn rings or cylinder walls, leaking head or intake manifold gaskets, restricted exhaust, stuck or burned valves, weak valve springs, improper ignition or valve timing and ignition problems.

2   Unfortunately, vacuum gauge readings are easy to misinterpret, so they should be used in conjunction with other tests to confirm the diagnosis.

3   Both the absolute readings and the rate of needle movement are important for accurate interpretation. Most gauges measure vacuum in inches of mercury (in-Hg). The following references to vacuum assume the diagnosis is being performed at sea level. As elevation increases (or atmospheric pressure decreases), the reading will decrease. For every 1,000 foot increase in elevation above approximately 2,000 feet, the gauge readings will decrease about one inch of mercury.

4   Connect the vacuum gauge directly to the intake manifold vacuum, not to ported (throttle body) vacuum. Be sure no hoses are left disconnected during the test or false readings will result.

5   Before you begin the test, allow the engine to warm up completely. Block the wheels and set the parking brake. With the transaxle in Park, start the engine and allow it to run at normal idle speed.
Warning: *Keep your hands and the vacuum gauge clear of the fans.*

6   Read the vacuum gauge; an average, healthy engine should normally produce about 17 to 22 in-Hg with a fairly steady needle (see illustration). Refer to the following vacuum gauge readings and what they indicate about

the engine's condition:

7   A low, steady reading usually indicates a leaking gasket between the intake manifold and cylinder head(s) or throttle body, a leaky vacuum hose, late ignition timing or incorrect camshaft timing. Check ignition timing with a timing light and eliminate all other possible causes, utilizing the tests provided in this Chapter before you remove the timing chain cover to check the timing marks.

8   If the reading is three to eight inches below normal and it fluctuates at that low reading, suspect an intake manifold gasket leak at an intake port or a faulty fuel injector.

9   If the needle has regular drops of about two-to-four inches at a steady rate, the valves are probably leaking. Perform a compression check or leak-down test to confirm this.

10   An irregular drop or down-flick of the needle can be caused by a sticking valve or an ignition misfire. Perform a compression check or leak-down test and read the spark plugs.

11   A rapid vibration of about four in-Hg vibration at idle combined with exhaust smoke indicates worn valve guides. Perform a leak-down test to confirm this. If the rapid vibration occurs with an increase in engine speed, check for a leaking intake manifold gasket or head gasket, weak valve springs, burned valves or ignition misfire.

12   A slight fluctuation, say one inch up and down, may mean ignition problems. Check all the usual tune-up items and, if necessary, run the engine on an ignition analyzer.

13   If there is a large fluctuation, perform a compression or leak-down test to look for a weak or dead cylinder or a blown head gasket.

14   If the needle moves slowly through a wide range, check for a clogged PCV system, incorrect idle fuel mixture, throttle body or intake manifold gasket leaks.

15   Check for a slow return after revving the engine by quickly snapping the throttle open until the engine reaches about 2,500 rpm and let it shut. Normally the reading should drop to near zero, rise above normal idle reading (about 5 in-Hg over) and then return to the previous idle reading. If the vacuum returns slowly and doesn't peak when the throttle is snapped shut, the rings may be worn. If there is a long delay, look for a restricted exhaust system (often the muffler or catalytic converter). An easy way to check this is to temporarily disconnect the exhaust ahead of the suspected part and redo the test.

5   Engine rebuilding alternatives

1   The do-it-yourselfer is faced with a number of options when purchasing a rebuilt engine. The major considerations are cost, warranty, parts availability and the time required for the rebuilder to complete the project. The decision to replace the engine block, piston/connecting rod assemblies and crankshaft depends on the final inspection results of your engine. Only then can you make a cost effective decision whether to have your

engine overhauled or simply purchase an exchange engine for your vehicle.

2   Some of the rebuilding alternatives include:

3   **Individual parts** - If the inspection procedures reveal that the engine block and most engine components are in reusable condition, purchasing individual parts and having a rebuilder rebuild your engine may be the most economical alternative. The block, crankshaft and piston/connecting rod assemblies should all be inspected carefully by a machine shop first.

4   **Short block** - A short block consists of an engine block with a crankshaft and piston/connecting rod assemblies already installed. All new bearings are incorporated and all clearances will be correct. The existing camshafts, valve train components, cylinder head and external parts can be bolted to the short block with little or no machine shop work necessary.

5   **Long block** - A long block consists of a short block plus an oil pump, oil pan, cylinder head, valve cover, camshaft and valve train components, timing sprockets and chain or gears and timing cover. All components are installed with new bearings, seals and gaskets incorporated throughout. The installation of manifolds and external parts is all that's necessary.

6   **Low mileage used engines** - Some companies now offer low mileage used engines which is a very cost effective way to get your vehicle up and running again. These engines often come from vehicles which have been in totaled in accidents or come from other countries which have a higher vehicle turnover rate. A low mileage used engine also usually has a similar warranty like the newly remanufactured engines.

7   Give careful thought to which alternative is best for you and discuss the situation with local automotive machine shops, auto parts dealers and experienced rebuilders before ordering or purchasing replacement parts.

6   Engine removal - methods and precautions

1   If you've decided that an engine must be removed for overhaul or major repair work, several preliminary steps should be taken.

2   Locating a suitable place to work is extremely important. Adequate work space, along with storage space for the vehicle, will be needed. If a shop or garage isn't available, at the very least a flat, level, clean work surface made of concrete or asphalt is required.

3   Cleaning the engine compartment and engine before beginning the removal procedure will help keep your tools and your hands clean.

4   An engine hoist or A-frame will also be necessary. Make sure the equipment is rated in excess of the combined weight of the engine and accessories. Safety is of primary importance, considering the potential hazards involved in lifting the engine out of the vehicle.

5   If the engine is being removed by a nov-

ice, a helper should be available. Advice and aid from someone more experienced would also be helpful. There are many instances when one person cannot simultaneously perform all of the operations required when lifting the engine out of the vehicle.

6   Plan the operation ahead of time. Arrange for or obtain all of the tools and equipment you'll need prior to beginning the job. Some of the equipment necessary to perform engine removal and installation safely and with relative ease are (in addition to an engine hoist) a heavy duty floor jack, complete sets of wrenches and sockets as described in the front of this manual, wooden blocks and plenty of rags and cleaning solvent for mopping up spilled oil, coolant and gasoline. If the hoist must be rented, make sure that you arrange for it in advance and perform all of the operations possible without it beforehand. This will save you money and time.

7   Plan for the vehicle to be out of use for quite a while. A machine shop will be required to perform some of the work which the do-it-yourselfer can't accomplish without special equipment. These shops often have a busy schedule, so it would be a good idea to consult them before removing the engine in order to accurately estimate the amount of time required to rebuild or repair components that may need work.

8   Always be extremely careful when removing and installing the engine. Serious injury can result from careless actions. Plan ahead, take your time and a job of this nature, although major, can be accomplished successfully.

7   Engine - removal and installation

Warning: *Gasoline is extremely flammable, so extra precautions must be taken when working on any part of the fuel system. DO NOT smoke or allow open flames or bare light bulbs near the vehicle. Also, don't work in a garage if a natural gas appliance with a pilot light is present. Disconnect the fuel lines running from the engine to the chassis (see Chapter 4). Plug or cap all open fittings/lines.*
Warning: *The air conditioning system is under high pressure! Have a dealer service department or service station discharge the system before disconnecting any system hoses or fittings.*

Removal

1   Relieve the fuel system pressure (fuel-injected models only) (see Chapter 4, Section 2), then disconnect the negative cable from the battery (see Chapter 5).

2   Cover the fenders and cowl (see Chapter 11). Special pads are available to protect the fenders, but an old bedspread or blanket will also work.

3   Remove the air cleaner assembly (see Chapter 4).

4   Drain the cooling system (see Chapter 1).

5   Label the vacuum lines, emissions sys-

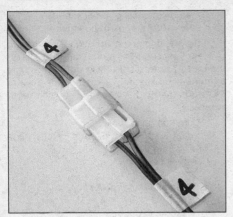

7.5a Label both ends of each wire before unplugging the connector

7.5b Remove the nut on the engine stud and disconnect the ground strap(s)

7.10 Set the power steering pump aside with the lines still connected - be sure it's upright so fluid won't spill

tem hoses, wiring connectors, ground strap(s) and fuel line(s) to ensure correct reinstallation (see illustration), then detach them (see illustration). If there's any possibility of confusion, make a sketch of the engine compartment and clearly label the lines, hoses and wires.

6   Label and detach all coolant hoses from the engine, including those attached to the engine oil cooler (if equipped).

7   Remove the cooling fan, shroud and radiator (see Chapter 3).

8   Remove the drivebelt(s) (see Chapter 1).

9   Disconnect the throttle linkage/cable (and TV linkage/cruise control cable, if equipped) from the engine (see Chapter 6). On 2007 and later models, the throttle body is operated electronically - there is no cable. Disconnect the large ETC connector at the throttle body.

10   On power steering equipped vehicles, unbolt the power steering pump (see Chapter 10). Leave the lines/hoses attached (see illustration) and make sure the pump is kept in an upright position in the engine compartment (use wire or rope to restrain it out of the way).

11   On air-conditioned vehicles, unbolt the compressor (see Chapter 3) and set it aside. Do not disconnect the hoses.

12   Drain the engine oil (see Chapter 1) and remove the oil filter.

13   On 2004 and later models, remove the battery and battery tray (see Chapter 5).

14   Remove the starter motor (see Chapter 5).

15   Remove the alternator (see Chapter 5). On 2007 and later models, remove the fasteners securing the two engine harnesses to the engine, disconnect the harness connectors and set the harnesses aside.

16   On 3.6L models, remove the upper intake manifold (see Chapter 2E).

17   Unbolt the exhaust system from the engine (see Chapter 4).

18   If you're working on a vehicle with an automatic transmission, refer to Chapter 7B and remove the torque converter-to-driveplate bolts. On 2007 and later models, remove the structural lower bellhousing cover.

19   Support the transmission with a jack. Position a block of wood between the jack and transmission to prevent damage to the transmission. Special transmission jacks with safety chains are available - use one if possible.

20   Attach an engine sling or a length of chain to the lifting brackets on the engine (see illustration).

21   Roll the hoist into position and connect the sling to it (see illustration). Take up the slack in the sling or chain, but don't lift the engine.

Warning: *DO NOT place any part of your body under the engine when it's supported only by a hoist or other lifting device.*

22   Remove the transmission-to-engine bolts.

23   Remove the engine mount-to-frame bolts.

24   Recheck to be sure nothing is still connecting the engine to the transmission or vehicle. Disconnect anything still remaining.

25   Raise the engine slightly. Carefully work it forward to separate it from the transmission. If you're working on a vehicle with an automatic transmission, be sure the torque converter stays in the transmission (clamp a pair of vise-grips to the housing to keep the converter from sliding out). If you're working on a vehicle with a manual transmission, the input shaft must be completely disengaged from the clutch. Slowly raise the engine out of the engine compartment (see illustration). Check carefully to make sure nothing is hanging up.

26   Remove the flywheel/driveplate and mount the engine on an engine stand.

7.20 Attach the chain to the lifting brackets (4.0L shown)

7.21 If possible, use the adjustable-angle type lifting sling (2.5L shown)

7.25 Pull the engine forward as far as possible to clear the transmission and then lift the engine high enough to clear the body

9.1 A ridge reamer is required to remove the ridge from the top of each cylinder - do this before removing the pistons!

9.4 Check the connecting rod side clearance with a feeler gauge as shown

Installation

27 Check the engine and transmission mounts. If they're worn or damaged, replace them.

28 If you're working on a vehicle with a manual transmission, install the clutch and pressure plate (see Chapter 8). Now is a good time to install a new clutch.

29 Carefully lower the engine into the engine compartment - make sure the engine mounts line up.

30 If you're working on a vehicle with an automatic transmission, guide the torque converter into the crankshaft following the procedure outlined in Chapter 7B.

31 If you're working on a vehicle with a manual transmission, apply a dab of high-temperature grease to the input shaft and guide it into the crankshaft pilot bearing until the bellhousing is flush with the engine block.

32 Install the transmission-to-engine bolts and tighten them securely.

Caution: *DO NOT use the bolts to force the transmission and engine together!*

33 Reinstall the remaining components in the reverse order of removal.

34 Add coolant, oil, power steering and transmission fluid as needed.

35 Run the engine and check for leaks and proper operation of all accessories, then install the hood and test drive the vehicle.

8 Engine overhaul - disassembly sequence

1 It's much easier to disassemble and work on the engine if it's mounted on a portable engine stand. A stand can often be rented quite cheaply from an equipment rental yard. Before the engine is mounted on a stand, the flywheel/driveplate should be removed from the engine.

2 If a stand isn't available, it's possible to disassemble the engine with it blocked up on the floor. Be extra careful not to tip or drop the engine when working without a stand.

3 If you're going to obtain a rebuilt engine, all external components must come off first to be transferred to the replacement engine, just as they will if you're doing a complete engine overhaul yourself. These include:

> Alternator and brackets
> Ignition system components
> Emissions control components
> Distributor, spark plug wires and spark plugs
> Thermostat and housing cover
> Water pump
> Fuel injection components or carburetor
> Intake/exhaust manifolds
> Oil filter
> Engine mounts
> Clutch and flywheel/driveplate
> Engine rear plate

Note: *When removing the external components from the engine, pay close attention to details that may be helpful or important during installation. Note the installed position of gaskets, seals, spacers, pins, brackets, washers, bolts and other small items.*

4 If you're obtaining a short block, which consists of the engine block, crankshaft, pistons and connecting rods all assembled, then the cylinder head(s), oil pan and oil pump will have to be removed as well. See *Engine rebuilding alternatives* for additional information regarding the different possibilities to be considered.

5 If you're planning a complete overhaul, the engine must be disassembled and the internal components removed in the following order:

> Valve cover
> Intake and exhaust manifolds
> Rocker arms and pushrods
> Cylinder head
> Valve lifters
> Timing chain cover
> Timing chain and sprockets
> Camshaft(s)
> Oil pan(s)
> Oil pump

> Piston/connecting rod assemblies
> Crankshaft and main bearings

6 Before beginning the disassembly and overhaul procedures, make sure the following items are available. Also, refer to Engine overhaul - reassembly sequence for a list of tools and materials needed for engine reassembly.

> Common hand tools
> Small cardboard boxes or plastic bags for storing parts
> Gasket scraper
> Ridge reamer
> Vibration damper puller
> micrometers
> Telescoping gauges
> Dial indicator set
> Valve spring compressor
> Cylinder hone
> Piston ring groove cleaning tool
> Electric drill motor
> Tap and die set
> Wire brushes
> Oil gallery brushes
> Cleaning solvent

9 Pistons and connecting rods - removal

Note: *Prior to removing the piston/connecting rod assemblies, remove the cylinder head, the oil pan and the oil pump by referring to the appropriate Sections in Chapter 2A, 2B, 2C, 2D or 2E.*

Note: *On 2.4L four-cylinder engines, the balance shaft carrier assembly must be removed before the piston/connecting rod assembly can be removed (see Section 10).*

Note: *On 3.6L V6 engines, new connecting rod cap bolts must be used when reassembling the engine, but save the old bolts for use when checking the connecting rod bearing oil clearance.*

1 Use your fingernail to feel if a ridge has formed at the upper limit of ring travel (about 1/4-inch down from the top of each cylinder). If carbon deposits or cylinder wear have produced ridges, they must be completely removed with a special tool (see illustration). Follow the manufacturer's instructions provided with the tool. Failure to remove the ridges before attempting to remove the piston/connecting rod assemblies may result in piston breakage.

2 After the cylinder ridges have been removed, turn the engine upside-down so the crankshaft is facing up.

3 On 3.6L V6 engines, remove the windage tray bolts in the reverse order of installation (see illustration 13.43a).

4 Before the connecting rods are removed, check the endplay with feeler gauges. Slide them between the first connecting rod and the crankshaft throw until the play is removed (see illustration). The endplay is equal to the thickness of the feeler gauge(s). If the endplay exceeds the service limit, new connect-

9.7 To prevent damage to the crankshaft journals and cylinder walls, slip sections of rubber or plastic hose over the rod bolts before removing the pistons

10.1 Checking crankshaft endplay with a dial indicator

ing rods will be required. If new rods (or a new crankshaft) are installed, the endplay may fall under the specified minimum (if it does, the rods will have to be machined to restore it - consult an automotive machine shop for advice if necessary). Repeat the procedure for the remaining connecting rods.

5   Check the connecting rods and caps for identification marks. If they aren't plainly marked, use a indelible marker or paint to make the appropriate number of indentations on each rod and cap (1, 2, 3, etc., depending on the cylinder they're associated with).

6   Loosen each of the connecting rod cap nuts 1/2-turn at a time until they can be removed by hand. Remove the number one connecting rod cap and bearing insert. Don't drop the bearing insert out of the cap.

7   Slip a short length of plastic or rubber hose over each connecting rod cap bolt to protect the crankshaft journal and cylinder wall as the piston is removed (see illustration).

10.3 Checking crankshaft endplay with a feeler gauge

8   Remove the bearing insert and push the connecting rod/piston assembly out through the top of the engine. Use a wooden hammer handle to push on the upper bearing surface in the connecting rod. If resistance is felt, double-check to make sure that all of the ridge was removed from the cylinder.

9   Repeat the procedure for the remaining cylinders.

10   After removal, reassemble the connecting rod caps and bearing inserts in their respective connecting rods and install the cap nuts finger-tight. Leaving the old bearing inserts in place until reassembly will help prevent the connecting rod bearing surfaces from being accidentally nicked or gouged.

11   Don't separate the pistons from the connecting rods (see Section for additional information).

10   Crankshaft - removal

Note: *The crankshaft can be removed only after the engine has been removed from the vehicle. It's assumed that the flywheel or driveplate, crankshaft pulley, timing chain(s), oil pan, oil pump body, oil filter and piston/connecting rod assemblies have already been removed. On 2.4L four-cylinder engines, the balance shaft carrier assembly must be removed (see Section 16). The rear main oil seal retainer must be unbolted and separated from the block before proceeding with crankshaft removal.*

1   Before the crankshaft is removed, measure the endplay. Mount a dial indicator with the indicator in line with the crankshaft and touching the end of the crankshaft as shown (see illustration).

2   Pry the crankshaft all the way to the rear and zero the dial indicator. Next, pry the crankshaft to the front as far as possible and check the reading on the dial indicator. The distance traveled is the endplay. A typical crankshaft endplay will fall between 0.003 and

0.010-inch (0.076 to 0.254 mm). If it's greater than that, check the crankshaft thrust surfaces for wear after it's removed. If no wear is evident, new main bearings should correct the endplay.

3   If a dial indicator isn't available, feeler gauges can be used. Gently pry the crankshaft all the way to the front of the engine. Slip feeler gauges between the crankshaft and the front face of the thrust bearing or washer to determine the clearance (see illustration).

4   On 3.6L V6 engines, remove the windage tray bolts in the reverse order of installation (see illustration 13.43a).

5   On 2.5L four-cylinder and six-cylinder engines, check the main bearing caps to see if they're marked to indicate their locations. They should be numbered consecutively from the front of the engine to the rear. If they aren't, mark them with number stamping dies or a center-punch (see illustrations). Main bearing caps generally have a cast-in arrow, which points to the front of the engine.

10.5a Use a center punch or number stamping dies to mark the main bearing caps to ensure installation in their original locations on the block (make the punch marks near one of the bolt heads)

10.5b The arrow on the main cap indicates the direction to the front of the engine while the stamped numbers indicate the specific journal (2.5L engine shown)

12.3 When checking piston ring end gap, the ring must be square in the cylinder bore (this is done by pushing the ring down with the top of a piston as shown)

6   On 2.4L four-cylinder engines, loosen the main bearing cap/bedplate fasteners 1/4- turn at a time each, until they can be removed by hand. Carefully and evenly pry the main bearing caps/bedplate off of the engine. Try not to drop the bearing inserts if they come out with the caps.
Caution: *Use the cast-in pry points on the bedplate. Do not pry on the block or bedplate mating surfaces, because damage to those surfaces can occur.*

7   On 3.6L V6 engines, remove the windage tray bolts main capbolts and cross-bolts (four on each side of the lower block). Purchase new main bearing cap bolts for reassembly. Tap the caps with a soft-face hammer, then separate them from the engine block. If necessary, use the bolts as levers to remove the caps. Try not to drop the bearing inserts if they come out with the caps.

8   On 2007 and later 3.8L V6 engines, remove the main cap cross-bolts (two on each side of the lower block). Purchase new cross-bolts for reassembly. On all other engines, tap the caps with a soft-face hammer, then sepa-

rate them from the engine block. If necessary, use the bolts as levers to remove the caps. Try not to drop the bearing inserts if they come out with the caps.

9   On all models, carefully lift the crankshaft out of the engine. It may be a good idea to have an assistant available, since the crankshaft is quite heavy and awkward to handle. With the bearing inserts in place inside the engine block and main bearing caps/bedplate, reinstall the main bearing caps/bedplate onto the engine block and tighten the fasteners finger-tight.

---

11   Engine overhaul - reassembly sequence

---

1   Before beginning engine reassembly, make sure you have all the necessary new parts, gaskets and seals as well as the following items on hand:

> Common hand tools
> *3/8-inch and 1/2-inch drive torque wrenches*
> *Piston ring installation tool*
> *Piston ring compressor*
> *Vibration damper installation tool*
> *Short lengths of rubber or plastic hose to fit over connecting rod bolts*
> *Plastigage*
> *Feeler gauges*
> *A fine-tooth file*
> *New engine oil*
> *Engine assembly lube or moly-base grease*
> *Gasket sealant*
> *Thread locking compound*

2   In order to save time and avoid problems, engine reassembly must be done in the following general order:

> *New camshaft bearings (must be done by automotive machine shop)*
> *Piston rings*

> *Crankshaft and main bearings*
> *Piston/connecting rod assemblies*
> *Oil pump*
> *Camshaft and lifters*
> *Oil pan*
> *Timing chain and sprockets*
> *Cylinder head, pushrods and rocker arms*
> *Timing cover*
> *Intake and exhaust manifolds*
> *Valve cover*
> *Engine rear plate*
> *Flywheel/driveplate*

---

12   Piston rings - installation

---

1   Before installing the new piston rings, the ring end gaps must be checked.

2   Lay out the piston/connecting rod assemblies and the new ring sets so the ring sets will be matched with the same piston and cylinder during the end gap measurement and engine assembly.

3   Insert the top (number one) ring into the first cylinder and square it up with the cylinder walls by pushing it in with the top of the piston (see illustration). The ring should be near the bottom of the cylinder, at the lower limit of ring travel.

4   To measure the end gap, slip feeler gauges between the ends of the ring until a gauge equal to the gap width is found (see illustration). The feeler gauge should slide between the ring ends with a slight amount of drag. Compare the measurement to the Specifications. If the gap is larger or smaller than specified, double-check to make sure you have the correct rings before proceeding.

5   If the gap is too small, it must be enlarged or the ring ends may come in contact with each other during engine operation, which can cause serious damage to the engine. The end gap can be increased by filing the ring

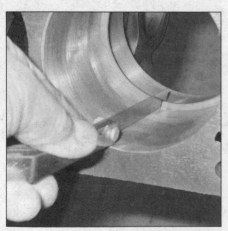

12.4 With the ring square in the cylinder, measure the end gap with a feeler gauge

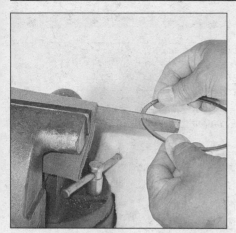

12.5 If the end gap is too small, clamp a file in a vise and file the ring ends (from the outside in only) to enlarge the gap slightly

12.9a Installing the spacer/expander in the oil control ring groove

12.9b DO NOT use a piston ring installation tool when Installing the oil ring side rails

ends very carefully with a fine file. Mount the file in a vise equipped with soft jaws, slip the ring over the file with the ends contacting the file face and slowly move the ring to remove material from the ends. When performing this operation, file only from the outside in (see illustration).

6   Excess end gap isn't critical unless it's greater than 0.040-inch. Again, double-check to make sure you have the correct rings for your engine.

7   Repeat the procedure for each ring that will be installed in the first cylinder and for each ring in the remaining cylinders. Remember to keep rings, pistons and cylinders matched up.

8   Once the ring end gaps have been checked/corrected, the rings can be installed on the pistons.

9   The oil control ring (lowest one on the piston) is usually installed first. It's normally composed of three separate components. Slip the spacer/expander into the groove (see illustration). If an anti-rotation tang is used, make sure it's inserted into the drilled hole in the ring groove. Next, install the lower side rail. Don't use a piston ring installation tool on the oil ring side rails, as they may be damaged. Instead, place one end of the side rail into the groove between the spacer/expander and the ring land, hold it firmly in place and slide a finger around the piston while pushing the rail into the groove (see illustration). Next, install the upper side rail in the same manner.

10   After the three oil ring components have been installed, check to make sure that both the upper and lower side rails can be turned smoothly in the ring groove.

11   The number two (middle) ring is installed next. It's usually stamped with a mark which must face up, toward the top of the piston.
Note: *Always follow the instructions printed on the ring package or box - different manufacturers may require different approaches. Do not mix up the top and middle rings, as they have different cross sections.*

12   Use a piston ring installation tool and make sure the identification mark is facing the top of the piston, then slip the ring into the middle groove on the piston (see illustration). Don't expand the ring any more than necessary to slide it over the piston.

13   Install the number one (top) ring in the same manner. Make sure the mark is facing up. Be careful not to confuse the number one and number two rings.

14   Repeat the procedure for the remaining pistons and rings.

13   Crankshaft - installation and main bearing oil clearance check

1   Crankshaft installation is the first step in engine reassembly. It's assumed at this point that the engine block and crankshaft have been cleaned, inspected and repaired or reconditioned.

2   Position the engine block with the bottom facing up.

3   Remove the main bearing cap bolts and lift out the caps (all but the 2.4L engine) or remove the mounting fasteners and lift off the main bearing caps/bedplate (2.4L engine). Lay the caps out in proper order.

4   If they're still in place, remove the original bearing inserts from the block and from the main bearing caps/bedplate. Wipe the bearing surfaces of the block and main bearing caps/bedplate with a clean, lint-free cloth. They must be kept spotlessly clean. This is critical for determining the correct bearing oil clearance.

Main bearing oil clearance check

5   Without mixing them up, clean the back sides of the new upper main bearing inserts (with grooves and oil holes) and lay one in each main bearing saddle in the block or bedplate. Each upper bearing has an oil groove and oil hole in it. On 2.4L four-cylinder

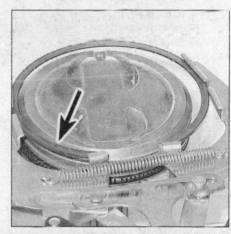

12.12 Installing the compression rings with a ring expander - the mark must face up

engines, install the grooved thrust bearing into the block saddle that has the machined surface. Clean the back sides of the lower main bearing inserts (without grooves) and lay them in the main bearing cap/bedplate saddles. Make sure the tab on the bearing insert fits into the recess in the block or main bearing cap/bedplate.
Caution: *The oil holes in the block must line up with the oil holes in the upper bearing inserts.*
Caution: *Do not hammer the bearing insert into place and don't nick or gouge the bearing faces. DO NOT apply any lubrication at this time.*

6   On 2.5L four-cylinder and all six-cylinder engines the flanged thrust bearing must be installed in the proper gap and saddle. On 2.5L four cylinder engines it is number two (counting from the front of the engine); on six-cylinder engines it's number three.

7   Clean the faces of the bearing inserts in the block and the crankshaft main bearing journals with a clean, lint-free cloth.

8   Check or clean the oil holes in the crank-

ENGINE BEARING ANALYSIS

Debris

Babbitt bearing embedded with debris from machinings

Microscopic detail of debris

Microscopic detail of gouges

Overplated copper alloy bearing gouged by cast iron debris

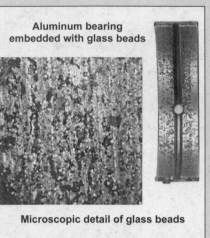

Aluminum bearing embedded with glass beads

Microscopic detail of glass beads

Damaged lining caused by dirt left on the bearing back

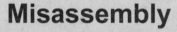

Misassembly

Result of a lower half assembled as an upper - blocking the oil flow

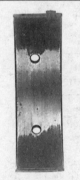

Excessive oil clearance is indicated by a short contact arc

Polished and oil-stained backs are a result of a poor fit in the housing bore

Result of a wrong, reversed, or shifted cap

Overloading

Damage from excessive idling which resulted in an oil film unable to support the load imposed

Damaged upper connecting rod bearings caused by engine lugging; the lower main bearings (not shown) were similarly affected

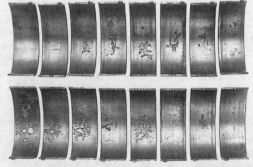

The damage shown in these upper and lower connecting rod bearings was caused by engine operation at a higher-than-rated speed under load

Misalignment

A warped crankshaft caused this pattern of severe wear in the center, diminishing toward the ends

A poorly finished crankshaft caused the equally spaced scoring shown

A tapered housing bore caused the damage along one edge of this pair

A bent connecting rod led to the damage in the "V" pattern

Lubrication

Result of dry start: The bearings on the left, farthest from the oil pump, show more damage

Result of a low oil supply or oil starvation

Severe wear as a result of inadequate oil clearance

Corrosion

Microscopic detail of corrosion

Corrosion is an acid attack on the bearing lining generally caused by inadequate maintenance, extremely hot or cold operation, or inferior oils or fuels

Microscopic detail of cavitation

Example of cavitation - a surface erosion caused by pressure changes in the oil film

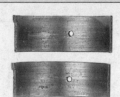

Damage from excessive thrust or insufficient axial clearance

Bearing affected by oil dilution caused by excessive blow-by or a rich mixture

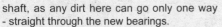

13.11 Lay the plastigage strip on the main bearing journals, parallel to the crankshaft centerline

13.15 Compare the width of the crushed Plastigage to the scale on the envelope to determine the main bearing oil clearance (always take the measurements at the widest point of the Plastigage); be sure to use the correct scale - standard and metric ones are included

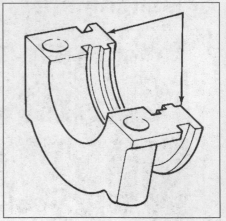

13.22a On 2.5L four-cylinder engines, apply a thin coat of sealant to the chamfered areas (arrows) of the rear bearing cap

shaft, as any dirt here can go only one way - straight through the new bearings.

9   Once you're certain the crankshaft is clean, carefully lay it in position in the cylinder block.

10   Before the crankshaft can be permanently installed, the main bearing oil clearance must be checked.

11   Cut several strips of the appropriate size of Plastigage (they must be slightly shorter than the width of the main bearing journal) and place one piece on each crankshaft main bearing journal, parallel with the journal axis, as shown (see illustration).

12   Clean the faces of the bearing inserts in the main bearing caps or bedplate. On 2.4L four-cylinder engines, hold the bearing inserts in place and install the main bearing cap/bedplate assembly onto the crankshaft and cylinder block. On all other engines install the caps in their respective positions (be careful not to mix them up!). DO NOT disturb the Plastigage.

13   Apply clean engine oil to all bolt threads prior to installation, then install all bolts finger-tight. On 2.4L engines tighten the bedplate fasteners in the proper sequence (see illustration 13.34), progressing in several steps, to the torque listed in this Chapter's Specifica-

tions. On all other engines, tighten the main bearing cap bolts by starting with the center main and working out towards the ends, tighten the main bearing cap bolts in three steps, to the torque listed in this Chapter's Specifications. DO NOT rotate the crankshaft at any time during this operation.

14   Remove the bolts in the reverse order of the tightening sequence and carefully lift the main bearing caps/bedplate straight up and off the block. Do not disturb the Plastigage or rotate the crankshaft. If any of the main bearing caps are difficult to remove, tap them gently from side-too-side with a soft-face hammer to loosen them.

15   Compare the width of the crushed Plastigage on each journal to the scale printed on the Plastigage envelope to determine the main bearing oil clearance (see illustration). A typical main bearing oil clearance should fall between 0.0015 to 0.0023-inch (0.038 to 0.058 mm). Check this Chapter's Specifications to make sure it's correct. You can also check with an automotive machine shop for the oil clearance for your engine.

16   If the clearance is not acceptable, the bearing inserts may be the wrong size (which means different ones will be required). Before deciding if different inserts are needed, make sure that no dirt or oil was between the bearing inserts and the main bearing caps/bedplate or block when the clearances were measured. If the Plastigage was wider at one end than the other, the crankshaft journal may be tapered (see Section). If the clearance still exceeds the limit specified, the bearing insert(s) will have to be replaced with an undersize bearing insert(s).

Caution: *When installing a new crankshaft, always install a standard bearing insert set.*

17   Carefully scrape all traces of the Plastigage material off the main bearing journals and/or the bearing insert faces. Be sure to remove all residue from the oil holes. Use your fingernail or the edge of a plastic card - don't nick or scratch the bearing faces.

18   Carefully lift the crankshaft out of the engine.

19   Clean the bearing insert faces in the cylinder block, then apply a thin, uniform layer of moly-base grease or engine assembly lube to each of the bearing surfaces. Be sure to coat the thrust faces of the thrust bearing/washers as well. (See Steps 5 and 6 for thrust washer/bearing locations.) On six cylinder engines, install the rear main oil seal sections in the block and rear main bearing cap.

Final crankshaft installation

20   Make sure the crankshaft journals are clean, then lay the crankshaft back in place in the cylinder block.

21   Clean the bearing insert faces and then apply the same lubricant to them.

22   On 2.5L four-cylinder engines, apply Loctite 515 sealant or equivalent to the chamfered area of the rear main bearing cap (see illustration). On 2.4L four-cylinder engines, apply Mopar Bedplate Sealant or equivalent to the bedplate sealing area on the block (see illustration). Hold the bearing inserts in place

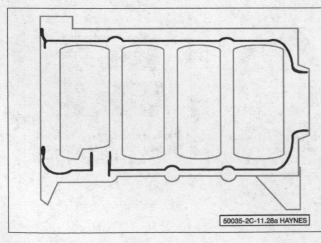

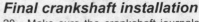

13.22b On 2.4L four-cylinder engines, apply Mopar Bedplate sealant or equivalent to the block-to-bedplate mating surface as shown

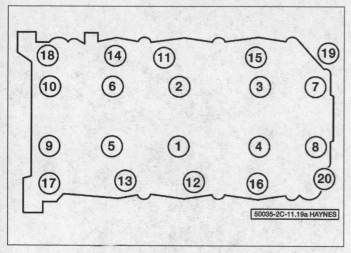

13.34 2.4L four cylinder main bearing cap/bedplate tightening sequence

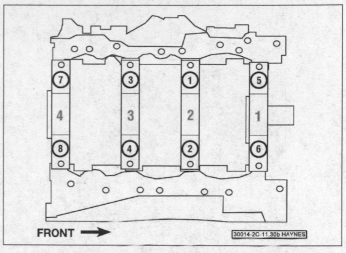

13.43a Main bearing cap inner bolt tightening sequence - 3.6L engines

and install the main bearing caps/bedplate on the crankshaft and cylinder block. Tap the main bearing caps/bedplate into place with a brass or a soft-face hammer.

23   Using NEW main bearing cap bolts, apply clean engine oil to the bolt threads, wipe off any excess oil and then install the fasteners finger-tight.

2.5L four-cylinder and Inline six-cylinder engines

24   Tighten all except the thrust bearing cap bolts to the specified torque (work from the center out and approach the final torque in three steps).

25   Tighten the thrust bearing cap bolts to 10-to-12 ft-lbs.

26   Tap the ends of the crankshaft forward and backward with a lead or brass hammer to line up the main bearing and crankshaft thrust surfaces

27   Retighten all main bearing cap bolts to the specified torque, starting with the center main and working out toward the ends.

28   On manual transmission equipped models, install a new pilot bearing in the end of the crankshaft (see Chapter 8).

29   Rotate the crankshaft a number of times by hand to check for obvious binding.

30   The final step is to check the crankshaft endplay with a feeler gauge or a dial indicator as described in Section 10. The endplay should be correct if the crankshaft thrust faces aren't worn or damaged and new bearings have been installed.

31   If you are working on an engine with a one-piece rear main oil seal, refer to Section 14 and install a new seal.

2.4L four-cylinder engines

32   Push the crankshaft forward using a screwdriver or prybar to seat the thrust bearing. Once the crankshaft is pushed fully forward to seat the thrust bearing, leave the screwdriver in position so that pressure stays

on the crankshaft until after all main bearing cap/bedplate fasteners have been tightened.

33   Tighten the main bearing cap/bedplate fasteners in the indicated sequence, to the torque listed in Step 1 of this Chapter's Specifications. Remove the screwdriver or prybar.

34   Tighten the main bearing bedplate fasteners in the indicated sequence to the torque and angle listed in the remaining steps of this Chapter's Specifications (see illustration).

35   Recheck crankshaft endplay with a feeler gauge or a dial indicator. The endplay should be correct if the crankshaft thrust faces aren't worn or damaged and if new bearings have been installed.

36   Rotate the crankshaft a number of times by hand to check for any obvious binding.

37   Install the new rear main oil seal (see Chapter 2A).

38   Reinstall the balance shaft carrier assembly (see Section 16).

3.8L V6 engines

39   Either use new bolts on the crankshaft

main caps, or examine your existing bolts. Hold a straightedge against the threaded portion of each bolt and hold them to the light. If you can see any section where the threads are not touching the straightedge, that section has stretched, and the bolt should be discarded. If any of your bolts show signs of stretch, replace the whole set with new bolts.

40   After the crankshaft main caps and bolts have been torqued for final assembly, install NEW cross-bolt/washer assemblies and tighten to the torque listed in this Chapter's Specifications.

3.6L V6 engines

41   Install the main bearing caps onto the designated journals.

42   Prior to installation, apply clean engine oil to the NEW bolt threads, wiping off any excess, then install all bolts finger-tight.

43   Tighten the cap bolts, in sequence (see illustrations), to the torque listed in this Chapter's Specifications.

44   Recheck crankshaft endplay with a feeler

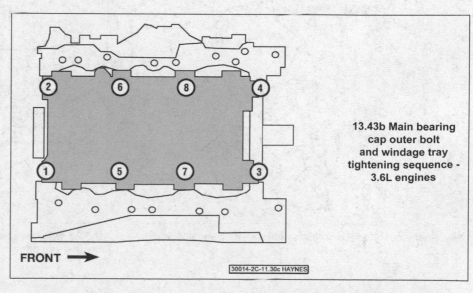

13.43b Main bearing cap outer bolt and windage tray tightening sequence - 3.6L engines

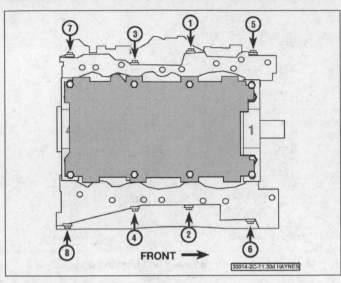

**13.43c Main bearing cap side bolt tightening sequence -
3.6L engines**

**14.3 Tap around the circumference of the oil seal with a hammer
and a punch to seat it squarely in the bore**

gauge or a dial indicator. The endplay should be correct if the crankshaft thrust faces aren't worn or damaged and if new bearings have been installed.

45   Rotate the crankshaft a number of times by hand to check for any obvious binding. It should rotate with a running torque of 50 in-lbs or less. If the running torque is too high, correct the problem at this time.

46   Install the new rear main oil seal (see Section 14).

14   Rear main oil seal installation

Note: *Refer to Chapter 2A, Section 19 or the 2.4L four-cylinder engine rear main oil seal re-placement procedure.*

2.5L engine

1   Clean the bore in the block/cap and the seal contact surface on the crankshaft. Check the crankshaft surface for scratches and nicks that could damage the new seal lip and cause oil leaks. If the crankshaft is damaged, the only alternative is a new or different crank-shaft.

2   Apply a light coat of engine oil or multi-purpose grease to the outer edge of the new seal, and to the seal lip.

3   Carefully work the seal lip over the end of the crankshaft and tap the seal in with a hammer and punch until it's seated in the bore (see illustration).

4.0L and 4.2L engines

4   Inspect the rear main bearing cap and engine block mating surfaces, as well as the seal grooves, for nicks, burrs and scratches. Remove any defects with a fine file or deburr-ing tool.

5   Install the semi-circular seal section in the block with the lip facing the front of the engine (see illustration).

6   Repeat the procedure to install the other seal half in the rear main bearing cap.

7   During final installation of the crankshaft (after the main bearing oil clearances have been checked with Plastigage) as described in Section 13, apply a thin, even coat of anaerobic type gasket sealant to the cham-fered areas of the cap or block (see illustra-tion). Don't get any sealant on the bearing face, crankshaft journal, seal ends or seal lips. Also, lubricate the seal lips with multi-purpose grease or engine assembly lube.

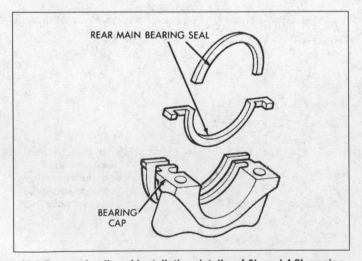

14.5 Rear main oil seal installation details - 4.0L and 4.2L engine

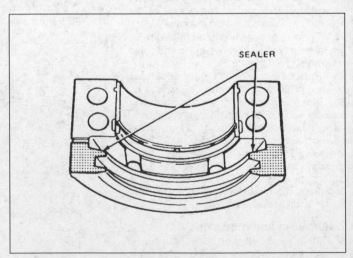

**14.7 Apply anaerobic sealant to the areas shown on the rear main
bearing cap prior to installation (don't get sealant in the grooves
or on the seal)**

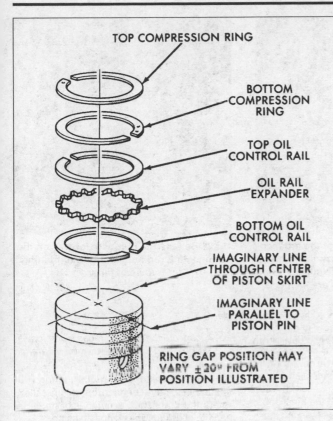

TOP COMPRESSION RING

BOTTOM COMPRESSION RING

TOP OIL CONTROL RAIL

OIL RAIL EXPANDER

BOTTOM OIL CONTROL RAIL

IMAGINARY LINE THROUGH CENTER OF PISTON SKIRT

IMAGINARY LINE PARALLEL TO PISTON PIN

RING GAP POSITION MAY VARY ±20° FROM POSITION ILLUSTRATED

15.5 Position the piston ring gaps as shown here before installing the piston/connecting rod assemblies in the engine

15.9 The arrow must point towards the front of the engine

5   Position the piston ring gaps at intervals around the piston (see illustration).

6   Slip a section of plastic or rubber hose over each connecting rod cap bolt.

7   Lubricate the piston and rings with clean engine oil and attach a piston ring compressor to the piston. Leave the skirt protruding about 1/4-inch to guide the piston into the cylinder. The rings must be compressed until they're flush with the piston.

8   Rotate the crankshaft until the number one connecting rod journal is at BDC (bottom dead center) and apply a coat of engine oil to the cylinder walls.

9   With the arrow or notch on top of the piston (see illustration) facing the front of the engine, gently insert the piston/connecting rod assembly into the number one cylinder bore and rest the bottom edge of the ring compressor on the engine block.

10   Tap the top edge of the ring compressor to make sure it's contacting the block around its entire circumference.

11   Gently tap on the top of the piston with the end of a wooden hammer handle (see illustration) while guiding the end of the connecting rod into place on the crankshaft journal. The piston rings may try to pop out of the ring compressor just before entering the cylinder bore, so keep some down pressure on

3.6L and 3.8L V6 engines

8   Use only a replacement rear seal that comes with a plastic alignment tool inside. The seal can not be centered properly without it.

9   Apply RTV sealant to the area where the seal cover will contact the oil pan surface.

10   Apply a bead of RTV sealant (1/4-inch) around the circumference of the seal retainer recess in the block, then install the seal and retainer over the crankshaft, making sure the two dowels align with the seal retainer. Install the bolts, but do not tighten them.

11   Once the seal is fully against the crankshaft, remove the plastic alignment tool and tighten the bolts to the torque listed in this Chapter's Specifications.

15   Pistons/connecting rods - installation and rod bearing oil clearance check

Caution: *On 3.6L V6 engines, new connecting rod cap bolts must be used when reassembling the engine, but use the old bolts when checking the connecting rod bearing oil clearance.*

1   Before installing the piston/connecting rod assemblies, the cylinder walls must be perfectly clean, the top edge of each cylinder must be chamfered, and the crankshaft must be in place.

2   Remove the cap from the end of the number one connecting rod (refer to the marks made during removal). Remove the original bearing inserts and wipe the bearing

surfaces of the connecting rod and cap with a clean, lint-free cloth. They must be kept spotlessly clean.

Connecting rod bearing oil clearance check

3   Clean the back side of the new upper bearing insert, then lay it in place in the connecting rod. Make sure the tab on the bearing fits into the recess in the rod. Don't hammer the bearing insert into place and be very careful not to nick or gouge the bearing face. Don't lubricate the bearing at this time.

4   Clean the back side of the other bearing insert and install it in the rod cap. Again, make sure the tab on the bearing fits into the recess in the cap, and don't apply any lubricant. It's critically important that the mating surfaces of the bearing and connecting rod are perfectly clean and oil free when they're assembled.

15.11 Drive the piston gently into the cylinder bore with the end of a wooden or plastic hammer handle

15.13 Lay the Plastigage strips on each rod bearing journal, parallel to the crankshaft centerline

15.17 Measuring the width of the crushed Plastigage to determine the rod bearing oil clearance (be sure to use the correct scale - standard and metric ones are included)

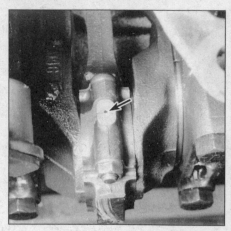

15.21 Be sure the numbers (arrow) on the connecting rod match before tightening the cap nuts

the ring compressor. Work slowly, and if any resistance is felt as the piston enters the cylinder, stop immediately. Find out what's hanging up and fix it before proceeding. Do not, for any reason, force the piston into the cylinder - you might break a ring and/or the piston.

12   Once the piston/connecting rod assembly is installed, the connecting rod bearing oil clearance must be checked before the rod cap is permanently bolted in place.

13   Cut a piece of the appropriate size Plastigage slightly shorter than the width of the connecting rod bearing and lay it in place on the number one connecting rod journal, parallel with the journal axis (see illustration).

14   Clean the connecting rod cap bearing face, remove the protective hoses from the connecting rod bolts and install the rod cap. Make sure the mating mark on the cap is on the same side as the mark on the connecting rod.

15   Install the nuts and tighten them to the torque listed in this Chapter's Specifcations, working up to it in three steps.

Note: *Use a thin-wall socket to avoid erroneous torque readings that can result if the socket is wedged between the rod cap and nut. If the socket tends to wedge itself between the nut and the cap, lift up on it slightly until it no longer contacts the cap. Do not rotate the crankshaft at any time during this operation.*

16   Remove the nuts or bolts and detach the rod cap, being very careful not to disturb the Plastigage. On 3.6L V6 engines, discard the cap bolts at this time as they cannot be reused.

Caution: *You MUST use new connecting rod bolts.*

17   Compare the width of the crushed Plastigage to the scale printed on the Plastigage envelope to obtain the oil clearance (see illustration). Compare it to the Specifications to make sure the clearance is correct.

18   If the clearance is not as specified, the bearing inserts may be the wrong size (which

means different ones will be required). Before deciding that different inserts are needed, make sure that no dirt or oil was between the bearing inserts and the connecting rod or cap when the clearance was measured. Also, recheck the journal diameter. If the Plastigage was wider at one end than the other, the journal may be tapered.

Final connecting rod installation

19   Carefully scrape all traces of the Plastigage material off the rod journal and/or bearing face. Be very careful not to scratch the bearing - use your fingernail or the edge of a credit card.

20   Make sure the bearing faces are perfectly clean, then apply a uniform layer of clean moly-base grease or engine assembly lube to both of them. You'll have to push the piston into the cylinder to expose the face of the bearing insert in the connecting rod - be sure to slip the protective hoses over the rod bolts first.

21   Slide the connecting rod back into place on the journal, remove the protective hoses from the rod cap bolts, install the rod cap and tighten the nuts or new bolts (3.6L V6 engines) to the torque listed in this Chapter's Specifications. Again, work up to the torque in three steps (see illustration).

22   Repeat the entire procedure for the remaining pistons/connecting rods.

23   The important points to remember are:

a) *Keep the back sides of the bearing inserts and the insides of the connecting rods and caps perfectly clean when assembling them.*

b) *Make sure you have the correct piston/ rod assembly for each cylinder.*

c) *The notch or mark on the piston must face the front of the engine.*

d) *Lubricate the cylinder walls with clean oil.*

e) *Lubricate the bearing faces when installing the rod caps after the oil clearance has been checked.*

24   After all the piston/connecting rod assemblies have been properly installed, rotate the crankshaft a number of times by hand to check for any obvious binding.

25   As a final step, the connecting rod endplay must be checked. Refer to Section 9 for this procedure.

26   Compare the measured endplay to the Specifications to make sure it's correct. If it was correct before disassembly and the original crankshaft and rods were reinstalled, it should still be right. If new rods or a new crankshaft were installed, the endplay may be inadequate. If so, the rods will have to be removed and taken to an automotive machine shop for resizing.

---

16   Balance shaft assembly - removal and installation (2.4L four-cylinder engine)

Removal

1   Remove the balance shaft assembly chain cover.

2   Remove the balance shaft sprocket bolt.

3   Loosen the balance shaft chain tensioner bolts.

4   Push the balance shaft inward, and pull or pry the balance shaft sprocket off of the shaft, so that the sprocket hangs freely. Remove the chain and sprocket.

5   Remove the balance shaft carrier-to-block bolts and remove the carrier assembly.

Installation

6   Install the carrier assembly and tighten the bolts to the torque listed in this Chapter's Specifications.

7   Remove the bolt from the other balance

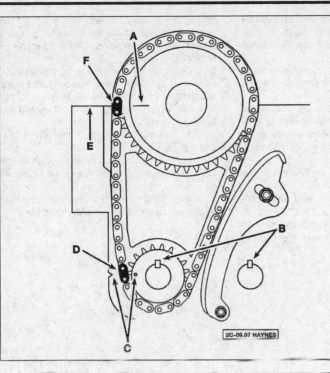

16.7 Rotate the crankshaft so that the No. 1 TDC mark on the crankshaft sprocket is aligned with the parting line of the main bearing cap/bedplate. When the balance shaft chain and balance shaft driven-sprocket are installed, they must also be aligned as shown

A   Mark on crankshaft sprocket
B   Balance shaft keyways pointing up
C   Alignment marks on counter balance sprocket and counter balance carrier case
D   Plated link on balance shaft chain
E   Parting line of main bearing cap/bedplate
F   Plated link on balance shaft chain

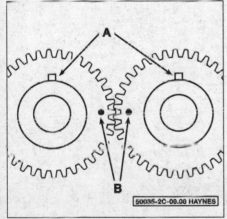

16.8 Align the balance shaft keyways and balance shaft gear marks as shown

A Balance shaft keyways pointing up
B Alignment marks on balance shaft gears

shaft and remove the gear cover. Rotate the crankshaft to the No. 1 top-dead-center (TDC) position, so that the No. 1 TDC timing mark on the crankshaft sprocket is aligned with the parting line of the main bearing cap (see illustration).

8   Align both balance shaft keyways at the 12 o'clock position (pointing toward the top of the engine) so that both balance shaft gear timing dots are pointed to each other (see illustration). Install the gear cover and tighten the bolt/stud to the torque listed in this Chapter's Specifications.

9   Install the chain so that the each of the plated links are aligned with each of the timing marks on the crankshaft and balance shaft sprockets, then slide the sprocket onto the balance shaft (see illustration 25.7).

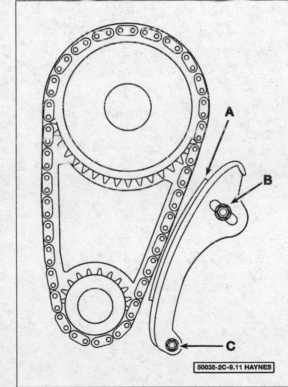

16.11 To adjust the balance shaft chain tensioner, position a 0.030-inch (1 mm) thick x 2.75-inch (70 mm) long shim spacer between the chain and tensioner, push on the tensioner firmly, then tighten the tensioner arm bolt and tensioner pivot bolt

A   0.039 (1 mm) thick shim
B   Tensioner adjuster bolt
C   Tensioner pivot bolt

10   Check the timing marks, plated links and keyways for correct alignment, then install both of the balance bolts and tighten to the torque listed in this Chapter's Specifications.
Note: *To prevent the crankshaft from rotating, wedge a wooden block between a crankshaft counterweight and the block.*

11   Position the chain tensioner and loosely install the tensioner bolts. Install the chain guide, making sure the tab is in the slot. Posi-tion a 0.039-inch thick x 2.75-inch long spac-er-shim between the tensioner and chain (see illustration). Push firmly on the tensioner, then tighten the top tensioner arm bolt, then tighten the lower tensioner pivot bolt - each to the torque listed in this Chapter's Specifications. Remove the spacer-shim.

12   Install the chain cover and tighten the bolts to the torque listed in this Chapter's Specifications.

17 Initial start-up and break-in after overhaul

Warning: *Have a fire extinguisher handy when starting the engine for the first time.*

1   Once the engine has been installed in the vehicle, double-check the engine oil and coolant levels.

2   With the spark plugs out of the engine and the ignition system disabled (see Section 3, Steps 4 and 5), crank the engine until oil pressure registers on the gauge or the light goes out.

3   Install the spark plugs, hook up the plug wires, if equipped, or install the ignition coils and restore the ignition and fuel system functions (see Chapter 1).

4   Start the engine. It may take a few moments for the fuel system to build up pressure, but the engine should start without a great deal of effort.

Note: *If backfiring occurs through the carburetor or throttle body, recheck the valve timing and ignition timing.*

5   After the engine starts, it should be allowed to warm up to normal operating temperature. While the engine is warming up, make a thorough check for fuel, oil and coolant leaks.

6   Shut the engine off and recheck the engine oil and coolant levels.

7   Drive the vehicle to an area with minimum traffic, accelerate at full throttle from 30 to 50 mph, then allow the vehicle to slow to 30 mph with the throttle closed. Repeat the procedure 10 or 12 times. This will load the piston rings and cause them to seat properly against the cylinder walls. Check again for oil and coolant leaks.

8   Drive the vehicle gently for the first 500 miles (no sustained high speeds) and keep a constant check on the oil level. It is not unusual for an engine to use oil during the break-in period.

9   At approximately 500 to 600 miles, change the oil and filter.

10   For the next few hundred miles, drive the vehicle normally. Do not pamper it or abuse it.

11   After 2000 miles, change the oil and filter again and consider the engine broken in.

Chapter 3
Cooling, heating and air conditioning systems

Contents

Specifications

General

Coolant capacity	See Chapter 1
Drivebelt tension	See Chapter 1
Radiator cap pressure rating	
2.4L engine	18 to 21 psi
2.5L engine	12 to 15 psi
Inline six-cylinder engines	16 to 18 psi
3.6L V6 engine	14 to 18 psi
3.8L V6 engine	18 to 21 psi
Thermostat rating (opening temperature)	192 to 195-degrees F
Refrigerant type	
1995 and earlier models	R-12
1997 through 2014 models	R-134a
2015 and later models	Either R-134a or R-1234yf (consult underhood label)
Refrigerant capacity	
1995 and earlier models	2.0 lbs
1997 through 2002 models	1.25 lbs
2003 through 2005 models	Refer to the underhood refrigeration label
2006 through 2010 models	1.125 lbs
2011 through 2014 models	1.38 lbs
2015 and later models	
R-134a systems	1.13 lbs
R-1234yf systems	1.25 lbs

Torque specifications — Ft-lbs (unless otherwise indicated)

Note: *One foot-pound (ft-lb) of torque is equivalent to 12 inch-pounds (in-lbs) of torque. Torque values below approximately 15 foot-pounds are expressed in inch-pounds, because most foot-pound torque wrenches are not accurate at these smaller values.*

2.4L engine	
Thermostat housing bolts	20
Water pump bolts	105 in-lbs
2.5L engine	
Fan clutch-to-water pump bolts	15 to 22
Fan-to-fan clutch nuts	18
Thermostat housing bolts	156 in-lbs
Water pump bolts	17
4.0L and 4.2L engines	
Fan clutch-to-water pump bolts	18
Fan-to-fan clutch nuts	18
Thermostat housing bolts	156 in-lbs
Water pump attaching bolts	9 to 18
3.6L V6 engine	
Thermostat housing bolts	108 in-lbs
Water inlet tube bolts	96 in-lbs
Water pump mounting bolts	96 in-lbs
3.8L V6	
Thermostat mounting bolts	17
Water pump mounting bolts	105 in-lbs

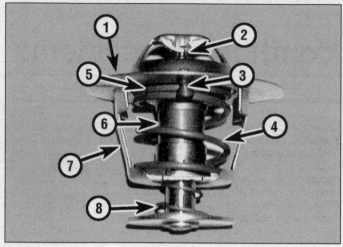

1.2 Typical thermostat

1	Flange	5	Valve seal
2	Piston	6	Valve
3	Jiggle valve	7	Frame
4	Main coil spring	8	Secondary coil spring

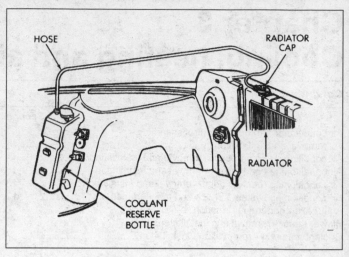

1.3 The coolant reserve system

1   General information

Engine cooling system

1   All vehicles covered by this manual employ a pressurized engine cooling system with thermostatically controlled coolant circulation. An impeller type water pump mounted on the front of the block pumps coolant through the engine. The coolant flows around each cylinder and toward the rear of the engine. Cast-in coolant passages direct coolant around the intake and exhaust ports, near the spark plug areas and in close proximity to the exhaust valve guides.

2   A wax pellet type thermostat is located in a housing near the front of the engine. During warm up, the closed thermostat allows the engine to reach operating temperature quickly. The thermostat maintains the normal operating temperature, and at the same time prevents the engine from overheating (see illustration).

3   The cooling system is sealed by a pressure-type radiator cap, which raises the boiling point of the coolant and increases the cooling efficiency of the radiator. If the system pressure exceeds the cap pressure relief value, the excess pressure in the system forces the spring-loaded valve inside the cap off its seat and allows the coolant to escape through the overflow tube into a coolant reservoir. When the system cools, the excess coolant is automatically drawn from the reservoir back into the radiator (see illustration).

4   The coolant reservoir does double duty as both the point at which fresh coolant is added to the cooling system to maintain the proper fluid level and as a holding tank for overheated coolant.

5   This type of cooling system is known as a closed design because coolant that escapes past the pressure cap is saved and reused.

Heating system

6   The heating system consists of a blower fan and heater core located in the heater box, the hoses connecting the heater core to the engine cooling system and the heater/air conditioning control head on the dashboard. Hot engine coolant is circulated through the heater core. When the heater mode is activated, a flap door opens to expose the heater box to the passenger compartment. A fan switch on the control head activates the blower motor, which forces air through the core, heating the air.

Air conditioning system

7   The air conditioning system consists of a condenser mounted in front of the radiator, an evaporator mounted adjacent to the heater core, a compressor mounted on the engine, a receiver/drier which contains a high pressure relief valve and the plumbing connecting all of the above components.

8   A blower fan forces the warmer air of the passenger compartment through the evaporator core (sort of a radiator-in-reverse), transferring the heat from the air to the refrigerant. The liquid refrigerant boils off into low pressure vapor, taking the heat with it when it leaves the evaporator.

2   Antifreeze - general information

Warning: *Do not allow antifreeze to come in contact with your skin or painted surfaces of the vehicle. Rinse off spills immediately with plenty of water. Never leave antifreeze lying around in an open container or in a puddle in the driveway or on the garage floor. Children and pets are attracted by its sweet smell. Antifreeze is fatal if ingested in sufficient quantity. Check with local authorities before disposing of used antifreeze. Many communities have collection centers which will see that antifreeze is disposed of safely. Antifreeze is also combustible, so don't store or use it near open flames.*

1   The cooling system should be filled with a water/ethylene glycol based antifreeze solution, which will prevent freezing down to at least negative 20-degrees F, or lower if local climate requires it. It also provides protection against corrosion and increases the coolant boiling point.

2   The cooling system should be drained, flushed and refilled at the specified intervals (see Chapter 1). Old or contaminated antifreeze solutions are likely to cause damage and encourage the formation of rust and scale in the system. Use distilled water with the antifreeze.

3   Before adding antifreeze, check all hose connections, because antifreeze tends to search out and leak through very minute openings. Engines don't normally consume coolant, so if the level goes down, find the cause and correct it.

4   The exact mixture of antifreeze-to-water which you should use depends on the relative weather conditions. The mixture should contain at least 50 percent antifreeze, but should never contain more than 70 percent antifreeze. Consult the mixture ratio chart on the antifreeze container before adding coolant. Hydrometers are available at most auto parts stores to test the coolant. Use antifreeze which meets the vehicle manufacturer's specifications.

3.9 Loosen the hose clamp, then detach the hose from the thermostat housing

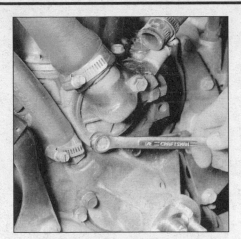

3.11a Remove the thermostat housing bolts

3.11b Thermostat assembly - 3.6L V6 engine

3 Thermostat - check and replacement

Warning: *Do not remove the radiator cap, drain the coolant or replace the thermostat until the engine has cooled completely.*

Check

1   Before assuming the thermostat is to blame for a cooling system problem, check the coolant level, drivebelt tension (see Chapter 1) and temperature gauge (or light) operation.

2   If the engine seems to be taking a long time to warm up (based on heater output or temperature gauge operation), the thermostat is probably stuck open. Replace the thermostat with a new one.

3   If the engine runs hot, use your hand to check the temperature of the upper radiator hose. If the hose isn't hot, but the engine is, the thermostat is probably stuck closed, preventing the coolant inside the engine from escaping to the radiator. Replace the thermostat.

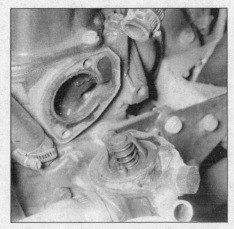

3.12 Note how the thermostat is installed

Caution: *Don't drive the vehicle without a thermostat. The computer may stay in open loop and emissions and fuel economy will suffer.*

4   If the upper radiator hose is hot, it means that the coolant is flowing and the thermostat is open. Consult the *Troubleshooting* section at the front of this manual for cooling system diagnosis.

Replacement

Note: *On 3.6L engines, the thermostat is an integral part of the housing and must be replaced as an assembly.*

5   Disconnect the cable from the negative terminal of the battery (see Chapter 5).

6   Drain the cooling system (see Chapter 1). If the coolant is relatively new or in good condition, save it and reuse it.

7   On 3.6L enignes, remove the air filter housing (see Chapter 4).

8   Follow the upper radiator hose to the engine to locate the thermostat housing.

Note: *On 3.6L engines, the thermostat is located at the right end of the engine, under the front valve cover.*

9   Loosen the hose clamp, then detach the hose from the fitting (see illustration). If it's stuck, grasp it near the end with a pair of adjustable pliers and twist it to break the seal, then pull it off. If the hose is old or deteriorated, cut it off and install a new one.

10   If the outer surface of the large fitting that mates with the hose is deteriorated (corroded, pitted, etc.) it may be damaged further by hose removal. If it is, the thermostat housing cover will have to be replaced.

11   Remove the bolts and detach the housing cover (see illustrations). If the cover is stuck, tap it with a soft-face hammer to jar it loose. Be prepared for some coolant to spill as the gasket seal is broken.

12   Note how it's installed (which end is facing into the cylinder head) (see illustration), then remove the thermostat.

13   Stuff a rag into the engine opening, then remove all traces of old gasket material and sealant from the housing and cover with a gasket scraper. Remove the rag from the opening and clean the gasket mating surfaces with lacquer thinner or acetone.

14   Install the new thermostat in the housing. Make sure the correct end faces up - the spring end is normally directed into the engine.

15   Apply a thin, uniform layer of RTV sealant to both sides of the new gasket and position it on the housing.

16   Install the cover and bolts. Tighten the bolts to the torque listed in this Chapter's Specifications.

17   Reattach the hose to the fitting and tighten the hose clamp securely.

18   Refill the cooling system (see Chapter 1).

19   Start the engine and allow it to reach normal operating temperature, then check for leaks and proper thermostat operation (as described in Steps 2 through 4).

4 Radiator - removal and installation

Warning: *The air conditioning system is under high pressure. Do not loosen any hose fittings or remove any components until after the system has been discharged by a dealer service department or service station. Always wear eye protection when disconnecting air conditioning system fittings.*

Warning: *Wait until the engine is completely cool before beginning this procedure.*

Removal

1   On 2012 and later models, have the air conditioning system discharged (see Warning above).

2   Disconnect the negative battery cable from the battery (see Chapter 5).

3   Drain the cooling system (see Chapter 1). If the coolant is relatively new or in good condition, save it and reuse it.

4   On 2012 and later models, remove the air filter housing (see Chapter 4).

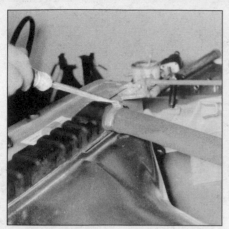

4.5a Loosen the upper radiator hose

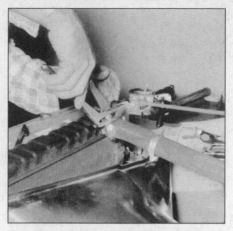

4.5b Grasp the hose with adjustable pliers and twist it to break the seal

4.8a Remove the bolts that attach the fan shroud to the radiator

4.8b Lift the fan shroud out of the engine compartment

4.9a Loosen the lower radiator hose clamp

4.9b Use retaining ring pliers to break the seal on the lower radiator hose

5   Loosen the hose clamps, then detach the upper radiator hose from the fitting (see illustration). If it's stuck, grasp the hose near the end with a pair of adjustable pliers and twist it to break the seal (see illustration), then pull it off - be careful not to distort the radiator fittings! If the hose is old or deteriorated, cut it off and install a new one.

6   On 2012 and later models, remove the side air deflector plastic push-pins and remove the air deflectors form the sides of the radiator then disconnect the lines to the condenser (see Section 15). Plug the lines and fittings.

7   Disconnect the reservoir hose from the radiator filler neck and, on 3.6L models, remove the coolant reservoir from the fan shroud. On 4.0L engines, set the coolant reservoir aside and unbolt and set aside the power steering fluid reservoir.

8   Remove the bolts that attach the shroud to the radiator and lift the shroud out of the engine compartment (see illustrations).

9   Loosen the clamp (see illustration) and detach the lower hose from the radiator. To ease and speed the removal of the lower radiator hose use retaining ring pliers (if available) to separate the hose from the radiator (see illustration).

10   If the vehicle is equipped with an automatic transmission, disconnect the cooler lines from the radiator. Use a drip pan to catch spilled fluid.

11   Plug the lines and fittings.

12   Remove the radiator mounting bolts (see illustration).

13   Carefully lift out the radiator (see illus-

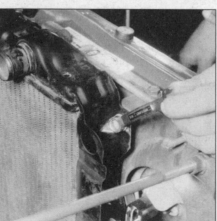

4.12 Remove the radiator mounting bolts

tration). Don't spill coolant on the vehicle or scratch the paint.

Note: *On 3.6L models, the condenser must be removed with the radiator, then unbolted once the assembly is out of the vehicle.*

14   With the radiator removed, it can be inspected for leaks and damage. If it needs repair, have a radiator shop or dealer service

4.13 Carefully lift the radiator out of the engine compartment

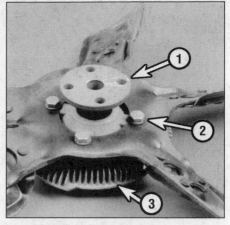

5.6 Remove the bolts attaching the clutch-fan to the water pump pulley

5.7 Remove the clutch-fan assembly out of the engine compartment

5.9 The clutch can now be unbolted from the fan

1   Mounting flange
2   Fan-to-clutch bolt
3   Fan clutch

department perform the work as special techniques are required.

15   Bugs and dirt can be removed from the radiator with compressed air and a soft brush. Don't bend the cooling fins as this is done.

16   Check the radiator mounts for deterioration and make sure there's nothing in them when the radiator is installed.

Installation

17   Installation is the reverse of the removal procedure.

18   After installation, fill the cooling system with the proper mixture of antifreeze and water. Refer to Chapter 1 if necessary.

19   Start the engine and check for leaks. Allow the engine to reach normal operating temperature, indicated by the upper radiator hose becoming hot. Recheck the coolant level and add more if required.

20   If you're working on an automatic transmission equipped vehicle, check and add fluid as needed.

21   On 2012 and later models, take the vehicle back to the shop that discharged it. Have the air conditioning system evacuated, charged and leak tested.

---

5   Engine cooling fan and clutch - check, removal and installation

Warning: *To avoid possible injury or damage, DO NOT operate the engine with a damaged fan. Do not attempt to repair fan blades - replace a damaged fan with a new one. All the vehicles covered in this manual are equipped with a temperature-controlled viscous fan clutch. It is driven by the water pump pulley and automatically increases or decreases the speed of the fan to provide the radiator proper cooling.*

Note: *2007 and later models have electric fans only.*

Belt driven fans
Check

1   Disconnect the negative battery cable and rock the fan back and forth by hand to check for excessive bearing play.

2   With the engine cold, turn the fan blades by hand. The fan should turn freely.

3   Visually inspect for substantial leakage from the clutch assembly. If problems are noted, replace the clutch assembly.

4   With the engine completely warmed up, turn off the ignition switch and disconnect the negative battery cable from the battery. Turn the fan by hand. Some drag should be evident. If the fan turns easily, replace the fan clutch.

Removal and installation

Caution: *4.0L models with the serpentine drivebelt are equipped with reverse-direction engine cooling fans. On these models, be sure to install only cooling fans and fan clutches marked REVERSE or the engine may be overheated and become damaged. However, keep in mind that the fan assembly drive nut is tightened clockwise.*

5   Disconnect the negative battery cable (see Chapter 5). Remove the fan shroud mounting screws and detach the shroud (see Section 4, 5).

6   Remove the fan clutch assembly:

a) *On conventional drivebelt models, remove the bolts/nuts attaching the fan clutch assembly to the water pump pulley (see illustration).*

b) *On serpentine drivebelt models, a special tool may be required to secure the water pump pulley while a large open-end wrench is used to loosen the fan drive nut. Sometimes it is possible to hold the water pump pulley by applying considerable hand pressure to the serpentine belt while the larger nut is loosened, but it may require the tool if the fan drive nut is excessively tight. Rotate the fan drive nut counterclockwise to loosen.*

7   Lift the fan/clutch assembly (and shroud, if necessary) out of the engine compartment (see illustration).

8   Carefully inspect the fan blades for damage and defects. Replace the fan if it's damaged.

9   At this point, the fan may be unbolted from the clutch, if necessary (see illustration). If the fan clutch is stored, position it with the radiator side facing down.

10   Installation is the reverse of removal.

a) *On conventional drivebelt models, tighten the fan clutch mounting bolts/nuts to the torque listed in this Chapter's Specifications.*

b) *On serpentine drivebelt models, tighten the fan drive nut securely. Rotate the fan drive nut clockwise to tighten.*

Electric fans (V6 engines)
Check

Note: *On 3.6L V6 engines, the electric fan is controlled by the Powertrain Control Module (PCM) and the electric cooling fan is not serviceable. Any failure of the fan blade, electric motor or fan shroud requires replacement of the fan shroud/module.*

3.8L V6 engine

11   If the engine is getting hot (or overheating) and the cooling fan is not coming on, check the fuse first. If the fuse is okay, unplug the electrical connector for the fan motor and apply battery voltage to the fan. Use a fused jumper wire on terminal A and another jumper wire going to ground on terminal B. If either fan motor doesn't come on, replace it.

Caution: *Do not apply battery power to the harness side of the connector.*

12   If the fan motors are okay, check the fan relay.

13   Locate the fan relays in the engine compartment fuse/relay box (see Chapter 12).

14   Test the relay (see Chapter 12).

15   If the fuse, motor and relay are func-

6.1a The temperature sending unit for the four-cylinder engine is at the back of the cylinder head

6.1b The temperature sending unit on inline six-cylinder engines is at the back of the cylinder head

8.4 The water pump weep hole will drip coolant when the seal on the pump shaft fails (pump removed from engine for clarity)

tional, check all wiring and connections to the fan motor. If no obvious problems are found, have the cooling fan system diagnosed by a dealer service department or repair shop with the proper diagnostic equipment.

Removal and installation

16   Drain the cooling system (see Chapter 1), then remove the upper radiator hose.
17   Remove the coolant reservoir.
18   Disconnect the fan electrical connector.
19   Remove the mounting fasteners for the fan assembly, then remove the assembly.
20   Installation is the reverse of removal. Be sure to tighten the fan assembly fasteners securely. Refer to Chapter 1 and refill the cooling system.

6   Coolant temperature sending unit - check and replacement

Note: *On 3.6L and 3.8L V6 engines, the temperature sending unit has been integrated into the coolant temperature sensor (see Chapter 6).*
Warning: *Wait until the engine is completely cool before beginning this procedure.*
1   The coolant temperature indicator system is composed of a light or temperature gauge mounted in the instrument panel and a coolant temperature sending unit mounted on the engine (see illustrations). Some vehicles have more than one sending unit, but only one is used for the indicator system.
2   If an overheating indication occurs, check the coolant level in the system and then make sure the wiring between the light or gauge and the sending unit is secure and all fuses are intact.
3   When the ignition switch is turned on and the starter motor is turning, the indicator light should be on (overheated engine indication).
4   If the light is not on, the bulb may be burned out, the ignition switch may be faulty or the circuit may be open. Test the circuit by grounding the wire to the sending unit while

the ignition is on (engine not running for safety). If the gauge deflects full scale or the light comes on, replace the sending unit.
5   As soon as the engine starts, the light should go out and remain out unless the engine overheats. Failure of the light to go out may be due to a grounded wire between the light and the sending unit, a defective sending unit or a faulty ignition switch. Check the coolant to make sure it's the proper type. Plain water may have too low a boiling point to activate the sending unit.
6   If the sending unit must be replaced, simply unscrew it from the engine and install the replacement.Use sealant on the threads. There will be some coolant loss as the unit is removed, so be prepared to catch it. Check the level after the unit has been installed.

7   Coolant reservoir - removal and installation

Warning: *Wait until the engine is completely cool before beginning this procedure.*
1   On 1995 and earlier models, remove the windshield washer fluid reservoir and its mounting bracket.
2   Loosen the hose clamps and detach the hose(s) from the reservoir.
3   Remove the screws or retaining strap and lift the reservoir from the vehicle.
Note: *On 2012 and later models, the reservoir clips onto the fan shroud and no fasteners are used.*
4   Installation is the reverse of removal.
5   Add coolant to the reservoir, run the engine until it reaches normal operating temperature, then allow it to cool. Recheck the coolant level, adding as necessary.

8   Water pump - check

1   A failure in the water pump can cause serious engine damage due to overheating.

2   There are three ways to check the operation of the water pump while it's installed on the engine. If the pump is defective, it should be replaced with a new or rebuilt unit.
3   With the engine running at normal operating temperature, squeeze the upper radiator hose. If the water pump is working properly, a pressure surge should be felt as the hose is released.
Warning: *Keep your hands away from the fan blades!*
4   Water pumps are equipped with weep or vent holes. If a failure occurs in the pump seal, coolant will leak from the hole. In most cases you'll need a flashlight to find the hole on the water pump from underneath to check for leaks (see illustration).
5   If the water pump shaft bearings fail there may be a howling sound at the front of the engine while it's running. Shaft wear can be felt if the water pump pulley is rocked up and down (see illustration). Don't mistake drivebelt slippage, which causes a squealing sound, for water pump bearing failure.

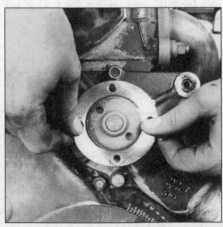

8.5 Grasp the water pump flange and try to rock the shaft back and forth for play (fan and pulley removed for clarity)

9.6 Remove the idler pulley (3.6L engine)

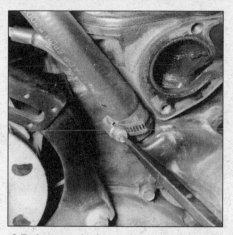

9.7a Loosen the hose clamps and detach the hoses from the water pump

9.7b Disconnect the bypass hose (A) and lower radiator hose (B) (3.6L engine)

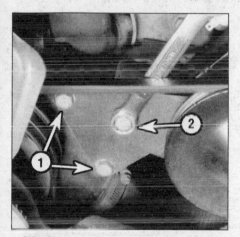

9.8a Remove the power steering pump (2.5L engine shown, 4.2L engine similar)

1   Mounting bolt
2   Adjusting bolt

9.8b Loosen the adjusting bolt on the alternator (2.5L engine shown, 4.2L engine similar)

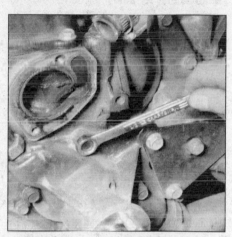

9.9a Remove the bolts and detach the water pump from the engine (four-cylinder engine shown, inline six-cylinder engines similar)

9   Water pump - replacement

Warning: *Wait until the engine is completely cool before beginning this procedure.*
Caution: *All 4.0L engines and some 2.5L and 4.2L engines have a reverse rotating water pump and viscous fan. This type of water pump can be identified by the words "RE-VERSE" imprinted on the viscous drive and/or inner side of the fan. On the body of the water pump "REV" is cast, and an "R" is stamped into the water pump impeller. The installation of the wrong pump will cause major engine damage.*

1   Disconnect the negative battery cable from the battery (see Chapter 5).
2   Drain the cooling system (see Chapter 3). If the coolant is relatively new or in good condition, save it and reuse it.
3   On 3.6L engines, remove the air filter housing and inlet housing (see Chapter 4).
4   Remove the cooling fan and shroud (see Section 5).

5   Remove the drivebelts (see Chapter 1) and the pulley at the end of the water pump shaft. On 2007 and later 3.8L engines, the pulley can remain with the water pump and on all 3.6L engines the pulley is not removable from the pump. Remove the pulley bolts, then shift the pulley around until all the water pump bolts can be accessed and removed, one at a time.
6   On 3.6L engines, remove the drivebelt idler pulley (see illustration).
7   Loosen the clamps and detach the hoses from the water pump (see illustrations). If they're stuck, grasp each hose near the end with a pair of adjustable pliers and twist it to break the seal, then pull it off. If the hoses are deteriorated, cut them off and install new ones.
8   Remove all accessory brackets from the water pump. When removing the power steering pump (see illustrations), and air conditioning compressor, don't disconnect the hoses. Tie the units aside with the hoses attached. On 2.4L four-cylinder engines, remove the

timing belt, timing belt idler pulley, camshaft sprockets and rear timing belt cover (see Chapter 2A).
9   Remove the bolts and detach the water pump from the engine. Note the locations of the various lengths and different types of bolts as they're removed to ensure correct installation (see illustrations).
10   Clean the bolt threads and the threaded holes in the engine to remove corrosion and sealant.
11   Compare the new pump to the old one to make sure they're identical (see illustrations).
12   Remove all traces of old gasket material from the engine with a gasket scraper.
13   Clean the engine and new water pump mating surfaces with lacquer thinner or acetone.
14   Apply a thin coat of RTV sealant to the engine side of the new gasket. On all V6 engines, the water pump is sealed with a rubber seal. Insert the rubber seal carefully before installing the pump, without using RTV sealant.

9.9b Note the location and various lengths and different types of bolts as they're removed (four-cylinder engine shown, inline six-cylinder engines similar)

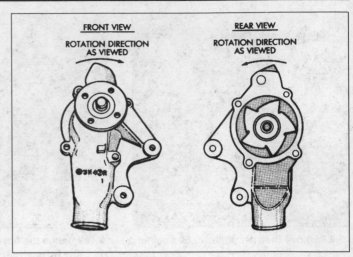

9.11a The water pump for the 2.5L and 4.2L engines with the "V" type drivebelts (forward rotating)

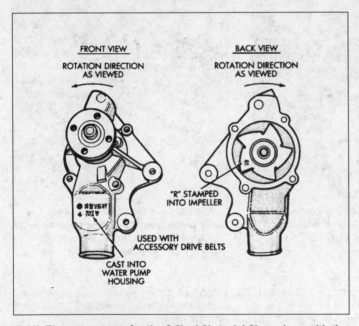

9.11b The water pump for the 2.5L, 4.0L and 4.2L engines with the serpentine drivebelt (reverse rotating)

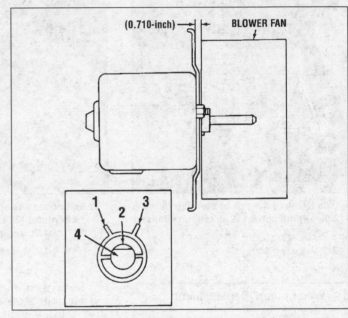

10.5 Pry the clip ears (1 and 3) off the flat surface (2) of the motor shaft (4) - bend the retaining clip like the original when installing it

15   Apply a thin layer of RTV sealant to the gasket mating surface of the new pump, then carefully mate the gasket and the pump. Slip a couple of bolts through the pump mounting holes to hold the gasket in place. On 2.4L four-cylinder engines, apply a thin coat of RTV sealant to the new water pump O-ring and position it in the grove on the back of the water pump.

Caution: *Make sure the O-ring is correctly seated in the water pump groove to avoid a coolant leak.*

16   Carefully attach the pump and gasket to the engine and thread the bolts into the holes finger-tight.

17   Install the remaining bolts. Tighten them to the torque listed in this Chapter's Specifica-

tions in 1/4-turn increments. Don't overtighten them or the pump may be distorted.

18   Reinstall all parts removed for access to the pump.

19   Refill the cooling system and check the drivebelt tension (see Chapter 1). Run the engine and check for leaks.

---

10   Blower motor - removal and installation

Warning: *Some models covered by this manual are equipped with airbags. Always disable the airbag system when working in the vicinity of airbag system components (see Chapter 12).*

1995 and earlier models

Heater blower motor

Warning: *Wait until the engine is completely cool before beginning this procedure.*

Removal

1   Disconnect the cable from the negative terminal of the battery (see Chapter 5).

2   Remove the heater core housing (see Section 11).

3   Disconnect the blower motor wires.

4   Unscrew the blower motor screws and remove the blower motor from the housing.

5   Detach the fan retainer clip from the fan hub (see illustration).

6   Slip the fan off the old motor shaft, remove the motor-to-cover attaching nuts and

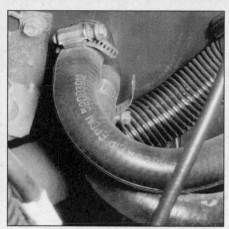

11.3 Disconnect the heater hoses at the heater core

11.4a Disconnect the heater control cable (right side)

11.4b Disconnect the heater control cable (center)

pull the motor off the cover.

7   Mount the new motor on the cover and slip the fan onto the shaft. Install the retainer clip.

Installation

8   Place the blower motor in position and install the mounting screws.

9   Install the heater core housing (see Section 11), if removed.

10   Reconnect the wires and battery cable. Test the motor in operation.

Air conditioning blower motor

Removal

11   Disconnect the negative cable from the battery (see Chapter 5).

12   Remove the mounting screws and lower the air conditioning evaporator core housing to access the blower motor attaching screws (it's not necessary to discharge the air conditioning system to remove the A/C blower motor) (see Section 11, Illustration 11.19).

13   Disconnect the blower motor wires.

14   Remove the blower motor mounting screws.

15   Lift the blower motor from the vehicle (see Steps 5 and 6 for replacing the blower motor).

Installation

16   Place the blower motor in position and install the mounting screws.

17   Raise the air conditioning evaporator core housing and install the mounting screws.

1997 through 2001 models

Note: *The blower motor on these models is removed from the passenger's side of the engine compartment.*

18   Remove the battery (see Chapter 5).

19   Remove the Powertrain Control Module (PCM) mounting screws, then pull the PCM out and reposition it.

20   Disconnect the electrical connector from the blower motor.

21   Remove the three blower motor mounting screws and detach the blower motor from the heater/evaporator core housing.

22   Installation is the reverse of removal.

2002 and later models

Note: *The blower motor on these models is removed from under the instrument panel.*

23   Disconnect the cable from the negative terminal of the battery (see Chapter 5).

24   Disconnect the electrical connector from the blower motor.

25   On 2002 through 2006 models, disengage the retaining tab and rotate the blower motor counterclockwise to remove it.

26   On 2007 and later models, remove the three mounting screws and lower the blower motor from the housing.

27   Installation is the reverse of removal.

11   Heater core and air conditioner evaporator core - replacement

Warning: *Wait until the engine is completely cool before beginning this procedure.*

Warning: *The air conditioning system is under high pressure. DO NOT disconnect any refrigerant fittings until after the system has been discharged by a dealer service department or service station.*

Warning: *Some models covered by this manual are equipped with airbags. Always disable the airbag system when working in the vicinity of airbag system components (see Chapter 12).*

Note: *On 1997 and later models, the HVAC unit must be removed from the vehicle in order to remove either the heater or the AC evaporator core.*

Heater core

Removal

1   Have the air conditioning system evacuated and the refrigerant recovered at a dealership or air conditioning service shop.

2   Disconnect the negative battery cable, then drain the cooling system (see Chapter 5).

3   Disconnect the heater hoses at the heater core inlet and outlet (see illustration). Disconnect the two refrigerant lines at the firewall.

4   Disconnect the heater control cables (see illustrations) and defroster duct.

5   On 1997 and later models, remove the instrument panel (see Chapter 11).

6   Disconnect the housing attaching nuts from the studs on the engine compartment side of the firewall (see illustration).

7   Tilt the heater housing assembly down and pull it to the rear. You can now remove the heater housing assembly from the vehicle.

8   Remove the retaining screws on the housing assembly and remove the heater core by pulling it straight out of the housing.

Installation

9   Reinstall the parts in the reverse order of removal.

Note: *Be sure the housing studs are extended through the firewall. Also avoid trapping wires between the housing fresh air inlet and the firewall and the heater housing.*

10   Refill the cooling system.

11   Start the engine and check for proper operation and leaks. Do not operate the air conditioning system until the system has been recharged by the shop that discharged it.

Evaporator core

Removal

Note: *On 1997 and later models, remove the instrument panel (see Chapter 11).*

12   Have the air conditioning system discharged (see the Warning at the beginning of this Section).

13   Disconnect the cable from the negative terminal of the battery (see Chapter 5).

14   On 1997 and later models, drain the cooling system (see Chapter 1).

15   Disconnect the inlet and receiver/drier-to-evaporator hoses.

16   Remove the retaining screws, hose clamps and dash grommet.

17   On older models, the housing is secured to the instrument panel's lower edge - lower the evaporator housing from the instrument panel (see illustration). On 1997 and later models, remove the HVAC housing from the

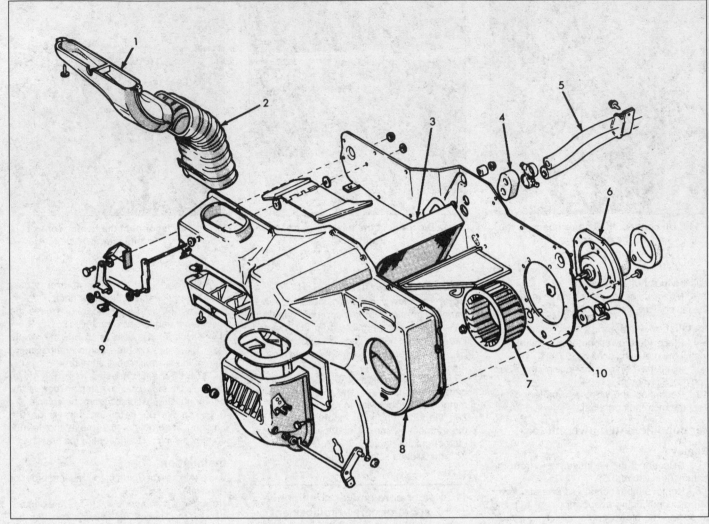

11.6 Heating system assembly (exploded view)

1	Defroster nozzle	5	Hose	9	Cable
2	Defroster duct	6	Blower motor	10	Heater housing cover
3	Heater core	7	Fan		
4	Seal	8	Heater housing		

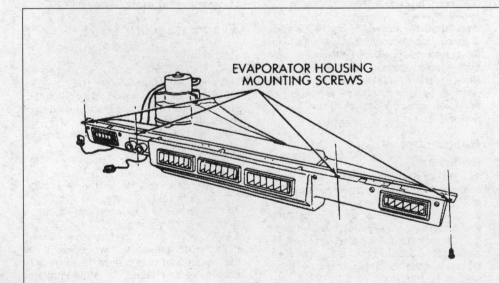

EVAPORATOR HOUSING
MOUNTING SCREWS

**11.17 Location of evaporative
housing-to-instrument panel
screws (early models)**

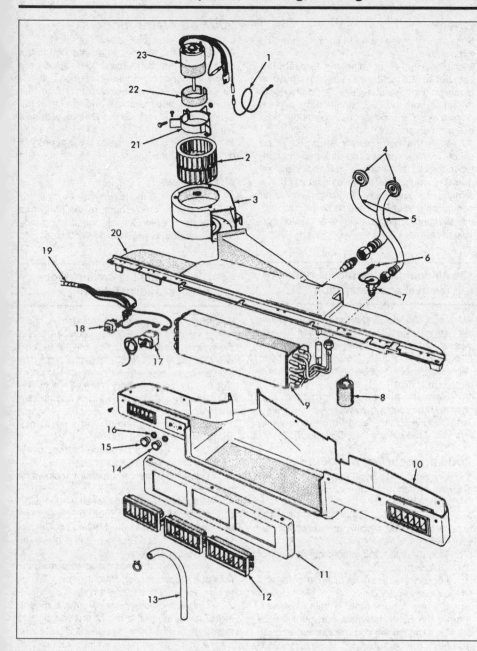

11.19 Evaporator housing assembly (early models)

1   Feed wire
2   Blower fan
3   Blower housing
4   Grommet
5   Hose
6   Capillary tube
7   Expansion valve
8   Insulation
9   Evaporative core
10 Lower housing
11 Louver panel
12 Louver
13 Drain tube
14 Temperature control knob
15 Fan control knob
16 Nut
17 Thermostat
18 Fan control switch
19 Switch harness
20 Upper housing
21 Bracket
22 Insulation
23 Blower motor

firewall, then release the clips securing the upper and lower halves of the housing to access the heater core or evaporator core.

18   Lower the evaporator housing from the dash panel. You can now remove the evaporator housing assembly from the vehicle.

19   Remove the retaining screws (see illustration), and remove the evaporator core by pulling it straight out of the housing.

Installation

20   Position the evaporator core in the housing and install the screws.

21   Reinstall the parts in the reverse order of removal.

22   Have the air conditioning system evacuated, recharged and leak tested.

23   Start the engine and check for proper operation.

12   Air conditioning system - check and maintenance

Warning: *The air conditioning system is under high pressure. Do not loosen any hose fittings or remove any components until after the system has been discharged by a dealer service department or service station. Always wear eye protection when disconnecting air conditioning system fittings.*

Note: *The air conditioning system on 1995 through 2014 models uses the non-ozone depleting refrigerant, referred to as R-134a. 2015 and later models use either R-134a or R-1234yf refrigerant. These refrigerants and their lubricating oils are not compatible with the R-12 system, and vice versa. Under no circumstances should the two different types*

of refrigerant and lubricating oil be intermixed. If mixed, it could result in costly compressor failure due to improper lubrication.

1   The following maintenance checks should be performed on a regular basis to ensure that the air conditioner continues to operate at peak efficiency.

a)   *Check the compressor drivebelt. If it's worn or deteriorated, replace it (see Chapter 1).*

b)   *Check the drivebelt tension and, if necessary, adjust it (see Chapter 1).*

c)   *Check the system hoses. Look for cracks, bubbles, hard spots and deterioration. Inspect the hoses and all fittings for oil bubbles and seepage. If there's any evidence of wear, damage or leaks, replace the hose(s).*

12.7 Inspect the sight glass - if the refrigerant looks foamy, it's low

d) Inspect the condenser fins for leaves, bugs and other debris. Use a "fin comb" or compressed air to clean the condenser.
e) Make sure the system has the correct refrigerant charge.

2   It's a good idea to operate the system for about 10 minutes at least once a month, particularly during the winter. Long term non-use can cause hardening, and subsequent failure, of the seals.

3   Because of the complexity of the air conditioning system and the special equipment necessary to service it, in-depth troubleshooting and repairs are not included in this manual. However, simple checks and component replacement procedures are provided in this Chapter. For more complete information on the air conditioning system, refer to the *Haynes Automotive Heating and Air Conditioning Manual*.

4   The most common cause of poor cooling is simply a low system refrigerant charge. If a noticeable drop in cool air output occurs, one of the following quick checks will help you determine if the refrigerant level is low.

13.3 Unplug the electrical connector (1) and unbolt the mounting bracket (2)

Check

5   Warm the engine up to normal operating temperature.

6   Place the air conditioning temperature selector at the coldest setting and put the blower at the highest setting. Open the doors (to make sure the air conditioning system doesn't cycle off as soon as it cools the passenger compartment).

7   With the compressor engaged - the clutch will make an audible click and the center of the clutch will rotate - inspect the sight glass, if equipped (see illustration). If the refrigerant looks foamy, it's low. Have the air conditioning system charged by an automotive air conditioning specialist or dealer service department.

---

13   Air conditioning receiver/drier - removal and installation

Warning: *The air conditioning system is under high pressure. DO NOT disassemble any part of the system (hoses, compressor, line fittings, etc.) until after the system has been depressurized by a dealer service department or service station.*

1   Have the air conditioning system discharged (see Warning above).

2   Disconnect the cable from the negative terminal of the battery (see Chapter 5).

2006 and earlier models

3   Unplug the electrical connector from the pressure switch near the top of the receiver/drier (see illustration).

4   Disconnect the refrigerant line from the receiver/drier. Use a back-up wrench to prevent twisting the tubing.

5   Plug the open fittings to prevent entry of dirt and moisture.

6   Loosen the mounting bracket bolts and lift the receiver/drier out.

7   If a new receiver/drier is being installed, remove the Schrader valve and pour the oil out into a measuring cup, noting the amount. Add fresh refrigerant oil to the new receiver/drier equal to the amount removed from the old unit plus one ounce.

2007 and later models

8   Remove the grille (see Chapter 11).

9   Locate the receiver/drier attached to the right side of the condenser, then remove the receiver/drier-to-condenser mounting bolt.

10   Disconnect the receiver/drier from the condenser and remove and discard the O-rings. Always replace the O-rings with new ones.

11   Plug the open fittings to prevent entry of dirt and moisture.

All models

12   Installation is the reverse of removal.

13   Take the vehicle back to the shop that discharged it. Have the air conditioning system evacuated, charged and leak tested.

---

14   Air conditioning compressor - removal and installation

Warning: *The air conditioning system is under high pressure. DO NOT disassemble any part of the system (hoses, compressor, line fittings, etc.) until after the system has been depressurized by a dealer service department or service station.*

Note: *The receiver/drier (see Section 13) should be replaced whenever the compressor is replaced.*

1   Have the air conditioning system discharged (see Warning above).

2   Disconnect the negative battery cable from the battery (see Chapter 5).

3   Disconnect the compressor clutch wiring harness.

4   Remove the drivebelt (see Chapter 1).

5   On 2012 and later models, disconnect the wiring harness to the Powertrain Control Module (PCM) (see Chapter 6) and move the harness out of the way.

6   Disconnect the refrigerant lines from the rear of the compressor. Plug the open fittings to prevent entry of dirt and moisture.

7   Unbolt the compressor from the mounting brackets and lift it out of the vehicle. On later 2.4L engines, the compressor is secured by one bolt and two nuts on studs. On 3.8L V6 models, there are three compressor mounting bolts and four mounting bolts on 3.6L engines (see illustrations).

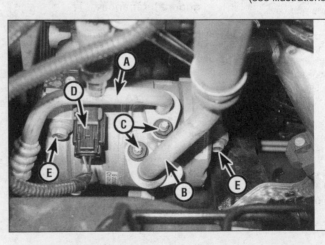

14.7a Air conditioning compressor mounting details - 2007 and later V6 engines

A   Discharge line
B   Suction line
C   Line mounting nuts
D   Electrical connector
E   Upper mounting bolts

14.7b Lower compressor mounting bolt - 2007 and later V6 engines

15.4a Disconnect the refrigerant lines from the condenser - be sure to use a back up wrench to avoid bending the line (use a flare nut wrench on the fitting if available).

15.4b The lower fitting can be reached through the grille opening

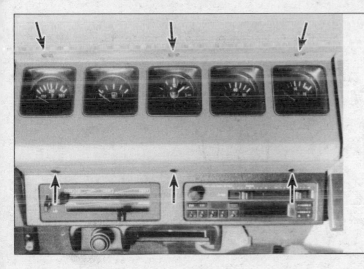

16.4 Remove the instrument panel mounting screws (typical)

8   If a new compressor is being installed, follow the directions with the compressor regarding the draining of excess oil prior to installation.

9   The clutch may have to be transferred from the original to the new compressor.

10   Installation is the reverse of removal. Replace all O-rings with new ones specifically made for air conditioning system use and lubricate them with refrigerant oil.

11   Have the system evacuated, recharged and leak tested by the shop that discharged it.

---

15   Air conditioning condenser - removal and installation

Warning: *The air conditioning system is under high pressure. DO NOT disassemble any part of the system (hoses, compressor, line fittings, etc.) until after the system has been depressurized by a dealer service department or service station.*

Warning: *Wait until the engine is completely*

cool before beginning this procedure.

1   Have the air conditioning system discharged (see Warning above).

2   Disconnect the negative battery cable from the battery (see Chapter 5).

3   Drain the cooling system (see Chapter 1).

4   Disconnect the refrigerant lines from the condenser (see illustrations).

Note: *On 3.6L models, the condenser refrigerant lines are accessible on the driver's side of the radiator.*

5   Remove the radiator (see Section 4). On 2007 through 2011 applications, remove the grille (see Chapter 11), then remove the radiator and condenser as a unit and separate the two components outside the vehicle.

6   Remove the mounting bolts from the condenser brackets.

7   Lift the condenser out of the vehicle and plug the lines to keep dirt and moisture out.

8   If the original condenser will be reinstalled, store it with the line fittings on top to prevent oil from draining out.

9   If a new condenser is being installed, pour one ounce of refrigerant oil into it prior to

installation.

10   Reinstall the components in the reverse order of removal. Be sure the rubber pads are in place under the condenser.

11   Have the system evacuated, recharged and leak tested by the shop that discharged it.

---

16   Air conditioner and heater control assembly - removal and installation

Warning: *Some models covered by this manual are equipped with airbags. Always disable the airbag system when working in the vicinity of airbag system components (see Chapter 12).*

1   Disconnect the negative cable from the battery (see Chapter 5).

2   Detach the instrument panel bezel (see Chapter 11).

3   Remove the radio (see Chapter 12).

4   On 1987 through 1995 models, remove the mounting screws from the center section of the instrument panel (see illustration). On 1997 through 2011 models, remove the glove box and on 2007 and later models the center bezel (2007 through 2010 models, see Chapter 11, Section 22 and Chapter 11, Section 24. On 2011 and later models, see Chapter 12, Section 20).

5   On 1987 through 1995 models, slide out the assembly and unplug the electrical connectors (see illustration).

6   On 1997 and later models, remove the four control assembly mounting bolts, pull out the assembly slightly, reach through the glove box opening and disconnect the two halves of the heater/air conditioning vacuum harness connector.

7   On 1987 through 1995 models, release the control cable locking tab with a screwdriver (see illustration).

8   On 1987 through 1995 models, detach

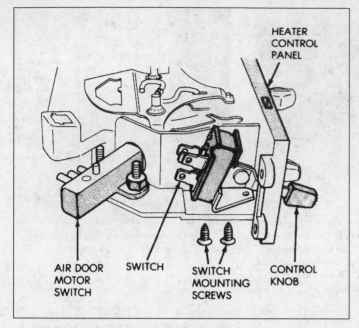

16.5 Unplug the electrical connectors and the vacuum lines

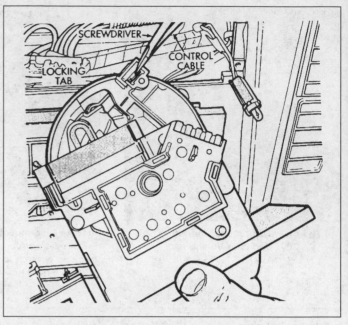

16.7 Release the control cable locking tab with a screwdriver

the ring on the end of the control cable from the arm on the bottom of the control panel (see illustration).

9   On 1997 and later models, pull out the heater/air conditioning assembly a little more and unplug the three electrical connectors from the backside of the assembly. Remove the heater/air conditioning assembly.

10   On 2012 and later models, the air conditioning and heater controller is mounted to the back side of the center bezel. Once the bezel is removed the controller mounting screws can be removed and the controller separated form the bezel.

11   Installation is the reverse of removal.

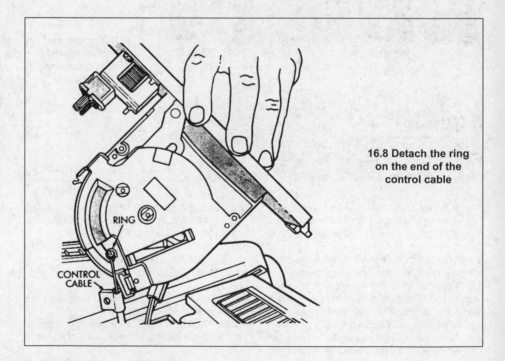

16.8 Detach the ring on the end of the control cable

Chapter 4
Fuel and exhaust systems

Contents

Specifications

Fuel pressure (at idle)

TBI systems	14 to 15 psi
MPI systems	
1996 and earlier models	
Vacuum hose connected	31 psi
Vacuum hose disconnected	39 psi
1997 through 2004 models	47.2 to 51.2 psi
2005 and later models	56 to 60 psi

Torque specifications

Ft-lbs (unless otherwise indicated)

Note: *One foot-pound (ft-lb) of torque is equivalent to 12 inch-pounds (in-lbs) of torque. Torque values below approximately 15 foot-pounds are expressed in inch-pounds, because most foot-pound torque wrenches are not accurate at these smaller values.*

Fuel pump (mechanical) mounting bolts	13 to 19
Carburetor-to-intake manifold mounting nuts	13 to 19
Throttle body mounting nuts	
TBI models	16
MPI models	
3.8L engines	65 in-lbs
3.6L engines	80 in-lbs
All other engines	100 in-lbs
Fuel rail mounting fasteners	
3.8L engines	17
3.6L engines	62 in-lbs
All other engines	100 in-lbs

1   General Information

Warning: *Gasoline is extremely flammable, so take extra precautions when you work on any part of the fuel system. Don't smoke or allow open flames or bare light bulbs near the work area, and don't work in a garage where a gas-type appliance (such as a water heater or a clothes dryer) is present. Since gasoline is carcinogenic, wear latex gloves when there's a possibility of being exposed to fuel, and, if you spill any fuel on your skin, rinse it off immediately with soap and water. Mop up any spills immediately and do not store fuel-soaked rags where they could ignite. The fuel system is under constant pressure, so, if any fuel lines are to be disconnected, the fuel pressure in the system must be relieved first. When you perform any kind of work on the fuel system, wear safety glasses and have a Class B type fire extinguisher on hand.*

1   The fuel system consists of the fuel tank, the fuel pump, the fuel filter, an air cleaner assembly and a carburetor or fuel injection system.

2   The pre-1991 2.5L engine is equipped with Throttle Body Injection (TBI). In 1991, the 2.5L engine became available with Multi-Port Injection (MPI). The 2.4L four-cylinder engine is also equipped with Multi-Port fuel injection.

3   The 4.2L engine is equipped with a two-barrel model BBD feedback carburetor. Wranglers equipped with this engine were manufactured from 1987 through 1990.

4   Vehicles with a 4.0L engine are equipped with a Multi-Port Injection (MPI) system. Wranglers equipped with this engine are manufactured from 1990 through 2006.

5   2007 and later models are equipped with either a 3.8L V6 engine (2007 through 2011) or a 3.6L V6 engine (2012 and later); both of these engines are also equipped with Multi-Port Injection.

6   The fuel pumps of carbureted models use a mechanical pump driven by an eccentric lobe on the camshaft. Fuel injected engines use a gear/rotor type pump driven by an electric motor. The mechanical pump is mounted on the engine block; electric pumps are installed inside the fuel tank. It should be noted that the electric pumps used with TBI and MPI systems are different and cannot be interchanged. For more information on the fuel feedback systems used on earlier models, refer to Chapter 6.

7   Later models covered by this manual are equipped with a sequential Multi-Port Injection (MPI) system. This system uses timed impulses to sequentially inject the fuel directly into the intake ports of each cylinder. The injectors are controlled by the Powertrain Control Module (PCM). The PCM monitors various engine parameters and delivers the exact amount of fuel, in the correct sequence, into the intake ports.

8   The fuel filters on 1997 and later models are extended-life parts and are not replaced during normal scheduled maintenance. They are generally only replaced when they are

2.6 To relieve the fuel pressure on an MPI-equipped vehicle, remove the cap from the pressure test port, place some shop towels underneath to absorb sprayed fuel…

shown to be plugged by fuel system troubleshooting. On 1995 and earlier models, a filter is mounted to the front of the fuel tank. On later models, the filter is integral with the fuel pump module; on these models the fuel pump module also contains the fuel pressure regulator. The fuel level sending unit is an integral component of the fuel pump and it must be removed from the fuel tank in the same manner. On vehicles that are not equipped with an access cover under the carpeting of the rear cargo area, it is necessary to lower the fuel tank for access to these fuel system components.

9   The exhaust system consists of exhaust manifold(s), a catalytic converter, an exhaust pipe and a muffler. Each of these components is replaceable. For further information regarding the catalytic converter, refer to Chapter 6. **Note:** *On 3.6L V6 models, the exhaust manifolds are integral with the cylinder heads.*

2   Fuel pressure relief (fuel-injected vehicles)

Warning: *Gasoline is extremely flammable, so take extra precautions when you work on any part of the fuel system. Don't smoke or allow open flames or bare light bulbs near the work area, and don't work in a garage where a gas-type appliance (such as a water heater or a clothes dryer) is present. Since gasoline is carcinogenic, wear fuel-resistant gloves when there's a possibility of being exposed to fuel, and, if you spill any fuel on your skin, rinse it off immediately with soap and water. Mop up any spills immediately and do not store fuel-soaked rags where they could ignite. The fuel system is under constant pressure, so, if any fuel lines are to be disconnected, the fuel pressure in the system must be relieved first. When you perform any kind of work on the fuel system, wear safety glasses and have a Class B type fire extinguisher on hand.*
Warning: *This procedure merely relieves the*

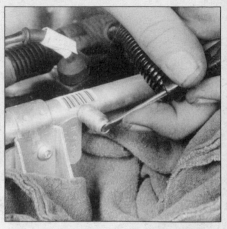

2.8 … then depress the valve in the test port with a small screwdriver or pin punch - wear safety goggles during pressure relief to protect your eyes from spraying fuel

pressure that the engine needs to run. But remember that fuel is still present in the system components, and take precautions accordingly before disconnecting any of them.
Note: *After the fuel pressure has been relieved, it's a good idea to lay a shop towel over any fuel connection to be disassembled, to absorb the residual fuel that may leak out when servicing the fuel system.*

Throttle Body Injection (TBI) equipped vehicles

1   The fuel system of vehicles equipped with Throttle Body Injection (TBI) is only under pressure when the fuel pump is operating. As long as the fuel pump is not operating (ignition key in the OFF position), TBI fuel system components can be removed without the need to release system pressure.

2   Disconnect the cable from the negative terminal of the battery before performing any work on the fuel system.

Multi-Port Injection (MPI) equipped vehicles

Models with a pressure test port

3   The MPI system is under a constant fuel pressure. Before attempting to service any fuel supply or return components on vehicles equipped with this system, release the fuel pressure.

4   Detach the cable from the negative battery terminal.

5   Remove the fuel tank filler cap to relieve fuel tank pressure.

6   Remove the cap from the pressure test port on the fuel rail (see illustration).

7   Place shop towels under and around the pressure test port to absorb fuel when the pressure is released from the fuel rail.

8   Using a small screwdriver or pin punch and push the test port valve in to relieve fuel pressure (see illustration). Absorb the spilled fuel with the shop towels.

9   Remove the shop towels.

10   Install the cap on the pressure test port.

11   Disconnect the cable from the negative terminal of the battery before performing any work on the fuel system.

Models without a pressure test port

12   Remove the gas cap. On 1997-1999 models and later models with "capless" fuel systems, hold the flapper open using a funnel or equivalent.

13   On 1997 through 2006 models, remove the fuel pump relay from the underhood fuse block. Use the diagram on the underside of the fuse block cover to locate the relay.

14   On 2007 and later models, remove the fuel pump fuse from the underhood fuse block. Use the diagram on the underside of the fuse block cover to locate the fuse.

15   On all models, start the engine and let it run until the engine stalls.

16   Turn the ignition off.

17   The fuel pressure is now relieved.

18   Disconnect the cable from the negative terminal of the battery before performing any work on the fuel system.

---

3   Fuel pump/fuel pressure - check

Warning: *Gasoline is extremely flammable, so take extra precautions when you work on any part of the fuel system. See the Warning at the beginning of Section 1.*

Mechanical pump (4.2L carbureted engines)

Quick check

1   Detach the cable from the negative battery terminal (see Chapter 5).

2   Remove the air cleaner assembly (see Section 7).

3   Detach the fuel inlet fitting from the carburetor and place the end of the inlet line in a metal or plastic container.

4   Attach the cable to the negative battery terminal.

5   Hook up a remote starter switch, if available, in accordance with the manufacturer's instructions. If you don't have a remote starter switch, you will need an assistant for the following procedures.

6   Disable the ignition coil by detaching the primary lead wires (see Chapter 5).

7   With the fuel line directed into the container, have an assistant turn the ignition key to Start and crank the engine for about ten seconds.

8   Fuel should be emitted from the fuel line in well-defined spurts. If it isn't, there is a problem somewhere in the fuel delivery system. The following tests will determine where the problem lies.

Pressure test

Note: *You will need a fuel pressure gauge, a hose restrictor and a section of flexible hose to perform the following procedures.*

9   Detach the fuel return hose at the fuel fil-

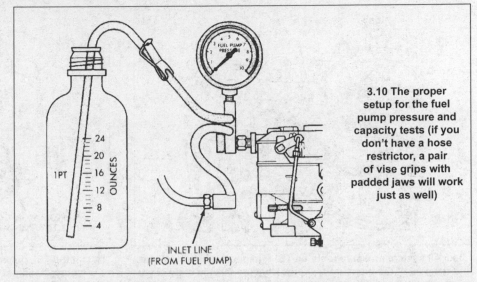

3.10 The proper setup for the fuel pump pressure and capacity tests (if you don't have a hose restrictor, a pair of vise grips with padded jaws will work just as well)

INLET LINE
(FROM FUEL PUMP)

ter (next to the carburetor) and plug the fitting on the filter.

10   Attach a pressure gauge, restrictor and flexible hose between the fuel inlet fitting or the fuel filter and the carburetor (see illustration).

11   Position the flexible hose and restrictor so fuel can be discharged into a graduated container.

12   Reattach the coil primary lead wires (the engine must be operated for the following test).

13   Start the engine (or have your assistant start it), let it run at curb idle rpm, then discharge the fuel into the container by momentarily opening the hose restrictor.

14   Close the hose restrictor, allow the pressure to stabilize and note the pressure. The gauge should indicate 4-to-5 psi.

   a)   *If the pump pressure is not within specification, and the fuel lines are in satisfactory condition, the pump is defective and should be replaced.*

   b)   *If the pump pressure is within specifications, perform the following tests for capacity and vacuum.*

Capacity test

15   Operate the engine at curb idle rpm.

16   Open the hose restrictor and allow fuel to discharge into a graduated container for 30 seconds, then close the restrictor. At least one pint of fuel should have been discharged.

   a)   *If the pump volume is less than one pint, repeat the test with an auxiliary fuel supply and a replacement fuel filter.*

   b)   *If the pump volume conforms to the specified amount while using the auxiliary fuel supply, look for a restriction in the fuel supply line from the tank and check the tank vent to make sure it's working properly.*

Direct connection vacuum test

17   You will need a vacuum gauge to perform the direct connection vacuum test. In this test, the vacuum test gauge is connected directly

to the fuel pump inlet to test the pump's ability to create a vacuum.

18   Detach the fuel inlet line at the fuel pump.

19   Attach a vacuum gauge to the fuel pump inlet.

20   Operate the engine at curb idle speed and note the vacuum gauge reading. It should indicate a vacuum of 10 in-Hg (the gauge will not indicate a vacuum until the fuel in the carburetor float bowl has been consumed and the pump begins to operate at full capacity).

21   If the pump vacuum is not within specification, the pump is defective. Replace it (see Section 4).

Indirect connection vacuum test

22   You will need a vacuum gauge and a T-fitting to perform the indirect connection vacuum test. In this test, a vacuum gauge is connected by a T-fitting into the pump inlet to determine whether an obstruction exists in the fuel line or the in-tank fuel filter.

23   Detach the fuel inlet line at the fuel pump.

24   Install a T-fitting between the disconnected fitting and the fuel pump inlet. Connect a vacuum gauge to the T-fitting.

25   Operate the engine at a speed of 1500 rpm for 30 seconds and note the reading on the vacuum gauge (again, the gauge will not indicate any vacuum until the fuel in the carburetor float bowl has been consumed and the pump begins to operate at full capacity). The indicated vacuum should not exceed 3 in-Hg.

26   If the indicated vacuum exceeds the specified vacuum, check the fuel line for a restriction. A partially clogged in-tank fuel filter can also cause excess vacuum.

Electric pump (1995 and earlier fuel-injected engines)

TBI pressure test

27   Detach the cable from the negative battery terminal.

28   Remove the pressure test port plug from

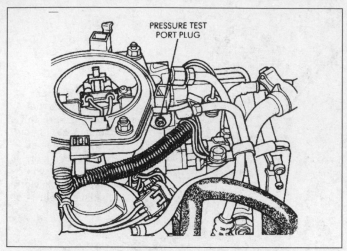

3.28 All system pressure tests on TBI-equipped vehicles require the removal of the pressure test port from the throttle body - in its place, install a special pressure test fitting (available at most auto parts stores)

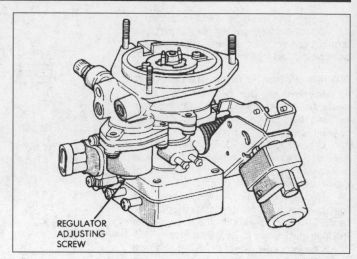

3.31 If the TBI system fuel pressure indicated on the test gauge is incorrect, adjust it by turning the regulator adjusting screw - turn the screw in (clockwise) to increase pressure or out (counterclockwise) to decrease pressure

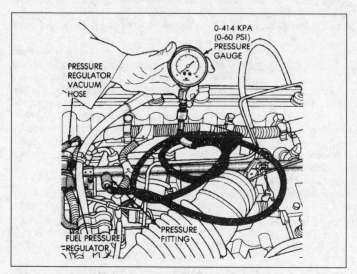

3.35 To test the MPI fuel system pressure, you will need to attach a 0-to-60 psi pressure gauge to the test port pressure fitting on the fuel rail

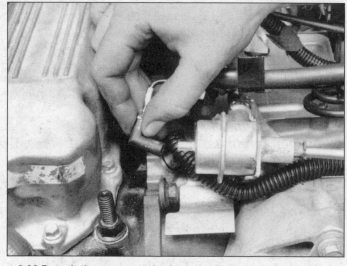

3.36 Detach the vacuum tube from the fuel pressure regulator, start the vehicle and note the gauge reading - with the vacuum line detached, fuel pressure should be about 30 psi

the throttle body (see illustration).

29   Install a pressure test fitting (available at a Jeep parts department) in place of the test port plug.

30   Attach a 0-to-30 psi fuel pressure gauge to the pressure test fitting (don't use a carburetor type 0-to-15 psi gauge).

31   Start the engine and let it idle. The pressure gauge should read 14-to-15 psi. If the pressure is incorrect, adjust it by turning the regulator adjusting screw (see illustration) to obtain the correct fuel pressure. Turn the screw at the bottom of the regulator in (clockwise) to increase pressure or out (counterclockwise) to decrease pressure.

32   If the fuel pressure is considerably higher than specified, and adjusting the regulator fails to lower it to the specified level, inspect the fuel return line for blockage.

33   If the fuel pressure is considerably below specification and adjusting the regulator fails to raise it to the specified level, momentarily pinch off the fuel return line and recheck the pressure.

a) If the fuel pressure has risen, replace the pressure regulator (see Section 16).

b) If the pressure has not risen, check the fuel filter (see Chapter 1) and fuel supply line for blockage. If they're OK, the fuel pump is probably faulty.

MPI pressure test

34   The MPI fuel system employs a vacuum-assisted pressure regulator. Fuel pressure should be about 8 to 10 psi higher with the vacuum line attached to the regulator than with the vacuum line disconnected. Fuel system pressure should be 31 psi with the vac-

uum line attached to the regulator and 39 psi with the line detached.

35   Attach a 0-to-60 psi fuel pressure gauge to the test port pressure fitting on the fuel rail (see illustration).

36   Detach and plug the vacuum tube from the fuel pressure regulator (see illustration).

37   Start the engine.

38   Note the gauge reading. With the vacuum line detached, fuel pressure should be about 39 psi.

39   Attach the vacuum line to the pressure regulator. Note the gauge reading. Fuel pressure should be about 31 psi.

40   If the indicated fuel pressure is not about 8-to-10 psi higher with the vacuum line removed from the regulator, inspect the pressure regulator vacuum line for leaks, kinks and blockage.

3.41 If the fuel pressure is below the specified level, momentarily pinch off the hose section of the fuel return line - fuel pressure will rise to 95 psi when the fuel return line is pinched, so turn the engine off immediately after pinching off the fuel return line

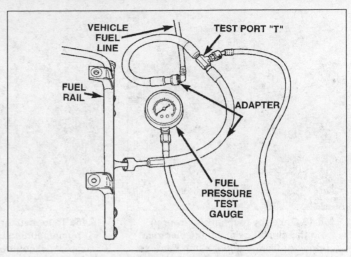

3.50 A special adapter hose with a T-fitting will be required for the fuel pressure checks

41 If the fuel pressure is below the specified level, momentarily pinch off the hose section of the return line (see illustration).

a) *The fuel pressure will rise to 95 psi when the fuel return line is pinched shut, so turn off the engine immediately after pinching off the fuel return line.*

b) *If the fuel pressure remains below specifications, inspect the fuel supply line, fuel filter (see Chapter 1) and fuel rail inlet (see Section 16) for blockage.*

c) *If the fuel pressure rises, replace the regulator.*

d) *If the fuel pressure is above specification, inspect the fuel return line for kinks and blockage.*

MPI fuel pressure leak-down test

42 If an abnormally long cranking period is required to restart a hot engine after the vehicle has been shut down for a short period of time, the fuel pressure may be leaking past the fuel pressure regulator or the check valve in the outlet end of the fuel pump.

43 With the engine off, attach a gauge capable of reading 0-to-100 psi to the pressure test port fitting on the fuel rail.

44 Start the vehicle and let the engine idle. Check the fuel pressure reading on the gauge. The fuel pressure should be within the specifications noted above.

45 Shut the engine off. Note the fuel pressure reading on the gauge. Leave the fuel pressure gauge connected. Allow the engine to sit for 30 minutes, then compare the fuel pressure reading on the gauge to the reading you took when you shut down the engine. A drop of 0-to-20 psi (to the 19-to-39 psi range) is acceptable. If the fuel pressure drop is within specification, the fuel pump outlet check valve and the fuel pressure regulator are both operating normally. If the fuel pressure drop is greater than 20 psi, restart the vehicle, let

the engine idle and momentarily pinch off the hose section of the fuel return line. The fuel pressure will rise to 95 psi when the fuel return line is pinched off, so shut the engine down immediately after pinching off the fuel return line. Note the pressure reading on the gauge. Allow the engine to sit for 30 minutes. Take another reading and compare it to the reading you took when you first shut down the engine.

a) *If the fuel pressure has dropped about 20 psi, replace the fuel pressure regulator.*

b) *If the fuel pressure has dropped considerably more than 20 psi, fuel pressure is bleeding off past the outlet check valve in the fuel pump. Replace the pump.*

Capacity test

46 Remove the cap from the pressure test port on the fuel rail (see illustration 2.5).

47 Attach a 0-to-60 psi fuel pressure gauge to the pressure fitting.

48 Start the engine. Pressure should be about 31 psi with the vacuum hose attached to the pressure regulator and 39 psi with the vacuum hose removed from the pressure regulator (see illustration 3.36). If the pressure is not within specifications, one of the following problems exists:

a) *There is a kink or other restriction in a fuel supply or return line hose. Inspect the lines and hoses.*

b) *The fuel pump flow rate is not sufficient. Take the vehicle to a dealer service department for proper checking of the fuel pump flow rate.*

c) *The fuel pressure regulator is malfunctioning. Take the vehicle to a dealer service department for proper checking (see Section 16 to replace the regulator).*

Electric pump (1997 and later models)

Note: *In order to perform the fuel pressure test, you will need a fuel pressure gauge capable of measuring high fuel pressure. The fuel gauge must be equipped with the proper fittings or adapters required to attach it to the fuel rail.*

49 Relieve the fuel pressure (see Section 2).

50 Remove the cap from the fuel pressure test port (if equipped) on the fuel rail or disconnect the fuel supply line from the fuel rail, and attach a fuel pressure gauge (see illustration).

Note: *A special adapter with a T-fitting will be required to perform the leakdown test described in Step 54.*

51 Start the engine and check the pressure on the gauge, comparing your reading with the pressure listed in this Chapter's Specifications.

52 If the fuel pressure is lower than specified, check the fuel lines and the fuel filter for restrictions. If no restriction is found, replace the fuel pump (see Section 4).

53 If fuel pressure is higher than specified, replace the fuel pressure regulator/fuel filter (see Section 16).

54 If the fuel pressure is within specifications, turn the engine off and monitor the fuel pressure for five minutes. The fuel pressure should not drop below 30 psi within five minutes. If it does, there is a leak in the fuel line, a fuel injector is leaking or the fuel pump module check valve is defective. To determine the problem area, perform the following:

Note: *A special fuel gauge adapter hose is required for the following tests, the fuel pressure gauge must be connected to the T-fitting (see illustration 3.50).*

55 Install the adapter hose, then turn on the ignition key to power-up the fuel system.

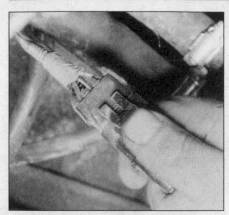

4.13 Once the fuel tank is lowered from the chassis, detach the electrical connector from the fuel pump harness

4.15a To loosen the lock ring for the fuel pump/sending unit assembly, turn it counterclockwise (1995 and earlier models)

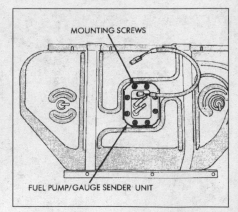

4.15b On vehicles equipped with a 20-gallon tank, the fuel pump/sending unit assembly is mounted with screws (1995 and earlier models)

Clamp off the adapter hose between the T-fitting and the line to the fuel pump, then turn the ignition key off. If the pressure drops below 30 psi within five minutes, a fuel injector (or injectors) is leaking (or the fuel rail may be leaking, but such a leak would be very apparent).

56   With the adapter hose installed, clamp off the adapter hose between the T-fitting and the fuel rail. Turn the ignition key on to energize the fuel pump, then turn the key off. If the pressure drops below 30 psi within five minutes, the fuel line is leaking, the check valve in the fuel pressure regulator is defective or the fuel pump is defective.

a) Check the entire length of the fuel line for leaks.
b) If no leaks are found in the fuel line and the pressure dropped quickly, replace the fuel pressure regulator/fuel filter.
c) If no leaks are found in the fuel line and the pressure dropped slowly, replace the fuel pump.

4   Fuel pump - removal and installation

Warning: Gasoline is extremely flammable, so take extra precautions when you work on any part of the fuel system. See the Warning at the beginning of Section 1.

Mechanical pump

1   Detach the cable from the negative battery terminal (see Chapter 5).
2   Remove the fuel tank filler cap to relieve fuel pressure.
3   Wrap shop towels around the fuel pump inlet hose and outlet line fitting to absorb any fuel spilled during fuel pump removal.
4   Detach the fuel inlet hose and outlet line fitting from the fuel pump.
5   Unscrew the fuel pump mounting bolts and remove the fuel pump and gasket.
6   Carefully scrape away any old gasket material from the fuel pump and engine block sealing surfaces.

7   Installation is the reverse of removal. Be sure to use a new gasket and tighten the fuel pump bolts to the torque listed in this Chapter's Specifications.

Electric pump

Note: Later 4WD models have two "fuel pump" modules. The secondary module on the right side of the vehicle contains only a level sensor and a fuel transfer fitting, but no pump (although the manufacturer refers to it as a fuel pump module). The primary fuel pump module is on the left side.

Removal

Note: The following procedure requires removal of the fuel tank.
8   Relieve the fuel system pressure (see Section 2).
9   Detach the cable from the negative battery terminal.
10   Raise the vehicle and place it securely on jackstands.
11   Remove the fuel tank (see Section 5).
12   Disconnect the fuel vent, supply and return hoses from the fittings on the fuel pump/sending unit.
13   Detach the fuel pump/sending unit elec-

trical harness connector from the main harness (see illustration).
14   The fuel pump/sending unit assembly is located inside the fuel tank. It's held in place by a cam lock ring mechanism consisting of an inner ring with three locking cams and an outer ring with three retaining tangs (1995 and earlier models) or a large plastic locknut (1997 and later models).
15   To unlock the fuel pump/sending unit assembly on 1995 and earlier models, turn the inner ring counterclockwise until the locking cams are free of the retaining tangs. If the rings are locked together too tightly to release them by hand, gently knock them loose with a wood dowel or a brass punch and hammer (see illustration). On vehicles equipped with the 20-gallon fuel tank, remove the mounting screws and then lift the fuel pump/sending unit assembly from the tank (see illustration).
16   On 1997 and later models, use a special lock ring tool or hammer and punch to turn the lock ring counterclockwise until it can be unscrewed by hand (see illustration).

Warning: Do not use a steel punch to knock the lock ring loose. A spark could cause an explosion!
17   Place a reference mark on the fuel

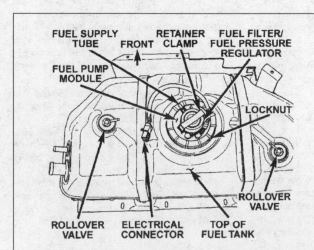

4.16 Fuel tank and fuel pump details - 1997 and later models

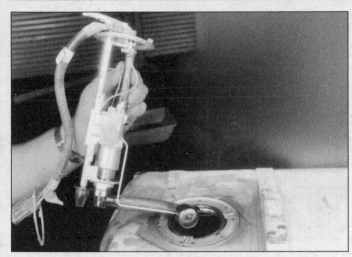

4.18 Carefully remove the fuel pump/sending unit assembly from the fuel tank

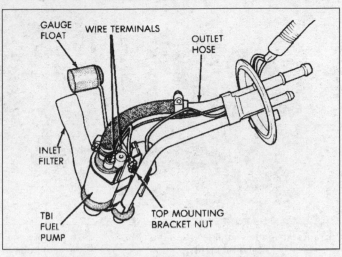

4.22a The TBI fuel pump/sending unit assembly

pump module and tank for the location before removing.

18 Extract the fuel pump/sending unit assembly from the fuel tank. The fuel level float and sending unit are delicate (see illustration). Do not bump them during removal or the accuracy of the sending unit may be affected.

Warning: *Fuel remains in the fuel pump module when removing. Use care and drain the fuel pump module once removed from the fuel tank.*

19 Inspect the condition of the gasket (O-ring) around the mouth of the lock ring mechanism. If it's dried, cracked or deformed, replace it.

20 Inspect the inside of the tank. Have it cleaned by a radiator shop if sediment is present.

21 If you are replacing the fuel pump, make sure you get the right pump. The TBI and MPI pumps look alike, but they're NOT interchangeable.

Disassembly and reassembly (1996 and earlier models only)

Note: *On 1997 and later models the fuel pump is not serviceable. In the event of failure, the complete fuel pump module assembly must be replaced.*

22 Remove and discard the fuel pump inlet filter (see illustrations).

23 Detach the fuel pump wires (the wire ends are different sizes and cannot be connected to the wrong terminal).

24 Detach the fuel pump outlet hose and clamp. Replace the hose if it shows signs of wear or deterioration.

25 Remove the fuel pump top mounting bracket nut. Remove the fuel pump.

26 Install a new inlet filter.

27 Place the fuel pump top mounting bracket over the top of the pump.

28 Position the fuel pump in the lower bracket. Slide the stud of the top bracket through the hole in the fuel pump side bracket.

Tighten the fuel pump top mounting nut.

29 Install the fuel pump outlet hose. Secure it with new clamps.

30 Connect the wire terminals to the motor.

Installation

31 Use a new o-ring on the fuel tank before installing the fuel pump module.

32 Insert the fuel pump/sending unit assembly into the fuel tank. On some models it is necessary to align the stopper (mounted on the fuel pump/sending unit assembly) with the cup located in the bottom of the fuel tank (see illustration).

33 On 1995 and earlier models, turn the inner lock ring clockwise until the locking cams are fully engaged by the retaining tangs. It may be necessary to push down on the inner lock ring until the locking cams slide under the retaining tangs. On 1997 and later models, tighten the lock ring securely.

34 Install the fuel tank.

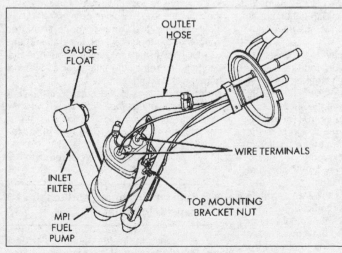

4.22b The MPI fuel pump/sending unit assembly

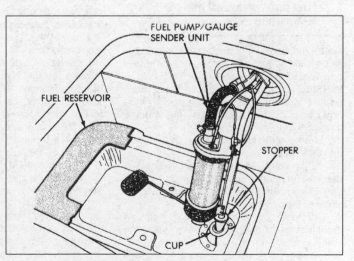

4.32 Fuel pump/gauge sender unit installation

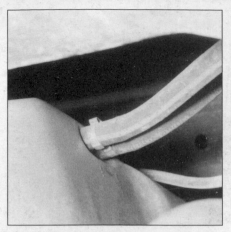

5.7a Remove the vent lines from the side of the fuel tank

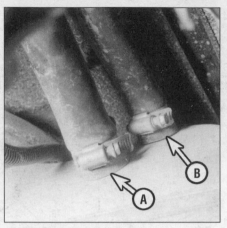

5.7b Remove the fuel supply line (A) and the vent hose (B) from the side of the fuel tank

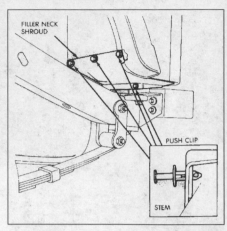

5.7c Pull the push clips OUT to separate the shroud from the chassis

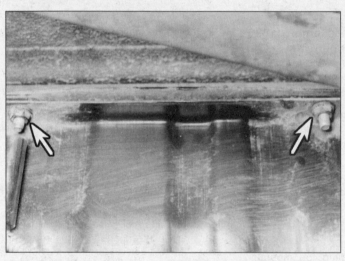

5.12a Remove the fuel tank mounting nuts on the front section ...

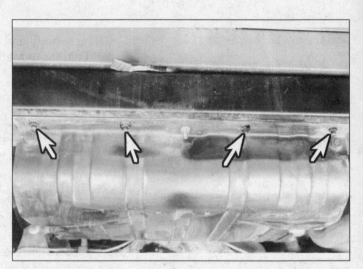

5.12b ... and remove the nuts from the rear section of the fuel tank

5   Fuel tank - removal and installation

Note: *The following procedure is much easier to perform if the fuel tank is empty. Run the engine until the tank is empty.*

Warning: *Gasoline is extremely flammable, so take extra precautions when you work on any part of the fuel system. See the Warning at the beginning of Section 1.*

1   Remove the fuel tank filler cap to relieve fuel tank pressure.

2   If the vehicle is fuel-injected, relieve the fuel system pressure (see Section 2).

3   Detach the cable from the negative terminal of the battery.

4   If the tank still has fuel in it, you can drain it at the fuel supply line after raising the vehicle.

5   Raise the vehicle and place it securely on jackstands.

6   Disconnect all hoses (see illustrations) and the electrical connector for the fuel gauge sending unit and electric fuel pump (if equipped) (see Section 4). Carefully label all hoses so you can reinstall them in their original locations.

7   On some models it may be necessary to remove the fuel filler neck shroud (see illustrations) from the left rear wheelwell in order to access the supply hose. Pull back the stem of the push clips and remove the shroud.

8   Using a mechanical pump (never by mouth), siphon the fuel from the tank at the fuel filler or fuel feed line, not the return line.

9   Ensure all fuel supply and EVAP quick-connect fitting and electrical connectors are disconnected from the fuel tank.

10   If necessary, remove the transfer case skid plate for access and/or removal.

11   Support the fuel tank with a floor jack or jackstands. Position a piece of wood between the jack head and the fuel tank to protect the tank.

Note: *The fuel tank skid plate and fuel tank may share the same fasteners and may need to be removed together. After tank removal, the tank and skid plate can be separated.*

12   Remove the nuts or bolts from the flanges of the fuel tank (see illustrations) and carefully lower the tank down enough to disconnect any remaining fittings or connectors from the fuel pump module.

Note: *Do not loosen the nuts from the tank straps. Remove the fuel tank along with the skid plate, if so equipped.*

13   Lower and remove the tank from the vehicle.

14   Installation is the reverse of removal.

6   Fuel tank cleaning and repair - general information

1   All repairs to the fuel tank or filler neck should be carried out by a professional who has experience in this critical and potentially

7.3 Use a small screwdriver and remove the clips from the air intake cover

7.5 Remove the mounting bolt located in the lower section of the housing

7.6 The warm air hose is located under the air cleaner housing

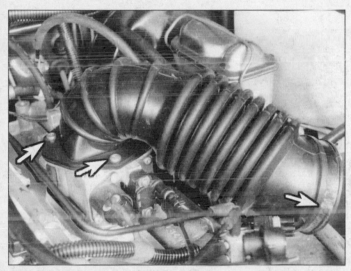

7.11a To remove the flexible air duct on a 4.0L MPI engine, loosen the hose clamp at one end (arrow) and remove the three attaching screws (arrows) from the other end - the third attaching screw is hidden by the duct in this photo

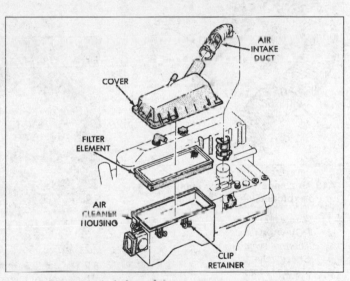

7.11b Exploded view of the air cleaner assembly on a 4.0L MPI engine

dangerous work. Even after cleaning and flushing of the fuel system, explosive fumes can remain and ignite during repair of the tank.

2   If the fuel tank is removed from the vehicle, it should not be placed in an area where sparks or open flames could ignite the fumes coming out of the tank. Be especially careful inside garages where a gas type appliance is located, because it could cause an explosion.

7   Air filter housing - removal and installation

2.5L engine

1   Detach the cable from the negative terminal of the battery.

2   Remove the air filter from the housing (see Chapter 1). Inspect the element for contamination by dirt and moisture. Replace it if necessary.

3   Lift up on the clips (see illustration) that hold the air intake assembly to the throttle body or remove the band clamp.

4   Remove the clamp that retains the air intake assembly to the housing and lift the air intake tube from the engine compartment.

5   Remove the nut from the bottom of the air cleaner housing (see illustration) and partially lift the air cleaner housing up.

6   Detach the warm air hose (see illustration) from the bottom of the housing.

7   Label and remove any vacuum hoses from the air cleaner housing.

8   Remove the air cleaner housing assembly.

9   Installation is the reverse of removal.

4.0L engine

10   Detach the cable from the negative battery terminal.

11   Loosen the hose clamp at one end and remove the three attaching screws at the other end of the flexible air duct between the air cleaner housing and the throttle body (see illustrations). Remove the duct.

12   Clearly label, then detach, all vacuum hoses from the air cleaner housing.

13   Detach the heat riser tube from the air cleaner housing.

14   Remove the upper half of the air cleaner housing lid, then remove the air filter element (see Chapter 1).

15   Remove the two bolts and one nut from the floor of the air cleaner housing. Remove the housing.

16   Installation is the reverse of removal.

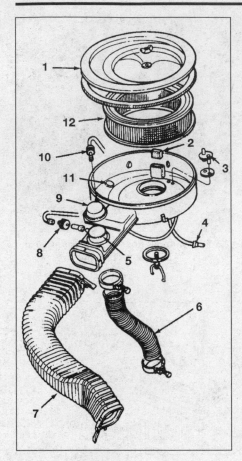

**7.18 Air cleaner assembly components -
exploded view (4.2L engine)**

1   Air cleaner cover
2   PCV valve filter
3   Thermal switch
4   Check valve
5   Vacuum motor
6   Heated air tube
7   Ambient air duct
8   Reverse delay valve
9   Trap door assembly
10   Reverse delay valve
11   Thermal vacuum switch
12   Filter element

4.2L engine

17   Detach the cable from the negative terminal of the battery.
18   Detach the flexible ambient air duct from the air cleaner housing snorkel (see illustration).
19   Remove the wing nut from the cover and remove the cover and filter element. Inspect the element for contamination by dirt and moisture. Replace it if necessary (see Chapter 1).
20   Clearly label, then detach, all hoses from the air cleaner housing.
21   Remove the air cleaner housing assembly.
22   Installation is the reverse of removal.

**7.25 Disconnect the IAT sensor (A), then
loosen the air intake tube clamp (B) -
V6 engine**

**8.2 The cable is retained by a plastic tang.
Use a pair of pliers and first squeeze the
tang and then push the cable through the
bracket (TBI engine shown)**

V6 engines

23   Detach the cable from the negative terminal of the battery.
24   Remove the engine cover.
25   Disconnect the IAT sensor connector at the air intake hose (see illustration).
26   Loosen and disconnect the crankcase ventilation hose from the top of the air cleaner housing.
27   Loosen the clamp securing the air intake hose to the throttle body and disconnect the hose.
28   On 3.6L engines, detach the coolant hose from the retainers on the shroud.
29   On all models, remove the mounting bolt(s) on the radiator shroud and lift the air cleaner housing from the one alignment pin.
30   Firmly pull the air filter housing, lid and intake hose as an assembly upwards to disengage the pin(s) from the inner fender and remove from the vehicle.
31   Installation is the reverse of removal.

**8.1 Use a small screwdriver to pry the
cable end off the throttle valve
(TBI engine shown)**

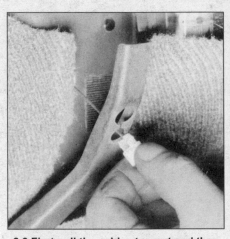

**8.3 First pull the cable stop out and then
lift it up and through the opening in the
pedal assembly (TBI engine shown)**

8   Accelerator cable - replacement

Note: *2007 and later models do not have an accelerator cable - the throttle body is controlled electronically by the Accelerator Pedal Position (APP) sensor (see Chapter 6, Section 10).*
1   Working inside the engine compartment, carefully pry the cable end from the throttle valve pivoting ball (see illustration) with a screwdriver.
2   Depress the cable-to-bracket fitting with a pair of pliers (see illustration) and then pull the cable through the bracket from the other side.
3   Working inside of the driver's compartment below the dash area, depress the throttle pedal and remove the cable stop through the larger opening (see illustration).
4   Remove the cable from the engine compartment. If the cable is equipped with a plas-

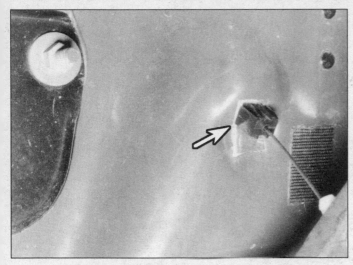

8.4 Squeeze the tang (arrow) with a pair of pliers and push the retainer through the opening

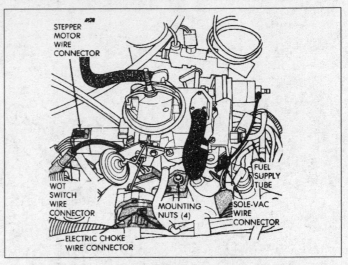

10.9 Remove the four mounting nuts from the base of the carburetor

tic retainer in the firewall (see illustration), squeeze the tang with a pair of pliers and push the retainer through the opening.

5　Installation is the reverse of removal.

9　Carburetor - adjustments

1　The carburetors used on the vehicles covered by this manual are protected by a Federally-mandated extended warranty (at the time this manual was written, the warranty was for 5 years/50,000 miles, whichever comes first - see your dealer for details).

2　We don't recommend carburetor adjustments while it's still under warranty. If you are having problems related to fuel delivery - and you have eliminated all other parts of the fuel delivery system as possible causes - take the vehicle to a dealer and have the carburetor professionally serviced.

3　Unless you really know what you're doing, we don't recommend you attempt to adjust an out-of-warranty carburetor either. The carburetors on these vehicles are expensive, complex and tricky to adjust. The adjustments are also totally interrelated, so it's impossible to do certain adjustments unless you have already done several others. Finally, by the time adjustments become necessary, the carburetor will probably be approaching the end of its service life and will be impossible to adjust to a like-new state of tune. At this point, you're better off buying a rebuilt or new carburetor.

10　Carburetor - removal and installation

Warning: *Gasoline is extremely flammable, so take extra precautions when you work on any part of the fuel system. See the Warning at the beginning of Section 1.*

Removal

1　Detach the cable from the negative battery terminal (see Chapter 5).

2　Remove the fuel filler cap to relieve fuel tank pressure.

3　Remove the air cleaner from the carburetor. Be sure to label all vacuum hoses attached to the air cleaner housing.

4　Disconnect the throttle cable from the throttle lever.

5　If the vehicle is equipped with an automatic transmission, disconnect the TV cable from the throttle lever (see Chapter 7B).

6　Clearly label all vacuum hoses and fittings, then disconnect the hoses.

7　Disconnect the fuel line from the carburetor.

8　Label the wires and terminals, then unplug all wire harness connectors.

9　Remove the mounting fasteners (see illustration) and detach the carburetor from the intake manifold. Remove the carburetor mounting gasket. Stuff a shop rag into the intake manifold openings.

Installation

10　Use a gasket scraper to remove all traces of gasket material and sealant from the intake manifold (and the carburetor, if it's being reinstalled), then remove the shop rag from the manifold openings. Clean the mating surfaces with lacquer thinner or acetone.

11　Place a new gasket on the intake manifold.

12　Position the carburetor on the gasket and install the mounting fasteners.

13　To prevent carburetor distortion or damage, tighten the fasteners to the torque listed in this Chapter's Specifications in a criss-cross pattern, 1/4-turn at a time.

14　The remaining installation steps are the reverse of removal.

15　Check and, if necessary, adjust the idle speed (see Chapter 1).

16　If the vehicle is equipped with an auto-

matic transmission, refer to Chapter 7B for the TV cable adjustment procedure.

17　Attach the negative battery cable.

18　Start the engine and check carefully for fuel leaks.

11　Carburetor - diagnosis and overhaul

Warning: *Gasoline is extremely flammable, so take extra precautions when you work on any part of the fuel system. See the Warning at the beginning of Section 1.*

Diagnosis

1　A thorough road test and check of carburetor adjustments should be done before any major carburetor service work. Specifications for some adjustments are listed on the Vehicle Emissions Control Information (VECI) label found in the engine compartment.

2　Carburetor problems usually show up as flooding, hard starting, stalling, severe backfiring and poor acceleration. A carburetor that's leaking fuel and/or covered with wet looking deposits definitely needs attention.

3　Some performance complaints directed at the carburetor are actually a result of loose, out-of-adjustment or malfunctioning engine or electrical components. Others develop when vacuum hoses leak, are disconnected or are incorrectly routed. The proper approach to analyzing carburetor problems should include the following items:

a) *Inspect all vacuum hoses and actuators for leaks and correct installation (see Chapters 1 and 6).*

b) *Tighten the intake manifold and carburetor mounting nuts/bolts evenly and securely.*

c) *Perform a cylinder compression test (see Chapter 2F).*

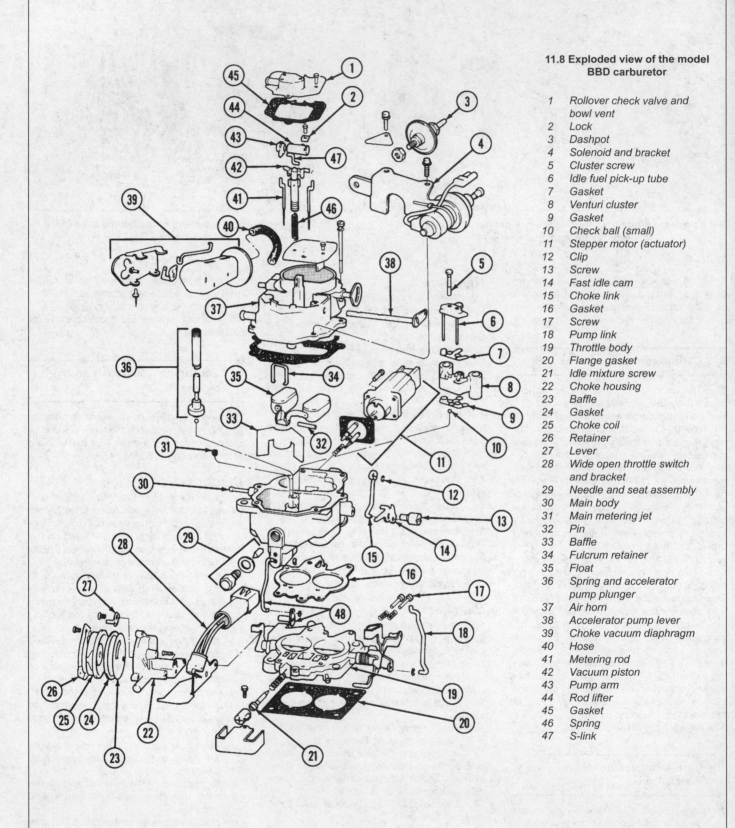

11.8 Exploded view of the model BBD carburetor

1   Rollover check valve and bowl vent
2   Lock
3   Dashpot
4   Solenoid and bracket
5   Cluster screw
6   Idle fuel pick-up tube
7   Gasket
8   Venturi cluster
9   Gasket
10 Check ball (small)
11 Stepper motor (actuator)
12 Clip
13 Screw
14 Fast idle cam
15 Choke link
16 Gasket
17 Screw
18 Pump link
19 Throttle body
20 Flange gasket
21 Idle mixture screw
22 Choke housing
23 Baffle
24 Gasket
25 Choke coil
26 Retainer
27 Lever
28 Wide open throttle switch and bracket
29 Needle and seat assembly
30 Main body
31 Main metering jet
32 Pin
33 Baffle
34 Fulcrum retainer
35 Float
36 Spring and accelerator pump plunger
37 Air horn
38 Accelerator pump lever
39 Choke vacuum diaphragm
40 Hose
41 Metering rod
42 Vacuum piston
43 Pump arm
44 Rod lifter
45 Gasket
46 Spring
47 S-link

d) Clean or replace the spark plugs as necessary (see Chapter 1).

e) Check the spark plug wires (see Chapter 1).

f) Inspect the ignition primary wires.

g) Check the ignition timing (follow the instructions printed on the Emissions Control Information label).

h) Check the fuel pump and fuel pressure (see Section 3).

i) Check the heat control valve in the air cleaner for proper operation (see Chapter 1).

j) Check/replace the air filter element (see Chapter 1).

k) Check the crankcase ventilation system (see Chapter 6).

l) Check/replace the fuel filter (see Chapter 1). Also, the filter in the tank could be restricted.

m) Check for a plugged exhaust system.

n) Check EGR valve operation (see Chapter 6).

o) Check the choke - it should be completely open at normal engine operating temperature (see Chapter 1).

p) Check for fuel leaks and kinked or dented fuel lines (see Chapters 1 and 4).

q) Check accelerator pump operation with the engine off (remove the air cleaner cover and operate the throttle as you look into the carburetor throat - you should see a stream of gasoline enter the carburetor).

r) Check for incorrect fuel or bad gasoline.

s) Have a dealer service department or repair shop check the electronic engine and carburetor controls.

4   Diagnosing carburetor problems may require that the engine be started and run with the air cleaner off. While running the engine without the air cleaner, backfires are possible. This situation is likely to occur if the carburetor is malfunctioning, but just the removal of the air cleaner can lean the fuel/air mixture enough to produce an engine backfire. **Warning:** *Do not position any part of your body, especially your face, directly over the carburetor during inspection and servicing procedures. Wear eye protection!*

Overhaul

5   Once it's determined that the carburetor needs an overhaul, several options are available. If you're going to attempt to overhaul the carburetor yourself, first obtain a good quality carburetor rebuild kit (which will include all necessary gaskets, internal parts, instructions and a parts list). You'll also need some special solvent and a means of blowing out the internal passages of the carburetor with air.

6   An alternative is to obtain a new or rebuilt carburetor. They are readily available from dealers and auto parts stores. Make absolutely sure the exchange carburetor is identical to the original. A tag is usually attached to the top of the carburetor or a number is stamped on the float bowl. It will help determine the exact type of carburetor you

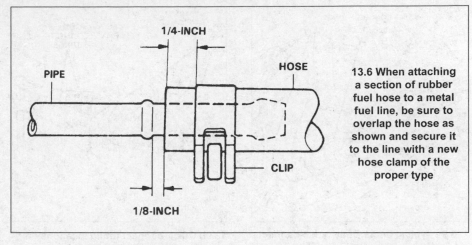

13.6 When attaching a section of rubber fuel hose to a metal fuel line, be sure to overlap the hose as shown and secure it to the line with a new hose clamp of the proper type

have. When obtaining a rebuilt carburetor or a rebuild kit, make sure the kit or carburetor matches your application exactly. Seemingly insignificant differences can make a large difference in engine performance.

7   If you choose to overhaul your own carburetor, allow enough time to disassemble it carefully, soak the necessary parts in the cleaning solvent (usually for at least one-half day or according to the instructions listed on the carburetor cleaner) and reassemble it, which will usually take much longer than disassembly. When disassembling the carburetor, match each part with the illustration in the carburetor kit and lay the parts out in order on a clean work surface. Overhauls by inexperienced mechanics can result in an engine which runs poorly or not at all. To avoid this, use care and patience when disassembling the carburetor so you can reassemble it correctly.

8   Because carburetor designs are constantly modified by the manufacturer in order to meet increasingly more stringent emissions regulations, it isn't feasible to include a step-by-step overhaul of each type. You'll receive a detailed, well illustrated set of instructions with any carburetor overhaul kit; they will apply in a more specific manner to the carburetor on your vehicle. An exploded view of the carburetor is included here (see illustration).

12   Fuel injection system - general information

1   Fuel-injected vehicles are equipped with either a Throttle Body Injection (TBI) system (2.5L engine) or a Multi-Port Injection (MPI) system (1991 and later 2.5L and all 4.0L six-cylinder, 3.8L V6 and 3.6L V6 engines). Both systems use an Electronic Control Unit (ECU) or Powertrain Control Module (PCM) to control pulse width.

2   The pulse width is the period of time during which the injector is energized (squirts fuel). The ECU/PCM, opens and closes the injector's ground path to control fuel injector pulse width and thus meter the amount of fuel available to the engine. By continually altering

the pulse width, the ECU/PCM adjusts the air-fuel ratio for varying operating conditions. For more information about the ECU/PCM, see Chapter 6.

3   Throttle Body Injection (TBI) is a single-point system that injects fuel through one electrically operated fuel injector into the throttle body above the throttle plate.

4   Multi-Port Injection (MPI) is a multi-injector, sequential system: Fuel is injected into the intake manifold upstream of each intake valve in precisely metered amounts through electrically operated injectors. The injectors are energized in a specific sequence by the ECU or PCM. There is no injector in the throttle body itself, as in a TBI system; the injectors are installed in the intake manifold. They receive pressurized fuel from a fuel rail attached to their upper ends.

5   System fuel pressure on both systems is provided by an in-tank electric fuel pump and is controlled by a fuel pressure regulator.

13   Fuel lines and fittings - inspection and replacement

Warning: *Gasoline is extremely flammable, so take extra precautions when you work on any part of the fuel system. See the Warning at the beginning of Section 1.*

Inspection and replacement

1   Check the fuel lines and all fittings and connections for cracks, leakage and deformation.

2   Check the fuel tank vapor vent system hoses and connections for looseness, sharp bends and damage.

3   Check the fuel tank for deformation, cracks, fuel leakage and tank band looseness.

4   Check the filler neck for damage and fuel leakage.

5   Repair or replace any damaged or deteriorated hoses or lines. If your vehicle is equipped with fuel injection, see below for information on replacing fuel line fittings.

6   When attaching hoses to metal lines, overlap them as shown (see illustration).

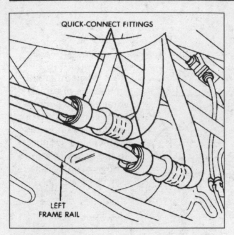

13.9a Typical under body quick-connect fittings (TBI-equipped vehicle)

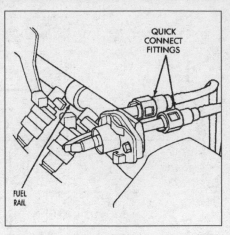

13.9b Quick-connect fitting locations (MPI-equipped vehicle)

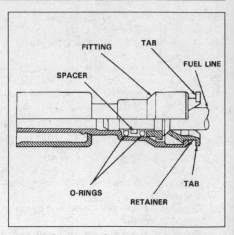

13.10 Cutaway of quick-connect fitting showing relationship of O-rings, spacer and retainer

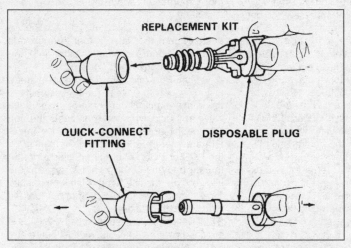

13.13 The new O-rings, spacer and retainer are already installed on a disposable plug - to install them in the quick-connect fitting, insert the plug into the fitting until you hear a click, then withdraw and discard the plug

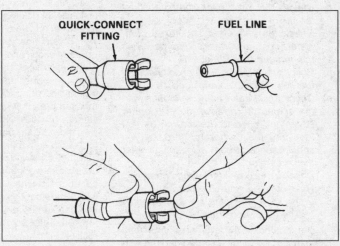

13.14 Once you've installed the new O-rings, spacer and retainer, push the fuel line into the fitting until you hear a click

Two-tab type fuel line fitting replacement (fuel-injected vehicles)

7   Remove the fuel tank filler cap to relieve fuel tank pressure.

8   If the vehicle is equipped with Multi-Port Injection (MPI), relieve the system pressure before proceeding (see Section 2). If the vehicle is equipped with Throttle Body Injection (TBI), system pressure is bled off when the fuel pump is not operating - you can disconnect fuel hoses and lines as soon as you have turned off the engine.

9   All fuel injected engines use special quick-connect fuel line fittings. On TBI-equipped vehicles, the fittings are located at the throttle body ends of the nylon reinforced hoses which connect the throttle body to the fuel supply and return lines and under the vehicle along the left frame rail (see illustration). On MPI-equipped engines, they're located at the fuel rail inlet port and at the

connection between the fuel return line and the fuel return hose (see illustration).

10   The fittings consist of two O-rings, a spacer between the two O-rings and a retainer (see illustration).

11   Every time you disconnect a quick-connect fitting, you must replace the O-rings, spacer and retainer. These parts are available as a repair kit through any dealer parts department.

Note: *On 2007 and later models, the O-rings in quick-connect fuel fittings are not serviceable. If the fitting is broken or leaking, the manufacturer suggests that the whole line be replaced.*

12   To disconnect a quick connect fitting, simply pinch the two retainer tabs together and pull the fitting apart. The retainer, O-rings and spacer will come out of the fitting when you pull the fuel lines apart. Discard these parts.

13   The replacement kit (O-rings, spacer and retainer) is installed on a disposable plastic plug. To replace these parts, push the dis-

posable plug assembly into the quick connect fitting until you hear a "click" sound (see illustration). Then grasp the end of the disposable plug and pull it out of the fitting.

14   Push the fuel line into the refurbished quick-connect fitting until you hear a "click" sound (see illustration).

15   Verify that the connection is secure by pulling firmly back on the fuel line. It should be locked in place.

Single-tab type fuel line fitting replacement (fuel-injected models)

Caution: *Do not try to repair damaged fittings or fuel lines. If repair is necessary, replace the complete fuel line quick-connect fitting assembly.*

16   Relieve the system pressure before proceeding (see Section 2).

17   The fittings consist of O-rings, spacers and a pull tab. The O-rings and spacers can't be serviced separately, but new pull tabs are

available and must be used.

18   To disconnect the fitting, simply press the release tab on the side of the fitting, use a screwdriver to pry up the pull tab and pull the fitting apart (see illustrations). Discard the old pull tab.

19   Apply a light coat of clean engine oil to the inner surface of the fitting.

20   Insert the quick-connect fitting into the fuel line until the built-in stop on the fuel line rests on the back of the fitting.

21   Push the new pull tab down until it locks into place in the quick-connect fitting.

22   Verify the connection is secure by pulling firmly back on the fuel line. It should be locked in place. Run the engine and check for fuel leaks.

Plastic retainer ring type fuel line fitting replacement (fuel-injected models)

Caution: *Do not try to repair damaged fittings or fuel lines. If repair is necessary, replace the complete fuel line quick-connect fitting assembly.*

23   Relieve the system pressure before proceeding (see Section 2).

24   The fittings consist of O-rings, spacers and a plastic retainer. The O-rings and spacers can't be serviced separately.

25   To disconnect a quick-connect fitting, simply push the fitting toward the component being serviced while pushing the plastic retaining ring squarely into the fitting (see illustration). While the plastic retaining ring is depressed, pull the fitting from the component.

26   Apply a light coat of clean engine oil to the inner surface of the fitting.

27   Insert the quick-connect fitting into the fuel line until you hear a "click" sound.

28   Verify the connection is secure by pulling

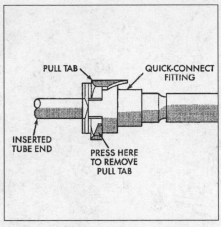
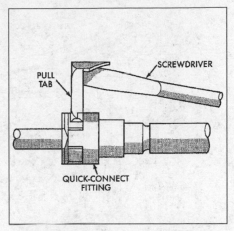

13.18a On single-tab fittings, use your fingers to press the release tabs on the sides of the fitting...

13.18b ... then, while pressing the tabs, pry up the pull tab with a screwdriver, then pull the fitting apart

firmly back on the fuel line. It should be locked in place. Run the engine and check for fuel leaks.

14   Throttle body (TBI-equipped vehicles) - removal and installation

Warning: *Gasoline is extremely flammable, so take extra precautions when you work on any part of the fuel system. See the Warning at the beginning of Section 1.*

1   Detach the cable from the negative battery terminal.

2   Detach the vacuum hoses from the throttle body upper bonnet. Release the mounting clips and remove the upper bonnet.

3   Remove the three mounting nuts and lift off the lower bonnet (see illustrations).

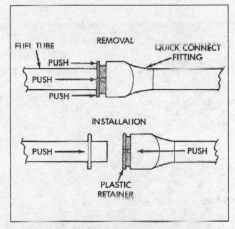

13.25 On models with plastic retainer rings, press the ring squarely into the fitting body, making sure the ring doesn't get cocked and, if necessary, use an open-end wrench on the plastic retaining ring shoulder to help pull the fitting free

14.3a Remove the mounting nuts, then detach the lower bonnet ...

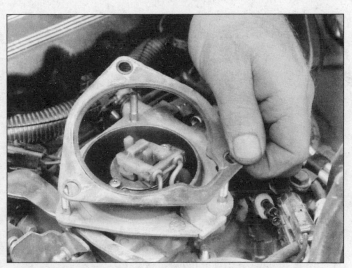

14.3b ... then remove the gasket from the rim of the throttle body

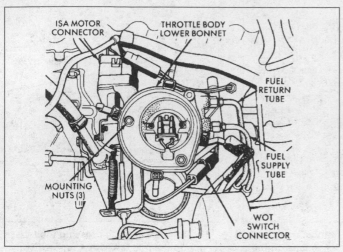

14.4 Disconnect the ISA motor connector from the throttle body

14.5 Use a back-up wrench to keep the fitting on the TBI unit stationary while loosening the fuel line

14.8 Identify and tag the vacuum tubes at the back of the throttle body, then detach them

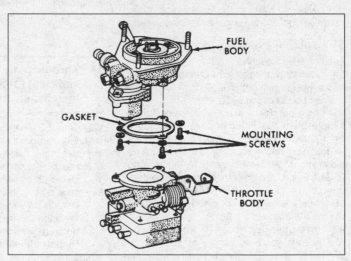

15.3 An exploded view of the fuel body assembly

4   Disconnect the ISA motor harness connector (see illustration).
5   Detach the fuel supply and return lines (see illustration) from the throttle body.
6   Remove the accelerator cable and return spring (see Section 8).
7   Detach the wire harness connector from the injector by compressing the lock tabs and lifting up.
8   Identify and label the vacuum tubes at the back of the throttle body so you can install them in their original locations. Detach the vacuum tubes from the throttle body (see illustration).
9   Detach the TPS connector (two connectors on automatics).
10   Remove the throttle body mounting nuts and remove the throttle body.
11   Remove any old gasket material or dirt from the mating surfaces of the intake manifold and the throttle body.
12   If you are replacing the throttle body

assembly, remove the ISA motor and throttle position sensor. Install them on the replacement throttle body and adjust them (see Section 15).
13   Installation is the reverse of removal. Be sure to use a new gasket and tighten the mounting nuts to the torque listed in this Chapter's Specifications.

---

15   Throttle body injection (TBI) system - component replacement

Warning: *Gasoline is extremely flammable, so take extra precautions when you work on any part of the fuel system. See the Warning at the beginning of Section 1.*

Fuel body

1   Detach the cable from the negative battery terminal.

2   Remove the throttle body (see Section 14).
3   Remove the three Torx head screws that attach the fuel body to the throttle body (see illustration).
4   Remove the original gasket and discard it.
5   Installation is the reverse of removal.

Fuel injector
Removal

6   Remove the throttle body upper bonnet (see Section 14).
7   Remove the throttle body lower bonnet (see Section 14).
8   Detach the injector connector (see illustration) by compressing the lock tabs and lifting up.
9   Remove the screws and lift off the retainer (see illustration).
10   Using a small screwdriver, gently pry

15.8 To remove the injector connector on TBI-equipped vehicles, compress the tabs and lift up

15.9 First remove the screws (Torx 15) from the retainer and...

15.10 ... gently pry the center with a screwdriver and carefully extract the injector by rocking it back and forth while lifting up - do not twist it during removal

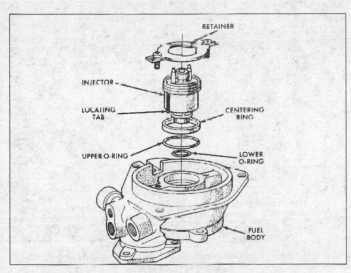

15.12 An exploded view of TBI fuel injector components

15.21 Remove the three Torx screws from the fuel pressure regulator housing (TBI unit removed for clarity)

the center collar of the injector and carefully remove the injector by rocking it back and forth with your fingers while lifting up (see illustration) with the screwdriver.

Caution: *Do not twist the injector during removal or its locating tab will be damaged.*

11   Remove and discard the centering ring and upper and lower O-rings.

Caution: *Do not re-use these rings or fuel leakage and poor driveability may occur.*

Installation

12   Lubricate the replacement lower O-ring with light oil. Install the replacement lower O-ring in the bottom of the fuel injector housing bore (see illustration).

13   Lubricate the replacement upper O-ring with light oil. Install it in the fuel injector housing bore.

14   Install the centering ring on top of the upper O-ring.

15   Align the locating tab on the bottom of the injector (see illustration 15.12) with the slot in the bottom of the housing and install the injector.

16   Install the retainer and tighten the screws securely.

17   Attach the injector connector.

18   Install the lower and upper bonnets.

19   Attach the negative battery cable.

Fuel pressure regulator

20   Remove the throttle body (see Section 14).

21   Remove the pressure regulator mounting screws (see illustration).

Warning: *The regulator is under spring pressure. To prevent possible injury from the regulator flying off, keep the regulator forced against the throttle body while you're removing the screws.*

22   Remove the housing, spring, spring seats, diaphragm and pivot (see illustration).

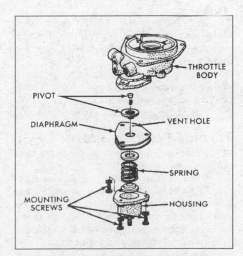

15.22 An exploded view of the fuel pressure regulator assembly

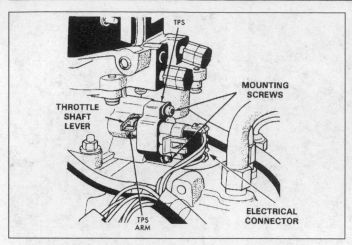

15.28 To remove the throttle position sensor (TPS), unplug the electrical connector and remove the two mounting screws

15.29 Remove the two Torx screws from the TPS housing (TBI unit removed for clarity)

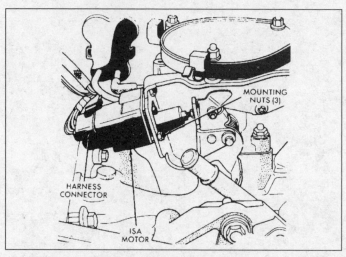

15.33 Disconnect the ISA motor harness connector; to remove the motor, unscrew the three mounting nuts - use a back-up wrench to avoid damaging the motor

16.4 Idle speed stepper motor connector (left) and TPS connector (right) - typical shown

23   Remove any foreign material from the housing.

24   Installation is the reverse of removal. Make sure you install the diaphragm so its vent hole is aligned with the vent holes in the throttle body and housing.

25   After you have replaced the regulator and installed the throttle body on the engine, start the engine and check for leaks.

26   Adjust the fuel pressure (see Section 3).

Throttle Position Sensor (TPS)

27   Remove the upper and lower air inlet bonnets (see Section 14).

28   Remove the throttle body (see Section 14). This is not absolutely necessary, but it makes it easier to get at the TPS. If you don't remove the throttle body, unplug the TPS connector (see illustration). Note that the TPS used on vehicles with automatic transmissions has two connectors.

29   Remove the TPS mounting screws (see illustration).

30   Remove the TPS from the throttle shaft lever.

31   Installation is the reverse of removal. Be sure the TPS arm is underneath the throttle shaft lever.

32   Have the TPS adjusted by a dealer service department.

Idle speed actuator (ISA) motor

33   Remove the ISA motor harness connector (see illustration).

34   Detach the throttle return spring.

35   Remove the three ISA motor-to-bracket mounting nuts (see illustration 15.33). Use a back-up wrench to prevent the studs which hold the ISA motor together from turning.

Caution: *Don't attempt to remove the ISA motor-to-bracket nuts without using a back-up wrench on the stud nuts. ISA motor internal components may be damaged if the studs disengage.*

36   Remove the ISA motor from the bracket.

37   Installation is the reverse of removal.

38   After you have replaced the ISA motor, have it adjusted by a qualified repair facility.

16   Multi-Point Injection (MPI) - component replacement

Warning: *Gasoline is extremely flammable, so take extra precautions when you work on any part of the fuel system. See the Warning at the beginning of Section 1.*

Throttle body

1   Detach the cable from the negative battery terminal.

2   Relieve the fuel pressure (see Section 2).

3   Disconnect the flexible air duct from the throttle body (see Section 7).

2006 and earlier models

4   Detach the idle speed stepper motor and throttle position sensor wire connectors (see illustration).

16.5 Use a small screwdriver to pry the MAP sensor vacuum tube from the back of the throttle body

16.6 To detach the linkage from the throttle arm, insert a screwdriver between the linkage and the arm and pop it loose

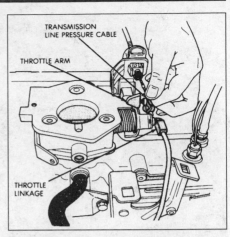

16.7 If the vehicle is equipped with an automatic transmission, detach the line pressure cable at the throttle arm

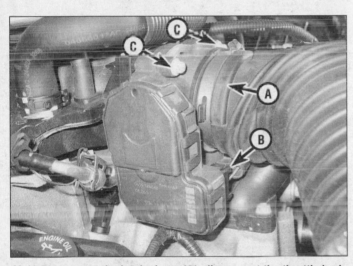

16.10 Disconnect the intake hose (A), disconnect the throttle body electrical connector (B), and remove the mounting bolts (C, two indicated here)

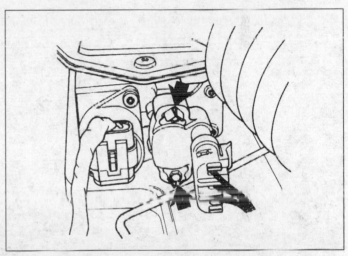

16.18 To remove the TPS, remove the retaining screws (arrows), then pull the TPS from the throttle assembly - if the screws are secured by lock tabs (as shown here), bend the tabs back - use new tabs when reinstalling the screws (manual transmission shown)

5   Detach the MAP sensor vacuum tube from the back of the throttle body (see illustration).
6   Detach the throttle linkage at the throttle arm (see illustration).
7   If equipped an with automatic transmission, detach the line pressure cable at the throttle arm (see illustration).
8   Remove the mounting bolts, throttle body and gasket. Discard the old gasket and clean the gasket mating surfaces on the throttle body and intake manifold.
9   Installation is the reverse of removal.

2007 and later models
10   Disconnect the throttle body electrical connector (see illustration).
11   Remove the mounting bolts and the throttle body. Check the condition of the throttle body seal. If the seal is OK, it can be reused.
12   Installation is the reverse of removal.

Idle speed stepper motor (2006 and earlier models)
13   Detach the cable from the negative battery terminal (see Chapter 5).
14   Unplug the wire connector from the idle speed stepper motor, remove the retaining screws, then pull off the idle speed stepper motor (see illustration 16.4).
15   Installation is the reverse of removal.

Throttle position sensor (2006 and earlier models)
16   Detach the cable from the negative battery terminal (see Chapter 5).
17   Unplug the TPS wire connector (see illustration 16.4).

18   Bend back the TPS lock tabs, if equipped (see illustration). Remove the retaining screws, then detach the TPS from the throttle plate assembly.
19   Installation is the reverse of removal.
Note: *When installing, the tab on the throttle shaft will need to be lined up with the inside of the TPS. To do this, then installing, rotate the TPS to engage the tab, then rotate to install the screws and tighten. The TPS will have slight tension on it when in position to install the screws.*

Fuel injector rail assembly
20   Remove the fuel filler cap to relieve fuel tank pressure.
21   Relieve the fuel pressure (see Section 2).
22   Detach the cable from the negative battery terminal (see Chapter 5).

16.23a Numerically label the injector harness connectors so you don't mix them up during reassembly

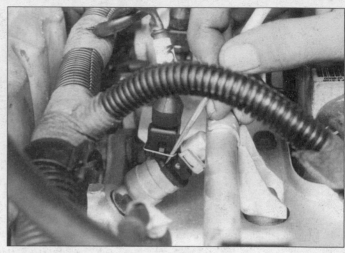

16.23b Use a scribe (shown) or a small screwdriver to pop loose the retaining clip that attaches the harness connector to each injector

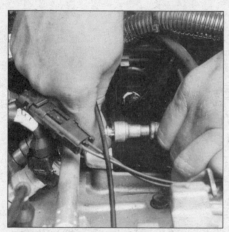

16.25a Detach the fuel supply hose from the fuel rail

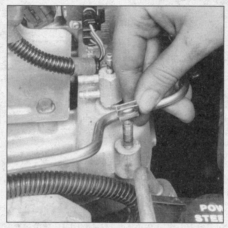

16.25b Remove the nut from the fuel return line bracket and slide the bracket off its mounting stud…

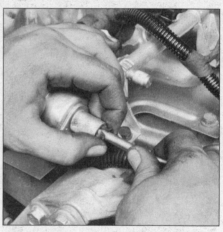

16.25c … then detach the fuel return line from the fuel pressure regulator

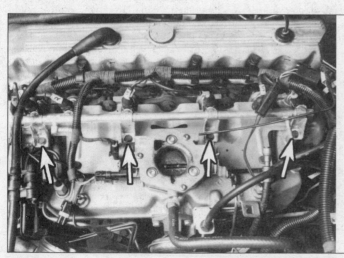

16.26 Remove the fuel rail mounting bolts (typical)

2006 and earlier models

23   Numerically label, then unplug, the injector harness connectors (see illustrations). On 2004 and later models, the harness connectors are factory-numbered, and you must push back a red slider at each harness connector to release it.

24   If equipped, detach the vacuum hose from the fuel pressure regulator (see illustration 3.36).

25   Detach the fuel supply hose from the fuel rail, the fuel return line from the intake manifold, then the fuel return line from the fuel pressure regulator (see illustrations). Refer to Section 13 for information on removing and replacing fuel line fittings.

26   Remove the fuel rail mounting bolts (see illustration).

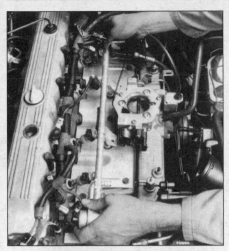

16.29 Before installing the fuel rail mounting bolts, position the tip of each injector over its respective bore in the intake manifold, then push down on the injectors to seat them completely (4.0L engine shown)

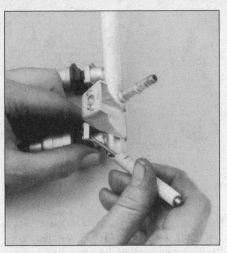

16.43 Use a small screwdriver (shown) or scribe to pop loose the clip that secures the injector to the fuel rail assembly

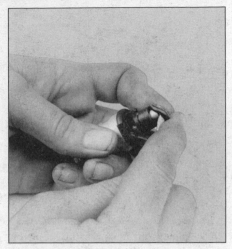

16.44 Be sure to remove the old O-ring and seal from the injector (a replacement kit, available at most auto parts stores, includes O-rings and seals - enough O-rings and seals for all injectors and an extra seal for the fuel pressure regulator)

27   If the vehicle is equipped with an automatic transmission, it may be necessary to remove the automatic transmission line pressure cable and bracket to remove the fuel rail assembly (see illustration 16.7).

28   Remove the fuel rail by simultaneously rocking and pulling up on it until all injectors are out of the intake manifold. Work slowly and carefully so you don't damage the assembly.

29   Installation is the reverse of removal, but be sure to do the following:

a) Before attempting to reattach the fuel rail assembly mounting bolts, position the tip of each injector above its corresponding bore in the intake manifold (see illustration), then seat the injectors by pushing down on them. You must seat the injectors properly before you tighten the fuel rail mounting bolts.

b) When you reattach the fuel lines, be sure to use a new O-ring, spacer and retainer repair kit (see Section 13).

2007 and later models

30   Remove the upper intake manifold (see Chapter 2D, Section 6 or Chapter 2E, Section 5).

31   Remove the insulator from the driver side valve cover.

32   Disconnect the fuel injector electrical connectors. Slide the connector lock to the unlock position before attempting to disconnect.

33   Disconnect the fuel supply line quick-connect fitting at the fuel rail.

34   Remove the four bolts and the fuel rail. Pull carefully but firmly to remove the injectors from the lower intake manifold. On 2007 through 2011 models, remove the fuel rail one side at a time.

Note: The injectors may stay in the lower intake manifold and may need to be removed after removing the fuel rail.

35   Remove the injectors from the fuel rail by pulling firmly.

36   Installation is reverse of removal.

37   Replace the injector O-rings before installing the injectors and fuel rail.

38   Tighten the fasteners to the torque listed in this Chapter's Specifications.

Fuel injectors

39   Remove the fuel filler cap to relieve fuel tank pressure.

40   Relieve the system fuel pressure (see Section 2).

41   Detach the cable from the negative battery terminal (see Chapter 5).

42   Remove the fuel injector rail assembly as described earlier in this Section.

2006 and earlier models

43   Remove the retaining clip(s) that attach the injector(s) to the rail assembly (see illustration).

44   If you are servicing a leaking injector, remove the old O-rings and seals (see illustration).

45   An O-ring kit is available from a dealer parts department for both the 2.5L and the 4.0L engines. For example, a kit for a 4.0L engine consists of 6 brown and 7 black seals. The brown seals fit on the injector tips; the black seals fit on the rail end of the injectors. Do not switch the brown and black O-rings - they're different in design and composition. The extra black seal is for the fuel pressure regulator.

46   Because the O-ring kit includes enough O-rings for all six injectors (they're not available individually), it's a good idea to replace the upper and lower O-rings on all injectors, even if only one or two are actually leaking at the time you service them. Otherwise, you will probably find yourself repeating this entire procedure down the road - to fix other leaky injectors.

47   Installation is the reverse of removal. Be sure to coat the injector O-rings with a little fuel before installing the injector.

2007 and later models

48   Firmly pull the fuel injectors from the fuel rail to detach the retainer. The retainer will stay on the injector.

Note: Injectors may remain in the lower intake manifold when the fuel rail is removed, using a twisting motion, remove the fuel injector from the manifold.

49   An O-ring kit is available from a dealer parts department. Different O-rings are used on the upper and lower ends of the injector. Do not switch the O-rings - they're different in design and composition.

50   Installation is the reverse of removal. Be sure to coat the injector O-rings with a little fuel before installing the injector.

Fuel pressure regulator

Note: On 2007 and later models, the fuel pressure regulator is part of the fuel pump module and replaced as a unit.

1996 and earlier models

Note: On these models the fuel pressure regulator is located on the fuel rail.

51   Remove the fuel filler cap to relieve fuel tank pressure.

52   Relieve the system fuel pressure (see Section 2).

53   Detach the cable from the negative battery terminal (see Chapter 5).

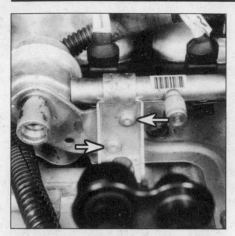

16.54 Remove the fuel pressure regulator retaining screws

16.55 Pull the fuel pressure regulator off the end of the fuel rail

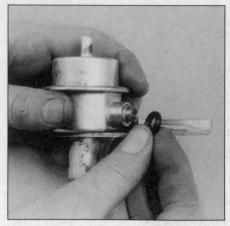

16.56 Always install a new O-ring on the pressure regulator

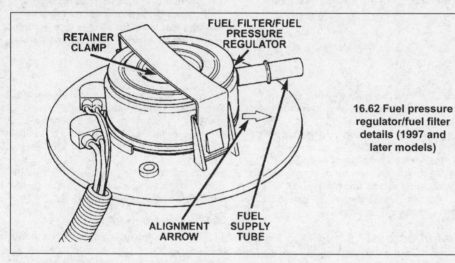

16.62 Fuel pressure regulator/fuel filter details (1997 and later models)

RETAINER CLAMP

FUEL FILTER/FUEL PRESSURE REGULATOR

ALIGNMENT ARROW

FUEL SUPPLY TUBE

54   Remove the fuel pressure regulator retaining screws (see illustration).

55   Pull the regulator off the fuel rail (see illustration).

56   Whenever you remove the fuel pressure regulator, always install a new O-ring (see illustration). This O-ring is available as part of an O-ring kit for the injectors (see Step 34 above).

57   Installation is the reverse of removal.

1997 through 2004 models

Note: *These models are equipped with a "returnless" fuel system. The fuel pressure regulator is mounted on top of the fuel pump/fuel level sending unit assembly.*

Note: *The fuel filter requires service only when a fuel contamination problem is suspected.*

58   Relieve the fuel system pressure (see Section 2).

59   Detach the cable from the negative battery terminal (see Chapter 5).

60   Remove the fuel tank (see Section 5).

61   Detach the fuel line from the fuel pressure regulator.

62   Unsnap the clamp from the top of the fuel filter/pressure regulator assembly (see illustration).

63   Remove the fuel pressure regulator/fuel filter by gently prying the unit from the fuel pump module. Remove the gasket from under the regulator.

64   Check the regulator to make sure that both O-rings came off with it (there's a small one at the end of the regulator and a larger one up a little higher). If both of them aren't present, retrieve the missing one(s) from the fuel pump module.

65   Installation is the reverse of removal. Lubricate the O-rings with clean engine oil, and be sure to install a new gasket to the top of the fuel pump module. The arrow on the top of the pressure regulator should point to the front of the vehicle. Also, a new regulator retaining clamp should be used.

---

17   Exhaust system servicing - general information

Warning: *Inspection and repair of exhaust system components should be done only after enough time has elapsed after driving the vehicle to allow the system components to cool completely. Also, when working under the ve-*hicle, make sure it is securely supported on jackstands.

1   The exhaust system (see illustrations) consists of the exhaust manifold(s), the catalytic converter, the muffler, the tailpipe and all connecting pipes, brackets, hangers and clamps. The exhaust system is attached to the body with mounting brackets and rubber hangers. If any of the parts are improperly installed, excessive noise and vibration will be transmitted to the body.

2   Conduct regular inspections of the exhaust system to keep it safe and quiet. Look for any damaged or bent parts, open seams, holes, loose connections, excessive corrosion or other defects which could allow exhaust fumes to enter the vehicle. Deteriorated exhaust system components should not be repaired; they should be replaced with new parts.

3   If the exhaust system components are extremely corroded or rusted together, welding equipment will probably be required to remove them. The convenient way to accomplish this is to have a muffler repair shop remove the corroded sections with a cutting torch. If, however, you want to save money by doing it yourself (and you don't have a welding outfit with a cutting torch), simply cut off the old components with a hacksaw. If you have compressed air, special pneumatic cutting chisels can also be used. If you do decide to tackle the job at home, be sure to wear safety goggles to protect your eyes from metal chips and work gloves to protect your hands.

4   Here are some simple guidelines to follow when repairing the exhaust system:

Work from the back to the front when removing exhaust system components.

a) *Apply penetrating oil to the exhaust system component fasteners to make them easier to remove.*

b) *Use new gaskets, hangers and clamps when installing exhaust systems components.*

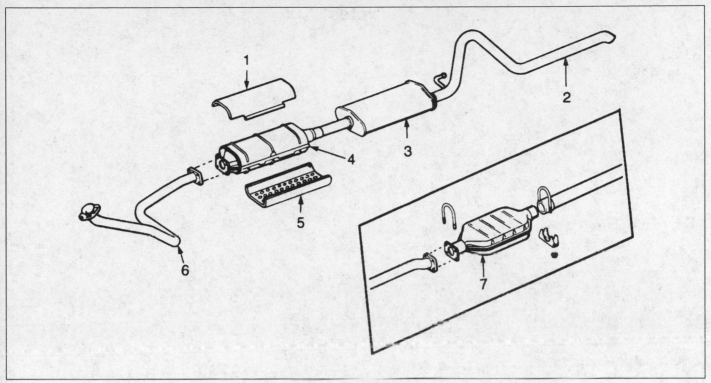

17.1a Exploded view of a typical exhaust system for a four-cylinder engine

1 Upper heat shield
2 Tail pipe
3 Muffler
4 Catalytic converter
5 Lower heat shield
6 Exhaust pipe
7 Resonator (Canada only)

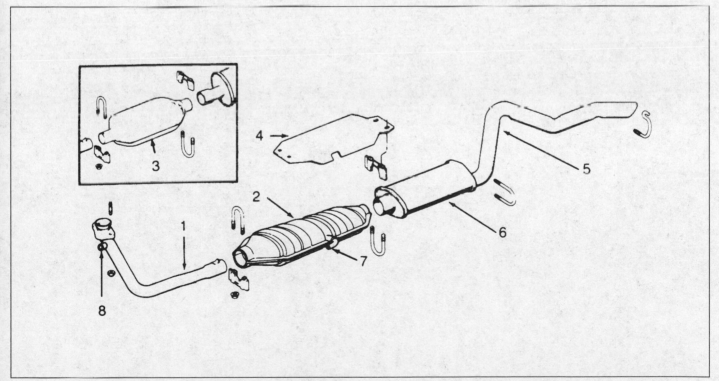

17.1b Exploded view of a typical exhaust system for an in-line six-cylinder engine

1 Front exhaust pipe
2 Catalytic converter
3 Resonator (Canada only)
4 Converter heat-shield
5 Tailpipe
6 Muffler
7 Downstream air injection tube port
8 Upstream air injection tube port

Notes

Chapter 5
Engine electrical systems

Contents

Specifications

Ignition coil resistance

1987 through 1990 four-cylinder models	
Primary	0.4 to 0.8 ohms
Secondary	2500 to 4000 ohms
Carbureted models	
Primary	1.13 to 1.23 ohms
Secondary	77 to 93 K-ohms
1991 and later models (except 2000 six-cylinder models)	
Diamond	
Primary	0.97 to 1.18 ohms
Secondary	11.3 to 15.3 K-ohms
Toyodenso	
Primary	0.95 to 1.20 ohms
Secondary	11.3 to 13.3 K-ohms
2000 through 2006 six-cylinder models (Primary only)	0.71 to 0.88 ohms
2007 and later models	
Primary	0.6 to 0.9 ohms
Secondary	6000 to 9000 ohms
Ignition coil wire resistance (all except 2000 six-cylinder models)	3 to 10 K-ohms

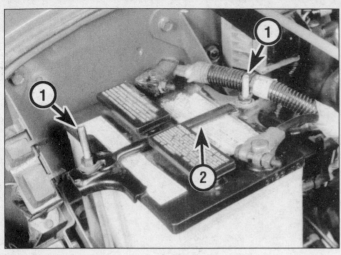

2.3a Unscrew the nuts (1) and lift the clamp (2) off the battery (early models)

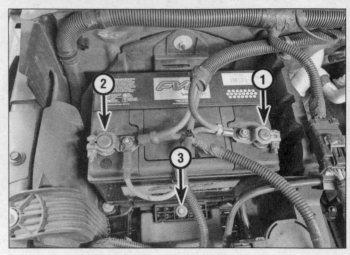

2.3b Battery mounting details (later models)

1	*Negative terminal*	3 *Hold-down bolt/clamp*
2	*Positive terminal*	

1   General information

1   The engine electrical systems include all ignition, charging and starting components. Because of their engine-related functions, these components are discussed separately from chassis electrical devices such as the lights, the instruments, etc. (which are included in Chapter 12).

2   Always observe the following precautions when working on the electrical systems:

a) *Be extremely careful when servicing engine electrical components. They are easily damaged if checked, connected or handled improperly.*

b) *Never leave the ignition switch on for long periods of time with the engine off.*

c) *Don't disconnect the battery cables while the engine is running.*

d) *Maintain correct polarity when connecting a battery cable from another vehicle during jump starting.*

e) *Always disconnect the negative cable first and hook it up last or the battery may be shorted by the tool being used to loosen the cable clamps.*

3   It's also a good idea to review the safety-related information regarding the engine electrical systems located in the Safety first! section near the front of this manual before beginning any operation included in this Chapter.

2   Battery - removal and installation

Caution: *Always disconnect the negative cable first and hook it up last or the battery may be shorted by the tool being used to loosen the cable clamps.*

1   Disconnect the negative (-) battery cable from the negative (-) battery terminal.

2   Disconnect the positive (+) battery cable from the positive (+) battery terminal.

3   Remove the battery hold-down clamp (see illustrations).

4   Lift out the battery. Be careful - it's heavy.

5   While the battery is out, inspect the carrier (tray) for corrosion (early models with a metal tray).

6   If you are replacing the battery, make sure you get one that's identical, with the same dimensions, amperage rating, cold cranking rating, etc.

7   On models so equipped, transfer the thermal guard to the new battery.

8   Installation is the reverse of removal.

9   Connect the positive (+) battery cable first, then the negative (-) battery cable second.

3   Battery cables - check and replacement

1   Periodically inspect the entire length of each battery cable for damage, cracked or burned insulation and corrosion. Poor battery connections can cause starting problems and decreased engine performance.

2   Check the cable-to-terminal connections at the ends of the cables for cracks, loose wire strands and corrosion. The presence of white, fluffy deposits under the insulation at the cable terminal connection is a sign that the cable is corroded and should be replaced. Check the terminals for distortion, missing mounting bolts and corrosion.

3   When removing the cables, always disconnect the negative cable first and hook it up last or the battery may be shorted by the tool used to loosen the cable clamps. Even if only the positive cable is being replaced, be sure to disconnect the negative cable from the battery first.

4   Disconnect the old cables from the battery, then trace each of them to their opposite ends and detach them from the starter solenoid and ground terminals. Note the routing of each cable to ensure correct installation.

5   If you are replacing either or both of the old cables, take them with you when buying new cables. It is vitally important that you replace the cables with identical parts. Cables have characteristics that make them easy to identify: positive cables are usually red, larger in cross-section and have a larger diameter battery post clamp; ground cables are usually black, smaller in cross-section and have a slightly smaller diameter clamp for the negative post.

6   Clean the threads of the solenoid or ground connection with a wire brush to remove rust and corrosion. Apply a light coat of battery terminal corrosion inhibitor, or petroleum jelly, to the threads to prevent future corrosion.

7   Attach the cable to the solenoid or ground connection and tighten the mounting nut/bolt securely.

8   Before connecting a new cable to the battery, make sure that it reaches the battery post without having to be stretched.

9   Connect the positive cable first, followed by the negative cable.

4   Ignition system - general information

1990 and earlier four-cylinder engine

1   These models are equipped with an ignition system consisting of a solid state Ignition Control Module (ICM), an electronic distributor, an Electronic Control Unit (ECU), a specially machined flywheel and a Top Dead Center (TDC) sensor.

2   The solid state ICM is located in the engine compartment on the right (passen-

ger's) side of the firewall in the engine compartment, consists of a solid state ignition circuit and an integrated ignition coil that can be removed and serviced separately if necessary. The ICM controls ignition timing, using signals from the ECU.

3   The ECU gets its information regarding TDC, BDC and engine speed from a TDC sensor mounted on the flywheel/driveplate housing. The flywheel has two teeth machined off every 180-degrees to define a precise point 90-degrees before TDC and BDC.

Carbureted six-cylinder engine

4   The Solid State Ignition (SSI) system used on these models is made up of the Micro Computer Unit (MCU), located in the passenger compartment, conventional distributor which uses vacuum to control timing and a coil and an ignition control module located on the passenger's side firewall in the engine compartment.

1991 though 1999 models

5   1991 through 1999 four- and six-cylinder engines use the same ignition system. It consists of an engine computer (located on the driver's side firewall, behind the windshield washer reservoir), a distributor and a coil mounted on the engine block next to the distributor. On 1991 and 1992 models, the engine computer is referred to as the Engine Control Module (ECM). On 1993 and later models, it is referred to as the Powertrain Control Module (PCM).

2000 and later models

6   The 2000 and later models are equipped with a distributorless ignition system. The ignition system consists of the battery, ignition coils, spark plugs, camshaft position sensor, crankshaft position sensor and the Powertrain Control Module (PCM). The PCM controls the ignition timing and spark advance characteristics for the engine. The ignition timing is not adjustable.

7   The PCM controls the ignition system by opening and closing the ignition coil ground circuit. The computerized ignition system provides complete control of the ignition timing by determining the optimum timing in response to engine speed, coolant temperature, throttle position and vacuum pressure in the intake manifold. These parameters are relayed to the PCM by the camshaft position sensor, crankshaft position sensor, throttle position sensor and the manifold absolute pressure sensor. The PCM and crankshaft position sensors are very important components of the ignition system. The ignition system will not operate and the engine will not start if the PCM or the crankshaft position sensor are defective. Refer to Chapter 6 for additional information on the various sensors.

2000 through 2006 in-line six-cylinder models

8   The ignition system uses a "waste spark" method of spark distribution. The system uti-

5.1 To use a calibrated ignition tester (available at most auto parts stores), simply disconnect a spark plug wire, attach the wire to the tester and clip the tester to a good ground - if there is enough power to fire the plug, sparks will be clearly visible between the electrode tip and the tester body as the engine is turned over

lizes three ignition coils in a coil rail assembly. Each coil is paired with the opposite cylinder in the firing order (1-6, 5-2, 3-4) so one cylinder under compression fires simultaneously with its opposing cylinder, where the piston is on the exhaust stroke. Since the cylinder on the exhaust stroke requires very little of the available voltage to fire its plug, most of the voltage is used to fire the plug of the cylinder on the compression stroke. Conventional ignition coils have one end of the secondary winding connected to the engine ground. On a waste spark system, neither end of the secondary winding is grounded - instead one end of the coil's secondary winding is directly attached to the spark plug and the other end is attached to the spark plug of the companion cylinder.

2007 though 2011 models

9   2007 though 2011 models are equipped with single coil for all cylinders. Each cylinder has a spark plug wire that connects the coil terminal to the corresponding spark plug. The coil is fired by the PCM.

2012 and later models

10   2012 and later models are equipped with coil-on-plug ignition. Each cylinder has an ignition coil bolted to the valve cover, connected to the spark plug. The coil is fired by the PCM.

---

5   Ignition system - check

2002 and earlier four-cylinder models and 1999 and earlier six-cylinder models

Warning: *Because of the high voltage generated by the ignition system, extreme care should be taken when this check is performed.*

1   If the engine turns over but won't start, disconnect the spark plug wire from any spark plug and attach it to a calibrated ignition tester (available at most auto parts stores). Connect the clip on the tester to a bolt or metal bracket on the engine (see illustration). If you're

unable to obtain a calibrated ignition tester, remove the wire from one of the spark plugs and, using an insulated tool, hold the end of the wire about 1/4-inch from a good ground.

2   Crank the engine and watch the end of the tester or spark plug to see if bright blue, well-defined sparks occur. If you're not using a calibrated tester, have an assistant crank the engine for you.

3   If sparks occur, sufficient voltage is reaching the plug to fire it (repeat the check at the remaining plug wires to verify that the distributor cap and rotor are OK). However, the plugs themselves might be fouled, so remove and check them as described in Chapter 1.

4   If no sparks or intermittent sparks occur, remove the distributor cap and check the cap and rotor as described in Chapter 1. If moisture is present, dry out the cap and rotor, then reinstall the cap and repeat the spark test.

5   If there's still no spark, detach the coil secondary wire from the distributor cap and hook it up to the tester (reattach the plug wire to the spark plug), then repeat the spark check. Again, if you don't have a tester, hold the end of the wire about 1/4-inch from a good ground.

6   If sparks now occur, the distributor cap, rotor or plug wire(s) may be defective.

7   If no sparks occur, check the primary wire connections at the coil to make sure they're clean and tight. Check for voltage at the coil. Make any necessary repairs, then repeat the check again.

8   If there's still no spark, the coil-to-cap wire may be bad (check the resistance with an ohmmeter and compare it to this Chapter's Specifications). If a known good wire doesn't make any difference in the test results, the ignition coil may be defective.

2000 through 2006 six-cylinder models

Caution: *Because of the ignition system design on the six-cylinder models of this vintage, a special set of spark plug wires must be obtained or fabricated before the ignition system check can be performed. A test set can be fabricated from bulk spark plug wire and ter-*

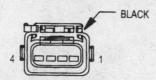

CAV	CIRCUIT	FUNCTION
1	K91 16TN/RD	COIL DRIVER NO. 1
2	A142 16DG/OR	AUTOMATIC SHUT DOWN RELAY OUTPUT
3	K92 16TN/PK	COIL DRIVER NO. 2
4	K93 16TN/OR	COIL DRIVER NO. 3

5.14 Ignition coil rail electrical connector terminal identification (harness side) - 2000 six-cylinder engine

6.2a The ignition coil on 1987 through 1990 fuel-injected models is located on the right (passenger's) side of the firewall in the engine compartment - when removing the coil, unscrew the mounting bracket bolts

minals available at most auto parts stores. As an alternative, individual jumper wires can be used to ground the spark plug terminals not being tested. Whichever method you choose, make sure all the spark plug terminals are either connected to a spark plug or grounded to the engine block before cranking the engine or damage to the ignition coils may result.

9   Disable the fuel system by removing the fuel pump relay from the power distribution center (see Chapter 12).

10   On inline six-cylinder models, remove the bolts retaining the ignition coil rail (see Section 6). Carefully detach the coil rail from the spark plug, turn the coil rail over and place it in a secure location. Do not disconnect the electrical connector from the ignition coil rail.

11   Attach a calibrated ignition system tester (available at most auto parts stores) to one of the spark plug boots. Using a heavy gauge jumper wire, connect the clip on the tester to the bolt or bare metal bracket on the engine. Connect the remaining ignition coil spark plug terminals to the spark plugs or ground them to the engine. Crank the engine and watch the end of the tester to see if a bright blue, well-defined spark occurs (weak spark, or intermittent spark could also be an indication of problems).

12   If a spark occurs, sufficient voltage is reaching the plug to fire it (repeat the check at the remaining spark plug terminals to verify that the ignition coils are good). If the ignition system is operating properly the problem lies elsewhere; i.e., a mechanical or fuel system problem. However, the spark pugs may be fouled, so remove and check them as described in Chapter 1.

13   If a spark occurs at one or more of the coils, remove the ignition coil rail and measure the primary resistance of the ignition coils (see Section 6). Check the spring inside each spark plug boot for corrosion or damage. Replace the ignition coil rail if defective.

14   If no spark occurs at all coils, disconnect the electrical connector from the coil rail and check for battery voltage to the ignition coil rail from the auto shut-down relay and power distribution center. Attach a 12 volt test light or voltmeter to a good engine ground point

and check for power at the dark green/orange wire terminal of the ignition coil rail harness connector (see illustration). Battery voltage should be available with the ignition key on. If there is no battery voltage present at the coil rail connector, check the auto shut-down relay (see Chapter 12) and circuits between the power distribution center and ignition coil rail (don't forget to check the fuses). Also check the auto shut-down relay control circuit from the relay to the PCM for continuity.

15   If the previous checks are correct, check for a trigger signal from the Powertrain Control Module. Attach a test light to the dark green/orange wire terminal and one of the other terminals of the coil rail harness connector. Crank the engine. The test light should blink with the engine cranking if a trigger signal is present. Check for a trigger signal between the dark green/orange wire terminal and each of the other terminals in the connector. If a trigger signal is present at the coil rail connector, the Powertrain Control Module and the crankshaft position sensor are functioning properly. If a trigger signal is not present at the coil terminals, check the crankshaft position sensor (see Chapter 6). If the crankshaft position sensor is good, have the PCM checked by a dealer service department or other qualified repair shop.

2007 and later models

16   The best way to diagnose the ignition system on these models is to connect a scan tool and check for Diagnostic Trouble Codes (see Chapter 6).

6   Ignition coil - check and replacement

1999 and earlier models

1   Detach the cable from the negative battery terminal.

2   Mark the wires and terminals with pieces of numbered tape, then remove the primary wires and the high-tension cable from the coil (see illustrations). Disconnect the coil mount-

6.2b On six-cylinder carbureted models, the coil is mounted next to the distributor - to remove the electrical connector, grasp it securely and pull it straight off the terminals

ing bracket, remove the coil/bracket assembly, clean the outer case and check it for cracks and other damage.

3   Clean the coil primary terminals and check the coil tower terminal for corrosion. Clean it with a wire brush if any corrosion is found.

4   Check the coil primary resistance by attaching the leads of an ohmmeter to the positive and negative terminals (see illustrations). Compare your readings to the primary resistance listed in this Chapter's Specifications.

5   Check the coil secondary resistance by hooking one of the ohmmeter leads to the primary terminals and the other to ohmmeter lead to the large center (high-tension) terminal (see illustrations). Compare your readings to the secondary resistance listed in this Chapter's Specifications.

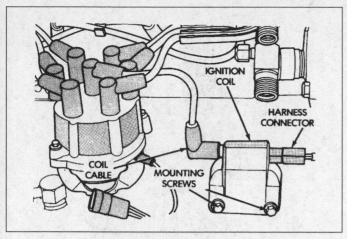

6.2c On 1991 and later models, the coil is mounted in front of the distributor

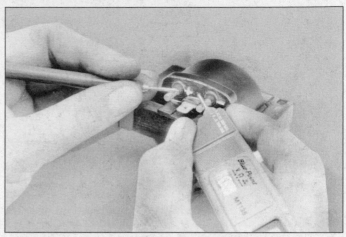

6.4a To check the coil primary resistance on 1987 through 1990 fuel-injected models, touch the ohmmeter leads to the positive and negative terminals and compare this reading to the coil primary resistance listed in this Chapter's Specifications

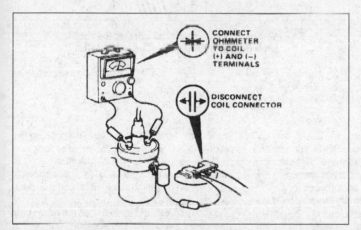

6.4b To check the coil primary resistance on carbureted models, touch the leads of an ohmmeter to the positive and negative terminals, then compare the reading with the coil primary resistance in this Chapter's Specifications

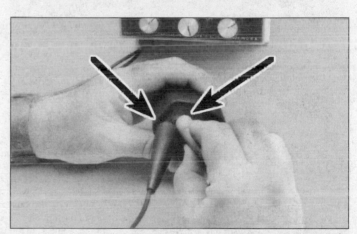

6.4c On 1991 and later models, connect the leads of an ohmmeter to the positive and negative primary terminals and compare the reading with the coil primary resistance in this Chapter's Specifications

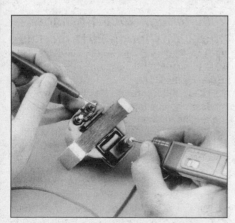

6.5a To check the coil secondary resistance on 1987 through 1990 fuel-injected models, touch one lead of the ohmmeter to one of the primary terminals and the other lead to the high tension terminal, then compare the reading to the coil secondary resistance listed in this Chapter's Specifications

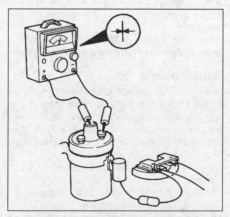

6.5b On carbureted models, check the coil secondary resistance by touching one lead of the ohmmeter to one of the primary terminals and the other lead to the high tension terminal; compare this reading to the coil secondary resistance listed in this Chapter's Specifications

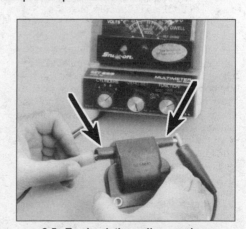

6.5c To check the coil secondary resistance on 1991 and later models, touch one lead of the ohmmeter to one of the primary terminals and the other lead to the high tension terminal, then compare the reading to the coil secondary resistance listed in this Chapter's Specifications

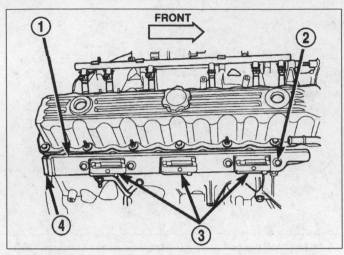

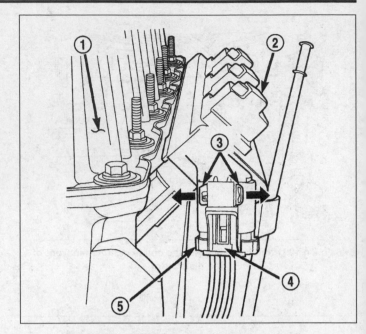

**6.15 Ignition coil rail installation details - 2000 through 2006
six-cylinder models**

1　Coil rail
2　Mounting bolts (1 of 4)
3　Ignition coils
4　Electrical connector

**6.17 Ignition coil rail electrical connector details -
2000 through 2006 six-cylinder models**

2　Ignition coil rail
3　Slide tab
4　Release lock
5　Electrical connector

**6.24 The coilpack on 2007 though 2012
V6 engines is located over the
left valve cover**

6　If the measured resistances are not as specified, the coil is probably defective and should be replaced with a new one. The best method of diagnosing the ignition system on later models is to connect a scan tool and check for Diagnostic Trouble Codes related to the ignition system.

7　For proper ignition system operation, all coil terminals and lead wires should be kept clean and dry.

8　Install the coil in the vehicle and hook up the wires.

9　Attach the cable to the negative battery terminal.

2000 through 2006 six-cylinder models

Check

10　Remove the ignition coil rail assembly (see Replacement procedure).

11　Clean the three outer cases and check for cracks or other damage. Clean the coil primary terminals and check the springs and spark plug boots for damage. If either the springs or spark plug boots are damaged, the coil rail assembly must be replaced.

12　Check the coil primary resistance. Connect an ohmmeter to terminals no. 2 and 1; 2 and 3; 2 and 4; of the coil connector. Each measurement is the primary resistance of one of the three coils in the coil rail assembly.

13　Compare your measurements to the resistance values in this Chapter's Specifications. If either measured resistance value is not as specified, replace the ignition coil rail assembly.

Note: *The entire ignition coil rail assembly must be replaced if only one coil is defective.*

Replacement

Note: *The ignition coil rail assembly consists of the three ignition coils, spark plug boots, springs, electrical connector and internal wiring. None of the components are serviced separately. The entire assembly is removed and replaced as a unit.*

14　The coil rail is located above the spark plugs.

15　Remove the ignition coil rail assembly mounting bolts (see illustration).

16　Carefully work the spark plug boots off the spark plugs by alternately prying at one end of the coil rail, then the other. If difficulty is encountered, twist the spark plug boots with a spark plug boot removal tool to loosen the seal.

17　Position the coil rail to access the electrical connection. Disconnect the electrical connector from the coil rail by first pushing the slide tab up, then press the release lock and pull the connector off (see illustration).

18　Remove the ignition coil rail assembly.

19　When installing the ignition coil rail, position all of the spark plug boots over the spark plugs and press the ignition coil rail down until the boots are completely seated.

20　Install the mounting bolts and tighten them in stages until secure.

21　Connect the electrical connector and slide the tab down until locked in place.

2000 though 2006 4-cylinder and 2007 though 2011 models

22　All 2007 and later models are equipped with a distributorless ignition system controlled by the PCM.

23　On 2000 through 2006 four-cylinder models, the coilpack is located on the top of the engine, near the throttle body.

24　On 2007 to 2011 V6 models, the coilpack is attached to a bracket over the left valve cover (see illustration).

25　Spark plug wires go directly from the coil to the designated spark plugs. All wires and their coil terminals are factory-marked.

26　If the wires are not marked, mark them with pieces of numbered tape. If you're working on a four-cylinder model, remove the air intake duct from the throttle body. On all models, disconnect the wires from the coil pack, remove the mounting bolts, then detach the coil from its bracket.

27　Installation is the reverse of removal.

2012 and later models

28   Disconnect the negative battery cable (see Section 2).
29   To remove the engine cover, at the front, pull upwards firmly to disengage the retainers, then pull the cover forward to remove.
30   If removing the coils on the driver's side of the vehicle, remove the upper intake manifold (see Chapter 2D, Section 6 or Chapter 2E, Section 5).
31   Unlock the connector lock and disconnect the electrical connector from the coil.
32   Remove the bolt attaching the coil to the valve cover.
33   While using a twisting motion to break the coil loose from the spark plug without damage, remove the ignition coil.
34   The spark plugs may now be serviced.
35   Installation is reverse of removal.

---

7   Ignition control module - check and replacement (1990 and earlier four-cylinder models and carbureted six-cylinder models)

Check

1   You need an approved ignition control module tester (Tester J-24642E or equivalent) to test the ignition control modules used with any of the vehicles covered by this manual. Without this equipment, module testing is beyond the scope of the home mechanic. If you have access to the necessary tool, the instructions for testing the module are provided by the manufacturer.

Replacement
Four-cylinder models
2   Remove the ignition coil (see Section 6).
3   Remove the two screws that attach the module to the coil frame. Pull off the module.
4   Installation is the reverse of removal.

Six-cylinder models
5   Disconnect the electrical connectors from the module.
6   Remove the mounting screws and remove the module from the firewall.
7   Installation is the reverse of removal.

---

8   Trigger wheel and/or pickup coil assembly - removal and installation (carbureted models only)

Removal

1   Detach the cable from the negative battery terminal.
2   The following procedure may be easier if you remove the distributor (see Section 11) but it's not absolutely necessary that you do so.
3   If you do decide to remove the distributor, place it in a bench vise.

4   Remove the distributor cap and rotor (see Chapter 1).
5   Using the trigger wheel puller tool, available at most auto parts stores, remove the trigger wheel (see illustration). Use a flat washer to prevent the puller from contacting the inner shaft. Remove the pin.
6   Remove the pickup coil assembly retainer and washers from the pivot pin on the base plate.
7   Remove the two pickup coil plate screws.
8   Lift the pickup coil assembly from the distributor housing.

Installation

9   Position the pickup coil assembly into the distributor housing.
10   Make sure the pin on the pickup coil assembly fits into the hole in the vacuum advance mechanism link.
11   Install the washers and retainer on the pivot pin to secure the pickup coil assembly to the base plate.
12   Position the wiring harness in the slot in the distributor housing. Install the two pickup coil plate screws and tighten them securely.
13   Install the trigger wheel on the shaft with hand pressure. The long portion of the teeth must face up. When the trigger wheel and slot in the shaft are properly aligned, use a pin punch and a small hammer to tap the pin into the locating groove in the trigger wheel and shaft. If the distributor is not installed in the engine, support the shaft while installing the trigger wheel pin.
14   Install the rotor and the distributor cap.
15   Attach the cable to the negative battery terminal.

---

9   Vacuum advance mechanism - check and replacement (carbureted models only)

Check

1   Hook up a timing light in accordance with the manufacturer's instructions.
2   Make sure the vacuum hose is attached to the vacuum advance mechanism (see illustration 8.5).
3   Run the engine until it reaches normal operating temperature.
4   With the engine idling, watch the timing marks at the front of the engine with the timing light (see Chapter 1 for more information).
Note: *The white paint mark on the timing degree scale identifies the specified timing degrees Before Top Dead Center (BTDC) at 1600 rpm; it does not identify TDC.*
5   Slowly increase the engine speed to 2000 rpm, noticing how quickly the ignition timing advances. Disconnect and plug the vacuum hose from the vacuum advance mechanism. Again, increase the engine speed to 2000 rpm and notice how quickly the ignition timing advances. With the hose connected, the ignition timing should advance more quickly

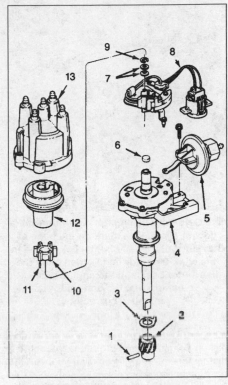

8.5 Exploded view of the distributor assembly used on carbureted models

1   Pin
2   Gear
3   Washer
4   Distributor body
5   Vacuum advance mechanism
6   Wick
7   Washer
8   Pickup coil
9   Pickup coil retainer
10   Trigger wheel
11   Pin
12   Rotor
13   Cap

than it does with the hose disconnected. If it doesn't, replace the vacuum advance mechanism.
Note: *A defective Micro Computer Unit (MCU) can also alter ignition timing.*
6   Unplug and reconnect the hose to the vacuum advance mechanism.

Replacement

7   Detach the cable from the negative battery terminal (see Section 2).
8   Remove the distributor cap and rotor (see Chapter 1).
9   The following procedure is easier if you remove the distributor (see Section 11), but it's not absolutely necessary that you do so.
10   If you do decide to remove the distributor, place it in a bench vise.
11   Remove the pickup coil (see Section 8).
12   Remove the vacuum hose and attaching screws from the vacuum advance mechanism (see illustration 8.5). Tilt the vacuum advance

11.6 Before loosening the distributor hold-down bolt, make a mark on the edge of the distributor base directly below, and in line with, the rotor tip (1), then mark the distributor base and the engine block (2) to ensure that the distributor is installed correctly

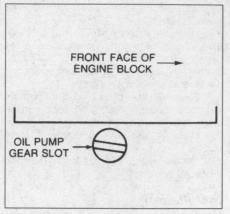

11.10a To seat the distributor on a 1987 through 1994 four-cylinder engine, use a screwdriver to rotate the oil pump gear so the slot is slightly past the three o'clock position…

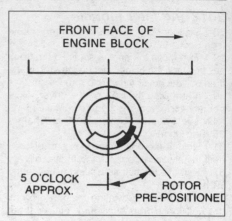

11.10b … then, with the distributor cap removed, install the distributor with the rotor pointing toward the five o'clock position

mechanism to disengage the link from the pickup coil pin, which protrudes through the distributor housing. If necessary, loosen the base plate screws to get more clearance. Lift the vacuum advance mechanism out of the distributor housing.

13   To calibrate a new vacuum advance mechanism:

a)   *Insert an appropriately sized Allen wrench into the vacuum hose tube of the old vacuum advance mechanism; count the number of clockwise turns necessary to bottom the adjusting screw.*

b)   *Turn the adjusting screw of the replacement vacuum advance mechanism clockwise to bottom it, then turn it counterclockwise the same number of turns you counted above.*

14   Install the advance mechanism on the distributor housing. Make sure the link is engaged on the pin of the pickup coil.

15   Install and tighten the vacuum advance mechanism attaching screws. If you loosened the base plate screws, tighten them too.

16   Install the pickup coil (see Section 8).

17   Install the distributor (see Section 11).

18   Install the distributor cap and rotor (see Chapter 1).

19   Attach the cable to the negative battery terminal.

20   Check the ignition timing and adjust it, if necessary (see Chapter 1).

21   Attach the vacuum hose to the vacuum advance mechanism.

10   Centrifugal advance mechanism - check and replacement (carbureted models only)

1   Detach the vacuum hose from the vacuum advance mechanism and plug it (see illustration 8.5).

2   Hook up a timing light and tachometer in accordance with the manufacturer's instructions.

3   Start the engine and, with the engine idling, watch the timing marks at the front of the engine with the timing light (see Chapter 1 for more information).

4   Slowly increase engine speed to 2000 rpm. Timing should advance smoothly as engine speed increases. If it advances unevenly, the centrifugal advance mechanism is faulty. Replace the distributor (see Section 11). You will need to switch the following parts to the replacement distributor:

a)   *Cap and rotor (see Chapter 1).*

b)   *Trigger wheel and/or pickup coil assembly (see Section 8).*

c)   *Vacuum advance mechanism (see Section 9).*

11   Distributor - removal and installation

Removal

1   Detach the cable from the negative battery terminal (see Section 2).

2   Detach the primary lead from the coil.

3   Disconnect all electrical wires from the distributor. If the wires don't unplug at the distributor, follow the wires as they exit the distributor to find the connector.

4   Look for a raised "1" on the distributor cap. This marks the location for the number one cylinder spark plug wire terminal. If the cap does not have a mark for the number one terminal, locate the number one spark plug and trace the wire back to its corresponding terminal on the cap.

5   Remove the distributor cap (see Chapter 1) and turn the engine over until the rotor is pointing toward the number one spark plug terminal (see locating TDC procedure in Chapter 2B or 2C).

6   Make a mark on the edge of the distribu-

tor base directly below the rotor tip and in line with it (if the rotor on your engine has more than one tip, use the center one for reference). Also, mark the distributor base and the engine block to ensure that the distributor is installed correctly (see illustration).

7   Remove the distributor hold-down bolt and clamp, then pull the distributor straight up to remove it.

Caution: *DO NOT turn the crankshaft while the distributor is out of the engine, or the alignment marks will be useless.*

Installation

Note: *If the crankshaft has been moved while the distributor is out, the number one piston must be repositioned at TDC. This can be done by feeling for compression pressure at the number one plug hole as the crankshaft is turned. Once compression is felt, align the ignition timing zero mark with the pointer.*

8   Insert the distributor into the engine in exactly the same relationship to the block that it was in when removed.

9   To mesh the helical gears on the camshaft and the distributor, it may be necessary to turn the rotor slightly. Recheck the alignment marks between the distributor base and the block to verify that the distributor is in the same position it was in before removal. Also check the rotor to see if it's aligned with the mark you made on the edge of the distributor base.

Seating the distributor

Note: *If you have difficulty seating the distributor on the engine block, use the appropriate Step (10, 11 or 12 below) for the type of engine you have. If the distributor seats properly, with the flange flush with the engine block, proceed to Step 13.*

10   If you have difficulty getting the distributor to seat properly on a 1987 through 1994 four-cylinder engine, use the following procedure:

a)   *Make sure the number one piston is at TDC (see Chapter 2B).*

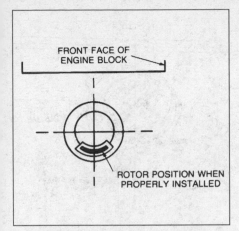

11.10c When the 1987 through 1994 four-cylinder distributor is completely and correctly seated (engaged), the rotor should be at the six o'clock position

b) Working over the right side (passenger) fender, look into the hole in the engine block where the distributor mounts. You should see the oil pump gear slot (see illustration 11.10a). Put a screwdriver into the slot and rotate the oil pump gear so the gear slot is slightly past the three o'clock position.
c) With the distributor cap removed, install the distributor with the rotor pointing to the five o'clock position (see illustration 11.10b).
d) With the distributor fully engaged in its correct location, the rotor should be pointing to the six o'clock position (see illustration).
e) If the distributor is still not installed correctly, repeat this procedure.

11   If you are having difficulty getting the distributor to seat properly on a 1995 four-cylinder engine, use the following procedure:

a) Make sure the number one cylinder is at TDC (see Chapter 2B).
b) Look into the hole in the engine block where the distributor mounts. You should see the oil pump gear slot (see illustration 11.11a). Put a screwdriver into the hole and rotate the oil pump gear so the gear slot is slightly before the ten o'clock position.
c) The pulse ring must be locked in place to hold the rotor in the number one cylinder firing position during installation. Lift the camshaft position sensor straight up and out of the distributor. Rotate the distributor shaft and install a 3/16 inch drift pin punch tool through the correct alignment hole in the plastic ring and into the mating hole in the distributor housing (see illustration 11.11b). This will prevent the distributor shaft and rotor from rotating during installation.
d) Install the rotor onto the shaft.
e) Visually line up the distributor with the centerline of the base slot in the one o'clock position (see illustration 11.11c).

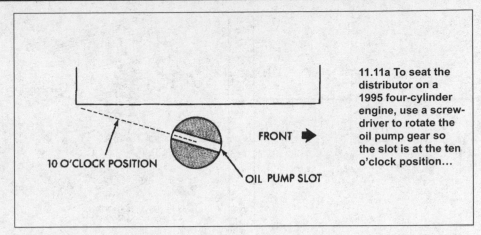

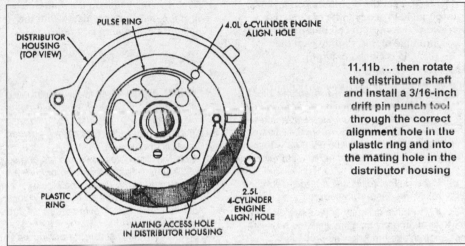

11.11a To seat the distributor on a 1995 four-cylinder engine, use a screwdriver to rotate the oil pump gear so the slot is at the ten o'clock position…

11.11b … then rotate the distributor shaft and install a 3/16-inch drift pin punch tool through the correct alignment hole in the plastic ring and into the mating hole in the distributor housing

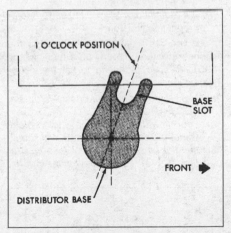

11.11c Visually line up the distributor with the centerline of the base slot in the one o'clock position

f) Install the distributor. It will rotate clockwise during installation and when the distributor is fully installed the centerline of the base slot will be aligned with the clamp bolt hole on the engine (see illustration 11.11d). The rotor should also be pointing to slightly past (clockwise of) the three o'clock position.

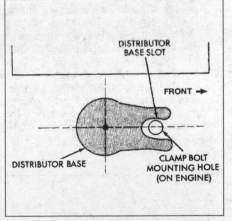

11.11d When the distributor is installed correctly, the centerline of the base slot will be aligned with the clamp bolt hole on the engine

g) If the distributor is still not installed correctly, repeat this procedure.

12   If you have difficulty getting the distributor to seat properly on a carbureted six-cylinder engine, use the following procedure:

a) Make sure the number one piston is at TDC (see Chapter 2C).

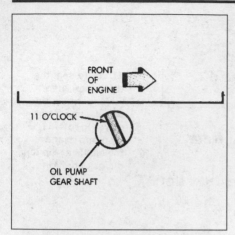

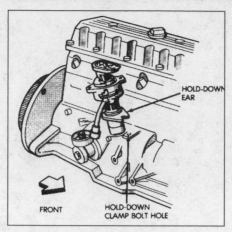

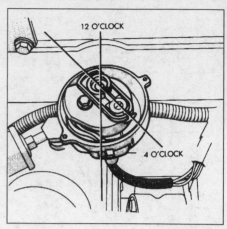

11.13a To seat the distributor on a 1987 through 1994 six-cylinder engine, use a screwdriver to turn the oil pump gearshaft until the slot is slightly past the 11 o'clock position...

11.13b ... visually line up the hold-down ear of the distributor housing with the hold-down clamp bolt hole...

11.13c ... turn the rotor to the four o'clock position, then slide the distributor down into the block until it seats

b) *Look into the hole in the engine block where the distributor mounts. You should see the oil pump gear slot. Put a screwdriver into the slot and rotate the oil pump gear so the rotor will be lined up with the number 1 terminal when the distributor is inserted.*
c) *If the distributor is still not installed correctly, repeat this procedure.*

13 If you have difficulty getting the distributor to seat properly on a fuel-injected six-cylinder engine, use the following procedure:

a) *Look into the hole in the engine block where the distributor mounts. You should see the oil pump gear shaft (see illustration 11.13a). Put a screwdriver into the slot in the oil pump gear shaft and rotate the shaft until the slot is slightly past the 11 o'clock position.*
b) *If you removed it, Install the rotor.*
c) *Without engaging the distributor gear with the camshaft gear in the engine, position the distributor in the hole in the engine block. Be sure the distributor gasket is installed.*

d) *Visually line up the hold-down ear of the distributor housing with the hold-down clamp bolt hole (see illustration 11.13b).*
e) *Turn the rotor to the four o'clock position (see illustration 11.13c).*
f) *Slide the distributor down into the engine block until it seats. Keep the hold-down ear aligned to the hole in the block.*
g) *The rotor should be in the five o'clock position with the trailing edge of the rotor blade lined up with the mark you scribed on the distributor housing prior to removal (the number one spark plug wire post location).*
h) *If the distributor still won't seat properly, repeat this procedure.*

14 If you are having difficulty getting the distributor to seat properly on a fuel-injected 1995 inline six-cylinder engine, use the following procedure:

a) *Make sure the number one cylinder is at TDC (see Chapter 2C).*
b) *Look into the hole in the engine block where the distributor mounts. You should see the oil pump gear slot (see illustration 11.14a). Put a screwdriver into the*

hole and rotate the oil pump gear so the gear slot is slightly before the eleven o'clock position.
c) *The pulse ring must be locked in place to hold the rotor in the number one cylinder firing position during installation. Lift the camshaft position sensor straight up and out of the distributor. Rotate the distributor shaft and install a 3/16 inch drift pin punch tool through the correct alignment hole in the plastic ring and into the mating hole in the distributor housing (see illustration 11.11b). This will prevent the distributor shaft and rotor from rotating during installation.*
d) *Install the rotor onto the shaft.*
e) *Visually line up the distributor with the centerline of the base slot in the one o'clock position (see illustration 11.11c).*
f) *Install the distributor. It will rotate clockwise during installation and when the distributor is fully installed the centerline of the base slot will be aligned with the clamp bolt hole on the engine (see illustration 11.14b). The rotor should also be pointing to slightly past (clockwise of) the five o'clock position.*
g) *If the distributor is still not installed correctly, repeat this procedure.*

15 Place the hold-down clamp in position and loosely install the bolt.
16 On 1995 four-cylinder and inline 6-cylinder models, remove the pin punch tool from the distributor. Install the camshaft position sensor onto the distributor and align the wiring harness grommet with the notch in the distributor. Install the rotor.
17 Attach the electrical wires to the distributor.
18 Reattach the spark plug wires to the plugs (if removed).
19 Connect the cable to the negative terminal of the battery.
20 Check the ignition timing (see Chapter 1) and tighten the distributor hold-down bolt securely.

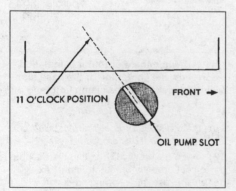

11.14a To seat the distributor on a 1995 inline six-cylinder engine, use a screwdriver to rotate the oil pump gear so the slot is at the 11 o'clock position

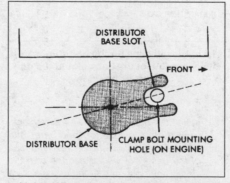
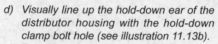

11.14b When the distributor is installed correctly, the centerline of the base slot will be aligned with the clamp bolt hole on the engine

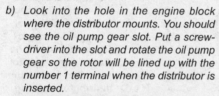

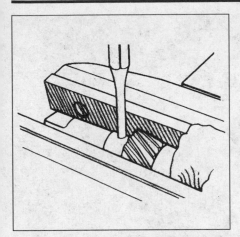

12.4 Use a small punch and hammer to drive out the retaining pin, then remove the distributor gear from the shaft

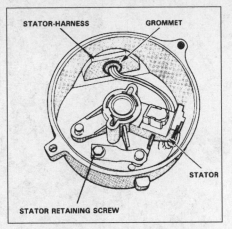

12.6 After marking the position of the stator assembly, remove the retaining screw, push the grommet through the distributor housing and remove the stator (1991 through 1994)

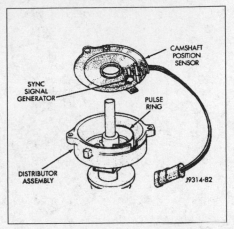

12.12 Lift the stator (camshaft position sensor) from the distributor housing

12 Stator (Camshaft Position Sensor) - replacement (1991 through 2002 four-cylinder models/1991 through 1999 six-cylinder models)

Note: *The stator is also referred to as the SYNC signal generator on 1991 models, and the Camshaft Position Sensor on 1992 through 2002 four-cylinder/1992 through 1999 six-cylinder models.*

1991 through 1994 models

1   Remove the distributor from the engine (see Section 11).
2   Remove the distributor cap and rotor (see Chapter 1).
3   Secure the distributor shaft gear in a bench vise. Wrap a rag around the shaft to prevent damage from the vise jaws.
4   Use a small punch and hammer to drive out the retaining pin, then remove the distributor gear from the shaft (see illustration).
5   Remove the distributor shaft from the distributor housing.
6   Mark the location of the stator (see illustration) so you can return it to the same location during reassembly.
7   Remove the stator retaining screw.
8   Remove the stator harness by pushing the grommet through the distributor housing. Remove the stator assembly.

1995 and later models

9   Disconnect the cable from the negative battery terminal (see Section 2).
10   Remove the distributor cap and rotor (see Chapter 1).
11   Disconnect the sensor's electrical connector.
12   Lift the stator (camshaft position sensor) from the distributor housing (see illustration).
13   Installation is the reverse of removal.

13 Charging system - general information and precautions

1   The charging system includes the alternator, an internal voltage regulator, a charge indicator, the battery, a fusible link and the wiring between all the components. The charging system supplies electrical power for the ignition system, the lights, the radio, etc. The alternator is driven by a drivebelt at the front of the engine.
2   The purpose of the voltage regulator is to limit the alternator's voltage to a preset value. This prevents power surges, circuit overloads, etc., during peak voltage output.
3   The fusible link is a short length of insulated wire integral with the engine compartment wiring harness. Production fusible links are identified by the flag color. See Chapter 12 for additional information regarding fusible links.
4   The charging system doesn't ordinarily require periodic maintenance. However, the drivebelt, battery, battery cables and connections should be inspected at the intervals outlined in Chapter 1.
5   The dashboard warning light should come on when the ignition key is turned to Start, then go off immediately. If it remains on, there is a malfunction in the charging system (see Section 14). Some vehicles are also equipped with a voltmeter. If the voltmeter indicates abnormally high or low voltage, check the charging system (see Section 14).
6   Be very careful when making electrical circuit connections to a vehicle equipped with an alternator and note the following:

a) *When reconnecting wires to the alternator from the battery, be sure to note the polarity.*
b) *Before using arc welding equipment to repair any part of the vehicle, disconnect the wires from the alternator and the battery terminals.*
c) *Never start the engine with a battery charger connected.*
d) *Always disconnect both battery leads before using a battery charger.*
e) *The alternator is turned by an engine drivebelt which could cause serious injury if your hands, hair or clothes become entangled in it with the engine running.*
f) *Because the alternator is connected directly to the battery, it could arc or cause a fire if overloaded or shorted out.*
g) *Wrap a plastic bag over the alternator and secure it with rubberbands before steam cleaning the engine.*

14 Charging system - check

1   If a malfunction occurs in the charging circuit, don't automatically assume that the alternator is causing the problem. First check the following items:

a) *Check the drivebelt tension and condition (see Chapter 1). Replace it if it's worn or deteriorated.*
b) *Make sure the alternator mounting and adjustment bolts are tight.*
c) *Inspect the alternator wiring harness and the connectors at the alternator and voltage regulator. They must be in good condition and tight.*
d) *Check the fusible link (if equipped) located between the starter solenoid and the alternator. If it's burned, determine the cause, repair the circuit and replace the link (the vehicle won't start and/or the accessories won't work if the fusible link blows). Sometimes a fusible link may look good, but still be bad. If in doubt, remove it and check for continuity with an ohmmeter or test light.*
e) *Start the engine and check the alternator for abnormal noises (a shrieking or squealing sound indicates a bad bearing).*

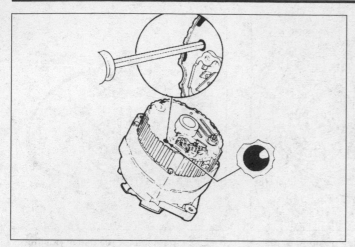

14.5 To seat the Delco alternator, locate the test hole in the back, ground the tab that's located inside the hole by inserting a screwdriver blade into the hole and touching the tab and the case at the same time

15.4 To remove the alternator, detach the electrical connectors (earlier models)...

15.5a ... loosen the alternator adjustment bolt...

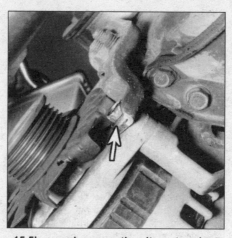

15.5b ... and remove the alternator pivot bolt from below

hole and touching the tab and the case at the same time (see illustration).

Caution: *Do not run the engine with the tab grounded any longer than necessary to obtain a voltmeter reading. If the alternator is charging, it is running unregulated during the test. This condition may overload the electrical system and cause damage to the components.*

6   The reading on the voltmeter should be 15-volts or higher with the tab in the test hole grounded.

7   If the voltmeter indicates low battery voltage, the alternator is faulty and should be replaced with a new one (see Section 15).

8   If the voltage reading is 15-volts or higher and a no charge condition is present, the regulator or field circuit is the problem. Remove the alternator (see Section) and have it checked further by an auto electric shop.

15   Alternator - removal and installation

1   Detach the cable from the negative terminal of the battery (see Section 2).

2   Remove the engine cover if necessary.

3   On 2007 and later models, remove the air intake hose and air filter housing (see Chapter 4, Section 7).

4   On all models, detach the electrical connectors from the alternator (see illustration).

Note: *It may be necessary to remove one of the alternator mounting bolts to pivot the alternator and access the electrical connectors.*

5   On older models, loosen the alternator adjustment and pivot bolts (see illustrations) and detach the drivebelt. On 2003 and later models, rotate the automatic belt tensioner to remove the drivebelt.

6   On older models, remove the adjustment and pivot bolts and separate the alternator from the engine. On 2007 and later models, remove the upper and lower mounting bolts (see illustrations).

f) *Check the specific gravity of the battery electrolyte. If it's low, charge the battery (doesn't apply to maintenance-free batteries).*

g) *Make sure the battery is fully charged (one bad cell in a battery can cause overcharging by the alternator).*

h) *Disconnect the battery cables (negative first, then positive). Inspect the battery posts and the cable clamps for corrosion. Clean them thoroughly if necessary (see Chapter 1). Reconnect the cable to the negative terminal.*

i) *With the key off, connect a test light between the negative battery post and the disconnected negative cable clamp.*

j) *If the test light does not come on, reattach the clamp and proceed to the next step.*

k) *If the test light comes on, there is a short (drain) in the electrical system of the vehicle. The short must be repaired before the charging system can be checked.*

l) *Disconnect the alternator wiring harness.*

m) *If the light goes out, the alternator is bad.*

n) *If the light stays on, pull each fuse until the light goes out (this will tell you which component is shorted).*

2   Using a voltmeter, check the battery voltage with the engine off. If should be at least 12.66 volts.

3   Start the engine and check the battery voltage again. It should now be approximately 13.5 to 15 volts.

4   On Delco alternators, locate the test hole in the back of the alternator.

Note: *If there is no test hole, the vehicle is equipped with a newer CS type alternator. Further testing of this type of alternator must be done by a dealer service department or automotive electrical shop. Nippondenso alternators (used on later models) have no test hole.*

5   Ground the tab that is located inside the hole by inserting a screwdriver blade into the

15.6a Remove the two lower mounting bolts - 2007 and later models

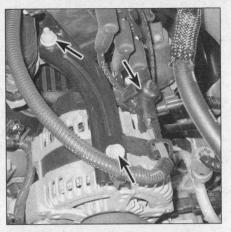

15.6b From above, disconnect the electrical connector, then remove the mounting nut and bolt (later models)

16.2 Mark the front and rear end frame housings with a scribe or paint mark before separating them

7   If you are replacing the alternator, take the old one with you when purchasing a replacement unit. Make sure the new/rebuilt unit looks identical to the old alternator. Look at the terminals - they should be the same in number, size and location as the terminals on the old alternator. Finally, look at the identification numbers - they will be stamped into the housing or printed on a tag attached to the housing. Make sure the numbers are the same on both alternators.

8   Many new/rebuilt alternators DO NOT have a pulley installed, so you may have to switch the pulley from the old unit to the new/rebuilt one. When buying an alternator, find out the shop's policy regarding pulleys - some shops will perform this service free of charge.

9   Installation is the reverse of removal.

10   After the alternator is installed, adjust the drivebelt tension (see Chapter 1).

11   Check the charging voltage to verify proper operation of the alternator (see Section 14).

16.4a Carefully separate the drive end frame and the rectifier end frame

16.5 After removing the bolts holding the stator assembly to the end frame, remove the stator

16 Alternator brushes - replacement

1   Remove the alternator from the vehicle (see Section).

Delco alternator

Note: *The following procedure applies only to SI type alternators. CS types have riveted housings and cannot be disassembled.*

2   Scribe or paint marks on the front and rear end frame housings of the alternator to facilitate reassembly (see illustration).

3   Remove the four through-bolts holding the front and rear end frames together.

4   Separate the drive end frame from the rectifier end frame (see illustrations).

5   Remove the bolts holding the stator to the rear end frame and separate the stator from the end frame (see illustration).

6   Remove the nuts attaching the diode trio to the rectifier bridge and remove the trio (see illustration).

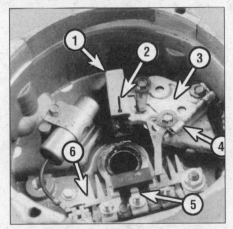

16.4b Inside a typical Delco alternator

1   *Brush holder*
2   *Paper clip*
     (holding the brushes in place)
3   *Regulator*
4   *Resistor (not all models)*
5   *Diode trio*
6   *Rectifier bridge*

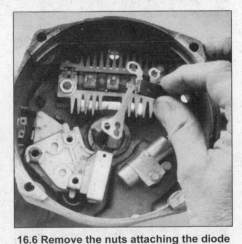

16.6 Remove the nuts attaching the diode trio to the rectifier bridge and remove the trio

16.7 After removing the screws that attach the regulator, brush holder and the resistor (if equipped) to the end frame, remove the regulator

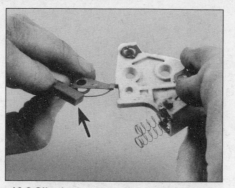

16.8 Slip the brush retainer off the brush holder and remove the brushes (arrow)

16.11 To hold the brushes in place during reassembly, insert a paper clip through the hole in the rear end frame nearest rotor shaft

16.12 To replace the brushes on Nippondenso alternators, remove the B+ terminal nut, washer and insulator (arrow)

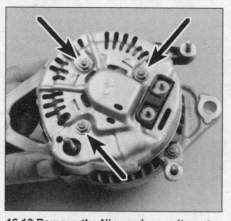

16.13 Remove the Nippondenso alternator rear cover attaching nuts (arrows) and remove the cover

16.14a Remove the brush holder attaching nuts…

7   Remove the screws attaching the resistor (not used on all models) and regulator and brush holder to the end frame and remove the regulator (see illustration).

8   Remove the brushes from the brush holder by slipping the brush retainer off the holder (see illustration).

9   Remove the springs from the brush holder.

10   Installation is the reverse of the removal procedure, but be sure to note the following:

11   When installing the brushes in the brush holder, install the brush closest to the end frame first. Slip a paper clip through the rear of the end frame to hold the brush, then insert the second brush and push the paper clip in to hold both brushes while reassembly is completed (see illustration). The paper clip should not be removed until the front and rear end frames have been bolted together.

Nippondenso alternator

12   With the alternator removed from the vehicle (see Section 15), remove the B+ insulator nut and insulator (see illustration).

13   Remove the rear cover attaching nuts and remove the rear cover (see illustration).

14   Remove the brush holder attaching screws and lift the brush holder from the alternator (see illustrations).

15   Before installing the new brush holder assembly, check for continuity between each brush and the appropriate field terminal (see illustration).

16   To install the brush holder assembly, use your finger to depress the brushes (see illustration), then slide the holder over the commutator slip rings and screw it into place.

17   Installation is otherwise the reverse of removal. When installing the B+ insulator, be sure to align the guide tang with the hole in the rear cover.

17   Starting system - general information and precautions

1   The sole function of the starting system is to turn over the engine quickly enough to

16.14b … and remove the brush holder assembly (Nippondenso alternator)

16.15 Using an ohmmeter, check for continuity between each brush and appropriate field terminal (if there's no continuity, switch one of the leads to the other field terminal or brush)

16.16 Depress the brushes with your index finger as you slide the brush holder into place

19.3a Pry off the pressed-metal nut...

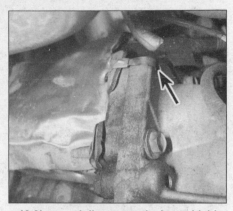

19.3b ... and disengage the heat shield retaining clip

allow it to start.

2   The starting system consists of the battery, the starter motor, the starter solenoid, a remote starter relay (on some models) and the wires connecting them. A number of different starter motors - including Bosch, Mitsubishi and Motorcraft - are used on the vehicles covered by this manual. If you replace the starter motor, be sure to take the old starter with you to the parts department to make sure you get the right replacement. The solenoid is mounted directly on the starter motor or, on Motorcraft units, is a separate component located in the engine compartment.

3   The solenoid/starter motor assembly is installed on the lower part of the engine, next to the transmission bellhousing.

4   When the ignition key is turned to the Start position, the starter solenoid is actuated through the starter control circuit. The starter solenoid then connects the battery to the starter. The battery supplies the electrical energy to the starter motor, which does the actual work of cranking the engine.

5   The starter on a vehicle equipped with an automatic transmission can only be operated when the transmission selector lever is in Park or Neutral.

6   Always observe the following precautions when working on the starting system:

a) *Excessive cranking of the starter motor can overheat it and cause serious damage. Never operate the starter motor for more than 15 seconds at a time without pausing to allow it to cool for at least two minutes.*

b) *The starter is connected directly to the battery and could arc or cause a fire if mishandled, overloaded or shorted out.*

c) *Always detach the cable from the negative terminal of the battery before working on the starting system.*

---

18   Starter motor - testing in vehicle

Note: *Before diagnosing starter problems, make sure the battery is fully charged.*

1   If the starter motor does not operate at all when the switch is turned to Start, make sure the shift lever is in Neutral or Park (automatic transmission).

2   Make sure that the battery is charged and that all cables, both at the battery and starter solenoid terminals, are clean and secure.

3   If the starter motor spins but the engine is not cranking, the overrunning clutch in the starter motor is slipping and the starter motor must be replaced.

4   If, when the switch is actuated, the starter motor does not operate at all but the solenoid clicks, then the problem lies with either the battery, the starter relay (if equipped), the main solenoid contacts or the starter motor itself (or the engine is seized).

5   If the solenoid plunger cannot be heard when the switch is actuated, the battery is bad, the fusible link is burned (the circuit is open) or the solenoid itself is defective.

6   To check the solenoid, connect a jumper lead between the battery (+) and the ignition switch wire terminal (the small terminal) on the solenoid. If the starter motor now operates, the solenoid is OK and the problem is in the ignition switch, neutral start switch or the wiring.

7   If the starter motor still does not operate, remove the starter/solenoid assembly for disassembly, testing and repair.

8   If the starter motor cranks the engine at an abnormally slow speed, first make sure that the battery is charged and that all terminal connections are tight. If the engine is partially seized, or has the wrong viscosity oil in it, it will crank slowly.

9   Run the engine until normal operating temperature is reached, then disconnect the coil wire from the distributor cap and ground it.

10   Connect a voltmeter positive lead to the positive battery post and connect the negative lead to the negative post.

11   Crank the engine and take the voltmeter readings as soon as a steady figure is indicated. Do not allow the starter motor to turn for more than 15 seconds at a time. A reading of 9-volts or more, with the starter motor turning at normal cranking speed, is normal. If

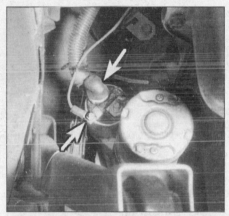

19.4 Before unbolting the starter motor assembly, detach the wires (arrows) from the solenoid (or from the starter motor itself, on some models) - be sure the battery is disconnected

the reading is 9-volts or more but the cranking speed is slow, the motor is faulty. If the reading is less than 9-volts and the cranking speed is slow, the solenoid contacts are probably burned, the starter motor is bad, the battery is discharged or there is a bad connection.

---

19   Starter motor - removal and installation

Note: *On some vehicles, it may be necessary to remove the exhaust pipe(s) or frame crossmember to gain access to the starter motor. In extreme cases it may even be necessary to unbolt the mounts and raise the engine slightly to get the starter out.*

1   Detach the cable from the negative terminal of the battery (see Section 2).

2   Raise the vehicle and support it securely on jackstands.

3   If equipped, remove the fasteners and the starter shield (see illustrations).

4   Clearly label, then disconnect the wires from the terminals on the starter motor and solenoid (if mounted on the starter) (see illustration).

19.5a The starter lower mounting bolt (in-line six-cylinder model shown)

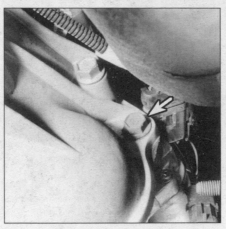

19.5b The starter upper mounting bolt (in-line six-cylinder engine) - view is from the front, looking toward the rear

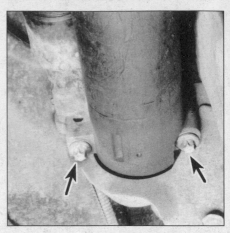

19.5c On some four-cylinder engines, the starter is held in place by E-12 Torx-head bolts which will require a special socket

20.3 Before removing the solenoid from the starter motor, detach the starter motor terminal strap - Mitsubishi starter shown

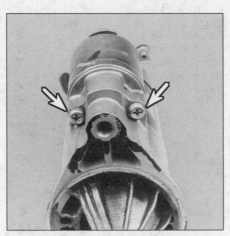

20.4 To detach the solenoid from the starter motor, remove the solenoid attaching screws from the front of the starter solenoid mount (Mitsubishi starter shown) - Bosch starters only have one screw

20.7 If you have a Motorcraft starter solenoid, it's located near the battery - to remove it, detach the wires and remove the mounting bracket bolts - be sure the battery is disconnected!

5   Remove the mounting bolts (see illustrations) and detach the starter.
6   Installation is the reverse of removal.

---

20   Starter solenoid - removal and installation

Note: *The procedure applies to 1993 and earlier models only. On 1994 and later models, the solenoid is not serviceable; if it fails, the starter must be replaced.*
1   Disconnect the cable from the negative terminal of the battery (see Section 2).

All solenoids except Motorcraft

2   Remove the starter motor (see Section 19).
3   Disconnect the strap from the solenoid to the starter motor terminal (see illustration).
4   Remove the screws which secure the solenoid to the starter motor (see illustration).
5   On some models it may be necessary to twist the solenoid in a clockwise direction to disengage the flange from the starter body.
6   Installation is the reverse of removal.

Motorcraft solenoid

7   Locate the solenoid - it's mounted in the engine compartment near the battery (see illustration). Detach the electrical wires from the starter solenoid terminals. Label them to assure proper reassembly.
8   Remove the solenoid mounting bracket bolts and detach the solenoid.
9   Installation is the reverse of removal.

Chapter 6
Emissions and engine control systems

Contents

1   General Information

1   To prevent pollution of the atmosphere from incompletely burned and evaporating gases, and to maintain good driveability and fuel economy, a number of emission control systems are incorporated. The principal systems are:

Positive Crankcase Ventilation
  (PCV) system
Closed Crankcase Ventilation
  (CCV) system
Evaporative emissions control
  (EVAP) system
Thermostatically controlled Air Cleaner
  (TAC) system
Exhaust Gas Recirculation (EGR) system
Catalytic converter
Engine management system

2   The sections in this Chapter include descriptions, checking procedures within the scope of the home mechanic and component replacement procedures (when possible) for each of the systems listed above.

3   Before assuming an emissions control system is malfunctioning, check the fuel and ignition systems carefully. The diagnosis of some emission control devices requires specialized tools, equipment and training. If checking and servicing becomes too diffi-cult or if a procedure is beyond your ability, consult a dealer service department or other qualified shop. Remember, the most frequent cause of emissions problems is simply a loose or broken vacuum hose or wire, so always check the hose and wiring connections first.

4   This doesn't mean, however, that emission control systems are particularly difficult to maintain and repair. You can quickly and easily perform many checks and do most of the regular maintenance at home with common tune-up and hand tools.

Note: *Because of a Federally-mandated extended warranty which covers the emission control system components, check with your*

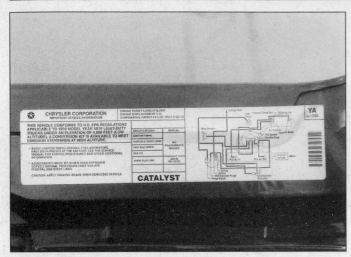

1.6 A typical Vehicle Emissions Control Information (VECI) label (1990 model with a four-cylinder engine shown)

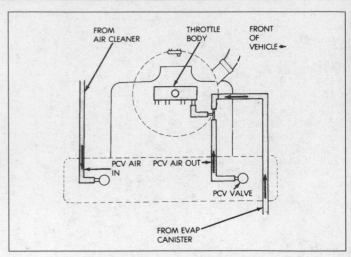

2.1a Positive Crankcase Ventilation (PCV) system (four-cylinder engine)

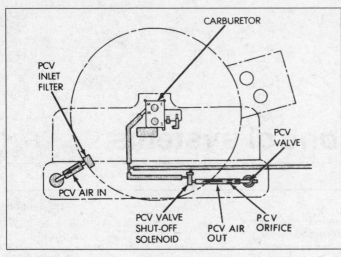

2.1b Positive Crankcase Ventilation (PCV) system (4.2L six-cylinder engine)

2.3 Locating the PCV valve on 2007 through 2011 models with 3.8L V6 engines

dealer about warranty coverage before working on any emissions-related systems. Once the warranty has expired, you may wish to perform some of the component checks and/ or replacement procedures in this Chapter to save money.

5   Pay close attention to any special precautions outlined in this Chapter. It should be noted that the illustrations of the various systems may not exactly match the system installed on your vehicle because of changes made by the manufacturer during production or from year-to-year.

6   The Vehicle Emissions Control Information (VECI) label is located in the engine compartment (see illustration). This label contains important emissions specifications and, if applicable, adjustment information. When servicing the engine or emissions systems, the

VECI label in your particular vehicle should always be checked for up-to-date information.

2   Crankcase ventilation systems

Positive Crankcase Ventilation (PCV) system

1   The Positive Crankcase Ventilation (PCV) system (see illustrations) reduces hydrocarbon emissions by scavenging crankcase vapors. It does this by circulating fresh air from the air cleaner through the crankcase, where it mixes with blow-by gases and is rerouted through a PCV valve to the intake manifold.

2   The main components of the PCV system

are the PCV valve, a fresh air filtered inlet and the vacuum hoses connecting these two components with the engine. 4.2L six-cylinder engines also have a PCV shut-off solenoid to shut off the flow of crankcase vapors to the intake manifold under certain operating conditions.

3   On 2007 through 2011 models, the PCV valve is located in the driver's side valve cover, near the ignition coil (see illustration). On 2012 and later models, the PCV valve is attached to the rear of the passenger's side valve cover with Torx screws.

4   To maintain idle quality, the PCV valve restricts the flow when the intake manifold vacuum is high. If abnormal operating conditions (such as piston ring problems) arise, the system is designed to allow excessive amounts of blow-by gases to flow back through the crankcase vent tube into the air

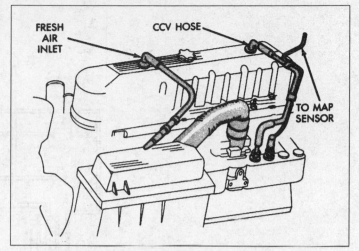

2.6a Closed Crankcase Ventilation (CCV) system (four-cylinder engine)

2.6b Close Crankcase Ventilation (CCV) system (4.0L six-cylinder engine)

cleaner to be consumed by normal combustion.

5   Checking and replacement of the PCV valve and filter is covered in Chapter 1.

Closed Crankcase Ventilation (CCV) system

6   1997 though 2006 models are equipped with a Closed Crankcase Ventilation (CCV) system (see illustrations). The CCV system performs the same function as a conventional PCV system but does not use a vacuum controlled valve. A molded vacuum tube connects manifold vacuum to a grommet on the front of the valve cover (four-cylinder engine) or top rear of the cover (4.0L six-cylinder engine). The grommet contains a calibrated orifice that meters the amount of crankcase vapors drawn out of the engine.

7   A fresh air supply hose from the air cleaner is connected to the rear of the valve cover (four-cylinder engine) or the top front of the cover (4.0L six-cylinder engine). When the engine is operating, fresh air enters the engine and mixes with the crankcase vapors. Manifold vacuum draws the vapor/air mixture through the calibrated orifice and into the intake manifold. The vapors are consumed during combustion.

3   Evaporative emissions control system

General description

1   This system is designed to trap and store fuel that evaporates from the fuel system that would normally enter the atmosphere in the form of hydrocarbon (HC) emissions.

2   The system is very simple and consists of a charcoal-filled canister, canister purge

3.3 A typical evaporative emissions charcoal-filtered canister - the arrow points to the purge valve

valve (and canister purge solenoid on some models), a combination rollover/pressure relief valve and connecting lines and hoses.

3   When the pressure in the fuel tank exceeds 3 psi (caused by fuel evaporation), a pressure relief/rollover valve opens, preventing excessive pressure build-up in the tank and allowing the fuel vapors to flow to an evaporative canister containing charcoal that absorbs the fuel vapors (see illustration). On carbureted models, the carburetor float bowl is also vented to the evaporative canister to allow vapors from the float bowl to flow to the canister. When the engine is started (cold), the charcoal continues to absorb and store fuel vapor. As the engine warms up, the stored vapors are routed to the intake manifold or air cleaner and combustion chambers where they are burned

during normal engine operation.

4   A canister purge valve controls when the stored vapors are allowed to flow to the intake manifold or air cleaner. This valve is actuated by intake manifold vacuum. On some models, system purging is not computer controlled and a coolant temperature switch in line between the intake manifold (or air cleaner) and canister purge valve assures that purging occurs only when coolant temperature is above 70-degrees F. On some models, the computer controls a solenoid that's in line between the intake manifold (or air cleaner) and purge valve. This solenoid serves the same function as the coolant temperature switch.

5   The relief valve, which is mounted in the fuel filler cap, opens to vent excessive pressure or vacuum in the fuel tank.

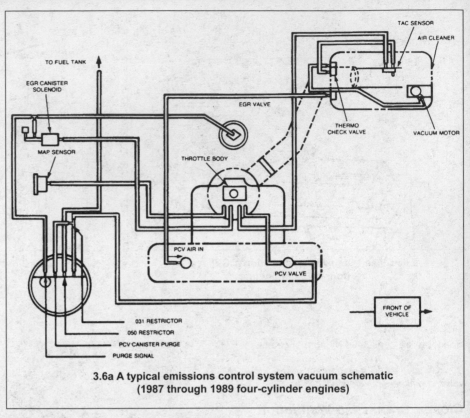

3.6a A typical emissions control system vacuum schematic
(1987 through 1989 four-cylinder engines)

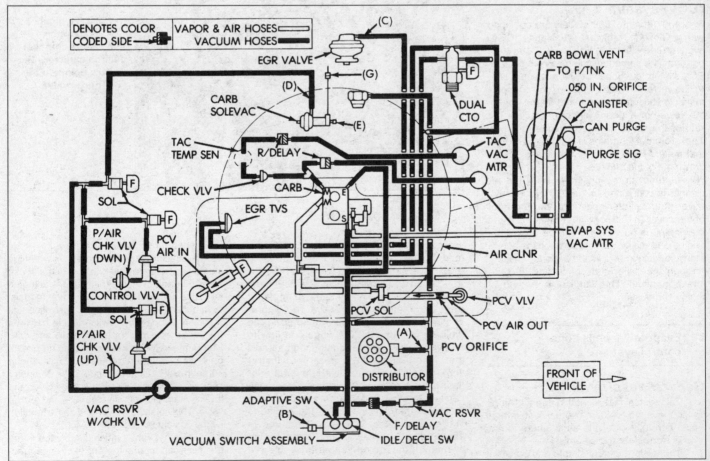

3.6b A typical emissions control system vacuum schematic (4.2L six-cylinder engine)

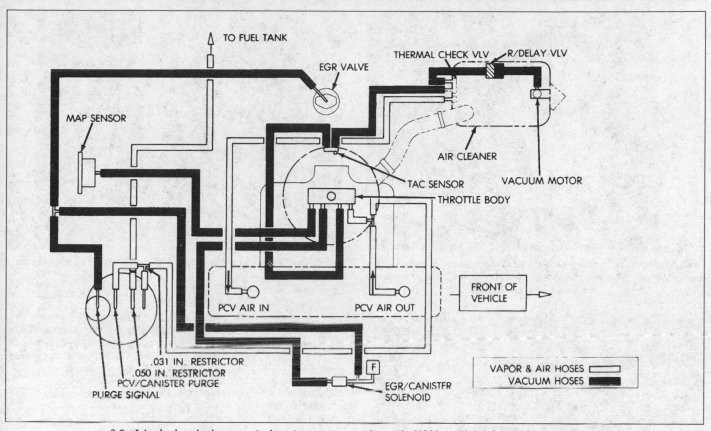

3.6c A typical emissions control system vacuum schematic (1990 and later four-cylinder engine)

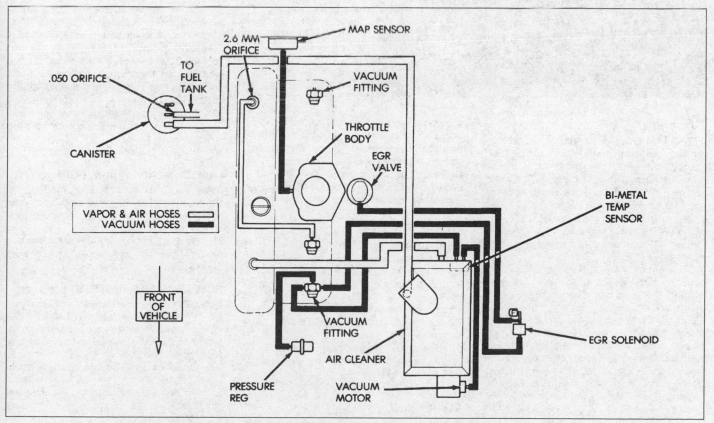

3.6d A typical emissions control system vacuum schematic (4.0L six-cylinder engine)

3.8 A typical evaporative emissions system purge solenoid - on some models (like the one shown here) the solenoid also controls vacuum to the EGR valve

3.10 On 2007 and later models, pull the valve off of the bracket

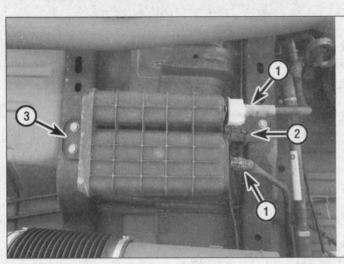

3.17 Disconnect the quick-disconnect fittings and hoses (1), electrical connectors (2) and (on 2007 and later models) remove the bolts securing the bracket (3) (2011 model shown)

Checking

6   Check hoses and lines for misrouting, cracks, deterioration and other damage (see illustrations). Check the fuel filler cap gasket for deformation and other damage. The most common symptom of a problem with this system is a fuel odor under the hood (2002 and earlier models) or coming from under the rear of the vehicle (2003 and later models), which is most often caused by a damaged canister or hoses.

7   To check the purge valve, unplug the upper vacuum hose from the valve (see illustration 3.3) and connect a hand vacuum pump in its place. Also unplug the purge hose leading to the intake manifold or air cleaner and attach a short piece of vacuum hose in its place. When vacuum is applied with the vacuum pump, you should be able to blow through the length of vacuum hose attached to the purge hose port. When no vacuum is applied, you should not be able to blow through the hose.

8   To check the purge solenoid (models so equipped) (see illustration),

unplug the electrical connector from the solenoid and apply battery voltage to the terminals using two jumper wires. You should hear a click if the solenoid is operating properly.
Caution: *Don't leave the jumper wires connected to the solenoid any longer than necessary to perform this check.*

Replacement

Canister purge valve

Note: *On 2007 and later models, the canister purge valve is located near the battery.*

9   Disconnect the negative battery cable (see Chapter 5).
10   Locate the canister purge valve and pull the purge valve up and out of the bracket (see illustration).
11   Disconnect the electrical connector.
12   Disconnect the quick-connect fittings from the purge valve.
13   Installation is reverse of removal.

EVAP canister

Note: *On 2002 and earlier models, the EVAP canister is located in the engine compart-*

ment. On 2003 through 2006 models, the EVAP canister, leak detection pump and pump filter are attached to a bracket behind the passenger rear wheel. On 2007 and later models, the EVAP canister is located under the vehicle, near the rear driveshaft.

14   Disconnect the negative battery cable (see Chapter 5).
15   On 2000 and later models, raise and support the vehicle on jack stands.
16   On 2003 through 2006 models, remove the right rear wheel and inner fender liner.
17   On all models, locate the EVAP canister and disconnect the electrical connectors, quick-disconnect fittings and hoses (see illustration).
18   On 2003 through 2006 models, disconnect the Leak Detection Pump connector and any hoses that may prevent removal of the canister and bracket.
19   On all models, remove the bolts and remove the bracket and/or canister from the vehicle.
20   Installation is reverse of removal.

Leak Detection Pump (LDP)

Note: *On 2003 through 2006 models, the EVAP canister, leak detection pump and pump filter are attached to a bracket behind the passenger rear wheel.*

21   On 2003 through 2006 models, remove the EVAP canister and remove the LDP from the bracket.

Fuel Tank Pressure (FTP) sensor

Note: *2012 and later models are equipped with a Fuel Tank Pressure (FTP) sensor. The FTP sensor is located above the fuel tank, attached to the EVAP hoses, near the fuel tank filler hose.*

22   Disconnect the negative battery cable (see Chapter 5).
23   Raise and support the vehicle on jackstands.
24   Remove the gas cap to relieve fuel tank pressure.

25   Locate the FTP sensor and disconnect the electrical connector.
26   Release the retaining tab and rotate the FTP sensor clockwise, pull up and remove.
27   Inspect the seal. Replace if damaged.
28   Installation is the reverse of removal. Lubricate the seal with clean motor oil.

4   Thermostatically controlled Air Cleaner (TAC) system (carburetor and TBI-equipped models through 1990)

General description

1   The Thermostatic Air Cleaner (TAC) provides heated intake air during warmup, then maintains the inlet air temperature within a 70-degrees F to 105-degrees F operating range by mixing warm and cool air. This allows leaner fuel/air mixture settings for the carburetor or throttle body, which reduces emissions and improves driveability (see illustration).
2   The TAC system is comprised of the following major components:
   A heat shroud that partially encloses the exhaust manifold.
   A heated air tube.
   A special air cleaner assembly equipped with a bi-metal temperature sensor.
   A time delay valve.
   A check valve.
   A vacuum motor.
   A heat duct valve assembly.
3   A vacuum motor, which operates a heat duct valve in the air cleaner, etc., maintains a balance between two fresh air inlets - one hot and one cold - and is actuated by the intake manifold vacuum.
4   When the engine temperature is cold, warm air radiating off the exhaust manifold is routed, by a shroud which fits over the manifold, up through a heated air tube and into the air cleaner. This provides warm air for the carburetor or TBI, resulting in better driveability and faster warmup. As the temperature inside the air cleaner rises, the heat duct valve is gradually closed by the vacuum motor (which, in turn is controlled by a bi-metal temperature sensor inside the air cleaner) and the air cleaner draws air through a cold (ambient) air duct instead. The result is a consistent intake air temperature.
5   On some models, a trap door system opens in a similar manner to close off the air cleaner from the outside air when the engine is inoperative.

Checking

General operation
Note: *Make sure the engine is cold before beginning this test.*
6   Always check the vacuum source and the integrity of all vacuum hoses between the source and the vacuum motor before beginning the following test. Do not proceed until

all cracked and broken hoses have been replaced.
7   Apply the parking brake and block the wheels.
8   Detach the flexible duct (if equipped) from the air cleaner snorkel (see Chapter 4).
9   With the engine off, observe the heat duct valve inside the air cleaner snorkel. It should be fully open to cold air. If it isn't, it might be binding or sticking. Make sure it's not rusted in an open or closed position by attempting to move it by hand. If it's rusted, it can usually be freed by cleaning and oiling the hinge. If it fails to work properly after servicing, replace it.
10   Start the engine. Note the position of the heat duct valve. Now it should be fully closed to incoming cold air.
11   Have an assistant rapidly depress and release the accelerator 1/2 to 3/4 of its travel. The heat duct valve should briefly remain stationary, then move to the cold air position, then back to the heated air position.
12   Loosely attach the flexible duct to the air cleaner and warm the engine to normal operating temperature. Remove the flexible duct and observe the heat duct valve. It should be either fully open or at a mixture position (half open) that provides the correct temperature for the inlet air to the carburetor or TBI.
13   Stop the engine and connect the flexible duct to the air cleaner.
14   If the heat duct valve does not function as described above, look for a mechanical bind in the linkage and disconnected vacuum hoses or air leaks at the vacuum motor, bi-metal sensor, time delay valve, check valve, intake manifold or vacuum hoses.
15   If the heat duct valve manually operates freely and you cannot find any hose disconnections or leaks, attach a hose from an intake manifold vacuum source directly to the vacuum motor and start the engine.
If the heat duct valve closes, either the thermal switch, time delay valve or check valve is defective.
If the heat duct valve does not close, replace the vacuum motor.

Bi-metal temperature sensor
16   Detach the two vacuum hoses from the sensor.
17   If necessary, remove the sensor (see replacement procedure below) and cool it below 40-degrees F in a freezer.
18   Attach a vacuum pump to one of the sensor's vacuum fittings and a vacuum gauge to the other fitting.
19   Apply 14 in-Hg. vacuum to the sensor.
20   With the sensor at a temperature below 40-degrees F, the gauge should indicate a vacuum. Disconnect the vacuum pump momentarily to relieve the vacuum.
21   Warm the sensor above 55-degrees F and again attempt to apply vacuum. There should not be steady vacuum reading on the gauge.
22   Replace the sensor if it's defective.

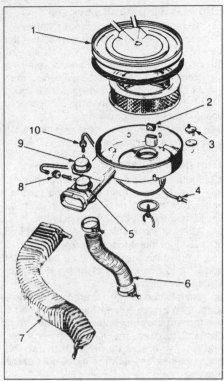

4.1 A typical thermostatically controlled air cleaner (six-cylinder engine shown, four-cylinder engine similar)

1   Air cleaner cover
2   PCV valve filter
3   Bi-metal temperature sensor
4   Check valve
5   Vacuum motor
6   Heated air tube
7   Ambient body (cold) air duct
8   Time delay valve
9   Trap door assembly (not on all models)
10   Trap door time delay valve (not on all models)

Component replacement

Note: *Before replacing the following components, check on parts availability. On some models the components can only be replaced with a complete air cleaner assembly.*

Heat duct valve vacuum motor
23   Remove the air cleaner (see Chapter 4).
24   Clearly label, then detach the vacuum hose from the heat duct valve vacuum motor.
25   Drill out the rivet which secures the heat duct valve vacuum motor to the air cleaner snorkel.
26   Lift the motor and tilt it to one side to detach the motor linkage from the heat duct valve assembly. Remove the motor.
27   Installation is the reverse of removal. If you don't have a rivet tool, you'll need a self-tapping sheet-metal screw of the correct diameter to attach the vacuum motor to the snorkel. Make sure the rivet (or the screw) does not interfere with the movement of the duct valve.

Bi-metal temperature sensor

28   Remove the air cleaner (see Chapter 4).
29   Detach the two vacuum hoses from the sensor.
30   Pry up the tabs on the sensor retaining clip. Remove the clip, gasket and sensor from the air cleaner. Before removing the sensor, note its position in relation to the air cleaner to ensure proper reassembly.
31   Installation is the reverse of removal. Be sure to use a new gasket.

Trap door vacuum motor

32   Remove the air cleaner (see Chapter 4).
33   Clearly label, then detach the vacuum hoses from the heat duct valve motor, bi-metal sensor and the trap door vacuum motor.
34   Drill out the rivet which secures the trap door vacuum motor to the bracket.
35   Lift the vacuum motor from the bracket and tilt it to one side to clear the door arm. Remove the motor.
36   Installation is the reverse of removal. If you don't have a rivet tool, you'll need a self-tapping sheet-metal screw of the correct diameter to attach the vacuum motor to the bracket. Make sure the rivet (or the screw) does not interfere with the movement of the trap door.

5   Pulse air system

General description

1   The Pulse Air system, used on earlier models, uses the alternating pressure and vacuum pulsation created in the exhaust system to draw air into the exhaust system. This additional air aids in further burning of exhaust gasses in the exhaust system, resulting in lower emissions. Air is supplied from the filtered side of the air cleaner through a hose to the air control valve, which is controlled by the computer. When opened by the air switch solenoid, the air valve allows air to flow to the air injection check valve, through which it enters the exhaust system. The following explains the components of the system:

a) *The air injection check valve is a reed valve that is opened and closed by the vacuum and pressure exhaust pulsations. During vacuum pulsations, atmospheric pressure opens the check valve and forces air into the exhaust system.*

b) *The air control valve controls the supply of filtered air routed to the air injection check valve. The valve is opened and closed by the air switch solenoid.*

c) *The air switch solenoid controls the air control valve by switching vacuum to the air control valve on and off during varying operating conditions. The solenoid is controlled by the computer.*

d) *Vacuum is stored in the vacuum storage reservoir until it's released by the air switch solenoid.*

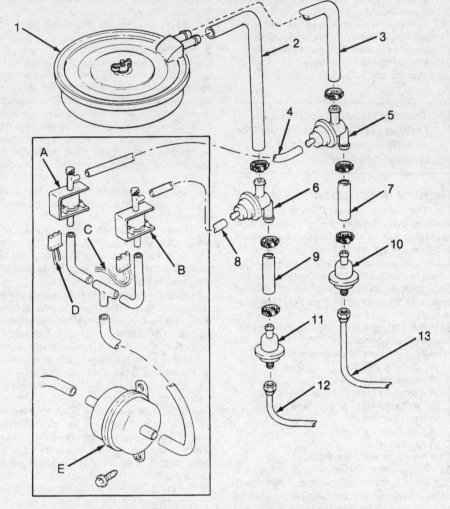

5.3 An exploded view of a typical Pulse Air System

1	Air cleaner	10	Upstream check valve
2	Air cleaner-to-downstream air control valve vacuum hose	11	Downstream check valve
3	Air cleaner-to-upstream air control valve vacuum hose	12	Downstream tube-to-converter
		13	Upstream tube-to-exhaust pipe
4	Upstream vacuum hose	A	Air switch solenoid (upstream)
5	Upstream air control valve	B	Air switch solenoid (downstream)
6	Downstream air control valve	C	Control wires from computer (downstream)
7	Upstream check valve hose	D	Control wires from computer (upstream)
8	Downstream vacuum hose		
9	Downstream check valve hose	E	Vacuum storage reservoir

e) *Depending on operating conditions, the computer switches the air injection point to and from the exhaust manifold and catalytic converter. The computer does this by energizing and de-energizing the air switch solenoids.*

Checking

2   Because of the complexity of the Pulse Air system, it is difficult to diagnose a malfunctioning system at home. However, if you suspect the system is malfunctioning, a simple inspection is as follows:

a) *Inspect all hoses, vacuum lines and wires. Be sure they are in good condition and all connections are clean and tight.*

b) *If there is still a malfunction in the system take the vehicle to a dealer service department or a certified emission control repair shop for testing.*

Component replacement

3   To replace Pulse Air system components, refer to the accompanying exploded view of the Pulse Air system (see illustration).

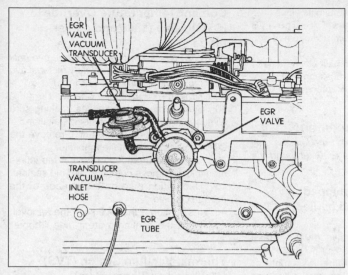

6.2 A typical EGR valve and vacuum transducer on a six-cylinder engine (4.0L six-cylinder shown)

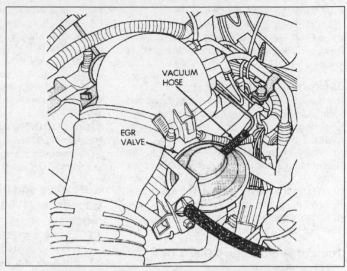

6.8 Location of the EGR valve on four-cylinder models - when checking the valve, remove the vacuum hose and connect a hand vacuum pump

6 Exhaust Gas Recirculation (EGR) system (1987 through 1990 and 2007 through 2011 models)

Caution: *Do not operate the engine (other than temporarily for testing) with any EGR system components disconnected or not operating as designed. Doing so can lead to severe engine damage from detonation.*

General description

1 This system recirculates a portion of the exhaust gases into the intake manifold to reduce the combustion temperatures and thus decrease the amount of oxides of nitrogen (NOx) in the exhaust.

2 The main component in the system is the EGR valve. The EGR valve is a vacuum-controlled device which regulates the amount of exhaust gas bled into the intake. Some six-cylinder engines use a backpressure transducer (normally mounted near the EGR valve) (see illustration). The backpressure transducer measures the amount of exhaust gas backpressure on the exhaust side of the EGR valve and varies the strength of the vacuum signal to the EGR valve based on backpressure. The transducer uses this signal to provide the correct amount of recirculated exhaust gas under various conditions.

3 The EGR valves on later four-cylinder and all 4.0L six-cylinder engines use an EGR solenoid. The EGR solenoid is controlled by the computer. When energized by the computer, the solenoid closes and prevents vacuum from reaching the EGR valve. When it's not energized, the solenoid is open and vacuum is applied to the EGR valve. The computer monitors engine coolant temperature and other operating conditions to determine when EGR operation is desired. On many four-cylinder engines, one solenoid controls

vacuum to both the EGR valve and the canister purge valve (see illustration 3.8).

4 EGR systems on earlier four-cylinder and all 4.2L six-cylinder engines are not computer controlled. They use a Coolant Temperature Override (CTO) valve and a Thermal Vacuum Switch (TVS). The CTO restricts vacuum flow to the EGR valve when coolant temperature is below about 115-degrees F. The TVS, located in the air cleaner, restricts vacuum flow to the EGR valve when intake air temperature is below about 50-degrees F.

5 2007 through 2011 models use an electronic EGR valve bolted to the rear of the passenger cylinder head. The PCM opens and closes the EGR valve.

6 Common engine problems associated with the EGR system are rough idling, stalling at idle, rough engine performance during light throttle application and stalling during deceleration. Keep in mind that changes in exhaust system backpressure (caused by blockage or leaks) can cause the EGR system to malfunction, sometimes resulting in driveability problems.

Checking

Warning: *Use extreme caution when the engine is running. Do not stand in line with the engine cooling fan. Keep your hands away from the pulleys, belts or fan. Do not wear loose clothing.*

General (1990 and earlier models only)

7 With the engine at normal operating temperature, the parking brake set and the wheels blocked, have an assistant raise the engine speed to approximately 1500 rpm while you watch the EGR valve stem. It should move, indicating the EGR valve is opening. If it does not open, the EGR valve is not receiving vacuum or the EGR valve is malfunctioning.

8 Disconnect the vacuum hose from the

EGR valve and connect a hand vacuum pump in its place (see the accompanying illustration or illustration 6.2). With the engine idling, apply about 15 in-Hg of vacuum. The valve should hold vacuum, it should open and the engine should run roughly or stall.

a) If the valve holds vacuum and opens, but the engine does not run roughly or stall, the EGR valve and/or passages (in the intake manifold) are clogged or the EGR tube is corroded, damaged or clogged. Remove the components and clean or replace them as necessary.

b) If the valve does not hold vacuum, the valve diaphragm is ruptured. Replace the valve.

c) If the valve holds vacuum but does not open, the valve is stuck. Replace it.

EGR solenoid

1990 and earlier models

9 Apply the parking brake and block the wheels.

10 Warm the engine to normal operating temperature and perform the following checks with the engine idling.

11 Check the vacuum to the solenoid (it should be 15 in-Hg minimum). If vacuum is low or non-existent, check for kinks, twists or loose connections of the vacuum hoses and lines.

12 If the vacuum is OK, reconnect the vacuum line to the input port and connect a vacuum gauge to the solenoid output port.

13 If vacuum reads zero, go to the next step. If the gauge is reading a vacuum, have the solenoid and the ECU checked by the dealer service department or other qualified shop.

14 Disconnect the electrical connector at the solenoid. There should now be vacuum at the output port. If not, replace the EGR valve solenoid.

2007 through 2011 models

15 To check EGR operation of the electronic EGR valve, a diagnostic scan tool with the capabilities to perform functional checks is required.

Backpressure transducer

16 Disconnect the vacuum output, input and backpressure lines. Remove the transducer.

17 Plug the output port, connect a hand-operated vacuum pump to the input port.

18 Apply 1 to 2 psi of air pressure to the backpressure port with a hand-operated air pump.

19 Using the hand-operated vacuum pump, apply 12 in-Hg of vacuum.

20 The transducer must be replaced if it does not hold a vacuum.

Coolant Temperature Override (CTO) valve

21 Inspect vacuum hoses for air leaks, correct routing and loose connections.

22 Disconnect the outlet hose from the CTO (leading to the TVS) and connect a vacuum gauge to the outlet port on the CTO (see illustration).

23 Start the engine and run at approximately 1500 rpm (engine cold). No vacuum should be present.

24 Replace the CTO valve if vacuum is indicated.

25 Run the engine until coolant temperature reaches or exceeds 115-degrees F.

26 With the engine rpm at 1500, vacuum should be indicated. If not, replace the CTO valve.

Thermal Vacuum Switch (TVS)

27 The TVS is located in the air cleaner. Cool the TVS to approximately 40-degrees F (it may be necessary to remove the switch and refrigerate it), disconnect the vacuum hose from the TVS inner port and connect a hand-operated vacuum pump in its place.

28 Apply vacuum to the TVS. The TVS check valve should maintain a vacuum. If not, replace the TVS.

29 Start the engine. When air cleaner intake air temperature is above 50-degrees F, vacuum should not remain. Replace the TVS if vacuum is maintained.

Component replacement

Note: *On 2007 through 2011 models, the only EGR components are the EGR tube and the electronic EGR valve.*

EGR valve and (if equipped) transducer (1990 and earlier models)

30 Locate the EGR valve on the intake manifold (see illustration 6.2 or 6.7).

31 Remove the air cleaner assembly or the air intake hose from the throttle body as needed for access (see Chapter 4).

32 Detach the vacuum hose from the EGR valve or EGR valve transducer.

33 Remove the two EGR valve mounting bolts.

34 On 2007 through 2011 models, remove the upper intake manifold (see Chapter 2D, Section 6) to access the EGR valve, which is mounted to the rear of the right cylinder head.

35 Remove the EGR valve, the old gasket and restrictor plate (if so equipped). Discard the old gasket.

36 Clean the gasket mating surfaces of the intake manifold and the EGR valve (if you're not installing a new one). Use a gasket scraper, then clean the surfaces with lacquer thinner or acetone.

37 Clean all exhaust passages in the intake manifold to insure a free flow.

38 Installation is the reverse of removal. Be sure to use a new gasket.

Coolant Temperature Override (CTO) valve (1990 and earlier models)

Warning: *Never remove the radiator cap until the engine has cooled completely (at least five hours after the engine has been run).*

39 Drain the coolant (see Chapter 1).

40 Detach the vacuum hoses, making sure all hoses are marked for easier installation.

41 Using an open-end wrench, remove the CTO valve from the intake manifold.

42 Clean the threaded of hole in the intake manifold to remove corrosion and old sealant.

43 Use Teflon tape on the threads of the new CTO valve.

44 Installation is the reverse of the removal.

45 Refill the cooling system (see Chapter 1).

Thermal Vacuum Switch (TVS) (1990 and earlier models)

46 Remove the air cleaner.

47 Detach and label the vacuum hoses from the TVS.

48 Detach the retaining clip(s) attaching the TVS to the air cleaner.

49 Remove the TVS from the air cleaner.

50 Installation is the reverse of the removal.

EGR tube (1990 and earlier models)

Four-cylinder engines

51 Remove the EGR tube-to-exhaust manifold bolts (see illustration).

52 Using a flare-nut wrench (if available), unscrew the EGR tube nut at the intake manifold.

53 Remove the tube and discard the gasket.

54 Clean the gasket mating surface with a scraper, then wipe it with a rag soaked in lacquer thinner or acetone.

55 Install the EGR tube. Install the EGR

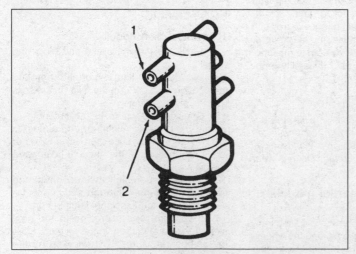

6.22 A typical CTO valve - it is normally threaded into the intake manifold

1 *Inlet port (to a ported vacuum source)*
2 *Outlet port (to the TVS)*

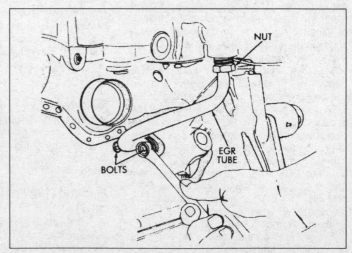

6.51 EGR tube removal (four-cylinder engine)

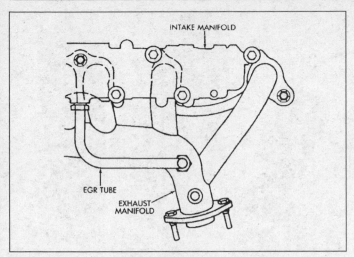

6.58 Typical six-cylinder engine EGR tube installation details (4.0L six-cylinder engine shown, 4.2L six-cylinder engine similar)

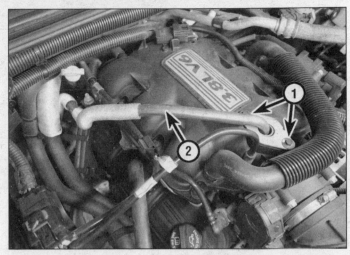

6.65 Remove the bolts (1) attaching the EGR tube (2) to the upper intake manifold

tube line nut to the intake manifold first.

56 Connect the EGR tube to the exhaust manifold. Be sure to use a new gasket.

In-line six-cylinder engines

57 To remove the EGR tube, it may be necessary to loosen the exhaust manifold mounting bolts (see Chapter 2C).

58 Using a flare-nut wrench (if available), loosen the EGR tube line nuts at the intake and exhaust manifolds (see illustration).

59 Remove the EGR tube.

60 Install the EGR tube, but don't tighten the line nuts at this time.

61 Tighten the intake manifold line nut first.

62 Tighten the exhaust manifold line nut next.

63 If loosened, tighten the exhaust manifold bolts to the torque listed in the Specifications in Chapter 2C.

EGR valve and tube (2007 through 2011 models)

64 Near the valve cover on the passenger side, remove the nut and EVAP tube bracket from the EGR bracket. Remove the stud attaching the EGR tube bracket to the cylinder head.

65 Remove the two bolts attaching the EGR tube to the upper intake manifold (see illustration).

66 Detach the spark plug wires from the spark plugs on the right cylinder bank, then remove the fasteners and detach the spark plug wire bracket from the valve cover studs.

67 Disconnect the electrical connector from the EGR valve.

68 If the vehicle is equipped with an automatic transmission, remove the dipstick tube bolt and pull the dipstick tube from the transmission.

69 Remove the bolts attaching the EGR tube to the EGR valve on the rear of the passenger's cylinder head.

70 Remove the EGR valve mounting bolts and detach the EGR valve.

71 Installation is reverse of removal. Use new gaskets during installation.

7 Catalytic converter

Note: *Because of a Federally mandated extended warranty which covers emissions-related components such as the catalytic converter, check with a dealer service department before replacing the converter at your own expense.*

General description

1 The catalytic converter is an emissions control device added to the exhaust system to reduce pollutants from the exhaust gas stream. Two types of converters are used. Your vehicle may be equipped with either of the two. The conventional oxidation catalyst reduces the levels of hydrocarbon (HC) and carbon monoxide (CO). The three-way catalyst lowers the levels of oxides of nitrogen (NOx) as well as HC and CO.

Checking

2 The test equipment for a catalytic converter is expensive and highly sophisticated. If you suspect that the converter on your vehicle is malfunctioning, take it to a dealer or authorized emissions inspection facility for diagnosis and repair.

3 Whenever the vehicle is raised for servicing of underbody components, check the converter for leaks, corrosion, dents and other damage. Check the welds/flange bolts that attach the front and rear ends of the converter to the exhaust system. If damage is discovered, the converter should be replaced.

4 Although catalytic converters don't break too often, they do become plugged. The easiest way to check for a restricted converter is to use a vacuum gauge to diagnose the effect of a blocked exhaust on intake vacuum.

a) Open the throttle until the engine speed is about 2000 rpm
b) Release the throttle quickly.
c) If there is no restriction, the gauge will quickly drop to not more than 2 in-Hg or more above its normal reading.
d) If the gauge does not show 5 in-Hg or more above its normal reading, or seems to momentarily hover around its highest reading for a moment before it returns, the exhaust system, or the converter, is plugged (or an exhaust pipe is bent or dented, or the core inside the muffler has shifted)

Component replacement

5 Refer to the information on exhaust system component replacement in Chapter 4.

8 Computerized Emission Control (CEC) systems

1 These vehicles are equipped with a computer to monitor and control engine functions. The computer goes by various names on the models covered by this manual:

Micro Computer Unit (MCU)
(1987 through 1989 models)
Electronic Control Unit (ECU) (1990 and 1991 models)
Single Board Engine Controller (SBEC) (1990 and 1991 models)
Single Board Engine Controller II (SBEC II) (1992 and later models)
Powertrain Control Module (PCM) (1993 and later models).

2 These systems monitor various engine operating conditions and adjust the air/fuel mixture, ignition timing, engine idle speed, etc., to promote better fuel economy, improve driveability and reduce exhaust emissions.

3 Each of the systems used on the various models covered by this manual includes

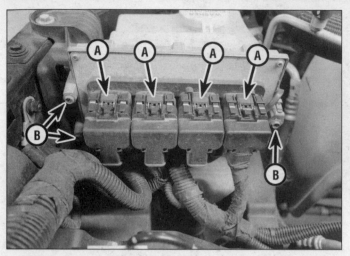

8.13 Disengage the connector locks (A) and depress the tabs to disconnect the electrical connectors, then remove the PCM mounting bolts (B)

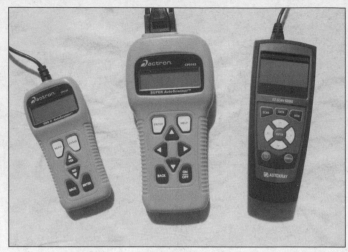

9.2 Scanners like these from Actron and AutoXray are powerful diagnostic aids - they can tell you just about anything you want to know about your engine management system

a computer and many information sensors and output actuators. The information sensors inform the computer of the vehicle's current operating parameters, the computer compares this information to its "map" (which tells what these parameters should be), and, if the information does not match the map, the computer sends signals to the output actuators to alter engine operation to match the map. Information sensors are discussed in Section 10 of this Chapter. Output actuators include the following:

a) *Carburetor mixture control solenoid or fuel injector(s) (see Chapter 4).*
b) *EGR/evaporative emissions solenoid(s) (see Sections 3 and 6).*
c) *Ignition control module (see Chapter 5).*
d) *Pulse air switch solenoids (see Section 5).*
e) *Automatic Idle Speed (AIS) motor or idle stepper motor (see Chapter 4).*
f) *Fuel pump relay.*

4   Complete diagnosis of the computerized emission control system is beyond the scope the home mechanic. Fortunately, all of these systems are protected by a Federally mandated extended warranty (5 years/ 50,000 miles, or whichever comes first, at the time this manual was written). This warranty covers all emissions control components (EGR, PCV, CCV, Pulse Air, evaporative control systems, information sensors, the catalytic converter, etc.). It also covers emissions related parts like the carburetor, certain fuel injection components, exhaust manifold and major ignition system components (the distributor, ignition wires and coil, spark plugs, etc.). Contact a dealer service department for further details regarding the coverage for your vehicle; he is obligated by Federal law to provide you with a detailed list of the emission related parts on your vehicle which are protected by the Federal warranty.

5   If your vehicle is out of warranty and you suspect a problem with the computer-

ized emissions control system, the next two Sections in this Chapter are designed to help you diagnose the system. If you are uncertain what the problem is after using these two Sections, take the vehicle to a dealer service department or other qualified shop that has the special equipment and expertise to diagnose these systems completely.

Powertrain Control Module (PCM) - replacement

1999 and earlier models

6   Disconnect the negative battery cable.
7   Locate the PCM and unlock the electrical connector locks (if equipped).
8   Disconnect the PCM connectors.
9   Remove the bolts/screws and remove the PCM from the vehicle.
10   Installation is reverse of removal.

2000 and later models

Caution: *The PCM can be replaced easily, however, on later models, data in the PCM that is particular for the vehicle to start and run must be downloaded from the old PCM prior to removal and uploaded to the NEW PCM before the vehicle will operate. This procedure must be performed by a qualified technical or repair facility using specialized diagnostic and programming equipment. Failure to do this may result in the vehicle not starting or running or run correctly or problems with other systems. It is highly recommended to have the PCM replaced and programmed by a qualified repair facility.*
Note: *The following procedure is intended only for removing/repositioning the existing PCM for access to other components.*
Note: The PCM is mounted to a bracket near the windshield washer fluid reservoir at the left front corner of the engine compartment.
11   Disconnect the cable from the negative terminal of the battery (see Chapter 5).
12   Remove the plastic shields from the

electrical connectors, if equipped.
13   Disconnect the electrical connectors from the PCM (see illustration).
14   Remove the mounting bolts and detach the PCM from the bracket.
15   Installation is the reverse of removal.

9   Diagnostic Trouble Codes (DTCs) (1991 and later models) - description and code retrieving

Note: *The diagnostic trouble codes on all models can be extracted from the Powertrain Control Module (PCM) using a trouble code reader or scan tool. On 1991 THROUGH 1995 models only, the PCM can be placed in the diagnostic mode and the trouble codes flashed on the Check Engine light. On 1997 and later models, have the vehicle diagnosed by a dealer service department or other qualified automotive repair facility if the proper SCAN tool is not available.*

1   The PCM will illuminate the CHECK ENGINE light (also known as the Malfunction Indicator Lamp) on the dash if it recognizes a fault in the system. The light will remain illuminated until the problem is repaired and the code is cleared or the PCM does not detect any malfunction for several consecutive drive cycles.
2   The diagnostic codes for the On Board Diagnostic (OBD) system can be extracted from the PCM using a SCAN tool on all models (see illustration). On 1991 through 1995 models only, the system can be accessed to flash the trouble codes on the CHECK ENGINE light. To extract the diagnostic trouble codes on 1991 through 1995 models using this method, proceed as follows:

a) *Without starting the engine, turn the ignition key On, Off, On, Off and finally On. The CHECK ENGINE light on the dash will begin to flash.*

Self-diagnostic codes

Code	Probable cause
11	Ignition
13	Manifold Absolute Pressure (MAP) sensor vacuum
14	Manifold Absolute Pressure (MAP) sensor electrical
15	Distance sensor or circuit
17	Engine running too cool
21	Oxygen sensor or circuit
22	Coolant temperature sensor or circuit
23	MAT sensor or circuit
24	Throttle Position Sensor (TPS) sensor or circuit
25	Automatic Idle Speed (AIS) circuit
27	Fuel injector control
31	EVAP solenoid or circuit

Code	Probable cause
33	Air conditioning clutch relay
41	Alternator field
42	Automatic shutdown relay
44	Battery temperature sensor
46	Battery over voltage
47	Battery under voltage
51	Oxygen sensor – lean condition indicated
52	Oxygen sensor – rich condition indicated
53	Internal engine controller fault
54	Distributor sync pickup
55	End of Code Output
62	Emissions Maintenance Reminder (EMR) mileage accumulator
63	Controller failure EEPROM write denied

Trouble code chart - 1991 through 1995 models

b) If any trouble codes are stored in the PCM memory, the CHECK ENGINE light will flash the number of the first digit, pause and flash the number of the second digit. For example: Code 23, air temperature sensor circuit would be indicated by two flashes, pause, three flashes. A long pause will appear between individual codes if more than one code is present. Carefully observe the flashes and record the exact code number(s) onto paper.

c) After the stored codes have been indicated (or if everything in the self diagnosis system is functioning properly), the CHECK ENGINE light will flash a Code 55. Refer to the accompanying charts for trouble code identification.

d) If the ignition key is turned Off during the code extraction process and possibly turned back ON, the self diagnostic system will automatically invalidate the procedure. Restart the procedure to extract the codes.

Note: *The self diagnostic system cannot be accessed with the engine running.*

3 The preferred code extraction method requires a special trouble code reader or scan tool that interfaces with the OBD system by plugging into the diagnostic connector. Trouble code readers are more economical, but only have the capability of reading and erasing trouble codes. A scan scan tool has the ability to diagnose in-depth driveability problems and it allows freeze frame data to be retrieved from the PCM stored memory. Freeze frame data is an OBD II PCM feature that records all related sensor and actuator activity on the PCM data stream whenever an engine control or emissions fault is detected and a trouble code is set. This ability to look at the circuit conditions and values when the malfunction occurs provides a valuable tool when trying to diagnose intermittent driveability problems. If the tool is not available and intermittent driveability problems exist, have the vehicle checked at a dealer service department or other qualified repair shop.

Clearing diagnostic trouble codes

Note: *Always clear the codes from the PCM before starting the engine after a new elec-*tronic engine control component (information sensor or output actuator) is installed. The PCM stores the operating parameters of each sensor. The PCM may set a trouble code if a new sensor is allowed to operate before the parameters from the old sensor have been erased.

1991 through 1995 models

4 On these models the trouble codes can be erased by disconnecting the cable from the negative terminal of the battery for at least 15 seconds. Certain driveability problems may be encountered for a while after doing this, as the computer must "relearn" its operating parameters.

1997 and later models

5 After the system has been repaired, the codes must be cleared from the PCM memory using a code reader or scan tool.

Note: *Do not disconnect the battery from the vehicle in an attempt to clear the codes. If necessary, have the codes cleared by a dealer service department or other qualified repair facility.*

Diagnostic Trouble Code chart - 1997 and later models

Note: *Not all DTCs that may display are listed in the table below. Some DTCs are manufacturer specific while some are generic OBD-II DTCs.*

Code	Possible cause
P0010	Bank 1 camshaft 1 - position actuator circuit open
P0013	Bank 1 camshaft 2 - position actuator circuit open
P0016	Crankshaft/camshaft timing misalignment (bank 1 sensor 1)
P0017	Crankshaft/camshaft timing misalignment (bank 1 sensor 2)
P0018	Crankshaft position - camshaft position correlation (bank 2 sensor 1)
P0019	Crankshaft position - camshaft position correlation (bank 2 sensor 2)
P0020	Bank 2 camshaft 1 - position actuator circuit open
P0023	Bank 2 camshaft 2 - position actuator circuit open
P0031	HO2S heater control circuit low (bank 1, sensor 1)
P0032	HO2S heater control circuit high (bank 1, sensor 1)
P0037	HO2S heater control circuit low (bank 1, sensor 2)
P0038	HO2S heater control circuit high (bank 1, sensor 2)
P0051	HO2S heater control circuit low (bank 2, sensor 1)
P0052	HO2S heater control circuit high (bank 2, sensor 1)
P0057	HO2S heater control circuit low (bank 2, sensor 2)
P0058	HO2S heater control circuit high (bank 2, sensor 2)
P0068	Throttle position (TP) sensor inconsistent with mass air flow (MAF) sensor
P0071	Ambient air temperature sensor range/performance problem
P0072	Ambient air temperature sensor circuit low input
P0073	Ambient air temperature sensor circuit high input
P0107	Manifold absolute pressure or barometric pressure circuit, low input
P0108	Manifold absolute pressure or barometric pressure circuit, high input
P0111	Intake air temperature circuit, range or performance problem

Code	Possible cause
P0112	Intake air temperature circuit, low input
P013A	HO2S slow response – rich to lean (bank 1, sensor 2)
P013C	HO2S slow response – rich to lean (bank 2, sensor 2)
P0113	Intake air temperature circuit, high input
P0116	Engine coolant temperature circuit range/performance problem
P0117	Engine coolant temperature circuit, low input
P0118	Engine coolant temperature circuit, high input
P0121	Throttle position or pedal position sensor/switch circuit, range or performance problem
P0122	Throttle position or pedal position sensor/switch circuit, low input
P0123	Throttle position or pedal position sensor/switch circuit, high input
P0124	Throttle position or pedal position sensor/switch circuit, intermittent
P0125	Insufficient coolant temperature for closed loop fuel control
P0128	Coolant thermostat (coolant temperature below thermostat regulating temperature)
P0129	Barometric pressure - too low
P0131	O2 sensor circuit, low voltage (bank 1, sensor 1)
P0132	O2 sensor circuit, high voltage (bank 1, sensor 1)
P0133	O2 sensor circuit, slow response (bank 1, sensor 1)
P0135	O2 sensor heater circuit malfunction (bank 1, sensor 1)
P0136	O2 sensor circuit malfunction (bank 1, sensor 2)
P0137	O2 sensor circuit, low voltage (bank 1, sensor 2)
P0138	O2 sensor circuit, high voltage (bank 1, sensor 2)
P0139	O2 sensor circuit, slow response (bank 1, sensor 2)
P0141	O2 sensor heater circuit malfunction (bank 1, sensor 2)
P0147	O2 sensor heater circuit malfunction (bank 1, sensor 3)
P0151	O2 sensor circuit, low voltage (bank 2, sensor 1)
P0152	O2 sensor circuit, high voltage (bank 2, sensor 1)

Diagnostic Trouble Code chart - 1997 and later models (continued)

Note: *Not all DTCs that may display are listed in the table below. Some DTCs are manufacturer specific while some are generic OBD-II DTCs.*

Code	Possible cause
P0153	O2 sensor circuit, slow response (bank 2, sensor 1)
P0154	O2 sensor circuit - no activity detected (bank 2, sensor 1)
P0155	O2 sensor heater circuit malfunction (bank 2, sensor 1)
P0157	O2 sensor circuit, low voltage (bank 2, sensor 2)
P0158	O2 sensor circuit, high voltage (bank 2, sensor 2)
P0159	O2 sensor circuit, slow response (bank 2, sensor 2)
P0161	O2 sensor heater circuit malfunction (bank 2, sensor 2)
P0171	System too lean (bank 1 sensor 1)
P0172	System too rich (bank 1 sensor 1)
P0174	System too lean (bank 2 sensor 1)
P0175	System too rich (bank 2 sensor 1)
P0196	Engine oil temperature sensor circuit performance
P0197	Engine oil temperature sensor circuit high
P0198	Engine oil temperature sensor circuit low
P0201	Injector circuit malfunction - cylinder no. 1
P0202	Injector circuit malfunction - cylinder no. 2
P0203	Injector circuit malfunction - cylinder no. 3
P0204	Injector circuit malfunction - cylinder no. 4
P0205	Injector circuit malfunction - cylinder no. 5
P0206	Injector circuit malfunction - cylinder no. 6
P0218	Transmission overheating condition
P0221	Throttle position or pedal position sensor/switch B, range or performance problem
P0222	Throttle position or pedal position sensor/switch B circuit, low input
P0223	Throttle position or pedal position sensor/switch B circuit, high input
P0300	Random/multiple cylinder misfire detected
P0301	Cylinder no. 1 misfire detected

Code	Possible cause
P0302	Cylinder no. 2 misfire detected
P0303	Cylinder no. 3 misfire detected
P0304	Cylinder no. 4 misfire detected
P0305	Cylinder no. 5 misfire detected
P0306	Cylinder no. 6 misfire detected
P0315	Crankshaft position system - variation not learned
P0320	Crankshaft position (CKP) sensor/engine speed (RPM) sensor - circuit malfunction
P0325	Knock sensor no. 1 circuit malfunction (bank 1 or single sensor)
P0330	Knock sensor no. 2 circuit malfunction (bank 2)
P0335	Crankshaft position sensor "A" circuit malfunction
P0336	Crankshaft position sensor performance
P0339	Crankshaft position sensor "A" - circuit intermittent
P0340	Camshaft position sensor circuit malfunction (bank 1 sensor 1)
P0344	Camshaft position sensor circuit intermittent (bank 1 sensor 1)
P0345	Camshaft position sensor circuit malfunction (bank 2 sensor 1)
P0349	Camshaft position sensor circuit intermittent (bank 2 sensor 1)
P0365	Camshaft position sensor circuit malfunction (bank 1 sensor 2)
P0369	Camshaft position sensor circuit intermittent (bank 1 sensor 2)
P0390	Camshaft position sensor circuit malfunction (bank 2 sensor 2)
P0394	Camshaft position sensor circuit intermittent (bank 2 sensor 2)
P0351	Ignition coil A primary or secondary circuit malfunction
P0352	Ignition coil B primary or secondary circuit malfunction
P0353	Ignition coil C primary or secondary circuit malfunction
P0401	Exhaust gas recirculation - insufficient flow detected
P0403	Exhaust gas recirculation - circuit malfunction

Diagnostic Trouble Code chart - 1997 and later models (continued)

Note: *Not all DTCs that may display are listed in the table below. Some DTCs are manufacturer specific while some are generic OBD-II DTCs.*

Code	Possible cause
P0404	Exhaust gas recirculation - range or performance problem
P0405	Exhaust gas recirculation valve position sensor A - circuit low
P0406	Exhaust gas recirculation valve position sensor A - circuit high
P0420	Catalyst system efficiency below threshold (bank 1)
P0421	Warm-up catalyst efficiency below threshold (bank 1)
P0430	Catalyst system efficiency below threshold (bank 2)
P0431	Warm-up catalyst efficiency below threshold (bank 2)
P0432	Main catalyst efficiency below threshold (bank 2)
P0440	Evaporative emission control system malfunction
P0441	Evaporative emission control system, incorrect purge flow
P0442	Evaporative emission control system, small leak detected
P0443	Evaporative emission control system, purge control valve circuit malfunction
P0452 low input	Evaporative emission control system, pressure sensor
P0453	Evaporative emission control system, pressure sensor high input
P0455	Evaporative emission (EVAP) control system leak detected (no purge flow or large leak)
P0456	Evaporative emission (EVAP) control system leak detected (very small leak)
P0457	Evaporative emission control system leak detected (fuel cap loose/off)
P0460	Fuel level sensor circuit malfunction
P0461	Fuel level sensor circuit, range or performance problem
P0462	Fuel level sensor circuit, low input
P0463	Fuel level sensor circuit, high input
P0480	Cooling fan no. 1, control circuit malfunction

Code	Possible cause
P0481	Cooling fan no. 2, control circuit malfunction
P0498	Evaporative emission system, vent control - circuit low
P0499	Evaporative emission system, vent control - circuit high
P050B	Cold start ignition timing performance
P050D	Cold start rough idle
P0500	Vehicle speed sensor malfunction
P0501	Vehicle speed sensor, range or performance problem
P0503	Vehicle speed sensor circuit, intermittent, erratic or high input
P0505	Idle control system malfunction
P0506	Idle control system, rpm lower than expected
P0507	Idle control system, rpm higher than expected
P0508	Idle control system circuit low
P0509	Idle control system circuit high
P0513	Incorrect immobilizer key
P0516	Battery temperature sensor circuit low
P0517	Battery temperature sensor circuit high
P0522	Engine oil pressure sensor/switch circuit, low voltage
P0523	Engine oil pressure sensor/switch circuit, high voltage
P0532	A/C refrigerant pressure sensor, low input
P0533	A/C refrigerant pressure sensor, high input
P0551	Power steering pressure sensor circuit, range or performance problem
P0562	System voltage low
P0563	System voltage high
P0571	Cruise control/brake switch A, circuit malfunction
P0572	Cruise control/brake switch A, circuit low
P0573	Cruise control/brake switch A, circuit high
P0579	Cruise control system, multi-function input "A" - circuit range/performance problem
P0580	Cruise control system, multi-function input "A" - circuit low

Diagnostic Trouble Code chart - 1997 and later models (continued)

Note: *Not all DTCs that may display are listed in the table below. Some DTCs are manufacturer specific while some are generic OBD-II DTCs.*

Code	Possible cause
P0581	Cruise control system, multi-function input "A" - circuit high
P0582	Cruise control system, vacuum control - circuit open
P0585	Cruise control system, multi-function input A/B - correlation
P0586	Cruise control system, vent control - circuit open
P0591	Cruise control system, multi-function input B - circuit range/performance problem
P0592	Cruise control system, multi-function, input B - circuit low
P0593	Cruise control system, multi-function input B - circuit high
P0594	Cruise control system, servo control - circuit open
P060B	Electronic Throttle Control (ETC) A to D ground performance
P060D	Electronic Throttle Control (ETC) level 2 Accelerator Pedal Position Sensor (APPS) performance
P060E	Electronic Throttle Control (ETC) level 2 Throttle Position Sensor (TPS) performance
P060F	Electronic Throttle Control (ETC) level 2 ECT performance
P0600	Serial communication link malfunction
P0601	Internal control module, memory check sum error
P0602	Control module, programming error
P0604	Internal control module, random access memory (RAM) error
P0605	Internal control module, read only memory (ROM) error
P0606	PCM processor fault
P061A	Electronic Throttle Control (ETC) level 2 torque performance
P061C	Electronic Throttle Control (ETC) level 2 RPM performance
P0613	Transmission control module (TCM) processor error
P062C	Electronic Throttle Control (ETC) level 2 MPH performance

Code	Possible cause
P0622	Generator lamp F, control circuit malfunction
P0627	Fuel pump control - circuit open
P063A	Genreator voltage sense circuit
P0630	VIN not programmed or mismatch - ECM/PCM
P0632	Odometer not programmed - ECM
P0633	Immobilizer key not programmed – ECM
P0642	Engine control module (ECM), knock control - defective
P0643	Sensor reference voltage A - circuit high
P0645	A/C clutch relay control circuit
P0652	Sensor reference voltage B - circuit low
P0653	Sensor reference voltage D - circuit high
P0685	EGM power relay, control - circuit open
P0688	Engine, control relay - short to positive
P0691	Engine coolant blower motor 1 - short to ground
P0692	Engine coolant blower motor 1 - short to positive
P0693	Engine coolant blower motor 2 - short to ground
P0694	Engine coolant blower motor 2 - short to positive
P0700	Transmission control system malfunction
P0703	Torque converter/brake switch B, circuit malfunction
P0706	Transmission range sensor circuit, range or performance problem
P0711	Transmission fluid temperature sensor circuit, range or performance problem
P0712	Transmission fluid temperature sensor circuit, low input
P0713	Transmission fluid temperature sensor circuit, high input
P0714	Transmission fluid temperature sensor circuit, intermittent input
P0715	Input/turbine speed sensor circuit malfunction
P0716	Input/turbine speed sensor circuit, range or performance problem
P0720	Output speed sensor malfunction
P0721	Output speed sensor circuit, range or performance problem

Diagnostic Trouble Code chart - 1997 and later models (continued)

Note: *Not all DTCs that may display are listed in the table below. Some DTCs are manufacturer specific while some are generic OBD-II DTCs.*

Code	Possible cause
P0725	Engine speed input circuit malfunction
P0726	Engine speed input circuit, range or performance problem
P0731	Incorrect gear ratio, first gear
P0732	Incorrect gear ratio, second gear
P0733	Incorrect gear ratio, third gear
P0734	Incorrect gear ratio, fourth gear
P0736	Incorrect gear ratio, reverse gear
P0740	Torque converter clutch, circuit malfunction
P0750	Shift solenoid A malfunction
P0755	Shift solenoid B malfunction
P0760	Shift solenoid C malfunction
P0765	Shift solenoid D malfunction
P0783	Third-to-fourth shift malfunction
P0817	Starter disable (park/neutral) circuit open
P0841	Transmission fluid pressure sensor/switch "A" circuit range/performance problem
P0845	Transmission fluid pressure sensor/switch "B" circuit malfunction
P0846	Transmission fluid pressure sensor/switch "B" circuit range/performance problem
P0850	Park/neutral position (PNP) switch - input circuit malfunction
P0853	Drive switch - input circuit malfunction

Code	Possible cause
P0868	Transmission fluid pressure (TFP) sensor - low
P0869	Transmission fluid pressure (TFP) sensor- high
P0870	Transmission fluid pressure (TFP) circuit malfunction - sensor/switch C
P0871	Transmission fluid pressure (TFP) sensor C - range/ performance problem
P0882	Transmission control module (TCM) power input signal low
P0883	Transmission control module (TCM) power input signal high
P0884	Transmission control module (TCM) power input signal intermittent malfunction
P0888	Transmission control module (TCM) power relay sense circuit malfunction
P0890	Transmission control module (TCM) power relay - sense circuit low
P0891	Transmission control module (TCM) power relay - sense circuit high
P0897	Transmission fluid deteriorated
P0933	Hydraulic pressure sensor - range/performance problem
P0934	Hydraulic pressure sensor - circuit low input
P0935	Hydraulic pressure sensor - circuit high input
P0944	Hydraulic pressure unit - loss of pressure
P0992	Transmission fluid pressure (TFP) sensor F - circuit malfunction
P1524	Oil pressure out of range - camshaft advance/retard disabled
P1644	Incorrect variant/configuration

10 Information sensors

1   Information sensors inform the computer of the engine's current operating conditions so adjustments (air/fuel mixture, ignition timing, idle speed, etc.) can be made to achieve optimum driveability, lower emissions and improved fuel economy.

Note: *Because of a Federally mandated extended warranty which covers emissions-related components such as the information sensors, check with a dealer service department before replacing the sensors at your own expense.*

Oxygen sensor

2   Oxygen (O2) sensors are located in the exhaust manifold(s) or exhaust pipe(s). O2 sensors provide a variable voltage signal (about 0 to 1 volt) to the computer, based on the oxygen content in the exhaust. The computer uses this information to determine whether or not the fuel/air mixture needs to be altered by adjusting the pulse width of the fuel injectors or the carburetor mixture con-

trol solenoid.

3   Older models may be equipped with a single O2 sensor mounted in the exhaust manifold. A newer 4-cylinder equipped vehicle is equipped with two O2 sensors, one before the catalytic converters and one after. A newer in-line six or V6 equipped vehicle is equipped with four O2 sensors, two before the catalytic converters and two after, or mounted directly on the converter body.

4   The PCM uses the readings from the two sensors before and after the catalytic converter to determine the operating efficiency of the converter itself. A DTC for the catalyst can set if the readings do not meet requirements.

5   Checking the oxygen sensor is beyond the scope of the home mechanic. Take the vehicle to a dealer service department or other qualified shop for diagnosis.

Replacement

6   Locate the O2 sensor to be replaced (see illustrations).

Note: *It is recommended to spray a lubricant on the sensor where it screws or is bolted to the exhaust system to ease with removal.*

7   Disconnect the O2 electrical connector. The connectors may be protected by heat shields.

8   Using an O2 wrench, socket or similar, remove the O2 sensor (see illustration).

9   Installation is reverse of removal. Use anti-seize paste on the O2 sensor threads before installation. Use care not to contaminate the O2 sensor with the anti-seize material.

Knock sensor

General information

10   A knock sensor (see illustrations) is used on some models. The knock sensor on four-cylinder and 4.0L six-cylinder engines is on the left side of the engine block, above the oil pan. On 4.2L six-cylinder engines, it's in the intake manifold in front of the carburetor. On 3.8L V6 engines, it is on the passenger's side of the engine block, behind the engine mount. On 3.6L V6 engines, there are two knock sensors located below the lower intake manifold, bolted in the valley between the cylinder banks. The sensor is a piezoelectric crystal transducer that indicates detonation (knock)

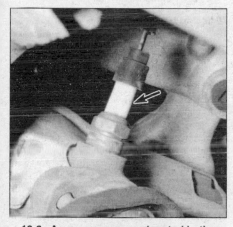

10.6a An oxygen sensor located in the exhaust manifold (2.5L four-cylinder engine)

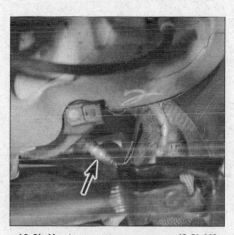

10.6b Upstream oxygen sensor (3.8L V6 engine, left cylinder bank, viewed from above)

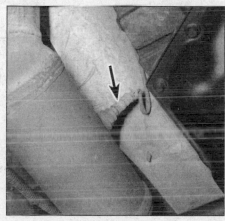

10.6c Downstream oxygen sensor (3.8L V6 engine, left cylinder bank, viewed from below)

10.6d Oxygen sensor details - 3.6L V6 engine, left cylinder bank

1   *Upstream O2 sensor*
2   *Downstream O2 sensor*

10.8 If available, it's a good idea to use an oxygen sensor socket

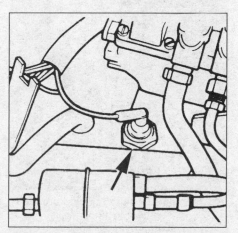

10.10a The knock sensor is located on the engine block or on the intake manifold, near the carburetor (as shown here on a 4.2L inline six-cylinder engine)

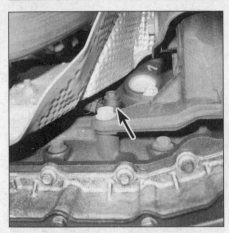

10.10b The knock sensor on 3.8L V6 engines is located on the passenger's side of the engine block near the engine mount

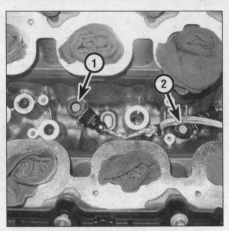

10.10c Knock sensor details - 3.6L V6 engine

1   Sensor one   *2   Sensor two*

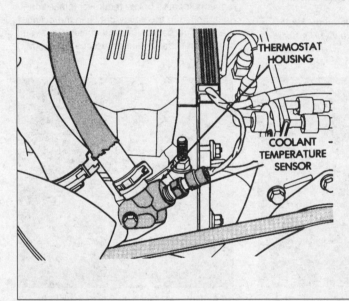

10.23a Engine Coolant Temperature (ECT) sensor location - 2.5L four-cylinder and inline six-cylinder engines

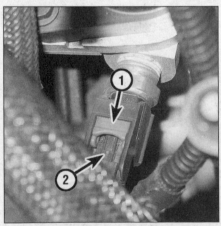

10.23b Engine Coolant Temperature (ECT) sensor location - 2.4L four-cylinder engines

1   Connector lock (slide away from sensor)
2   Retaining tab (squeeze, then unplug connector)

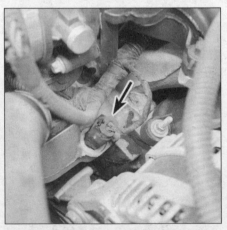

10.23c Engine Coolant Temperature (ECT) sensor location - 3.8L V6 engines

during engine operation. Electrical voltage from the sensor to the computer retards the ignition advance to eliminate detonation (knock).

Replacement

Note: *Checking the knock sensor is beyond the scope of the home mechanic. Take the vehicle to a dealer service department or other qualified shop for diagnosis.*

2011 and earlier models

11   If necessary for access to the sensor, raise the front of the vehicle and support it securely on jackstands.

12   Locate and disconnect the knock sensor electrical connector.

13   Carefully unscrew the sensor.

14   Clean the threaded hole of any corrosion and old sealant. Use Teflon tape on the threads of the new sensor.

15   Install the new knock sensor into the engine block or intake manifold. Torque it to 89 in-lbs. This torque is critical for the proper operation of the knock sensor.

16   Connect the electrical connector to the sensor.

17   Lower the vehicle.

2012 and later models

18   Remove the upper and lower intake manifolds and the oil filter housing (see Chapter 2E).

19   Disconnect the knock sensor(s) electrical connector.

20   Remove the bolt and knock sensor from the engine.

21   Installation is reverse of removal. Do not apply sealant or thread locker to the bolt threads.

22   Torque the knock sensor(s) bolt to 15 ft-lbs. This torque is critical for the proper operation of the knock sensor.

Engine Coolant Temperature (ECT) sensor

General information

23   The ECT sensor is a device that monitors the coolant temperature (see illustrations). On 2.5L four-cylinder and inline six-cylinder engines, it is mounted in the thermostat housing. On 2.4L four-cylinder engines it's mounted at the left-front corner of the cylinder head. On 3.8L V6 engines, it is mounted in the intake manifold below the throttle body. On 3.6L V6 engines, it is mounted in the driver's side cylinder head. As the coolant temperature changes, the resistance of the sensor changes, providing a varying input voltage to the computer. The computer uses information from the ECT to adjust fuel/air mixture, ignition timing and control EGR valve operation.

Replacement

Warning: *Wait until the engine is completely cool before replacing the ECT.*

24   Prepare the new sensor by wrapping the threads with Teflon tape or applying a non-hardening thread sealant. Open the radiator cap to release any residual pressure. Squeeze

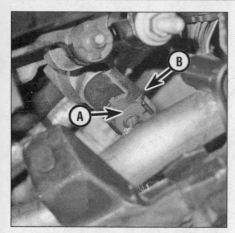

10.23d Engine Coolant Temperature (ECT) sensor location - 3.6L V6 engines

A   *Connector lock (slide up)*
B   *Retaining tab (squeeze, then unplug connector)*

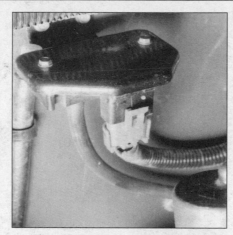

10.26a On early models, the Manifold Absolute Pressure (MAP) sensor is mounted on the firewall

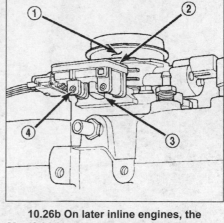

10.26b On later inline engines, the Manifold Absolute Pressure (MAP) sensor is mounted to the side of the throttle body

1   *Throttle body*
2   *MAP sensor*
3   *L-shaped rubber fitting*
4   *Mounting screws*

10.26c On 3.8L V6 engines, the MAP sensor is mounted to the rear of the upper intake manifold (rotate 1/4-turn counterclockwise to remove)

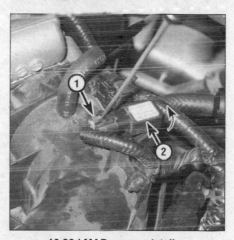

10.26d MAP sensor details - 3.6L V6 engine

1   *Connector lock (slide out, then depress and unplug connector)*
2   *MAP sensor (rotate 1/4-turn counterclockwise, then pull out)*

the upper radiator hose and reinstall the cap (this will create a slight vacuum in the cooling system, which will minimize coolant loss).

25   Place rags around the sensor to prevent spilling coolant. Unscrew the old sensor and immediately install the new one, tightening it securely. Plug in the electrical connector. Check the coolant level and add some, if necessary (see Chapter 1).

Manifold Absolute Pressure (MAP) sensor

General information

26   On early models, the MAP sensor is located on the firewall, near the valve cover (see illustration). It is connected electrically to the computer and to the throttle body by a vacuum hose. On later models, the MAP sensor is attached directly to the throttle body (see illustration) or to the intake manifold (see illustrations). The MAP sensor reads load (pressure) changes in the intake manifold. This causes electrical resistance changes in the MAP sensor, resulting in changing input voltage to the computer. The computer uses this information (input voltage) to vary the air/fuel mixture.

Checking

Early models

27   Inspect the vacuum hose connections from the throttle body to the MAP sensor. Replace a cracked or broken hose with a new one.

28   Disconnect the vacuum hose from the MAP sensor and connect a hand vacuum pump. Apply vacuum. The sensor should hold vacuum. If it does not, replace the sensor.

29   Further testing should be referred to a dealer service department or other qualified shop.

Later models

30   Check that the electrical connector is firmly connected to the MAP sensor. Also check that the fitting from the MAP sensor to the throttle body or intake manifold is securely connected.

Replacement

Early models (firewall mounted)

31   Disconnect the electrical connector from the MAP sensor.

32   Detach the vacuum hose from the MAP sensor.

33   Remove the two mounting nuts.

34   Remove the MAP sensor from the firewall.

35   Installation is the reverse of removal.

Later models (engine mounted)

36   Remove the engine cover (if equipped).

37   If necessary, detach the air filter intake tube from the throttle body.

38   Disconnect the electrical connector from the MAP sensor.

39   On 2006 and earlier in-line six-cylinder models, remove the MAP sensor mounting screws. Detach the MAP sensor from the throttle body. Slide the rubber L-shaped fitting from the throttle body. Remove the L-shaped fitting from the MAP sensor.

40   On 2006 and earlier 4-cylinder models, remove the MAP sensor mounting screw and remove the MAP sensor from the intake manifold.

41   On 2007 and later models, after the connector is removed, rotate the sensor 1/4 turn

10.44 On early models the Intake Air Temperature (IAT) sensor is mounted in the intake manifold (four-cylinder engine shown)

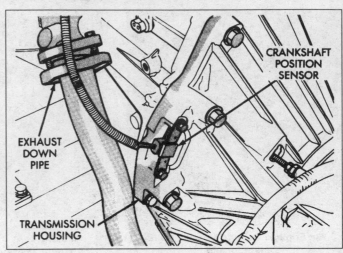

10.60a Bellhousing-mounted Crankshaft Position Sensor (CKP) (inline six-cylinder engine shown)

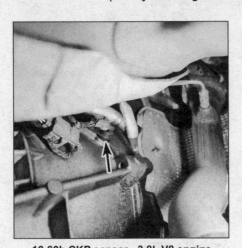

10.60b CKP sensor - 3.8L V8 engine

10.60c CKP sensor - 2.4L four-cylinder engine

1   Electrical connector
2   Mounting bolt

counterclockwise and pull out of the intake manifold.
42   If equipped, check the condition of the MAP sensor O-ring and replace if damaged.
43   Installation is the reverse or removal. Lubricate the O-ring with clean motor oil.
Note: *On 2007 and later models, the connector prevents the MAP sensor from rotating and becoming loose.*

Intake Air Temperature (IAT) sensor

General information
44   The IAT sensor sends the inlet air temperature to the PCM. The IAT sensor is installed in the intake manifold (see illustration) or air intake hose near the throttle body (2007 and later models). Its sensor element extends into the air stream. The sensor resistance changes as the air stream temperature changes, sending a varied input voltage to the

computer. The computer uses this information to alter the fuel/air mixture.

Replacement

2002 and earlier 4-cylinder models 2006 and earlier inline six-cylinder models
45   Remove the air cleaner (if necessary).
46   Disconnect the electrical connector from the MAT sensor.
47   Using a flare-nut wrench (if available), remove the MAT sensor from the intake manifold.
48   Clean the threaded hole to remove any corrosion or old sealant.
49   Use Teflon tape on the threads of the new MAT sensor.
50   Installation is the reverse of removal.

2003 and later 4-cylinder models and 2007 and later models
51   Disconnect the negative battery cable.
52   Remove the engine cover (if equipped).

53   Locate the IAT sensor and disconnect the electrical connector.
54   On 2007 through 2011 models, pull and twist the sensor to remove.
55   On 2003 and later 4-cylinder models, and 2012 and later models, lift the release tab and rotate the sensor 1/4 turn counterclockwise and pull out to remove.
56   Inspect the CKP O-ring and replace if damaged.
57   Installation is the reverse of removal. Rotate the IAT sensor clockwise until the release tab engages.

Throttle Position Sensor (TPS)
58   The Throttle Position Sensor (TPS), is mounted on the side of the carburetor or throttle body and connected directly to the throttle shaft on 2006 and earlier models. The TPS senses throttle movement and position, then transmits an electrical signal to the computer. This signal enables the computer to determine when the throttle is closed, in its normal cruise condition or wide open.
59   Checking the TPS is beyond the scope of the home mechanic. Take the vehicle to a dealer service department or other qualified shop for diagnosis. To replace the TPS, see Chapter 4, Section 15 and Chapter 4, Section 16.

Crankshaft Position Sensor (CKP)

General information
60   The CKP, used on later fuel-injected models, is attached to the transmission bellhousing on 2.5L four-cylinder, in-line six-cylinder and 3.8L V6 engines (see illustrations). On 2.4L four-cylinder engines, it is located on the engine block, slightly rearward of the right/front engine mount. On 3.6L V6 engines, it is located on the engine block, near the bellhousing. The CKP detects teeth on the flywheel as they pass the sensor during engine operation and provides the computer with information concerning engine speed and crankshaft

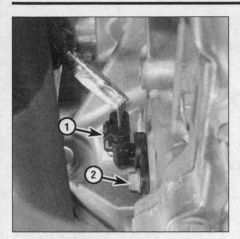

**10.60d CKP sensor details
(3.6L V6 engine)**

1   Electrical connector retaining tab
2   Mounting bolt

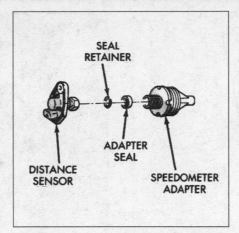

10.69 Distance sensor installation details

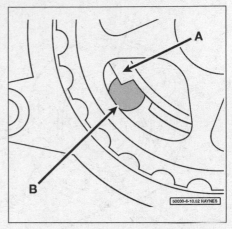

**10.74 CMP sensor adjustment details
(four-cylinder models)**

A   Target wheel
B   Camshaft Position Sensor (CMP)

angle. This information is used to advance or retard ignition timing and fuel injection.

Replacement

61   Raise and support the vehicle if necessary to access the CKP sensor.
62   Locate and disconnect the electrical connector from the CKP.
63   Removing the CKP bolt(s) and remove the CKP using a twisting motion.
64   Inspect the CKP O-ring and replace if damaged.
Caution: *On 2006 and earlier models, new sensors should be equipped with a paper spacer glued to the bottom of the sensor. If reinstalling an old sensor, a paper spacer must be installed to the bottom of the sensor. The spacer is ground off when the engine is started for the fist time after installation. If a spacer is not used, the sensor will be broken when the engine is started.*
65   Installation is the reverse of removal. Lubricate the O-ring with clean motor oil.
66   Ensure the CKP sensor is flush with the mounting surface before tightening the bolt(s).
67   On 2007 and later models, the cam/crank variation relearn procedure must be performed using a scan tool. The vehicle may run and drive without performing the procedure, however, the procedure should be performed as soon as possible by a qualified technician or repair facility.

Distance sensor

68   Some models are equipped with a distance sensor (instead of a speedometer cable) that sends a pulsating voltage signal to the computer that the computer converts to miles per hour.
69   To replace the distance sensor (located at the rear of the transfer case), raise the vehicle, support it securely on jackstands, disconnect the electrical connector from the sensor and unscrew it from the speedometer adapter (see illustration). Installation is the reverse of removal.

Camshaft position sensor (CMP)

70   The camshaft position sensor, in conjunction with the crankshaft position sensor, determines the timing for fuel injection on each cylinder. The camshaft position sensor is a Hall-effect device.

1991 through 2002 four-cylinder models and 1991 through 1999 six-cylinder models

71   See Chapter 5, Section 12 for the CMP/stator replacement procedure.

2003 and later four-cylinder models

Note: *On 2003 and later 4-cylinder models, the camshaft position sensor is mounted in the right-front side of the cylinder head. It reads the position of a target wheel that is located behind the exhaust camshaft drive gear, and sends a signal to the PCM every 180-degrees of rotation.*
72   Disconnect the electrical connector, then remove the mounting bolt and the sensor.
73   To install the CMP, it must be adjusted for depth (closeness to the target wheel). Disconnect the ECT sensor connector, then remove the mounting screws securing the upper timing belt cover.
74   With the key Off, rotate the engine with a socket and bar on the crankshaft pulley bolt until the target wheel behind the camshaft gear partially covers the sensor (see illustration). Install the sensor bolts finger-tight.
75   Insert a strip of 0.030-inch-thick brass shim stock between the sensor and the target wheel. Push the sensor lightly against the shim and tighten the sensor mounting bolts.
76   Reconnect the electrical connector to the sensor.

In-line six-cylinder models

Note: *On 2000 through 2006 in-line six-cylinder models, the camshaft position sensor is located on top of the oil pump drive assembly. It is possible to replace the camshaft position*

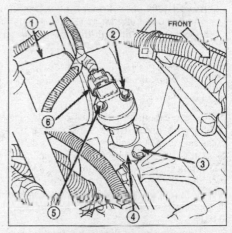

10.78 Camshaft position sensor installation details - 2000 through 2006 six-cylinder models

1   Oil filter
2   Camshaft position sensor
3   Clamp bolt
4   Oil pump drive clamp
5   Camshaft position sensor mounting bolts
6   Electrical connector

sensor without removing the oil pump drive assembly. If the oil pump drive assembly must be removed, the mounting flange must be precisely marked in relation to the engine block or it will be necessary to reset the camshaft position sensor with a scan tool.
77   Disconnect the electrical connector from the camshaft position sensor.
78   If removing the sensor only, remove the mounting bolts and remove the sensor from the oil pump drive (see illustration). Install the new sensor, tighten the bolts securely and connect the electrical connector.
79   If removing the oil pump drive assembly, position the number one cylinder at TDC on the compression stroke (see Chapter 2C).
80   Remove the sensor. Insert an appro-

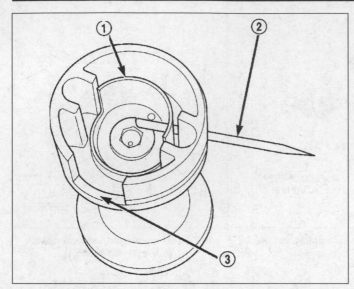

10.80 Before removing the camshaft position sensor on a 2000 through 2004 six-cylinder model, position the engine with the number one cylinder at TDC and install an appropriate size alignment pin through the hole in the base of the pulse ring

1   *Pulse ring*
2   *Alignment pin*
3   *Oil pump driveshaft assembly*

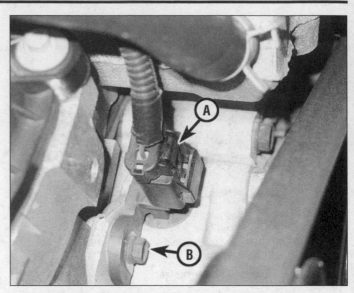

10.89 Disconnect the CMP sensor electrical connector (A), then remove the mounting bolt (B) - 3.8L V6 engines

priate size alignment pin (such as a drill bit) through the holes in the sensor base and pulse ring (see illustration). If the holes do not align, rotate the crankshaft until they do.

81   Mark the position of the oil pump drive mounting flange base to the engine block to ensure the oil pump drive can be re-installed in exactly the same position as originally installed.

82   Remove the oil pump drive hold-down bolt and withdraw the oil pump drive assembly. Remove and discard the O-ring.

83   If the crankshaft has been moved while the oil pump drive is out, the number one piston must be repositioned at TDC. This can be done by feeling for compression pressure at the number one spark plug hole as the crankshaft is rotated. Once compression is felt, continue rotating the crankshaft until the mark on the crankshaft damper is aligned with the zero or TDC mark on the timing indicator (see Chapter 2C).

84   On 2000 through 2004 models, turn the pulse ring until the hole in the pulse ring aligns horizontally with the hole in the housing. Insert an alignment pin through the holes (see illustration 10.80). Install a new O-ring on the oil pump drive assembly. On 2005 and 2006 models, there is a toothed wheel inside the oil pump drive. With the cover removed, insert an alignment tool or small screwdriver down vertically through the alignment hole in the toothed wheel, then the alignment hole in the housing behind it.

85   Insert the oil pump drive into the engine block and align the marks made in Step 81. Because of the helical-cut drive gear, the assembly will rotate clockwise as the gears

engage. Be sure to compensate by starting the installation with the drive gear assembly positioned counterclockwise from the desired finished position. Installing the oil pump drive assembly is very similar to installing a distributor. See Chapter 5 for additional information, if necessary. The oil pump drive must be installed in the same position as originally installed before removal. When properly installed, a line drawn through the center of the camshaft position sensor and electrical connector should be parallel with the centerline of the engine.

Note: *If the alignment marks are lost or poor driveability symptoms appear after installing the oil pump drive, take the vehicle to a dealer service department or other properly equipped repair facility and have the fuel system synchronization reset with a scan tool.*

86   Install the oil pump drive hold-down clamp and tighten the bolt to 17 ft-lbs.

87   The remainder of installation is the reverse of removal.

88   The cam/crank variation relearn procedure must be performed using a scan tool. The vehicle may run and drive without performing the procedure, however, the procedure should be performed as soon as possible by a qualified technician or repair facility.

3.8L V6 engines

Note: *On 2007 through 2011 3.8L V6 models, the CMP is located on the front timing cover, just above the water pump pulley.*

89   Disconnect the electrical connector from the engine harness above the CMP, then loosen, but do not remove, the CMP mounting bolt (see illustration). On 2007 models, the sensor has a pigtail wiring harness.

90   Pull upwards to remove the sensor.

91   Inspect the O-ring. Replace if damaged.

92   Installation is the reverse of removal. Lubricate the O-ring with clean motor oil.

93   The cam/crank variation relearn procedure must be performed using a scan tool. The vehicle may run and drive without performing the procedure, however, the procedure should be performed as soon as possible by a qualified technician or repair facility.

3.6L V6 engines

Note: *On 2012 and later 3.6L V6 models, the CMP(s) are located on top of the valve covers, at the rear.*

94   Disconnect the negative battery cable.

95   Remove the engine cover.

96   Disconnect the CMP electrical connector.

Note: *If all CMP sensors are going to be removed at one time and are to be reinstalled, mark their location to ensure they are installed in the original location from where they were removed.*

97   Loosen, but do not remove, the CMP mounting bolt (see illustration).

98   Remove the CMP with the bolt from the engine (see illustration).

99   Inspect the CMP seal. Replace if damaged.

100   Installation is the reverse of removal. Lubricate the seal with clean motor oil.

101   The cam/crank variation relearn procedure must be performed using a scan tool. The vehicle may run and drive without performing the procedure, however, the procedure should be performed as soon as possible by a qualified technician or repair facility.

10.97 CMP sensor mounting bolt

10.98 Pull the sensor straight out of the valve cover

11.7 Mark the positions of the VVT solenoids

Accelerator Pedal Position sensor (2007 and later models)

102 The accelerator pedal position sensor is an integral component of the accelerator pedal assembly. There is no accelerator cable. This accelerator pedal position sensor is a variable potentiometer that uses the position of the accelerator pedal as its input. The PCM uses this data to calculate the correct position for the throttle plate and directs the throttle motor inside the throttle body to open and close the throttle plate accordingly.

103 The accelerator pedal position sensor is an integral part of the accelerator pedal assembly. If diagnostic trouble codes indicate replacement is necessary, the entire pedal assembly must be replaced. Disconnect the sensor and unbolt the pedal assembly from the floor.

104 Working under the dashboard, disconnect the electrical connector and remove the two nuts securing the pedal assembly to the vehicle.

105 Installation is the reverse of removal.

11   Variable Valve Timing (VVT) system

1 The 3.6L V6 in 2012 and later models is equipped with Variable Valve Timing (VVT). The VVT system independently adjusts the timing of all four camshafts using solenoids and oil control valves to send oil pressure to the camshaft phaser assemblies. The four phasers are located on the front end of the camshafts, behind the VVT solenoids.

2 Each phaser has an Oil Control Valve (OCV). The OCV also bolts the Phaser to the camshaft. The OCV spool valve is spring loaded and moves freely in the OCV. The OCVs are identical in design but should be installed in the same location as when removed.

VVT solenoid replacement

3 Disconnect the negative battery cable (see Chapter 5).

4 Remove the engine cover.

5 For the driver's side solenoids, remove the throttle body (see Chapter 4). Remove the two nuts and three bolts and move the upper intake manifold support bracket out of the way.

6 For the passenger's side solenoids, remove the two nuts and detach the heater core tubes from the valve cover.

7 Locate the VVT solenoids on the front of the valve covers. If the solenoid(s) are to be reinstalled, mark their location to ensure they are installed in the original location from where they were removed (see illustration).

8 Disconnect the solenoid(s) electrical connector.

9 Remove the bolts and pull the solenoid out of the valve cover (see illustration).

10 Inspect the O-ring. Replace if damaged.

11 Installation is reverse of removal. Install the solenoid(s) in the same location as they were removed.

12 Perform the cam/crank variation relearn procedure using a scan tool. The vehicle may run and drive without performing the procedure, however, the procedure should be performed as soon as possible by a qualified

11.9 remove the Torx screws and twist the solenoid out of the valve cover

technician or repair facility.

Oil Control Valve (OCV) replacement

13 The OCVs are part of the camshaft sprockets and are attached to the ends of the camshafts. See Chapter 2E for the OCV replacement procedure.

14 After replacement, perform the cam/crank variation relearn procedure using a scan tool. The vehicle may run and drive without performing the procedure, however, the procedure should be performed as soon as possible by a qualified technician or repair facility.

Notes

Chapter 7 Part A
Manual transmission

Contents

Specifications

Lubricant type .... See Chapter 1

Torque specifications
Ft-lbs (unless otherwise indicated)

Note: *One foot-pound (ft-lb) of torque is equivalent to 12 inch-pounds (in-lbs) of torque. Torque values below approximately 15 foot-pounds are expressed in inch-pounds, because most foot-pound torque wrenches are not accurate at these smaller values.*

Transmission-to-engine bolts
    1999 and earlier (AX-5 and AX-15 transmissions) 28
    2000 to 2002 AX-5 and 2000 to 2004 NV3550 transmissions
        3/8-inch bolts 27
        7/16-inch bolts 43
        M12 bolts 55
    2003 to 2004
        2003 and 2004 NV1550 transmission 55
    2005 and 2006 (NSG370)
        4-cylinder
            Main bellhousing bolts 55
            Lower dust shield bolts 25
        6-cylinder
            Main bellhousing bolts 27
            Side and lower dust shield bolts 43
    2007 to 2011 (NSG370)
        Upper two bolts 30
        Two side bolts 50
        Four bottom bolts 40
    2012 and later (NSG370, all bellhousing bolts) 37
Shift lever tower bolts
    AX4/5, 15 transmission .... 75 in-lbs
    BA 10/5 transmission .... 156 in-lbs
    NV1550 transmission .... 100 in-lbs
    NV3550 transmission .... 62 to 88 in-lbs
    NSG370 transmission .... 120 in-lbs

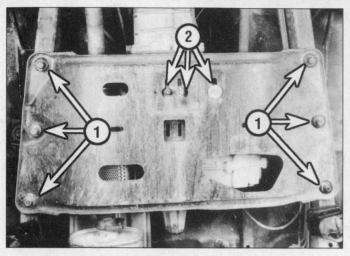

3.4a Crossmember installation details

1   Crossmember-to-frame nuts
2   Transmission mount nuts

3.4b On later models (2007 shown), remove the two mount-to-transmission bolts, then remove the two lower bolts through holes in the crossmember

1   General Information

1   All vehicles covered in this manual come equipped with either a four-, five- or six-speed manual transmission or a three- or four-speed automatic transmission. All information on the manual transmission is included in this Part of Chapter 7A. Information on the automatic transmission can be found in Part B of this Chapter. Information on the transfer case can be found in Part C of this Chapter.

2   Due to the complexity, unavailability of replacement parts and the special tools necessary, internal repair by the home mechanic is not recommended. The information in this Chapter is limited to general information and removal and installation of the transmission.

3   Depending on the expense involved in having a faulty transmission overhauled, it may be a good idea to replace the unit with either a new or rebuilt one. Your local dealer or transmission repair shop should be able to supply you with information concerning cost,

availability and exchange policy. Regardless of how you decide to remedy a transmission problem, you can still save a lot of money by removing and installing the unit yourself.

2   Shift knob - replacement

Note: *The following procedure applies to both the shift lever and range lever knobs. Information for all models was not available at time of publication.*

1   On 2006 and earlier models:

a) *Loosen the locknuts and unscrew the knob from the shift lever OR;*

b) *Remove the shift pattern plate from the top of the knob and remove the retaining nut, OR;*

c) *Unscrew the the shift knob from the shift lever.*

2   On 2007 and later models: Hold the shift lever rearwards, toward the rear of the vehicle, then pull the knob upwards using a

quick motion to remove it. If it is not possible to remove it by hand - cover the knob with a protective cloth, then, using a slide hammer with a 3-jaw puller attachment, remove the knob. To install, align and push the shift knob onto the shift lever until it is fully seated and does not pull off.

3   Shift lever assembly - removal and installation

AX 4/5 or 15 transmission

Note: *AX4 transmissions are used on 1995 and earlier models. AX5 transmissions are used on 2002 and earlier models. AX15 transmissions are used on 1999 and earlier models.*

1   Place the transmission into first or third gear.

2   Raise the vehicle and support it securely on jackstands.

3   Support the engine with a floor jack. Place a block of wood between the jack and the engine oil pan.

4   Remove the crossmember (see illustrations).

5   Lower the transmission/transfer case, but no more than three inches.

6   Reach around the right side of the transmission/transfer case and remove the dust boot from the shift tower and slide it up.

7   Press down on the retainer and turn it counterclockwise to release it (see illustrations). Remove the shift lever from the shift tower.

8   Installation is the reverse of removal.

BA 10/5 transmission

9   Remove the shift knob and locknuts from the shift lever.

10   Remove the screws from the shift lever boot retainer.

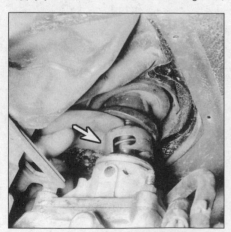

3.7a Press down on the retainer and turn it counterclockwise

3.7b The lugs (arrow) inside the shift tower engage with the slots in the retainer

4.1 Pry on the transmission/transfer case with a pry bar or a large screwdriver to check for excessive looseness

11   Remove the shift lever dust boot.
12   Detach the shaft retainer plate. Don't remove the stub shaft from the lever.
Note: *Some BA 10/5 transmission shift levers may be held in place with a snap-ring instead of a retainer plate.*
13   Installation is the reverse of removal.

NV1500 and NV3550 transmissions

Note: *NV1500 transmissions are used on 2003 through 2004 models. NV3550 transmissions are used on 2000 through 2004 models.*
14   Shift the transmission into first or third gear.
15   Unscrew and remove the shift lever extension from the shift lever assembly.
16   Remove the center console and shift boot
17   Remove the four bolts and the shift tower with the shift lever.
18   Remove the shift lever from the shift tower.
19   Installation is reverse of removal. If the seal is damaged, replace the seal for the shift tower.

NSG370 transmission

Note: *This transmission is used on 2005 and later models.*
20   Using a trim tool or tape-wrapped flat-tipped screwdriver, pry up the edges of the shift boot all around the console and pull the boot up. Use the same process to remove the secondary shift boot at the base of the shift lever at the transmission.
21   Remove the small bolt securing the shift lever to the shift stub on top of the transmission.
22   Installation is the reverse of removal.

4   Transmission mount - check and replacement

1   To check the condition of the mount, insert a large screwdriver or pry bar into the

5.12 AX 4/5 transmission/ transfer case with the crossmember removed

1   *Clutch bleed fitting*
2   *Clutch hydraulic line*
3   *AX 4/5 manual transmission*
4   *Transmission/ transfer case mount*
5   *Transfer case shift linkage*
6   *Transfer case*
7   *Speedometer cable*

space between the transfer case and the crossmember (see illustration). Try to pry the transmission/transfer case up slightly.
2   The transmission/transfer case should not move away from the insulator much at all. If it does, replace it.
3   To replace the mount, remove the nuts attaching it to the crossmember and the bolts attaching it to the transmission/transfer case (see illustrations 2.4a and 2.4b).
4   Raise the transmission/transfer case slightly with a jack and remove the mount, noting which holes are used in the crossmember for proper alignment during installation.
5   Installation is the reverse of the removal. Be sure to tighten the nuts/bolts securely.

5   Manual transmission - removal and Installation

Removal

Note: *The transmission and transfer case are removed as a single unit.*
1   Disconnect the negative cable from the battery.
2   Working inside the vehicle, remove the shift lever (see Section 3).
3   Raise the vehicle and support it securely on jackstands.
4   Remove the skid pates as necessary. Remove the catalytic converter/exhaust pipe assembly where necessary (see Chapter 4).
5   Now is a good time to drain the transmission fluid if needed (see Chapter 1).
6   Disconnect the speedometer cable and/ or speed sensor electrical connectors from the transmission. If equipped, remove the

crankshaft position sensor (see Chapter 6).
7   On 1993 and earlier and 2007 and later models, disconnect the clutch hydraulic line from the release cylinder (see Chapter 8, Section 7). Remove the two bolts and remove the release cylinder from the transmission.
8   On 1994 through 2006 models, unbolt the release cylinder from the transmission and secure out of the way - there's no need to disconnect the hydraulic line.
Caution: *Do not depress the clutch pedal while the transmission is out of the vehicle.*
9   On all models, remove the driveshafts (see Chapter 8). Use a plastic bag to cover the transfer case openings to prevent lubricant loss and contamination.
10   On 4WD models, it is recommended to remove the transfer case (see Chapter 7C, Section 7), however, if the transmission is being removed for a service such as clutch replacement, this may not be necessary.
11   Support the engine by placing a jack (with a block of wood as an insulator) under the engine oil pan. The engine should remain supported at all times while the transmission is out of the vehicle. Disconnect any remaining electrical connectors on the transmission case. Remove the starter (see Chapter 5).
12   Remove the nuts and bolts from the crossmember (see illustrations 2.4a and 2.4b), lower the crossmember and remove it from the vehicle (see illustration).
Warning: *The assembly is very heavy and awkward to remove - a transmission jack equipped with safety chains is highly recommended.*
13   Support the transmission with a jack - preferably a special jack made for this pur-

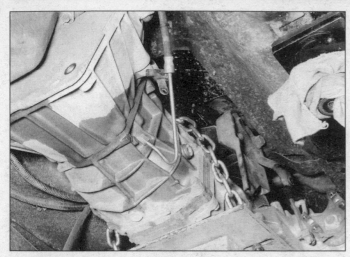

5.13 When removing the transmission/ transfer case, it's a good idea to use a transmission jack equipped with safety chains

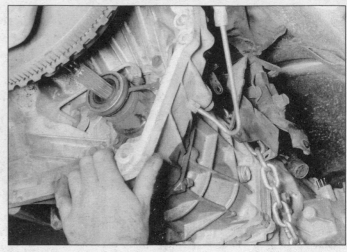

5.15 Move the transmission/transfer case toward the rear until the input shaft clears the clutch

pose. Safety chains will help steady the transmission on the jack (see illustration).

14   Remove the remaining transmission mount, where equipped, then remove the bolts securing the transmission bellhousing to the engine.

15   Make a final check that all wires and hoses have been disconnected from the transmission and then move the transmission and jack toward the rear of the vehicle until the transmission input shaft is clear of the clutch pressure plate. Keep the transmission level as this is done (see illustration).

16   Once the input shaft is clear, lower the transmission/transfer case and remove it from under the vehicle.

17   The clutch components can be inspected at this time by removing the clutch from the engine (see Chapter 8). In most cases, new clutch components should be routinely installed if the transmission is removed.

Installation

18   If removed, install the clutch components (see Chapter 8).

19   With the transmission/transfer case secured to the jack as on removal, raise the transmission/transfer case into position, then carefully slide it forward, engaging the input shaft with the clutch plate hub. DO NOT use excessive force to install the transmission / transfer case. If the input shaft does not slide into place, readjust the angle of the transmission so it is level and/or turn the input shaft so the splines engage properly with the clutch.

20   Install the bellhousing bolts, tightening them to the torque listed in this Chapter's Specifications. Also install the transmission mount (if equipped) and tighten the fasten-

ers securely.

21   Install the crossmember support. Inspect the mount and replace if necessary. Tighten the fasteners securely.

22   Remove the jacks supporting the engine and transmission.

23   Install the various items removed previously, referring to Chapter 8 for the installation of the driveshaft and Chapter 4 for installation of the exhaust components.

24   Make a final check that all wires, hoses and the speedometer cable have been connected and that the transmission has been filled with lubricant to the proper level (see Chapter 1). Lower the vehicle.

25   If the transmission fluid was drained, ensure fresh fluid of the correct specification is added to the proper level (see Chapter 1, Section 35).

26   Working inside the vehicle, install the shift lever (see Section 3) and the transfer case shift linkage (see Chapter 7C).

27   Connect the negative battery cable. Road test the vehicle for proper operation and check for leakage.

---

6   Manual transmission overhaul - general information

Note: *This overhaul procedure applies only to the specific transmissions mentioned below.*

1   Overhauling a manual transmission is a difficult job for the do-it-yourselfer. It involves the disassembly and reassembly of many small parts. Numerous clearances must be precisely measured and, if necessary, changed with select fit spacers and snap-rings. As a result, if transmission prob-

lems arise, it can be removed and installed by a competent do-it-yourselfer, but overhaul should be left to a transmission repair shop. Rebuilt transmissions may be available - check with your dealer parts department and auto parts stores. At any rate, the time and money involved in an overhaul is almost sure to exceed the cost of a rebuilt unit.

2   Nevertheless, it's not impossible for an inexperienced mechanic to rebuild a transmission if the special tools are available and the job is done in a deliberate step-by-step manner so nothing is overlooked.

3   The tools necessary for an overhaul include internal and external snap-ring pliers, a bearing puller, a slide hammer, a set of pin punches, a dial indicator and possibly a hydraulic press. In addition, a large, sturdy workbench and a vise or transmission stand will be required.

4   During disassembly of the transmission, make careful notes of how each piece comes off, where it fits in relation to other pieces and what holds it in place. Exploded views are included for the AX4/5, AX15, and BA10/15 as examples (see illustrations) to show where the parts go - but actually noting how they are installed when you remove the parts will make it much easier to get the transmission back together.

5   Before taking the transmission apart for repair, it will help if you have some idea what area of the transmission is malfunctioning. Certain problems can be closely tied to specific areas in the transmission, which can make component examination and replacement easier. Refer to the *Troubleshooting* section at the front of this manual for information regarding possible sources of trouble.

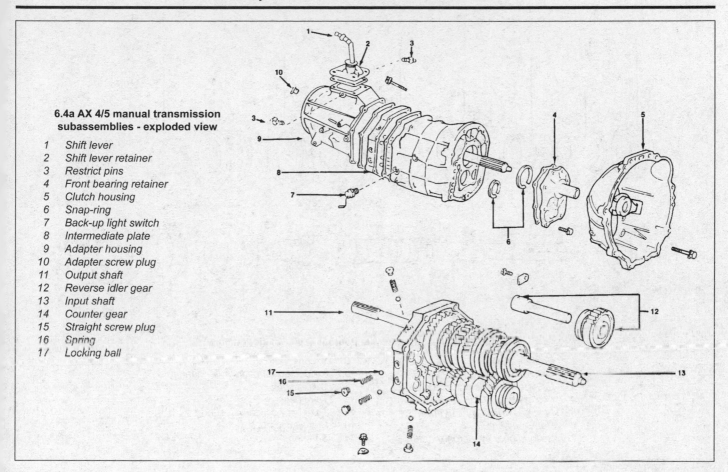

6.4a AX 4/5 manual transmission subassemblies - exploded view

1   Shift lever
2   Shift lever retainer
3   Restrict pins
4   Front bearing retainer
5   Clutch housing
6   Snap-ring
7   Back-up light switch
8   Intermediate plate
9   Adapter housing
10 Adapter screw plug
11 Output shaft
12 Reverse idler gear
13 Input shaft
14 Counter gear
15 Straight screw plug
16 Spring
17 Locking ball

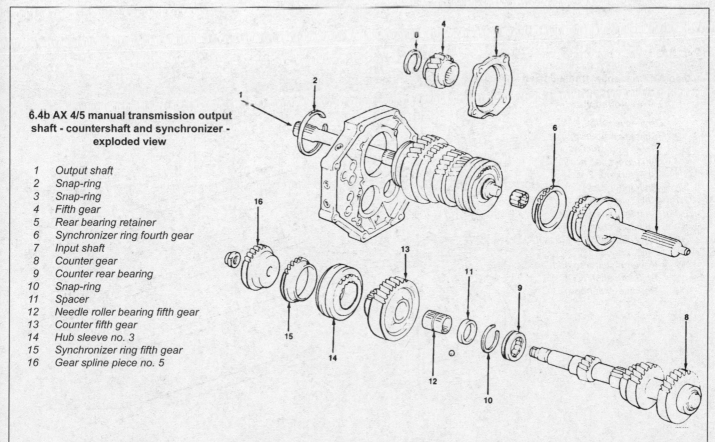

6.4b AX 4/5 manual transmission output shaft - countershaft and synchronizer - exploded view

1   Output shaft
2   Snap-ring
3   Snap-ring
4   Fifth gear
5   Rear bearing retainer
6   Synchronizer ring fourth gear
7   Input shaft
8   Counter gear
9   Counter rear bearing
10 Snap-ring
11 Spacer
12 Needle roller bearing fifth gear
13 Counter fifth gear
14 Hub sleeve no. 3
15 Synchronizer ring fifth gear
16 Gear spline piece no. 5

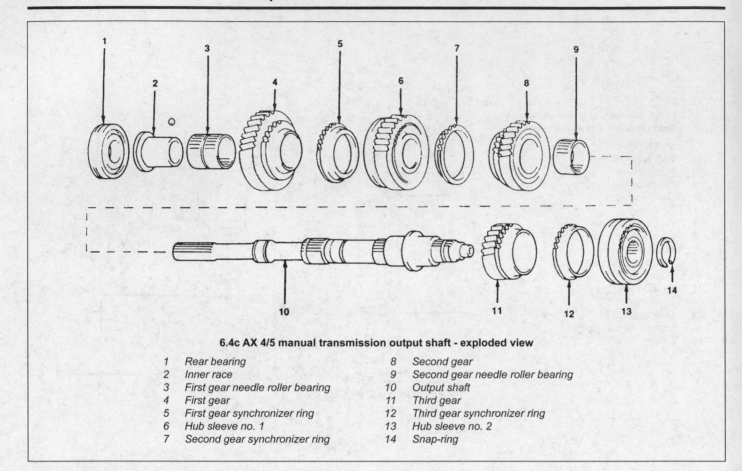

6.4c AX 4/5 manual transmission output shaft - exploded view

1	Rear bearing	8	Second gear
2	Inner race	9	Second gear needle roller bearing
3	First gear needle roller bearing	10	Output shaft
4	First gear	11	Third gear
5	First gear synchronizer ring	12	Third gear synchronizer ring
6	Hub sleeve no. 1	13	Hub sleeve no. 2
7	Second gear synchronizer ring	14	Snap-ring

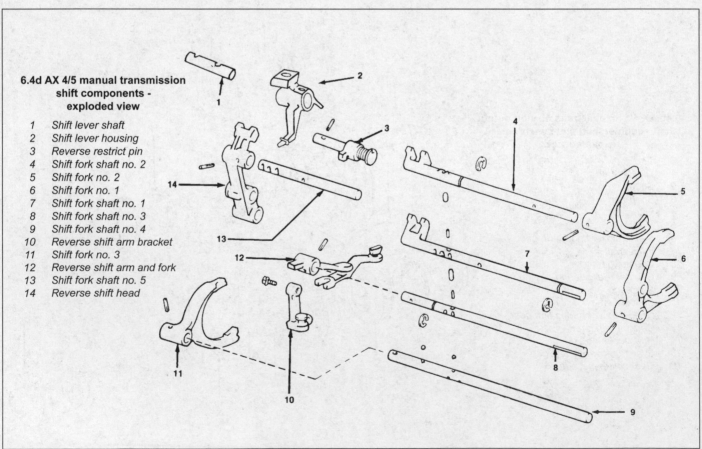

6.4d AX 4/5 manual transmission shift components - exploded view

1   Shift lever shaft
2   Shift lever housing
3   Reverse restrict pin
4   Shift fork shaft no. 2
5   Shift fork no. 2
6   Shift fork no. 1
7   Shift fork shaft no. 1
8   Shift fork shaft no. 3
9   Shift fork shaft no. 4
10   Reverse shift arm bracket
11   Shift fork no. 3
12   Reverse shift arm and fork
13   Shift fork shaft no. 5
14   Reverse shift head

**6.4e BA 10/15 manual transmission -
exploded view**

1   Fifth gear
2   Fifth gear roller bearing
3   Fifth gear
4   Fifth gear snap-ring
5   Reverse gear nut
6   Washer (not used in all models)
7   Reverse gear
8   Rear bearing retainer
9   Rear bearing race
10 Rear bearing
11 Rear bearing shim
12 Shim washer
13 First gear bearing
14 Bearing spacer
15 First gear
16 First-second synchronizer hub
17 Synchronizer hub
18 Second gear housing
19 Second gear
20 Mainshaft
21 Third gear bearing
22 Third gear
23 Third-fourth synchronizer
24 Synchronizer hub
25 Spring washer
26 Lock ring
27 Pilot bearing shims
28 Pilot bearing
29 Pilot bearing race
30 Input shaft
31 Front bearing
32 Front bearing race
33 Front bearing shims
34 Front bearing retainer
35 Oil seal
36 Mounting studs
37 Bearing race
38 Cluster front bearing
39 Front bearing race
40 Cluster gear
41 Cluster rear
42 Bearing race
43 Intermediate shaft
44 Synchronizer hub
45 Fifth gear synchronizer
46 Fifth intermediate rear
47 Fifth intermediate bear bearing
48 Thrust washer
49 Endplay shim
50 Intermediate shaft roller bearing race
51 Oil seal
52 Rear case
53 Fifth gear roller bearing race
54 Snap-ring
55 Intermediate shaft roller bearing
56 Alignment dowels
57 First-second lock spring and ball
58 Roll pin
59 Idler shaft
60 Reverse idler gear
61 Roll pin
62 Fifth-reverse shift fork
63 Fifth-reverse shift rail
64 First-second shift rail
65 Roll pin

66 First-second shift fork
67 Roll pin
68 Third-fourth shift fork
69 Third-fourth shift rail lock pin
70 Third-fourth shift rail
71 Detent plug
72 First-second detent spring
73 First-second detent ball
74 Interlock ball
75 Lock finger
76 Back-up light switch and washer

77 Alignment dowels
78 Front case - left half
79 Detent plug
80 Fifth-reverse detent spring
81 Fifth-reverse detent ball
82 Front case - right half
83 Intermediate case
84 Fill plug and washer
85 Drain plug and washer
86 Access plug

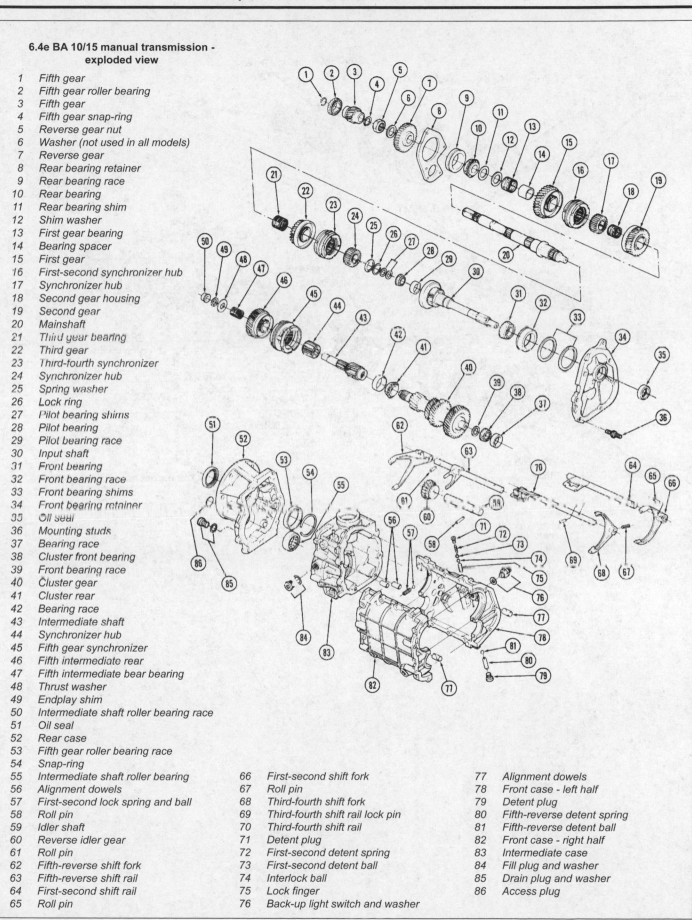

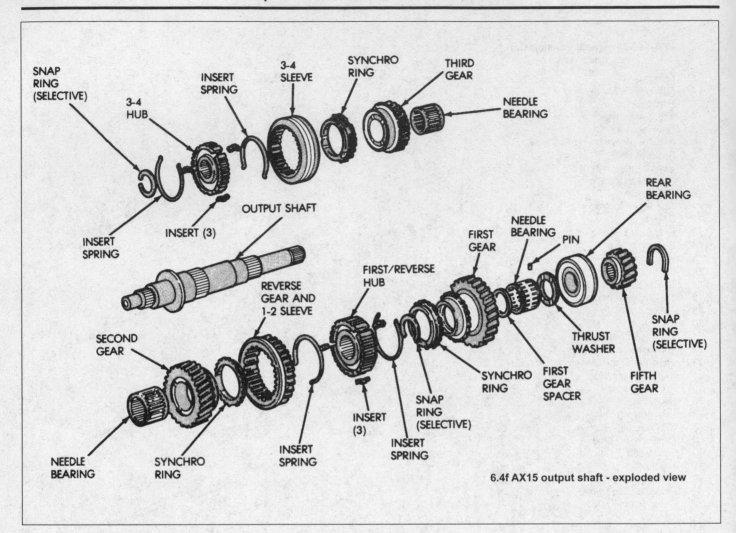

SNAP RING (SELECTIVE)

3-4 HUB

INSERT SPRING

3-4 SLEEVE

SYNCHRO RING

THIRD GEAR

NEEDLE BEARING

INSERT SPRING

INSERT (3)

OUTPUT SHAFT

REAR BEARING

FIRST GEAR

NEEDLE BEARING

PIN

SNAP RING (SELECTIVE)

THRUST WASHER

FIFTH GEAR

FIRST GEAR SPACER

SYNCHRO RING

REVERSE GEAR AND 1-2 SLEEVE

FIRST/REVERSE HUB

SECOND GEAR

SNAP RING (SELECTIVE)

INSERT SPRING

INSERT (3)

INSERT SPRING

NEEDLE BEARING

SYNCHRO RING

6.4f AX15 output shaft - exploded view

Chapter 7 Part B
Automatic transmission

Contents

Specifications

Torque specifications

Ft-lbs (unless otherwise indicated)

Note: *One foot-pound (ft-lb) of torque is equivalent to 12 inch-pounds (in-lbs) of torque. Torque values below approximately 15 ft-lbs are expressed in inch-pounds, since most foot-pound torque wrenches are not accurate at these smaller values.*

Front band adjusting screw - 2002 and earlier models
    With adapter .... 36 in-lbs
    Without adapter .... 72 in-lbs
Rear band adjusting screw - 2002 and earlier models .... 41 in-lbs
Neutral start switch 24
Converter-to-driveplate bolts
    2004 and earlier models 40
    2005 to 2011 models 65
    2012 and later models 27
Transmission bellhousing-to-engine mounting bolts
    2006 and earlier models 40
    2007 to 2011 models 95
    2012 and later models 37
Transmission output shaft flange nut 148

1   General Information

1   All vehicles covered in this manual come equipped with either a four-, five- or six-speed manual transmission or a three- or four-speed automatic transmission. Information on the automatic transmission is included in this Section. Information on the manual transmission can be found in Part A of this Chapter, and information on the transfer case can be found in Part C of this Chapter.

2   Due to the complexity of the automatic transmission and the need for specialized equipment to perform most service operations, this Chapter contains only general diagnosis, routine maintenance, adjustment and removal and installation procedures.

3   If the transmission requires major repair work, it should be left to a dealer service department or an automotive or transmission repair shop. You can, however, remove and install the transmission yourself and save the expense, even if the repair work is done by a transmission shop.

2   Diagnosis - general

Note: *Automatic transmission malfunctions may be caused by five general conditions: poor engine performance, improper adjustments, incorrect fluid level, hydraulic malfunctions or mechanical malfunctions. Diagnosis of these problems should always begin with a check of the easily repaired items: fluid level and condition (see Chapter 1), shift linkage adjustment and throttle linkage adjustment. Next, perform a road test to determine if the problem has been corrected or if more diagnosis is necessary. If the problem persists after the preliminary tests and corrections are completed, additional diagnosis should be done by a dealer service department or transmission repair shop. Refer to the Troubleshooting section at the front of this manual for information on symptoms of transmission problems.*

Preliminary checks

1   Drive the vehicle to warm the transmission to normal operating temperature.

2   Check the fluid level as described in Chapter 1 :

   a) *If the fluid level is unusually low, add enough fluid to bring the level within the designated area of the dipstick, then check for external leaks (see below).*

   b) *If the fluid is foaming, drain it and refill the transmission, then check for coolant in the fluid or a high fluid level.*

   c) *If the fluid level is abnormally high, drain off the excess, then check the drained fluid for contamination by coolant. The presence of engine coolant in the automatic transmission fluid indicates that a failure has occurred in the internal radiator walls that separate the coolant from the transmission fluid (see Chapter 1).*

3   Check the engine idle speed.
Note: *If the engine is malfunctioning, do not proceed with the preliminary checks until it has been repaired and runs normally.*

4   Check the Throttle Valve (TV) linkage or cable (earlier models) for freedom of movement. Adjust or replace it if necessary (see Section 10).
Note: *The TV linkage/cable may function properly when the engine is shut off and cold, but it may malfunction once the engine is hot. Check it cold and at normal engine operating temperature.*

5   Inspect the shift control linkage (see Section 9). Make sure that it's properly adjusted and that the linkage operates smoothly.

Fluid leak diagnosis

6   Most fluid leaks are easy to locate visually. Repair usually consists of replacing a seal or gasket. If a leak is difficult to find, the following procedure may help.

7   Identify the fluid. Make sure it's transmission fluid and not engine oil or brake fluid (automatic transmission fluid is a deep red color).

8   Try to pinpoint the source of the leak. Drive the vehicle several miles, then park it over a large sheet of cardboard. After a minute or two, you should be able to locate the leak by determining the source of the fluid dripping onto the cardboard.

9   Make a careful visual inspection of the suspected component and the area immediately around it. Pay particular attention to gasket mating surfaces. A mirror is often helpful for finding leaks in areas that are hard to see.

10   If the leak still cannot be found, clean the suspected area thoroughly with a degreaser or solvent, then dry it.

11   Drive the vehicle for several miles at normal operating temperature and varying speeds. After driving the vehicle, visually inspect the suspected component again.

12   Once the leak has been located, the cause must be determined before it can be properly repaired. If a gasket is replaced but the sealing flange is bent, the new gasket will not stop the leak. The bent flange must be straightened.

13   Before attempting to repair a leak, check to make sure that the following conditions are corrected or they may cause another leak.
Note: *Some of the following conditions cannot be fixed without highly specialized tools and expertise. Such problems must be referred to a transmission repair shop or a dealer service department.*

Gasket leaks

14   Check the pan periodically. Make sure the bolts are tight, no bolts are missing, the gasket is in good condition and the pan is flat (dents in the pan may indicate damage to the valve body inside).

15   If the pan gasket is leaking, the fluid level or the fluid pressure may be too high, the vent may be plugged, the pan bolts may be too tight, the pan sealing flange may be warped, the sealing surface of the transmission housing may be damaged, the gasket may be damaged or the transmission casting may be cracked or porous. If sealant instead of gasket material has been used to form a seal between the pan and the transmission housing, it may be the wrong sealant.

Seal leaks

16   If a transmission seal is leaking, the fluid level or pressure may be too high, the vent may be plugged, the seal bore may be damaged, the seal itself may be damaged or improperly installed, the surface of the shaft protruding through the seal may be damaged or a loose bearing may be causing excessive shaft movement.

17   Make sure the dipstick tube seal is in good condition and the tube is properly seated. Periodically check the area around the speedometer gear or sensor for leakage. If transmission fluid is evident, check the O-ring for damage.

Case leaks

18   If the case itself appears to be leaking, the casting is porous and will have to be repaired or replaced.

19   Make sure the oil cooler hose fittings are tight and in good condition.

Fluid comes out vent pipe or fill tube

20   If this condition occurs- the transmission is overfilled, there is coolant in the fluid, the case is porous, the dipstick is incorrect, the vent is plugged or the drain back holes are plugged.

3   Shift knob - replacement

2010 and earlier models
Note: *On 2010 and earlier models, removal procedures are not available.*

2011 and later models

1   Use a trim tool to separate the retaining ring from the bottom of the shift knob.

2   Remove the shift knob from the shift lever assembly.

3   Installation is reverse of removal.

4   Shift lever assembly - replacement and adjustment

Replacement

1   Place the shift lever into Park (P) position and remove the center console (see Chapter 11, Section 22).

2   Locate the shift cable on the shift lever assembly and disconnect the shift cable from the shift lever and shift lever assembly bracket (see Section 5).

3   Locate the shift interlock cable on the

shift lever assembly and disconnect it from the shift lever and bracket (see Section 6).

4   Disconnect the shift lever assembly electrical connectors.

5   Remove the nuts, bolts or screws attaching the shift lever assembly to the floorpan.

6   Remove the shift lever assembly from the vehicle.

7   Installation is reverse of removal. Be sure to adjust the shift cable and shift interlock cable.

Adjustment

Note: *The following procedure applies when the shift lever assembly or shift cable is removed or replaced.*

8   Place the shift lever into Park (P) position and remove the center console (see Chapter 11, Section 22).

9   On 2003 and later models, locate and loosen the adjustment nut on the shift cable lever (interior) enough to allow the cable to move freely for adjustment.

10   Raise and support the vehicle on jack stands.

11   On 2002 and earlier models, release the cable locking clamp and also release the cable bracket at the transmission, to allow the cable housing to move freely for adjustment.

12   Disconnect the shift cable end from the pivot on the shift lever at the transmission.

13   Move the transmission shift lever (at transmission) to park position by rotating it rearwards as far as it will go. Make sure the transmission is in the park position by attempting to rotate the rear driveshaft. Rotating the driveshaft will engage the parking pawl in the transmission and prevent the driveshaft from rotating.

14   Reconnect the cable end to the pivot on the shift lever at the transmission.

15   On 2002 and earlier models, attach the cable bracket and secure the cable locking clamp at the transmission.

16   Lower the vehicle.

17   Verify that the shift lever is in the Park (P) position.

18   On 2003 and later models, tighten the cable lever adjustment nut securely (interior).

19   Verify proper operation before installing the remaining interior components.

---

5   Shift cable - replacement and adjustment

---

1   On earlier models, the transmission is shifted via mechanical rods, rather than a cable.

Replacement

2   Place the shift lever into the Park (P) position.

3   Remove the center console (see Chapter 11, Section 22).

4   If necessary, remove the protective shield to better expose the shift cable connections.

5   Locate the shift cable on the shift lever

assembly, then disconnect the shift cable from the shift lever and shift lever assembly bracket.

6   Remove the shift cable grommet from the floorpan (or any retaining nuts holding the grommet in place, if equipped).

7   Raise and support the vehicle on jackstands.

8   Disconnect the shift cable from the transmission shift lever and bracket.

9   Remove the shift cable from the vehicle.

10   Installation is reverse of removal. Adjust the cable after installation for proper operation.

Adjustment

11   Refer to the adjustment procedure in Section 4.

---

6   Shift interlock cable - replacement and adjustment

Note: *This procedure applies to 2012 and later models.*

1   The shift interlock cable prevents the shift lever from being shifted from Park (P) position until the key is turned to any position EXCEPT LOCK. Once the shift lever is moved to any position EXCEPT Park (P), the key cannot be rotated to the lock position and removed. With the shift lever in Park (P), the key can be rotated to LOCK and removed.

2   On 2011 and earlier models, the Brake Transmission Shift Interlock (BTSI) solenoid is part of the cable (see Section 8).

Replacement

3   Lower the steering column to allow access to the shift interlock cable.

4   Turn the ignition switch to RUN.

5   Press the tab above the shift interlock cable and slide the cable bracket outward to disengage from the column.

6   Remove the cable end from the steering column.

7   Remove the center console (see Chapter 11, Section 22).

8   Locate the shift interlock cable on the shift lever assembly and disconnect it from the shift lever and bracket.

9   Remove the shift interlock cable from the vehicle, disconnecting it from any retaining clips.

10   Installation is reverse of removal. Adjust the cable after installation for proper operation.

Adjustment

Note: *The shift interlock cable is self-adjusting, but can be checked for proper self-adjustment operation.*

11   Remove the center console (see Chapter 11, Section 22).

12   Place the shift lever into Park (P) position, and turn the ignition switch to LOCK.

13   Pull the shift interlock cable adjustment lock up to allow the cable to move freely.

14   To verify proper self-adjustment of the cable, push the cable toward the rear, then release it. The cable should default to its original position. If the cable does not move freely, replace it.

15   Press the shift interlock cable adjustment lock down until a click is heard and the lock is secure.

16   Verify proper operation before installing the interior components.

---

7   Brake transmission shift interlock (BTSI) solenoid - override, check and replacement

---

Note: *This procedure applies to 2012 and later models.*

1   The BTSI solenoid requires the brake pedal to be depressed before the shift lever is shifted from the Park (P) position. When the brake pedal is pressed, the solenoid unlocks the shift lever assembly. No adjustment is required for the BTSI solenoid.

BTSI override

2   If the shift lever will not shift out of Park (P) with the brake pedal depressed, turn the ignition key to ACC or ON position.

3   Remove the cover to the right of the "D" indicator on the shift lever bezel.

4   Using a key or small screwdriver, insert into the opening and press down.

5   While holding the key or screwdriver down, move the shift lever out of the Park (P) position.

6   Install the cover once the issue is resolved.

Function check

7   Verify the ignition key can be rotated to LOCK position and can ONLY be removed from the ignition lock cylinder with the shift lever in Park (P) position.

8   Verify the ignition key cannot be rotated to the LOCK position with the shift lever in ANY position EXCEPT Park (P).

9   Verify the shift lever cannot be moved out of Park (P) position with the ignition key in ACC position and the brake pedal NOT pressed.

10   Verify the shift lever cannot be forcefully (using a light force) moved out of Park (P) position with the ignition key in ACC, RUN or START positions unless the brake pedal is pressed about 1/2" down.

11   Verify the shift lever cannot be moved out of Park (P) position with the ignition key in LOCK position and the brake pedal pressed.

12   Verify the shift lever can be moved between any position EXCEPT Park (P) or to Park (P) without pressing the brake pedal.

13   Verify the current transmission gear and the shift lever indicator match.

14   Verify the engine will start ONLY with the shift lever in Park (P) and Neutral (N) positions.

15   With the shift lever in Park (P) position,

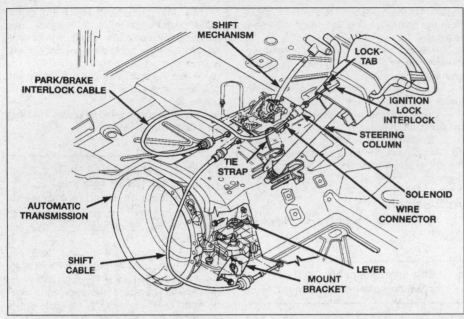

8.1 Details of the brake transmission shift interlock system (2011 and earlier models)

apply light pressure forward and rearward and confirm the engine starts.

16   With the shift lever in Neutral (N) position, the engine must start.

17   With the shift lever in Neutral (N) position and the engine running and brake pedal pressed, apply forward force to the shift lever (without pressing the shift knob). The shift lever should not move to Reverse (R) position.

18   If the vehicle does not respond as specified above, check adjustment of the shift cable and shift interlock cable.

Replacement

The BTSI solenoid is part of the shift lever assembly (see Section 4).

8   Brake transmission shift interlock cable - removal, installation and adjustment

Note: *This procedure applies to 2011 and earlier models.*

Warning: *Some models covered by this manual are equipped with airbags. Always disable the airbag system when working in the vicinity of airbag system components (see Chapter 12 Section 24).*

Removal and installation

1   Later models are equipped with a brake transmission shift interlock cable, which prevents the transmission from being shifted out of Park or Neutral unless the brake pedal is depressed. Here's how it works: When you depress the brake pedal, a switch down at the pedal closes the circuit to a solenoid that releases the park/brake interlock cable (see illustration). If you don't depress the brake pedal, the solenoid locks the park/brake interlock cable, which prevents the shift lever from being moved. This safety system is virtually trouble-free. However, the following procedure is included in the event that the cable should ever break, or should you have to disconnect it in order to service something else.

2   Remove the steering column lower shroud (see illustration 18.11a in Chapter 12), remove the headlight switch knob and shaft (only on some models, see Chapter 12, Section 13) and the steering column opening cover / knee bolster (Chapter 11, Section 24).

3   Remove the cable tie that secures the brake transmission shift interlock cable to the steering column. The cable tie is located in front of the solenoid (see illustration 8.1).

4   Unplug the electrical connector from the solenoid.

5   With the ignition key in the unlocked position, disengage the lock tab which connects the end of the cable to the steering column (see illustration) and detach the cable from the steering column.

6   Remove the center console assembly (see Chapter 11, Section 22).

7   Disconnect the cable end from the bellcrank on the shift lever.

8   Disconnect the cable from the shift lever bracket.

9   Remove the cable.

10   Installation is the reverse of removal. Be sure to adjust the cable before installing the center console.

Adjustment

11   Shift the transmission into Park. If you have just installed or replaced the cable, the center console and gear position indicator trim panel should still be off. If they're not, remove them now (see Chapter 11, Section 22).

12   Pull up the cable lock button (see illustration) to release the park/brake interlock cable.

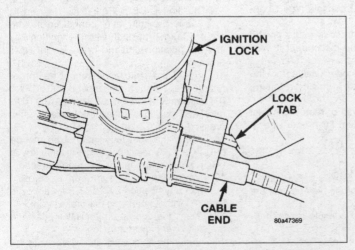

8.5 With the ignition key in the unlocked position, disengage the lock tab which connects the end of the cable to the steering column and detach the cable from the steering column

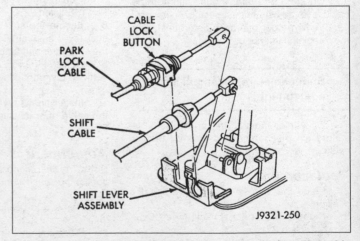

8.12 To release the park/brake interlock cable, pull up on the cable lock button

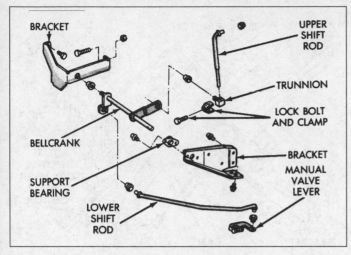

9.4 Shift linkage details

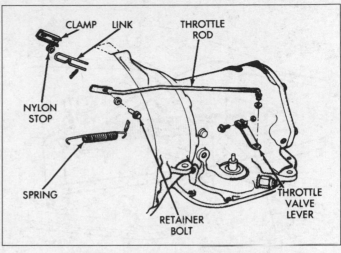

10.2a Throttle Valve (TV) linkage details

13   Turn the ignition switch to the LOCK position.

14   Using a suitable spacer, create a one-millimeter gap between the shifter pawl and the top of the shift gate.

15   Pull the cable forward, then release the cable and press down the cable lock button until it snaps into place.

16   Check your adjustment as follows:

a)   *Verify that you cannot press in the release button in the shift handle (floor shift) or move the release lever (column shift).*

b)   *Turn the ignition switch to the RUN position.*

c)   *Verify that you cannot shift out of PARK unless the brake pedal is applied.*

d)   *With the transmission shift lever out of PARK, release the brake pedal and the release button or release lever, then shift through all the gears. Verify that the ignition key doesn't go to the LOCK position.*

e)   *Verify that the shift lever can be returned to the PARK position without having to apply the brake.*

f)   *Move the shift lever back to the PARK position and verify that when the ignition key is turned to the LOCK position, the shift lever cannot be moved out of PARK.*

g)   *If the system operates as described, the adjustment is correct. If it doesn't, readjust the cable.*

17   Install the center console.

9   Shift linkage - check and adjustment

Check

1   Firmly apply the parking brake and try to momentarily operate the starter in each shift lever position. The starter should operate in Park and Neutral only. If the starter operates in any position other than Park or Neutral,

adjust the shift linkage (see below). If, after adjustment, the starter still operates in positions other than Park or Neutral, the neutral start switch is defective or in need of adjustment (see Section 12).

Note: *On 2004 and later models, the transmission is shifted via a cable, rather than mechanical rods.*

Adjustment

2   Place the shift lever in Park. Raise the vehicle and support it securely on jackstands.

3   Check the condition of the shift rods, bellcrank and the brackets (or the cable). Replace any worn or damaged parts. Do not adjust worn or damaged parts.

4   Loosen the trunnion lock bolt so that the bellcrank and shift rod slides freely (see illustration).

5   Be sure the shift lever on the transmission is all the way to the rear, in the last detent. This is the Park position.

6   Make sure the park lock is engaged by trying to rotate the driveshaft. The driveshaft will not rotate if the park lock is functioning properly.

7   When properly adjusted, there should be no lash in the shift linkage. Push up on the

bellcrank while pulling down on the shift rod. Tighten the lock bolt while holding the shift rod and bellcrank.

8   Lower the vehicle.

9   With the parking brake firmly applied, make sure the engine starts only in Park and Neutral. If the linkage is adjusted properly, but the starter operates in positions other than Park or Neutral, check the neutral start switch (see Section 12).

10   Check the steering wheel lock to make sure it operates smoothly.

10   Throttle Valve (TV) linkage/ cable (2003 and earlier models) - adjustment

1   The Throttle Valve (TV) linkage or cable can be adjusted to correct harsh, delayed or erratic shifting and lack of kickdown.

TV linkage

2   Remove the TV control rod spring (see illustration). Use the spring to hold the adjusting link against the nylon stop, in the forward position (see illustration).

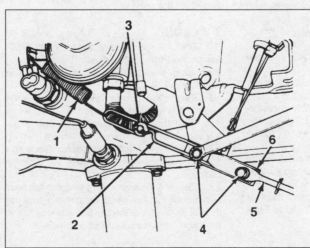

10.2b The Throttle Valve (TV) spring is used to hold the adjusting link against the nylon stop

1   *Spring*
2   *Link*
3   *Nylon stop*
4   *Bolt (clamp/retainer)*
5   *Throttle Valve (TV) control rod*
6   *Clamp*

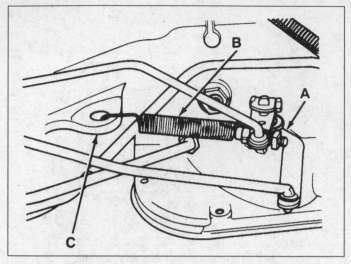

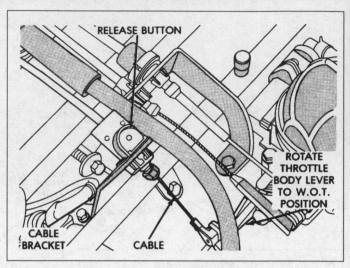

10.6 Use a spare spring to hold the Throttle Valve (TV) lever forward

A Lever   C Casting on bellhousing
B Spring

10.9a The TV cable adjuster is located along the valve cover, near the throttle body

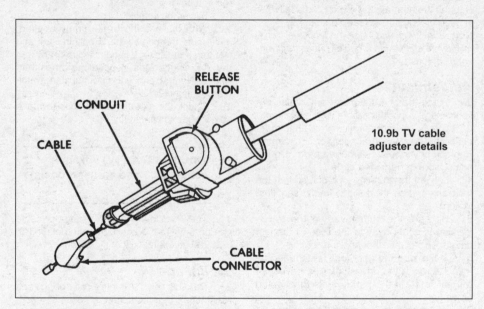

10.9b TV cable adjuster details

11 Bands (older models only) - adjustment

Note: *Band adjustment only applies to the 2002 and earlier models. There is no adjustment for the 2003 models, 42RLE 4-speed transmissions.*

1   The transmission bands should be adjusted at the specified intervals or when the upshifts or downshifts become consistently harsh and/or erratic.
2   Raise the vehicle and support it securely on jackstands.

Front band

3   The front band adjusting screw is located on the left side of the transmission, just above the Throttle Valve (TV) control levers.
4   Loosen the adjustment screw locknut and back out the adjusting screw five turns. Check the adjusting screw to make sure it turns freely in the case, lubricating it if necessary.
5   Using an inch-pound torque wrench and an adapter extension (if necessary) and a 5/16-inch 12-point socket, tighten the adjusting screw to the torque listed in this Chapter's Specifications (see illustration). If the adapter extension is used, be sure to apply the correct modified torque setting.
6   Back the adjuster screw out 2-1/2 turns for the 30RH transmission or 2-1/4 turns for the 32RH transmission.
7   Tighten the adjusting screw locknut securely while holding the screw with a socket or wrench so it does not rotate.

Rear band

8   The rear band adjusting screw is accessible after removing the oil pan (see illustration). Consequently, it's very convenient to make this adjustment at the time of the transmission fluid filter change (see Chapter 1).

3   Block the choke open and set the throttle off the fast idle cam. On models equipped with a throttle-operated solenoid valve, turn the ignition switch on (to energize the solenoid), and open the throttle half way to lock it. Return the throttle to the idle position.
4   Raise the vehicle and support it securely with jackstands.
5   Loosen the retainer and clamp bolts on the TV linkage adjusting link (see illustration 4.2b).
6   Use a spare spring to hold the transmission TV lever all the way forward, against the stop (see illustration). Hook the spring to the bellhousing boss.
7   Push on the end of the link to eliminate any lash, pull the clamp to the rear so the bolt bottoms in the rear of the rod slot. Tighten the clamp bolt. Pull the TV control rod to the rear until the rod bolt bottoms in the front rod slot and tighten the retainer bolt.

8   Install the TV control rod spring, remove the extra spring from the transmission lever and lower the vehicle.

TV cable

9   With the ignition switch in the Off position, retract the cable adjuster by depressing the button, then pushing the conduit in (see illustrations).
10   Rotate the throttle lever on the throttle body to the wide-open position.
11   Hold the throttle lever open and allow the cable conduit to extend all the way, which automatically adjusts the cable. Once the conduit is fully extended, release the adjuster button.
12   Depress the accelerator pedal to the floor and have an assistant check to make sure the throttle lever on the throttle body moves to the full-throttle position and doesn't bind.

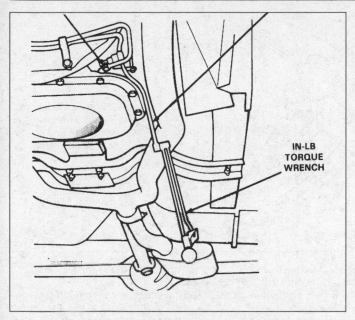

11.5 An adapter extension and inch-pound torque wrench are required to adjust the front transmission band

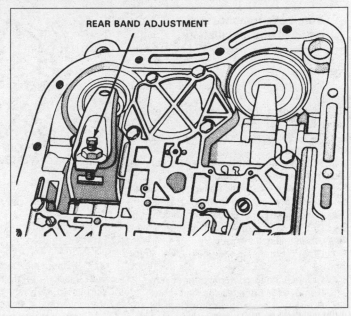

11.8 The rear band adjusting screw is accessible after removing the transmission oil pan

9   Remove the transmission oil pan (see Chapter 1).

10   Loosen the adjusting screw lock nut.

11   Tighten the adjusting screw with an inch-pound torque wrench and a 1/4-inch socket to the torque listed in this Chapter's Specifications.

12   Back out the adjusting screw seven turns for the 30RH transmission or four turns for the 32RH transmission. Install the locknut, hold the screw with a socket or wrench so it can't turn and tighten the locknut securely.

13   Install the transmission oil pan, then lower the vehicle.

14   Refill the transmission with transmission fluid to the proper level (see Chapter 1).

12   Neutral start switch (older models only) - check and replacement

Note: *On newer models, the Park Neutral Position (PNP) switch is located inside of the transmission.*

1   The neutral start and back-up light switches are combined into one unit. The switch has three terminals with the neutral switch being the center one. A ground for the starter solenoid circuit is provided through the shift lever in only the Neutral and Park positions.

2   Raise the vehicle and place it securely on jackstands. Detach the electrical connector from the Neutral start switch (see illustration) and test the switch for continuity. Continuity should exist between the center terminal and transmission case only when the shift lever is in Neutral and Park. If the switch appears to be

faulty, check the shift linkage (see Section 9) before replacing the switch.

3   Prior to replacing the switch, place a container under it to catch the transmission fluid.

4   Remove the switch and allow the fluid to drain into the container.

5   Place the shift lever in Park or Neutral and check the lever finger position, lever and shaft alignment with the switch opening.

6   Install the switch and seal, tighten the switch to the torque listed in this Chapter's Specifications.

7   Test the switch for continuity and plug in the connector.

8   Lower the vehicle and check the transmission fluid level (see Chapter 1), adding the specified fluid as necessary.

13   Output shaft oil seal - replacement

1   Remove the driveshaft (see Chapter 8, Section 11) or transfer case (see Chapter 7C, Section 7).

2   If the output shaft flange is bolted to the transmission, remove the fastener and the flange.

3   Carefully pry it out of the seal with a screwdriver or seal removal tool.

4   To install, use a large socket or oil seal driver tool.

5   Remaining installation is reverse of removal.

6   Top off the transmission fluid as necessary.

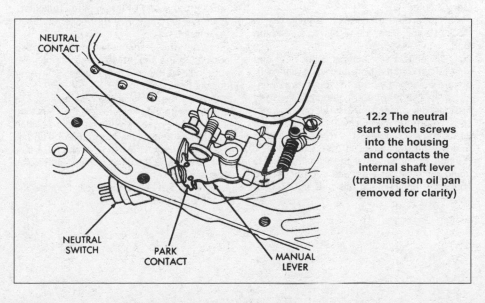

12.2 The neutral start switch screws into the housing and contacts the internal shaft lever (transmission oil pan removed for clarity)

14 Automatic transmission - removal and installation

Removal

1 Disconnect the negative cable from the battery.
2 Disconnect the upper bracket of the transmission filler tube.
3 Raise the vehicle and support it securely on jackstands.
4 Remove skid plates as necessary to allow access for transmission removal.
5 Remove the catalytic converter / exhaust pipe assembly (see Chapter 4). Be sure to disconnect the oxygen sensor connectors.
6 Drain the transmission fluid (see Chapter 1), then reinstall the pan.
7 Drain the transfer case fluid (see Chapter 1).
8 Remove the torque converter cover.
9 Remove the transmission filler tube.
10 Remove the starter motor (see Chapter 5, Section 19).
11 Mark the relationship of the torque converter to the driveplate so they can be installed in the same position (see illustration).
12 Remove the torque converter-to-driveplate nuts. Turn the crankshaft for access to each nut. Turn the crankshaft in a clockwise direction only (as viewed from the front).
13 Remove the driveshafts (see Chapter 8).
14 On older models, disconnect the speedometer cable.
15 Disconnect the transmission cooler lines and unclip the lines from the transmission. Plug the lines to prevent fluid loss. Note that this step may be easier once the transmission has been lowered slightly.
16 On 4.0L models, disconnect and remove the Crankshaft Position (CKP) sensor (see Chapter 6).
17 On 2003 and earlier models, disconnect the TV linkage or cable (see Section 10).
18 On all models, disconnect the shift linkage or cable (see previous section(s) in this Chapter) and the transfer case linkage/cable (see Chapter 7C).
19 Support the engine with a jack. Use a block of wood under the oil pan to spread the load.
20 Disconnect all electrical connectors and vent tubes from the transmission. Later models are equipped with a "bayonet" type connector, which is rotated counterclockwise in order to disconnect it. Also unbolt any heat shields covering the electrical connectors.
21 On 4WD models, it is recommended to remove the transfer case (see Chapter 7C, Section 7). However, if the transmission is being removed for a service such as torque converter replacement, this may not be necessary.

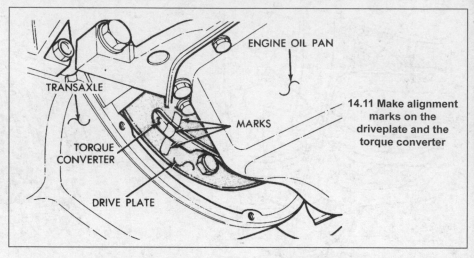

14.11 Make alignment marks on the driveplate and the torque converter

22 Support the transmission/transfer case with a jack - preferably a jack made for this purpose. Safety chains will help steady the transmission/transfer case on the jack.
23 Unbolt the transmission mount from the crossmember. Remove the crossmember-to-frame bolts.
24 Raise the transmission enough to allow removal of the crossmember.
25 Remove the bolts securing the transmission to the engine.
26 Lower the transmission slightly and ensure all electrical connections and lines have been disconnected.
27 Move the transmission/transfer case to the rear to disengage it from the engine block dowel pins and make sure the torque converter is detached from the driveplate. Secure the torque converter to the transmission so it won't fall out during removal (a pair of locking pliers clamped onto the bellhousing will work).

Installation

28 Prior to installation, rotate the torque converter back and forth to make sure the converter hub is securely engaged in the pump. Also apply a light film of high-temperature grease to the end of the engine crankshaft, where the torque converter pocket mates to the engine.
29 With the transmission/transfer case secured to the jack, raise it into position. Be sure to keep it level so the torque converter does not slide forward.
30 Align the holes in the bellhousing with the dowels on the engine block, then push the transmission assembly forward into position until it rests against the block. If it won't go all the way, find out why it isn't - don't force it or use the bolts to draw the transmission to the engine.
31 Install the bellhousing bolts. Tighten the

bolts to the torque listed in this Chapter's Specifications.
32 Turn the torque converter (by means of the crankshaft) clockwise to line up the threaded holes with the holes in the driveplate. The alignment mark on the torque converter and the driveplate made in Step 9 must line up.
33 Install the torque converter-to-driveplate bolts. Tighten them to the torque listed in this Chapter's Specifications.
34 Install the transfer case (if removed).
35 Connect the transmission cooler lines. Note that later models require new retaining clips to be used at the fittings.
36 Install the transmission/transfer case crossmember and tighten the fasteners securely.
37 Remove the jacks supporting the transmission/transfer case and the engine.
38 Install the dipstick tube and connect all breather hoses.
39 Install the starter motor (see Chapter 5).
40 Connect the shift linkage, TV linkage or cable. Also connect the transfer case shift linkage.
41 Plug in and secure the transmission electrical connectors. Install any heat shields to cover the connections and tighten the fasteners securely.
42 Install the torque converter cover, and any skid plates, where equipped.
43 Install the driveshafts (see Chapter 8).
44 Connect the speedometer cable (if equipped).
45 Adjust the shift linkage and TV linkage or cable (see Section 10).
46 Lower the vehicle.
47 Connect the cable to the negative terminal of the battery.
48 Fill the transmission with the specified fluid (see Chapter 1), run the engine and check for fluid leaks and correct transmission operation.

Chapter 7 Part C
Transfer case

Contents

Specifications

Torque specifications

	Ft-lbs
Front yoke (companion flange) nut	110
Rear companion flange nut	
2006 and earlier	90 to 130
2007 and later	210
Drain/fill plug	
2006 and earlier	15 to 25
2007 and later	20
Transfer case range position sensor	
2006 and earlier	16 to 25
2007 and later	20
Transfer case-to-transmission fasteners	26
Range lever	20 to 25

1   General information

1   The transfer case is a device (used on 4WD models) which passes power from the engine and transmission to the front and rear driveshafts.

2   Six transfer case options are used across the model year ranges: New Process (NP) 207, 231, 242 and New Venture (NV) 231, 241 (GenII and OR). All six units are the same part-time design with three operating ranges: 2WD high, 4WD high and 4WD low. The 4WD modes should only be engaged on unpaved surfaces, as the transfer case is undifferentiated.

2   Range lever assembly - replacement

1   Move the range lever to the 4L position before proceeding.

2006 and earlier models

2   Raise and support the vehicle on jackstands.

3   Loosen the shift linkage adjustment lock nut and slide the shift rod out of the pivot at the shifter. It is also possible to disconnect the shift rod from the pivot at the opposite end to remove.

4   Lower the vehicle.

5   Working inside the vehicle, remove the center console (see Chapter 11, Section 22).

6   Remove the screws attaching the range lever assembly to the floorpan.

7   Remove the range lever assembly from the vehicle.

8   Installation is reverse of removal. Adjust the shift linkage to ensure proper operation (see Section 4).

2007 and later models

9   Remove the center console (see Chapter 11, Section 22).

10   Carefully pry the shift cable from the

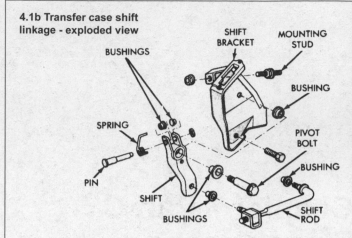

4.1b Transfer case shift linkage - exploded view

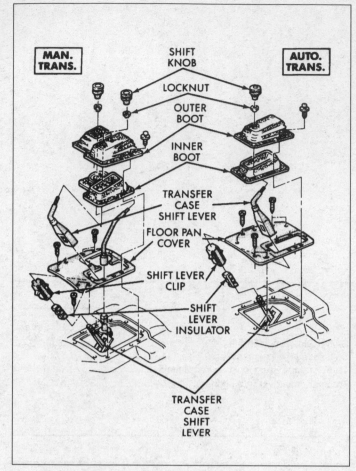

4.1a Transfer case range levers and boots - exploded view

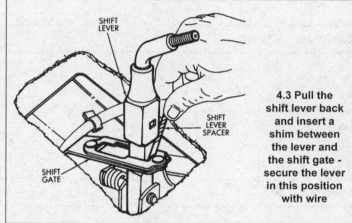

4.3 Pull the shift lever back and insert a shim between the lever and the shift gate - secure the lever in this position with wire

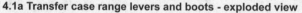

pivot on the shift lever.

11   Remove the clip and disconnect the shift cable housing from the bracket.

12   Remove the nuts securing the range lever assembly to the floor.

13   Remove the range lever assembly from the vehicle.

14   Installation is reverse of removal. Ensure

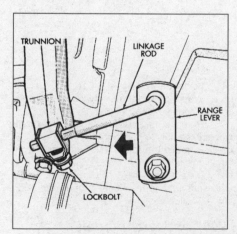

4.5 Loosen the lock bolt on the trunnion and adjust the rod so it slides freely in the trunnion

the range lever is in 4L position before connecting the cable.

---

3   Shift cable - replacement

Note: *The following procedure applies to 2007 and later models.*

1   On 2007 models, shift the range lever to 4L. On 2008 and later models, shift the range lever to Neutral (N).

2   Raise and support the vehicle on jackstands.

3   Remove the clip and disconnect the shift cable housing from the bracket.

4   Carefully pry the shift cable from the pivot on the shift lever.

5   Lower the vehicle, remove the center console (see Chapter 11), then disconnect the shift cable from the range lever assembly.

6   Detach the cable grommet from the floor of the vehicle and pull the cable through the opening to remove.

7   Installation is reverse of removal. On 2007 models, ensure the range lever and transfer case are in 4L position before connecting the cable. On 2008 and later models, ensure the range lever and transfer case are in Neutral (N) position before connecting the cable.

---

4   Shift linkage - adjustment

Note: *The following procedure applies to 2006 and earlier models only. 2007 and later models use a cable that does not have an adjustment.*

Warning: *Some models covered by this manual are equipped with airbags. Always disable the airbag system when working in the vicinity of airbag system components (see Chapter 12).*

1   The following images will assist in component identification (see illustrations).

2   Position the range lever as far to the rear as possible (4L position).

3   On 1994 and earlier models, insert a 1/8-inch drill bit between the shift lever and the shift gate (see illustration). Secure the shifter with wire and the drill bit with tape.

4   Raise the vehicle and support it securely on jackstands.

5   Under the vehicle, loosen the shift linage lock bolt so that the shift rod slides freely in the trunnion (see illustration).

6   With the range lever in 4L, shift the transfer case into the 4L position and tighten the lock bolt.

7   Lower the vehicle and check for proper operation.

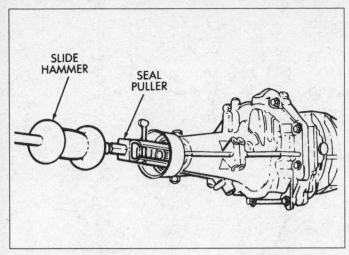

6.7 Removing the oil seal using a special tool

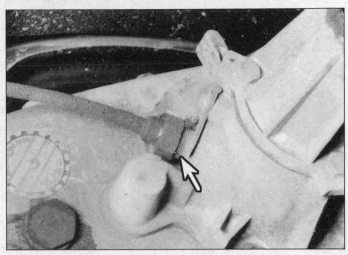

6.18a Location of the speedometer cable and drive gear housing on the transfer case (distance sensor similar)

5   Range position sensor - testing and replacement

Note: *Some models are equipped with both a range sensor and vehicle speed sensor, other models are only equipped with a vehicle speed sensor.*

Replacement

1   Raise and support the vehicle.
2   Locate the range position sensor near the shift lever on the transfer case housing.
3   Disconnect the electrical connector from the range sensor.
4   Unscrew the range sensor from the transfer case housing to remove.
5   Installation is reverse of removal. Replace the O-ring if necessary and tighten the sensor to the specified torque setting listed in this Chapter's Specifications.

Testing

6   The range sensor can be tested using a digital multimeter / ohm meter.
7   With the sensor removed, connect the ohm meter leads to the range sensor connector terminals.
8   Starting with the sensor's protrusion rod pushed in or at 10mm (position 1), compare the position 1 through 6 resistance readings with the table below.

Range position Resistance	(Ohms)
Position 1 (2H)	1124-1243
Position 2 (4H)	650-719
Position 3 (Neutral [N])	389-431
Position 4 (4L)	199-221
Position 5 (No gear used)	57-64
Position 6 (Rod fully extended at 20mm)	N/A

9   It may also be useful to test the sensor's resistance when installed in the transfer case, to be measured in conjunction with range lever operation (make sure the negative battery cable is disconnected and the sensor connector is unplugged).

6   Oil seals - replacement

1   Oil leaks frequently occur due to wear of the extension housing oil seal and/or the speedometer drive gear (or distance sensor) oil seal and O-ring. Replacement of these seals is relatively easy, since the repairs can usually be performed without removing the transmission or transfer case from the vehicle.

Extension housing oil seal

2   The extension housing oil seal is located at the extreme rear of the transfer case, where the rear driveshaft is attached. If leakage at the seal is suspected, raise the vehicle and support it securely on jackstands. If the seal is leaking, lubricant will be built up on the front of the driveshaft and may be dripping from the rear of the transfer case.
3   Refer to Chapter 8 for the removal of the driveshaft.
4   If equipped, remove the rear companion flange nut and companion flange.
5   Using a soft-faced hammer, carefully tap the dust shield (if equipped) to the rear and remove it. Be careful not to distort it.
6   Using a screwdriver or pry bar, carefully pry the oil seal out of the rear of the transfer case. Do not damage the splines on the output shaft.
7   If the oil seal cannot be removed with a screwdriver or pry bar, a special oil seal removal tool (available at auto parts stores) will be required (see illustration).
8   Using a large section of pipe or a very large deep socket as a drift, install the new oil seal. Drive it into the bore squarely and make

sure it's completely seated.
9   Reinstall the dust shield by carefully tapping it into place. Lubricate the splines of the transmission output shaft and the outside of the driveshaft yoke with lightweight grease.
10   If equipped, install the companion shaft and nut and tighten to the specified torque setting listed in this Chapter's Specifications.
11   Install the driveshaft (see Chapter 8). Be careful not to damage the lip of the seal.

Front output shaft oil seal

12   Raise and support the vehicle on jackstands.
13   Remove the front driveshaft.
14   Remove the output shaft companion flange nut and remove the flange from the transfer case.
15   Using a screwdriver or pry bar, carefully pry the oil seal out of the front of the transfer case. Do not damage the splines on the output shaft.
16   Using a large section of pipe or a very large deep socket as a drift, install the new oil seal. Drive it into the bore squarely and make sure it's completely seated.
17   The remainder of installation is reverse of removal. Tighten the front output shaft flange (yoke) nut to the torque setting listed in this Chapter's Specifications.

Speedometer cable/vehicle speed sensor O-ring/oil seal

Note: *Later models (up until 2006) do not have a speedometer cable. They use a vehicle speed sensor instead. 2007 and later models are not equipped with a vehicle speed sensor.*

18   The speedometer cable and drive gear (or vehicle speed sensor) housing is located on the back of the transfer case (see illustrations). Look for transmission oil around the cable housing to determine if the seal and O-ring are leaking.

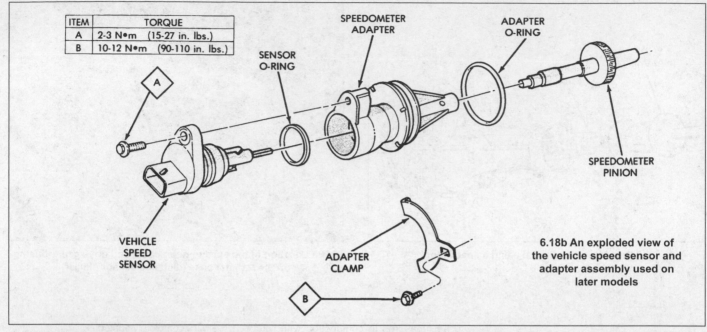

ITEM	TORQUE	
A	2-3 N•m	(15-27 in. lbs.)
B	10-12 N•m	(90-110 in. lbs.)

SENSOR O-RING

SPEEDOMETER ADAPTER

ADAPTER O-RING

ADAPTER O-RING

SPEEDOMETER PINION

A

VEHICLE SPEED SENSOR

ADAPTER CLAMP

B

6.18b An exploded view of the vehicle speed sensor and adapter assembly used on later models

6.20 Mark the relationship between the speedometer adapter housing (or vehicle speed sensor) and the transfer case - the adapter is offset and must be installed in the same relationship

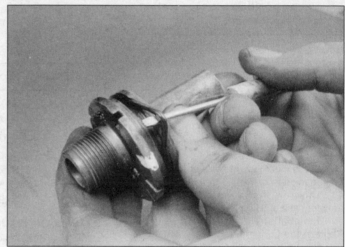

6.23a Use a small screwdriver to remove the O-ring from the groove…

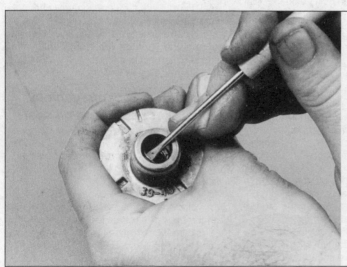

6.23b … then lift the adapter seal from the inside of the housing

19   Disconnect the speedometer cable (or unplug the electrical connector from the vehicle speed sensor).

20   Mark the relationship of the speedometer adapter to the transfer case (see illustration).

21   Remove the hold-down bolt and withdraw the adapter.

22   On models with a vehicle speed sensor, remove the speed sensor retaining screw and separate the sensor from the adapter, then remove the speedometer pinion from the adapter (see illustration 3.9b). On later models, push the sliding tab first in order to release the electrical connector.

23   Remove and discard the old O-rings. On models with a speedometer cable, there is an O-ring on the outside of the adapter and there's a seal inside the adapter housing (see illustrations). On models with a vehicle speed

sensor, there's an O-ring on the outside of the adapter and there's another O-ring on the vehicle speed sensor (see illustration 3.9b). Before installing the new O-ring(s)/seal, coat them with clean transmission fluid.

24   On models with a vehicle speed sensor, install the sensor in the adapter and tighten the sensor screw securely. On these models, count the number of teeth on the speedometer pinion, jot down this figure, then install the pinion in the adapter. Note the index number on the adapter body (see illustration). These numbers will correspond to the number of teeth on the pinion. Lubricate the pinion teeth with transmission fluid.

25   Install the adapter/speed sensor assembly in the transfer case and, on models with a speedometer cable, align the marks you made in Step 11, then install the hold-down clamp and bolt and tighten the bolt securely.

26   On models with a vehicle speed sensor, rotate the adapter until the correct (corresponding to the number of pinion teeth) range numbers are at the 6 o'clock position. Install the hold-down clamp and bolt and tighten the bolt securely.

27   Reconnect the speedometer cable or plug in the electrical connector.

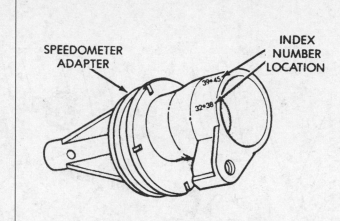

6.24 On models with a vehicle speed sensor, make sure that the correct range numbers (corresponding to the number of pinion teeth) are at the 6 o'clock position

---

7   Transfer case - removal and installation

Removal

1   Shift the transfer case to neutral (N) position.
2   Raise and support the vehicle.
3   Place reference marks on the yokes and driveshafts for installation, and disconnect the front and rear driveshafts from the transfer case yokes (see Chapter 8, Section 11).
4   Drain the transfer case lubricant.
5   Support the transmission using a jack or similar.
6   Remove the skid plate. On some automatic transmission models, the crossmember may require removal to remove the transfer case.
7   Disconnect the transfer case electrical connectors.
8   Disconnect the vent tube from the transaxle.
9   Disconnect the transfer case shift linkage/cable.

10   Support the transfer case with another jack and secure the transfer case to the jack.
11   Remove the nuts securing the transmission to the transfer case, then separate the two.
12   Remove the transfer case from the vehicle.

Installation

Caution: *DO NOT use excessive force to install the transfer case to the transmission - if the input shaft does not slide place, readjust the angle so it is level and/or turn the input or output shaft so the splines engage properly with the transmission.*

13   Installation is the reverse of removal. Be sure to tighten the transfer case-to-transmission nuts to the torque listed in this Chapter's Specifications.
14   On 2006 and earlier models, adjust the shift linkage (see Section 4).

---

8   Transfer case overhaul - general information

1   Overhauling a transfer case is a difficult job for the do-it-yourselfer. It involves the disassembly and reassembly of many small parts. Numerous clearances must be precisely measured and, if necessary, changed with select fit spacers and snap-rings. As a result, if transfer case problems arise, it can be removed and installed by a competent do-it-yourselfer, but overhaul should be

left to a transmission repair shop. Rebuilt transfer cases may be available - check with your dealer parts department and auto parts stores. At any rate, time and money involved in an overhaul is almost sure to exceed the cost of a rebuilt unit.
2   Nevertheless, it's not impossible for an inexperienced mechanic to rebuild a transfer case if the special tools are available and the job is done in a deliberate step-by-step manner so nothing is overlooked.
3   The tools necessary for an overhaul include internal and external snap-ring pliers, a bearing puller, a slide hammer, a set of pin punches, a dial indicator and possibly a hydraulic press. In addition, a large, sturdy workbench and vise or transmission stand will be required.
4   During disassembly of the transfer case, make careful notes of how each piece comes off, where it fits in relation to other pieces and what holds it in place. Exploded views are included for the NP 231 and 242 as reference only (see illustrations on the following pages) to show where the parts go - but actually noting how they are installed when you remove the parts will make it much easier to get the transfer case back together.
5   Before taking the transfer case apart for repair, it will help if you have some idea what area of the transfer case is malfunctioning. Certain problems can be closely tied to specific areas in the transfer case, which can make component examination and replacement easier.

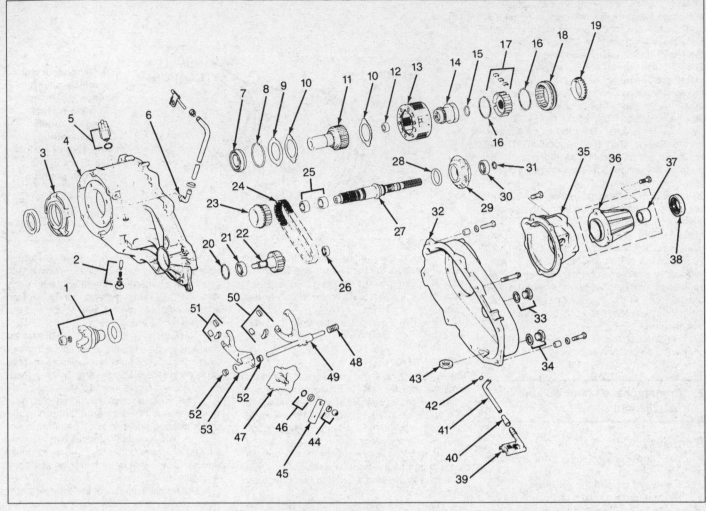

8.4a The NP 231 transfer case - exploded view

1	Front yoke nut, seal, washer, yoke and oil seal	18	Synchronizer sleeve
2	Shift detent plug, spring and pin	19	Synchronizer stop ring
3	Front retainer and seal	20	Snap-ring
4	Front case	21	Output shaft front bearing
5	Vacuum switch and seal	22	Output shaft (front)
6	Vent assembly	23	Drive sprocket
7	Input gear bearing and snap-ring	24	Drive chain
8	Low range gear snap-ring	25	Drive sprocket bearings
9	Input gear retainer	26	Output shaft rear bearing
10	Low range gear thrust washers	27	Mainshaft
11	Input gear	28	Oil seal
12	Input gear pilot bearing	29	Oil pump assembly
13	Low range gear	30	Rear bearing
14	Range fork shift hub	31	Snap-ring
15	Synchronizer hub snap-ring	32	Rear case
16	Synchronizer hub springs	33	Fill plug and gasket
17	Synchronizer hub and inserts	34	Drain plug and gasket
		35	Rear retainer

36	Extension housing
37	Bushing
38	Oil seal
39	Oil pick-up screen
40	Tube connector
41	Oil pick-up tube
42	Pick-up tube O-ring
43	Magnet
44	Range lever nut and washer
45	Ranger lever
46	O-ring and seal
47	Sector
48	Mode spring
49	Mode fork
50	Mode fork inserts
51	Range fork inserts
52	Range fork bushings
53	Range fork

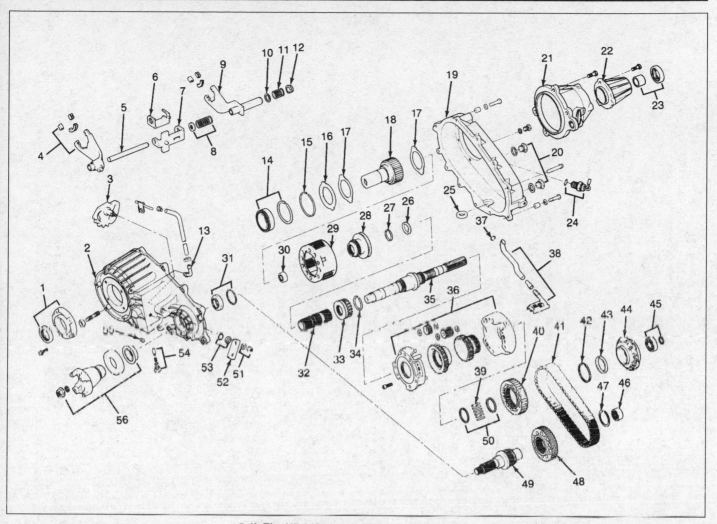

8.4b The NP 242 transfer case - exploded view

1	Front bearing retainer and seal
2	Front case
3	Shift sector
4	Low range fork inserts
5	Shift rail
6	Shift bracket
7	Slider bracket
8	Bushing and spring
9	Mode fork and inserts
10	Bushing
11	Fork spring
12	Bushing
13	Vent tube assembly
14	Input gear bearing and snap-ring
15	Low range gear snap-ring
16	Retainer, low range gear
17	Thrust washer, low range gear
18	Input gear
19	Rear case
20	Drain/fill plug
21	Rear bearing retainer
22	Extension housing
23	Bushing and oil seal
24	Vacuum switch
25	Magnet
26	Thrust ring
27	Snap-ring
28	Shift sleeve
29	Low range gear
30	Pilot bushing (input gear/mainshaft)
31	Front output shaft front bearing and snap-ring
32	Intermediate clutch shaft
33	Shift sleeve
34	Snap-ring
35	Mainshaft
36	Differential assembly
37	Oil pump tube O-ring
38	Oil pump pick-up tube and screen
39	Mainshaft bearing rollers
40	Drive sprocket
41	Drive chain
42	Snap-ring
43	Oil pump seal
44	Oil pump
45	Rear bearing and snap-ring
46	Front output shaft rear bearing
47	Snap-ring
48	Driven sprocket
49	Front output shaft
50	Mainshaft bearing spacers
51	Shift lever washer and nut
52	Shift lever
53	Sector O-ring and seal
54	Detent pin, spring and plug
55	Seal plug
56	Front yoke nut, seal, washer, yoke slinger and oil seal

Notes

Chapter 8
Clutch and drivetrain

Contents

Specifications

Clutch Fluid
Fluid type .... See Chapter 1

Torque specifications
Ft-lbs (unless otherwise indicated)

Note: *One foot-pound (ft-lb) of torque is equivalent to 12 inch-pounds (in-lbs) of torque. Torque values below approximately 15 ft-lbs are expressed in inch-pounds, since most foot-pound torque wrenches are not accurate at these smaller values.*

Clutch
Clutch master cylinder nuts or bolts
- 1987 through 1995 models 19
- 1996 and later models 28

Clutch slave cylinder nuts or bolts 17

Pressure plate-to-flywheel bolts
- Four-cylinder engine 23
- Six-cylinder and V6 engines
  - 1999 and earlier models 38
  - 2000 through 2006 models 37
  - 2007 and later models 24

Crossmember-to-frame bolts
- 2011 and earlier models 30
- 2012 and later models .... 106 in-lbs

Torque specifications (continued)

Ft-lbs (unless otherwise indicated)

Note: *One foot-pound (ft-lb) of torque is equivalent to 12 inch-pounds (in-lbs) of torque. Torque values below approximately 15 ft-lbs are expressed in inch-pounds, since most foot-pound torque wrenches are not accurate at these smaller values.*

Drivetrain

Crossmember-to-frame bolts	(See clutch specs.)
Front driveshaft	
2006 and earlier models	
U-joint strap bolts	168 in-lbs
Rear flange bolts	20
2007 and later models	
Transfer case flange bolts	15
Axle flange bolts	
Through 2010	81
2011 and later	89
Front differential pinion flange nut	
2000 and earlier models	
181 axle	Tighten to provide proper bearing preload
194 axle	200 to 350
2001 models (181 axle)	500 maximum
2002 models (181 axle)	260 maximum
2003 through 2006 models	
181 axle	160 to 500
216 axle	160 to 200
2007 and later models	
186 axle	160 to 400
216 axle	160 to 200
Rear axle pinion shaft lock bolt (older models)	168 in-lbs
Transmission output shaft flange nut	148
Front axle shift motor mounting bolts (older models)	108 in-lbs
Front axleshaft hub nut	
2006 and earlier models	175
2007 and later models	100
Front hub assembly-to-steering knuckle bolts	75
Rear axle control arm bolts/nuts (coil spring models)	
Upper	
2006 and earlier models	55
2007 to 2010 models	125
2011 and later models	142
Lower	
2002 and earlier models	130
2003 to 2006 models	150
2007 to 2010 models	125
2011 and later models	129

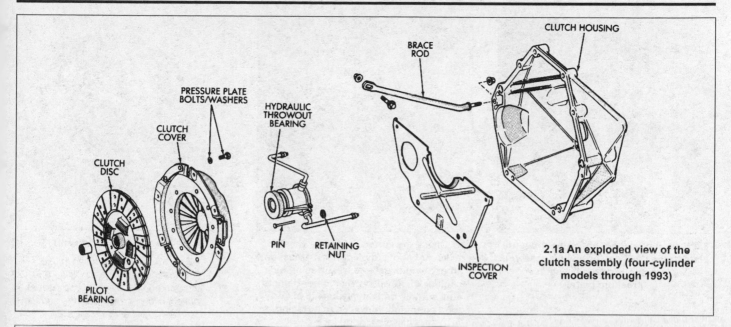

2.1a An exploded view of the clutch assembly (four-cylinder models through 1993)

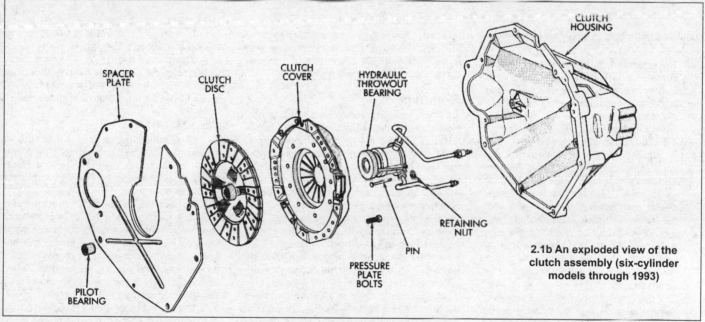

2.1b An exploded view of the clutch assembly (six-cylinder models through 1993)

1   General Information

1   The information in this Chapter deals with the components from the rear of the engine to the drive wheels, except for the transmission and transfer case, which are dealt with in the previous Chapter. For the purposes of this Chapter, these components are grouped into three categories; clutch, driveshaft and axles. Separate Sections within this Chapter offer general descriptions and checking procedures for components in each of the three groups.

2   Since nearly all the procedures covered in this Chapter involve working under the vehicle, make sure it's securely supported on sturdy jackstands or on a hoist where the vehicle can be easily raised and lowered.

2   Clutch - description and check

1   All vehicles with a manual transmission use a single dry plate, diaphragm spring type clutch (see illustrations). The clutch disc has a splined hub which allows it to slide along the splines of the transmission input shaft. The clutch and pressure plate are held in contact by spring pressure exerted by the diaphragm in the pressure plate.

2   The clutch release mechanism is operated by hydraulic pressure. The hydraulic release system consists of the clutch pedal, a master cylinder and fluid reservoir and the interconnecting hydraulic line. On 1987 through 1993 models, the hydraulic release bearing (combination release bearing/slave cylinder assembly) is mounted inside the clutch housing. On 1994 and later models, the slave cylinder is mounted outside the clutch housing and the release bearing and release lever are mounted inside the clutch housing.

3   When pressure is applied to the clutch pedal to release the clutch, hydraulic pressure is exerted against the release bearing through the clutch hydraulic line. The bearing pushes against the fingers of the diaphragm spring of the pressure plate assembly, releasing the clutch plate.

4   Terminology can be a problem when discussing the clutch components because commonly used terms may be different from those used by the manufacturer. For example, the driven plate is also called the clutch plate or disc, the clutch release bearing is sometimes called a throwout bearing or a concentric bearing, and so on.

5   Other than to replace components with obvious damage, some preliminary checks

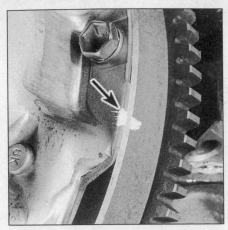

3.4 Mark the relationship of the pressure plate to the flywheel (arrow) (in case you are going to reuse the same pressure plate)

3.7 Check the surface of the flywheel for cracks, hot spots (dark colored areas) and other obvious defects; resurfacing by a machine shop will correct minor defects - the surface on this flywheel is in fairly good condition; however, resurfacing is always a good idea

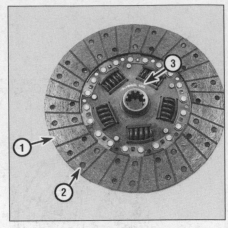

3.9 The clutch disc (typical)

1   *Lining - this will wear down in use*
2   *Rivets - these secure the lining and will damage the flywheel or pressure plate if allowed to contact the surface*
3   *Marks - "Flywheel side" or similar*

should be performed to diagnose clutch problems.

a) *The first check should be of the fluid level in the clutch master cylinder. If the fluid level is low, add fluid as necessary and inspect the hydraulic system for leaks. If the master cylinder reservoir has run dry, bleed the system as described in Section 8 and retest the clutch operation.*

b) *To check "clutch spin down time," run the engine at normal idle speed with the transmission in Neutral (clutch pedal up - engaged). Disengage the clutch (pedal down), wait several seconds and shift the transmission into Reverse. No grinding noise should be heard. A grinding noise would most likely indicate a problem in the pressure plate or the clutch disc (assuming the transmission is in good condition).*

c) *To check for complete clutch release, run the engine (with the parking brake applied to prevent movement) and hold the clutch pedal approximately 1/2-inch from the floor. Shift the transmission between 1st gear and Reverse several times. If the shift is rough, component failure is indicated.*

d) *Visually inspect the pivot bushing at the top of the clutch pedal to make sure there is no binding or excessive play.*

3   Clutch components - removal, inspection and installation

Warning: *Dust produced by clutch wear and deposited on clutch components is hazardous to your health. DO NOT blow it out with compressed air and DO NOT inhale it. DO NOT use gasoline or petroleum-based solvents to remove the dust. Brake system cleaner should*

be used to flush the dust into a drain pan. After the clutch components are wiped clean with a rag, dispose of the contaminated rags and cleaner in a covered, marked container.

Removal

1   Access to the clutch components is normally accomplished by removing the transmission, leaving the engine in the vehicle. If, of course, the engine is being removed for major overhaul, then check the clutch for wear and replace worn components as necessary. However, the relatively low cost of the clutch components compared to the time and trouble spent gaining access to them warrants their replacement anytime the engine or transmission is removed, unless they are new or in near perfect condition. The following procedures are based on the assumption the engine will stay in place.

2   Referring to Chapter 7A Part A, remove the transmission from the vehicle. Support the engine while the transmission is out. Preferably, an engine hoist should be used to support it from above. However, if a jack is used underneath the engine, make sure a piece of wood is positioned between the jack and oil pan to spread the load.

Caution: *The pick-up for the oil pump is very close to the bottom of the oil pan. If the pan is bent or distorted in any way, engine oil starvation could occur.*

3   To support the clutch disc during removal, install a clutch alignment tool through the clutch disc hub.

4   Carefully inspect the flywheel and pressure plate for indexing marks. The marks are usually an X, an O or a white letter. If they cannot be found, scribe marks yourself so the pressure plate and the flywheel will be in the same alignment during installation (see illustration).

5   Turning each bolt a little at a time, loosen the pressure plate-to-flywheel bolts. Work in a criss-cross pattern until all spring pressure is relieved. Then hold the pressure plate securely and completely remove the bolts, followed by the pressure plate and clutch disc.

Inspection

6   Ordinarily, when a problem occurs in the clutch, it can be attributed to wear of the clutch driven plate assembly (clutch disc). However, all components should be inspected at this time.

7   Inspect the flywheel for cracks, heat checking, grooves and other obvious defects (see illustration). If the imperfections are slight, a machine shop can machine the surface flat and smooth, which is highly recommended regardless of the surface appearance. Refer to Chapter 2F for the flywheel removal and installation procedure.

8   Inspect the pilot bearing (see Section 5).

9   Inspect the lining on the clutch disc. There should be at least 1/16-inch of lining above the rivet heads. Check for loose rivets, distortion, cracks, broken springs and other obvious damage (see illustration). As mentioned above, ordinarily the clutch disc is routinely replaced, so if in doubt about the condition, replace it with a new one.

10   Check the condition of the release bearing following the procedure in Section 4.

11   Check the machined surfaces and the diaphragm spring fingers of the pressure plate (see illustration). If the surface is grooved or otherwise damaged, replace the pressure plate. Also check for obvious damage, distortion, cracking, etc. Light glazing can be removed with medium grit emery cloth. If a new pressure plate is required, new and factory-rebuilt units are available.

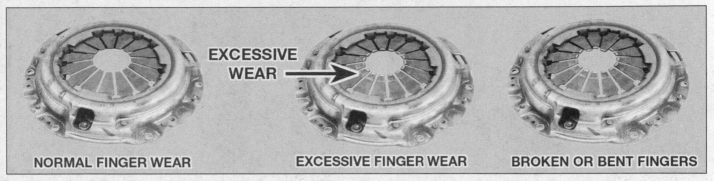

NORMAL FINGER WEAR   EXCESSIVE FINGER WEAR   BROKEN OR BENT FINGERS

3.11 Replace the pressure plate if excessive wear or damage is noted

3.13 Center the clutch disc in the pressure plate with an alignment tool before the bolts are tightened

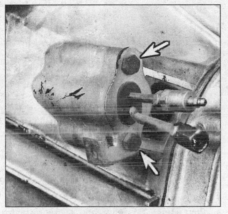

4.2 Remove the bolts (arrows), then slide the insulator plate and rubber insulator back on the lines (six-cylinder shown; on four-cylinder models, the bleeder line is on the other side of the transmission)

4.3 Remove the hydraulic release bearing retaining nut - be sure to use a new nut upon installation

Installation

12 Before installation, clean the flywheel and pressure plate machined surfaces with brake cleaner. It's important that no oil or grease is on these surfaces or the lining of the clutch disc. Handle the parts only with clean hands.

13 Position the clutch disc and pressure plate against the flywheel with the clutch held in place with an alignment tool (see illustration). Make sure it's installed properly (most replacement clutch plates will be marked "flywheel side" or something similar - if not marked, install the clutch disc with the damper springs toward the transmission).

14 Tighten the pressure plate-to-flywheel bolts only finger-tight, working around the pressure plate.

15 Center the clutch disc by ensuring the alignment tool extends through the splined hub and into the pilot bearing in the crankshaft. Wiggle the tool up, down or side-to-side as needed to bottom the tool in the pilot bearing. Tighten the pressure plate-to-flywheel bolts a little at a time, working in a criss-cross pattern to prevent distorting the cover. After all of the bolts are snug, tighten them to the specified torque mentioned in this Chapter's Specifications. Remove the alignment tool.

16 Using high-temperature grease, lubricate the inner groove of the release bearing (see

Section 4). Also place grease on the transmission input shaft bearing retainer.

17 Install the clutch release bearing as described in Section 4.

18 Install the transmission and all components removed previously. Tighten all fasteners to the proper torque specifications.

4 Clutch release bearing - removal, inspection and installation

Warning: *Dust produced by clutch wear and deposited on clutch components is hazardous to your health. DO NOT blow it out with compressed air and DO NOT inhale it. DO NOT use gasoline or petroleum-based solvents to remove the dust. Brake system cleaner should be used to flush the dust into a drain pan. After the clutch components are wiped clean with a rag, dispose of the contaminated rags and cleaner in a covered, marked container.*

1993 and earlier models
Removal

1 Following the appropriate procedure outlined in Chapter 7A, remove the transmission.

2 Unbolt the insulator plate from the clutch housing and slide the plate and rubber insulator off the lines (see illustration).

3 Remove the pressed metal retaining nut from the base of the hydraulic release bearing (see illustration) and slide the release bearing assembly off the transmission input shaft bearing retainer.

Inspection

4 Hold the center portion of the bearing stationary and rotate the outer portion while applying pressure. If the bearing doesn't turn smoothly or if it's noisy, replace it with a new one. Wipe the bearing with a clean rag and inspect it for damage and wear. Don't immerse the bearing in solvent - it is sealed for life and immersion would ruin it.

5 Hydraulic release bearings must also be checked for fluid leakage where the rubber seal meets the cylinder housing. If any leakage is evident, replace the entire assembly.

Installation

6 Installation is the reverse of the removal procedure, with a couple of points which must be noted.

7 Install a new pressed metal retaining nut.

Note: *When new, the hydraulic release bearing is retained in the compressed position by nylon straps - they are designed to break the first time the clutch pedal is depressed, so there is no need to remove them.*

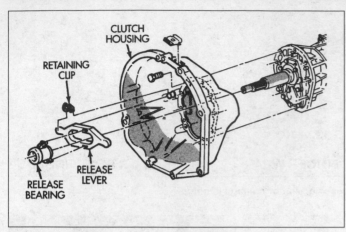

4.11 Disconnect the retaining clip securing the release lever, disconnect the release lever and slide the release bearing off the transmission input shaft (1994 models)

5.9 If you don't have an internal puller and slide hammer, pack the recess behind the pilot bearing with heavy grease and force it out hydraulically with a steel rod slightly smaller than the bore in the bearing - when the hammer strikes the rod, the bearing will pop out of the crankshaft

8   Install the transmission (see Chapter 7A).
9   Connect the hydraulic line and bleed the system as described in Section 8.

1994 and later models
Removal
10   Following the procedure outlined in Chapter 7A, remove the transmission.
11   Disconnect the release bearing from the release lever and slide the release bearing off the transmission input shaft (see illustration).

Inspection
12   Hold the center portion of the release bearing stationary and rotate the outer portion while applying pressure. If the bearing doesn't turn smoothly or if it's noisy, replace it with a new one. Wipe the bearing with a clean rag and inspect it for damage and wear. Don't immerse the bearing in solvent - it is sealed for life and immersion would ruin it.
13   Inspect the release fork and fork pivot. Make sure the fork pivot is secure in the clutch

housing and that it isn't bent or damaged.

Installation
14   Installation is the reverse of the removal procedure, with a couple of points that must be noted.
15   Fill the inner groove of the release bearing with high-temperature grease. Also apply a light coat of the same grease to the input shaft splines and to the face of the release bearing where it contacts the pressure plate diaphragm fingers.
16   Lightly lubricate the clutch release bearing where it contacts the release lever with the same grease.
17   Install the transmission (see Chapter 7A).
18   Bleed the system as described in Section 8.

5   Pilot bearing - inspection and replacement

Note: *On models equipped with a dual-mass (assembled) flywheel, it may be necessary to remove the flywheel in order to replace the pilot bearing.*
1   The clutch pilot bearing is a needle roller type bearing which is pressed into the rear of the crankshaft. Its primary purpose is to support the front of the transmission input shaft. The pilot bearing should be inspected whenever the clutch components are removed from the engine. Due to its inaccessibility, if you are in doubt as to its condition, replace it with a new one.
Note: *If the engine has been removed from the vehicle, disregard the following steps which do not apply.*
2   Remove the transmission (refer to Chapter 7A).
3   Remove the clutch components (see Section 3).
4   Inspect the bore of the pilot bearing for any excessive wear, scoring, lack of grease, dryness or obvious damage. If any of these conditions are noted, the bearing should be

replaced. A flashlight will be helpful to direct light into the recess.
5   Removal can be accomplished with a special internal puller and slide hammer, but an alternative method also works very well.
6   Find a solid steel bar which is slightly smaller in diameter than the bearing. Alternatives to a solid bar would be a wood dowel or a socket with a bolt fixed in place to make it solid.
7   Check the bar for fit - it should just slip into the bearing with very little clearance.
8   Pack the bearing and the area behind it (in the crankshaft recess) with heavy grease. Pack it tightly to eliminate as much air as possible.
9   Insert the bar into the bearing bore and strike the bar sharply with a hammer which will force the grease to the back side of the bearing and push it out (see illustration). Remove the bearing and clean all grease from the crankshaft recess.
10   To install the new bearing, pack the inside of the bearing and lightly lubricate the outside surface with wheel bearing grease. Drive the bearing into the recess with a bushing driver or an appropriately-sized socket. The seal must face out and the bearing must go in perfectly straight (see illustrations).

BEARING SEAL
MUST FACE
TRANSMISSION

4-CYL. BEARING

6-CYL. BEARING

5.10a The pilot bearing incorporates an O-ring seal which cannot be replaced separately (if any indication that the seal is leaking, or if the bearing is dry, replace it) - the bearing must be installed with the seal towards the transmission

5.10b Tap in the bearing with a bushing driver or a socket

11   Install the clutch components, transmission and all other components removed previously, tightening all fasteners properly.

6   Clutch master cylinder - removal and installation

Caution: *Before disconnecting any hydraulic lines or hoses, protect the vehicle from brake fluid, as the vehicle's finish can be damaged.*

1993 and earlier models
Removal

1   A pair of support rods are bolted into the engine compartment between the firewall and the front cross member. Loosen the locknut at the front of the left (driver's side) support rod and swing the rod to the side.
2   Although you can remove the clutch master cylinder without removing this support rod, you can't remove the reservoir cap to drain the clutch fluid or to refill the reservoir when you're done.
3   Remove the clutch master cylinder reservoir cap, and, using a suction gun or large syringe, suck out as much fluid as possible.
4   Disconnect the hydraulic line (see illustration) from the clutch master cylinder, using a flare nut wrench, if available.
5   Remove the master cylinder mounting nuts.
Note: *On some models, the lower nut faces forward and the upper nut faces to the rear (i.e., the bolt head faces forward); on these models, remove the upper nut from under the dash.*
6   Working under the dash, disconnect the pushrod from the clutch pedal. It is retained by a cotter pin, plastic washer and spring washer (see illustration).
7   Also from under the dash, remove the master cylinder upper mounting nut, if it faces to the rear (see illustration). Rather than attempt to loosen the nut from this position, it is much easier to simply hold the nut while an

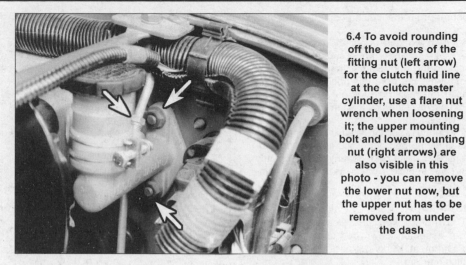

6.4 To avoid rounding off the corners of the fitting nut (left arrow) for the clutch fluid line at the clutch master cylinder, use a flare nut wrench when loosening it; the upper mounting bolt and lower mounting nut (right arrows) are also visible in this photo - you can remove the lower nut now, but the upper nut has to be removed from under the dash

assistant unscrews the bolt from the engine side of the firewall.
8   Pull the cylinder out of the hole in the firewall. Be careful not to let any of the fluid drip onto the vehicle's paint, as it will damage it.

Installation
9   Position the cylinder against the firewall and install the lower mounting nut, but don't tighten it fully yet.
10   Connect the hydraulic line to the cylinder, tightening the fitting by hand only. Since the cylinder is still loose, it can be wiggled around slightly to make it easier to align the fitting threads.
11   If the upper mounting nut faces to the rear, install the upper mounting bolt, again using an assistant to tighten the bolt while the nut is held stationary.
12   Connect the pushrod to the clutch pedal, install the washers and a new cotter pin.
13   Tighten the lower mounting nut.
14   Tighten the hydraulic line fitting securely.
15   Install the fluid reservoir if it was previously removed.
16   Fill the reservoir with brake fluid and

bleed the system as described in Section 8.

1994 through 2006 models
Note: *The clutch master cylinder, slave cylinder and connecting hydraulic line are serviced as an assembly. None of these components can be serviced separately, and all fittings are sealed. If any of the components are faulty, the entire assembly must be replaced.*

Removal
17   Raise the vehicle and place it securely on jackstands.
18   Remove the slave cylinder mounting nuts. Move the slave cylinder away from the clutch housing.
19   Disengage the hydraulic line from the body clips.
20   Lower the vehicle.
21   Make sure the master cylinder filler cap is secure.
22   Remove the lower master cylinder mounting nut.
Note: *The upper nut must be removed from under the dash.*
23   Working under the dash, disconnect the

6.6 Remove the cotter pin (arrow), plastic washer and spring washer, then disconnect the pushrod from the clutch pedal pin

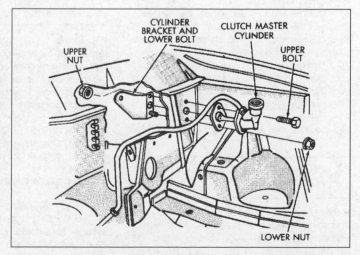

6.7 An exploded view of the clutch master cylinder assembly (note how the upper mounting nut faces to the rear of the unit)

pushrod from the clutch pedal. It is retained by a metal clip.

24   Also working under the dash, remove the master cylinder upper mounting nut that faces to the rear. Rather than attempting to loosen the nut from this position, it is much easier to simply hold the nut while an assistant unscrews the bolt from the engine side of the firewall.

25   Carefully pull the release/master cylinder assembly up and out of the engine compartment. Be careful not to let any of the fluid drip onto the vehicle's paint, as it will be damaged.

Installation

26   Carefully work the release/master cylinder assembly down and onto the engine compartment, working it past the engine and clutch housing.

27   Position the master cylinder against the firewall and install the lower mounting nut, but don't tighten it fully yet.

28   Install the upper mounting bolt, again using an assistant to tighten the bolt while the nut is held stationary.

29   Connect the pushrod to the clutch pedal and install the metal clip.

30   Tighten the lower mounting nut securely.

31   Raise the vehicle and place it securely on jackstands.

32   Insert the slave cylinder pushrod through the clutch opening and into the release lever. Be sure the cap on the end of the rod is securely engaged onto the lever, then install the mounting nuts. Tighten the nuts securely.

33   Attach the hydraulic line onto the body clips.

34   Fill the reservoir with brake fluid and bleed the system as described in Section 8.

2007 and later models

Note: *Once the hoses are disconnected, immediately plug them to prevent fluid loss.*

35   Pry the actuator rod from the clutch pedal arm.

36   Disconnect the reservoir supply hose at the clutch master cylinder.

37   Pull the clip and disconnect the hydraulic line from the clutch master cylinder.

38   Disconnect the clutch pedal position switch electrical connector.

39   Grasp the clutch master cylinder firmly and rotate clockwise 1/4 of a turn and remove from the brake booster mounting bracket.

40   Installation is reverse of removal.

41   Fill the reservoir with brake fluid and bleed the system as described in Section 8.

7   Clutch release (slave) cylinder - replacement

Note: *The following procedure applies to 2003 and earlier models and 2007 and later models. On 1994 though 2006 models, the clutch master cylinder, slave cylinder and connecting hydraulic line are serviced as an assembly. None of these components can be serviced*

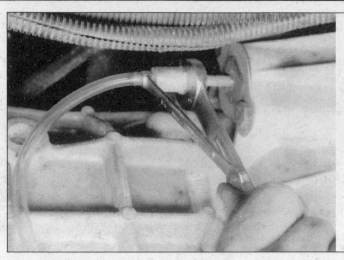

8.4 The bleeder screw is located on the right (passenger's) side of the transmission housing on four-cylinder models; on six-cylinder models, it's on the left side, immediately above the fitting for the clutch hydraulic line (see illustration 5.12 in Chapter 7A).

separately, and all fittings are sealed. If any of the components are faulty, the entire assembly must be replaced (see Section 6).

1   Place the transmission in neutral.

2   Raise and support the vehicle on jackstands.

3   Detach the clutch hydraulic line from the bracket.

4   Disconnect the clutch hydraulic line from the release cylinder.

5   Remove the fasteners attaching the release cylinder to the transmission.

Caution: *When removing the cylinder, be careful not to over-pivot or rotate the inner plunger, which will result in excessive fluid loss if the seal is broken. In other words, keep the cylinder as level as possible while removing.*

6   Remove the release cylinder from the transmission by pulling straight out until the actuator rod clears the transmission housing.

7   Installation is reverse of removal. Tighten the fasteners to the specified torque listed in this Chapter's Specifications.

8   Fill the reservoir with brake fluid and bleed the system as described in Section 8.

8   Clutch hydraulic system - bleeding

1   The hydraulic system should be bled to remove all air whenever any part of the system has been removed or if the fluid level has fallen so low that air has been drawn into the master cylinder. The procedure is very similar to bleeding a brake system.

2   Fill the master cylinder with new brake fluid conforming to DOT 3 specifications.

Caution: *Don't re-use any of the fluid coming from the system during the bleeding operation. Also, don't use fluid which has been inside an open container for an extended period of time.*

3   Raise the vehicle and place it securely on jackstands to gain access to the release cylinder (or bleeder screw), which is located on the side of the clutch housing.

Note: *On later models, the bleeder screw is located on top of the release (slave) cylinder.*

4   Remove the dust cap which fits over the bleeder screw (see illustration) and push a length of plastic hose over the screw. Place the other end of the hose in a clear container with about two inches of brake fluid. The hose end must be in the fluid at the bottom of the container.

5   Have an assistant depress the clutch pedal and hold it. Open the bleeder screw on the transmission, allowing fluid to flow through the hose. Close the bleeder screw when the flow of bubbles or old fluid ceases. Once closed, have your assistant release the pedal.

Note: *The bleeder screw used on four-cylinder models is on the right side of the transmission; the bleeder screw used on six-cylinder models is on the left side of the transmission, directly above the fitting for the clutch hydraulic line (see the transmission removal and installation procedure in Chapter 7A).*

6   Continue this process until all air is evacuated from the system, indicated by a solid stream of fluid being ejected from the bleeder screw each time with no air bubbles in the hose or container. Keep a close watch on the fluid level inside the master cylinder - if the level drops too low, air will be sucked back into the system and the process will have to be started all over again.

7   Lower the vehicle. Top off the fluid level and check carefully for proper operation before placing the vehicle in normal service.

9   Axles, axleshafts, differentials and driveshafts - general information

1   The models covered by this manual are equipped with Jeep's "Command-Trac" front axle (see illustration), which uses a two-piece (outer and intermediate) axleshaft in the right axle tube. The outer splines of the left axleshaft and the right (outer) axleshafts mesh with splines in the wheel hub. The front axleshafts have single cardan universal joints at their outer ends to allow the front wheels to turn left or right while transmitting torque.

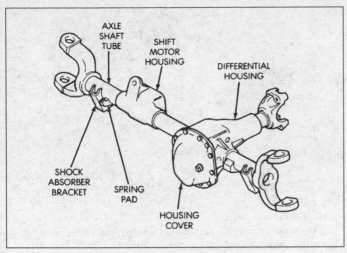

9.1 Front axle assembly

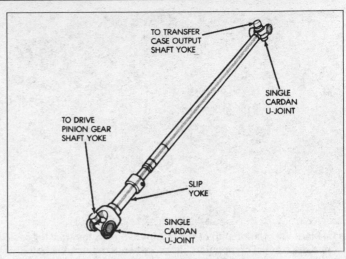

9.3a Front driveshaft assembly

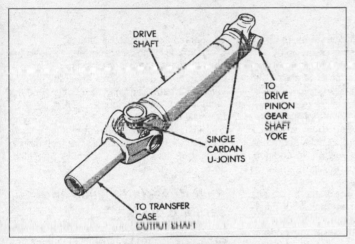

9.3b Rear driveshaft assembly

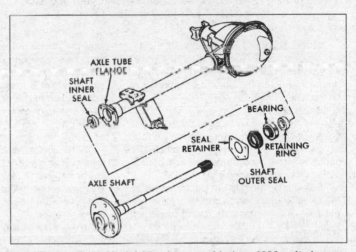

9.5a Typical Dana Model 35 axle assembly (pre-1990 unit shown; 1990 and later axles use a C-clip to connect the inner end of axleshafts to differential)

2   The inner end of the intermediate shaft is connected to the differential side gear by a snap-ring. When you select four-wheel drive operation by shifting the transfer case lever into one of the 4WD ranges, the two shafts are coupled together by a shift collar which engages matching splines located on the end of each axleshaft. The shift collar is controlled by a vacuum shift motor and shift fork, which are mounted on the right axle tube where the shift collar is located between the intermediate and outer axleshafts. When you select two-wheel drive, the vacuum shift motor and shift fork move the shift collar out of engagement with the two axleshaft splines. During two-wheel drive operation, the disengaged differential free-wheels instead of turning the ring gear, pinion and front driveshaft, saving unnecessary wear on these components.

3   The front driveshaft (see illustration) is equipped with single cardan universal joints at both ends and a slip yoke at its front end (the end which connects to the yoke at the drive pinion gear shaft). The rear driveshaft (see illustration) also has single cardan universal

joints at both ends. The rear driveshaft also has a slip yoke on its front end (the end that connects it to the transfer case output shaft yoke). Slip yokes and single cardan universal joints are equipped with "Zerk" type grease fittings; they should be lubricated at the recommended intervals (see Chapter 1).

4   The front and rear driveshafts are finely balanced by the manufacturer during assembly. If you remove or disassemble a driveshaft, carefully mark the relationship of the parts to ensure that you reassemble them so they're in the same relationship to each other as they were prior to disassembly. If you don't, the driveshafts can vibrate excessively.

5   The Model 35 rear axle (see illustration) has "semi-floating" axleshafts supported on their outer ends by the rear wheel bearings. The axle assembly is held in alignment to the body by the suspension leaf springs. The axle build date and manufacturer's number are stamped on right (passenger's side) axle tube near the housing cover; the axle assembly part number and ratio are on a tag attached to the left side of the housing cover (see illustration).

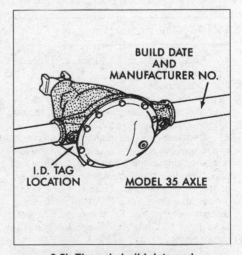

9.5b The axle build date and manufacturer's number are stamped on the passenger's side axle tube near the housing cover; the axle assembly part number and ratio are on a tag attached to the left side of the housing cover

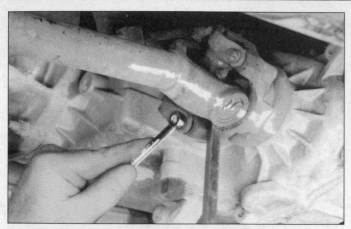

11.4 Mark the relationship of the U-joint flange to the transfer case and differential companion flange - when removing the bolts, insert a screwdriver through the U-joint to prevent the driveshaft from turning (2006 and earlier models shown, 2007 and later models are handled similarly)

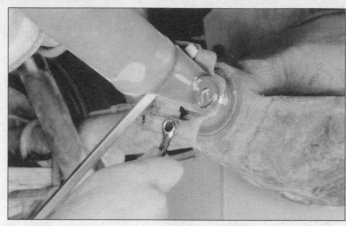

11.8 Mark the relationship of the U-joint flanges - when removing the bolts, insert a screwdriver through the U-joint to prevent the driveshaft from turning

6   The rear axle is equipped with a standard or an optional Trac-Lok (limited slip) differential. Trac-Lok differentials transfer torque from one wheel to the other if traction is lost and the wheel begins to spin.

7   Because of the complexity and critical nature of the differential adjustments, as well as the special equipment needed to perform the operations, disassembly of the differential should be done by a dealer service department or other repair shop.

8   Some later models are equipped with a Tru-Lok differential, which can lock either the front axle and/or rear axle for off-pavement driving in 4Low mode at speeds below 10 mph. A switch on the instrument panel allows the driver to select which axle is to be locked. When the switch is activated, an electric air pump actuates a diaphragm inside the differential that engages a dog clutch.

10   Driveline inspection

1   Raise the rear of the vehicle and support it securely on jackstands.

2   Crawl under the vehicle and visually inspect the driveshaft. Look for any dents or cracks in the tubing. If any are found, the driveshaft must be replaced.

3   Check for any oil leakage at the front and rear of the driveshaft. Leakage where the driveshaft enters the transmission or transfer case indicates a defective rear transmission or transfer case seal. Leakage where the driveshaft enters the differential indicates a defective pinion seal. For these repair operations refer to Chapter 7A and Section 13, respectively.

4   While under the vehicle, have an assistant turn the rear wheel so the driveshaft will rotate. As it does, make sure the universal joints are operating properly without binding, noise or looseness.

5   The universal joint can also be checked

with the driveshaft motionless, by gripping your hands on either side of the joint and attempting to twist the joint. Any movement at all in the joint is a sign of considerable wear. Lifting up on the shaft will also indicate movement in the universal joints.

6   Finally, check the driveshaft mounting bolts at the ends to make sure they are tight.

7   The above driveshaft checks should be repeated on the front driveshaft. In addition, check for grease leakage around the sleeve yoke, indicating failure of the yoke seal.

8   Check for leakage where the driveshafts connect to the transfer case and front differential. Leakage indicates worn oil seals.

9   Also check for leakage at the ends of the axle housings (at the drum brake backing plates), which would indicate a defective axle seal.

11   Driveshafts - removal and installation

Note: *Whenever a driveshaft is removed, new U-joint straps should be used during installation.*

1   Place the transmission and transfer case in Neutral with the parking brake off.

2   Raise the vehicle and support it securely on jackstands.

Front driveshaft (all models) / rear driveshaft (2006 Rubicon and all 2007 and later models)

3   Using white paint, chalk or a scribe, mark the relationship of the rear universal joint or flange to the transfer case companion flange. Also mark the relationship of the front U-joint or flange to the pinion shaft yoke at the front differential.

4   On 2006 and earlier models, remove the strap bolts from the front U-joint. Unbolt the rear U-joint flange from the transfer case

companion flange (see illustration).

5   On 2007 and later models, remove the bolts attaching the flanges together.

6   On all models, remove the shaft from the vehicle. On 2006 and earlier models, tape the bearing caps to the spider to prevent the caps from falling off.

7   Installation is the reverse of the removal procedure. Be sure to tighten the fasteners to the torque listed in this Chapter's Specifications.

Rear driveshaft - 2006 and earlier models

8   To ensure that the driveshaft maintains its balance, it must be reinstalled in the same position. Using a scribe, white paint or a hammer and punch, place alignment marks on the yokes at the drive pinion gear shaft and at the rear of the driveshaft (see illustration).

9   Remove the rear universal joint bolts and straps. Turn the driveshaft (or tires) as necessary to bring the bolts into the most accessible position.

10   Tape the bearing caps to the spider to prevent the caps from coming off during removal.

11   If equipped, loosen or cut the clamps attaching the boot to the slip yoke and differential.

12   Lower the rear of the driveshaft and then slide the slip yoke at the front out of the transmission or transfer case.

13   To prevent loss of fluid and protect against contamination while the driveshaft is out, wrap a plastic bag over the transmission or transfer case housing and hold it in place with a rubber band.

14   Remove the plastic bag from the transfer case and wipe the area clean. Inspect the oil seal carefully. Procedures for replacement of this seal can be found in Section 13.

15   Slide the slip yoke at the front of the driveshaft into the transfer case.

16   Raise the rear of the driveshaft into

12.2 A pair of needle-nose pliers can be used to remove the universal joint snap-rings

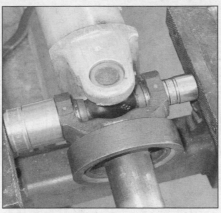

12.4 To press the universal joint out of the driveshaft yoke, set it up in a vise with the small socket pushing the joint and bearing cap into the large socket

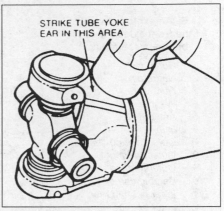

12.9 If the snap-ring will not seat in the groove, strike the yoke with a hammer - this will relieve tension that has set up in the yoke, and slightly spring the yoke ears (this should also be done if the joint feels tight when assembled)

position, checking to be sure the marks are in alignment. If not, turn the rear wheels to match the pinion flange and the driveshaft.

17   Remove the tape securing the bearing caps and install new straps and bolts. Tighten the bolts to the torque listed in this Chapter's Specifications.

12   Universal joints - replacement

Note: *A press or large vise will be required for this procedure. It may be a good idea to take the driveshaft to a repair or machine shop where the universal joints can be replaced for you, normally at a reasonable charge.*

1   Remove the driveshaft as outlined in the previous Section.

2   Using a small pair of pliers, remove the snap-rings from the spider (see illustration).

3   Supporting the driveshaft, place it in position on either an arbor press or on a workbench equipped with a vise.

4   Place a piece of pipe or a large socket with the same inside diameter over one of the bearing caps. Position a socket which is of slightly smaller diameter than the cap on the opposite bearing cap (see illustration) and use the vise or press to force the cap out (inside the pipe or large socket), stopping just before it comes completely out of the yoke. Use the vise or large pliers to work the cap the rest of the way out.

5   Transfer the sockets to the other side and press the opposite bearing cap out in the same manner.

6   Pack the new universal joint bearings with grease. Ordinarily, specific instructions for lubrication will be included with the universal joint servicing kit and should be followed carefully.

7   Position the spider in the yoke and partially install one bearing cap in the yoke. If the replacement spider is equipped with a grease fitting, be sure it's offset in the proper direction (toward the driveshaft).

13.6a Mark the relationship of the pinion shaft to the pinion shaft yoke

8   Start the spider into the bearing cap and then partially install the other cap. Align the spider and press the bearing caps into position, being careful not to damage the dust seals.

9   Install the snap-rings. If difficulty is encountered in seating the snap-rings, strike the driveshaft yoke sharply with a hammer. This will spring the yoke ears slightly and allow the snap-rings to seat in the groove (see illustration).

10   Install the grease fitting and fill the joint with grease. Be careful not to overfill the joint, as this could blow out the grease seals.

11   Install the driveshaft. Tighten the flange bolts to the specified torque.

13   Oil seals - replacement

Pinion seal

Note: *The following procedure applies to both front and rear differentials.*

1   A pinion shaft oil seal failure results in the leakage of differential gear lubricant past the

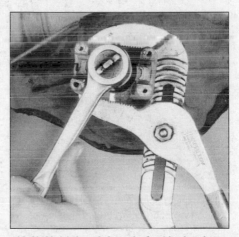

13.6b Hold the pinion shaft yoke in place and loosen the nut

seal and onto the driveshaft yoke or flange. The seal is replaceable without removing or disassembling the differential.

2   Loosen the front or rear wheel lug nuts, raise the vehicle and place it on jackstands.

3   Remove the front or rear wheels. If you're replacing the rear differential pinion seal, also remove the rear brake drums.

Note: *The wheels must be removed before you can obtain an accurate reading of the amount of torque required to turn the pinion.*

4   Disconnect the driveshaft from the pinion shaft yoke (see Section 11).

5   Using a torque wrench, slowly turn the pinion shaft nut and measure the torque required to turn the pinion.

Note: *On later models, the pinion shaft (flange surface) will need to be held in place with flange wrench instead of adjustable pliers, when removing the nut.*

6   Mark the relationship of the pinion shaft to the pinion shaft yoke (see illustration). Hold the pinion shaft yoke with a large pair of adjustable pliers, then remove the nut (see illustration).

**14.5a An exploded view
of the front axle hub and
bearing assembly**

1   Cotter pin
2   Nut retainer
3   Nut
4   Washer
5   Brake disc
6   Hub
7   Outer bearing seal
8   Outer bearing
9   Outer bearing race
10   Bearing carrier
11   Inner bearing race
12   Inner bearing
13   Inner bearing seal
14   Carrier seal
15   Disc brake splash
     shield
16   Axleshaft dust
     slinger
17   Bearing carrier bolts
18   Axleshaft

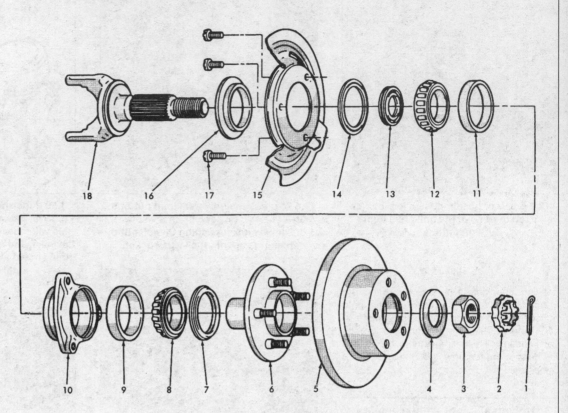

7   Remove the pinion shaft yoke from the shaft, using a puller if necessary.

8   After noting what the visible side of the oil seal looks like, carefully pry it out of the differential with a screwdriver or seal removal tool. Be careful not to damage the splines on the pinion shaft.

9   Lubricate the new seal lip with multi-purpose grease or differential lubricant and carefully install it in position in the differential. Using a seal driver or a short section of pipe of the proper diameter and a hammer, carefully drive the seal into place.

10   Clean the sealing lip contact surface of the pinion shaft yoke. Apply a thin coat of multi-purpose grease to the seal contact surface and the shaft spines and, using a soft-faced hammer, tap the pinion shaft yoke onto the shaft, making sure the match-marks line up.

11   Coat the threads of a new pinion shaft nut with multi-purpose grease and, using the holder to hold the flange, tighten the nut just enough to eliminate all end-play in the pinion shaft.

12   Turn the pinion shaft yoke several times to seat the bearing.

13   Using a torque wrench, see how much torque is required to turn the pinion shaft. The desired preload is the previously recorded torque value plus five inch-pounds. If the pre-load is less than desired, retighten the nut in small increments until the desired preload

is reached. If the maximum torque (add five inch-pounds to the torque required to loosen the nut on disassembly) is reached before the preload figure is obtained, the bearing spacer must be replaced by a repair shop.

Note: *Do not back-off the pinion nut to reduce the preload. After the preload is properly adjusted, proceed to the next Step.*

14   Connect the driveshaft to the pinion shaft yoke (see Section 11).

15   Install the brake drums or rotors and calipers, if you're working on the rear pinion seal, and the wheels, lower the vehicle to the ground and tighten the lug nuts to the torque listed in the this Chapter's Specifications.

16   Test drive the vehicle and check around the differential pinion shaft yoke for evidence of leakage.

Front axle seals

17   To replace the front axle seals, the differential carrier must be removed and the seals are serviced from inside of the differential housing. This job should be left to a dealer service department or repair shop.

Rear axle seals

18   The rear axle seals are part of the rear axle bearing assembly and are replaced by removing the axle and pressing the bearing and retainer off (see Section 18).

14   Front axle hub and bearings - removal, service and installation

Removal

1   Pry the bearing cap from the hub, remove the cotter pin and nut lock, then loosen the axle hub nut.

2   Loosen the front wheel lug nuts, raise the front of the vehicle and support it securely on jackstands. Remove the wheel.

3   Remove the disc brake caliper and disc (see Chapter 9).

4   Remove the ABS speed sensor if needed.

5   Remove the axle hub nut. Unbolt the hub assembly from the steering knuckle and pull it out of the knuckle bore (see illustrations). If the axle sticks in the hub splines, try tapping it loose with a dead blow hammer. If that doesn't work, push it out of the hub with a puller.

Service

6   On early models the hub bearings may be serviced, but due to the special tools and expertise required to separate and reassemble the hub and bearings, this job should be left to a dealer service department or repair shop. On later models, the hub and bearing assembly must be replaced as an assembly. Check with a parts specialist to determine parts availability for your model.

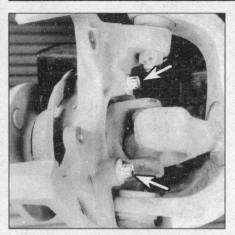

14.5b Remove the three bolts (front bolt not visible in this photo) that secure the hub assembly to the steering knuckle - a twelve-point socket will be necessary

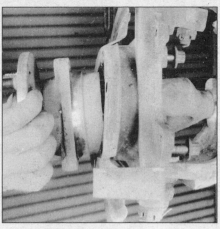

14.5c Carefully pull the hub assembly out of the steering knuckle

15.4 Once the hub and bearing assembly have been removed, the axleshaft can be pulled straight out of the housing

Installation

7   Using sandpaper or emery cloth, clean the opening in the steering knuckle to remove any rust or dirt that may be present. Lubricate the axleshaft splines with wheel bearing grease. Smear the opening in the steering knuckle with wheel bearing grease and install the hub assembly, tightening the bolts to the specified torque.

8   Install the washer and hub nut, tightening the nut securely. Install the brake disc and caliper (see Chapter 9), mount the wheel and lower the vehicle. Tighten the lug nuts to the torque listed in this Chapter's Specifications.

15 Front axleshafts - removal, overhaul and installation

Removal

Left or right outer axleshaft

1   Following the procedure described in Section 14, remove the front axle hub and bearing assembly.

2   Remove the disc brake backing plate (see illustration 14.5a).

3   If equipped with a shift motor and the right side axle is being removed, follow the procedure in Section 16 and remove the front axle shift motor.

4   Slide the axle straight out of the axle housing (see illustration).

Right side intermediate axleshaft (models with shift motor)

5   Remove the right side outer axleshaft (see above Steps).

6   Remove the differential cover (see the differential lubricant changing procedure in Chapter 1).

7   Remove the intermediate shaft retaining clip in the differential case (see illustration).

8   Slide the intermediate shaft out of the axle housing.

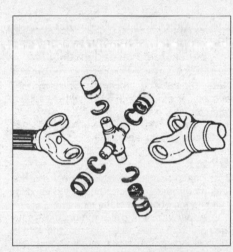

15.7 The right side intermediate axleshaft is held in the differential by a retaining clip

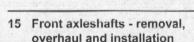

15.10a Exploded view of the front axleshaft U-joint assembly

9   Tighten the axle hub nut to the specified torque and install the nut lock and a new cotter pin. Install the hubcap.

U-joint overhaul

10   Follow the U-joint replacement procedure in Section 12, but note that the snap-rings are inboard of the yoke ears and fit into grooves in the bearing caps (see illustration). They are removed by driving them out with a screwdriver (see illustration).

Installation

11   Installation is the reverse of the removal procedure. If the intermediate axleshaft was removed, use a new gasket on the differential cover and fill the differential housing with the specified type of gear lubricant (see Chapter 1). If the front axle shift motor was removed, lubricate the axleshaft splines, shift collar and fork with wheel bearing grease.

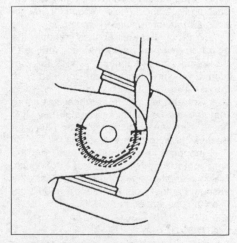

15.10b Push the snap-rings out of the groove in the U-joint bearings with a small screwdriver

16.8 Unplug the vacuum harness connectors (right three arrows), then remove the four bolts that retain the shift motor housing (left four arrows)

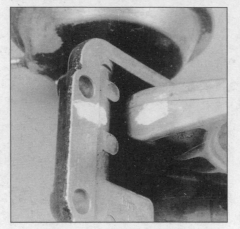

16.10a Mark the relationship of the shift fork to the housing so it will be reinstalled correctly

16.10b Remove the shift fork and motor retaining snap-ring (arrow is pointing to fork retaining snap-ring) and slide the motor out of the housing

16 Front axle shift actuator (motor) - check, removal and installation

Note: *The following procedure applies to 1990 and earlier models equipped with a vacuum operated shift actuator.*

1   Raise the front of the vehicle and support it securely on jackstands.

Check

2   Disconnect the vacuum line from the shift motor and connect a hand-held vacuum pump to the front port of the motor.

3   Apply vacuum to the motor and rotate the right front wheel to ensure that the axle is fully disengaged. The shift motor should hold vacuum for at least 30 seconds. If it leaks, replace it.

4   If the motor holds vacuum, connect the vacuum pump to the rear port on the shift motor. Plug the other ports and apply vacuum once again. It should hold vacuum for 30 seconds also. If not, replace the motor.

5   With vacuum still applied, remove the plug from the port where the vacuum line to the transfer case connects. Check for vacuum. If vacuum is not present, continue on to the next step.

6   Rotate the right front wheel to ensure that the axle has shifted completely. If it hasn't, remove the shift motor and check for freeness of the sliding shift collar.

7   Inspect the vacuum harness from the shift motor to the transfer case for kinks, cracks and other signs of damage. Check the vacuum harness connectors for a good, tight fit on the vacuum ports.

Removal

8   Unplug the vacuum harness from the shift motor (see illustration).

9   Remove the shift motor housing bolts and lift the shift motor housing, motor and fork from the axle housing. Remove all traces of

old gasket material.

10   Mark the relationship of the shift fork to the housing to return it to its original position upon reassembly (see illustration). Rotate the shift motor and remove the shift fork and motor retaining snap-rings (see illustration) by pushing them down with two screwdrivers. Pull the motor out of the housing.

Installation

11   Remove the O-ring from the shift motor and install a new one if the same motor is to be reinstalled.

12   Slide the shift motor into the housing and install the shift fork, lining up the previously applied match-marks. Install the snap-rings, making sure they are completely seated in their grooves.

13   Liberally coat the shift collar and axle-shaft splines with wheel bearing grease. Engage the shift fork with the shift collar and set the assembly into position on the axle housing. Be sure to use a new gasket. Install the bolts and tighten them to the specified torque.

14   Connect the vacuum harness and check the front differential lubricant level (see Chapter 1).

17 Front axle assembly - removal and installation

1   Loosen the front wheel lug nuts, raise the front of the vehicle and support it securely on jackstands positioned under the frame rails. Remove the front wheels.

2   Unbolt the front brake calipers and hang them out of the way with pieces of wire - don't let the calipers hang by the brake hose (see Chapter 9).

3   Remove the caliper brackets and brake discs (see Chapter 9).

4   Detach the brake lines from the axle

housing.

5   If equipped, remove the wheel speed sensors from the front hubs.

6   Disconnect the vacuum harness from the front axle shift motor (early models, see Section 16). On models with Tru-Lok, disconnect the electrical connectors at the front axle.

7   Mark the relationship of the front driveshaft to the front differential pinion shaft yoke, then disconnect the driveshaft from the yoke (see Section 11). On 1987 through 1995 models, discard the U-joint straps.

8   Position a hydraulic jack under the differential. If two jacks are available, place one under the right side axle tube to balance the assembly.

9   Disconnect the drag link (at the right side of the tie-rod), steering damper and track bar; disconnect the shock absorbers; loosen the stabilizer bar links at the stabilizer bar and disconnect the stabilizer bar links from the axle (see Chapter 10).

10   On leaf spring models, loosen the nuts and bolts that attach the spring rear eyes to the frame brackets; loosen the nuts and bolts that attach the front of the springs to the shackles (see Chapter 10).

11   On coil spring models, unbolt the upper and lower suspension arms from the axle (see Chapter 10).

12   On coil spring models, lower the differential enough to remove the springs.

13   On leaf spring models, raise the jack high enough to relieve the axle weight from the springs. Remove the spring shackle nuts and bolts and lower the front of the springs to the floor (see Chapter 10).

14   Remove the axle with the floor jack.

15   Installation is the reverse of the removal procedure. On 1987 through 1995 models, be sure to use new U-joint straps and tighten the bolts of the torque listed in this Chapter's Specifications. Be sure to tighten to the suspension fasteners to the torque values listed in Chapter 10 Specifications.

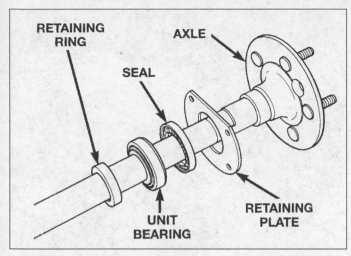

18.1 On models with the bearing pressed on the axleshaft, the axle is retained by a retaining plate bolted to the brake backing plate

18.2 Unscrew the four brake backing plate nuts using a socket on an extension passing through the hole in the axle flange.

Note: On models with disc brakes - the nuts are accessed from the back side.

18.3 Pull the axle from the housing using a slide hammer and axle flange adapter

18.5a Remove the inner axle seal from the housing using a slide hammer and internal puller jaw attachment

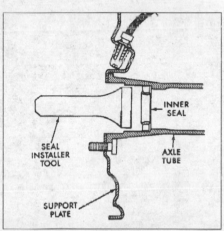

18.5b Lubricate the seal lip, then drive the seal into position with an installation tool or a piece of pipe with an outside diameter slightly smaller than the outside diameter of the seal

18   Rear axleshaft and bearing assembly - removal and installation

Note: Two types of axleshaft retaining methods are used on the models covered by this manual. On the first type, the axle bearing is pressed on the axleshaft and the axleshaft is retained in the tube by a bearing retaining plate (see illustration). On the second type, the axle bearing is pressed into the axle tube and the axleshaft is retained by C-clip locks in the differential. To determine which type you have, remove the brake drum and inspect the end of the axle tube behind the axleshaft flange. If a bearing retaining plate is visible, the axle bearing is pressed on the axleshaft. Models equipped with C-clips are not equipped with a bearing retaining plate, the end of the axle tube and the axleshaft seal will be visible.

1   Loosen the wheel lug nuts, raise the rear of the vehicle and support it securely on jackstands. Remove the wheel. Remove the brake drum or disc.

Models with a bearing retainer

Note: This procedure applies to some 2006 and earlier models and all 2007 and later models.

Removal

2   Remove the nuts attaching the bearing retainer (and brake backing plate) to the axle tube flange (see illustration).
3   Connect a slide hammer and adapter to the axle flange and pull the axleshaft assembly from the axle housing (see illustration).
4   If the bearing must be replaced, take the assembly to a dealer service department or a repair shop to have the old bearing and outer seal removed and new ones installed.

If a new bearing is installed, be sure to also replace the inner seal (see next Step).
5   If the brake backing plate shows evidence of leaking differential lubricant, the inner axleshaft seal should be replaced. Remove the seal using the slide hammer with an internal puller jaw attachment (see illustration). Install the new seal using a seal driver or piece of pipe (see illustration).

Installation

6   Wipe the bearing bore in the axle housing clean. Pack the bearing with wheel bearing grease and apply a thin coat of grease to the outer surface of the bearing.
7   Smear the lips of the inner seal with grease, then guide the axleshaft straight into the axle housing, being careful not to damage the seal.
8   Install the retaining nuts for the brake backing plate and bearing retainer, and tighten them to the torque listed in this Chap-

18.12a Rotate the axleshaft until you can see the lock bolt for the differential pinion shaft and remove the lock bolt...

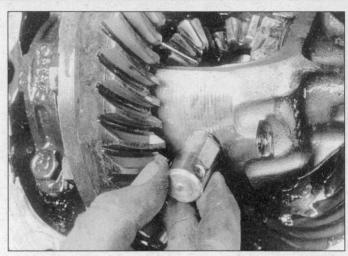

18.12b ... and then carefully remove the pinion shaft from the differential carrier (don't turn the wheels or the carrier after the shaft has been removed, or the spider gears might fall out)

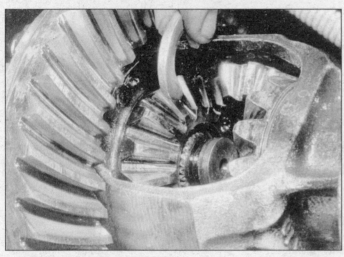

18.13 Push in the axle flange, remove the C-clip lock from the inner end of the axleshaft

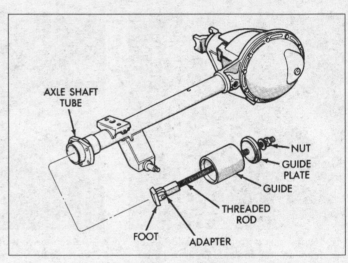

18.17 An exploded view of a special bearing removal tool, with which you can remove the axleshaft bearing and seal simultaneously

ter's Specifications. Slide the brake drum over the axle flange.

9   Install the wheel and lug nuts, tightening the lug nuts securely. Lower the vehicle and tighten the lug nuts to the torque listed in Chapter 1 Specifications.

Models with a C-clip

Note: *Some 2006 and earlier models are equipped with C-clips that retain the axle in the housing.*

Removal

10   Clean away all foreign material from the area where the differential housing cover mates with the differential housing.

11   Loosen the differential housing cover bolts and drain the differential lubricant from the housing (see Chapter 1). Remove the housing cover.

12   Rotate an axleshaft until you can see the lock bolt for the differential pinion shaft. Remove the lock bolt and the pinion shaft from the differential carrier (see illustrations).

Caution: *Don't turn the wheels or the carrier after the shaft has been removed, or the spider gears might fall out.*

13   Push in on the axleshaft (toward the differential) and remove the axleshaft C-clip lock from its recessed groove in the axleshaft (see illustration). If you need a screwdriver to pry it up far enough to pull it out, make sure you don't damage the gear teeth.

14   Slide the axleshaft out of the axle tube. Use care to prevent damage to the axleshaft bearing and seal, which will remain in the axle tube.

15   Inspect the bearing contact surface on the axleshaft. It should be a dull gray in appearance and may even appear to be slightly dented. But if you see signs of brinelling, pitting and spalling, the axleshaft AND

the bearing must be replaced.

16   Even if there are no signs of extreme bearing/axleshaft wear, the brake backing plate may be leaking differential lubricant. If it is, replace the outer axleshaft seal by prying it out of the axle tube with a small pry bar or a large screwdriver.

17   If you're going to install a new bearing, you can remove the seal at the same time as the bearing, provided you use Bearing Removal Tool Set 6310, or a similar setup (see illustration). Use the adapter tool with the smallest "foot" from the removal tool set. Thread the adapter onto the threaded rod. With the foot parallel to the adapter bracket, insert it through the bearing bore and pivot it 90-degrees (i.e., pivot it perpendicular to the bracket) with a suitable device. Position the guide against the axleshaft tube and turn the nut against the guide plate to remove the bearing.

Installation

18   Thoroughly wipe clean the axleshaft bearing bore in the axle tube.

19   Position the new axleshaft bearing on the "pilot" of your bearing installation tool. Insert the axleshaft bearing into the axle tube bore (make sure the bearing isn't cocked in the bore). Gently tap the driver handle until the bearing is seated firmly against the shoulder in the axle tube.

Caution: *Don't use the new axleshaft seal to seat the bearing in the axle tube bore; this could damage the seal and cause lubricant to leak from the axle tube.*

20   Install the new seal using a special seal installation seal driver, available at most auto parts stores (see illustration), or a suitably sized section of pipe. When the installation tool contacts the axle tube "face," the seal will be positioned at the proper depth in the bore.

21   Wipe the bearing bore in the axle housing clean. Pack the bearing with wheel bearing grease and apply a thin coat of grease to the outer surface of the bearing.

22   Lubricate the bearing bore and the seal lip, then guide the axleshaft straight into the axle tube and engage its splines with the splines in the differential side gear. Make sure you don't damage the axleshaft seal lip.

23   Push in on the axleshaft and install the C-clip lock in the recessed groove on the inner end of the axleshaft. To seat the C-clip, lock into the counterbore in the differential side gear and pull the axleshaft out.

24   Insert the pinion shaft into the differential carrier through the thrust washers and the pinion gears. Align the hole in the shaft with the lock bolt hole in the carrier, install the lock bolt and tighten it to the torque listed in this Chapter's Specifications.

25   Install the differential housing cover (see Chapter 1).

26   Install the brake drum (see Chapter 9).

27   Install the wheel and lug nuts. Tighten the lug nuts securely. Lower the vehicle and tighten the lug nuts to the torque listed in Chapter 1 Specifications.

28   Refill the differential housing with the specified lubricant (see Chapter 1).

29   Test drive the vehicle to make sure the brakes and axle are operating properly. If the vehicle has Trac-Lok (i.e., a limited slip differential), make 10 to 12 slow, figure-eight turns to ensure that the new lubricant is pumped through the clutch discs.

19   Rear axle assembly - removal and installation

Leaf-spring models

1   Loosen the rear wheel lug nuts. Raise the vehicle and support it securely on jackstands placed underneath the frame rails, either adjacent to or slightly in front of the rear spring front eyes.

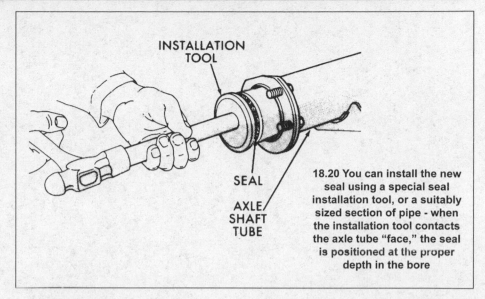

18.20 You can install the new seal using a special seal installation tool, or a suitably sized section of pipe - when the installation tool contacts the axle tube "face," the seal is positioned at the proper depth in the bore

2   Remove the wheels.

3   Disconnect the driveshaft from the differential pinion shaft yoke and hang the rear of the driveshaft from the underbody with a piece of wire (see Section 11).

4   Unbolt the rear track bar from the axle tube (see Chapter 10).

5   Disconnect the axle vent tube from its fitting.

6   Disconnect the parking brake cables from the equalizer (see Chapter 9).

7   Position a floor jack under the differential. If two jacks are available, place one under each side axle to balance the assembly.

8   Disconnect the shock absorbers from the axle (see Chapter 10).

9   Disconnect the flexible brake hose from the floorpan fitting. Plug the end of the hose or wrap a plastic bag tightly around it to prevent excessive fluid loss and contamination.

10   Loosen, but don't remove, the bolts that attach the spring eyes to the frame brackets and shackles (see Chapter 10).

11   Remove the U-bolt nuts from the leaf spring tie plates (see Chapter 10).

12   Raise the rear axle assembly slightly, then unbolt the springs from the shackles (see Chapter 10) and lower the rear ends of the springs to the floor (only on models with the axle housing mounted above the spring).

13   Lower the jack and move the axle assembly out from under the vehicle.

14   Installation is the reverse of the removal procedure. Be sure to tighten the U-bolt nuts and the U-joint strap bolts to the torque values listed in Chapter 10 Specifications.

Coil-spring models

15   Raise and support the vehicle securely on jackstands.

16   Remove the rear wheels.

17   Position a floor jack under the differential. If two jacks are available, place one under each side axle to balance the assembly.

18   Remove the ABS wheels speed sensors (if equipped) from the rear of the brake backing plates. Disconnect the parking brake cables from the rear axle, then remove the calipers and brake discs (see Chapter 9). Also, if equipped, disconnect the brake sensor connector(s). On models with Tru-Lok rear differentials, disconnect the Tru-Lok electrical connectors at the rear axle. The calipers can be tied out of the way with mechanic's wire, without disconnecting the brake fluid lines.

19   Disconnect the vent tube from the axle housing and make match marks on the rear of the driveshaft and the pinion flange of the rear axle, then remove/disconnect the driveshaft from the axle. The driveshaft can temporarily be suspended with mechanic's wire, instead of being removed completely at both ends.

20   Disconnect the links of the rear stabilizer bar. The stabilizer bar can be removed from the vehicle still attached to the rear axle, if necessary. If the rear axle is to be replaced, remove the stabilizer bar bushing clamps from the rear axle and remove the stabilizer bar.

21   Remove the shock absorbers (see Chapter 10).

22   Remove the bolts securing the upper and lower control arms to the rear axle housing.

23   Remove the two mounting bolts and the rear track bar.

24   Swing the control arms out of the way, then lower the axle until the rear coil springs can be removed. Remove the rear axle.

25   Installation is the reverse of removal, with the following Steps in mind. Before fully tightening the track bar or control arms mounting bolts, the rear axle assembly should be raised until the rear axle is at its ride height relative to the chassis. Tighten the track bar and control arm bolts to the torque listed in this Chapter's Specifications. Tighten all other fasteners to the torque settings listed in their respective Chapter's Specifications.

Notes

Chapter 9
Brakes

Contents

Specifications

General
Brake fluid type .... See Chapter 1

Disc brakes
Disc minimum thickness	Stamped or cast into disc
Disc runout (maximum)	
1989 and earlier models	0.004 inch
1990 and 1991 models	0.005 inch
1992 through 2002 models	0.003 inch
2003 through 2006 models	0.004 inch
2007 and later models	0.0008 inch
Thickness variation	0.0005 inch
2011 and earlier models	0.0005 inch
2012 and later models	0.00035 inch
Brake pad minimum thickness	See Chapter 1

Drum brakes
Drum maximum diameter (refinish limit)	Stamped or cast into drum

Torque specifications   Ft-lbs (unless otherwise indicated)
Note: One foot-pound (ft-lb) of torque is equivalent to 12 inch-pounds (in-lbs) of torque. Torque values below approximately 15 ft-lbs are expressed in inch-pounds, since most foot-pound torque wrenches are not accurate at these smaller values.

Power brake booster pushrod nuts (pre-1991 models)	
Inner nut	25
Outer nut	75 in-lbs
Power brake booster mounting nuts	
2002 and earlier models	25 to 29
2003 through 2006 models	29
2007 and later models	18
Master cylinder mounting nuts	
1996 and earlier models	15
1997 through 2002 models	13 to 18
2003 and later models	156 in-lbs
Caliper mounting pins (bolts)	
Front	
1993 and earlier models	30
1994 through 2006 models	132 in-lbs
2007 and later models	26
Rear	
2003 and earlier models	132 in-lbs
2004 through 2006 models	18
2007 and later models	26
Caliper mounting bracket bolts (2007 and later)	
Front	
2007 through 2010 models	120
2011 and later models	100
Rear	77
Brake hose banjo bolt (front and rear calipers)	23 to 24
Wheel cylinder mounting bolts	84 in-lbs
Wheel lug nuts	See Chapter 1
Wheel speed sensor mounting bolt	90 in-lbs

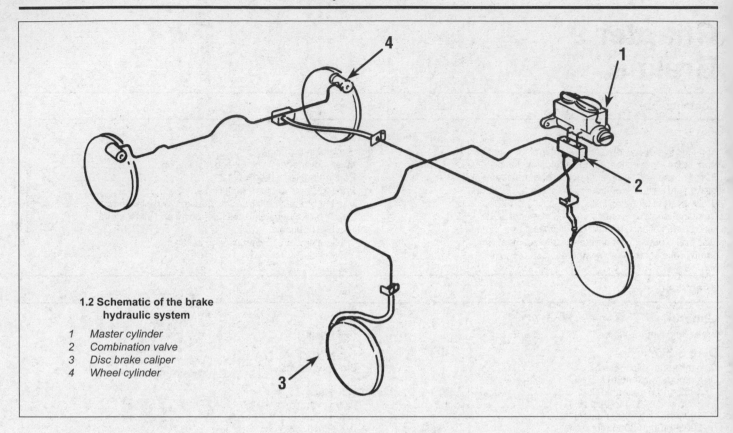

1.2 Schematic of the brake hydraulic system

1   Master cylinder
2   Combination valve
3   Disc brake caliper
4   Wheel cylinder

1   General information

1   The vehicles covered by this manual are equipped with hydraulically operated front and rear brake systems. The front brakes are ventilated discs; the rear brakes are either drums (models through 2002) or solid discs (2003 and later models). Both the front and rear brakes are self-adjusting. The front and rear disc brakes automatically compensate for pad wear, while the rear drum brakes incorporate an adjustment mechanism, which is activated as the brakes are applied when the vehicle is stopped in reverse. Anti-lock brakes are optional on most models.

Hydraulic circuits

2   The hydraulic system consists of two separate circuits (see illustration); if a leak or failure occurs in one hydraulic circuit, the other circuit will remain operative. The master cylinder has separate reservoirs for each circuit. A visual warning of circuit failure or air in the system is given by a warning light activated by displacement of the piston in the pressure differential switch portion of the combination valve (on non-ABS systems) from its normal "in balance" position.

Master cylinder/reservoir assembly

3   Early models use a cast-iron master cylinder with an integral reservoir. Later models use an aluminum type cylinder with a nylon reservoir; it is not rebuildable. If found to be defective, it must be replaced. (The reservoir grommets are replaceable, however).

Combination valve

4   The combination valve, used on non-ABS models, performs two functions. A proportioning valve controls front-to-rear brake action during rapid stops.
5   A brake pressure differential switch continuously compares the front and rear brake pressures. If a failure occurs somewhere in the system, a red warning light on the instrument cluster comes on. Once a failure has occurred, the warning light remains on until the system has been repaired.
6   On ABS-equipped vehicles, the ABS unit performs the functions of the combination valve.

Power brake booster

7   A dual-diaphragm, vacuum-operated power brake booster, mounted between the firewall and the master cylinder, utilizes engine manifold vacuum and atmospheric pressure to provide assistance to the hydraulic brake system.

Anti-lock Brake System (ABS)

8   Some later models have an Anti-lock Braking System (ABS) that aids vehicle stability during heavy braking or on wet or uneven surfaces.

Parking brake

9   The parking brake system consists of a pedal (1995 and earlier models) or a lever between the front seats (1997 and later models), the cables connecting the pedal or lever to the rear brakes, an equalizer for balancing the tension of the two rear cables, and the brake shoes (on all models with rear drums; the parking brake system utilizes the brake shoes themselves). On models with rear disc brakes, small parking brake shoes are housed inside the rear disc assemblies.

Service

10   After completing any operation involving disassembly of any part of the brake system, always test drive the vehicle to check for proper braking performance before resuming normal driving. When testing the brakes, perform the tests on a clean, dry flat surface. Conditions other than these can lead to inaccurate test results.
11   Test the brakes at various speeds with both light and heavy pedal pressure. The vehicle should stop evenly without pulling to one side or the other. Avoid locking the brakes because this slides the tires and diminishes braking efficiency and control of the vehicle.
12   Tires, vehicle load and front-end alignment are factors which also affect braking performance.

Precautions

13   There are some general cautions and

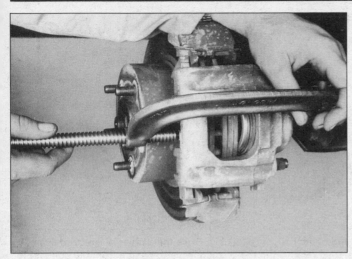

2.5a If you've got a 1987 through 1995 or 2007 and later model, use a large C-clamp to push the piston back into the caliper bore - note that one end of the clamp is on the flat area on the backside of the caliper and the other end (screw end) is pressing against the outer brake pad

2.5b A C-clamp is hard to use on the calipers used on 1997 through 2006 models; use a screwdriver to lever the piston back into the caliper bore

2.6 Before removing the caliper, wash off all traces of brake dust with brake system cleaner

tering mask should be worn when working on the brakes. Do not, under any circumstances, use petroleum-based solvents to clean brake parts. Use brake system cleaner or clean brake fluid only!

Note: When servicing the disc brakes, use only high quality, nationally recognized name brand pads.

1   Remove the cover or cap from the brake fluid reservoir.

2   Loosen the wheel lug nuts, raise the front of the vehicle and support it securely on jackstands.

3   Remove the front wheels. Work on one brake assembly at a time, using the assembled brake for reference if necessary.

4   Inspect the brake disc carefully as outlined in Section 4. If machining is necessary, follow the information in that Section to remove the disc, at which time the pads can be removed from the calipers as well.

5   Push the piston back into the bore to provide room for the new brake pads. A C-clamp can be used to accomplish this on 1995 and earlier models and 2007 and later models (see illustration); on 1997 through 2006 and later models, use a screwdriver to lever the piston into its bore (see illustration). As the piston is depressed to the bottom of the caliper bore, the fluid in the master cylinder will rise. Make sure it doesn't overflow. If necessary, siphon off some of the fluid.

6   Before removing the caliper, wash off all traces of brake dust with brake system cleaner (see illustration).

1987 through 1995 models

7   To replace the brake pads on a 1995 or earlier model model, see illustrations 2.7a through 2.7j. Don't skip any steps - follow the instructions, in the exact sequence shown, in the caption under each illustration.

warnings involving the brake system on this vehicle:

a) *Use only brake fluid conforming to DOT 3 specifications.*

b) *The brake pads and linings contain fibers that are hazardous to your health if inhaled. Whenever you work on brake system components, clean all parts with brake system cleaner. Do not allow the fine dust to become airborne. Also, wear an approved filtering mask.*

c) *Safety should be paramount whenever any servicing of the brake components is performed. Do not use parts or fasteners that are not in perfect condition, and be sure that all clearances and torque specifications are adhered to. If you are at all unsure about a certain procedure, seek professional advice. Upon completion of any brake system work, test the brakes carefully in a controlled area before putting the vehicle into normal service. If a*

problem is suspected in the brake system, don't drive the vehicle until it's fixed.

d) *Used brake fluid is considered a hazardous waste and it must be disposed of in accordance with federal, state and local laws. DO NOT pour it down the sink, into septic tanks or storm drains, or on the ground. Clean up any spilled brake fluid immediately and then wash the area with large amounts of water. This is especially true for any finished or painted surfaces.*

2   Disc brake pads (front and rear) - replacement

Warning: *Disc brake pads must be replaced on both front wheels at the same time - never replace the pads on only one wheel. Also, the dust created by the brake system is harmful to your health. Never blow it out with compressed air and don't inhale any of it. An approved fil-*

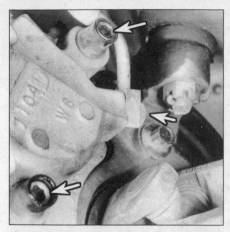

2.7a Using an Allen wrench, unscrew the two caliper mounting pins - do not disconnect the brake hose banjo bolt (center arrow) unless you're removing the caliper to overhaul it

2.7b Swing the upper end of the caliper out of the anchor plate, then remove the caliper completely. Take this opportunity to check for fluid leakage around the caliper piston boot, which would indicate the need to overhaul the calipers

2.7c Once the caliper is removed from the anchor plate, hang it from the coil spring with a piece of wire or a tie-strap - DON'T let it hang by the brake hose

2.7d Pry down the lower anti-rattle clip and remove the outer brake pad

2.7e Pull the anti-rattle clips away from the pad with your index fingers and force the inner brake pads out with your thumbs

2.7f Before installing the brake pads, clean the sliding surfaces on the caliper and anchor plate and apply a thin coat of high-temperature grease to the anchor plate in the area shown

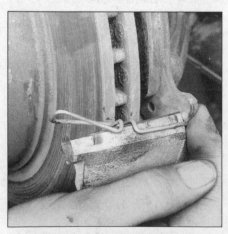

2.7g Position the anti-rattle clips on the anchor plate and install the inner brake pad

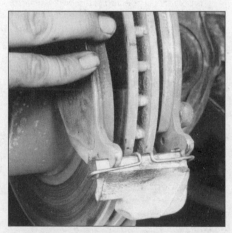

2.7h Place the lower end of the outer pad on the anchor plate and push it down against the anti-rattle clip, then lift up on the upper anti-rattle clip and swing the pad into position

2.7i Engage the notch in the lower end of the caliper with the anchor plate, then rotate it over the pads

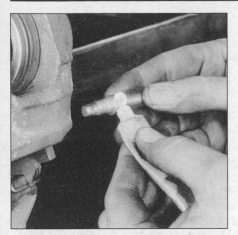

2.7j Lubricate the mounting pins with high-temperature grease, push them into the caliper and tighten them to the torque listed in this Chapter's Specifications

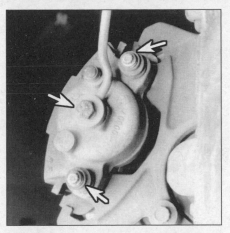

2.8a Remove the caliper pins (upper and lower arrows) with a box-end wrench or socket - do NOT remove the brake hose banjo bolt (middle arrow) unless you are removing the caliper for overhaul

2.8b Slide the caliper assembly off the disc

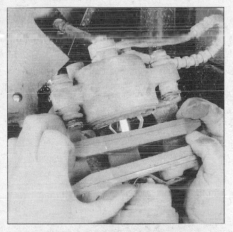

2.8c Grasp the caliper between your hands like this and pull the inner pad off with your fingers

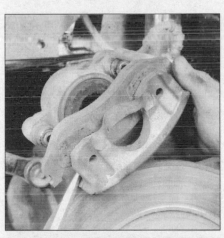

2.8d Pry off the outer pad with a screwdriver

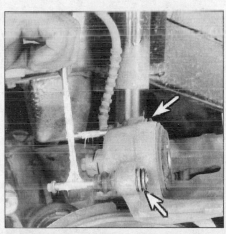

2.8e Inspect the rubber dust boots for the caliper pins and replace them if they're torn or damaged, then lubricate the caliper pins with high temperature grease

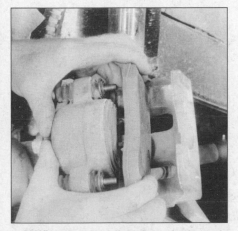

2.8f When you install the inner brake pad, make sure the retaining clips on the back of the pad are pushed into the hole in the caliper piston as far as they'll go (the back of the pad should be seated firmly against the piston)

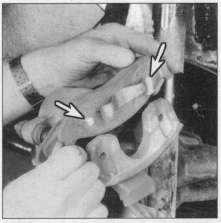

2.8g When you install the outer brake pad, make sure the retaining clip on the back of the pad is pushed all the way down onto the caliper…

1997 through 2006 models

8   To replace the brake pads on a 1997 through 2006 model, see illustrations 2.8a through 2.8k. Don't skip any steps - follow the instructions, in the exact sequence shown, in the caption under each illustration.

2007 and later models

9   To replace the brake pads on a 2007 or later model, see illustrations 2.9a through 2.9n. Don't skip any steps - follow the instructions, in the exact sequence shown, in the caption under each illustration.

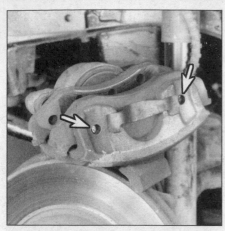

2.8h … and the locating lugs (arrows in previous photos) are aligned with their respective holes in the caliper

2.8i Before installing the caliper, lubricate the sliding surfaces (upper arrows) on the lower edges of the brake pads and on the steering knuckle (lower arrow) with high temperature grease

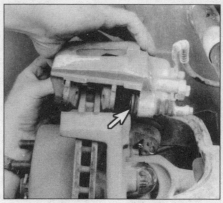

2.8j When you install the caliper and pad assembly back onto the brake disc rotor, make sure you don't damage the new pads, and make sure the bushings (arrow points to lower bushing, upper bushing not visible in this photo) don't snag on the steering knuckle and tear (view shown is from underneath looking straight up)

2.8k Make sure the notches in the lower edges of the brake pads (upper arrow) are properly seated onto the sliding surface of the steering knuckle (lower arrow) - clean and lubricate the anti-rattle clips (later models)

2.9a Unscrew the upper and lower caliper mounting bolts while holding the slide pins with an open-end wrench

2.9b Remove the caliper from its mounting bracket and support it with a length of wire - don't let it hang by the brake hose!

2.9c Remove the inner pad from the caliper mounting bracket…

2.9d … and the outer pad

2.9e Remove the pad support plates from the caliper mounting bracket. Check them for cracks and wear. It's a good idea to replace them whenever changing the pads

2.9f Remove the upper and lower slide pins from the caliper mounting bracket. Clean them…

2.9g … and lubricate them with high-temperature brake grease

2.9h Reinstall the slide pins in the mounting bracket, making sure the boots seat properly

2.9i Lubricate the pad support plates with high-temperature grease where the pad ears will contact them…

2.9j … then install the support plates in the mounting bracket

2.9k Install the outer brake pad…

2.9l … and the inner brake pad to the mounting bracket

2.9m Place the caliper into position over the pads

2.9n Install the caliper mounting bolts and tighten them to the torque listed in this Chapter's Specifications.

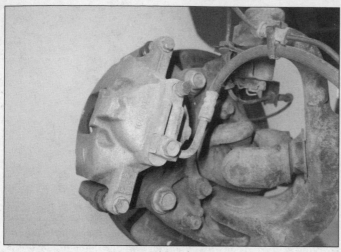

3.4 Brake hose-to-caliper banjo bolt (2011 JK model shown)

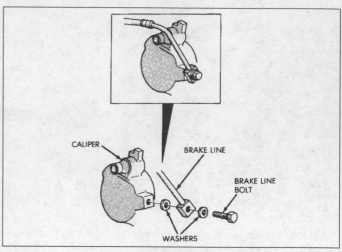

3.9 Be sure to use NEW copper sealing washers on both sides of the banjo fitting when reattaching the brake hose (earlier style caliper shown, later style similar)

All models

10   When reinstalling the caliper, be sure to tighten the mounting pins/bolts to the torque listed in this Chapter's Specifications. After the job has been completed, firmly depress the brake pedal a few times to bring the pads into contact with the disc.

11   Install the wheels and lug nuts. Lower the vehicle and tighten the lug nuts to the torque listed in the Chapter 1 Specifications.

12   Check the brake fluid level, adding as necessary (see Chapter 1).

13   Check for fluid leakage and make sure the brakes operate normally before driving in traffic.

---

3   Disc brake caliper - removal and installation

Warning: *Dust created by the brake system is harmful to your health. Never blow it out with compressed air and don't inhale any of it. An approved filtering mask should be worn when working on the brakes. Do not, under any circumstances, use petroleum-based solvents to clean brake parts. Use brake system cleaner or clean brake fluid only!*

Note: *If an overhaul is indicated (usually because of fluid leakage) explore all options before beginning the job. New and factory rebuilt calipers are available on an exchange basis, which makes this job quite easy. If it's decided to rebuild the calipers, make sure a rebuild kit is available before proceeding. Always rebuild the calipers in pairs - never rebuild just one of them.*

Removal

1   Remove the cover from the brake fluid reservoir, siphon off two thirds of the fluid into a container and discard it.

2   Loosen the wheel lug nuts, raise the vehicle and support it securely on jackstands. Remove the wheels.

3   Bottom the piston in the caliper bore (see illustrations 2.5a or 2.5b).

4   Remove the brake hose banjo bolt and detach the hose (see illustration). Have a rag handy to catch spilled fluid and wrap a plastic bag tightly around the end of the hose to prevent fluid loss and contamination.

Note: *Do not remove the brake hose from the caliper if you are only removing the caliper for access to other components.*

5   Unscrew the two caliper pins/mounting bolts and detach the caliper from the torque plate/mounting bracket (refer to Section 2 if necessary).

Installation

6   Inspect the caliper pins/mounting bolts for excessive corrosion. Replace them if necessary.

7   Clean the sliding surfaces of the caliper and the anchor plate/mounting bracket.

8   Install the caliper (see Section 2).

9   Install the brake hose and banjo bolt. Be sure to use new copper sealing washers (see illustration). Tighten the bolt to the torque listed in this Chapter's Specifications.

10   If the brake hose was disconnected, be sure to bleed the brakes (see Section 10).

11   Install the wheels and lower the vehicle. Tighten the wheel lug nuts to the torque listed in the Chapter 1 Specifications.

12   After the job has been completed, firmly depress the brake pedal a few times to bring the pads into contact with the disc.

13   Check brake operation before driving the vehicle in traffic.

---

4   Brake disc - inspection, removal and installation

Inspection

1   Loosen the wheel lug nuts, raise the vehicle and support it securely on jackstands.

4.4a Use a dial indicator to check disc runout - if the reading exceeds the specified allowable runout limit, the disc will have to be machined or replaced

Remove the wheel.

2   Remove the brake caliper as described in Section 2. It's not necessary to disconnect the brake hose. After removing the caliper mounting pins, suspend the caliper out of the way as shown in illustration 2.7c. Don't let the caliper hang by the hose and don't stretch or twist the hose. Reinstall two of the lug nuts to hold the disc in place.

3   Visually check the disc surface for score marks and other damage. Light scratches and shallow grooves are normal after use and may not always be detrimental to brake operation, but deep score marks - over 0.015-inch (0.38 mm) - require disc removal and refinishing by an automotive machine shop. Be sure to check both sides of the disc. If pulsating has been noticed during application of the brakes, suspect disc runout. Be sure to check the wheel bearings to make sure they're properly adjusted.

4   To check disc runout, place a dial indicator at a point about 1/2-inch from the outer edge of the disc (see illustration). Set the indi-

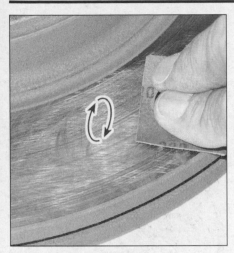

4.4b Using a swirling motion, remove the glaze from the disc surface with sandpaper or emery cloth

4.5a The minimum thickness is cast into the inside of the disc

4.5b Use a micrometer to measure disc thickness at several points

cator to zero and turn the disc. The indicator reading should not exceed the specified allowable runout limit. If it does, the disc should be refinished by an automotive machine shop.

Note: *Professionals recommend resurfacing of brake discs regardless of the dial indicator reading (to produce a smooth, flat surface that will eliminate brake pedal pulsations and other undesirable symptoms related to questionable discs). At the very least, if you elect not to have the discs resurfaced, deglaze them with sandpaper or emery cloth (use a swirling motion to ensure a nondirectional finish) (see illustration).*

5   The disc must not be machined to a thickness less than the specified minimum refinish thickness. The minimum (or discard) thickness is cast into the inside of the disc (see illustration). The disc thickness can be checked with a micrometer (see illustration).

Removal

6   Remove the two lug nuts that were installed to hold the disc in place, then slide the disc off the hub (see illustration). If you're working on a 2007 or later model, the caliper mounting bracket must be removed to remove the brake disc.

Installation

7   Place the disc over the wheel studs on the hub.

8   If you're working on a 2007 or later model, install the caliper anchor bracket and tighten the bolts to the torque listed in this Chapter's Specifications. Install the brake pads and caliper over the disc (refer to Section 2 for the caliper installation procedure, if necessary). Tighten the caliper mounting pins to the specified torque.

9   Install the wheel, then lower the vehicle to the ground. Depress the brake pedal a few times to bring the brake pads into contact with the disc. Bleeding of the system will not

be necessary unless the brake hose was disconnected from the caliper. Check the operation of the brakes carefully before placing the vehicle into normal service.

5   Drum brake shoes - replacement

Warning: *Drum brake shoes must be replaced on both wheels at the same time - never replace the shoes on only one wheel. Also, the dust created by the brake system is harmful to your health. Never blow it out with compressed air and don't inhale any of it. An approved filtering mask should be worn when working on the brakes. Do not, under any circumstances, use petroleum-based solvents to clean brake parts. Use brake system cleaner or clean brake fluid only!*

Caution: *Whenever the brake shoes are replaced, the retracting and hold-down springs should also be replaced. Due to the continuous heating/cooling cycle that the springs are subjected to, they lose their tension over a pe-*

riod of time and may allow the shoes to drag on the drum and wear at a much faster rate than normal. When replacing the rear brake shoes, use only high quality nationally recognized brand name parts.

Note: *The Wrangler has been equipped with two types of drum brake: the 10-inch drum brake and the 9-inch drum brake. The primary difference is the design of the adjuster cable and lever. Compare the brake on your vehicle with the illustrations to determine which procedure to use.*

1   Loosen the wheel lug nuts, raise the rear of the vehicle and support it securely on jackstands. Block the front wheels to keep the vehicle from rolling.

2   Release the parking brake.

3   Remove the wheel.

Note: *All four rear brake shoes must be replaced at the same time, but to avoid mixing up parts, work on only one brake assembly at a time.*

4   Remove the rear drums. If either brake drum is difficult to pull off the axle and shoe

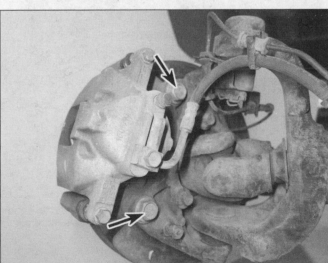

4.6 Caliper mounting bracket bolts - 2007 and later (JK) models

assembly, make sure the parking brake is completely released, then apply some penetrating oil at the hub-to-drum joint. Allow the oil to soak in and try to pull off the drum. If you still can't pull it off, retract the brake shoes (see illustration 5.9a).

10-inch drum brake

5   Follow illustrations 5.5a through 5.5y for the 10-inch drum brake shoe replacement procedure. Don't skip around - follow the instructions, in the sequence shown, in the captions accompanying the illustration.

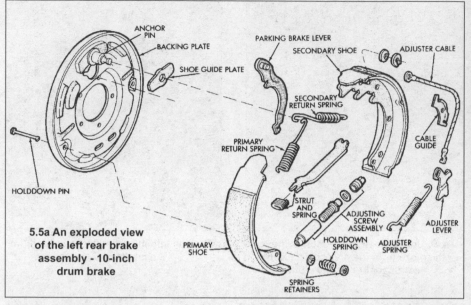

5.5a An exploded view of the left rear brake assembly - 10-inch drum brake

5.5b Wash off the brake assembly with brake cleaner and allow it to dry before you disassemble anything (position a drain pan under the brake to catch the runoff) - DO NOT USE COMPRESSED AIR TO BLOW THE BRAKE DUST FROM THE PARTS!

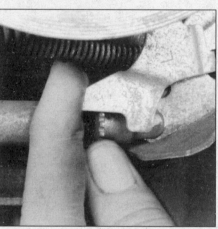

5.5c Pull out on the adjuster lever and turn the star wheel to retract the brake shoes

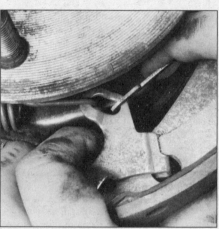

5.5d Pull back on the self-adjuster cable and push the adjusting lever toward the rear, unhooking it from the secondary brake shoe

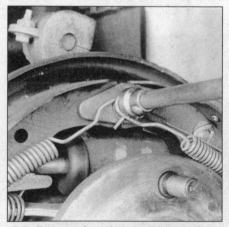

5.5e Remove the primary and secondary shoe retracting springs - the spring removal tool shown here can be purchased at most auto parts stores and greatly simplifies this step

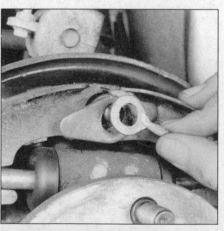

5.5f Remove the self-adjuster cable and anchor pin plate from the anchor pin

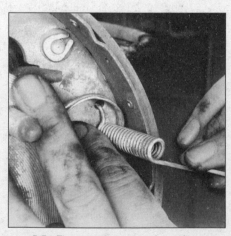

5.5g Remove the secondary shoe retracting spring and cable guide from the secondary shoe

5.5h Remove the primary shoe holddown spring and pin...

5.5i ... then lift the primary shoe and adjusting screw from the backing plate

5.5j Remove the parking brake link

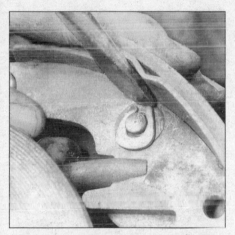

5.5k Remove the secondary shoe hold-down spring and pin, then lift the shoe from the backing plate - pry the parking brake lever retaining clip off the pivot pin...

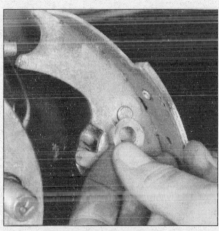

5.5l ... then separate the lever from the secondary shoe - be careful not to lose the spring washer

5.5m Lubricate the brake shoe contact areas with high-temperature grease

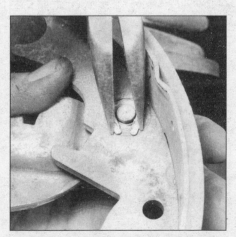

5.5n Attach the new shoe to the parking brake lever, install the spring washer and retaining clip on the pivot pin, then crimp the clip closed with a pair of pliers

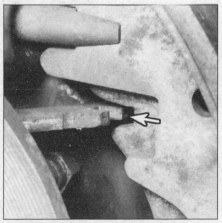

5.5o Install the secondary shoe and hold-down spring to the backing plate, then position the end of the parking brake link into the notch

5.5p Lubricate the adjusting screw with high temperature multi-purpose grease

5.5q Place the primary shoe against the backing plate, then install the hold-down spring - make sure the parking brake strut and wheel cylinder pushrods engage in the brake shoe slots

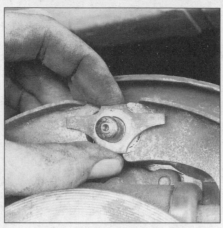

5.5r Install the anchor pin plate...

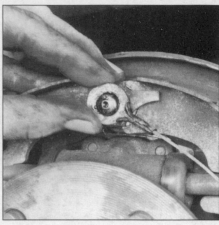

5.5s ... and the self-adjuster cable

5.5t Hook the end of the secondary shoe retractor spring through the cable guide and into the hole in the shoe, then stretch the spring over the anchor pin

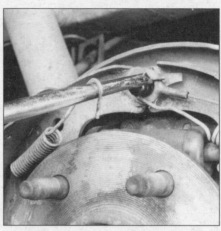

5.5u Install the primary shoe retractor spring – the tool shown here is available at most auto parts stores and makes this step much easier and safer

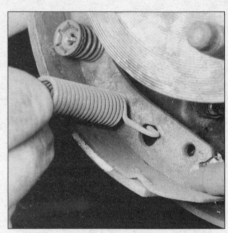

5.5v Hook the adjuster lever spring into the hole at the bottom of the primary shoe

5.5w Hook the adjuster lever spring and cable into the adjuster lever and pull the cable down and to the rear, inserting the hook on the lever into the hole in the secondary shoe

5.5x Wiggle the assembly to ensure the shoes are centered on the backing plate

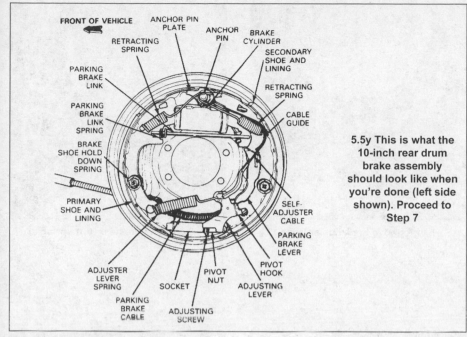

FRONT OF VEHICLE · ANCHOR PIN PLATE · ANCHOR PIN · BRAKE CYLINDER · RETRACTING SPRING · SECONDARY SHOE AND LINING · PARKING BRAKE LINK · RETRACTING SPRING · PARKING BRAKE LINK SPRING · CABLE GUIDE · BRAKE SHOE HOLD DOWN SPRING · PRIMARY SHOE AND LINING · SELF-ADJUSTER CABLE · PARKING BRAKE LEVER · ADJUSTER LEVER SPRING · SOCKET · PIVOT NUT · PIVOT HOOK · ADJUSTING LEVER · PARKING BRAKE CABLE · ADJUSTING SCREW

5.5y This is what the 10-inch rear drum brake assembly should look like when you're done (left side shown). Proceed to Step 7

9-inch drum brake

6   Follow illustrations 5.6a through 5.6ee for the 9-inch drum brake shoe replacement procedure. Don't skip around - follow the instructions, in the sequence shown, in the captions accompanying the illustrations.

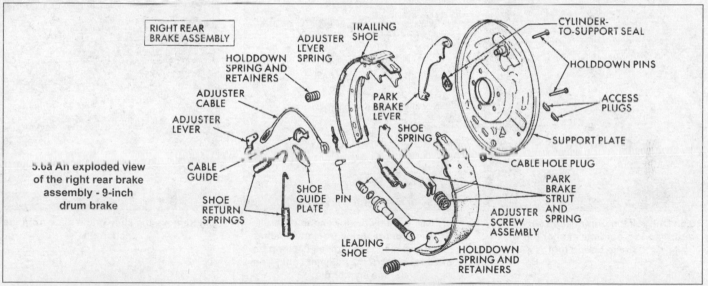

RIGHT REAR BRAKE ASSEMBLY · TRAILING SHOE · CYLINDER-TO-SUPPORT SEAL · ADJUSTER LEVER SPRING · HOLDDOWN SPRING AND RETAINERS · HOLDDOWN PINS · ADJUSTER CABLE · PARK BRAKE LEVER · ACCESS PLUGS · ADJUSTER LEVER · SHOE SPRING · SUPPORT PLATE · CABLE GUIDE · CABLE HOLE PLUG · SHOE RETURN SPRINGS · SHOE GUIDE PLATE · PIN · ADJUSTER SCREW ASSEMBLY · PARK BRAKE STRUT AND SPRING · LEADING SHOE · HOLDDOWN SPRING AND RETAINERS

5.6a An exploded view of the right rear brake assembly - 9-inch drum brake

5.6b Wash off the brake assembly with brake cleaner and allow it to dry before you disassemble anything (position a drain pan under the brake to catch the runoff) - DO NOT USE COMPRESSED AIR TO BLOW THE BRAKE DUST FROM THE PARTS!

5.6c Pry the adjuster lever up and off the star wheel on the adjuster screw and turn the star wheel to retract the brake shoes

5.6d Unhook the adjuster cable from its hole (arrow) in the adjuster lever and let it hang out of the way

5.6e Unhook the adjuster lever spring from the adjuster lever (before you remove it, make sure you have a clear mental image of how it looks when it's correctly installed on the pivot pin for the parking brake lever, with its lower end hooked around the front edge of the adjuster lever and its other, unhooked end pressing against the inside circumference of the trailing shoe)

5.6f Remove the adjuster lever

5.6g Remove the return spring

5.6h Unhook the primary and secondary return spring from the anchor pin with a brake spring tool

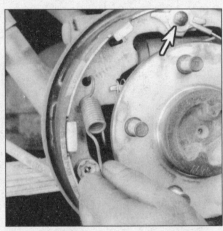

5.6i Unhook the lower end of the primary return spring from the leading shoe and disconnect the metal loop on the upper end of the adjuster cable from the anchor pin

5.6j Remove the shoe guide plate from the anchor pin

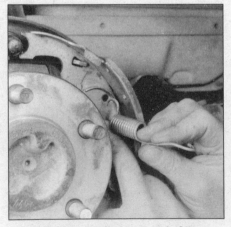

5.6k Remove the lower end of the secondary return spring from the trailing shoe

5.6l Remove the cable guide

5.6m Depress the retainer for the hold-down spring on the leading shoe and give it a slight twist to release it from the hold-down pin...

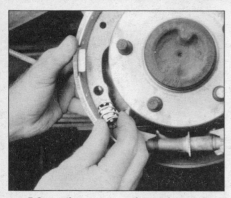

5.6n … then remove the spring and retainer from the leading shoe (it's a good idea to remove the hold-down pin by pulling it out from the back side of the brake backing plate to ensure you don't lose it) - now remove the retainer, hold-down spring and pin from the trailing shoe in the same fashion

5.6o Disengage the notch in the front end of the parking brake strut from its corresponding notch in the leading shoe and remove the strut and spring

5.6p Spread the leading and trailing shoes apart and remove them from the brake support plate with the spring and adjuster screw assembly still attached (you can disconnect and remove the spring and adjuster screw assembly first, but the shoes will fall off; by keeping everything together this way during removal, you can see how the spring and adjuster fit between the two shoes)

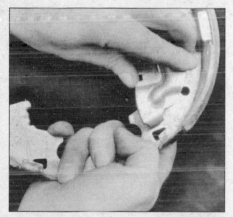

5.6q Disengage the parking brake lever from the back side of the trailing shoe (if you need to detach the parking brake cable from the parking brake lever, see Section 13)

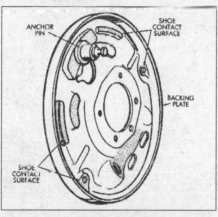

5.6r Lubricate the brake support plate with high temperature grease at the indicated (shaded) areas

5.6s Lubricate the adjusting screw threads with high temperature multi-purpose grease (see illustration 5.5p), install the adjuster screw and spring between the new leading and trailing shoes as shown and install the shoe assembly back onto the support plate

5.6t When you install the parking brake strut between the two shoes, make sure the notch in the rear end of the strut seats properly into its corresponding notch in the trailing shoe

5.6u Push the hold-down pin through the brake support plate from the back side of the plate, install the hold-down spring and retainer, depress the retainer, give it a little twist and release spring pressure - now tug on the retainer and make sure it doesn't pop loose from the flanged head on the hold-down pin

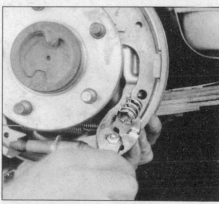

5.6v Install the hold-down pin, spring and retainer for the trailing shoe in exactly the same way you just installed the hold-down spring assembly for the leading shoe, then check it to make sure it's properly installed

5.6w Engage the hooked end closer to the coiled part of the front return spring with its hole in the leading shoe - engage the hooked end closer to the coiled part of the rear return spring into its hole in the adjuster cable guide and install the cable guide onto the trailing shoe

5.6x Install the shoe guide plate and the upper end of the adjuster onto the anchor pin

5.6y Install the hooked end that's farther away from the coiled part of the front return spring to the anchor pin with a brake spring installation tool

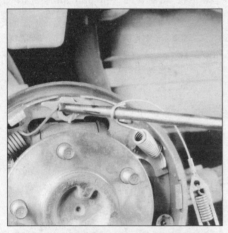

5.6z Install the hooked end that's farther away from the coiled part of the rear return spring to the anchor pin with a brake spring installation tool

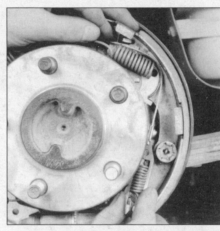

5.6aa Route the lower end of the adjuster cable into its groove in the cable guide

5.6bb Install the adjuster lever spring on the pivot for the parking brake lever - make sure it's installed exactly the way it was before, with the loop in the spring facing up, the hooked end facing forward and down, and the straight end facing to the rear and up against the inside circumference of the trailing shoe

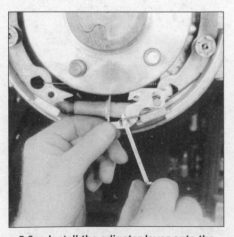

5.6cc Install the adjuster lever onto the pivot for the parking brake lever, then engage the hooked end of the adjuster lever spring over the forward end of the lever with a small screwdriver

5.6dd Hook the lower end of the adjuster cable over its corresponding notch in the adjuster lever

5.6ee The rear brake assembly should look like this when you're done!

5.7 The maximum allowable drum diameter is cast into the drum

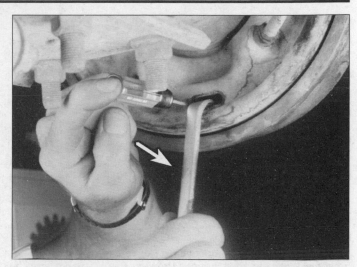

5.9a To adjust the brakes, remove the rubber plug from the adjustment hole in the backing plate, lift the adjuster lever off the star wheel on the adjuster screw with a narrow screwdriver and, using a brake adjuster tool or another screwdriver...

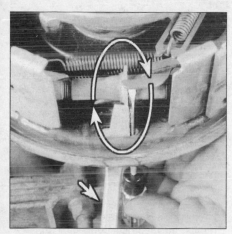

5.9b ... turn the adjuster wheel in the direction shown until the shoes drag on the brake drum, then turn the wheel in the opposite direction until the drum turns freely again; make sure you keep the adjuster lever off the star wheel while you're turning the wheel (drum removed for clarity in this photo)

All models

7   Before reinstalling the drum, check it for cracks, score marks, deep scratches and hard spots, which will appear as small discolored areas. If the hard spots can't be removed with fine emery cloth, or if any of the other conditions listed above exist, take the drum to an automotive machine shop to have it turned. **Note:** *Professionals recommend resurfacing the drums whenever a brake job is done. Resurfacing will eliminate the possibility of out-of-round drums. If the drums are worn so much that they can't be resurfaced without exceeding the maximum allowable diameter (stamped into the drum) (see illustration), then new ones will be required. At the very least, if you elect*

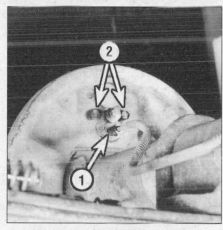

6.4 To remove the wheel cylinder, disconnect the brake line fitting (1), then remove the two wheel cylinder mounting bolts (2)

not to have the drums resurfaced, remove the glazing from the surface with medium-grit emery cloth using a swirling motion.
8   Once the new shoes are in place, install the drums on the axle flanges.
9   Remove the rubber plugs from the brake backing plates. Pull the lever off the adjusting star wheel with one narrow screwdriver and turn the adjusting wheel with a brake adjuster tool (or another screwdriver), moving the shoes away from the drum (see illustrations). Turn the star wheel until the brakes drag slightly as the drum is turned, then turn the wheel in the opposite direction until the drum turns freely again.
Note: *You must keep the adjuster lever off the star wheel while you're turning it or it won't turn.*
10   Repeat this adjustment on the opposite wheel and install the backing plate plugs.

11   Mount the wheel, install the lug nuts, then lower the vehicle. Tighten the lug nuts to the torque listed in the Chapter 1 Specifications.
12   Make a number of forward and reverse stops to allow the brakes to self-adjust themselves.
13   Check brake operation before driving the vehicle in traffic.

6   Wheel cylinder - removal and installation

Removal

1   Raise the rear of the vehicle and support it securely on jackstands. Block the front wheels to keep the vehicle from rolling.
2   Remove the brake shoe assembly (see Section 5).
3   Remove all dirt and foreign material from around the wheel cylinder.
4   Completely loosen the brake line fitting (see illustration). Don't pull the brake line away from the wheel cylinder.
5   Remove the wheel cylinder mounting bolts.
6   Detach the wheel cylinder from the brake backing plate and place it on a clean workbench. Immediately plug the brake line to prevent fluid loss and contamination.
Note: *If the brake shoe linings are contaminated with brake fluid, install new brake shoes.*

Installation

7   Place the wheel cylinder in position and install the bolts.
8   Connect the brake line and tighten the fitting. Install the brake shoe assembly.
9   Bleed the brakes (see Section 10).
10   Check brake operation before driving the vehicle in traffic.

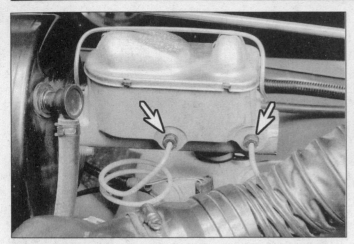

7.2 To disconnect the brake lines from the master cylinder, unscrew these threaded fittings (arrows) – use a flare nut wrench if you have one, to prevent rounding off the corners of the nuts

7.4 To detach the master cylinder assembly from the brake booster, remove these nuts (arrows)

7 Master cylinder - removal and installation

Removal

1 Place rags under the brake line fittings and prepare caps or plastic bags to cover the ends of the lines once they are disconnected. **Caution:** *Brake fluid will damage paint. Cover all body parts and be careful not to spill fluid during this procedure.*

2 Loosen the threaded fittings (see illustration) that connect the brake lines to the master cylinder. To prevent rounding off the flats on these nuts, a flare-nut wrench, which wraps around the nut, should be used. On 2006 and earlier models, unbolt and set aside the EVAP canister for master cylinder access.

3 Pull the brake lines away from the master cylinder slightly and plug the ends to prevent contamination. On 2007 and later models, disconnect the electrical connector for the brake fluid level indicator at the fluid reservoir.

4 Remove the two master cylinder mounting nuts (see illustration) and remove the master cylinder from the vehicle.

5 Remove the reservoir cover, then discard any fluid remaining in the reservoir.

Installation

6 Carefully install the master cylinder by reversing the removal steps, then bleed the brakes (see Section 10).

8 Combination valve - check and replacement

Note: *This procedure only applies to models without an Anti-lock Braking System (ABS).*

Check

1 Disconnect the wire connector from the pressure differential switch (see illustration).

Note: *When unplugging the connector, squeeze the side lock releases, moving the inside tabs away from the switch, then pull up. Pliers may be used as an aid if necessary.*

2 Using a jumper wire, connect the switch wire to a good ground, such as the engine block.

3 Turn the ignition key to the On position. The warning light in the instrument panel should light.

4 If the warning light does not light, either the bulb is burned out or the electrical circuit is defective. Replace the bulb or repair the electrical circuit as necessary.

5 When the warning light functions correctly, turn the ignition switch off,

6 Disconnect the jumper wire and reconnect the wire to the switch terminal.

7 Make sure the master cylinder reservoirs are full, then attach a bleeder hose to one of the rear wheel bleeder valves and immerse the other end of the hose in a container partially filled with clean brake fluid.

8 Turn on the ignition switch.

9 Open the bleeder valve while a helper applies moderate pressure to the brake pedal. The brake warning light on the instrument panel should light.

10 Close the bleeder valve before the helper releases the brake pedal.

11 Reapply the brake pedal with moderate to heavy pressure. The brake warning light should go out.

12 Attach the bleeder hose to one of the front brake bleeder valves and repeat Steps 8 through 10. The warning light should react in the same manner as in Steps 8 and 10.

13 Turn off the ignition switch.

14 If the warning light did not come on in Steps 8 and 11, but does light when a jumper is connected to ground, the warning light switch portion of the combination valve is defective and the combination valve must be replaced (the components of the combination valve are not individually serviceable).

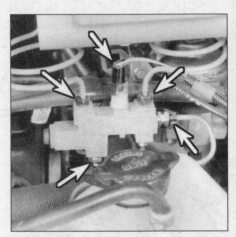

8.1 To test the pressure differential switch, unplug the electrical connector (upper arrow); to remove the combination valve, loosen the four threaded fittings (lower arrows) with a flare-nut wrench and detach the hydraulic lines

Replacement

15 Place a container under the combination valve and protect all painted surfaces with newspapers or rags.

16 To disconnect the hydraulic lines from the combination valve, use a flare-nut wrench to loosen the threaded fittings at the valve (see illustration 8.1). Plug the lines to prevent further loss of fluid and to protect the lines from contamination.

17 Disconnect the electrical connector from the pressure differential switch.

18 Remove the bolt holding the valve to the mounting bracket and remove the valve from the vehicle.

19 Installation is the reverse of the removal procedure.

20 Bleed the entire brake system (see Section 10).

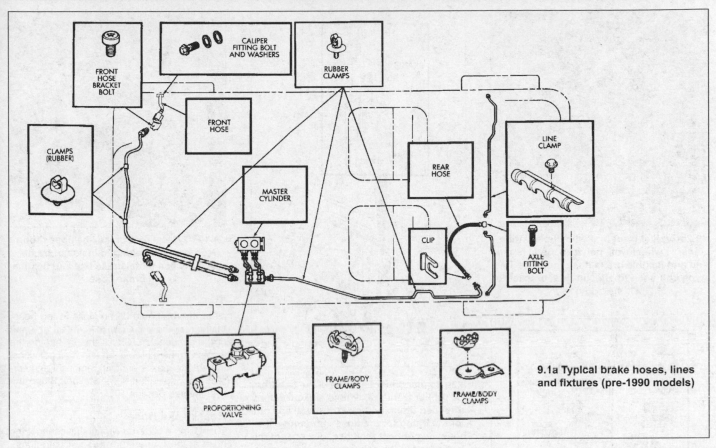

9.1a Typical brake hoses, lines and fixtures (pre-1990 models)

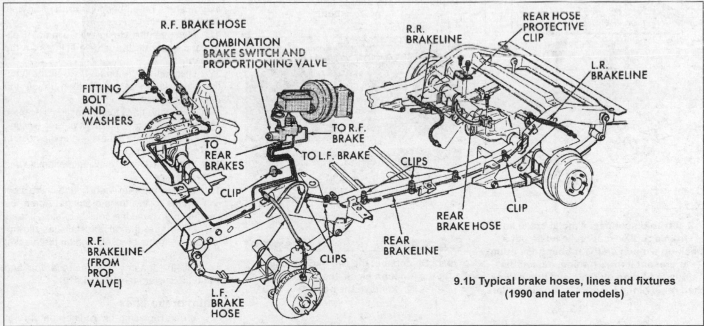

9.1b Typical brake hoses, lines and fixtures (1990 and later models)

9 Brake hoses and lines - inspection and replacement

Inspection

1   About every six months, with the vehicle raised and supported securely on jackstands, the rubber hoses (see illustrations) which con-nect the steel brake lines with the front and rear brake assemblies should be inspected for cracks, chafing of the outer cover, leaks, blisters and other damage. These are impor-tant and vulnerable parts of the brake system and inspection should be complete. A light and mirror will be helpful for a thorough check. If a hose exhibits any of the above conditions, replace it with a new one.

Replacement

Front brake hose

2   Disconnect the brake line from the hose fitting, being careful not to bend the frame bracket or brake line (see illustrations). Use a flare nut wrench, if you have one, to pro-tect the corners of the fitting from becoming rounded off.

9.2a Typical front brake line/hose fitting - inside wheel well, between metal brake line and flexible brake hose (note the Torx type bolt used to affix integral bracket to the body)

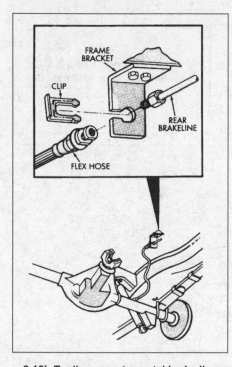

9.10b To disconnect a metal brake line from a rubber rear brake hose, put a back-up wrench on the rubber hose fitting to prevent it from turning, loosen the threaded fitting on the metal brake line, then remove the U-clip with a pair of pliers

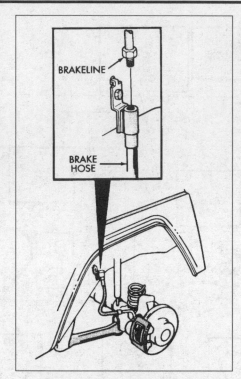

9.2b To disconnect a metal brake line from a rubber front brake hose, unscrew the threaded fitting and pull the metal line out of the fitting for the hose - to remove the hose, disconnect the hose, disconnect the banjo bolt at the caliper end, then remove the Torx bolt

9.12 Disconnect the two hydraulic lines at the junction block, then unbolt and remove the hose

9.10a Typical rear brake line/hose fitting - on bracket welded to inside of frame rail, between metal brake line and flexible brake hose

plete, there should be no kinks in the hose. Make sure the hose doesn't contact any part of the suspension. Check this by turning the wheels to the extreme left and right positions. If the hose makes contact, remove it and correct the installation as necessary. Bleed the system (see Section 10).

Rear brake hose

10   Using a back-up wrench, disconnect the hose at the frame bracket (see illustrations), being careful not to bend the bracket or steel lines.

11   Remove the U-clip with a pair of pliers and separate the female fitting from the bracket.

12   Disconnect the brake hose at the junction block (see illustration), then unbolt and remove the hose.

13   Attach the hose to the junction block and tighten the fitting securely. Without twisting the hose, install the female end of the hose in the frame bracket.

14   Install the U-clip retaining the female end to the bracket.

15   Using a back-up wrench, attach the steel line fittings to the female fittings. Again, be careful not to bend the bracket or steel line.

16   Make sure the hose installation did not loosen the frame bracket. Tighten the bracket if necessary.

17   Fill the master cylinder reservoir and bleed the system (see Section 10).

Metal brake lines

18   When replacing brake lines be sure to use the correct parts. Don't use copper tubing for any brake system components. Purchase steel brake lines from a dealer or auto parts store.

19   Prefabricated brake line, with the tube ends already flared and fittings installed, is available at auto parts stores and dealers. These lines are also bent to the proper shapes.

20   When installing the new line, make sure

3   Detach the integral hose bracket from the frame (you'll need a Torx drive socket of the correct size to remove the bracket bolts on some vehicles).

4   Remove the inlet fitting bolt from the brake caliper (see illustration 2.7a or 2.8a) and separate the hose from the caliper. Discard the sealing washers.

5   To install the hose, first attach it to the caliper, using new sealing washers on both sides of the fitting. Tighten the inlet fitting bolt

to the torque listed in this Chapter's Specifications.

6   Without twisting the hose, screw the brake line threaded fitting into the hose fitting, but don't tighten it yet.

7   Install the bolt which attaches the integral hose bracket to the frame and tighten it securely.

8   Tighten the brake line threaded fitting securely.

9   When the brake hose installation is com-

it's securely supported in the brackets and has plenty of clearance between moving or hot components.

21   After installation, check the master cylinder fluid level and add fluid as necessary. Bleed the brake system as outlined in the next Section and test the brakes carefully before driving the vehicle in traffic.

10   Brake system bleeding

Warning: *Wear eye protection when bleeding the brake system. If the fluid comes in contact with your eyes, immediately rinse them with water and seek medical attention.*
Note: *Bleeding the hydraulic system is necessary to remove any air that manages to find its way into the system when it's been opened during removal and installation of a hose, line, caliper or master cylinder.*

1   It will probably be necessary to bleed the system at all four brakes if air has entered the system due to low fluid level, or if the brake lines have been disconnected at the master cylinder.
2   If a brake line was disconnected only at a wheel, then only that caliper or wheel cylinder must be bled.
3   If a brake line is disconnected at a fitting located between the master cylinder and any of the brakes, that part of the system served by the disconnected line must be bled.
4   Remove any residual vacuum from the brake power booster by applying the brake several times with the engine off.
5   Remove the master cylinder reservoir cover and fill the reservoir with brake fluid. Reinstall the cover.
Note: *Check the fluid level often during the bleeding operation and add fluid as necessary to prevent the fluid level from falling low enough to allow air bubbles into the master cylinder.*
6   Have an assistant on hand, as well as a supply of new brake fluid, a clear container partially filled with clean brake fluid, a length of 3/16-inch plastic, rubber or vinyl hose to fit over the bleeder valve and a wrench to open and close the bleeder valve.
7   Beginning at the right rear wheel, loosen the bleeder valve slightly, then tighten it to a point where it is snug but can still be loosened quickly and easily.
8   Place one end of the hose over the bleeder valve and submerge the other end in brake fluid in the container (see illustration).
9   Have the assistant pump the brakes slowly a few times to get pressure in the system, then hold the pedal firmly depressed.
10   While the pedal is held depressed, open the bleeder valve just enough to allow a flow of fluid to leave the valve. Watch for air bubbles to exit the submerged end of the tube. When the fluid flow slows after a couple of seconds, close the valve and have your assistant release the pedal.
11   Repeat Steps 9 and 10 until no more air is seen leaving the tube, then tighten the bleeder valve and proceed to the left rear

10.8 When bleeding the brakes, a hose is connected to the bleeder valve at the caliper or wheel cylinder and then submerged in brake fluid. Air will be seen as bubbles in the tube and container. All air must be expelled before moving to the next wheel.

wheel, the right front wheel and the left front wheel, in that order, and perform the same procedure. Be sure to check the fluid in the master cylinder reservoir frequently.
12   Never use old brake fluid. It contains moisture which will deteriorate the brake system components.
13   Refill the master cylinder with fluid at the end of the operation.
14   Check the operation of the brakes. The pedal should feel solid when depressed, with no sponginess. If necessary, repeat the entire process.
Warning: *Do not operate the vehicle if you are in doubt about the effectiveness of the brake system.*

11   Power brake booster - check, removal and installation

Operating check

1   Depress the brake pedal several times with the engine off and make sure that there is no change in the pedal reserve distance.
2   Depress the pedal and start the engine. If the pedal goes down slightly, operation is normal.

Airtightness check

3   Start the engine and turn it off after one or two minutes. Depress the brake pedal several times slowly. If the pedal goes down farther the first time but gradually rises after the second or third depression, the booster is airtight.
4   Depress the brake pedal while the engine is running, then stop the engine with the pedal depressed. If there is no change in the pedal reserve travel after holding the pedal for 30 seconds, the booster is airtight.

11.9a Unplug the electrical connector from the brake light switch (arrow) - if the vehicle is a pre-1991 model, remove the two booster pushrod nuts (arrows) and slide out the pushrod bolt; BE SURE TO NOTE WHICH SIDE OF THE BOLT IS INSERTED FROM - YOU MUST INSERT IT FROM THE SAME DIRECTION DURING REASSEMBLY OR THE BRAKE PEDAL COULD BIND

Removal

5   Power brake booster units should not be disassembled. They require special tools not normally found in most service stations or shops. They are fairly complex and because of their critical relationship to brake performance it is best to replace a defective booster unit with a new or rebuilt one.
6   To remove the booster, first unbolt the brake master cylinder from the booster (see Section 7) and carefully pull it forward.
7   Disconnect the vacuum hose leading from the engine to the booster. Be careful not to damage the hose when removing it from the booster fitting.
8   Locate the pushrod connecting the booster to the brake pedal, underneath the dash.
9   Unplug the brake light switch wire connector (see illustration) and, on pre-1991 models, remove the pushrod bolt nuts and pull out the bolt. Discard the bolt and nuts. On 1991 and later models, the pushrod is attached to a small stud on the brake pedal and secured to the stud with a retaining clip. Remove this clip (see illustration).
10   Remove the four nuts holding the brake booster to the firewall (see illustrations). You may need a light to see these nuts - they're located fairly high up the firewall, under the dash. On 2007 and later models, the booster is mounted to an adapter plate, which is secured to the engine side of the firewall with four nuts; there are no fasteners on the interior side of the firewall.
11   Slide the booster straight out from the firewall until the bolts clear the holes and remove the booster assembly, bracket and spacer gasket(s).
12   Detach the old booster assembly from

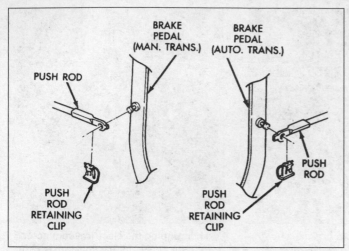

11.9b On 1991 and later models, the booster pushrod is secured to the brake pedal assembly with a retaining clip instead of nuts (note that the pushrod is attached to the left side of the pedal on manual transmission models and the right side on automatic transmission models)

11.10a These four bolts attach the brake booster bracket to the firewall, but you have to remove the nuts for these bolts from inside the vehicle, up under the dash

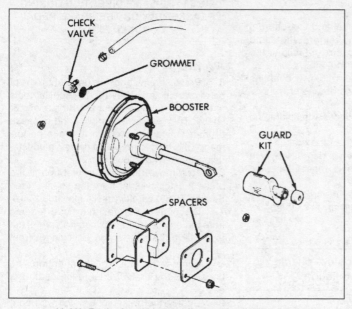

11.10b Brake booster installation details (typical)

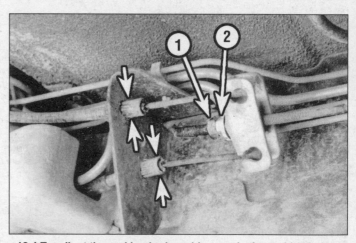

12.4 To adjust the parking brake cables, apply the parking brake, loosen the equalizer locknut (1) and - holding the equalizer rod with a pair of locking pliers to prevent it from turning - turn the adjuster nut (2) until the cable tension is fairly taut; when you're satisfied that the cable tension is correct, tighten the locknut; if you're replacing either rear cable, you'll have to compress the cable housing retainer tangs (arrows) to free the cable from the bracket

the mounting bracket and install the bracket onto the new booster unit. Tighten the mounting nuts securely.

Installation

13   Installation procedures are basically the reverse of those for removal. Don't forget to reinstall the spacer gasket(s) between the booster mounting bracket and the firewall. Tighten the pushrod nuts, booster mounting nuts and the master cylinder mounting nuts to the torque listed in this Chapter's Specifications.
Warning: *On pre-1991 models, when you install the bolt that attaches the booster pushrod to the brake pedal, insert it from the same side as it was originally installed (usually from the right side on manual transmission models*

and from the left side on automatic transmission models). And make sure the bolt passes through the brake pedal first, THEN the pushrod on these models.

12   Parking brake - adjustment

1   The adjustment of the parking brake, often overlooked or put off by many motorists, is actually a fairly critical adjustment. If the parking brake cables are too slack, the brake won't hold the vehicle on an incline - if they're too tight, the brakes may drag, causing them to wear prematurely. Another detrimental side effect of a tightly adjusted parking brake cable is the restriction of the automatic adjuster

assembly on the rear drum brakes, which will not allow them to function properly.
2   The first step in adjusting slack parking brake cables is to ensure the correct adjustment of the rear drum brakes. This can be accomplished by making a series of forward and reverse stops, which will bring the brake shoes into proper relationship with the brake drums.
3   Fully apply and release the parking brake four or five times, then set the parking brake lever or pedal to the fifth notch.
4   Raise the rear of the vehicle and support it securely on jackstands. While holding the equalizer rod with a pair of locking pliers, loosen the equalizer locknut and turn the equalizer adjuster nut (see illustration) until the cables are fairly taut.

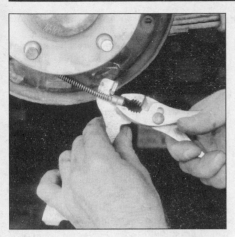

13.3 To disconnect the cable end from the parking brake lever, pull back on the return spring and maneuver the cable out of the slot in the lever

13.4 Compress the retainer tangs (arrows) to free the cable and housing from the brake support plate

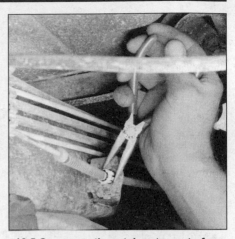

13.5 Compress the retainer tangs to free the cable and housing from the frame bracket

5   Release the parking brake and apply it, making sure it travels five to seven clicks. If it travels too far, tighten the adjuster nut a little more. If the travel is less than five clicks, the locknut will have to be loosened.

6   After the parking brake has been properly adjusted, tighten the locknut, then place the handle or pedal in the released position and rotate the rear wheels, making sure the brakes don't drag.

7   Lower the vehicle and test the operation of the parking brake on an incline.

13   Parking brake cables - replacement

1   Release the parking brake. Loosen the rear wheel lug nuts, raise the rear of the vehicle and support it securely on jackstands.

2   Remove the rear wheel and brake drum (or caliper and disc). Loosen the equalizer nut fully (see illustration 12.4).

3   On drum-brake models, following the procedure in Section 5, remove the brake shoes, then disconnect the parking brake cable end from the parking brake lever (see illustration).

4   Compress the cable housing retainer tangs at the brake support plate (see illustration) and push the cable and housing through the backing plate or bracket. On disc-brake models, unhook the cable end from the actuator lever.

5   Compress the cable housing retainer tang at the bracket on the frame (see illustration) and pry the housing out of the frame bracket, then compress the cable housing retainer tang at the bracket right behind the equalizer and slide the forward end of the cable out of its slot in the equalizer (see illustration 12.4).

6   Installation is the reverse of the removal procedure. Be sure to adjust the parking brake as described in Section 12.

14   Brake light switch - replacement

1   Disconnect the cable from the negative terminal of the battery.

2011 and earlier models

2   From under the dash, unplug the brake light switch electrical connector and remove the pushrod bolt (pre-1991 models) or the retaining clip (1991 and later models) (see Section 11). Remove the brake light switch, noting the positions of the bushings, spacers and sleeves (see illustrations).

3   Lubricate the switch bushings, spacers and sleeves with a light coat of multi-purpose

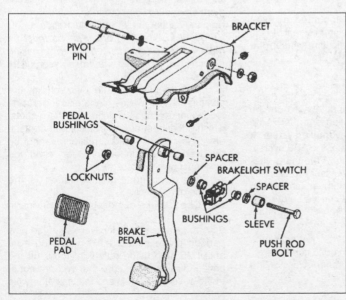

14.2a An exploded view of the non-adjustable brake light switch assembly on pre-1991 models

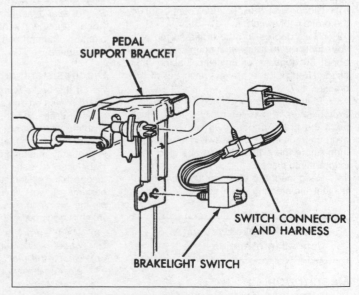

14.2b An exploded view of the adjustable brake light switch assembly used on 1991 and later models

grease and position the switch against the brake pedal. Install the pushrod bolt and nuts or retaining clip (see Section 11). On pre-1991 models, be sure to tighten the nuts to the torque listed in this Chapter's Specifications.

4   Plug in the electrical connector and reconnect the battery.

5   On pre-1991 models, the switch is not adjustable. On 1991 and later models, it is adjustable.

6   To check the switch adjustment on 1991 and later models, move the brake pedal forward by hand and watch the switch plunger. It should be fully extended at the point at which pedal freeplay is taken up and brake application begins. A clearance of about 1/8-inch should exist between the plunger and the pedal at this point.

7   If the plunger-to-pedal clearance is correct and the brake lights are operating, no adjustment is necessary. If the plunger doesn't fully extend and the clearance between the pedal and switch barrel is insufficient, adjust the switch.

Note: *On 2007 and later models, if the brake-light switch is removed, it can not be reused. A new switch must be installed.*

8   To adjust the switch, grasp the brake pedal and pull it to the rear as far as possible. The switch plunger barrel will "ratchet" to the rear in its retaining clip to the correct position. Measure the plunger-to-pedal clearance to make sure it's correct and verify that the brake lights are still operating correctly.

Warning: *Make SURE the brake pedal returns to its fully released position after adjustment. The switch can interfere with full pedal return if it's too far forward, resulting in dragging brakes caused by partial brake application.*

2012 and later models

9   Disconnect the negative battery cable from the battery terminal.

10   Remove the steering column covers (see Chapter 11).

11   Disconnect the electrical connector to the brake light switch.

12   While depressing the brake switch with your foot, rotate the switch counterclockwise about 30 degrees or until the locking tabs align. Then pull the brake switch out of the bracket.

13   To install, be sure to have the brake light switch lever arm extended out fully. Then push the brake pedal down with your foot, align the tabs to the brake switch and bracket then rotate the switch 30 degrees clockwise to lock it into place.

14   Reconnect the electrical connector and reinstall the steering wheel covers.

15 Anti-lock Brake System (ABS) - general information

Description

1   Some 1994 models have an Anti-lock Brake System (ABS) designed to maintain vehicle maneuverability, directional stability and optimum deceleration under severe braking conditions on most road surfaces. It does so by monitoring the rotational speed of all four wheels and controlling the brake line pressure to all four wheels during braking. This prevents the wheels from locking up prematurely during hard braking.

Components

Pump

2   The pump, which is driven by an electric motor, provides high-pressure brake fluid to the hydraulic assembly, where it is stored in the hydraulic bladder accumulator.

Hydraulic assembly

3   The integral hydraulic assembly includes a booster/master cylinder, modulator, hydraulic bladder accumulator and fluid reservoir. Basically, the assembly regulates hydraulic pressure (stored in the accumulator) to meet the demands of the braking system. The hydraulic assembly is located on the fenderwell on the driver's side of the vehicle.

Electronic control unit

4   The electronic control unit is mounted to the right of the steering column under the dash and is the "brain" for the system. The function of the control unit is to accept and process information received from the wheel speed sensors to control the hydraulic line pressure, avoiding wheel lock up. The control unit also constantly monitors the system, even under normal driving conditions, to find faults with the system.

5   If a problem develops within the system, the brake warning light will glow on the dashboard. A diagnostic code will also be stored, which, when retrieved by a service technician, will indicate the problem area or component.

Wheel speed sensors

6   A speed sensor is mounted at each wheel. The speed sensors send signals to the electronic control unit, indicating wheel rotational speed.

Diagnosis and repair

7   If the brake warning light on the dashboard comes on and stays on, make sure the parking brake is not applied and there's no problem with the brake hydraulic system. If neither of these is the cause, the ABS system is probably malfunctioning. Although a special electronic tester is necessary to properly diagnose the system, the home mechanic can perform a few preliminary checks before taking the vehicle to a dealer service department which is equipped with this tester.

    a) *Make sure the brakes, calipers and wheel cylinders are in good condition.*

    b) *Check the electrical connectors at the electronic control unit.*

    c) *Check the fuses.*

    d) *Follow the wiring harness to the speed sensors and brake light switch and make sure all connections are secure and the wiring isn't damaged.*

8   If the above preliminary checks don't rectify the problem, the vehicle should be diagnosed by a dealer service department.

16 Parking brake shoes (rear disc brakes) - replacement

Warning: *Dust created by the brake system is harmful to your health. Never blow it out with compressed air and don't inhale any of it. An approved filtering mask should be worn when working on the brakes. Do not, under any circumstances, use petroleum-based solvents to clean brake parts. Use brake system cleaner only!*

1   Loosen the wheel lug nuts, release the parking brake, raise the rear of the vehicle and support it securely on jackstands. Block the front wheels to keep the vehicle from rolling. Remove the rear wheels.

2   Remove the rear brake calipers (don't disconnect the hoses). Hang them with a length of wire.

3   Remove the wheel stud clips and slide the rear brake discs off the studs.

Note: *If the brake disc cannot be easily pulled off the axle and shoe assembly, make sure that the parking brake is completely released, then apply some penetrating oil at the hub-to-disc joint. Allow the oil to soak in and try to pull the disc off.*

4   Remove the center console (see Chapter 11). Pull the parking brake cable up (see illustration). Move the spring until the two tabs pass each other and then insert a screwdriver into the side hole. Release the tension on the spring.

5   Clean the parking brake shoe assembly with brake system cleaner then follow the accompanying illustrations (16.5a through 16.5o) for the parking brake shoe replacement procedure. Be sure to stay in order and read the caption under each illustration.

Note: *All four parking brake shoes must be replaced at the same time, but to avoid mixing up parts, work on only one brake assembly at a time.*

6   Before installing the disc, check the parking brake surfaces of the disc for cracks, score marks, deep scratches and hard spots, which will appear as small discolored areas. If any of the above listed conditions cannot be removed with sandpaper or emery cloth, the disc must be replaced.

7   The remainder of installation is the reverse of removal.

8   Check brake operation before driving in traffic.

9   To increase the effectiveness of the new parking brake shoes, make one stop from about 25 mph using only light force on the parking brake. Make sure that you are not in traffic while you do this and that it is otherwise safe.

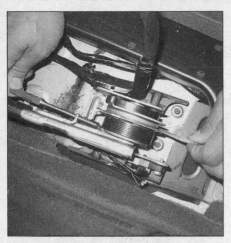

16.4 Pull the cable up as shown, then place a punch or screwdriver in the hole

16.5a Pushing on the pin from the backing plate side with your finger, pry the front hold-down clip loose, then pull the pin out

16.5b Remove the rear hold-down clip and pin the same way

16.5c Disengage the lower spring from the parking brake shoes

16.5d Remove the adjuster

16.5e Disengage the upper spring from the rear parking brake shoe

16.5f Remove both parking brake shoes

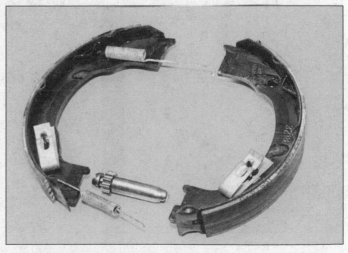

16.5g Here's how the shoes, springs and adjuster go together

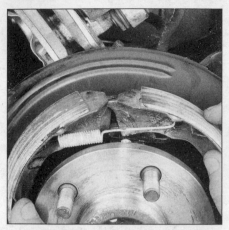

16.5h Holding them together with the upper spring, install the new shoes

16.5i Spread the upper ends of the shoes apart and engage them with the anchor as shown

16.5j Install the adjuster

16.5k Make sure the adjuster is engaged with the shoes as shown

16.5l Install the lower spring

16.5m Make sure the coils of the lower spring are facing down, away from the adjuster

16.5n Install the rear pin and hold-down clip as shown, with the head of the pin firmly seated into the lower, smaller part of the hole in the clip

16.5o Install the front pin and hold-down clip the same way

17   Troubleshooting

PROBABLE CAUSE	CORRECTIVE ACTION

No brakes - pedal travels to floor

1 Low fluid level 2 Air in system	1 and 2 Low fluid level and air in the system are symptoms of another problem a leak somewhere in the hydraulic system. Locate and repair the leak
3 Defective seals in master cylinder	3 Replace master cylinder
4 Fluid overheated and vaporized due to heavy braking	4 Bleed hydraulic system (temporary fix). Replace brake fluid (proper fix)

Brake pedal slowly travels to floor under braking or at a stop

1 Defective seals in master cylinder	1 Replace master cylinder
2 Leak in a hose, line, caliper or wheel cylinder	2 Locate and repair leak
3 Air in hydraulic system	3 Bleed the system, inspect system for a leak

Brake pedal feels spongy when depressed

1 Air in hydraulic system	1 Bleed the system, inspect system for a leak
2 Master cylinder or power booster loose	2 Tighten fasteners
3 Brake fluid overheated (beginning to boil)	3 Bleed the system (temporary fix). Replace the brake fluid (proper fix)
4 Deteriorated brake hoses (ballooning under pressure)	4 Inspect hoses, replace as necessary (it's a good idea to replace all of them if one hose shows signs of deterioration)

Brake pedal feels hard when depressed and/or excessive effort required to stop vehicle

1 Power booster faulty	1 Replace booster
2 Engine not producing sufficient vacuum, or hose to booster clogged collapsed or cracked	2 Check vacuum to booster with a vacuum gauge. Replace hose if cracked or clogged, repair engine if vacuum is extremely low
3 Brake linings contaminated by grease or brake fluid	3 Locate and repair source of contamination, replace brake pads or shoes
4 Brake linings glazed	4 Replace brake pads or shoes, check discs and drums for glazing, service as necessary
5 Caliper piston(s) or wheel cylinder(s) binding or frozen	5 Replace calipers or wheel cylinders
6 Brakes wet	6 Apply pedal to boil-off water (this should only be a momentary problem)
7 Kinked, clogged or internally split brake hose or line	7 Inspect lines and hoses, replace as necessary

Excessive brake pedal travel (but will pump up)

1 Drum brakes out of adjustment	1 Adjust brakes
2 Air in hydraulic system	2 Bleed system, inspect system for a leak

Excessive brake pedal travel (but will not pump up)

1 Master cylinder pushrod misadjusted	1 Adjust pushrod
2 Master cylinder seals defective	2 Replace master cylinder
3 Brake linings worn out	3 Inspect brakes, replace pads and/or shoes
4 Hydraulic system leak	4 Locate and repair leak

Brake pedal doesn't return

1 Brake pedal binding	1 Inspect pivot bushing and pushrod, repair or lubricate
2 Defective master cylinder	2 Replace master cylinder

Troubleshooting (continued)

PROBABLE CAUSE	CORRECTIVE ACTION

Brake pedal pulsates during brake application

1 Brake drums out-of-round	1 Have drums machined by an automotive machine shop
2 Excessive brake disc runout or disc surfaces out-of-parallel	2 Have discs machined by an automotive machine shop
3 Loose or worn wheel bearings	3 Adjust or replace wheel bearings
4 Loose lug nuts	4 Tighten lug nuts

Brakes slow to release

1 Malfunctioning power booster	1 Replace booster
2 Pedal linkage binding	2 Inspect pedal pivot bushing and pushrod, repair/lubricate
3 Malfunctioning proportioning valve	3 Replace proportioning valve
4 Sticking caliper or wheel cylinder	4 Repair or replace calipers or wheel cylinders
5 Kinked or internally split brake hose	5 Locate and replace faulty brake hose

Brakes grab (one or more wheels)

1 Grease or brake fluid on brake lining	1 Locate and repair cause of contamination, replace lining
2 Brake lining glazed	2 Replace lining, deglaze disc or drum

Vehicle pulls to one side during braking

1 Grease or brake fluid on brake lining	1 Locate and repair cause of contamination, replace lining
2 Brake lining glazed	2 Deglaze or replace lining, deglaze disc or drum
3 Restricted brake line or hose	3 Repair line or replace hose
4 Tire pressures incorrect	4 Adjust tire pressures
5 Caliper or wheel cylinder sticking	5 Repair or replace calipers or wheel cylinders
6 Wheels out of alignment	6 Have wheels aligned
7 Weak suspension spring	7 Replace springs
8 Weak or broken shock absorber	8 Replace shock absorbers

Brakes drag (indicated by sluggish engine performance or wheels being very hot after driving)

1 Brake pedal pushrod incorrectly adjusted	1 Adjust pushrod
2 Master cylinder pushrod (between booster and master cylinder)	2 Adjust pushrod incorrectly adjusted
3 Obstructed compensating port in master cylinder	3 Replace master cylinder
4 Master cylinder piston seized in bore	4 Replace master cylinder
5 Contaminated fluid causing swollen seals throughout system	5 Flush system, replace all hydraulic components
6 Clogged brake lines or internally split brake hose(s)	6 Flush hydraulic system, replace defective hose(s)
7 Sticking caliper(s) or wheel cylinder(s)	7 Replace calipers or wheel cylinders
8 Parking brake not releasing	8 Inspect parking brake linkage and parking brake mechanism, repair as required
9 Improper shoe-to-drum clearance	9 Adjust brake shoes
10 Faulty proportioning valve	10 Replace proportioning valve

PROBABLE CAUSE	CORRECTIVE ACTION

Brakes fade (due to excessive heat)

1 Brake linings excessively worn or glazed	1 Deglaze or replace brake pads and/or shoes
2 Excessive use of brakes	2 Downshift into a lower gear, maintain a constant slower speed (going down hills)
3 Vehicle overloaded	3 Reduce load
4 Brake drums or discs worn too thin	4 Measure drum diameter and disc thickness, replace drums or discs as required
5 Contaminated brake fluid	5 Flush system, replace fluid
6 Brakes drag	6 Repair cause of dragging brakes
7 Driver resting left foot on brake pedal	7 Don't ride the brakes

Brakes noisy (high-pitched squeal)

1 Glazed lining	1 Deglaze or replace lining
2 Contaminated lining (brake fluid, grease, etc.)	2 Repair source of contamination, replace linings
3 Weak or broken brake shoe hold-down or return spring	3 Replace springs
4 Rivets securing lining to shoe or backing plate loose	4 Replace shoes or pads
5 Excessive dust buildup on brake linings	5 Wash brakes off with brake system cleaner
6 Brake drums worn too thin	6 Measure diameter of drums, replace if necessary
7 Wear indicator on disc brake pads contacting disc	7 Replace brake pads
8 Anti-squeal shims missing or installed improperly	8 Install shims correctly

Brakes noisy (scraping sound)

1 Brake pads or shoes worn out; rivets, backing plate or brake	1 Replace linings, have discs and/or drums machined (or replace) shoe metal contacting disc or drum

Brakes chatter

1 Worn brake lining	1 Inspect brakes, replace shoes or pads as necessary
2 Glazed or scored discs or drums	2 Deglaze discs or drums with sandpaper (if glazing is severe, machining will be required)
3 Drums or discs heat checked	3 Check discs and/or drums for hard spots, heat checking, etc. Have discs/drums machined or replace them
4 Disc runout or drum out-of-round excessive	4 Measure disc runout and/or drum out-of-round, have discs or drums machined or replace them
5 Loose or worn wheel bearings	5 Adjust or replace wheel bearings
6 Loose or bent brake backing plate (drum brakes)	6 Tighten or replace backing plate
7 Grooves worn in discs or drums	7 Have discs or drums machined, if within limits (if not, replace them)
8 Brake linings contaminated (brake fluid, grease, etc.)	8 Locate and repair source of contamination, replace pads or shoes
9 Excessive dust buildup on linings	9 Wash brakes with brake system cleaner
10 Surface finish on discs or drums too rough after machining	10 Have discs or drums properly machined (especially on vehicles with sliding calipers)
11 Brake pads or shoes glazed	11 Deglaze or replace brake pads or shoes

Brake pads or shoes click

1 Shoe support pads on brake backing plate grooved or	1 Replace brake backing plate excessively worn
2 Brake pads loose in caliper	2 Loose pad retainers or anti-rattle clips
3 Also see items listed under Brakes chatter	

Troubleshooting (continued)

PROBABLE CAUSE	CORRECTIVE ACTION

Brakes make groaning noise at end of stop

PROBABLE CAUSE	CORRECTIVE ACTION
1 Brake pads and/or shoes worn out	1 Replace pads and/or shoes
2 Brake linings contaminated (brake fluid, grease, etc.)	2 Locate and repair cause of contamination, replace brake pads or shoes
3 Brake linings glazed	3 Deglaze or replace brake pads or shoes
4 Excessive dust buildup on linings	4 Wash brakes with brake system cleaner
5 Scored or heat-checked discs or drums	5 Inspect discs/drums, have machined if within limits (if not, replace discs or drums)
6 Broken or missing brake shoe attaching hardware	6 Inspect drum brakes, replace missing hardware

Rear brakes lock up under light brake application

PROBABLE CAUSE	CORRECTIVE ACTION
1 Tire pressures too high	1 Adjust tire pressures
2 Tires excessively worn	2 Replace tires
3 Defective proportioning valve	3 Replace proportioning valve

Brake warning light on instrument panel comes on (or stays on)

PROBABLE CAUSE	CORRECTIVE ACTION
1 Low fluid level in master cylinder reservoir (reservoirs with fluid level sensor)	1 Add fluid, inspect system for leak, check the thickness of the brake pads and shoes
2 Failure in one half of the hydraulic system	2 Inspect hydraulic system for a leak
3 Piston in pressure differential warning valve not centered	3 Center piston by bleeding one circuit or the other (close bleeder valve as soon as the light goes out)
4 Defective pressure differential valve or warning switch	4 Replace valve or switch
5 Air in the hydraulic system	5 Bleed the system, check for leaks
6 Brake pads worn out (vehicles with electric wear sensors - small	6 Replace brake pads (and sensors) probes that fit into the brake pads and ground out on the disc when the pads get thin)

Brakes do not self adjust

Disc brakes

PROBABLE CAUSE	CORRECTIVE ACTION
1 Defective caliper piston seals	1 Replace calipers. Also, possible contaminated fluid causing soft or swollen seals (flush system and fill with new fluid if in doubt)
2 Corroded caliper piston(s)	2 Same as above

Drum brakes

PROBABLE CAUSE	CORRECTIVE ACTION
1 Adjuster screw frozen	1 Remove adjuster, disassemble, clean and lubricate with high-temperature grease
2 Adjuster lever does not contact star wheel or is binding	2 Inspect drum brakes, assemble correctly or clean or replace parts as required
3 Adjusters mixed up (installed on wrong wheels after brake job)	3 Reassemble correctly
4 Adjuster cable broken or installed incorrectly (cable-type adjusters)	4 Install new cable or assemble correctly

Rapid brake lining wear

PROBABLE CAUSE	CORRECTIVE ACTION
1 Driver resting left foot on brake pedal	1 Don't ride the brakes
2 Surface finish on discs or drums too rough	2 Have discs or drums properly machined
3 Also see Brakes drag	

Chapter 10
Suspension and steering systems

Contents

Specifications

Torque specifications

Ft-lbs (unless otherwise indicated)

Note: *One foot-pound (ft-lb) of torque is equivalent to 12 inch-pounds (in-lbs) of torque. Torque values below approximately 15 ft-lbs are expressed in inch-pounds, since most foot-pound torque wrenches are not accurate at these smaller values.*

Front suspension (1995 and earlier models)

Leaf spring
- Spring eye-to-shackle bolt nuts ... 95
- Spring eye-to-frame bracket bolt nuts ... 105
- Tie plate U-bolt nuts ... 90

Shock absorber
- Upper nut ... 45
- Lower eye bolt nut ... 45

Stabilizer bar
- Stabilizer bar-to-link bolt nut ... 45
- Stabilizer bar-to-frame bracket nuts ... 30
- Stabilizer bar link-to-tie plate nut ... 45

Track bar
- Axle bracket nut
  - 1987 through 1993 ... 74
  - 1994 ... 125
  - 1995 ... 105
- Frame bracket nut
  - 1987 through 1994 ... 125
  - 1995 ... 105

Steering knuckle-to-axle balljoint stud nuts ... 100

Torque specifications (continued)   **Ft-lbs (unless otherwise indicated)**

Note: *One foot-pound (ft-lb) of torque is equivalent to 12 inch-pounds (in-lbs) of torque. Torque values below approximately 15 ft-lbs are expressed in inch-pounds, since most foot-pound torque wrenches are not accurate at these smaller values.*

Front suspension (1997 and later models)

Shock absorber
  Upper nut
    1995 and earlier models .... 108 in-lbs
    1997 through 2006 models... 17
    2007 and later models 20
  Lower nuts
    1995 and earlier models 45
    1997 through 2006 models... 21
    2007 through 2010 models... 56
    2011 and 2012 models 65
    2013 and later models 72
Stabilizer bar
  Stabilizer bar bushing clamp bolts 45
  Stabilizer bar link upper nut
    2006 and earlier models 45
    2007 and later models 75
  Stabilizer bar lower link bolt 75
Suspension arm bolts and nuts
  Upper arm, both ends
    2006 and earlier models 55
    2007 and later models 75
  Lower arm
    Axle bracket nut
      2003 and earlier models.. 85
      2004 through 2006 models.. 130
      2007 and later models
        Original, without caster adjusting kit................................ 125
        With caster adjusting kit installed 63
    Frame bracket nut... 130
Track bar
  Ball stud-to-frame bracket nut
    2006 and earlier models 65
    2007 and later models 125
  Bolt/nut at axle housing bracket
    2002 and earlier models 55
    2003 through 2006 models... 40
    2007 and later models 125
Steering knuckle balljoint nuts
  2006 and earlier models
    Upper.. 75
    Lower.. 80
  2007 and later models... 70

Rear suspension (1995 and earlier models)

Leaf spring
  Spring-to-shackle bolt nuts.. 95
  Spring-to-frame bracket bolt nuts.. 105
  Tie plate U-bolt nuts.. 90
Shock absorber nuts.. 44
Track bar nuts.. 125

Rear suspension (1997 and later models)

Shock absorber
  Upper bolts
    2006 and earlier models 23
    2007 and later models 37
  Lower nut
    2006 and earlier models 74
    2007 and later models 56
Stabilizer bar
  Stabilizer-to-link nut
    2006 and earlier models 40
    2007 and later models 66
  Stabilizer bushing clamp bolts... 45

Torque specifications (continued)   Ft-lbs (unless otherwise indicated)

Note: *One foot-pound (ft-lb) of torque is equivalent to 12 inch-pounds (in-lbs) of torque. Torque values below approximately 15 ft-lbs are expressed in inch-pounds, since most foot-pound torque wrenches are not accurate at these smaller values.*

Rear suspension (1997 and later models) (continued)
Suspension arm bolts and nuts
    Upper arms (both ends)
        2006 and earlier models 55
        2007 and later models 125
    Lower arm (both ends)
        2003 and earlier models 103
        2004 through 2006 models 150
        2007 and later models 125
Track bar bolts/nuts
    2006 and earlier models 74
    2007 and later models 125

Steering
Airbag module arming screw (1995 models) .... 10 to 15 in-lbs
Airbag module-to-steering wheel
    Nuts (1995 models) .... 100 in-lbs
    Screws (1997 through 2006 models) .... 90 in-lbs
    Screws (2011 and later models) .... 120 in-lbs
    Steering wheel nut
        1995 and earlier 25
        1997 and later 40
Intermediate shaft pinch bolt
    2006 and earlier models 33
    2007 and later models 36
Steering gear mounting bolts
    1995 and earlier models 65
    1997 through 2006 models 70
    2007 and later models 87
Pitman arm-to-Pitman arm shaft nut 185
Drag link-to-Pitman arm nut
    2006 and earlier models 60
    2007 and later models 77
Drag link clamp bolts/nuts
    2000 and earlier models 36
    2007 and later models 26
Drag link ballstud nuts, 2006 and earlier models 55
Drag link-to-tie rod nut, early models 35
Drag link-to-knuckle nut, 2007 and later models 63
Steering damper lock nut
    2003 and earlier models 30
    2004 through 2006 models 55
    2007 and later models 63
Tie-rod-to-steering knuckle nuts
    2006 and earlier models 35
    2007 and later models 63
Tie-rod adjustment sleeve clamp bolt nut
    2006 and earlier models .... 168 in-lbs
    2007 and later models 45
Steering damper-to-tie-rod nut 53
Steering damper-to-axle bracket bolt 55
Wheel lug nuts .... See Chapter 1

1.1 Front suspension and steering components (1987 through 1995 models)

1	Drag link end	8	Pitman arm	15	Shift motor
2	Stabilizer bar clamp	9	Leaf spring	16	Shock absorber
3	Stabilizer bar	10	Tie rod adjustment sleeve	17	Stabilizer bar-to-leaf spring bracket
4	Drag link	11	Leaf spring bracket and U-bolts		connecting link
5	Track bar	12	Tie rod	18	Steering knuckle
6	Steering gear	13	Front axle assembly	19	Lower balljoint
7	Leaf spring shackles	14	Steering damper		

1 General information and precautions

1   The front suspension on 1987 through 1995 models (see illustration) consists of a solid front axle, suspended by two semi-elliptic, multi-leaf springs and a pair of hydraulic shock absorbers. The leaf springs are attached to the axle by U-bolts and tie plates which are positioned by spring saddles welded to the axle tubes. The rear end of each spring is attached to a frame bracket with a bolts and nut; the front end of each spring is attached to a pair of shackle plates with a nut and bolt. A rubber bushing, pressed into the ends of the springs, acts as an insulator between the spring and the bolt. Clips are bolted to the springs to align the leafs with each other and keep them together.

A stabilizer bar reduces body roll and a track bar prevents lateral movement.

2   The rear suspension on 1987 through 1995 models (see illustration) is virtually identical to the front: It also uses a solid rear axle, two semi-elliptic, multi-leaf springs and a pair of shock absorbers. The springs are attached to the axle and the frame in identical fashion to the front setup. Again, a track bar prevents lateral movement. However, no stabilizer bar is employed at the rear.

3   On 1997 and later models, the front axle is suspended by a pair of shock absorbers and two coil springs. Four control arms allow the axle to move vertically; a track bar prevents lateral movement. A stabilizer bar controls body roll. Each steering knuckle is positioned by a pair of balljoints pressed into the upper and lower ends of a yoke welded to

the end of the axle. The rear suspension on 1997 and later models is virtually identical to the front suspension (see illustrations).

4   Steering is either manual or power-assisted. An intermediate shaft connects the steering column to a recirculating-ball type steering gearbox. The steering gear transmits turning motion through a pitman arm to a drag link attached to a tie rod. The ends of the tie rod are connected to the steering knuckles. All steering linkage connections - pitman arm to drag link, drag link to tie rod and tie rod to steering knuckles - are balljoints. The steering knuckles themselves are also attached to the axle with upper and lower balljoints. A steering damper between the frame and the tie rod reduces "bump steer" (the slight turning of a wheel away from its normal direction of travel as it moves through its suspension travel).

1.2 Rear suspension components (1987 through 1995 models)

1	Leaf spring shackle	3	Track bar	5	Shock absorber
2	Leaf spring	4	Rear axle assembly	6	Leaf spring bracket and U-bolts

1.3a Front suspension and steering components (1997 and later 4WD models)

1	Stabilizer bar	7	Track bar	12	Lower yoke-to-steering knuckle balljoint
2	Stabilizer bar link	8	Lower suspension arm (upper arms		(upper balljoints not visible in this photo)
3	Coil spring		not visible in this photo)	13	Axleshaft CV joint
4	Adjuster tube for right tie-rod	9	Differential	14	Left tie-rod end
5	Drag link	10	Axle tube	15	Adjuster tube for left tie-rod
6	Steering damper	11	Axle tube yoke	16	Tie-rod

1.3b Rear suspension components (1997 and later models; 4WD model shown; 2WD models similar)

1	Shock absorber	4	Axle tube	7	Lower suspension arm (upper arms
2	Coil spring	5	Differential		not visible in this photo)
3	Track bar	6	Stabilizer bar		

Precautions

5   When working on the suspension or steering system components, you'll often run into fasteners which seem impossible to loosen. That's because they're continually subjected to water, road grime, mud, etc., and can become rusted or "frozen," making them extremely difficult to remove. To loosen stubborn fasteners, use plenty of penetrating oil and allow it to soak in for a while.

6   Sometimes a sharp blow with a hammer and punch is effective in breaking the bond between the nut and the bolt threads, but make sure the punch doesn't slip off the fastener and ruin the threads. Heating a frozen fastener with a torch sometimes helps too, but we don't recommend this method because of the danger of starting a fire. Long breaker bars or "cheater" (extension) pipes increase your leverage, but they can also

break off bolts and ball studs if too much force is applied. And never use a cheater pipe on a ratchet. If you do, the extra leverage provided by the cheater could damage the ratcheting mechanism. Sometimes, it's easier to break loose a frozen fastener if you first turn the nut or bolt in the tightening (clockwise) direction. Nuts are also easier to remove if you clean the exposed threads of bolts and ball studs with a wire brush. Cleaning up the threads also protects them from damage during removal of a rusted or frozen nut. Always discard fasteners that require drastic measures to unscrew and replace them with new fasteners during reassembly.

7   Always inspect steering and suspension fasteners any time they're loosened or removed. If necessary, replace them with new parts with the same part number or of original equipment quality and design. For your

safety, observe all torque values listed in this Chapter's Specifications to ensure that suspension and steering assemblies don't come apart. Never attempt to heat or straighten any suspension or steering components. Instead, replace any bent or damaged part with a new one.

8   Most of the procedures in this Chapter involve jacking up the vehicle and working partly or totally underneath it, so get a good pair of jackstands and use them to support the vehicle any time it's elevated. It's also helpful to have a hydraulic floor jack to lift the vehicle; floor jacks are also handy for supporting components such as axle assemblies during certain procedures. **Warning:** Never, under any circumstances, rely on a jack as the sole means of support while working on or under the vehicle.

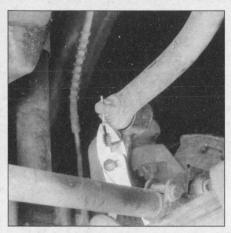

2.2a Remove the cotter pins from the bolts that attach the stabilizer bar to the links, remove the nuts and disconnect the ends of the bar from the links

2.2b If the stabilizer bar proves difficult to separate from the links at either end, remove this nut and washer, and disconnect the link(s) from the leaf spring tie plate(s)

2.3a To detach the stabilizer bar from the vehicle, remove these two bolts from the left bracket

2 Stabilizer bar and bushings - removal and installation

1   Apply the parking brake. Raise the front of the vehicle and support it securely on jackstands.

1987 through 1995 models

2   Remove the cotter pins (see illustration) from the stabilizer bar-to-link bolts, then remove the stabilizer bar-to-link nuts. If the bolts are difficult to remove, disconnect the lower ends of the links from the leaf spring tie plates (see illustration).

3   Remove the stabilizer bar bracket bolts (see illustrations) and detach the bar from the vehicle.

4   Pull the brackets off the stabilizer bar and inspect the bushings for cracks, hardness and other signs of deterioration. If the bushings are damaged, replace them.

5   Position the stabilizer bar bushings on the bar (see illustration).

6   Push the brackets over the bushings and raise the bar up to the frame. Install the bracket bolts but don't tighten them completely at this time.

7   Install the stabilizer bar-to-link nuts, washers, spacers and rubber bushings and tighten the nuts securely. Install a new cotter pin in each bolt.

8   If you disconnected the lower ends of the links from the leaf spring tie plates, reattach them and tighten the nuts securely.

9   Tighten the bracket bolts securely.

1997 and later models

10   Remove the stabilizer bar-to-link nuts (see illustration). If it is necessary to remove the links, simply unbolt them from the axle brackets.

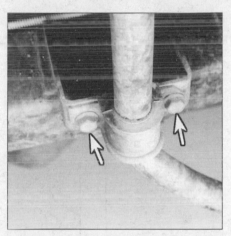

2.3b ... then detach the right bracket bolts and remove the bar and brackets; while the bar is off the vehicle, pull the rubber bushings off the bar and inspect them for hardness, cracks or other damage - replace them if they are hard, cracked or otherwise deformed

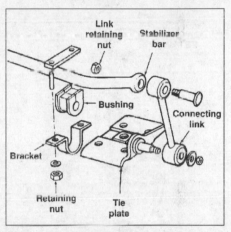

2.5 An exploded view of the stabilizer bar, a bracket and a link (right end shown)

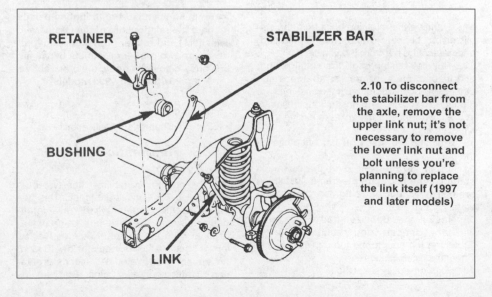

2.10 To disconnect the stabilizer bar from the axle, remove the upper link nut; it's not necessary to remove the lower link nut and bolt unless you're planning to replace the link itself (1997 and later models)

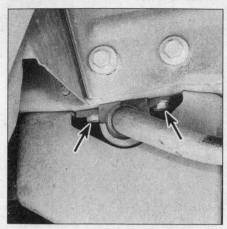

2.11 To disconnect the stabilizer bar from the frame, remove the bushing clamp bolts (arrows); inspect the rubber bushings and replace them if they're hard, cracked or otherwise deformed (1997 and later models)

3.2 To detach the upper end of the shock absorber from the vehicle, remove the upper nut (arrow), washer and rubber grommet (1987 through 1995 models)

3.3a To detach the lower end of the shock absorber from the axle, remove this bolt and nut (1987 through 1995 models)

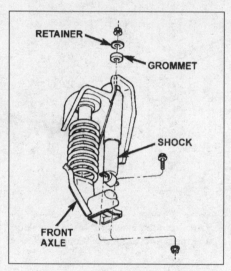

3.3b Front shock absorber mounting details (1997 and later models)

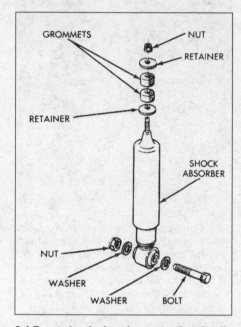

3.4 Front shock absorber mounting details - note the relationship of the retainers (washers) and rubber grommets - up top, there are two rubber grommets because one goes below the body, the other above it (1987 through 1995 models)

11   Remove the retaining bolts from the stabilizer bar bushing clamps (see illustration) and detach the bar from the vehicle.
12   Pull the bushings off the stabilizer bar and inspect them for cracks, hardness and other signs of deterioration. If the bushings are damaged, replace them. Inspect the bushings in the lower ends of the links, replacing them if necessary.
13   Position the stabilizer bar bushings on the bar.
14   Push the brackets over the bushings and raise the bar up to the frame. Install the bracket bolts but don't tighten them completely at this time.
15   Install the stabilizer bar-to-link nuts, washers, spacers and rubber bushings, tightening the nuts to the torque listed in this Chapter's Specifications.
16   Tighten the bracket bolts to the torque

listed in this Chapter's Specifications.

ASBS - Automatic Stabilizer Bar System

17   The automatic stabilizer bar system is available on 2007 and later models. This system allows for a greater wheel travel in off-road conditions. The system relies on operator input from the control switch as well as vehicle speed. At low speeds (below 15 mph) the system is activated. At speeds greater than 15 mph the system automatically returns

to the normal "connected" configuration.
18   No diagnostics or removal procedures have been provided because of the complexities of the system. Diagnostics require the use of an oscilloscope and a diagnostic scanner. Some basic checks such as checking fuses, ground leads and electrical connectors can be performed.

3   Front shock absorbers - removal and installation

Removal

1   Loosen the wheel lug nuts, raise the vehicle and support it securely on jackstands. Apply the parking brake. Remove the wheel.
2   Remove the upper shock absorber stem nut (see illustration). Use an open end wrench to keep the stem from turning. If the nut won't loosen because of rust, squirt some penetrating oil on the stem threads and allow it to soak in for awhile. It may be necessary to keep the stem from turning with a pair of locking pliers, since the flats provided for a wrench are quite small.
3   Remove the lower shock mounting nut and bolt (see illustrations) and pull the shock absorber out from the wheel well. Remove the washers and the rubber grommets from the top of the shock absorber.

Installation

4   Extend the new shock absorber as far as possible. Position a new washer and rubber grommet (see illustration) on the stem and guide the shock up into the upper mount.
5   Install the upper rubber grommet and washer and wiggle the stem back-and-forth to ensure the grommets are centered in the mount. Tighten the stem nut securely.
6   Install the lower mounting bolts and nuts and tighten them securely.

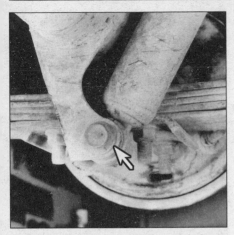

4.3 To remove a rear shock, remove this bolt, both washers and the nut (not visible in this photo)…

4.4a … then remove the upper mounting nut and washer from the upper mounting stud and slide the upper shock eye off the stud (1987 through 1995 models)

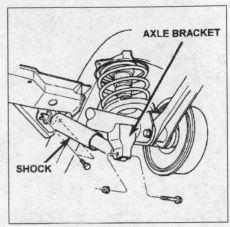

4.4b Rear shock absorber mounting details (1997 and later models)

4   Rear shock absorbers - removal and installation

1   Raise the rear of the vehicle and support it securely on jackstands.

2   Support the rear axle assembly with a floor jack placed under the differential. Raise the jack just enough to take the spring pressure off the shock absorbers (the shock absorbers limit down travel of the suspension).

3   Remove the shock absorber lower retaining nut, washers and bolt (see illustration).

4   Remove the upper mounting nut and washer (see illustrations) and slide the shock off the upper mounting stud. On 2007 and later models, the top of the rear shock is secured with two bolts.

5   Installation is the reverse of the removal procedure (see illustration). Be sure to place a washer on either side of the eye at the lower end of the shock and tighten the nuts to the torque listed in this Chapter's Specifications.

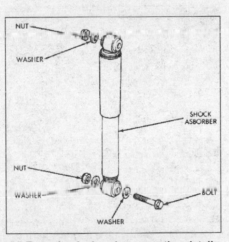

4.5 Rear shock absorber mounting details - be sure to place a washer on each side of the lower shock eye during installation (1987 through 1995 models)

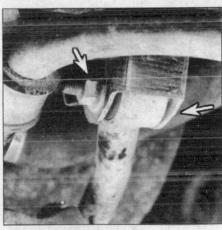

5.2a To disconnect the upper end of the front track bar from the frame bracket, remove this nut and bolt (arrows)

5   Track bar - removal and installation

Note: *This procedure applies to the front and rear track bars.*

1   Raise the front of the vehicle and support it securely on jackstands.

2   Remove the retaining nut and bolt from the frame rail bracket (see illustrations).

3   Remove the bolt and nut (see illustrations) from the axle bracket end of the bar and remove the bar from the vehicle.

4   Installation is the reverse of the removal procedure. Be sure to tighten the fasteners to the torque listed in this Chapter's Specifications.

Note: *After installation, do not fully tighten the fasteners. Lower the vehicle to the ground and tighten the fasteners to the torque listed in this Chapter's Specifications, with the full weight of the vehicle on the suspension.*

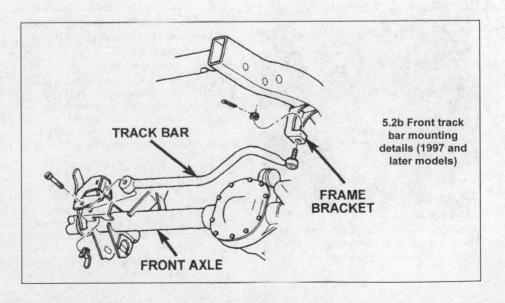

5.2b Front track bar mounting details (1997 and later models)

5.2c To disconnect the upper end of the rear track bar from the frame bracket, remove this nut and bolt (arrows)

5.3a To disconnect the lower end of the front track bar from the front axle bracket, remove this nut (not visible in this photo) and bolt (arrow)

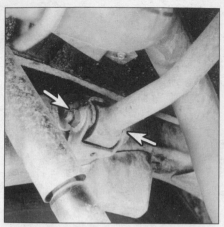

5.3b To disconnect the lower end of the rear track bar from the rear axle bracket, remove this nut (arrow) and bolt

6.3 If you're removing a front leaf spring, remove the stabilizer bar link nut (left arrow), then remove these four nuts (right arrows) and the tie plate

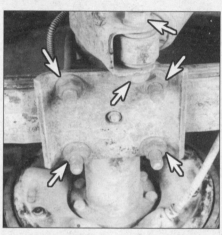

6.4 If you're removing a rear leaf spring, remove the lower shock eye nut and bolt (top and upper center arrows), then remove the four remaining nuts (arrows) and the tie plate

6.6a If you're removing a front leaf spring, remove this nut and bolt from the shackle at the front crossmember

6.6b If you're removing a rear leaf spring, remove this nut and bolt from the shackle at the rear crossmember

6 Leaf springs and bushings (1987 through 1995 models) - removal and installation

Note: *This procedure applies to front and rear leaf spring assemblies. It also applies to both ends of each axle, but we recommend that you do one side at a time, to keep the axle under control and so you'll have one side to use as a "guide" to reassembly.*

Bushing check

1   All models are equipped with silent-block type rubber bushings which are pressed into the spring eyes. The bushings should be inspected for cracks, damage and looseness indicating excessive wear. To check for wear, jack up the frame until the weight is removed from the spring bushing. Pry the spring eye up-and-down to check for movement. If there is considerable movement, the bushing is worn and should be replaced.

Spring removal

2   Loosen the front or rear wheel lug nuts, raise the front or rear of the vehicle and support it securely on jackstands. Remove the wheel. Support the front or rear axle assembly with a floor jack positioned underneath the differential. Raise the axle just enough to take the axle weight off the spring.

3   If you're removing a front leaf spring, remove the stabilizer bar link nut at the spring tie plate (see illustration).

4   If you're removing a rear leaf spring, disconnect the rear shock absorber from the axle tube bracket (see illustration).

5   Unscrew the U-bolt nuts, the spring tie plate and the U-bolts from the axle.

6   Remove the spring-to-shackle bolt (see illustrations).

6.7a If you're removing a front leaf spring, remove this nut and bolt from the frame bracket

6.7b If you're removing a rear leaf spring, remove this nut and bolt from the frame bracket

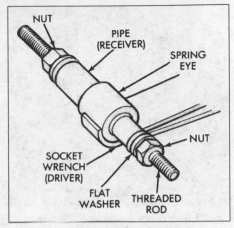

6.13 A threaded rod and two approximately-sized sockets can be used to remove and install the spring eye bushings

7   Remove the spring eye-to-frame bracket bolt (see illustrations) and remove the spring from the vehicle.

Bushing replacement

8   The bushings are of two different sizes and tools can be fabricated from threaded rod for pressing them out. For small diameter bushings, cut an eight inch length of 3/8-inch diameter threaded rod and, for the large diameter bushings, cut an eleven-inch length of 1/2-inch diameter threaded rod.

9   Insert the threaded rod through the bushing.

10   Place a socket over one end of the rod with the open end toward the bushing to serve as a driver. The socket must be large enough to bear against the bushing outer sleeve and small enough to pass through the spring eye.

11   Install a flat washer and hex nut on the rod behind the socket.

12   On the opposite end of the threaded rod, install a piece of pipe to serve as a receiver. The inside diameter of the pipe must be large enough to accommodate the bushing while still seating against the spring eye surface. It must also be long enough to accept the entire bushing.

13   Secure the pipe section on the rod with a flat washer and nut (see illustration). The washer must be large enough to properly support the pipe.

14   Tighten the nuts finger-tight to align the components. The socket must be positioned in the spring eye and aligned with the bushing and the pipe must butt against the eye surface so the bushing can pass through it.

15   Press the bushing out of the spring eye by tightening the nut at the socket end of the rod.

16   Remove the bushing and tool from the spring eye.

17   Install the new bushing on the threaded rod and assemble and align the tools as previously described.

18   Line up the bushing with the spring eye and press the new bushing into position.

19   Loosen the nuts and check to make sure the bushing is centered in the spring eye with the ends of the bushing flush with or slightly below the sides of the eye. If necessary, reinstall the tools and adjust the bushing position.

Spring installation

20   Installation is the reverse of the removal procedure. Be sure to tighten the spring mounting bolts and the spring tie plate U-bolt nuts to the torque listed in this Chapter's Specifications.

Note: *The vehicle must be standing at normal ride height before tightening the front and rear mounting bolts.*

7   Suspension arms (1997 and later models) - removal and installation

Note: *Remove and install only one suspension arm at a time to avoid the possibility of the axle housing shifting out of position, which would make reassembly much more difficult. If it is absolutely necessary to remove more*

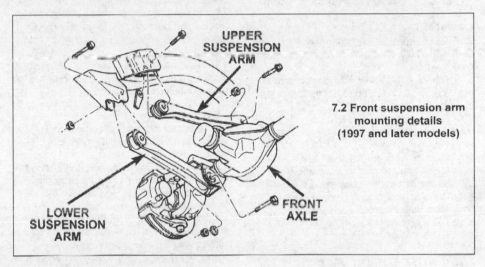

7.2 Front suspension arm mounting details (1997 and later models)

than one at a time, support the axle with a floor jack.

Front suspension arms

1   Raise the front of the vehicle and support it securely on jackstands.

Upper arm

2   Remove the nut and bolt securing the upper suspension arm to the axle housing bracket (see illustration).

3   Remove the bolt and nut connecting the upper suspension arm to the frame bracket and remove the arm from the vehicle.

4   Check the arm for distortion and cracks. If the arm is damaged, replace it.

5   Inspect the bushing in the axle housing (upper arm only) for cracking, hardness and general deterioration. If it is in need of replacement, take the arm to a dealer service department or an automotive machine shop to have it replaced.

6   Installation is the reverse of removal. Be sure to tighten the fasteners to the torque listed in this Chapter's Specifications.

Note: *The fasteners should be tightened after the vehicle has been lowered.*

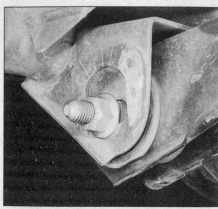

7.7 Before disconnecting the lower suspension arm from the axle housing bracket, mark the relationship of the cam adjuster to the bracket, then remove the nut and pull out the bolt (1997 and later models)

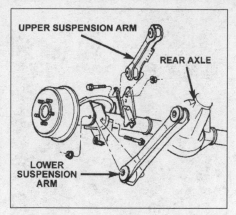

7.12a Rear suspension arm-to-axle mounting details (1997 and later models)

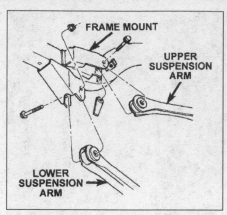

7.12b Rear suspension arm-to-frame mounting details (1997 and later models)

Lower arm

7   Paint or scribe alignment marks on the cam adjusters to insure proper reassembly (see illustration).
8   Remove the lower suspension arm nut, the cam and the cam bolt from the bracket on the axle housing.
9   Remove the nut and bolt from the frame rail bracket and remove the lower suspension arm.
10   Installation is the reverse of removal. Be sure to re-align the marks you made between the cam adjuster and the suspension arm and tighten the fasteners to the torque listed in this Chapter's Specifications.
Note: *The fasteners should be tightened after the vehicle has been lowered.*

Rear suspension arms

11   Raise the rear of the vehicle and support it securely on jackstands.

Upper arm

12   Remove the nut and bolt securing the upper suspension arm to the axle housing bracket (see illustrations).
13   Remove the nut and bolt connecting

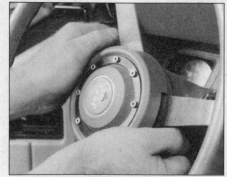

9.2 To remove the horn pad, pull it straight off with both hands - don't use a screwdriver or any other tool to pry the pad off; it's unnecessary and you'll damage or scratch something

the upper suspension arm to the frame rail bracket and remove the arm from the vehicle.
14   Check the arm for distortion and cracks. Inspect the bushings for tears and cracks. If the arm or either bushing is damaged, replace the arm.
15   Installation is the reverse of removal. Be sure to tighten all fasteners to the torque listed in this Chapter's Specifications.

Lower arm

16   Remove the nut and bolt connecting the lower suspension arm to the axle bracket (see illustration 7.12a).
17   Remove the nut and bolt connecting the lower suspension arm to the frame rail bracket (see illustration 7.12b) and remove the lower suspension arm.
18   Installation is the reverse of removal. Be sure to tighten the fasteners to the torque listed in this Chapter's Specifications.
Note: *The fasteners should be tightened after the vehicle has been lowered.*

8   Coil spring (1997 and later models) - removal and installation

Note: *This procedure applies to the front and rear coil springs.*
1   Loosen the front wheel lug nuts, raise the front of the vehicle and support it securely on jackstands. Remove the wheels.
2   Mark and disconnect the front driveshaft from the front differential pinion shaft yoke (see Chapter 8), then hang the driveshaft out of the way with a piece of wire.
3   Support the axle assembly with either a floor jack under the differential or, preferably, two jacks, one at each end of the axle (the latter option provides better balance). Unbolt the lower suspension arms from the axle (see Section 7).
4   Unbolt the stabilizer bar links (see Section 2) and the shock absorbers at the front axle housing (see Section 3 or Section 4).
5   Disconnect the track bar at the axle bracket (see Section 5).

6   If you're servicing a front coil spring, separate the drag link from the Pitman arm (see Section 12).
7   Slowly lower the axle assembly until the coil springs are fully extended. If you are using only one jack, have an assistant support the right side of the axle as it's lowered. Remove the spring from the vehicle.
8   Check the spring for deep nicks and corrosion, which will cause premature failure of the spring. Replace the spring if these or any other questionable conditions are evident.
9   Position the coil spring on the axle housing, place the spring retainer over the bottom coil of the spring and tighten the spring retainer bolt securely.
10   Raise the axle up into position and connect the lower suspension arms to the axle housing. Tighten the fasteners to the specified torque.
11   If you're servicing a front coil spring, connect the drag link to the Pitman arm.
12   Connect the track bar to its bracket on the axle.
13   Connect the stabilizer bar links and the shock absorbers to the front axle housing.
14   Connect the front driveshaft to the differential pinion shaft yoke (see Chapter 8).
15   Install the wheels and lug nuts and lower the vehicle. Tighten the lug nuts to the torque listed in the Chapter 1 Specifications.

9   Steering wheel - removal and installation

1   Disconnect the cable from the negative terminal of the battery (see Chapter 5).

Models without an airbag

2   Detach the horn pad from the steering wheel and disconnect the wires to the horn switch (see illustration).
3   Remove the steering wheel retaining nut, then mark the relationship of the steering shaft to the hub (if marks don't already exist or don't line up) to simplify installation and ensure steering wheel alignment (see illustration). Remove the three screws and detach the horn contact

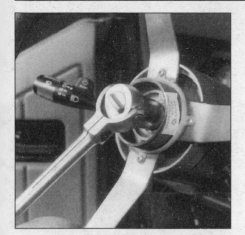

9.3a Remove the steering wheel retaining nut

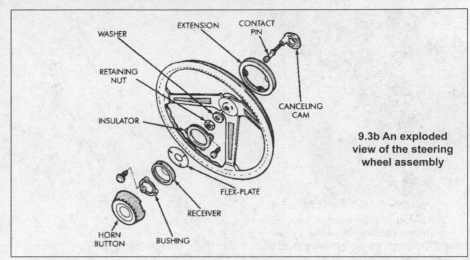

9.3b An exploded view of the steering wheel assembly

9.4 You may be able to separate the steering wheel from the steering shaft by hand, but if the splines are frozen, remove the wheel from the shaft with a puller - DO NOT HAMMER ON THE SHAFT!

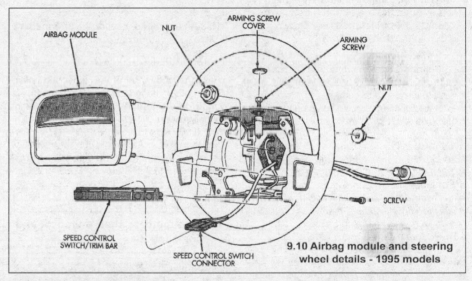

9.10 Airbag module and steering wheel details - 1995 models

components (see illustration).

4 Use a puller to detach the steering wheel from the shaft (see illustration). Don't hammer on the shaft to dislodge the steering wheel.

5 To install the wheel, align the mark on the steering wheel hub with the mark on the shaft and slip the wheel onto the shaft. Install the nut and tighten it to the specified torque.

6 Connect the horn wire and install the horn pad.

7 Connect the negative battery cable.

Models with an airbag

8 If you're working on a 1995 model, roll down the driver's side window.

9 Disconnect the cable from the negative terminal of the battery. Wait at least two minutes before proceeding (this will disable the airbag system on 1997 and later models; proceed to the next Step for the airbag disarming procedure on 1995 models).

10 If you're working on a 1995 model, pry off the small cover from the top of the steering wheel hub. Get out of the vehicle, reach into the vehicle and, using an 8 mm socket, unscrew the arming screw until it stops (it

should protrude approximately one inch from the surface of the steering wheel trim) (see illustration). The airbag is now disarmed.

11 Remove the airbag module fasteners from the backside of the steering wheel. On 2007 through 2010 models, the driver's airbag is retained by three wire clips. The steering wheel has three openings in the Instrument panel side. Rotate each opening until it is at the 12 o'clock position, where you can use a screwdriver to release the clip from the pro-

jections on the back of the airbag to release the clips. Rotate the wheel again to align and disconnect the clips on the remaining two projections. Lift the airbag module away from the wheel. On 1997 and later models, unplug the electrical connectors from the module (see illustration). Set the module aside in an isolated location.

Warning: *Carry the module with the trim side facing away from your body, and set it down with the trim side facing up.*

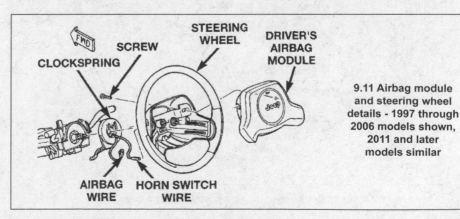

9.11 Airbag module and steering wheel details - 1997 through 2006 models shown, 2011 and later models similar

10.2 Using white paint, mark the relationship of the upper and lower universal joints to the steering shaft and steering gear input shaft, respectively; then remove the upper pinch bolt (arrow) and lower pinch bolt (not shown, but identical)

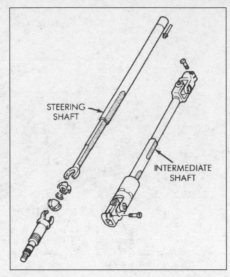

10.3 An exploded view of the intermediate shaft assembly

12   Pull the airbag module and horn switch away from the steering wheel far enough to gain access to the electrical connections. Disconnect the connectors and remove the air bag.

Note: *The air bag connectors use two types of fasteners to secure the connector to the airbag as well as to ensure a proper connection. Lift the center part of the connector up to release the CPA (Connector Position Assurance) tabs, then disconnect the main clips on either side of the connector. When installing, push the clip into place, then press the CPA tab down to secure the connector.*

13   Perform Steps 3 and 4 of this Section.
14   To install the wheel, refer to Step 5.

Warning: *If the clockspring for the airbag system was inadvertently turned, refer to Chapter 12, Section 24 for the centering procedure (1997 and later models only). Be sure to carefully thread the wiring harness for the cruise control, airbag (1997 and later models) and horn through the proper openings in the steering wheel.*

15   Position the airbag module over the steering wheel, plug in the electrical connectors and install the module. On 2007 through 2010 models, engage the lower wire loop with the hook on the steering wheel hub, then press the upper part of the airbag into place. On all other models, tighten the module fasteners to the torque listed in this Chapter's Specifications.
16   If you're working on a 1995 model, close the door and, reaching through the window, screw in the arming screw, tightening it to the torque listed in this Chapter's Specifications.
17   Connect the negative battery cable.

10   Intermediate shaft - removal and installation

Warning: *On 1997 and later models, make sure the steering shaft is not turned while the intermediate shaft is removed or you could damage the airbag system. To prevent the shaft from turning, position the wheels pointing straight ahead, thread the seat belt through the steering wheel and fasten it into its latch. If the steering wheel is inadvertently turned, remove the steering wheel and center the clockspring (see Chapter 12).*

1   Turn the front wheels to the straight ahead position.
2   Using white paint, mark the relationship of the upper universal joint to the steering shaft and the lower universal joint to the steering gear input shaft (see illustration).
3   Remove the upper and lower universal-joint pinch bolts (see illustration). Some designs require the steering gear to be loosened (bolts removed) and repositioned to allow shaft removal (see Section 11).
4   Pry the intermediate shaft out of the steering shaft universal joint with a large screwdriver, then pull the shaft from the steering gearbox.
5   Installation is the reverse of the removal procedure. Be sure to align the marks and tighten the pinch bolts to the torque listed in this Chapter's Specifications.

11   Steering gear - removal and installation

Warning: *On 1997 and later models, make sure the steering shaft is not turned while the steering gear is removed or you could damage the airbag system. To prevent the shaft from turning, position the wheels pointing straight ahead, thread the seat belt through the steering wheel and fasten it into its latch. If the steering wheel is inadvertently turned, remove the steering wheel and center the clockspring (see Chapter 12).*

Removal

1   Raise the front of the vehicle and support it securely on jackstands. Apply the parking brake.
2   Place a drain pan under the steering gear (power steering only). Disconnect the hoses/lines (see illustration) and cap the ends to prevent excessive fluid loss and contamination. If available, use a flare-nut wrench to disconnect the hoses/lines.
3   Mark the relationship of the intermediate shaft lower universal joint to the steering gear input shaft. Remove the intermediate shaft lower pinch bolt (see Section 10).
4   Remove the Pitman arm nut and washer (see illustration). Mark the relationship of the

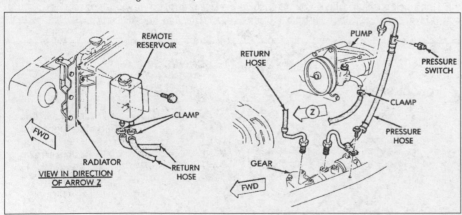

11.2 An exploded view of the power steering lines and hoses

11.4a Remove the Pitman arm nut and washer...

Pitman arm to the shaft so it can be installed in the same position (see illustration).

5   Separate the Pitman arm from the shaft with a two-jaw puller (see illustration).

6   Support the steering gear and remove the mounting bolts (see illustration). Lower the unit, separate the intermediate shaft from the steering gear input shaft and remove the steering gear from the vehicle.

Installation

7   Raise the steering gear into position and connect the intermediate shaft, aligning the marks.

8   Install the steering gear mounting bolts and washers and tighten them to the torque listed in this Chapter's Specifications.

9   Slide the Pitman arm onto the shaft. Make sure the marks are aligned. Install the washer and nut and tighten the nut to the specified torque.

10   Install the intermediate shaft lower pinch bolt and tighten it to the torque listed in this Chapter's Specifications.

11   Connect the power steering hoses/lines to the steering gear and fill the power steering pump reservoir with the recommended fluid (see Chapter 1).

12   Lower the vehicle and bleed the steering system (see Section 16)

---

12   Steering linkage - Inspection, removal and installation

Caution: *DO NOT use a "pickle fork" type balljoint separator - it may damage the balljoint seals.*

Inspection

1   The steering linkage (see illustration) connects the steering gear to the front wheels and keeps the wheels in proper relation to each other. The linkage consists of the Pitman

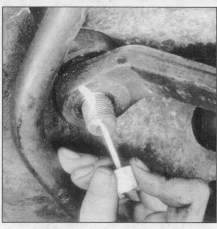

11.4b ... then, before removing the Pitman arm, mark its relationship to the steering gear shaft

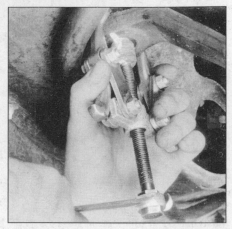

11.5 Use a two-jaw puller to separate the Pitman arm from the steering gear shaft

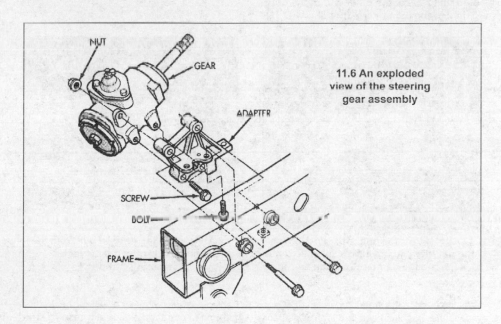

11.6 An exploded view of the steering gear assembly

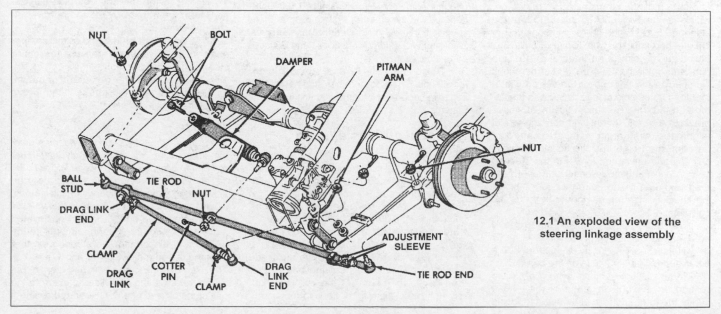

12.1 An exploded view of the steering linkage assembly

12.6a Remove the cotter pin from the castellated nut which retains the drag link ball stud to the tie-rod (shown) and loosen - but don't remove - the nut, remove the cotter pin and loosen the nut on the ball stud that retains the other end of the drag link to the pitman arm (not shown)…

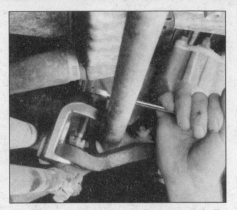

12.6b … then attach a puller to each ball stud, separate the ball studs from the pitman arm (shown) and the tie-rod (not shown) and remove the drag link

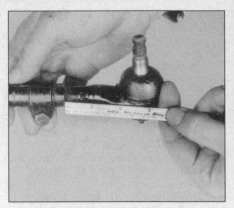

12.7 If the drag link or tie-rod ends must be replaced, measure the distance from the end of the drag link/tie-rod end to the center of the ball stud so the new drag link/tie-rod end can be set to this dimension

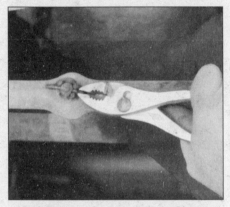

12.10 Remove the cotter pin and loosen the nut, then install a two-jaw puller and separate the damper from the tie-rod

12.11 Remove the nut and bolt from the frame bracket and remove the steering damper

arm, fastened to the steering gear shaft, which moves the drag link back and forth. This back and-forth motion is transmitted to the tie rod, which itself moves back-and-forth to turn the steering knuckle. The tie-rod is connected to the steering knuckles with a pair of balljoints. The right balljoint is an integral part of the right end of the tie rod. The left tie-rod end is clamped to the left end of the tie-rod with a threaded adjustable sleeve. Used with the tie-rod and the drag link, this adjustment sleeve provides toe adjustment and steering wheel alignment. A steering damper, connected between the frame and the tie-rod, reduces shimmy and unwanted forces to the steering gear. All critical connections - pitman-arm-to-drag link, drag link-to-tie-rod, tie-rod-to-steering knuckle, steering damper-to-tie-rod - use balljoints.

2   Set the wheels in the straight ahead position and lock the steering wheel.

3   Raise one side of the vehicle until the tire is approximately 1-inch off the ground.

4   Mount a dial indicator with the needle resting on the outside edge of the wheel. Grasp the front and rear of the tire and, using light pressure, wiggle the wheel back-and-forth and note the dial indicator reading. The gauge reading should be less than 0.108-inch. If the play in the steering system is more than specified, inspect each steering linkage pivot point and ball stud for looseness and replace parts if necessary.

5   Raise the vehicle and support it on jackstands. Check for torn ball stud boots, frozen joints and bent or damaged linkage components.

Removal and installation

Drag link

6   Remove the cotter pins (see illustration) from the castellated nuts, loosen the nuts, separate the ball studs from both ends of the drag link with a two-jaw puller (see illustration) and remove the drag link.

Note: *If only one drag link end needs replacing, separate the ballstud at that end only.*

7   If either drag link end must be replaced, measure the distance from the end of the drag link to the center of the ball stud and record it (see illustration). Loosen the clamp

bolt and unscrew the drag link end. The number of threads showing on the inner and outer drag link ends should be equal within three threads. Don't tighten the clamps yet.

8   Installation is the reverse of removal. When you install the drag link, insert the drag link ends into the pitman arm and the tie-rod until they're fully seated. Install the castellated nuts and tighten them to the torque listed in this Chapter's Specifications. Install new cotter pins. You may have to tighten the nuts slightly to align a slot in the nut with the hole in each ball stud.

9   Tighten the clamp nuts to the torque listed in this Chapter's Specifications.

Steering damper

10   Remove the cotter pin from the castellated nut that attaches the steering damper ball stud to the tie rod (see illustration), loosen the nut, install a two-jaw puller and separate the steering damper from the tie rod.

11   Remove the nut and bolt (see illustration) from the frame bracket and remove the steering damper.

12   If the balljoint on the end of the damper shaft must be replaced, replace the entire steering damper assembly.

13   Installation is the reverse of removal. Tighten the nuts to the torque listed in this Chapter's Specifications.

Tie-rod

Note: *If only the left tie-rod end needs replacing, ignore Step 15, separate only the left tie-rod end in Step 16, then proceed to Step 18.*

14   Loosen the wheel lug nuts, raise the vehicle and support it securely on jackstands. Apply the parking brake. Remove the wheels.

15   Remove the cotter pin and castellated nut that connect the steering damper to the tie-rod and disconnect the steering damper from the tie rod (see Steps 10 and 11).

16   Remove the cotter pins and loosen, but do not remove, the castellated nuts from the ball studs on each end of the tie-rod. Using a

13.2 To disconnect the tie-rod from the steering knuckle, remove the cotter pin from the castellated nut, loosen - but don't remove - the nut (to prevent the parts from separating violently), install a small two-jaw puller and press the ballstud out of the knuckle

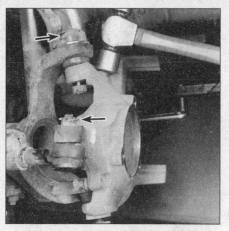

13.5 To remove the steering knuckle, remove the cotter pins, loosen the castellated nuts on the upper and lower balls studs (arrows) and strike the top of the knuckle with a hammer

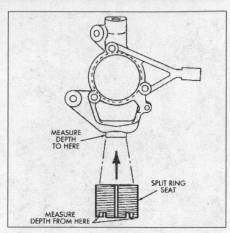

13.8a Cutaway of the split-ring seat used to adjust height of lower balljoint (which determines amount of vertical freeplay of steering knuckle) on steering knuckles used on pre-1990 models

two-jaw puller, loosen the right tie-rod balljoint and the left tie-rod end from the steering knuckle and the drag link ball stud from the tie-rod (see Step 6). Remove the castellated nuts. Pull the drag link ball stud from the tie rod, pull the right tie-rod balljoint and the left tie-rod end from the steering knuckles, and remove the tie rod.

17   If the right tie-rod balljoint must be replaced, replace the entire tie-rod.

18   If the left tie-rod end must be replaced, measure the distance from the end of the tie-rod to the center of the ball stud and record it (see illustration 12.7). Loosen the adjustment sleeve clamp and unscrew the tie-rod end.

19   Lubricate the threaded portion of the left tie-rod end with chassis grease. Screw the new tie-rod end into the adjuster tube and adjust the distance from the tube to the ball stud to the previously measured dimension. Don't tighten the clamp yet.

20   To install the tie-rod, insert the balljoint studs into the steering knuckles until they're seated. Install the nuts and tighten them to the torque listed in this Chapter's Specifications. If a ball stud spins when attempting to tighten the nut, force it into the tapered hole with a large pair of pliers.

21   Install new cotter pins. If necessary, tighten the nuts slightly to align a slot in each nut with a hole in its respective ball stud.

22   Tighten the clamp nuts to the torque listed in this Chapter's Specifications.

23   Install the wheel and lug nuts, lower the vehicle and tighten the lug nuts to the torque listed in the Chapter 1 Specifications. Have the front end alignment checked and, if necessary, adjusted.

Pitman arm

24   See Section 11 for this procedure.

13   Steering knuckle - removal and installation

Removal

1   Loosen the wheel lug nuts, raise the vehicle and support it securely on jackstands. Remove the wheel.

2   Disconnect the tie-rod end from the steering knuckle (see illustration).

3   Remove the brake caliper and disc (see Chapter 9).

4   Remove the front axle hub and bearing assembly and remove the axleshaft (see Chapter 8).

5   Remove the cotter pins and loosen the castellated nuts on the balljoint studs (see illustration).

6   Using a large hammer, tap the steering knuckle at the top to separate it from the balljoint studs.

7   Carefully check the steering knuckle for cracks, especially around the steering arm and spindle mounting area. Check for elongated balljoint stud holes. Replace the steering knuckle if any of these conditions are found.

Installation

8   If you're replacing the steering knuckle on a 1990 or later model, proceed to Step 10; if you're replacing the steering knuckle on a pre-1990 model, unscrew the split ring seat (see illustration) from the lower mount and transfer it to the new knuckle. Also remove the disc anchor plate from the old knuckle (see illustration).

9   Measure the depth of the split ring seat in the knuckle using a depth micrometer or vernier caliper (see illustration). Screw the split ring seat in or out to attain the proper depth of 0.206 inch.

10   Position the steering knuckle on the axle housing, inserting the balljoint studs into the holes in the knuckle. Install the nuts and

13.8b If you're installing a new steering knuckle on a pre-1990 model, remove the anchor plate bolts (arrows), remove the anchor plate and install it on the new knuckle

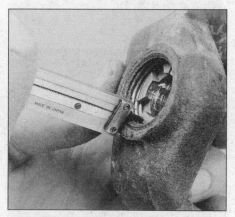

13.9 On pre-1990 models, the split ring seat must be screwed in to a depth of 0.206 inch, measured from the spindle boss to the flats of the seat; you can make this measurement with a depth micrometer, or a vernier caliper (as shown here)

15.2 Before you remove the power steering pump mounting bolts, unplug the power steering pressure switch (A), and disconnect the high pressure line (B) and the return hose (C) (this unit has an integral reservoir - some models use a remote reservoir bolted to the radiator, as shown in illustration 11.2)

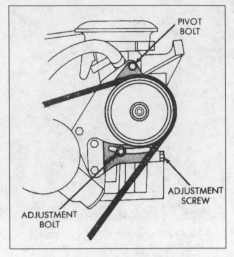

15.3a Front power steering pump mounting bolts

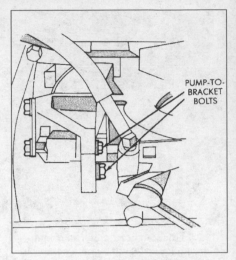

15.3b Rear power steering pump mounting bolts

tighten them to the torque listed in this Chapter's Specifications. Remember to use new cotter pins.

11   Install the axleshaft (see Chapter 8).

12   Install the front axle hub and bearing assembly (see Chapter 8).

13   If you removed the caliper mounting bracket from the steering knuckle, install it on the new knuckle and tighten the bolts to the torque listed in the Chapter 9 Specifications.

14   Install the brake disc and caliper (see Chapter 9).

15   Connect the tie-rod to the steering knuckle and tighten the nut to the torque listed in this Chapter's Specifications. Install a new cotter pin.

16   Install the wheel and lug nuts. Lower the vehicle and tighten the lug nuts to the torque listed in the Chapter 1 Specifications.

14   Balljoints - replacement

1   The balljoints are a press fit in the front axle housing, which necessitates the use of a special press tool and receiver cup to remove and install them. The tools are available at most auto parts stores to rent for a nominal fee. Directions on the use of the tool should be read completely before attempting to use it. If you cannot find the proper tool to perform this procedure we recommended that the steering knuckle be removed and taken to an automotive machine shop or other qualified repair facility to have the balljoints replaced.

15   Power steering pump - removal and installation

Removal

1   Loosen the pump drivebelt and slip the belt over the pulley (see Chapter 1).

2   Unplug the power steering pressure switch (see illustration). Using a suction gun, suck out as much power steering fluid from the reservoir as possible. Position a drain pan under the pump and disconnect the high pressure line and fluid return hose. It may be necessary to remove the air cleaner housing for access to the return hose (if so, see Chapter 4). Cap the ends of the lines to prevent excessive fluid leakage and the entry of contaminants.This is a good time to inspect and, if necessary, replace the power steering hoses/lines (see illustration 11.2).

3   Remove the front and rear pump mounting bolts (see illustrations), then lift the pump from the engine. On 2003 and later models, the front pump-mounting bolts can be accessed through the holes in the pulley (see illustration).

4   If it is necessary to remove the pulley from the pump, first measure how far the pump shaft protrudes from the face of the pulley hub. Remove the pulley from the shaft with a special power steering pump pulley removal tool (see illustration). This tool can be purchased at most auto parts stores.

Installation

5   A special pulley installation tool is available for pressing the pulley back onto the pump shaft, but an alternate tool can be fabricated from a long bolt, nut, washer and a socket of the same diameter as the pulley hub (see illustration). Push the pulley onto the shaft until the shaft protrudes from the hub the previously recorded amount.

6   Installation of the power steering pump is the reverse of the removal procedure (see illustration). Be sure to bleed the power steering system following the procedure in Section 16.

15.3c Access the pump mounting bolts through the holes in the pulley

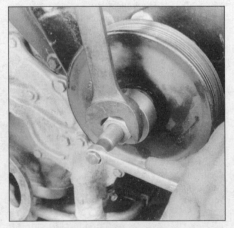

15.4 This special tool, designed for removing power steering pump pulleys, is available at most auto parts stores

15.5 To install the pulley on the shaft, use a long bolt with the same thread pitch as the internal threads of the power steering pump shaft, a nut, washer and a socket that's the same diameter as the pulley hub

16 Power steering system - bleeding

1   Following any operation in which the power steering fluid lines have been disconnected, the power steering system must be bled to remove all air and obtain proper steering performance.

2   With the front wheels in the straight ahead position, check the power steering fluid level and, if low, add fluid until it reaches the Cold (C) mark on the dipstick.

3   Start the engine and allow it to run at fast idle. Recheck the fluid level and add more if necessary to reach the Cold (C) mark on the dipstick.

4   Bleed the system by turning the wheels from side-to-side, without hitting the stops. This will work the air out of the system. Keep the reservoir full of fluid as this is done.

5   When the air is worked out of the system, return the wheels to the straight ahead position and leave the vehicle running for several more minutes before shutting it off.

6   Road test the vehicle to be sure the steering system is functioning normally and noise free.

7   Recheck the fluid level to be sure it is up to the Hot (H) mark on the dipstick while the engine is at normal operating temperature. Add fluid if necessary (see Chapter 1).

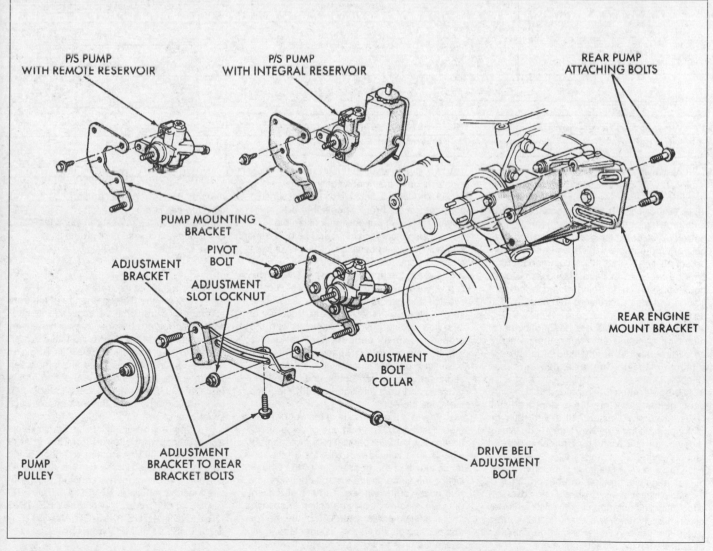

15.6 An exploded view of a typical late-model power steering pump/reservoir assembly (some models use a remote reservoir as shown in illustration 11.2)

METRIC TIRE SIZES
P 185 / 80 R 13

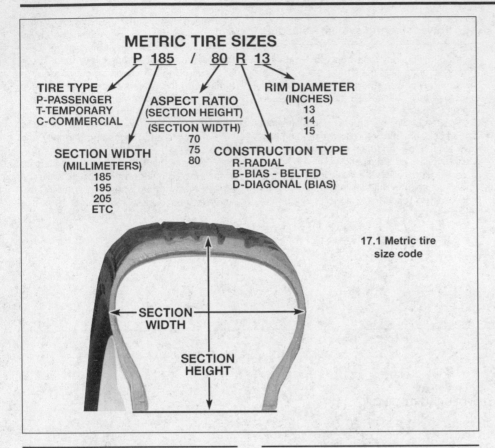

TIRE TYPE
P-PASSENGER
T-TEMPORARY
C-COMMERCIAL

ASPECT RATIO
(SECTION HEIGHT)
─────────────
(SECTION WIDTH)
70
75
80

RIM DIAMETER
(INCHES)
13
14
15

SECTION WIDTH
(MILLIMETERS)
185
195
205
ETC

CONSTRUCTION TYPE
R-RADIAL
B-BIAS - BELTED
D-DIAGONAL (BIAS)

17.1 Metric tire size code

SECTION WIDTH

SECTION HEIGHT

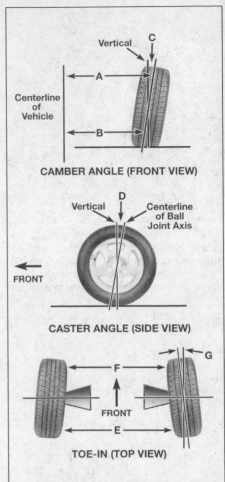

CAMBER ANGLE (FRONT VIEW)

CASTER ANGLE (SIDE VIEW)

TOE-IN (TOP VIEW)

18.3 Front end alignment details

A minus B = C (degrees camber)
D = Degrees caster
E minus F = toe-in (measured in inches)
G = toe-in (expressed in degrees)

17 Wheels and tires - general information

1   All vehicles covered by this manual are equipped with metric-sized fiberglass or steel belted radial tires (see illustration). Use of other size or type of tires may affect the ride and handling of the vehicle. Don't mix different types of tires, such as radials and bias belted, on the same vehicle as handling may be seriously affected. It's recommended that tires be replaced in pairs on the same axle, but if only one tire is being replaced, be sure it's the same size, structure and tread design as the other.

2   Because tire pressure has a substantial effect on handling and wear, the pressure on all tires should be checked at least once a month or before any extended trips (see Chapter 1).

3   Wheels must be replaced if they are bent, dented, leak air, have elongated bolt holes, are heavily rusted, out of vertical symmetry or if the lug nuts won't stay tight. Wheel repairs that use welding or peening are not recommended.

4   Tire and wheel balance is important to the overall handling, braking and performance of the vehicle. Unbalanced wheels can adversely affect handling and ride characteristics as well as tire life. Whenever a tire is installed on a wheel, the tire and wheel should be balanced by a shop with the proper equipment.

18 Front end alignment - general information

1   A front end alignment refers to the adjustments made to the front wheels so they are in proper angular relationship to the suspension and the ground. Front wheels that are out of proper alignment not only affect steering control, but also increase tire wear. The only front end adjustments possible on these vehicles are caster and toe-in.

2   Getting the proper front wheel alignment is a very exacting process, one in which complicated and expensive machines are necessary to perform the job properly. Because of this, you should have a technician with the proper equipment perform these tasks. We will, however, use this space to give you a basic idea of what is involved with front end alignment so you can better understand the process and deal intelligently with the shop that does the work.

3   Toe-in is the turning in of the front wheels (see illustration). The purpose of a toe specification is to ensure parallel rolling of the front wheels. In a vehicle with zero toe-in, the distance between the front edges of the wheels will be the same as the distance between the rear edges of the wheels. The actual amount of toe-in is normally only a fraction of an inch. Toe-in adjustment is controlled by the tie-rod end position on the tie-rod. Incorrect toe-in will cause the tires to wear improperly by making them scrub against the road surface.

4   Caster is the tilting of the top of the front steering axis from the vertical (see illustration). A tilt toward the rear is positive caster and a tilt toward the front is negative caster. On 1995 and earlier models this angle is adjusted by installing tapered shims between the front axle pads and the leaf spring brackets. On 1997 and later models it's adjusted by an adjusting cam at the axle-end of each lower control arm.

5   Camber (the tilting of the front wheels from vertical when viewed from the front of the vehicle) is factory present at 0-degree and cannot be adjusted. If the camber angle isn't correct, the components causing the problem must be replaced. NEVER ATTEMPT TO ADJUST THE CAMBER ANGLE BY HEATING OR BENDING THE AXLE OR ANY OTHER SUSPENSION COMPONENT!

Chapter 11
Body

Contents

1   General Information

Warning: *Some models covered by this manual are equipped with Supplemental Restraint Systems (SRS), more commonly known as airbags. Always disable the airbag system before working in the vicinity of any airbag system components to avoid the possibility of accidental deployment of the airbags, which could cause personal injury (see Chapter 12).*

1   Certain body components are particularly vulnerable to accident damage and can be unbolted and repaired or replaced. Among these parts are the hood, doors, tailgate, liftgate, bumpers and front fenders.

2   Only general body maintenance practices and body panel repair procedures within the scope of the do-it-yourselfer are included in this Chapter.

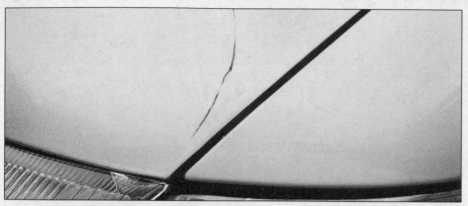

Make sure the damaged area is perfectly clean and rust free. If the touch-up kit has a wire brush, use it to clean the scratch or chip. Or use fine steel wool wrapped around the end of a pencil. Clean the scratched or chipped surface only, not the good paint surrounding it. Rinse the area with water and allow it to dry thoroughly

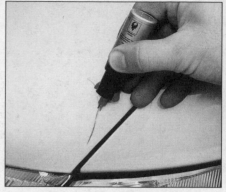

Thoroughly mix the paint, then apply a small amount with the touch-up kit brush or a very fine artist's brush. Brush in one direction as you fill the scratch area. Do not build up the paint higher than the surrounding paint

2 Body - maintenance

1   The condition of your vehicle's body is very important, because the resale value depends a great deal on it. It's much more difficult to repair a neglected or damaged body than it is to repair mechanical components. The hidden areas of the body, such as the wheel wells, the frame and the engine compartment, are equally important, although they don't require as frequent attention as the rest of the body.

2   Once a year, or every 12,000 miles, it's a good idea to have the underside of the body steam cleaned. All traces of dirt and oil will be removed and the area can then be inspected carefully for rust, damaged brake lines, frayed electrical wires, damaged cables and other problems. The front suspension components should be greased after completion of this job.

3   At the same time, clean the engine and the engine compartment with a steam cleaner or water soluble degreaser.

4   The wheel wells should be given close attention, since undercoating can peel away and stones and dirt thrown up by the tires can cause the paint to chip and flake, allowing rust to set in. If rust is found, clean down to the bare metal and apply an anti-rust paint.

5   The body should be washed about once a week. Wet the vehicle thoroughly to soften the dirt, then wash it down with a soft sponge and plenty of clean soapy water. If the surplus dirt is not washed off very carefully, it can wear down the paint.

6   Spots of tar or asphalt thrown up from the road should be removed with a cloth soaked in solvent.

7   Once every six months, wax the body and chrome trim. If a chrome cleaner is used to remove rust from any of the vehicle's plated parts, remember that the cleaner also removes part of the chrome, so use it sparingly.

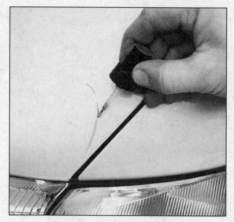

If the vehicle has a two-coat finish, apply the clear coat after the color coat has dried

3 Vinyl trim - maintenance

1   Don't clean vinyl trim with detergents, caustic soap or petroleum-based cleaners. Plain soap and water works just fine, with a soft brush to clean dirt that may be ingrained. Wash the vinyl as frequently as the rest of the vehicle.

2   After cleaning, application of a high quality rubber and vinyl protectant will help prevent oxidation and cracks. The protectant can also be applied to weatherstripping, vacuum lines and rubber hoses, which often fail as a result of chemical degradation, and to the tires.

4 Upholstery and carpets - maintenance

1   Every three months remove the carpets or mats and clean the interior of the vehicle (more frequently if necessary). Vacuum the upholstery and carpets to remove loose dirt and dust.

2   Leather upholstery requires special care. Stains should be removed with warm water

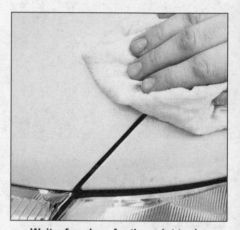

Wait a few days for the paint to dry thoroughly, then rub out the repainted area with a polishing compound to blend the new paint with the surrounding area. When you're happy with your work, wash and polish the area

and a very mild soap solution. Use a clean, damp cloth to remove the soap, then wipe again with a dry cloth. Never use alcohol, gasoline, nail polish remover or thinner to clean leather upholstery.

3   After cleaning, regularly treat leather upholstery with a leather wax. Never use car wax on leather upholstery.

4   In areas where the interior of the vehicle is subject to bright sunlight, cover leather seats with a sheet if the vehicle is to be left out for any length of time.

5 Body repair - minor damage

1   See photo sequences

Repair of minor scratches

2   If the scratch is superficial and does not penetrate to the metal of the body, repair is very simple. Lightly rub the scratched area

with a fine rubbing compound to remove loose paint and built up wax. Rinse the area with clean water.

3   Apply touch-up paint to the scratch, using a small brush. Continue to apply thin layers of paint until the surface of the paint in the scratch is level with the surrounding paint. Allow the new paint at least two weeks to harden, then blend it into the surrounding paint by rubbing with a very fine rubbing compound. Finally, apply a coat of wax to the scratch area.

4   If the scratch has penetrated the paint and exposed the metal of the body, causing the metal to rust, a different repair technique is required. Remove all loose rust from the bottom of the scratch with a pocket knife, then apply rust inhibiting paint to prevent the formation of rust in the future. Using a rubber or nylon applicator, coat the scratched area with glaze-type filler. If required, the filler can be mixed with thinner to provide a very thin paste, which is ideal for filling narrow scratches. Before the glaze filler in the scratch hardens, wrap a piece of smooth cotton cloth around the tip of a finger. Dip the cloth in thinner and then quickly wipe it along the surface of the scratch. This will ensure that the surface of the filler is slightly hollow. The scratch can now be painted over as described earlier in this section.

Repairing simple dents

Note: *These photos illustrate a method of repairing simple dents. They are intended to supplement* Body repair - minor damage *in this Chapter and should not be used as the sole instructions for body repair on these vehicles.*

5   When repairing dents, the first job is to pull the dent out until the affected area is as close as possible to its original shape. There is no point in trying to restore the original shape completely as the metal in the damaged area will have stretched on impact and cannot be restored to its original contours. It is better to bring the level of the dent up to a point which is about 1/8-inch below the level of the surrounding metal. In cases where the dent is very shallow, it is not worth trying to pull it out at all.

6   If the back side of the dent is accessible, it can be hammered out gently from behind using a soft-face hammer. While doing this, hold a block of wood firmly against the opposite side of the metal to absorb the hammer blows and prevent the metal from being stretched.

7   If the dent is in a section of the body which has double layers, or some other factor makes it inaccessible from behind, a different technique is required. Drill several small holes through the metal inside the damaged area, particularly in the deeper sections. Screw long, self tapping screws into the holes just enough for them to get a good grip in the metal. Now the dent can be pulled out by pulling on the protruding heads of the screws with locking pliers.

8   The next stage of repair is the removal of paint from the damaged area and from

an inch or so of the surrounding metal. This is easily done with a wire brush or sanding disk in a drill motor, although it can be done just as effectively by hand with sandpaper. To complete the preparation for filling, score the surface of the bare metal with a screwdriver or the tang of a file or drill small holes in the affected area. This will provide a good grip for the filler material. To complete the repair, see the Section on filling and painting.

Repair of rust holes or gashes

9   Remove all paint from the affected area and from an inch or so of the surrounding metal using a sanding disk or wire brush mounted in a drill motor. If these are not available, a few sheets of sandpaper will do the job just as effectively.

10   With the paint removed, you will be able to determine the severity of the corrosion and decide whether to replace the whole panel, if possible, or repair the affected area. New body panels are not as expensive as most people think and it is often quicker to install a new panel than to repair large areas of rust.

11   Remove all trim pieces from the affected area except those which will act as a guide to the original shape of the damaged body, such as headlight shells, etc. Using metal snips or a hacksaw blade, remove all loose metal and any other metal that is badly affected by rust. Hammer the edges of the hole inward to create a slight depression for the filler material.

12   Wire brush the affected area to remove the powdery rust from the surface of the metal. If the back of the rusted area is accessible, treat it with rust inhibiting paint.

13   Before filling is done, block the hole in some way. This can be done with sheet metal riveted or screwed into place, or by stuffing the hole with wire mesh.

14   Once the hole is blocked off, the affected area can be filled and painted. See the following subsection on filling and painting.

Filling and painting

15   Many types of body fillers are available, but generally speaking, body repair kits which contain filler paste and a tube of resin hardener are best for this type of repair work. A wide, flexible plastic or nylon applicator will be necessary for imparting a smooth and contoured finish to the surface of the filler material. Mix up a small amount of filler on a clean piece of wood or cardboard (use the hardener sparingly). Follow the manufacturer's instructions on the package, otherwise the filler will set incorrectly.

16   Using the applicator, apply the filler paste to the prepared area. Draw the applicator across the surface of the filler to achieve the desired contour and to level the filler surface. As soon as a contour that approximates the original one is achieved, stop working the paste. If you continue, the paste will begin to stick to the applicator. Continue to add thin layers of paste at 20-minute intervals until the level of the filler is just above the surrounding metal.

17   Once the filler has hardened, the excess

can be removed with a body file. From then on, progressively finer grades of sandpaper should be used, starting with a 180-grit paper and finishing with 600-grit wet-or-dry paper. Always wrap the sandpaper around a flat rubber or wooden block, otherwise the surface of the filler will not be completely flat. During the sanding of the filler surface, the wet-or-dry paper should be periodically rinsed in water. This will ensure that a very smooth finish is produced in the final stage.

18   At this point, the repair area should be surrounded by a ring of bare metal, which in turn should be encircled by the finely feathered edge of good paint. Rinse the repair area with clean water until all of the dust produced by the sanding operation is gone.

19   Spray the entire area with a light coat of primer. This will reveal any imperfections in the surface of the filler. Repair the imperfections with fresh filler paste or glaze filler and once more smooth the surface with sandpaper. Repeat this spray-and-repair procedure until you are satisfied that the surface of the filler and the feathered edge of the paint are perfect. Rinse the area with clean water and allow it to dry completely.

20   The repair area is now ready for painting. Spray painting must be carried out in a warm, dry, windless and dust free atmosphere. These conditions can be created if you have access to a large indoor work area, but if you are forced to work in the open, you will have to pick the day very carefully. If you are working indoors, dousing the floor in the work area with water will help settle the dust which would otherwise be in the air. If the repair area is confined to one body panel, mask off the surrounding panels. This will help minimize the effects of a slight mismatch in paint color. Trim pieces such as chrome strips, door handles, etc., will also need to be masked off or removed. Use masking tape and several thicknesses of newspaper for the masking operations.

21   Before spraying, shake the paint can thoroughly, then spray a test area until the spray painting technique is mastered. Cover the repair area with a thick coat of primer. The thickness should be built up using several thin layers of primer rather than one thick one. Using 600-grit wet-or-dry sandpaper, rub down the surface of the primer until it is very smooth. While doing this, the work area should be thoroughly rinsed with water and the wet-or-dry sandpaper periodically rinsed as well. Allow the primer to dry before spraying additional coats.

22   Spray on the top coat, again building up the thickness by using several thin layers of paint. Begin spraying in the center of the repair area and then, using a circular motion, work out until the whole repair area and about two inches of the surrounding original paint is covered. Remove all masking material 10 to 15 minutes after spraying on the final coat of paint. Allow the new paint at least two weeks to harden, then use a very fine rubbing compound to blend the edges of the new paint into the existing paint. Finally, apply a coat of wax.

These photos illustrate a method of repairing simple dents. They are intended to supplement *Body repair - minor damage* in this Chapter and should not be used as the sole instructions for body repair on these vehicles.

1 If you can't access the backside of the body panel to hammer out the dent, pull it out with a slide-hammer-type dent puller. Tap with a hammer near the edge of the dent to help 'pop' the metal back to its original shape, about 1/8-inch below the surface of the surrounding metal

2 Using coarse-grit sandpaper, remove the paint down to the bare metal. Clean the repair area with wax/silicone remover.

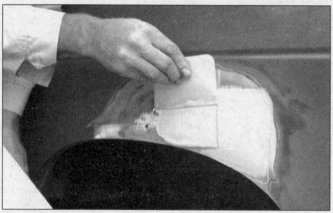

3 Following label instructions, mix up a batch of plastic filler and hardener, then quickly press it into the metal with a plastic applicator. Work the filler until it matches the original contour and is slightly above the surrounding metal

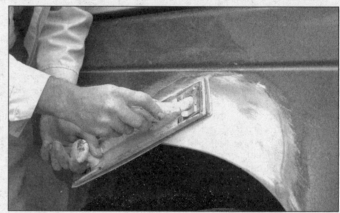

4 Let the filler harden until you can just dent it with your fingernail. File, then sand the filler down until it's smooth and even. Work down to finer grits of sandpaper - always using a board or block - ending up with 360 or 400 grit

5 When the area is smooth to the touch, clean the area and mask around it. Apply several layers of primer to the area. A professional-type spray gun is being used here, but aerosol spray primer works fine

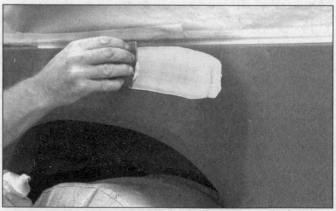

6 Fill imperfections or scratches with glazing compound. Sand with 360 or 400-grit and re-spray. Finish sand the primer with 600 grit, clean thoroughly, then apply the finish coat. Don't attempt to rub out or wax the repair area until the paint has dried completely (at least two weeks)

6   Body repair - major damage

1   Major damage must be repaired by an auto body shop specifically equipped to perform major repairs. These shops have the specialized equipment required to do the job properly.

2   If the damage is extensive, the body must be checked for proper alignment or the vehicle's handling characteristics may be adversely affected and other components may wear at an accelerated rate.

3   Due to the fact that all of the major body components (hood, fenders, etc.) are separate and replaceable units, any seriously damaged components should be replaced rather than repaired. Sometimes the components can be found in a wrecking yard that specializes in used vehicle components, often at considerable savings over the cost of new parts.

7   Hinges and locks - maintenance

1   Once every 3000 miles, or every three months, the hinges and latch assemblies on the doors, hood, liftgate and tailgate should be given a few drops of light oil or lock lubricant. The door latch strikers should also be lubricated with a thin coat of grease to reduce wear and ensure free movement. Lubricate the door and liftgate locks with spray-on graphite lubricant.

8   Fixed glass - replacement

1   Replacement of the windshield and fixed glass requires the use of special fast-setting adhesive/caulk materials and some specialized tools and techniques. These operations should be left to a dealer service department or a shop specializing in glass work.

9   Radiator grille panel - removal and installation

Warning: *The air conditioning system is under high pressure. Do not loosen any hose fittings or remove any components until the system has been discharged. Air conditioning refrigerant should be properly discharged into an EPA-approved recovery/recycling unit by a dealer service department or an automotive air conditioning repair facility. Always wear eye protection when disconnecting air conditioning system fittings.*

1987 through 1995 models

1   On air conditioned models, take the vehicle to a properly equipped shop and have the air conditioning discharged before beginning work.

2   Remove the bolts and detach the radiator and shroud from the grille panel (see Chapter 3).

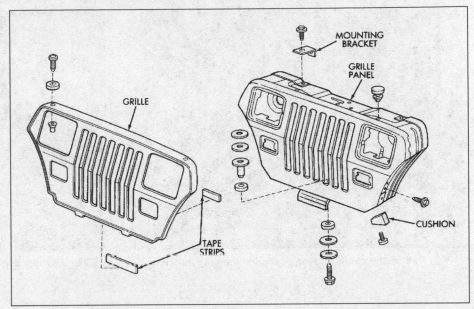

9.3 Typical radiator grille and panel details (1987 through 1995 models)

9.4 Loosen the nuts (arrow) and detach the support rods

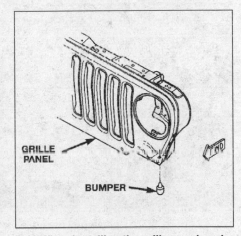

9.19 When installing the grille panel, make sure that the bumpers are correctly aligned

3   Remove the bolts attaching the grille panel to the crossmember and fenders (see illustration).

4   Loosen the support rod nuts, detach the rod, then lift the grille panel up and tilt it forward, then disconnect the wiring harness (see illustration).

5   With air conditioning disconnected (see Step 1), disconnect the high pressure hose from the sight glass and cap it.

6   Remove grille panel from the vehicle.

7   Installation is the reverse of removal.

1997 through 2006 models

8   If the vehicle is air-conditioned, have the air conditioning system evacuated before proceeding.

9   Remove the front crossmember cover.

10   Remove the crossmember valance cover.

11   Remove the cooling system reservoir.

12   Remove the bolts that secure the radiator and shroud to the grille panel.

13   If the vehicle is air conditioned, disconnect the high-pressure and low-pressure lines at the quick-disconnect fittings. Cap the lines to prevent contamination.

14   Remove the bolts radiator support rod-to-grille panel bolts.

15   Unplug the electrical connectors for the headlights, turn signals, side markers and horns.

16   Remove the fender-to-grille panel bolts.

17   Remove the grille-to-frame mount bolt.

18   Detach the grille from the vehicle.

19   Installation is the reverse of removal. When placing the grille in position, make sure that the rubber support bumpers (see illustration) are aligned.

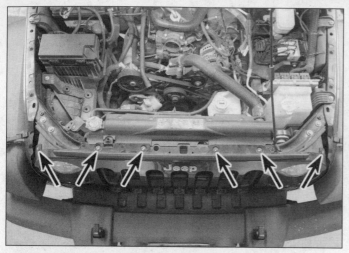

9.21 Pull up the centers of the pushpins, then pry them out

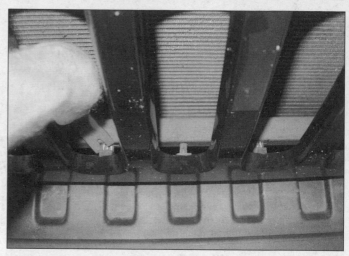

9.22a Carefully pry the retaining clips along the bottom edge of the grille…

9.22b … then pull the grille panel out

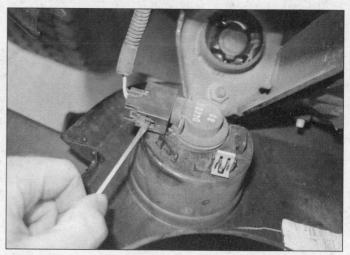

9.23 Release the connector lock, then depress the tab to disconnect the electrical connectors from the fog lights

10.3 Use a grease pencil to mark the hood hinge location - the marks can be easily cleaned later

2007 and later models

20   Disconnect the cable from the negative battery terminal.
21   Release the six pushpins along the top of the grille panel (see illustration).
22   Using a plastic trim tool, release the tabs on the five plastic clips along the bottom/rear edge of the grille panel (see illustrations).
23   Pull the grille panel out enough to disconnect the electrical connectors. Remove the grille panel (see illustration).
24   Installation is the reverse of removal.

10   Hood - removal, installation and adjustment

Note: *The hood is heavy and somewhat awkward to remove and install - at least two people should perform this procedure.*

Removal and installation

1   Use blankets or pads to cover the cowl area of the body and the fenders. This will protect the body and paint as the hood is lifted off.
2   Disconnect any cables or wire harnesses which will interfere with removal. Disconnect the windshield washer nozzles. Disconnect the ground strap.
3   Close the hood and scribe alignment marks around the hinge with a grease pencil (so the marks can be cleaned off later) to ensure proper alignment during installation (see illustration).
4   Using a #40 Torx head bit, remove the hinge-to-hood bolts, then lift the hinges up out of the way.
5   Lift off the hood (see illustration).
6   Installation is the reverse of removal. Be sure to line up the hinges with the grease pencil marks and tighten the hinge-to-hood bolts securely.

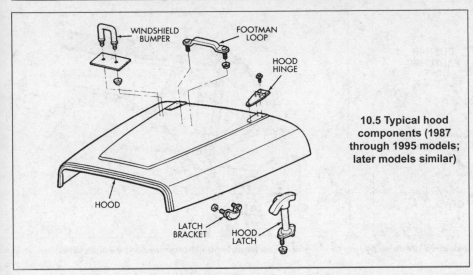

10.5 Typical hood components (1987 through 1995 models; later models similar)

11.2 Use wood blocks to prop up the hardtop

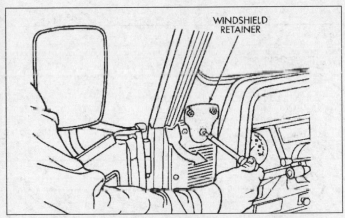

11.3a A Torx tool will be required to remove the windshield retaining bolts

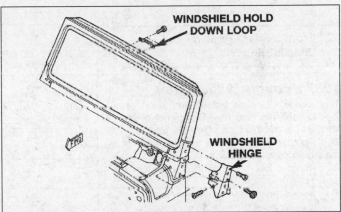

11.3b Windshield hinge installation details (1997 through 2006 models, later models similar)

Adjustment

7   Fore-and-aft and side-to-side adjustment of the hood is done by moving the hood in relation to the hinge plate after loosening the bolts.
8   Loosen the bolts and move the hood into correct alignment. Move it only a little at a time. Tighten the hood bolts, then open and close the hood to check the alignment.

11 Framed windshield assembly - removal and installation

Note: On all models, the windshield glass is fixed (bonded) to the windshield frame. It should only be replaced by a professional glass technician.

1   Remove the windshield wiper assemblies. First mark the position of each wiper arm on the wiper pivot shaft to ensure correct reassembly. Next, insert an ice-pick-type tool through the hole that's just above the pivot shaft on the wiper arm. Grasp the wiper arm at the pivot shaft and pull off the assembly.
2   Detach the convertible or hardtop from the windshield frame. The hardtop can be propped up out of the way on wood blocks after loosen-

ing the attaching bolts (see illustration).
3   On 1987 through 1995 models, remove the windshield retainers (see illustration). On 1997 through 2006 models, remove the pivot screw closest to the hinge pivot point (see illustration) and tilt the windshield forward. On 2007 and later models, remove the bolts securing the front of the sport bars to the top

corners of the windshield frame.
Note: 2007 and later models require the removal of the cowl top panel in order to access the lower-middle hinge fasteners (see Section 26)
4   Remove the hinge screws and lift the windshield frame assembly off the vehicle (see illustrations).
5   Installation is the reverse of removal.

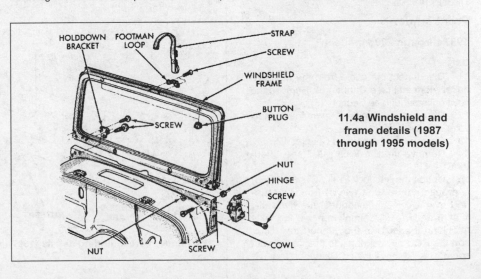

11.4a Windshield and frame details (1987 through 1995 models)

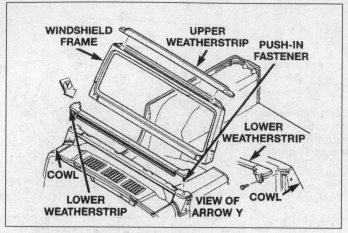

11.4b Windshield and frame details (1997 through 2006 models, later models similar)

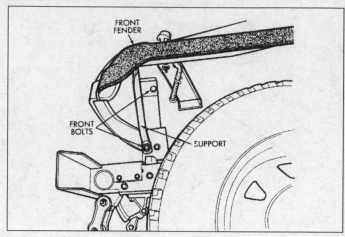

12.3 The front fender bolts are easily accessible

12   Front fender - removal and installation

1987 through 1995 models

1   Release the hood hold-down.
2   Detach the side marker lamp and disconnect the radio antenna (see Chapter 12).
3   Remove the bolts from the front edge of the fender (see illustration).
4   Remove the rear support and fender-to-body bolts (see illustration).
5   Detach the fender from the vehicle.
6   Installation is the reverse of removal.

And later models

Front fender flare

7   Remove the side marker lamp (see Chapter 12).
8   Remove the flare-to-fender retaining screws (see illustration).
9   Detach the flare from the front fender.
10   Installation is the reverse of removal. Make sure that the surface between the fender and the flare is clean before reattaching the flare.

Front fender

1997 through 2006 models

Left

11   Disconnect the cable from the negative battery terminal (see Chapter 5). Remove the cowl grille panel (see Section 26).
12   Remove the windshield washer reservoir.
13   Remove the horns (see Chapter 12).
14   Remove the EVAP canister (see Chapter 6).
15   Unbolt the Anti-lock Brake System (ABS) hydraulic control unit (HCU) from the support tray. Do NOT disconnect the hydraulic lines from the HCU; simply remove the bolts attaching the HCU to the support tray. Support the HCU by securing it to the firewall with some wire. Remove the HCU support tray.

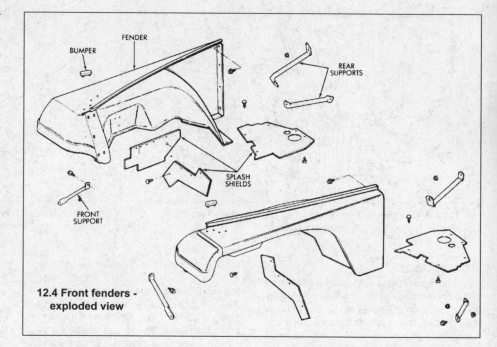

12.4 Front fenders - exploded view

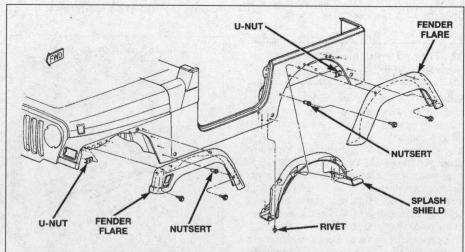

12.8 Fender flare mounting details (1997 through 2006 models, later models similar)

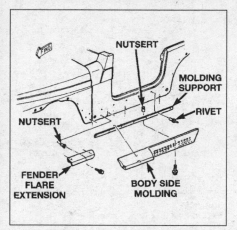

12.19 Body side molding installation details (1997 and later mosdels)

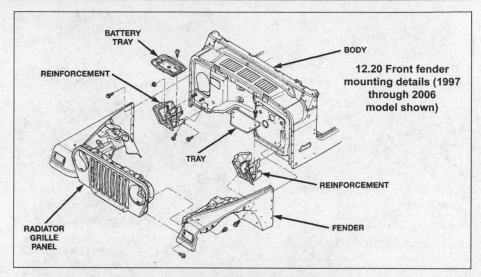

12.20 Front fender mounting details (1997 through 2006 model shown)

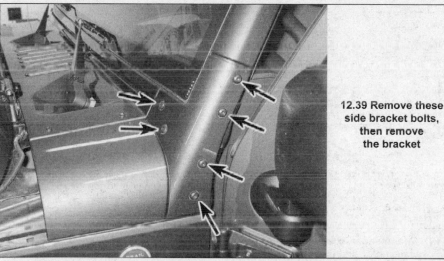

12.39 Remove these side bracket bolts, then remove the bracket

16   Detach the forward wiring harness clips from the fender. Detach the headlight connector.
17   Thread the wire harness for the fog lamp (if equipped), the parking light and the side marker light through the access hole in the fender well.
18   Remove the fender flare, If equipped (see Steps 7 through 9 above).
19   Remove the body side molding, if equipped, as follows: Remove the bolts from the underside of the body molding (see illustration). Lift up the molding to disengage it from the molding support. (If it's necessary to romove tho molding support, you'll have to drill out and discard the rivets. Use new rivets when installing the molding support.)
20   Remove the fender-to body bolts, tho fender-to-HCU tray support bracket bolts and the fender-to-grille bolts (see illustration).
21   Installation is the reverse of removal. To install the body side molding correctly, put the upper edge of the molding over the upper edge of the molding support and slide it down.

Right

22   Remove the battery (see Chapter 5).
23   Remove the air cleaner housing (see Chapter 4).
24   Remove the bolts that attach the Power Distribution Center (PDC) to the fender (see Chapter 12). Detach the PDC wire harness clips from the battery tray and from the fender. Move the PDC and support it from the firewall with a piece of wire.
25   Detach the air conditioning high pressure line retainer from the fender.
26   Detach the forward wiring harness clips from the fender.
27   Remove the battery tray.
28   Detach the connector for the battery temperature sensor.
29   Disconnect the vacuum line from the reservoir located under the battery tray reinforcement bracket.
30   Thread the wire harness for the fog lamp (if equipped), the parking light and the side marker light through the access hole in the

fender well.
31   Remove the fender flare, if equipped (see Steps 7 through 9).
32   Remove the body side molding, if equipped (see Step 18 above).
33   Remove the fender-to-body bolts, the fender-to-battery tray support brackct bolts and the fender-to-grille bolts (see illustration 12.19).
34   Installation is the reverse of removal. To install the body side molding correctly, put the upper edge of the molding over the upper edge of the molding support and slide it down.

2007 and later models - left or right side

35   Disconnect the cable from the negative battery terminal (see Chapter 5).
36   Remove the cowl top panel (see Section 26).
37   Remove the front fender flares (see previous Steps).
38   Remove the front fenderwell splash shield pushpin and bolt fasteners, detach the ABS sensor wire harness from the splash shield, then remove the shield.
39   Remove the bracket retaining the windshield frame and fender (see illustration).
40   Remove the 3 upper fender bolts, and

the 2 fender bolts exposed by the removed cowl panel.
41   With the door open, remove the 2 rear fender bolts (one bolt is facing horizontally, the other is facing down).
42   Remove the 2 lower fender bolts.
43   Working in the fenderwell- remove the front fender bolt, then remove the fender. Also remove the antenna from the appropriate side fender.
44   Installation is the reverse of removal. Install the fender retaining bolts loosely at first to allow for proper alignment; once even alignment has been achieved, tighten all the fender retaining bolts securely.

13   Bumpers - removal and installation

Through 1995 models

1   Disconnect any wiring or other components that would interfere with bumper removal.
2   Support the bumper with a jack or jackstand. Alternatively, have an assistant support the bumper as the bolts are removed.

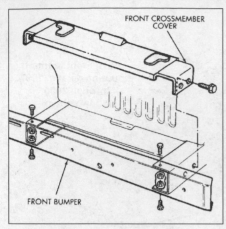

13.3a Front bumper details

13.3b The rear bumper is welded to the frame, but the bumperette bolts (arrows) are easily accessible

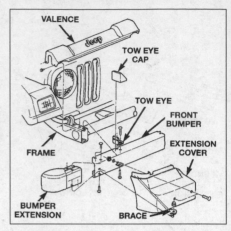

13.7a Front bumper extension mounting details (1997 and later models)

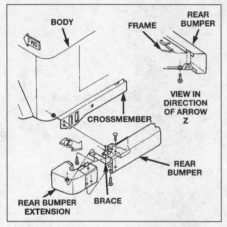

13.7b Rear bumper extension mounting details (1997 and later models)

14.1 Partially close the door and lift the return strap off the pin

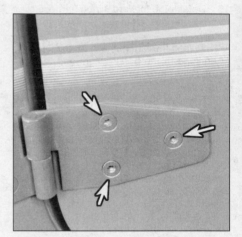

14.3 After marking the hinge location with a grease pencil, remove the bolts (arrows) with a Torx-head tool

14.4 Remove the nut (arrow) and pull the hinge pin out

3   Remove the bolts that secure the bumper mounting brackets to the frame, then detach the bumper (see illustrations).
4   Installation is the reverse of removal.
5   Tighten the retaining bolts securely.
6   Install any components that were removed.

And later models

Note: *For 2007 and later models- the front bumper is comprised of 2 components - the structural metal bumper and the bumper cover. Both components are fastened by the same mounting bolts and can be separated once removed from the vehicle. There are a total of 8 mounting bolts - 2 sets accessed from the fenderwell on the outside, and 2 sets accessed from the inside of the frame (with the bumper top trim panel removed).*

7   The bumpers on these models are equipped with extensions (see illustrations) which can be replaced without removing the bumpers.
8   Removing and installing the bumpers is otherwise similar to the procedure for earlier models (see Steps 1 through 6).

14   Door - removal, installation and adjustment

Note: *The procedure is the same for full-doors or half-doors.*

1   Remove the door trim panel (see Sec-

tion 17). Disconnect any wire harness connectors and push them through the door opening so they won't interfere with door removal. Detach the door return strap (see illustration). On 2007 and later models, remove the front kick panel to access the electrical connector. Disconnect the connector.
2   Place a jack or jackstand under the door or have an assistant on hand to support it when the hinge bolts are removed.
Note: *If a jack or jackstand is used, place a rag between it and the door to protect the door's painted surfaces.*

Convertible

3   Scribe around the lower door hinge with a grease pencil (so the marks can removed later), then remove the bolts with a Torx head tool (see illustration).
4   Remove the upper door hinge pin nut, extract the pin and lift the door off the vehicle (see illustration).

Hardtop

5   Remove the hinge pin nuts, extract the pins and remove the door from the vehicle (see illustration 14.4).

All models

6   Installation is the reverse of removal. Tighten the hinge-to-door bolts and hinge nuts securely.

7   Following installation of the door, check the alignment and adjust it if necessary as follows:

  a) *Forward-and-backward adjustments are made by loosening the lower door hinge-to-body bolts.*

  b) *Forward-and-backward and up-and-down adjustments can be made by loosening the hinge-to-door bolts*

  c) *The door lock striker can also be adjusted in-and-out.*

15   Liftgate - removal, installation and adjustment (hardtop models only)

1   Open the liftgate and cover the upper body area around the opening with pads or cloths to protect the painted surfaces when the liftgate is removed.

2   Unplug the dome lamp and defroster electrical connector from the liftgate wiring harness.

3   Remove the rear wiper motor cover and unplug the electrical harness and washer hose. Remove the wiper arm by pulling the tab away from the pivot shaft and pulling the arm off the shaft (see illustration).

4   Scribe around the hinge flanges with a grease pencil so the liftgate can be easily adjusted when installed.

5   While an assistant supports the liftgate, pry off the clips and detach the support struts.

6   Remove the hinge bolts and detach the liftgate from the vehicle (see illustration).

7   Installation is the reverse of removal. Tighten the hinge bolts securely.

8   After installation, close the liftgate and make sure it's in proper alignment with the surrounding body panels.

9   The engagement of the liftgate can be adjusted by removing the screws and the striker and adding or removing shims underneath to raise or lower it (see illustration). If you add or remove shims, tighten the striker screws securely (on 2006 and earlier models so equipped).

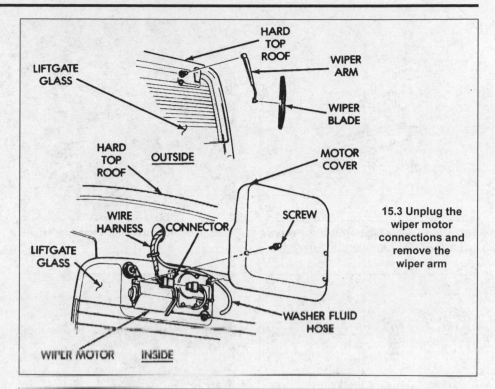

15.3 Unplug the wiper motor connections and remove the wiper arm

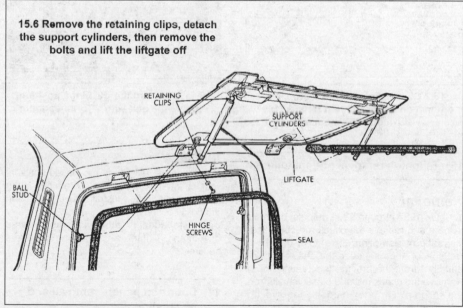

15.6 Remove the retaining clips, detach the support cylinders, then remove the bolts and lift the liftgate off

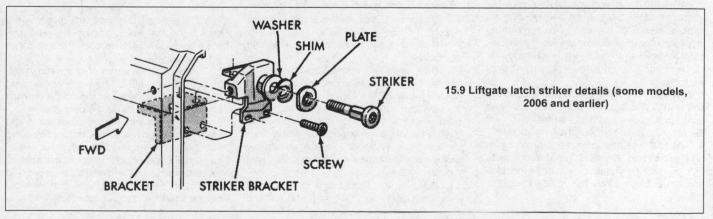

15.9 Liftgate latch striker details (some models, 2006 and earlier)

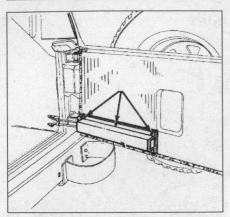

16.1a Remove the check rod cover screws (arrows) (1987 through 1995 models)

16.1b Remove the check rod spacer…

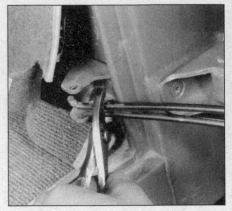

16.1c … and squeeze the rod to detach it from the bracket

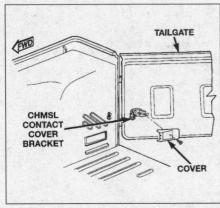

16.2 Center high-mounted stoplight contact cover installation details (1997 through 2006 models)

16.4a After marking the hinge position, remove the bolt with a Torx-head tool

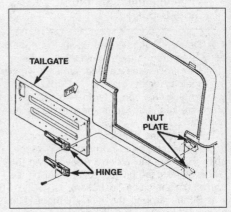

16.4b Tailgate hinge assembly mounting details (1997 and later models)

16 Tailgate - removal and installation

Removal

1   On 1987 through 1995 models, open the tailgate and remove the check rod cover (see illustration). Use pliers to remove the check rod spacer, then squeeze the check rod and detach it from the bracket (see illustrations). Remove the check rod and plastic shield from the tailgate. On later models, remove the check rod mounting bolts.

2   On 1997 and later models, remove the spare tire, open the tailgate and remove the contact cover for the center high-mounted stoplight (see illustration). Unplug the electrical connectors for the center high-mounted stoplight and disengage the wire harness from the tailgate.

3   Close the tailgate and scribe around the body hinge with a grease pencil. On 2007 and later models, use a plastic trim tool to pry off the hinge covers to access the hinge bolts.

4   With the tailgate closed and/or an assistant supporting it, use a Torx-head tool to remove the hinge bolts, then release the latch and lift the tailgate from the vehicle (see illustrations).

Installation

5   Place the tailgate in the closed position, with the latch engaged. Place the hinge in the marked position and install the bolts. Tighten the bolts securely.

6   Installation is otherwise the reverse of removal. Tighten all remaining fasteners securely.

17 Door trim panel - removal and installation

1   Disconnect the negative cable from the battery.

2   Remove the armrest and door handle assemblies.

3   On models with manual crank windows, remove the Allen head screw and detach the window regulator handle.

4   On convertible top models, unzip the plastic window, then push down and pull up sharply to detach the window assembly from the door (see illustration). Rotate the window grommets and lift them out of the door panel (see illustration).

5   Insert a flat, forked tool or a padded screwdriver between the trim panel and the door and disengage the plastic clip (see illustration). Work around the outer edge until the panel is free. On convertible models, insert a screwdriver into the grommet holes and detach the upper door panel clips (see illustration). On 2007 and later models with full doors, remove the plastic trim covers from the inside handle area, remove the various retaining bolts and screws from the door panel, then disengage the pushpins securing the door panel with a trim tool.

6   For access to the inner door on hardtop models, carefully peel back the plastic watershield.

7   Once all of the clips are disengaged, detach the trim panel, unplug any wire harness connectors and remove the trim panel from the vehicle.

8   Prior to installation of the door panel, be sure to reinstall any retainers in the panel which may have come out during the removal procedure and remain in the door itself.

9   Plug in the wire harness connectors and place the panel in position in the door. Press the door panel into place until the clips are seated and install the handle and armrest assemblies. Install the trim panel retaining bolts/screws and trim covers (as equipped). Install the manual regulator window crank (if equipped).

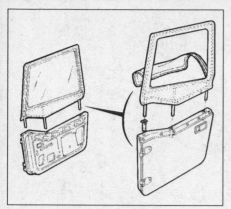

17.4a Convertible door details

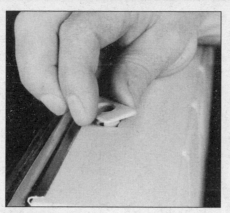

17.4b Rotate the window grommets and lift them out of the door

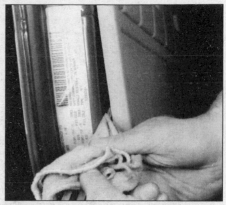

17.5a A flat, forked tool or a screwdriver padded with a rag makes the job of prying the panel retainers loose much easier

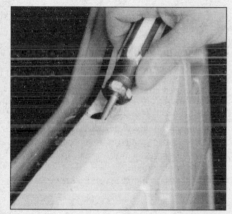

17.5b On convertible models, work through the window retainer grommet holes to pry the upper door trim clips loose

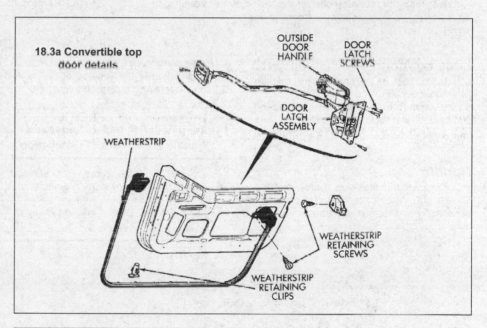

18.3a Convertible top door details

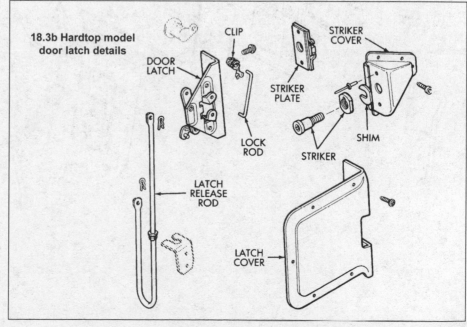

18.3b Hardtop model door latch details

18   Door latch, lock cylinder and handle - removal and installation

1   Remove the door trim panel and water-shield (see Section 17).

2   On hardtop models, remove the door window glass (see Section 23). On 2007 and later models with full doors, remove the glass and separate the stamped-metal door carrier by disconnecting the wiring harness and removing one screw (accessible when a rubber plug on the door is removed), and the perimeter mounting screws. The latch is now accessible.

Door latch

3   Remove the three door latch retaining screws from the end of the door, disconnect the links or cables, disconnect the electrical connector (if equipped), then remove the latch (see illustrations). On later models, the latch is retained by upper and lower tabs that need to be depressed instead of being retained by bolts.

4   Installation is the reverse of removal. Tighten the door latch retaining screws securely.

18.6 Push the retaining clip off the lock cylinder housing to release it from the door

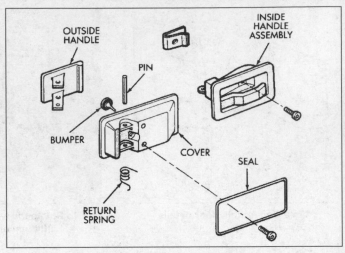

18.7 Hardtop door handle details (earlier models shown)

Lock cylinder

5   Disconnect the link from the lock cylinder (where necessary).

6   Use pliers to slide the retaining clip off and remove the lock cylinder from the door (see illustration). Installation is the reverse of removal.

Handle

7   Remove the retaining nut(s), pull the handle out, detach the control rod (where necessary) and remove the handle from the door (see illustration).

8   Installation is the reverse of removal. Tighten the retaining nut(s) securely.

19   Tailgate latch, lock cylinder and handle - removal and installation

1   Open the tailgate, remove the screws and detach the latch cover (see illustration). On 2007 and later models, remove the latch trim with a trim tool, located toward the end of the tailgate.

2   Remove the clip and detach the latch rod(s) (see illustration).

3   Remove the latch retaining screws, disconnect the lock cylinder rod, remove the retaining clip and detach the lock cylinder, if necessary (see illustration).

4   Remove the latch handle screws, disengage the handle from the latch, then remove the latch mechanism.

5   Installation is the reverse of removal.

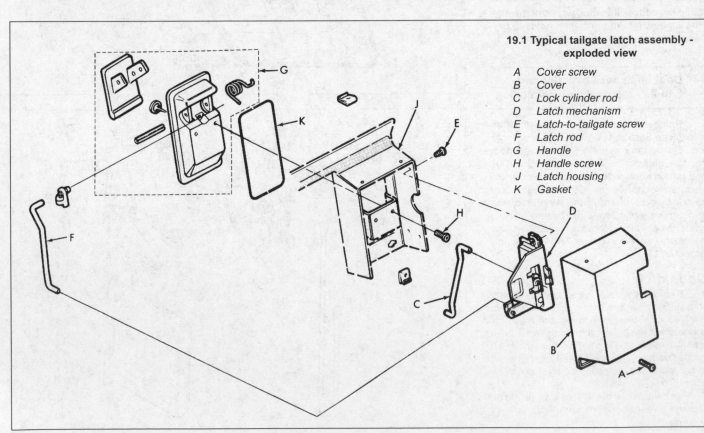

19.1 Typical tailgate latch assembly - exploded view

A   Cover screw
B   Cover
C   Lock cylinder rod
D   Latch mechanism
E   Latch-to-tailgate screw
F   Latch rod
G   Handle
H   Handle screw
J   Latch housing
K   Gasket

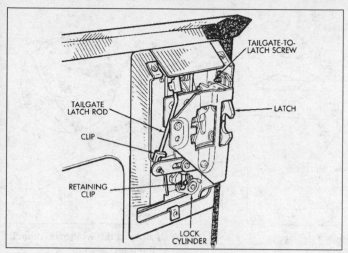

19.2 Detach the clip and disconnect the latch rod - 2007 and later models will have more than one rod to detach

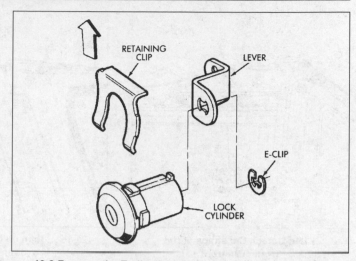

19.3 Remove the E-clip, detach the lever, then remove the lock cylinder

20 Hardtop - removal and installation

Earlier models

1   Remove the hardtop-to-windshield frame screw.

2   Remove the hardtop-to-body bolts and washers (see illustration).

3   Unplug any electrical connectors that would interfere with removal.

4   With the help of an assistant, lift the hard top off the vehicle, taking care not to damage the foam sealer used between the top and body.

5   Installation is the reverse of removal.

Later model 3-piece hardtops

6   On 2007 and later models, there are two removable front sections of the hardtop. To remove them, first release the handle clamps that secure the two panels to each other and the vehicle. Next, remove the 2 rear thumbscrews.

7   Release the two front clamps above the windshield frame, then lift out the two removable front panels, one at a time from outside the vehicle.

8   The main hardtop can be removed by taking out the three allen bolts along each side at the rear interior (and two upper bolts on each side (exterior) at the front of the top on four door models).

9   Disconnect the electrical connector and windshield washer supply hose.

10   The hardtop rear section is awkward and heavy, have an assistant or two help with removal.

11   Installation is the reverse of removal.

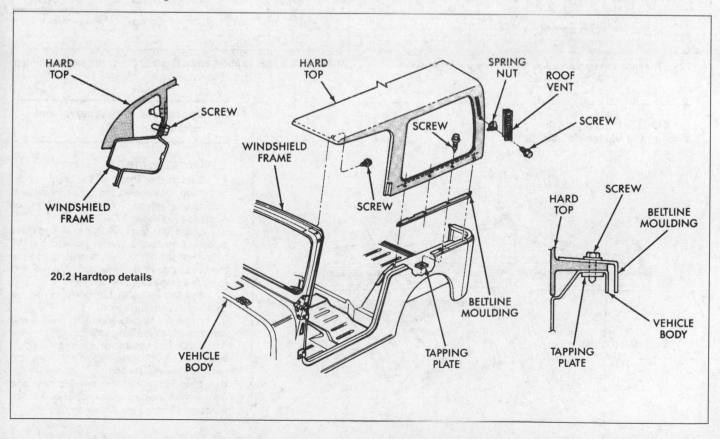

20.2 Hardtop details

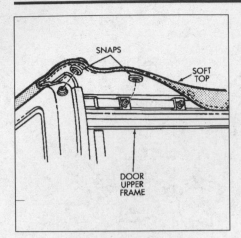

21.1a Detach the snaps at the front corners…

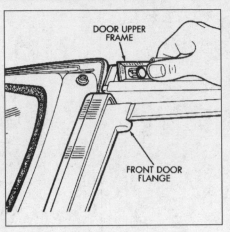

21.1b … then disconnect the upper door frame

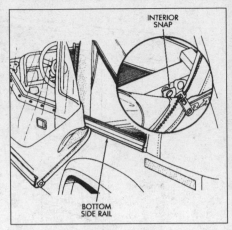

21.2 After unzipping the windows, detach the interior snap

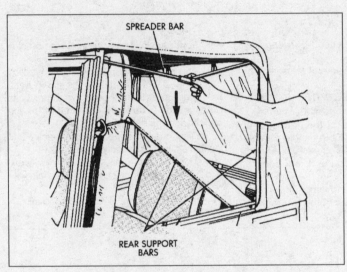

21.3 Release the spreader bar tension by pulling it down

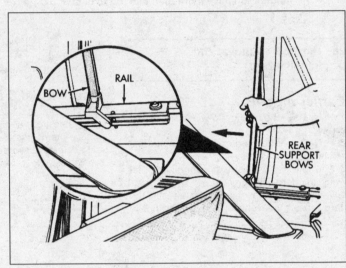

21.5 Push the rear support bows forward out of the side rail notch

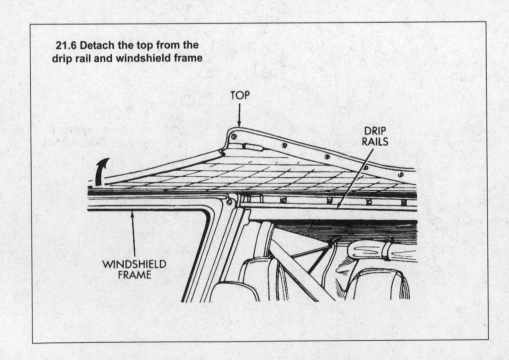

21.6 Detach the top from the drip rail and windshield frame

21 Convertible top - removal and installation

Earlier models

1   Detach the snaps at the front corner of the top, disconnect the upper frame and unsnap the fasteners, then remove the door windows (see illustrations).

2   Unzip the front and rear side curtain zippers, unsnap the interior tab and pull the bottom edges out of the channel, then slide the front edge of the side curtain down and remove it (see illustration).

3   Pull the spreader bar down to release the tension (see illustration).

4   Open the tailgate and unzip the top and side zippers on the rear curtains.

5   Push the bottom of the rear support bows forward about two-inches out of the side rail notch (see illustration).

6   Detach the top from the drip rails and from the retainer along the upper end of the windshield frame (see illustration).

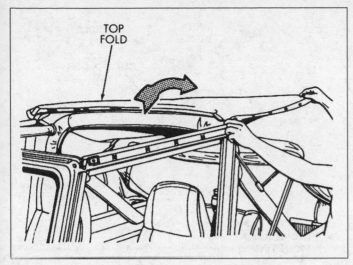

21.7 Fold the top back to the first bow

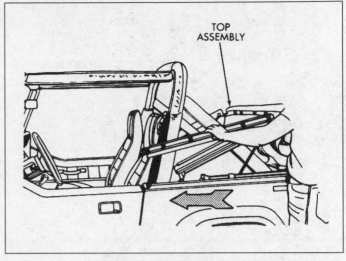

21.8 Slide the top assembly to the rear so the bottom of the bows move forward and fold under

7   Fold the top back at the front support bow (see illustration).

8   Slide the drip rail lock forward, pull it off the lockpin on the windshield frame, then slide the whole assembly to the rear so the bottom of the rear support bows move forward and fold under the bows and drip rails (see illustration).

9   Slide the front support bow out of the side rail, then remove the convertible top assembly from the vehicle.

10   Installation is the reverse of removal.

And later models

Note: *The procedure is similar for both two-door and four-door models.*

11   Undo the hook-and-loop straps on the quarter windows, then release the windows from the side rails.

12   Unzip the rear window and release the two retainers where the window is secured to the tailgate.

13   Undo the two clamps above the windshield frame and pull back the top enough to release the soft-top retainers from the upper and lower rail retainers.

14   Fold the top down.

15   If the top is to be completely removed from the vehicle, remove the bolts and release the knuckles at the top-pivot brackets.

16   Installation is the reverse of removal.

22   Center console and bezel - removal and installation

Through 1995 models

1   Disconnect the negative cable at the battery.

2   Open the console door for access.

3   Remove the retaining screws (see illustration).

4   Detach the console and lift it from the vehicle.

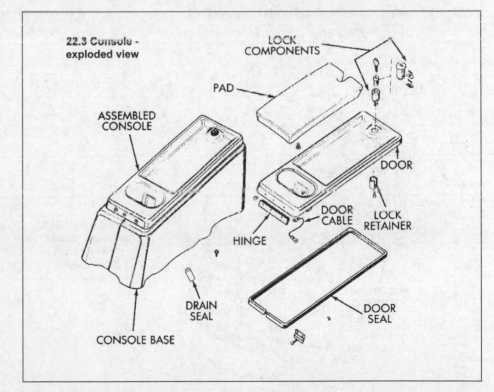

22.3 Console - exploded view

5   Installation is the reverse of removal.

1997 through 2017 models

Warning: *Some models covered by this manual are equipped with airbags. Always disable the airbag system when working in the vicinity of airbag system components (see Chapter 12).*

Center console

6   Move the seats to the full rearward position. Place the passenger seat in the fully reclining position.

7   On vehicles with an automatic transmission, grasp the shift handle firmly and yank it upward to remove it from the shift lever. On

4WD models, remove the transfer case shift knob in the same manner (see Chapter 7B for more info).

8   Using a plastic trim tool, remove the trim panel from the rear of the center console and disconnect any electrical connectors (later models).

9   On vehicles with an automatic transmission, use a small flat-bladed screwdriver to pry up the gear position indicator trim panel.

10   On vehicles with a manual transmission, pry up the shift boot and remove the shifter handle mounting bolt and the shift handle.

11   On vehicles with a mini console, remove the trim disc from the bottom of the cup holder.

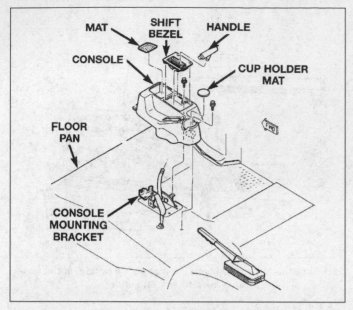

22.12a Mini console mounting details (1997 through 2006 models)

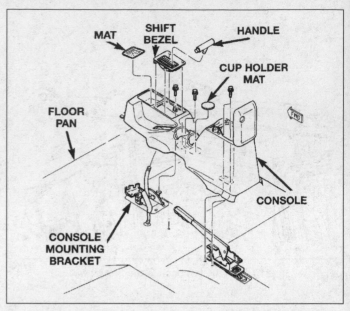

22.12b Full console mounting details (1997 through 2006 models)

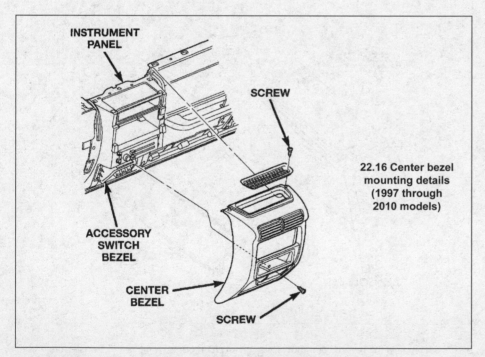

22.16 Center bezel mounting details (1997 through 2010 models)

12   On 2007 through 2017 models, pry up the console top trim piece with a plastic trim tool. Remove the console retaining bolts (see illustrations). 2007 and later model consoles are retained by 4 bolts, accessed from the front and rear sides.

13   Shift the transfer case to the 4L position and engage the parking brake.

14   Where equipped, disconnect the electrical connectors. Lift up the console, rotate it if necessary, and remove it through the passenger door.

Instrument panel center bezel

Note: *For 2011 and later models, see Chapter 12, Section 20.*

15   Remove the instrument panel top cover (see Step 28 in Section 24).

16   Remove the ash tray. Remove the screw in the back of the ash tray that attaches the center bezel to the lower instrument panel (see illustration).

17   Remove the two screws that attach the center bezel to the top of the instrument panel.

18   Using a wide, flat-bladed tool, carefully pry the lower edge of the center bezel away from the instrument panel.

19   Lift up the lower edge of the center bezel to release the four snap clip retainers that secure it to the instrument panel.

20   Remove the center bezel.

21   Installation is the reverse of removal.

---

23   Door window glass - removal and installation (hardtop models only)

---

1   Remove the door trim panel and watershield (see Section 17).

2   Lower the window glass.

Through 1995 models

Vent glass

3   Remove the division channel upper screw and the lower adjustment screw (see illustration).

4   Detach the front three inches of weatherstripping from the upper door frame, then remove the division channel and tilt the glass out of the frame.

5   Installation is the reverse of removal.

Window glass

6   Remove the glass channel stop bumper (see illustration 23.3).

7   Remove the screws attaching the window regulator arm guide to the glass, then remove the guide assembly (see illustration 23.3).

8   Lower the glass to the bottom of the door, then remove the vent glass division channel screws. Pull out about three inches of weatherstripping from the upper door frame, then remove the division channel.

9   Raise the glass and tilt it toward the hinge side of the door, then detach it from the rear channel. Remove the glass by pulling it up and out of the door.

10   Installation is the reverse of removal. The amount of effort required to raise and lower the window glass can be adjusted by moving the lower end of the division channel fore-and-aft before tightening the lower adjustment screw.

1997 through 2017 models

11   Pull the door glass run channel from the door sail. On 2007 and later models, remove the door carrier assembly (see Section 17).

12   Roll the glass all the way down.

13   Remove the door sail panel screws and remove the sail (see illustrations).

14   Roll up the glass 1/4-turn to access the regulator arm guide. On 2007 and later models, remove the nut securing the rear glass run-channel and move the channel aside, then rotate the glass 90 degrees forward (so the front of the glass is now down) and remove the glass upward from the door.

15   Remove the screws that attach the regulator arm guide to the glass.

16   Lift the glass upward while tilting it inward, then remove it from the door.

17   Installation is the reverse of removal.

24   Instrument panel - removal and installation

1995 and earlier models

1   Disconnect the negative battery cable.

2   Remove the screws from the instrument panel (see illustrations).

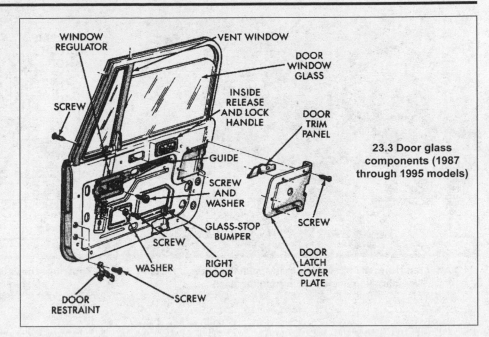

23.3 Door glass components (1987 through 1995 models)

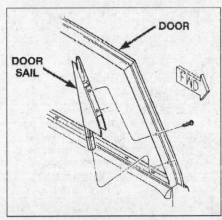

23.13a Remove the door sail panel screws…

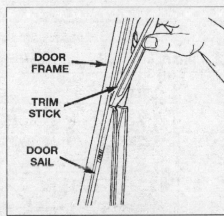

23.13b … then pry the sail panel loose with a small stick (1997 through 2010 models)

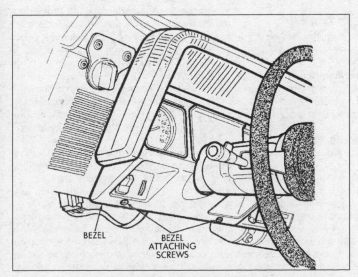

24.2a Remove the two lower instrument panel screws under the steering column with a Phillips screwdriver

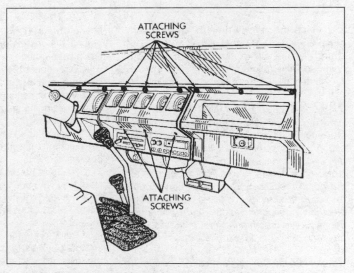

24.2b The upper and lower instrument panel screws run the length of the dash

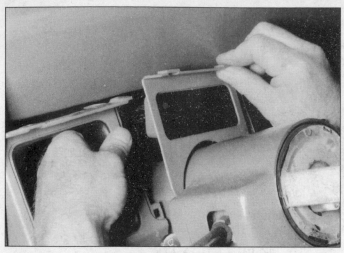

24.3 After removing the attaching screws, pull the bezel parts out sharply to detach them from the dash

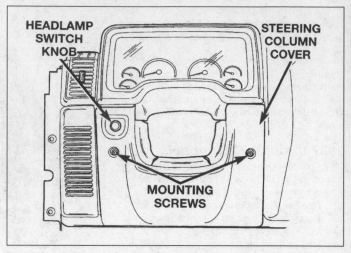

24.8 Remove these two screws from the cover for the steering column opening and remove the cover (1997 through 2010 models)

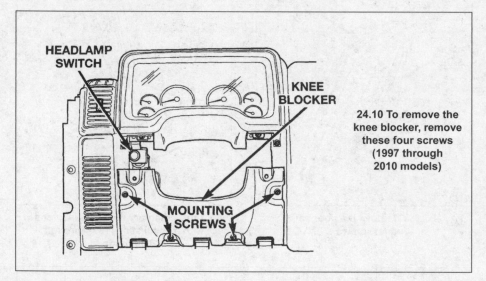

24.10 To remove the knee blocker, remove these four screws (1997 through 2010 models)

3   Once the screws have been removed, grasp the individual panel pieces and pull out sharply at the top to detach them from the dash (see illustration).

4   Installation is the reverse of removal.

1997 through 2010 models

Warning: *Some models covered by this manual are equipped with airbags. Always disable the airbag system when working in the vicinity of airbag system components (see Chapter 12).*

Note: *Note 1: This is a difficult procedure for the home mechanic. There are many hidden fasteners, difficult angles to work in and many electrical connectors to tag and disconnect/connect. We recommend that this procedure be done only by an experienced do-it-yourselfer.*

Note: *Note 2: During removal of the instrument panel, make careful notes of how each piece comes off, where it fits in relation to other pieces and what holds it in place. If you note*

how each part is installed before removing it, getting the instrument panel back together again will be much easier.

5   Disconnect the cable from the negative battery terminal. On 2007 and later models, have the air conditioning refrigerant recovered before beginning the procedure, and drain the cooling system.

6   If the vehicle is equipped with a tilt steering column, raise the column to its highest position.

7   Remove the headlight switch knob and shaft (see Chapter 12, Section 13).

8   Remove the two screws that retain the cover for the steering column opening (see illustration).

9   Pull the steering column opening cover straight back as far back as it will go. Work the lower edge of the cover rearward to disengage the hooks on the lower edge of the cover from the pivots on the lower edge of the instrument panel. Remove the cover.

10   Remove the four screws that attach the knee blocker to the instrument panel (see illustration). Remove the knee blocker.

11   Insert the key in the ignition switch and turn the key to the On position.

12   On 2006 and earlier models, insert a pin punch (or a small screwdriver) through the access hole in the lower steering column cover, then depress the retainer tang in the key lock cylinder and pull the lock cylinder out of the ignition switch lock housing (see Chapter 12, Section 18).

13   Remove the three screws that attach the lower steering column cover to the upper column cover (see Chapter 12).

14   If the vehicle is equipped with a tilt steering column, lower the column to its lowest position. If the vehicle is equipped with a non-tilt steering column, loosen the two nuts that attach the upper steering column bracket to the steering column support bracket studs on the dash panel, then lower the column enough to remove the upper steering column cover.

15   Remove the upper and lower steering column covers.

16   If the vehicle is equipped with a tilt steering column, disconnect the tilt mechanism control cable from the tilt lever to facilitate access to the steering column electrical connectors.

17   Unplug the electrical connectors to the multi-function switch, wiper/washer switch, ignition switch, anti-theft system, etc.

18   Detach the steering column wiring harness retainer from the steering column.

19   It's not absolutely necessary to remove the steering wheel in order to remove the steering column, but it is recommended since it reduces the chance of damaging the airbag system. (If you prefer to separate the airbag, steering wheel and steering column/steering shaft into three components, refer to Chapter 12 for instructions on disabling and removing

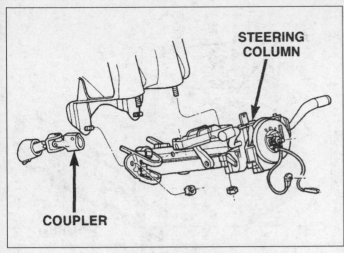

**24.20 Steering column mounting details
(1997 through 2010 models)**

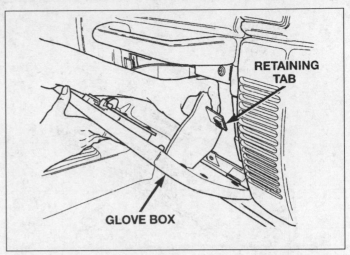

**24.24a Support the glove box door with one hand, reach inside
the glove box, depress the tab and pull the door open until the tab
clears the glove box opening (1997 through 2010 models)**

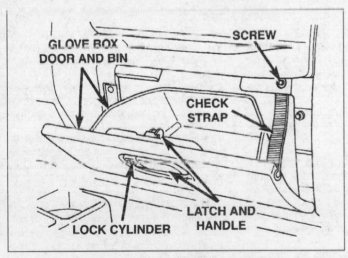

**24.24b On 1998 and later models, support the glove box door with
one hand, grasp the check strap as close to the glove box door
as possible and slide the rolled end of the check strap out of the
edge of the door (1997 through 2010 models)**

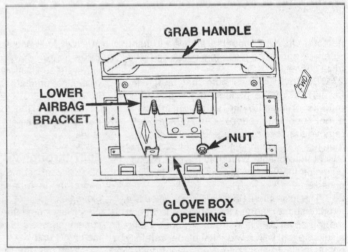

**24.27 Remove the two nuts that attach the lower side of the
passenger's side airbag module bracket to the studs on the dash
panel (1997 through 2010 models)**

the airbag and refer to Chapter 10 for steering wheel removal.) If you opt to leave the steering wheel installed, it's critical that the steering wheel not be allowed to move in relation to the steering column. The steering wheel must remain indexed to the steering column because of the "clockspring" under the steering wheel. The clockspring, which is part of the driver's side airbag circuit, carries current from the main harness to the steering wheel-mounted airbag, in the event of an accident. Using cable ties, immobilize the steering wheel and the steering column so that they cannot be moved in relation to one another.
Warning: *Failure to prevent steering wheel rotation can damage the clockspring, which can cause the airbag system to fail.*

20   Remove the pinch bolt from the upper half of the steering shaft coupler (see illustration).

21   Remove the four nuts that attach the steering column mounts to the steering column support bracket. Lower the steering column mounts off the support bracket studs and remove the column/steering wheel assembly.
Warning: *If the steering wheel is still installed, do NOT lay the steering column/steering wheel assembly on the airbag.*

22   Reach through the steering column opening and clearly label and unplug all electrical connectors.

23   Disconnect the heater/air conditioning temperature control cable from the blend-air door lever.

24   Release the glove box latch and open the glove box door. On 1997 models, support the glove box door with one hand, reach inside the glove box, depress the tab (see illustration), then pull the door open until the tab clears the glove box opening. On 1998 and later models, support the glove box door with one hand, grasp the check strap as close to the glove box door as possible and slide the rolled end of the check strap out of the edge of the door (see illustration).

25   Lower the glove box door and disengage the hooks on the lower edge of the glove box door from the slots on the instrument panel. Remove the glove box.

26   Reach through the glove box opening and clearly label and unplug all electrical con-

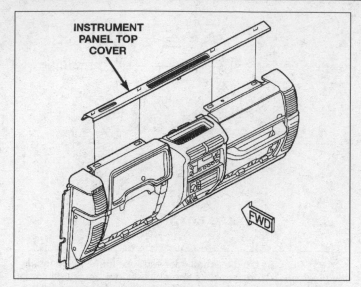

24.28 To separate the instrument panel top cover from the instrument panel, pry it off with a suitable wide, flat-bladed tool (1997 through 2010 models)

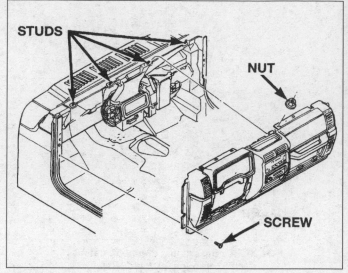

24.30 The instrument panel is attached to the door hinge pillar by three screws at each end and to the dash panel studs by four nuts across the top (1997 through 2010 models)

nectors. On 2007 models, remove the right-side kick-panel and disconnect the large electrical connector.

27   Remove the two nuts that attach the lower side of the passenger's side airbag module bracket to the studs on the dash panel (see illustration). On 2007 models, remove the floor console and center console, then tag and disconnect the electrical connectors at the console. You may have to release pushpins that secure the harness to the floor console.

28   The instrument panel top cover uses five equally spaced snap clip retainers to attach the top cover to the instrument panel. Using a suitable tool with a wide, flat blade, carefully pry up the instrument panel top cover from the instrument panel (see illustration). On 2007 models, use a plastic trim tool to release the clips securing the center instrument panel finish panels (the lower panel first, then the uppermost panel), then disconnect the electrical connector from the top panel. The lower panel houses the HVAC controls; disconnect the cables and electrical connectors at the control unit to remove the panel. Remove the audio unit. Use the trim tool to also remove the end caps from each side of the instrument panel.

Note: *It will be helpful to have both doors open as wide as possible during instrument panel removal.*

29   It's not absolutely necessary to remove the instrument cluster from the instrument panel, but if you're planning to replace the instrument panel, now would be a good time to remove the instrument cluster bezel and the cluster (see Chapter 12). The instrument panel is also lighter (and therefore easier to maneuver) with the cluster removed.

30   On 2006 and earlier models, remove the three instrument panel-to-door hinge pillar screws (see illustration) that attach each end of the instrument panel to the door hinge pillars.

31   Remove the four nuts that attach the top of the instrument panel to the dash panel studs.

2007 through 2010 models only

32   Disconnect the antenna lead at the right end of the instrument panel and remove the glove box.

33   Disconnect the electrical connectors, coolant hoses, and refrigerant line-block from the HVAC unit.

34   Remove the two top nuts securing the brake booster to the engine compartment side of the firewall and set aside the electrical harness.

35   Remove the battery and battery tray (see Chapter 5).

36   At the center of the instrument panel, remove the mounting screws securing the frame for the center finish panels.

37   At the right side of the firewall, pull back the large grommet over the main wiring harness, away from the firewall.

38   Remove the plastic caps over the fasteners at the top of the instrument panel and remove the fasteners.

39   Remove the instrument panel fasteners at each side of the panel (where the end caps go).

40   Pull the main electrical harness at the right side through the firewall to allow removal of the instrument panel.

All 2010 and earlier models

41   Have an assistant to help you remove the instrument panel, particularly if you left the steering column attached to the instrument panel.

Caution: *Before removing the instrument panel fully, watch for any cables or electrical connectors you might have missed, and disconnect them.*

42   Installation is the reverse of removal. Be sure to torque the steering column fasteners to 17 ft-lbs, and the intermediate shaft coupler bolt to 33 ft-lbs.

2011 and later models

Warning: *These models are equipped with airbags. Always disable the airbag system when working around airbag system components (see Chapter 12).*

Note: *This is a difficult procedure for the home mechanic. There are many hidden fasteners, difficult angles in which to work and many wiring connectors to tag and disconnect. We recommend that this procedure only be done by an experienced do-it-yourselfer.*

Note: *During removal of the instrument panel, make careful notes of how each piece comes off, where it fits in relation to other parts and what it holds in place. If you note how each part is installed before removing it, reassembly will be much easier.*

Instrument panel air outlets

Note: *For more detailed info on removing the air outlets, refer to Chapter 12, Section 20.*

43   Turn the louvers of the air outlet to the eleven o'clock position (near vertical). Move the louvers down so that you can reach up inside at an upward angle.

44   Put a small screwdriver into the small square hole that should now be near the one o'clock position.

45   Gently pry the tab toward the center of the outlet while twisting the housing counterclockwise. Pull the outlet out of the instrument panel.

46   To install it, push the air outlet into place and turn it clockwise.

Instrument main trim panel

Note: *For more detailed info on removing the main instrument trim panel, refer to Chapter 12, Section 20.*

47   Remove the left and center air outlets (see previous Steps).

48   Adjust the steering wheel to the lowest position.

49   Remove the cover from the lower steering column opening (see Steps 74 and 75).

50   On vehicles with power windows, use a plastic trim tool or a screwdriver wrapped with tape to gently pry out the switch module. Disconnect the wiring and remove the switch assembly.

51   If the vehicle has manual windows, use the plastic tool to pry out the storage bin.

52   Remove the mat from the bottom of the storage bin at the top center of the instrument panel. Remove the screw from beneath the mat.

53   Remove the screw from under the power window switch/storage bin area.

54   Remove the two screws from the area of the steering column.

55   Reach into the air outlet openings at the center lower part of the main trim panel and firmly pull out on the reinforcement ring to release the clips. Don't try to use tools to do this.

56   Carefully release each of the remaining retaining clips around the perimeter of the main trim panel using a plastic trim removal tool or a screwdriver wrapped with tape. Remove the main trim panel.

57   Installation is the reverse of removal.

Instrument panel center trim panel

58   Remove the instrument main trim panel (see Steps 47 through 56).

59   Use a plastic trim tool or a screwdriver wrapped with tape to release the clips of the center bezel and lower it.

60   Disconnect the wiring connectors and remove the bezel.

61   Installation is the reverse of removal.

Instrument panel cover

62   Refer to Section 22 and remove the center console.

63   Label, then disconnect the wiring and move it out of the way.

64   Use a plastic trim tool or a screwdriver wrapped with tape to pry off the end caps of the instrument panel.

65   Remove the center trim panel (see Steps 58 through 60).

66   Refer to Chapter and remove the radio.

67   Remove the glove box (see Steps 77 and 78).

68   Use a plastic trim tool or a screwdriver wrapped with tape to pry out, disconnect and remove the instrument panel tweeter speakers.

69   Remove the instrument main trim panel (see Step 47).

70   Refer to Chapter and remove the passenger airbag.

71   Remove the glove box striker.

72   Remove the screws that retain the instrument panel cover to the reinforcement and remove it.

73   Installation is the reverse of removal.

Steering column lower cover

74   Use a plastic trim tool or a screwdriver wrapped with tape to pry out and release the upper ears of the cover.

75   Pull the upper part of the cover rearward and disconnect the lower tabs. The reinforcement plate under the cover can now be removed if necessary.

76   Installation is the reverse of removal.

Glove box

77   Open the glove box, then pull the side inward. Lower the glove box.

78   Release the hinges and remove the glove box.

79   Installation is the reverse of removal.

Grab bar

80   Use a plastic trim tool or a screwdriver wrapped with tape to pry out the decorative trim.

81   Remove the bolts and the grab handle.

82   Installation is the reverse of removal.

Instrument panel assembly

Warning: *The air conditioning system is under high pressure. DO NOT disconnect any refrigerant fittings until after the system has been discharged by a dealer service department or service station.*

83   Have the air conditioning system discharged by an authorized shop.

84   Disconnect the wiring connector, then detach the door check straps. Open the doors as far as possible for clearance.

85   Disconnect the cable from the negative battery terminal (see Chapter 5). Disconnect the positive cable and the right side ground wire. Remove the battery and the battery tray.

86   Refer to Section 22 and remove the center console. Label and disconnect the wiring under the console. Detach the wiring harnesses and move them aside.

87   Remove the steering column lower cover (see Step 74 and 75).

88   Remove the audio system amplifier (see Chapter 12).

89   Unbolt and lower the steering column as required (see Chapter 10).

90   Use a plastic trim tool or a screwdriver wrapped with tape to pry the end caps from the instrument panel.

91   On vehicles with automatic transmissions, remove the shifter assembly (see Chapter 7B).

92   Remove the transfer case shifter on vehicles with 4WD (see Chapter 7C).

93   Remove the radio (see Chapter 12).

94   Remove the lower brackets that secure the center instrument panel support.

95   On vehicles with manual transmissions, disconnect the clutch push rod from the pedal arm.

96   Disconnect the brake push rod from the brake pedal arm.

97   Disconnect the ground wires at the right end of the instrument panel.

98   Disconnect the wiring connectors at both sides of the instrument panel.

99   Disconnect the antenna cable at the right side of the instrument panel.

100   Remove the glove box (see Steps 77 and 78).

101   Detach the power steering reservoir and move it out of the way.

102   Drain the engine coolant (see Chapter 1).

103   Remove the interfering EGR tube from the area of the heater hoses at the firewall.

104   Refer to Chapter 2E and remove the upper intake manifold.

105   Disconnect the heater hoses from the firewall connections. Seal the ends to prevent contamination.

106   Disconnect the air conditioning hoses from the firewall fitting. Seal the open ends to prevent contamination.

107   Move the wiring harness near the brake booster out of the way.

108   Remove the two upper nuts from the brake booster bracket.

109   Release the large wiring harness grommet at the right side of the firewall. Detach any retainers from the wiring harness.

110   Remove the trim caps along the top edge of the instrument panel, then remove the nuts under them.

111   Remove the side bolts from each end of the instrument panel assembly near the door jambs. Move the instrument panel rearward.

112   Pull the main wiring harness through the hole in the firewall.

113   With the help of an assistant, remove the instrument panel from the vehicle.

114   Installation is the reverse of removal. Have the air conditioning system serviced at the facility that discharged it. Make sure to refill the cooling system (see Chapter 1).

25   Seats - removal and installation

Warning: *1995 and later models are equipped with a Supplemental Restraint System (SRS), more commonly known as airbags. This system is designed to protect the driver and, on 1997 and later models, the front seat passenger, from serious injury in the event of a head-on or frontal collision. It consists of an airbag module in the center of the steering wheel, and, on 1997 and later models, the right side of the instrument panel. Wait at least 5 minutes after the battery has been disconnected before beginning work on or near any airbag system components.*

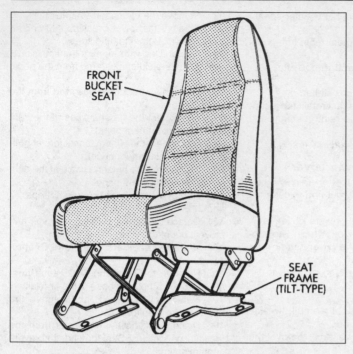

25.3a The front bucket seat frame bolts to the floor

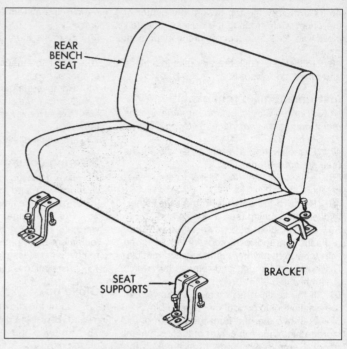

25.3b Typical rear bench seat details

1   Disconnect the cable from the negative battery terminal (see Chapter 5).

2   If necessary, remove the trim cover and seat belt anchor bolt from the seat.

3   Remove the retaining bolts and lift the seats from the vehicle (see illustrations).

4   On models so equipped, tilt the seat rearward and disconnect any electrical connectors.

5   Installation is the reverse of removal. Tighten the retaining bolts securely.

26 Cowl top panel - removal and installation

1   Disconnect the cable from the negative battery terminal.

2   Remove the windshield wiper arms (see Chapter 12), and raise and support the hood.

3   Remove the top bolts from the cowl panel, then remove the pushpins securing the front edge of the panel (see illustration). Lift the panel from the vehicle, being careful not to scratch the cowl top panel paint on the wiper assembly.

4   Installation is the reverse of removal.

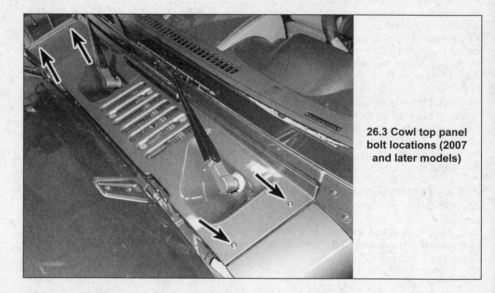

26.3 Cowl top panel bolt locations (2007 and later models)

Chapter 12
Chassis electrical system

Contents

Specifications

Torque specifications

Note: *One foot-pound (ft-lb) of torque is equivalent to 12 inch-pounds (in-lbs) of torque. Torque values below approximately 15 ft-lbs are expressed in inch-pounds, since most foot-pound torque wrenches are not accurate at these smaller values.*

Airbag controller retaining nuts	
2000 and earlier models	95 in-lbs
2001 through 2006 models	125 in-lbs
2007 through 2012 models	80 in-lbs
2013 and later models	97 in-lbs
Airbag module retaining fasteners	
Driver's side	See Chapter 10
Passenger's airbag	
2006 and earlier models	105 in-lbs
2007 and later models	55 in-lbs
Front impact sensor mounting fasteners	70 in-lbs

1   General information

1   The electrical system is a 12–volt, negative ground type. Power for the lights and all electrical accessories is supplied by a lead/acid-type battery which is charged by the alternator.
2   This Chapter covers repair and service procedures for the various electrical components not associated with the engine. Information on the battery, alternator, distributor and starter motor can be found in Chapter 5.
3   It should be noted that when portions of the electrical system are serviced, the negative battery cable should be disconnected from the battery to prevent electrical shorts and/or fires.

2   Electrical troubleshooting - general information

1   A typical electrical circuit consists of an electrical component, any switches, relays, motors, fuses, fusible links or circuit breakers related to that component and the wiring and connectors that link the component to both the battery and the chassis. To help you pinpoint an electrical circuit problem, wiring diagrams are included at the end of this book.
2   Before tackling any troublesome electrical circuit, first study the appropriate wiring diagrams to get a complete understanding of what makes up that individual circuit. Trouble spots, for instance, can often be narrowed down by noting if other components related to the circuit are operating properly. If several components or circuits fail at one time, chances are the problem is in a fuse or ground connection, because several circuits are often routed through the same fuse and ground connections.
3   Electrical problems usually stem from simple causes, such as loose or corroded connections, a blown fuse, a melted fusible link or a bad relay. Visually inspect the condition of all fuses, wires and connections in a problem circuit before troubleshooting it.
4   If testing instruments are going to be utilized, use the diagrams to plan ahead of time

where you will make the necessary connections in order to accurately pinpoint the trouble spot.
5   The basic tools needed for electrical troubleshooting include a circuit tester or voltmeter (a 12–volt bulb with a set of test leads can also be used), a continuity tester, which includes a bulb, battery and set of test leads, and a jumper wire, preferably with a circuit breaker incorporated, which can be used to bypass electrical components. Before attempting to locate a problem with test instruments, use the wiring diagram(s) to decide where to make the connections.

Voltage checks

6   Voltage checks should be performed if a circuit is not functioning properly. Connect one lead of a circuit tester to either the negative battery terminal or a known good ground. Connect the other lead to a connector in the circuit being tested, preferably nearest to the battery or fuse. If the bulb of the tester lights, voltage is present, which means that the part of the circuit between the connector and the battery is problem free. Continue checking the rest of the circuit in the same fashion. When you reach a point at which no voltage is present, the problem lies between that point and the last test point with voltage. Most of the time the problem can be traced to a loose connection.
Note: *Keep in mind that some circuits receive voltage only when the ignition key is in the Accessory or Run position.*

Finding a short

7   One method of finding shorts in a circuit is to remove the fuse and connect a test light or voltmeter in its place to the fuse terminals. There should be no voltage present in the circuit. Move the wiring harness from side-to-side while watching the test light. If the bulb goes on, there is a short to ground somewhere in that area, probably where the insulation has rubbed through. The same test can be performed on each component in the circuit, even a switch.

Ground check

8   Perform a ground test to check whether

a component is properly grounded. Disconnect the battery and connect one lead of a self-powered test light, known as a continuity tester, to a known good ground. Connect the other lead to the wire or ground connection being tested. If the bulb goes on, the ground is good. If the bulb does not go on, the ground is not good.

Continuity check

9   A continuity check is done to determine if there are any breaks in a circuit - if it is passing electricity properly. With the circuit off (no power in the circuit), a self-powered continuity tester can be used to check the circuit. Connect the test leads to both ends of the circuit (or to the "power" end and a good ground), and if the test light comes on the circuit is passing current properly. If the light doesn't come on, there is a break somewhere in the circuit. The same procedure can be used to test a switch, by connecting the continuity tester to the switch terminals. With the switch turned On, the test light should come on.

Finding an open circuit

10   When diagnosing possible open circuits, it is often difficult to locate them by sight because oxidation or terminal misalignment are hidden by the connectors. Merely wiggling a connector on a sensor or in the wiring harness may correct the open circuit condition. Remember this when an open circuit is indicated when troubleshooting a circuit. Intermittent problems may also be caused by oxidized or loose connections.
11   Electrical troubleshooting is simple if you keep in mind that all electrical circuits are basically electricity running from the battery, through the wires, switches, relays, fuses and fusible links to each electrical component (light bulb, motor, etc.) and to ground, from which it is passed back to the battery.
12   Any electrical problem is an interruption in the flow of electricity to and from the battery.

3   Fuses - general information

1   The electrical circuits of the vehicle are protected by a combination of fuses, circuit breakers and fusible links. The fuse block is located in different locations depending on model year (see illustrations).
1987 through 1995 models: Under the left side of the instrument panel.
1997 through 2006 models: Behind the glove box.
2007 and later models: In the right side of the engine compartment, next to the battery. On these models the fuse/relay box is called the Totally Integrated Power Module (TIPM), and incorporates solid state circuitry that takes the place of certain relays.
Note: *In addition to the fuse block, 2006 and earlier models have a fuse/relay block called the Power Distribution Center (PDC) in the right side of the engine compartment.*

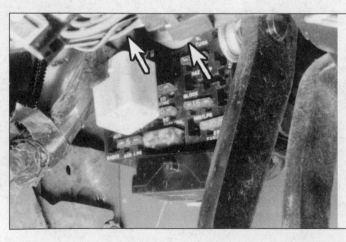

3.1a On 1995 and earlier models, the fuse block is located under the left side of the instrument panel, next to the parking brake mechanism (turn signal and hazard flashers are located at the top)

3.1b On 1997 through 2006 models, there is a fuse block behind the glove box and a fuse/relay block located at the right side of the engine compartment (2007 and later models just have the fuse/relay block in the engine compartment, called the Totally Integrated Power Module [TIPM])

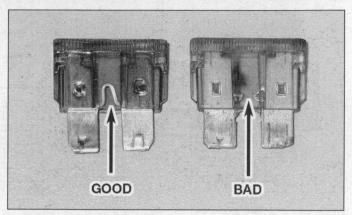

3.3 When a fuse blows, the element between the terminals melts

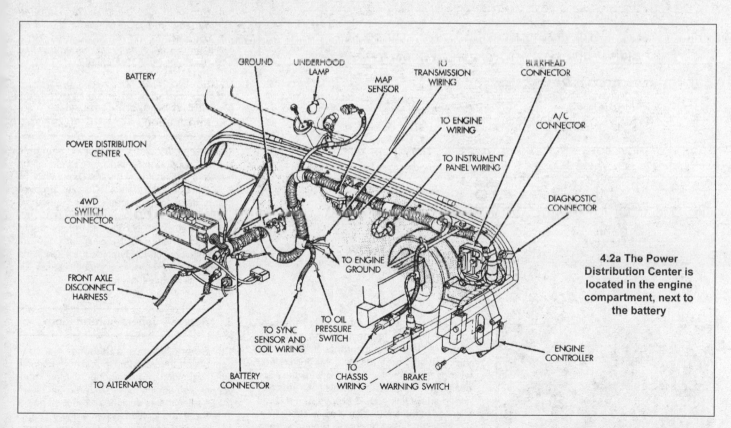

4.2a The Power Distribution Center is located in the engine compartment, next to the battery

2   Each of the fuses is designed to protect a specific circuit, and the various circuits are identified on the fuse box cover.

3   Miniaturized fuses are employed in the fuse block. These compact fuses, with blade terminal design, allow fingertip removal and replacement. If an electrical component fails, always check the fuse first. The easiest way to check fuses is with a test light. Check for power at the exposed terminal tips of each fuse. If power is present on one side of the fuse but not the other, the fuse is blown. A blown fuse can also be confirmed by visually inspecting it (see illustration).

4   Be sure to replace blown fuses with the correct type. Fuses of different ratings are physically interchangeable, but only fuses of the proper rating should be used. Replacing a fuse with one of a higher or lower value than specified is not recommended. Each electrical circuit needs a specific amount of protection. The amperage value of each fuse is molded into the fuse body.

5   If the replacement fuse immediately fails, don't replace it again until the cause of the problem is isolated and corrected. In most cases, the cause will be a short circuit in the wiring caused by a broken or deteriorated wire.

4   Fusible links - general information

1   Some circuits are protected by fusible links. The links are used in circuits which are not ordinarily fused, such as the charging circuit.

2   Later models are equipped with a Power Distribution Center (PDC) located next to the battery (see illustrations). The PDC uses maxi fuses instead of fusible links for some high-amperage circuits. These maxi fuses are checked visually, just like standard fuses (see illustration).

4.2b Like standard fuses, the maxi fuses can be checked visually

FUSIBLE LINK CHART

Wire Gauge	Color Code	Color
12 Ga.	BK	Black
14 Ga.	RD	Red
16 Ga.	DB	Dark Blue
18 Ga.	GY	Gray
20 Ga.	OR	Orange
30 Ga.	LG	Light Green

4.2c Always replace a burned-out fusible link with one of the same color code

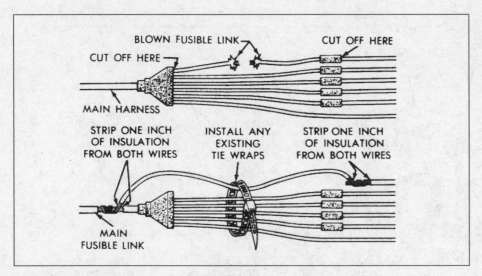

4.4 Fusible link repair details

g) Use plenty of electrical tape around the soldered joint. No wires should be exposed.

h) Connect the battery ground cable. Test the circuit for proper operation.

5   Circuit breakers - general information

1   Circuit breakers protect components such as wipers and headlights. Some circuit breakers are located in the fuse box.

2   On some models the circuit breaker resets itself automatically, so an electrical overload in a circuit breaker protected system will cause the circuit to fail momentarily, then come back on. If the circuit does not come back on, check it immediately. Once the condition is corrected, the circuit breaker will resume its normal function.

6   Relays - general information

1   Several electrical accessories and components on the vehicle use relays to transmit electrical signals to components. Most models are also equipped with an Auto Shutdown (ASD) relay that is designed to shut off power to the fuel and ignition systems under certain conditions. If a relay is defective, that component will not operate properly.

2   On early models, the various relays are grouped together in several locations (see illustration). On later models to 2006, the relays are contained within the Power Distribution Center (PDC) located under the hood (see illustration). On 2007 and later models, the relays are located in the Totally Integrated Power Module (TIPM) next to the battery; some of the relays are replaceable, while others are integral to the TIPM.

3   If a faulty relay is suspected, it can be removed and tested by a dealer service department or repair shop. Defective relays must be replaced as a unit.

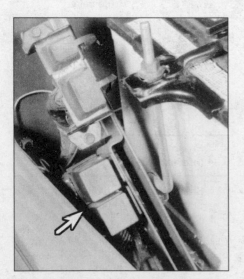

6.2a On early models, various relays are located next to the battery

3   Although wire-type fusible links appear to be a heavier gauge than the wire they are protecting, the appearance is due to the thick insulation. All fusible links are several wire gauges smaller than the wire they are designed to protect. The fusible links are color coded and a link should always be replaced with one of the same color (see illustration).

4   Fusible links cannot be repaired, but a new link of the gauge can be put in its place. The procedure is as follows:

a) Disconnect the negative cable from the battery.

b) Disconnect the fusible link from the wiring harness.

c) Cut the damaged fusible link out of the wiring just behind the connector.

d) Strip the insulation back approximately 1–inch (see illustration).

e) Position the connector on the new fusible link and twist or crimp it into place.

f) Use rosin core solder at each end of the new link to obtain a good solder joint.

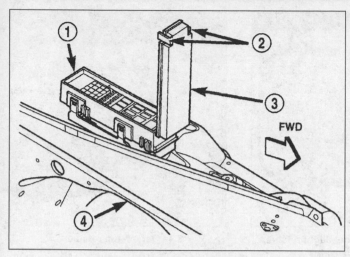

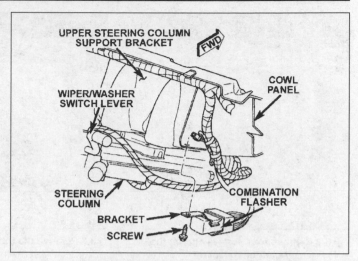

6.2b On later models to 2006, the relays are contained within the power distribution center

1 Power distribution center
2 Latches
3 Cover
4 Right side front fender

7.15 Combination flasher unit installation details (1997 model shown)

7 Turn signal and hazard flashers - check and replacement

Warning: *The models covered by this manual are equipped with a Supplemental Restraint System (SRS), more commonly known as airbags. Always disconnect the negative battery cable(s) and wait two minutes before working in the vicinity of any airbag system component to avoid the possibility of accidental deployment of the airbag, which could cause personal injury (see Section 24).*

1987 through 1995 models

Turn signal flasher

1   The turn signal flasher, a small canister–shaped unit located in the fuse block, flashes the turn signals (see illustration 3.1).
2   When the flasher unit is functioning properly, an audible click can be heard during its operation. If the turn signals fail on one side or the other and the flasher unit does not make its characteristic clicking sound, a faulty turn signal bulb is indicated.
3   If both turn signals fail to blink, the problem may be due to a blown fuse, a faulty flasher unit, a broken switch or a loose or open connection. If a quick check of the fuse box indicates that the turn signal fuse has blown, check the wiring for a short before installing a new fuse.
4   To replace the flasher, simply pull it out of the fuse block.
5   Make sure that the replacement unit is identical to the original. Compare the old one to the new one before installing it.
6   Installation is the reverse of removal.

Hazard flasher

7   The hazard flasher, a small canister-shaped unit located in the fuse block (see

illustration 3.1), flashes all four turn signals simultaneously when activated.
8   The hazard flasher is checked in a fashion similar to the turn signal flasher (see Steps 2 and 3).
9   To replace the hazard flasher, pull it out of the fuse block.
10   Make sure the replacement unit is identical to the one it replaces. Compare the old one to the new one before installing it.
11   Installation is the reverse of removal.

1997 through 2006 models

12   On these models, the turn signal flasher and hazard flasher are combined into a single unit.
13   Disconnect the cable from the negative battery cable.

1997 through 2000 models

14   Remove the knee blocker from the instrument panel (see Chapter 11, Section 24).
15   Reach through the right side of the steering column opening in the instrument panel and unscrew the combination flasher bracket from the upper steering column mounting bracket (to the right of the steering column) (see illustration).
16   Lower the combination flasher and mounting bracket slightly, then disconnect the combination flasher from the wiring harness connector.
17   Remove the combination flasher and mounting bracket as a single assembly. Don't bother to separate the old flasher unit from the bracket. The new flasher comes with a new bracket.
18   Installation is the reverse of removal.

2001 through 2006 models

19   Remove the lower steering column cover (see Chapter 11).

20   Lower the steering column all the way, leaving the lever in the released position, then remove the upper steering column cover.
21   Pull the flasher unit from the left multi-function switch.
22   Installation is the reverse of removal.

2007 and later models

23   The turn signal and hazard flasher functions on these models is incorporated into the Totally Integrated Power Module (TIPM) - there is no replaceable flasher unit.

8 Headlight bulb - replacement

1987 through 1995 models

1   Detach the electrical connector from the headlight (see illustration).

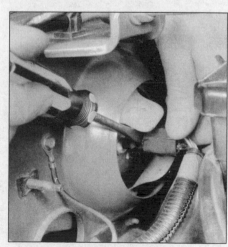

8.1 Use a screwdriver to detach the headlight connector

8.2 Remove four screws and lift the headlight bezel off

8.3 Remove the four headlight retainer screws (arrows)

8.4a Detach the retainer...

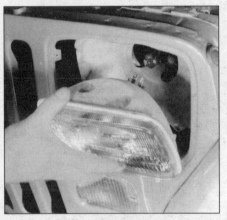

8.4b ... then lower the headlight from the opening

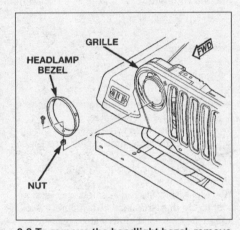

8.8 To remove the headlight bezel, remove the bezel retaining screws (1997 and later models)

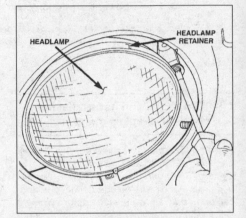

8.9 To remove the headlight retaining ring, remove the retaining ring screws (1997 and later models)

2   Remove the four screws and detach the headlight bezel (see illustration).
3   Remove the retainer screws, taking care not to disturb the adjusting screws (see illustration).
4   Detach the retainer and remove the headlight (see illustrations).
5   Place the headlight in position and install

the retainer and screws. Tighten the screws securely.
6   Place the bezel in position and install the retaining screws.
7   Plug in the electrical connector and reconnect the battery cable.

1997 through 2006 models

8   Remove the headlight bezel screws and detach the headlight bezel (see illustration).
9   Remove the headlight retaining ring screws (see illustration). Remove the headlight retaining ring.
10   On 2006 and earlier models, pull out the headlight and disconnect the electrical connector.
11   Installation is the reverse of removal.

2007 and later models

12   Remove the radiator grille (see Chapter 11).
13   Remove the screws and detach the headlight retainer, then remove the headlight housing and disconnect the electrical connector (see illustration).
14   Rotate the bulb holder counterclockwise to remove it from the headlight housing (see illustration).

Caution: *Oils from your fingers will shorten the bulb life. Do not touch the bulb with your fingers; use a lint-free cotton cloth. If anything gets on the bulb, clean it with rubbing alcohol before installation.*

15   When you're done, check and, if necessary, adjust the headlight beam alignment (see Section 9).

8.14 Turn the bulb holder counterclockwise and pull the bulb from the housing

8.13 Headlight housing retainer screws

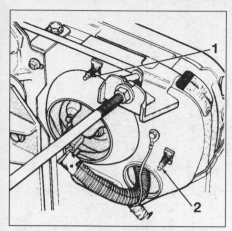

9.1a Headlight adjusting screw locations (1987 through 1995 models)

1   *Vertical*   2   *Horizontal*

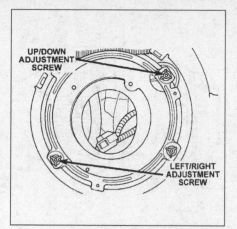

9.1b Headlight adjusting screw locations (1997 through 2006 models).

9.1c 2007 and later models only have vertical adjustment screws

9   Headlights - adjustment

Note: *The headlights must be aimed correctly. If adjusted incorrectly they could blind the driver of an oncoming vehicle and cause a serious accident or seriously reduce your ability to see the road. The headlights should be checked for proper aim every 12 months and any time a new headlight is installed or front end body work is performed. It should be emphasized that the following procedure is only an interim step which will provide temporary adjustment until the headlights can be adjusted by a properly equipped shop.*

1   Headlights have two spring loaded adjusting screws, one on the top controlling up-and-down movement and one on the side controlling left-and-right movement accessible from the back of the headlights, in the engine compartment (see illustrations).

2   There are several methods of adjusting the headlights. The simplest method requires a blank wall 25 feet in front of the vehicle and a level floor (see illustration).

3   Position masking tape vertically on the wall in reference to the vehicle centerline and the centerlines of both headlights.

4   Position a horizontal tape line in reference to the centerline of all the headlights.

Note: *It may be easier to position the tape on the wall with the vehicle parked only a few inches away.*

5   Adjustment should be made with the vehicle sitting level, the gas tank half-full and no unusually heavy load in the vehicle.

6   Starting with the low beam adjustment, position the high intensity zone so it is two inches below the horizontal line and two inches to the side of the headlight vertical line away from oncoming traffic. Adjustment is made by turning the top adjusting screw clockwise to raise the beam and counterclockwise to lower the beam. The adjusting screw on the side should be used in the same manner to

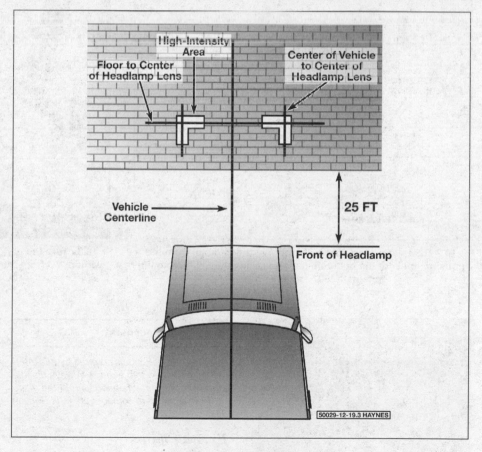

9.2 Headlight aiming details

move the beam left or right (2006 and earlier models only).

7   With the high beams on, the high intensity zone should be vertically centered with the exact center just below the horizontal line.

Note: *It may not be possible to position the headlight aim exactly for both high and low*

beams. *If a compromise must be made, keep in mind that the low beams are the most used and have the greatest effect on driver safety.*

8   Have the headlights adjusted by a dealer service department or service station at the earliest opportunity.

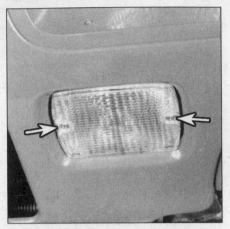

10.1a The front parking light bulbs are accessible after removing the screws and lens…

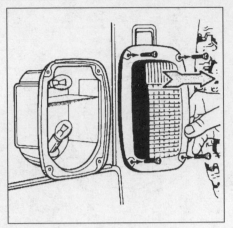

10.1b … as are the taillight bulbs…

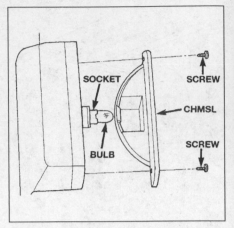

10.1c … and the center high-mount stop light bulb (1997 and later models)

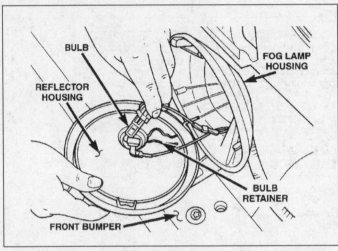

10.2 To replace a fog light bulb, remove the reflector from the housing, pull out the bulb retainer and remove the bulb from the retainer (1997 and later models)

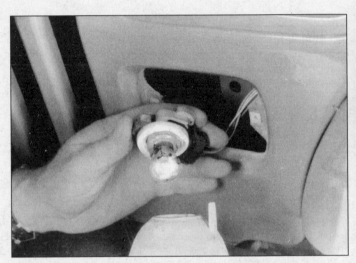

10.3a Turn the parking light bulb holder to align the tabs, then withdraw it from the bezel housing - push the bulb in and turn it counterclockwise to remove it

10.3b The tail light bulb is also removed by turning it counterclockwise and withdrawing it

10   Bulb replacement

Warning: *Some models covered by this manual are equipped with airbags. Always disable the airbag system when working in the vicinity of airbag system components (see Section 24).*

Exterior lights

1   The lenses of many lights are held in place by screws, which makes it a simple procedure to gain access to the bulbs (see illustrations). On some lights the lenses are held in place by clips. The lenses can be removed either by unsnapping them or by using a small screwdriver to pry them off.

2   To replace a fog light bulb, remove the reflector-to-fog light housing screws, pull the reflector assembly out of the housing (see illustration), squeeze the bulb retainer together, pull it out of the reflector and remove the bulb from the retainer. Installation is the reverse of removal.

3   Several types of bulbs are used. Some are removed by pushing in and turning them counterclockwise (see illustrations). Others can simply be unclipped from the terminals or pulled straight out of the socket.

Interior lights

Instrument panel lights

4   To gain access to the instrument panel lights, the instrument cluster will have to be removed first (see Section 20) (see illustration).

Dome light

5   Access to the dome light bulbs is accomplished by prying the lens off (see illustrations).

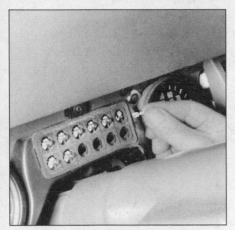

10.4 After removing the instrument cluster, simply pull the bulbs out to remove them

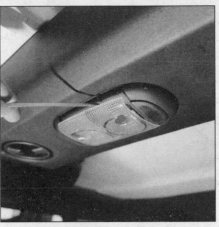

10.5a Carefully pry the dome light lens off…

10.5b … then pull the bulb(s) straight out of the socket

10.6a Pry the notched end of the lens down from the housing…

10.6b … then remove the bulb from the terminals

11.4 Support the radio and unplug the electrical connector and antenna cable

Cargo light

6   Insert a small screwdriver into the notch in the light housing and pry the lens down for access to the bulb (see illustrations).
Warning: *Do not pry on the glass portion of the bulb - only pry on the ends.*

11   Radio and speakers - removal and installation

Warning: *Some models covered by this manual are equipped with airbags. Always disable the airbag system when working in the vicinity of airbag system components (see Section 24).*

Radio

1   Disconnect the negative cable at the battery.
2   On 1987 through 1995 models, remove the instrument panel (see Chapter 11). On 1997 through 2010 models, remove the center bezel (see Chapter 11, Section 24).
3   On 2007 through 2010 models, use a trim stick to carefully pry off upper and lower center trim panels. On 2011 and later models, remove the instrument panel center trim panel (see Chapter 11). On 2011 and later models, remove the instrument cluster bezel (see Section 20). On all models, remove the radio retaining screws.
Note: *If the radio is REQ or RET type, press the Set and Scan buttons at the same time. The words "transportation mode" should display on the screen, indicating that the radio may be removed.*
Note: *If the radio is equipped with an internal HDD (Hard Disk Drive), perform a complete users data backup (a scan tool is required for this).*
Note: *On the radios that are equipped with an HDD, failure to perform the users data backup means that all the preset radio stations, stored music and personal preferences will not be stored when the memory power has been removed. Another method (without a scanner) is to write down all of the preset stations and re-enter them after the job has been completed.*
4   Slide the radio out and support it, disconnect the ground cable, antenna and electrical connectors, then remove the assembly from the instrument panel (see illustration).
5   Installation is the reverse of removal. If the radio is REQ or RET type, after installing the radio, remove the radio from "transportation mode." With the ignition switch in the OFF position, pull up the J13 fuse that's located in the fuse and relay box (see Section 3), into the pre-stage position. After a few seconds, push the IOD fuse down until its fully seated. The radio should no longer be in "transportation mode."
Note: *If the radio is equipped with an internal HDD (Hard Disk Drive), establish communication with the HDD using the USB connection and load the customer data back into the radio (scan tool required).*

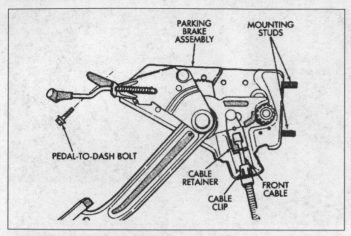

11.10 The parking brake assembly will have to be unbolted and moved out of the way for access to the driver's side speaker

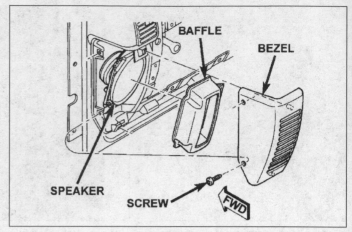

11.14 Speaker mounting details (1997 and later models)

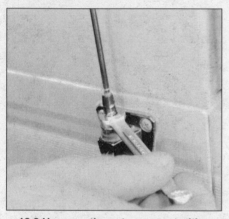

12.2 Unscrew the antenna mast with a small wrench

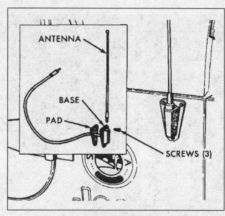

12.6 Remove the screws and pull the cable out through the holes in the body

Speakers

1987 through 1995 models

Passenger's side

6　Reach up behind the right side of the instrument panel and remove the four nuts retaining the speaker in place.

7　Detach the speaker and pull it out for access to the electrical connector. Unplug the connector and remove the speaker.

8　Installation is the reverse of removal.

Driver's side

9　In the engine compartment, remove the nuts from the two parking brake assembly studs which project through the firewall.

10　In the passenger compartment, remove the bolt holding the parking brake assembly to the instrument panel, then lower the assembly out of the way (see illustration).

11　With the speaker now accessible, remove the retaining nuts.

12　Unplug the connector and remove the speaker.

13　Installation is the reverse of removal. On hardtop models, make sure to install the ground wire when installing the parking brake assembly bolt.

1997 and later models

Instrument panel speakers

14　On 2006 and earlier models, remove the two speaker bezel-to-instrument panel screws (see illustration). On 2007 and later models, remove the steering column opening cover, and remove the fasteners securing the amplifier. Disconnect and remove the amplifier. Remove the instrument panel end caps to access the fasteners and connectors for the instrument panel speakers.

15　Using a wide, flat-bladed tool, carefully pry the upper and lower edges of the speaker bezel off the instrument panel to release the two snap clip retainers that attach the bezel to the instrument panel. Remove the speaker bezel from the instrument panel.

16　Remove the foam rubber speaker baffle from the speaker (see illustration 11.14).

17　Remove the four screws that attach the speaker to the instrument panel. Pull out the speaker, unplug the electrical connector from the speaker and remove the speaker. On 2007 and later models, there is also a small tweeter attached to the top of the instrument panel. Remove the mounting screw and the tweeter.

18　Installation is the reverse of removal.

Sound bar speakers

19　Remove the four screws that attach the speaker grille and speaker to the sound bar. Lower the speaker and grille and unplug the electrical connector from the speaker. Remove the speaker and grille.

20　Installation is the reverse of removal.

12　Antenna - removal and installation

Warning: *Some models covered by this manual are equipped with airbags. Always disable the airbag system when working in the vicinity of airbag system components (see Section 24).*

Antenna mast

1　The antenna mast can be unscrewed and replaced with a new one in the event it is damaged.

2　Use a small wrench to unscrew the mast (see illustration).

3　Install the new antenna mast finger-tight and tighten it securely with the wrench.

Antenna and cable

4　Disconnect the cable from the negative battery terminal (see Chapter 5).

5　Remove the radio and disconnect the antenna cable (see Section 11). Connect a string or wire to the radio end of the cable.

Note: *On 1997 and later models, the antenna mast must be unscrewed and the cover removed from the base for access to the base screws.*

6　Remove the antenna pad and mast assembly and pull the cable out through the hole in the body (see illustration).

7　Connect the string or wire to the new cable and pull it into the passenger compartment.

8　Install the antenna pad and mast assembly.

9　Connect the cable to the radio, then install the radio.

10　Connect the battery negative cable.

13   Headlight switch and dash illumination rheostat - removal and installation

Warning: *Some models covered by this manual are equipped with airbags. Always disable the airbag system when working in the vicinity of airbag system components (see Section 24).*

1987 through 1995 models

1   Disconnect the cable from the negative battery terminal (see Chapter 5).
2   Remove the instrument cluster bezel (see Chapter 11).
3   Remove the instrument cluster indicator bezel.
4   Remove the switch or rheostat screws, pull the switch or rheostat assembly out, then unplug the electrical connector (see illustrations).
5   Plug in the new switch or rheostat securely, then place it in position and install the screws. The remainder of installation is the reverse of removal.

1997 through 2006 models

6   Disconnect the cable from the negative battery terminal (see Chapter 5).
7   Pull out the headlight switch control knob to the ON position.
8   Reach up under the instrument panel to the left of the steering column and push the headlight switch retainer button (see illustration 13.10). While holding the button down, pull out the headlight switch control knob and shaft.
9   Remove the steering column cover and knee blocker (see Chapter 11, Section 24).
10   Remove the spanner nut that attaches the headlight switch to the instrument panel (see illustration).
11   Separate the headlight switch from the instrument panel and unplug the electrical connector. Remove the switch.
12   Installation is the reverse of removal.

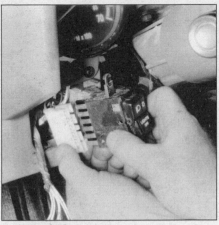

13.4a After removing the screws, grasp the switch securely and unplug it from the electrical connector

2007 and later models

13   The headlight switch and instrument panel light dimming functions are part of the circuitry for the left multi-function switch. For troubleshooting, use a scan tool to pinpoint the problem with either multi-function switch. The multi-function switch cannot be repaired; if there is a problem, the switch must be replaced as a unit (see Section 17).

14   Headlight dimmer switch (1987 through 1995 models) - removal and installation

Warning: *Some models covered by this manual are equipped with airbags. Always disable the airbag system when working in the vicinity of airbag system components (see Section 24).*

1   On 1997 and later models, the headlight dimmer switch is incorporated into the left multi-function switch (see Section 17).
2   Disconnect the cable from the negative

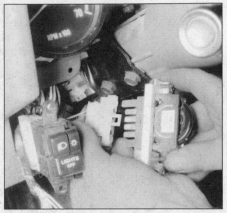

13.4b The dash illumination rheostat is removed in the same way as the headlight switch - unplug it from the connector and remove the screws

terminal of the battery (see Chapter 5).
3   Remove the instrument cluster bezel (see Chapter 11, Section 24).
4   On air-conditioned models, remove the attaching screws and detach the evaporator housing and bracket from the instrument panel for access to the switch.
5   Tape the switch actuating rod to the steering column to prevent disengagement.
6   Remove the two bolts, detach the rod, unplug the electrical connector and lower the switch from the steering column.
7   Engage the new switch with the rod and place it in position, then install the mounting bolts finger-tight.
8   Remove the securing tape from the rod, then insert a 3/32-inch drill bit into the adjustment hole (see illustration). Push the switch toward the steering wheel to take up the slack in the actuator control rod, then tighten the bolts securely.
9   Remove the drill bit, plug in the connector and install any components which were removed.
10   Connect the negative battery cable.

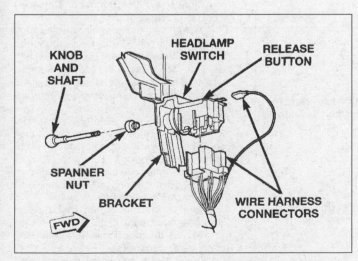

13.10 Headlight switch mounting details (1997 and later models)

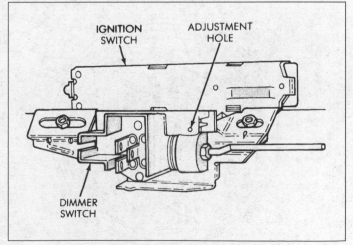

14.8 Dimmer switch adjustment details

15.3 Turn signal electrical connector

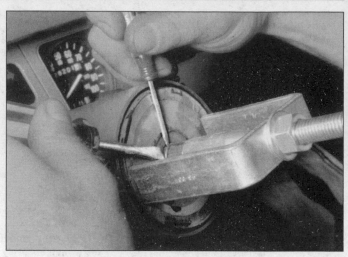

15.4 The retaining ring can be removed with a screwdriver after depressing the lock plate with a special tool

15.5 With the lock plate removed, the canceling cam and spring can be lifted off

15.7 Use a Phillips screwdriver to remove the multi-function actuator screw

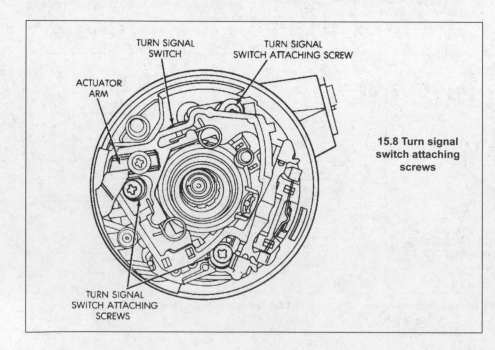

15.8 Turn signal switch attaching screws

15 Turn signal/hazard warning switch (1987 through 2006 models) - removal and installation

Warning: *Some models covered by this manual are equipped with airbags. Always disable the airbag system when working in the vicinity of airbag system components (see Section 24).*

Note: *On 2007 and later models, the hazard switch is a part of the instrument panel switch assembly, just below the HVAC controls at the center of the instrument panel. If the hazard switch or any other switch on this panel is faulty, the entire switch assembly must be replaced. Use a scan tool to determine if the switch panel must be replaced.*

1   The turn signal/hazard switch is located at the top end of the steering column and is operated by the multi-function control stalk.

2   Disconnect the negative battery cable (see Chapter 5), then remove the steering wheel (see Chapter 10).

3   Unplug the turn signal electrical connector (see illustration). Wrap tape around the connector to prevent snagging when the harness is pulled up out of the column. Remove the plastic harness cover by pulling it up and off the weld nuts, then sliding it off the harness.

4   Depress the lock plate using a special tool, available at most auto parts stores, then use a small screwdriver to pry out the retaining ring (see illustration).

5   Remove the lock plate, canceling cam and upper bearing spring (see illustration).

6   Remove the hazard switch knob.

7   Remove the turn signal actuator arm screw (see illustration).

8   Remove the turn signal switch attaching screws (see illustration).

9   Remove the instrument cluster bezel (see Chapter 11).

10   Remove the steering column attaching nuts and bolts, then lower the column.

11   Lift the switch out and guide the wiring harness up through the steering column opening.

12   Installation is the reverse of removal. After installation, it may be necessary to adjust the dimmer switch (1995 and earlier models) (see Section 14).

16   Windshield wiper/washer switch (1987 through 1995 models) - check and replacement

Warning: *Some models covered by this manual are equipped with airbags. Always disable the airbag system when working in the vicinity of airbag system components (see Section 24).*

Note: *On 1997 and later models, the windshield wiper/washer switch is incorporated into the multi-function switch (see Section 17).*

1   These models are equipped with a multi-function lever located on the left side of the steering column which controls the wiper/washer, turn signal and dimmer switches. The wipers are two-speed with an optional intermittent feature.

Check

2   Disconnect the cable from the negative terminal of the battery (see Chapter 5).

3   Unplug the electrical connector from the switch.

4   Use an ohmmeter or self-powered test light to check for continuity between the switch terminals at the electrical connector with the switch in the indicated positions (see illustrations).

5   Replace the wiper/washer switch if the continuity is not as specified.

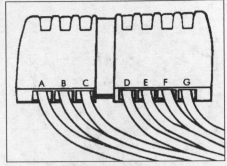

16.4a Wiper/washer connector terminal details

A   *Delay - dark green (intermittent only)*
B   *Washer - pink*
C   *High - violet*
D   *Ignition - white*
E   *Low/park - grey*
F   *Off/park - yellow*
G   *Delay - brown (intermittent only)*

SWITCH POSITION	TERMINALS	ZERO OHMS
Off	E and F	Yes
	All Others	No
Lo	D and E	Yes
	All Others	No
Hi	C and D	Yes
	All Others	No
Wash	B and D	Yes
	D and E	Yes
	All Others	No

16.4b Two-speed wiper switch check chart - ohmmeter readings should be as specified in the three switch positions

SWITCH POSITION	TERMINALS	ZERO OHMS
Off	E and F	Yes
	All Others	No
Lo	D and E	Yes
	All Others	No
Hi	C and D	Yes
	All Others	No
Wash/Mist	B and D	Yes
	D and E	Yes
	All Others	No
Delay	A and G	152-480K ohms

16.4c Intermittent wiper switch check chart - ohmmeter should be as specified in each switch position

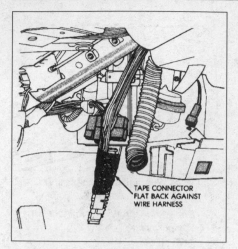

16.6 Unplug the connector at the bottom of the steering column and wrap it with tape, as shown

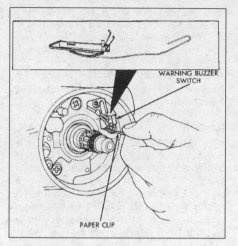

16.9 With the key in the On position, hook a piece of wire (a straightened paper clip works well) under the spring retainer and remove the key buzzer switch

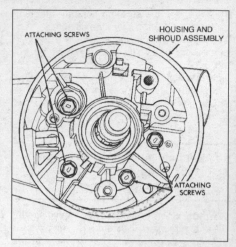

16.10 The housing and shroud assembly is held in place by four attaching screws or bolts

Replacement

6   Unplug the electrical connector and tape it flat against the harness (see illustration).

7   Remove the turn signal switch as described in Section 15, except that it won't be necessary to pull the connector out of the column, only to pull it up far enough for access to the housing screws.

8   Remove the ignition lock cylinder (see Section 18).

9   Bend the end of a straightened paper clip into a hook, insert it into the loop of the key warning buzzer switch, then lift the switch out (see illustration).

10   Remove the four screws or bolts and lift the housing and shroud assembly off the column (see illustration).

11   Remove the wiper/washer switch actuating lever by pulling it straight out.

12   Remove the switch cover, then remove the pivot screw and detach the wiper/washer switch (see illustration).

13   Install the new switch and cover.

14   Push on the dimmer switch rod to make sure it's connected. Place the housing and shroud assembly in position on the steering column with the lock pin forward of the slot in the lock rack, then position the first tooth with the most forward gear of the lock rack (see illustration).

15   Install the screws and carefully mate the housing and shroud assembly.

16   Install the key and lock cylinder assembly and make sure the lock pin extends fully when the key is in the lock position (see illustration 16.14).

17   Installation is the reverse of removal.

17   Multi-function switch (1997 and later models) - removal and installation

1997 through 2000 models

Warning: *Some models covered by this manual are equipped with airbags. Always disable the airbag system when working in the vicinity of airbag system components (see Section 24).*

1   On these models, the headlight dimmer, turn signal and hazard flasher and windshield wiper/washer switches are integrated into one switch assembly on the steering column. This switch is known as a multi-function switch.

2   Disconnect the cable from the negative battery terminal (see Chapter 5).

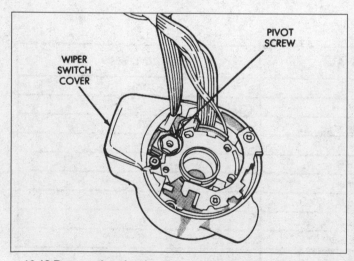

16.12 Remove the wiper/washer switch cover and pivot screw

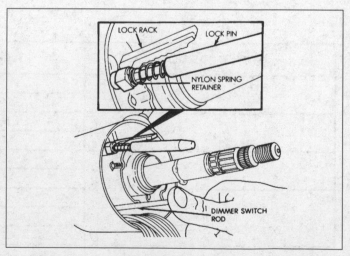

16.14 Make sure the dimmer switch rod is secure by pushing on it and that the nylon spring retainer is forward of the lock rack

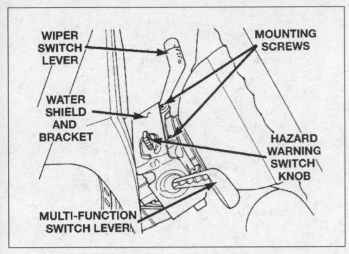

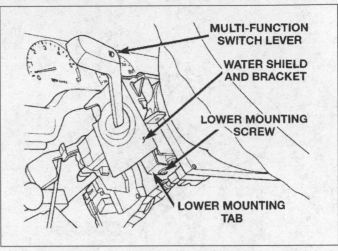

17.8a To detach the switch water shield and bracket from the steering column, remove the two screws on the top of the switch shield...

17.8b ... and the screw on the bottom of the bracket (1997 through 2000 models)

3   Remove the knee blocker (see Chapter 11, Section 24).

4   Place the tilt column, if equipped, in the fully raised position.

5   Insert a small screwdriver or pin punch through the access hole in the lower steering column cover and push in the ignition key lock cylinder retaining tumbler (see Section 18). While depressing the retaining tumbler, pull the ignition lock cylinder and key out of the ignition lock housing.

6   Remove the three screws that attach the lower steering column cover to the upper cover.

7   On vehicles with a non-tilt steering column, loosen the two nuts that secure the column upper mounting bracket to the dash panel steering column bracket studs. Lower the column far enough to remove the upper steering column cover.

8   Remove the three screws (two on the top of and one on the side of the switch water shield) that attach the switch water shield and bracket to the steering column (see illustrations).

9   Carefully pull the lower mounting tab on the switch water shield bracket away from the steering column far enough to clear the screw boss below the multi-function switch lever.

10   Remove the water shield and bracket and the multi-function switch from the steering column and unplug the electrical connectors. (On vehicles equipped with a tilt steering column, lifting up on the tilt release lever will provide extra clearance for switch removal.)

11   Carefully remove the water shield by pulling it off over the hazard warning switch knob and the multi-function switch lever. This left half of the multi-function switch includes the headlight dimmer switch and the hazard warning flasher and turn signal switch.

12   To remove the windshield wiper and washer switch (the right half of the multi-function switch), carefully pull the windshield wiper and washer switch up and away from the right side of the steering column and unplug the electrical connector from the switch.

13   Installation is the reverse of removal.

2001 through 2006 models

14   The multi-function switch consists of a main body that fits over the top of the steering column and two stalks. One stalk is on the left of the column and controls the lighting functions such as the headlights and interior lights, the other is on the right of the column and controls the front and rear wiper and washer systems.

15   The switch can be removed and taken to the dealer for diagnosis if necessary.

16   Disconnect the cable from the negative terminal of the battery (see Chapter 5).

17   On vehicles with tilt steering columns, lower the column as much as possible and allow the tilt lever to remain in the released position.

18   Remove the steering column covers (see Chapter 11).

19   Disconnect both electrical connectors from the switch.

20   Grasp the switch and pull it upward while wiggling it gently to release it from the locating tabs.

21   Installation is the reverse of the removal procedure.

2007 and later models

22   On these models there are left and right multi-function switches. These switches mount to each side of the airbag clockspring housing.

23   Disconnect the cable from the negative terminal of the battery (see Chapter 5).

24   Remove the steering column covers (see Chapter 11).

25   Remove the screw securing the switch to the clockspring housing, then slide the switch out from the housing and disconnect the electrical connectors (see illustrations). Remove the switch from the housing.

26   Installation is the reverse of removal.

17.25a Remove the switch mounting screw...

17.25b ... then separate the switch from the clockspring housing and detach the electrical connectors

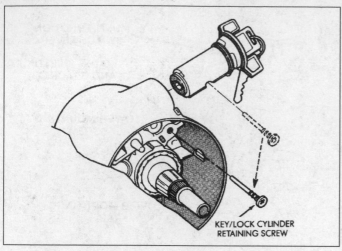

18.5 Remove the screw and pull the lock cylinder out (1990 and earlier models)

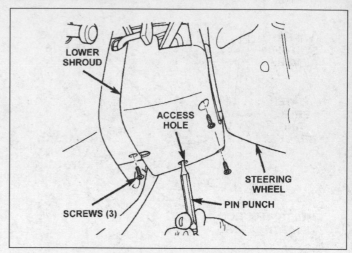

18.11a To release the ignition key lock cylinder, insert a pin punch through the access hole in the lower steering column cover, depress the release tang in the lock cylinder and pull out the cylinder; to remove the lower steering column cover, remove these three screws (1997 and later models)

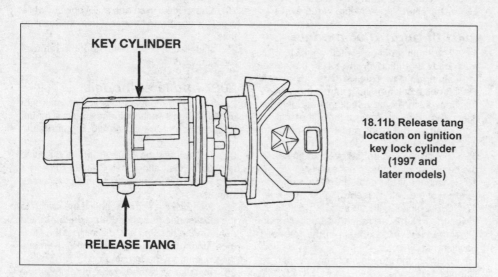

18.11b Release tang location on ignition key lock cylinder (1997 and later models)

18   Ignition lock cylinder - removal and installation

Warning: *Some models covered by this manual are equipped with airbags. Always disable the airbag system when working in the vicinity of airbag system components (see Section 24).*

1987 through 1995 models

1   Disconnect the cable from the negative battery terminal (see Chapter 5).
2   Remove the turn signal/hazard warning switches (see Section 15).
3   Remove the ignition key lamp assembly.
4   Place the lock cylinder in the On position.
5   On 1990 and earlier models, remove the retaining screw and withdraw the cylinder from the steering column (see illustration). On 1991 and later models, insert a thin screwdriver in the slot adjacent to the screw and press against the spring latch to remove the cylinder.
6   Insert the lock cylinder into position and install the screw (1990 and earlier models only). Tighten the screw securely.
7   Installation is the reverse of removal.

1997 through 2000 models

8   Disconnect the cable from the negative battery terminal (see Chapter 5).
9   If the vehicle is equipped with an automatic transmission, put the shift lever in the PARK position.
10   Turn the key to the ON position.
11   Insert a small screwdriver or pin punch through the access hole in the lower steering column cover (see illustration) and depress the release tang (see illustration) on the bottom of the key lock cylinder. While pushing up on the release tang, pull out the key lock cylinder.
12   Installation is the reverse of removal. Be sure to push in the key lock cylinder until it snaps into place.

2001 and later models

Note: *On later models, if the key is difficult to turn, the problem may not be in the switch or lock cylinder. On automatic transmission vehicles with floor console-mounted shifters, the shifter interlock cable may be out of adjustment. If it is defective inside the steering column, the steering column must be replaced. On manual transmission vehicles, the small button behind the key cylinder may be defective. If it is defective, the steering column must be replaced.*

13   Disconnect the cable from the negative battery terminal (see Chapter 5).
14   Put the key into the lock cylinder.
15   On vehicles equipped with an automatic transmission, place the shifter in Park.
16   Remove the steering column covers.
17   Turn the key to the On position. On models with a keyless-entry system, remove the halo ring and keyless entry module.
18   Push a small punch or a similar tool into the hole in the bottom of the switch.
19   Pull out on the key while pushing in on the punch. The cylinder will slide out with the key.
20   To install a new cylinder, first put the key into it. Turn it to the On position.
21   Line the cylinder up in the correct "On" orientation with the housing and slide it in. It will snap into place.
22   Turn the key to the Lock position.
23   The remainder of installation is the reverse of removal.

POSITION	CIRCUIT	
START	I-1, B-1 & S	CONNECTED
	G-1, G-2	GROUNDED
ON	I-1 & B-1	CONNECTED
	A & B-2	CONNECTED
	I-3 & B-3	CONNECTED
OFF	OPEN	
OFF-LOCK	OPEN	
ACC.	A & B-2	CONNECTED

19.4a Terminal details and schematic diagram of the ignition switch

19   Ignition switch - check and replacement

Warning: *Some models covered by this manual are equipped with airbags. Always disable the airbag system when working in the vicinity of airbag system components (see Section 24).*

1987 through 1995 models

1   Disconnect the cable from the negative battery terminal (see Chapter 5).
2   The ignition switch is located on the steering column and is actuated by a rod attached to the key lock cylinder.

Check

3   Remove the switch (see Steps 6 through 9).
4   Use an ohmmeter or self-powered test light and the accompanying illustration and check chart to check for continuity between the switch terminals (see illustrations).
5   If the switch does not have correct continuity, replace it.

Replacement

6   Disconnect the cable from the negative

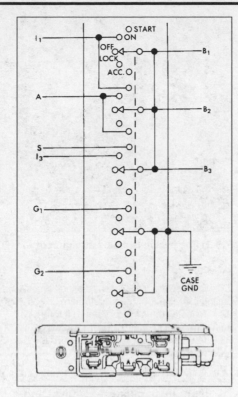

19.4b Ignition switch continuity chart - continuity should be as specified in each switch position

battery terminal (see Chapter 5).
7   Insert the key into the lock cylinder and turn it to the Off-Lock position.
8   On models so equipped, remove the intermittent wiper module.
9   Unplug the electrical connector, remove the bolts, then detach the switch from the actuator rod and lower it from the steering column.
10   Installation is the reverse of removal. Move the switch slider to the Accessory position. On standard steering columns, this is all the way to the left (steering wheel side), on tilt

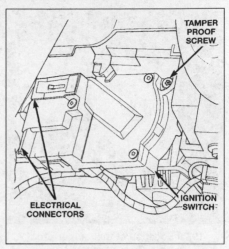

19.14 Remove the ignition switch retaining screw (the tamper-proof Torx type) (1997 through 2000 models)

columns, all the way to the right (away from the steering wheel). As the switch is engaged to the actuator rod, push the switch down the steering column to remove any slack from the rod before fully tightening the bolts.

1997 through 2000 models

11   Remove the ignition key lock cylinder (see Section 18).
12   Remove the lower steering column cover screws (see illustration 18.11a) and remove the cover.
13   Unplug the two electrical connectors from the ignition switch.
14   Remove the ignition switch retaining screw (see illustration). (The screw is a tamper-proof Torx type.)
15   Using a small screwdriver, depress the locking tab (see illustration) and remove the ignition switch from the steering column.
16   Installation is the reverse of removal. Before installing the switch, rotate the slot in the switch to the ON position (see illustration).

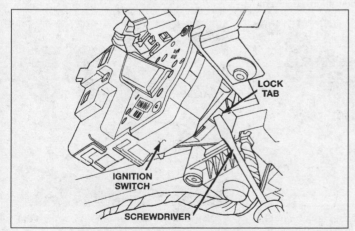

19.15 Using a small screwdriver, depress the lock tab and remove the ignition switch from the steering column (1997 through 2000 models)

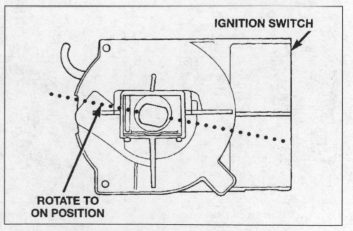

19.16 Before installing the switch, be sure to rotate the slot in the switch to the ON position (1997 through 2000 models)

19.20 Location of the tamper-proof Torx screw

19.21 The switch is pulled straight out to release it

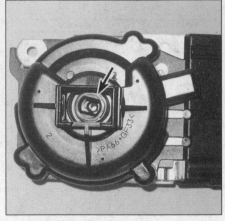

19.22 This is the switch turned to the ON position (it must be in this position before it can be installed)

2001 and later models

17   Remove the ignition key lock cylinder.
18   Remove the multi-function switch.
19   Disconnect the wiring from the switch.
20   Use a tamper-proof Torx screwdriver to remove the screw securing the switch (see illustration).

21   Release the switch from the lock tabs by pulling it straight out (see illustration).
22   To install the switch, first turn it to the On position (see illustration).
23   The remainder of installation is the reverse of removal.

20   Instrument cluster - removal and installation

Warning: *Some models covered by this manual are equipped with airbags. Always disable the airbag system when working in the vicinity of airbag system components (see Section 24).*

1987 through 1995 models

1   Disconnect the cable from the negative battery terminal (see Chapter 5).
2   Remove the instrument cluster bezel (see Chapter 11, Section 24).
3   On 1991 and earlier models, remove the retaining screws and detach the indicator bezel (see illustration).
4   Remove the cluster and switch panel screws and pull the cluster out far enough for access to the electrical and speedometer connectors (see illustration). On some

models it may be necessary to disconnect the speedometer cable at the transmission or cruise control adapter to provide sufficient slack so the cluster can be pulled out (see Section 21).
5   Unplug the connectors, detach the speedometer cable (later models) and remove the cluster (see illustrations).
6   Installation is the reverse of removal.

1997 through 2006 models

7   Disconnect the cable from the negative battery terminal (see Chapter 5).
8   Remove the headlight switch knob and shaft (see Section 13).
9   Remove the two screws that retain the cover for the steering column opening (see illustration 24.8 in Chapter 11). Pull the steering column opening cover straight back as far back as it will go. Work the lower edge of the cover rearward to disengage the hooks on the lower edge of the cover from the pivots on the lower edge of the instrument panel. Remove the cover.
10   The instrument panel top cover uses five equally-spaced snap clip retainers to attach the top cover to the instrument panel. Using

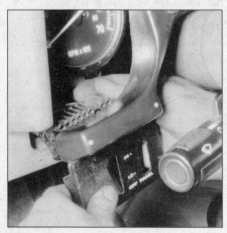

20.3 Remove the screws and detach the indicator bezel

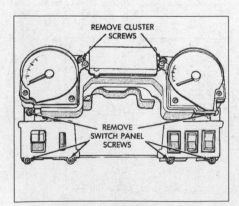

20.4 Cluster and switch panel screw locations

REMOVE CLUSTER SCREWS

REMOVE SWITCH PANEL SCREWS

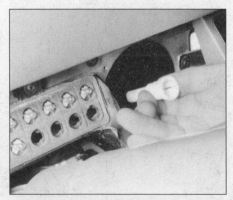

20.5a On later models, the speedometer is part of the cluster and you'll have to disconnect the speedometer cable by squeezing the release lever as shown here

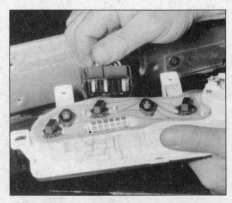

20.5b Pull the cluster out and detach the electrical connector

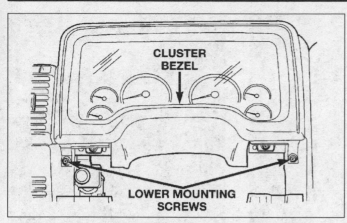

20.11a To detach the instrument cluster bezel, remove these two screws from the lower edge of the cluster…

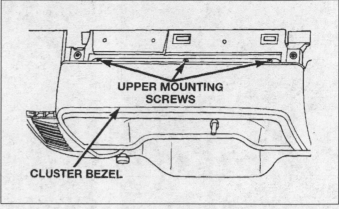

20.11b … and remove these three screws from the upper edge (1997 and later models)

a suitable tool with a wide, flat blade, carefully pry up the instrument panel top cover from the instrument panel (see illustration 24.28 in Chapter 11).

11   Remove the two screws that attach the lower edge of the cluster to the instrument panel and remove the three screws that attach the upper edge of the cluster to the instrument panel (see illustrations). Pull off the cluster bezel and remove it from the instrument panel.

12   Remove the four screws that attach the instrument cluster to the instrument panel (see illustration).

13   Pull the instrument cluster back and disconnect it from the two "self-docking" electrical connectors.

14   Installation is the reverse of removal. (The two self-docking connectors are rigidly mounted and are aligned with their corresponding connector halves in the back of the cluster. When the cluster is placed in position and pushed back into place, it will automatically plug into the connectors.)

2007 through 2010 models

15   Disconnect the cable from the negative battery terminal (see Chapter 5).

16   Using a plastic trim tool, pry the top of the lower steering column opening cover, then swing the cover back and detach the tabs at the bottom of the cover from the instrument panel reinforcement.

17   Using a plastic trim tool, pry out the top of the cover directly below the steering column, then swing the cover back and detach the tabs at the bottom from the instrument panel reinforcement.

18   Remove the two bolts and detach the knee bolster reinforcement plate from the instrument panel.

19   Remove the two screws at the bottom of the instrument cluster bezel and remove the bezel.

20   Remove the four instrument cluster screws, pull the cluster back, then disconnect the electrical connectors from the cluster and remove the cluster from the instrument panel.

21   Installation is the reverse of removal.

2011 and later models

22   Disconnect the cable from the negative battery terminal (see Chapter 5).

23   Remove the left HVAC register from the instrument panel. To do this, rotate the register so the louvers are pointing to the 11 o'clock position, angle them down slightly, then insert a screwdriver into the register at the 12: 30 position and pry the retaining tab inwards while rotating the register counterclockwise (see illustration).

24   Remove the two HVAC registers from the center bezel using the same technique.

25   Remove the trim panel below the steering column (see illustration).

26   If equipped, push the power window switch out from behind and unplug it. If not equipped with power windows, pry out the

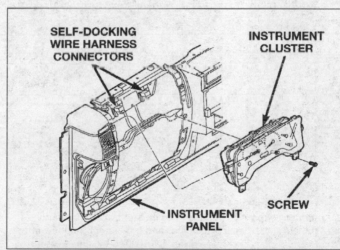

20.12 To detach the instrument cluster from the instrument panel, remove the four retaining screws (1997 and later models)

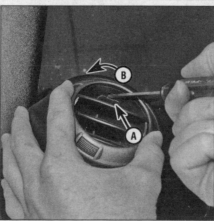

20.23 Pry the register retaining tab (A) inward and rotate the register counterclockwise to free it (B)

20.25 Steering column trim panel screws

20.26 Remove the screw from behind the power window switch or storage bin, as applicable

20.27 Remove the screw from below the upper storage tray mat

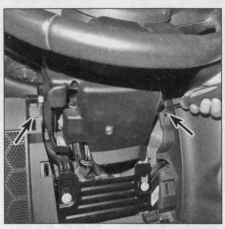

20.28 Remove the cluster bezel screws from the steering column opening

storage bin from the center bezel. Remove the screw from the opening (see illustration).

27   Remove the upper storage tray mat from the center of the instrument panel, then remove the screw underneath (see illustration).

28   Remove the two screws from the instrument cluster bezel below the steering column (see illustration).

29   Carefully pull the center lower part of the bezel from the instrument panel (see illustration).

30   Carefully free the remaining clips around the perimeter of the bezel and detach the bezel from the instrument panel (see illustration).

31   Unscrew the instrument cluster screws and pull it from the instrument panel, then disconnect the electrical connectors and remove the cluster (see illustration).

32   Installation is the reverse of removal.

21   Speedometer cable (1987 through 1995 models) - removal and installation

Warning: *Some models covered by this manual are equipped with airbags. Always disable the airbag system when working in the vicinity of airbag system components (see Section 24).*

1   Disconnect the cable from the negative battery terminal (see Chapter 5).

2   Disconnect the speedometer cable from the transmission/transfer case or cruise control adapter (see illustration).

3   Detach the cable from the routing clips in the engine compartment and pull the cable up

20.29 Free the lower bezel retaining clips from the instrument panel

20.30 The cluster bezel, which covers the center and left side of the instrument panel, is retained by clips around its perimeter

20.31 Instrument cluster mounting screws

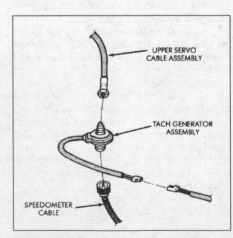

21.2 Unscrew the collar and pull the speedometer cable out of the cruise control adapter (shown) or transmission/ transfer case housing, as applicable

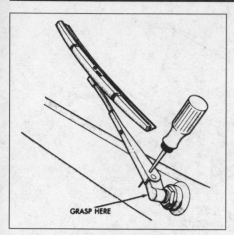

22.2 After marking the position, grasp the wiper arm, insert a punch or ice pick in the release clip hole and pull the arm assembly off the spindle

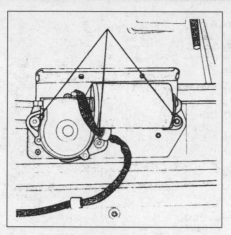

22.3 Wiper motor bolt location

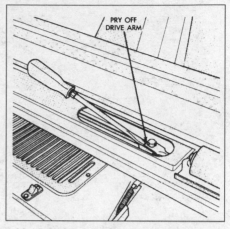

22.4 Pry the wiper linkage drive arm off with a screwdriver

to provide enough slack to allow disconnection from the speedometer.

4   Remove the instrument cluster screws, pull the cluster out and disconnect the speedometer cable from the back of the cluster (see illustration 20.6a).

5   Remove the cable from the vehicle.

6   Prior to installation, lubricate the speedometer end of the cable with spray-on speedometer cable lubricant (available at auto parts stores).

7   Installation is the reverse of removal.

22   Windshield wiper motor - removal and installation

1   Disconnect the cable from the negative battery terminal (see Chapter 5).

1987 through 1995 models
Removal

2   Use a pencil or marking pen to mark the

arm-to-spindle relationship, remove the windshield wiper arms (see illustration).

3   Remove the hold-down bolts at the corners and fold the windshield forward, out of the way. Remove the wiper motor screws or bolts (see illustration).

4   Use a screwdriver to disconnect the wiper linkage drive arm (see illustration).

5   Grasp the motor securely, lift it out through the access hole and detach the drive arm by prying it off the pivot (DO NOT remove the pivot nut) (see illustration).

6   On models with intermittent wipers, remove the two screws and detach the wiper module from the instrument panel.

7   Reach up under the instrument panel in the passenger's compartment and unplug the motor electrical connector, then remove the wiper motor from the vehicle.

Installation

8   Insert the wiring harness through the access hole and plug it in. Install the intermittent wiper module.

9   Turn the wiper motor on to cycle it to the Park position, shut it off, then connect the wiper linkage drive arm to the motor (see illustration).

10   Lower the motor and arm assembly into position and install the screws/bolts. Tighten the screws/bolts securely.

11   Connect the drive arm to the pivot shaft (see illustration).

12   The remainder of installation is the reverse of removal.

1997 and later models
Front motor

13   Remove the screw that attaches the center of the cowl plenum cover/grille panel to the cowl plenum (see illustration).

14   Open and support the hood.

15   On 2002 and earlier models, peel the ends of the cowl-to-hood seal away from the metal flange where the dash panel and cowl plenum panel meet. Pull back the seal far enough to access the screws that secure the outer ends of the cowl plenum cover/grille

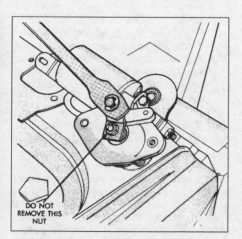

22.5 Pry the drive arm off the pivot with a screwdriver - DO NOT remove the nut

22.9 Use large pliers to press the drive arm onto the shaft

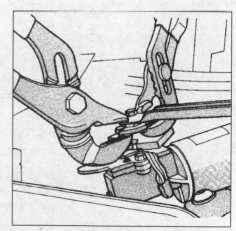

22.11 Press the drive arm evenly onto the wiper motor shaft using two pairs of pliers

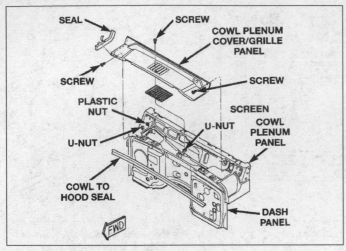

22.13 Cowl plenum cover/grille panel mounting details (1997 and later models)

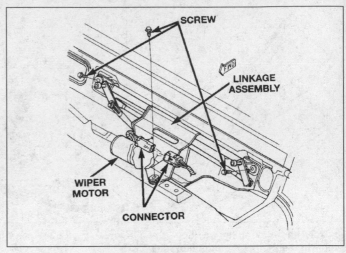

22.19 Front windshield wiper motor mounting details (1997 and later models)

panel to the cowl plenum panel.

16   Remove the screw that attaches each outer end of the cowl plenum cover/grille panel to the cowl plenum panel.

17   Remove the cowl plenum cover/grille panel. Be careful not to damage the paint around the pivot openings of the panel.

18   Reach into the cowl plenum and unplug the wiper motor electrical connector.

19   Remove the wiper module mounting bracket screws (see illustration).

20   Remove the wiper module from the cowl plenum as a unit. On 2007 and later models, pull the assembly upward to disengage the rubber isolator from the front of the cowl opening.

21   Release the retainer that secures the wiper motor electrical harness to the wiper module bracket.

22   Turn over the wiper module and remove the nut that attaches the wiper linkage crank arm to the wiper motor output shaft.

23   Remove the three screws that attach the wiper motor to the wiper module mounting bracket.

24   Installation is the reverse of removal.

Rear motor

25   From the outside of the liftgate glass, remove the rear wiper motor output shaft nut and bezel (see illustration).

26   From the outside of the liftgate glass, remove the rear wiper motor output shaft rubber gasket.

27   From the inside of the liftgate glass, remove the three screws that attach the rear wiper motor cover to the motor.

28   Disconnect the electrical connector from the motor.

29   Loosen - but don't remove - the right liftgate glass hinge nut.

30   From the inside of the liftgate glass, carefully separate the wiper motor from the liftgate glass until the output shaft clears the hole in the glass.

31   Move the motor to the right until the slotted hole in the motor mounting bracket clears the grommet under the right liftgate glass hinge nut.

32   Remove the rear wiper motor.

33   Installation is the reverse of removal.

23   Cruise control system - description and check

2006 and earlier models

1   The cruise control system maintains vehicle speed with a vacuum actuated servo motor located in the engine compartment, which is connected to the throttle linkage by a cable. The system consists of the servo motor, clutch switch, brake switch, control switches, a relay and associated vacuum hoses.

2   Because of the complexity of the cruise control system and the special tools and techniques required for diagnosis, repair should be left to a dealer service department or a repair shop. However, it is possible for the home mechanic to make simple checks of the wiring and vacuum connections for minor faults which can be easily repaired. These include:

a)   Inspect the cruise control actuating switches for broken wires and loose connections.

b)   Check the cruise control fuse.

c)   The cruise control system is operated by vacuum so it's critical that all vacuum switches, hoses and connections are secure. Check the hoses in the engine compartment for tight connections, cracks and obvious vacuum leaks.

2007 and later models

3   On these models, the Powertrain Control Module (PCM) controls the cruise control system electronically via the electronic throttle control system. If you have problems with the cruise control system, check for the presence of trouble codes stored in the PCM (see Chapter 6). If that doesn't turn up any problems, have it checked by a dealer service department or other qualified repair shop.

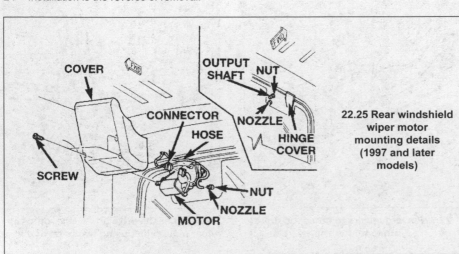

22.25 Rear windshield wiper motor mounting details (1997 and later models)

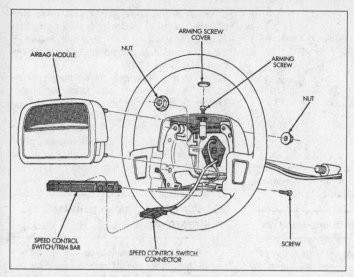

24.5 Airbag module and steering wheel details - 1995 models

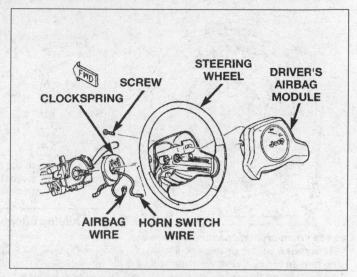

24.15a Airbag module, steering wheel and clockspring details - 1997 and later models

24   Airbag system (1995 and later models) - general information

1   1995 and later models are equipped with a Supplemental Restraint System (SRS), more commonly known as airbags. This system is designed to protect the driver and, on 1997 and later models, the front seat passenger, from serious injury in the event of a head-on or frontal collision. It consists of an airbag module in the center of the steering wheel, and, on 1997 and later models, the right side of the instrument panel. 1995 models have a self-contained system, in which the impact sensor is housed within the airbag module on the steering wheel. The system on 1997 and later models utilizes a control module (which contains an impact sensor) mounted on the forward part of the transmission tunnel, under the heater/air conditioner floor duct, a "clockspring" under the steering wheel which can transmit current to the driver's side airbag module regardless of steering wheel position, and a passenger's side airbag module mounted above the glove box.
2   Additionally, 2007 and later models could be equipped with optional side-impact airbags mounted in the outboard sides of the seat backs.
3   Whenever working in the vicinity of any airbag system components it is important to disable the system to prevent accidental deployment of the airbag(s), which could cause personal injury.

1995 models
Disarming the system
4   Roll down the driver's side window.
5   Pry off the small cover from the top of the steering wheel hub. Get out of the vehicle and close the door, then using an 8 mm socket, reach in and unscrew the arming screw until

it stops (it should protrude approximately one inch from the surface of the steering wheel trim) (see illustration). The airbag is now disarmed.

Arming the system
6   Reach through the driver's window and turn the arming screw until it is seated (tighten it to approximately 15 in-lbs). Install the arming screw cover on the steering wheel hub.

Airbag module removal and installation
7   Disarm the airbag system as described earlier in this Section.
8   Removal of the driver's side airbag is covered in Chapter 10, Section 9.

1997 and later models
Disarming the system
9   Turn the ignition switch to the Off position. Disconnect the cable from the negative terminal of the battery. Make sure the battery cable cannot accidentally come into contact with the battery terminal.
10   Wait at least two minutes for the back-up power supply to be depleted before beginning work.

Arming the system
11   Make sure the ignition switch is in the Off position.
12   Connect the cable to the negative terminal of the battery.
13   Turn the ignition switch to the On position. Confirm that the airbag warning light glows for 6 to 8 seconds, then goes out, indicating the system is functioning properly.

Centering the clockspring
14   If the airbag system clockspring becomes uncentered (during steering wheel removal, for example), it must be centered to prevent it

from breaking.

1997 through 2006 models
15   With the steering wheel removed, turn the clockspring rotor clockwise until it stops (don't apply too much force) (see illustrations).
16   Turn the clockspring rotor counterclockwise about 2-1/2 turns; the flats on the rotor should be horizontal and the wiring harness should be positioned at the bottom. If it isn't, turn the clockspring an additional 1/2 turn counterclockwise.

2007 and later models
17   With the steering wheel removed, turn the clockspring rotor clockwise until it stops (don't apply too much force).
18   Turn the clockspring rotor counterclockwise about 2-1/2 turns. Adjust the clockspring rotor counterclockwise or clockwise, as necessary, so the wiring harness is positioned at the top, and the drive pin (dowel) is positioned at the bottom.

All models
19   Install the steering wheel following the procedure described in Chapter 10.

Airbag module removal and installation
Driver's side
20   Disarm the airbag system as described earlier in this Section.
21   Removal of the driver's side airbag is covered in Chapter 10, Section 9.

Passenger's side - 2006 and earlier models
22   Disarm the airbag system as described earlier in this Section.
23   Remove the instrument panel (see Chapter 11).
24   Prop the instrument panel up on its side.

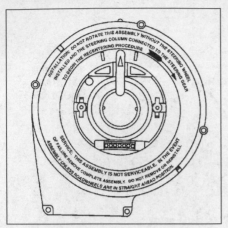

24.15b When properly centered, the airbag clockspring will be positioned like this; the flats in the center of the rotor will be horizontal, and the wiring harness will be positioned at the bottom

Remove the three nuts that attach the airbag module to the instrument panel (see illustration).

25   Remove the airbag module.

26   Installation is the reverse of removal. Be sure to tighten the airbag module retaining screws to the torque listed in this Chapter's Specifications.

Passenger's side - 2007 and later models

27   Disable the airbag system as described earlier in this Section.

28   Remove the passenger's grab-handle from the top of the instrument panel. Pry up the small plastic covers to reveal the mounting bolts.

29   Between the airbag cover and the windshield, remove the small plastic cover to access and remove the one nut securing the airbag assembly.

30   Remove the glovebox (see Chapter 11, Section 24).

31   Remove the two nuts securing the airbag to the brace, on either side of the glovebox latch.

32   From inside the glovebox opening, remove the lower airbag mounting nuts.

33   Use a plastic trim tool to gently pry the airbag and its cover toward the rear of the vehicle until the assembly is free of the snaps securing it to the instrument panel, then pull the assembly rearward enough to access and disconnect the two airbag electrical connectors.

34   Installation is the reverse of removal. When connecting the airbag module electrical connectors (they are color-coded for their location), be sure to engage the CPA (Connector Position Assurance) clips after the connectors are attached. Make sure the studs on the airbag assembly align with the proper holes before installing any of the mounting nuts.

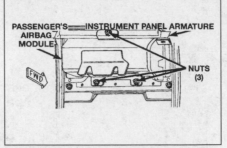

24.24 To detach the passenger side airbag module from the instrument panel, remove these three nuts

---

25   Adding aftermarket accessories

1   Customizing your Wrangler is a big part of owning one. Electrical additions are a big part of that too. But, you should also keep in mind the factory systems that are installed have been designed to carry the electrical load as they were designed from the factory and not for additional systems you'd like to add. Piggybacking lighting onto the factory lighting wire system can overload the factory wiring system.

2   Do not overlap an aftermarket system within the factory wiring or a factory dedicated system. Always start at the battery and add your own fuse or breaker, then to a switch and relay provided with the aftermarket system. For example, a lot of aftermarket spot lights can get very warm after just a few minutes of use. The warmer the bulb gets the more resistance is built up. The more resistance creates

a barrier to the current flow. This raises the current pressure which can mean possible switch, relay, connection, or wiring failure IF those components are not up to handling the load requirements.

3   With any aftermarket accessory, such as stereo, lights, winches, etc., follow the manufacturer's specifications and directions for installation to avoid any future electrical problems.

4   Securely mount your aftermarket components properly to avoid wire chafing and to ensure that they have a solid path to ground.

---

26   Wiring diagrams - general information

1   Since it isn't possible to include all wiring diagrams for every year covered by this manual, the following diagrams are those that are typical and most commonly needed.

2   Prior to troubleshooting any circuits, check the fuse and circuit breakers (if equipped) to make sure they're in good condition. Make sure the battery is properly charged and check the cable connections (see Chapter 1).

3   When checking a circuit, make sure that all connectors are clean, with no broken or loose terminals. When unplugging a connector, do not pull on the wires. Pull only on the connector housings themselves.

4   Refer to the accompanying chart for the wire color codes applicable to your vehicle (see illustration).

COLOR CODE	COLOR	STANDARD TRACER COLOR	COLOR CODE	COLOR	STANDARD TRACER CODE
BL	BLUE	WT	OR	ORANGE	BK
BK	BLACK	WT	PK	PINK	BK OR WT
BR	BROWN	WT	RD	RED	WT
DB	DARK BLUE	WT	TN	TAN	WT
DG	DARK GREEN	WT	VT	VIOLET	WT
GY	GRAY	BK	WT	WHITE	BK
LB	LIGHT BLUE	BK	YL	YELLOW	BK
LG	LIGHT GREEN	BK	*	WITH TRACER	

26.4 Wiring diagram color codes

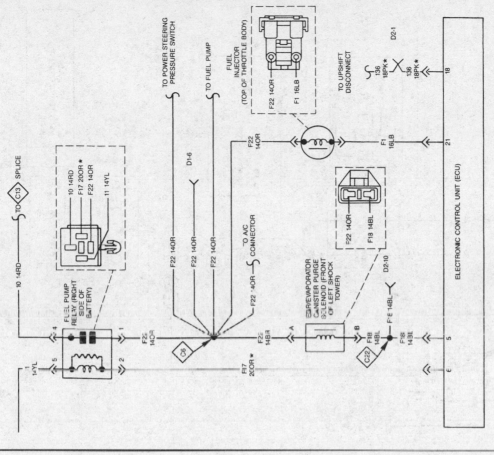

2.5L engine fuel injection system wiring diagram - 1987 through 1995 models (2 of 3)

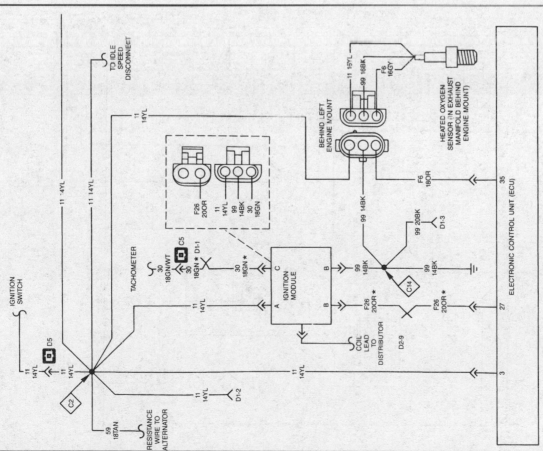

2.5L engine fuel injection system wiring diagram - 1987 through 1995 models (1 of 3)

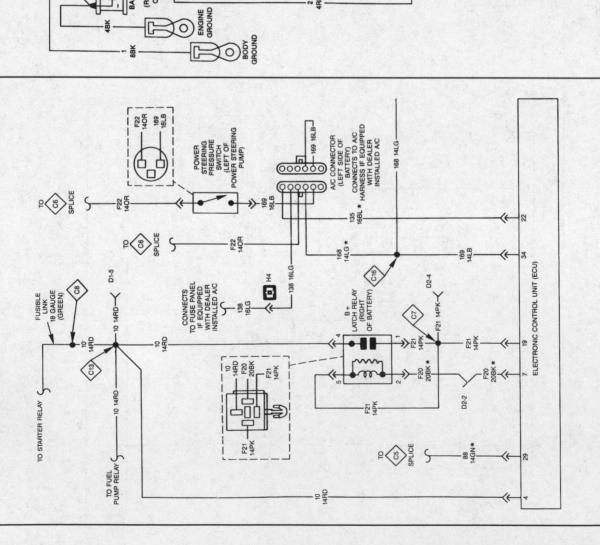

Starting system wiring diagram - 1987 through 1995 models

2.5L engine fuel injection system wiring diagram - 1987 through 1995 models (3 of 3)

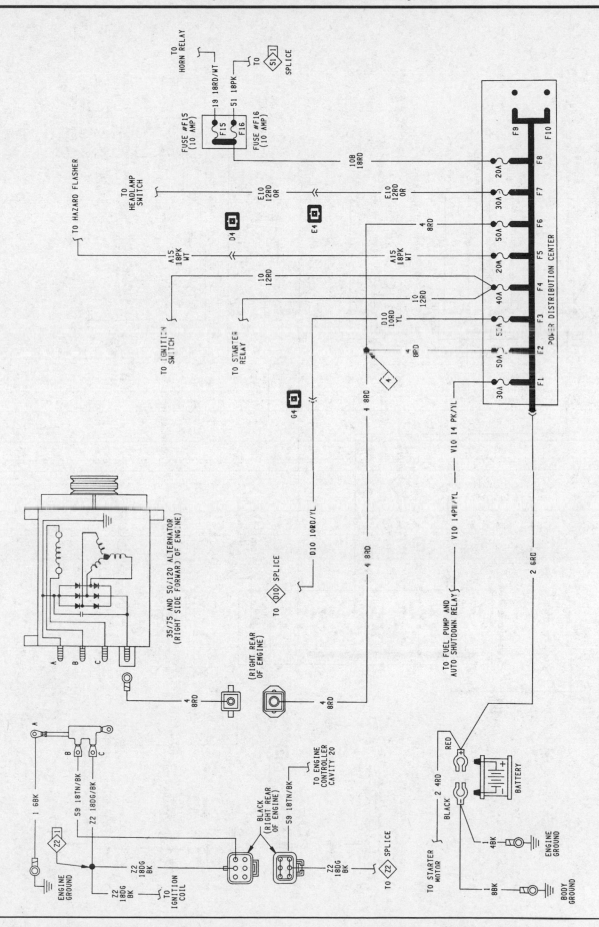

Charging system wiring diagram - 1987 through 1995 models

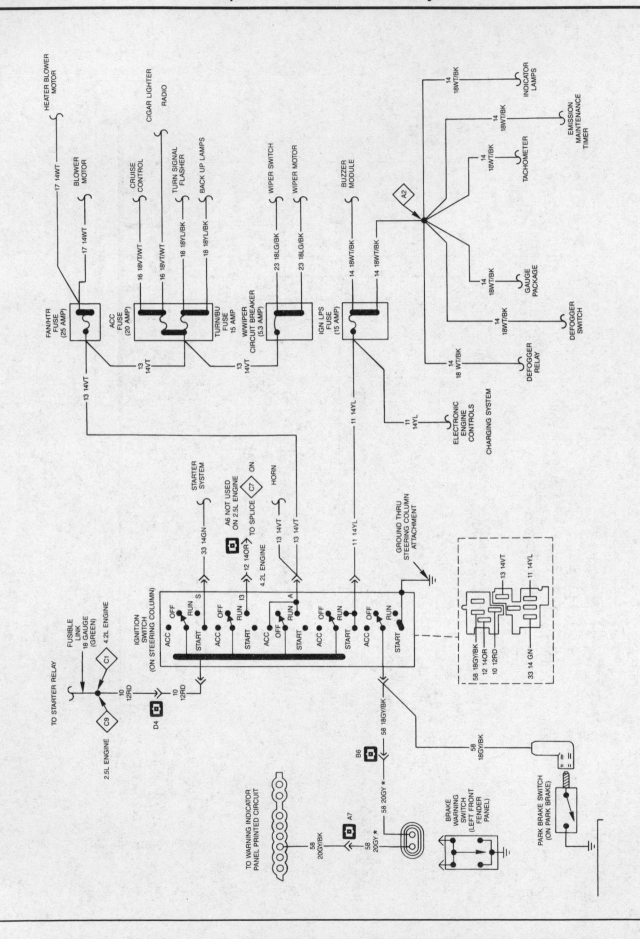

Ignition switch wiring diagram - 1987 through 1995 models

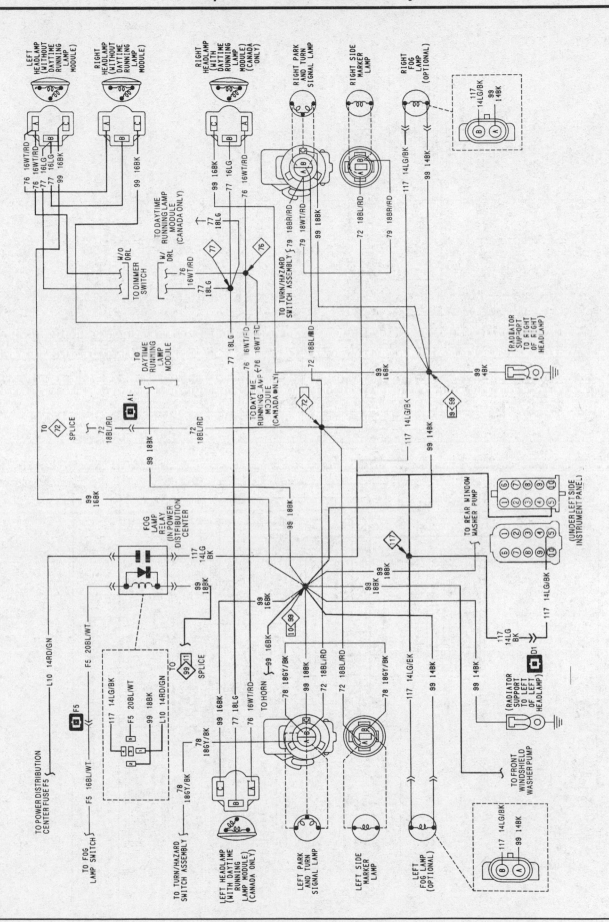

Front end lighting wiring diagram - 1987 through 1995 models

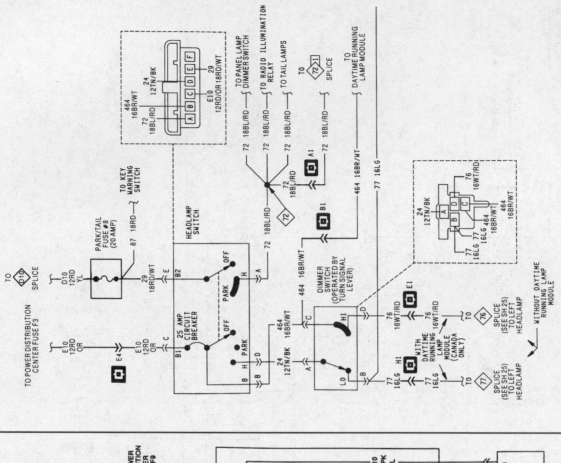

Headlight switch wiring diagram - 1987 through 1995 models

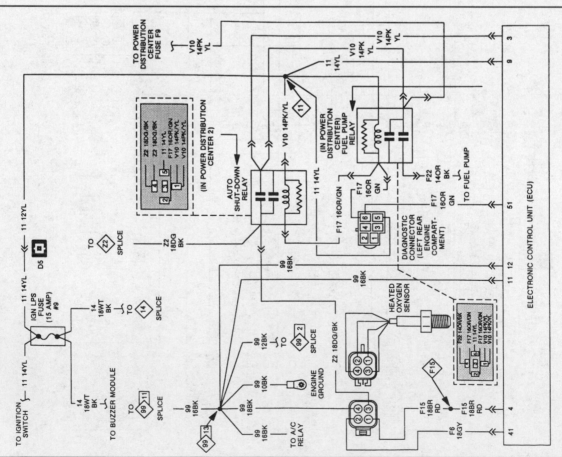

4.0L engine fuel injection system wiring diagram - 1987 through 1995 models

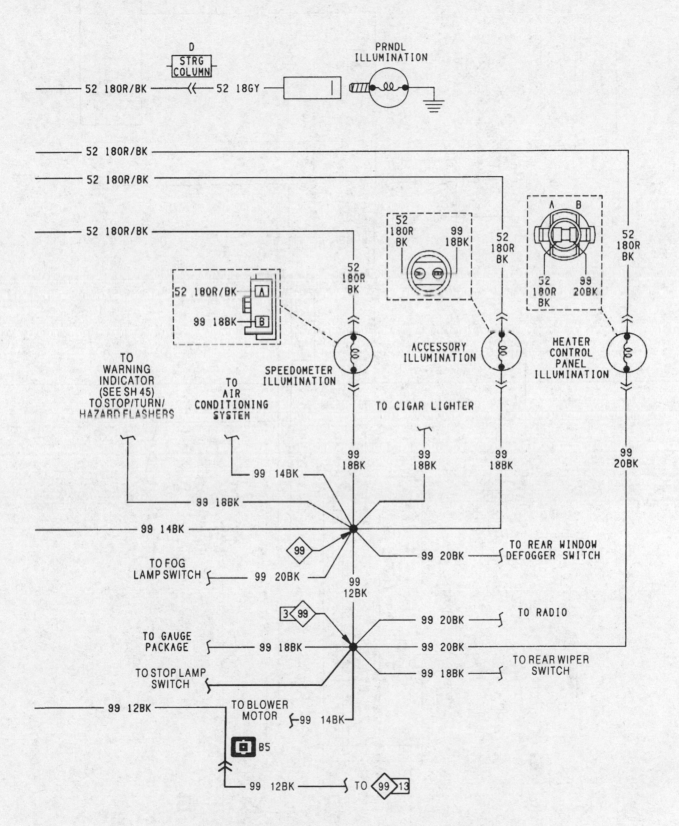

instrument panel lighting wiring diagram - 1987 through 1995 models

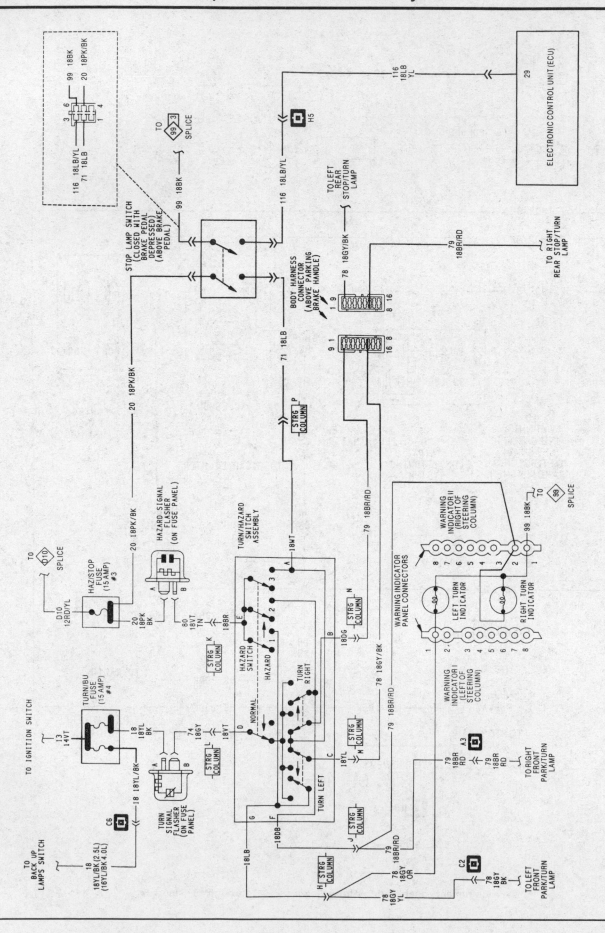

Stop/turn and hazard flasher system wiring diagram - 1987 through 1995 models

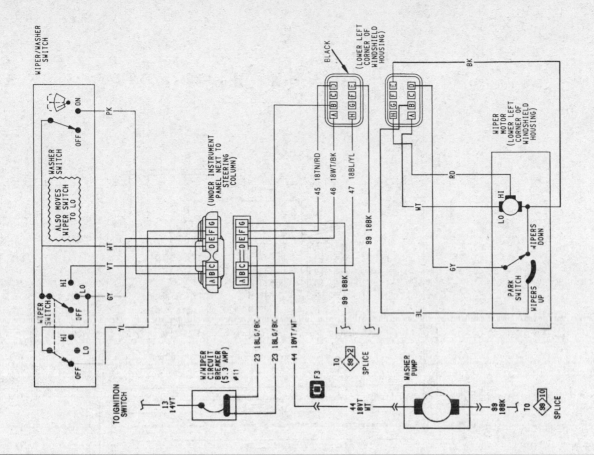

Windshield washer/wiper system wiring diagram (standard) - 1987 through 1995 models

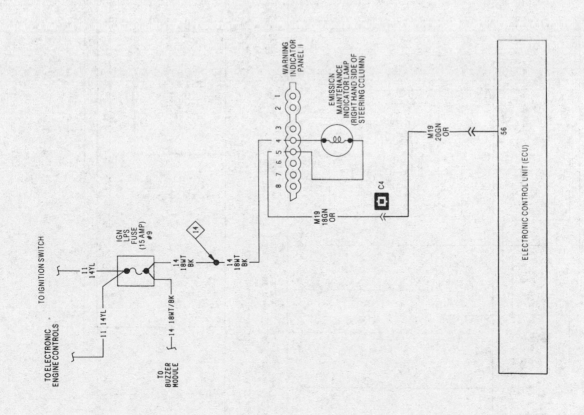

Emission maintenance reminder wiring diagram - 1987 through 1995 models

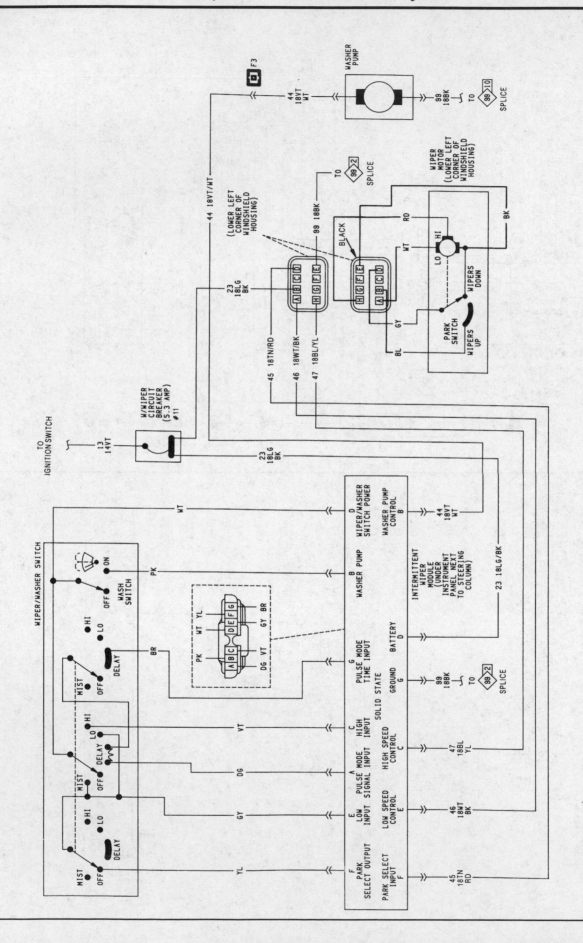

Windshield washer/wiper system wiring diagram (intermittent) - 1987 through 1995 models

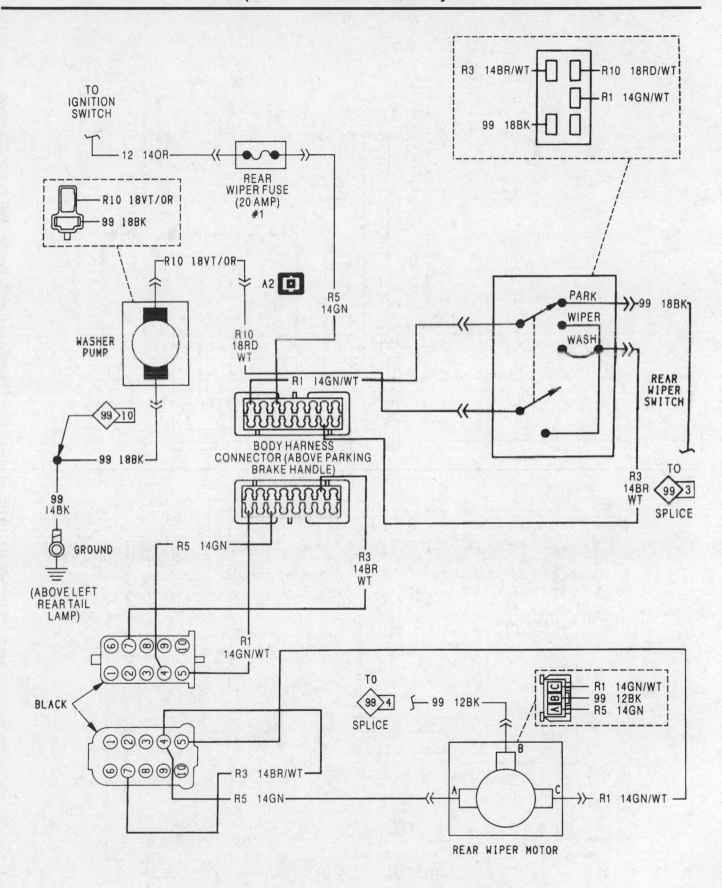

Rear washer/wiper system wiring diagram - 1987 through 1995 models

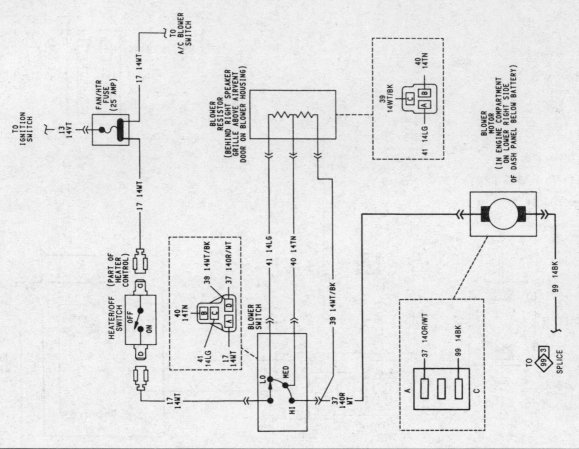

Heater system wiring diagram - 1987 through 1995 models

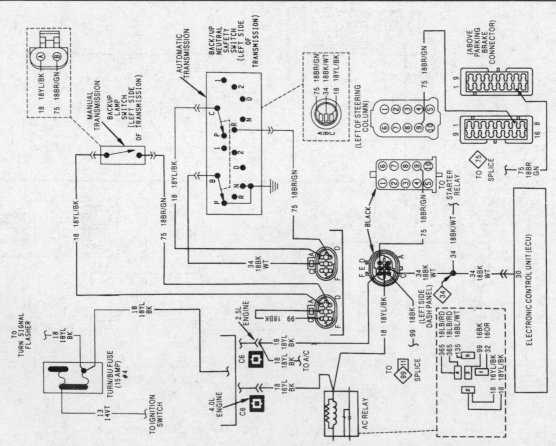

Back-up lamp/neutral safety switch wiring diagram - 1987 through 1995 models

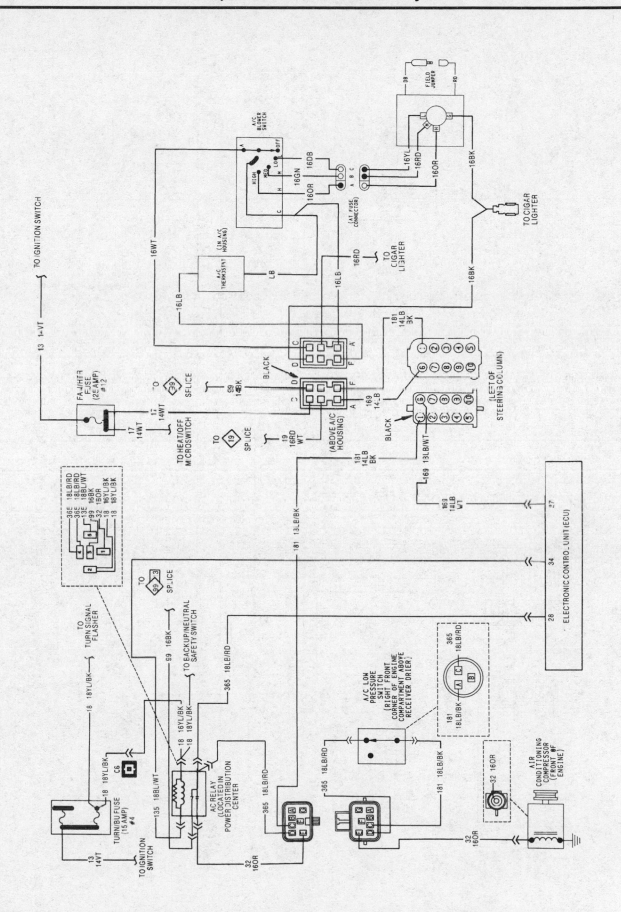

Air conditioning system wiring diagram - 1987 through 1995 models

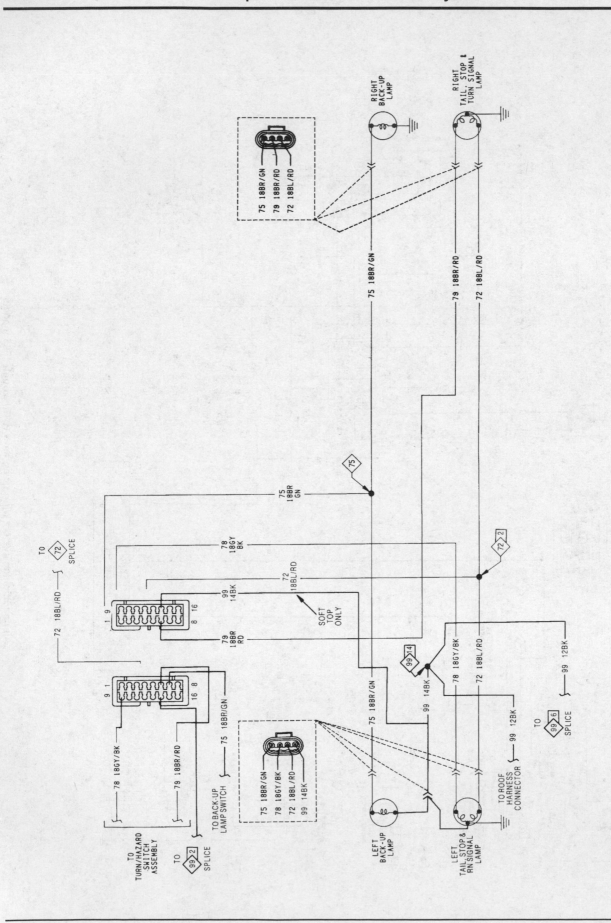

Rear lighting wiring diagram - 1987 through 1995 models

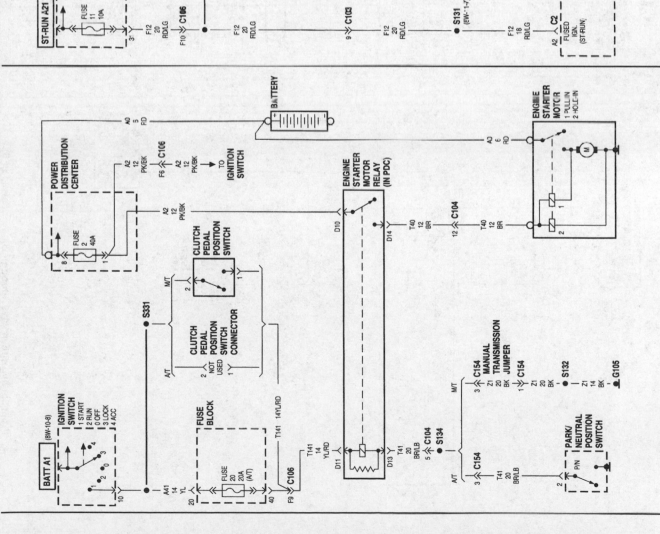
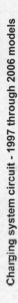

Charging system circuit - 1997 through 2006 models

Starting system circuit - 1997 through 2006 models

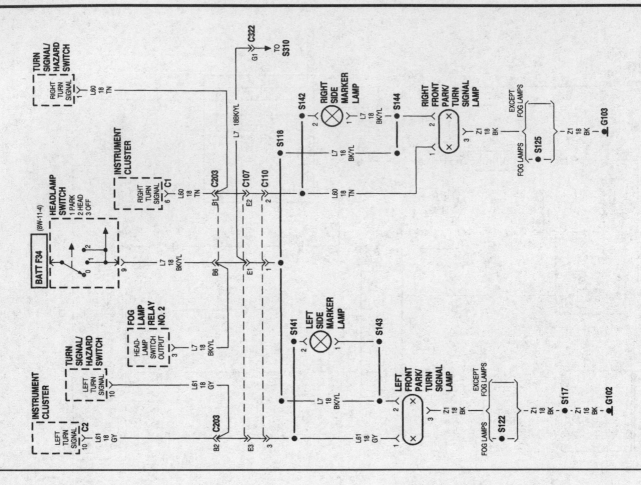

Front lighting circuit -1997 through 2006 models (2 of 5)

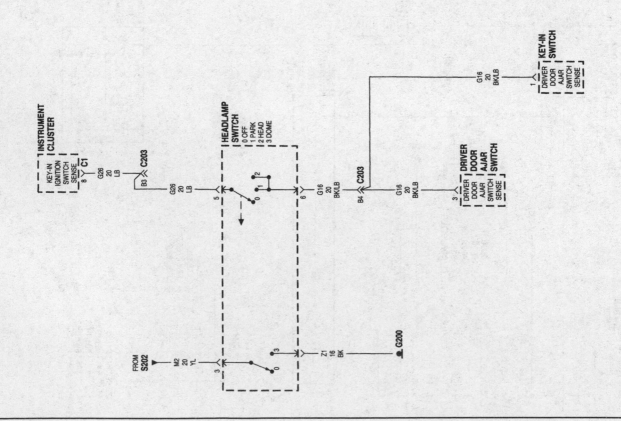

Front lighting circuit - 1997 through 2006 models (1 of 5)

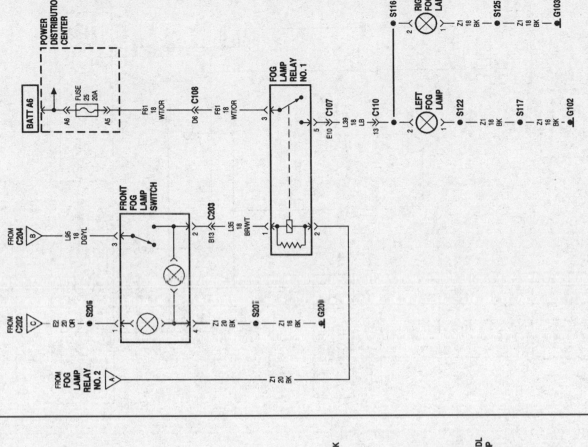

Front lighting circuit - 1997 through 2006 models (4 of 5)

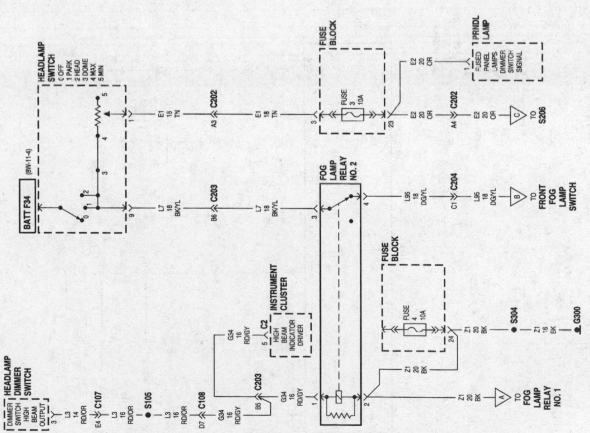

Front lighting circuit - 1997 through 2006 models (3 of 5)

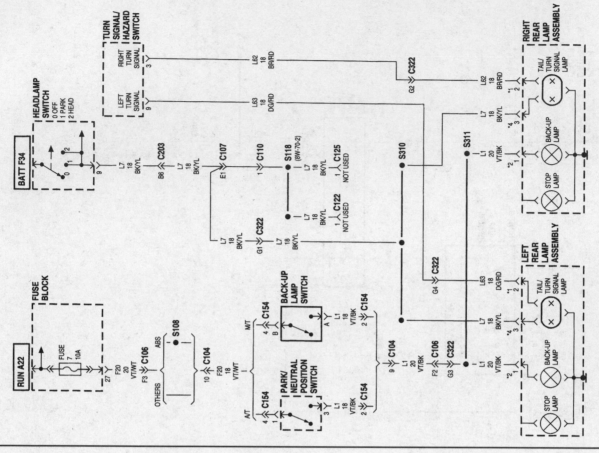

Rear lighting circuit - 1997 through 2006 models (1 of 3)

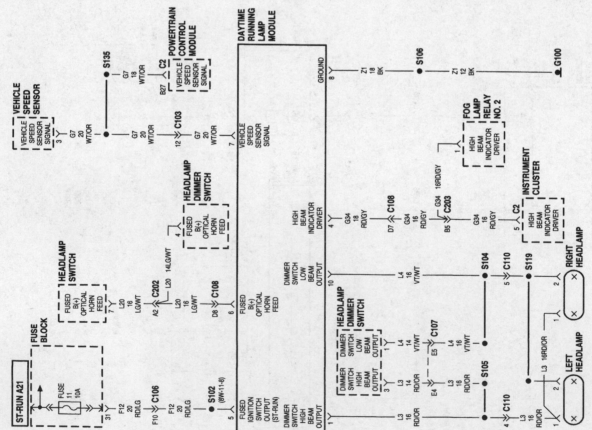

Front lighting circuit - 1997 through 2006 models (5 of 5)

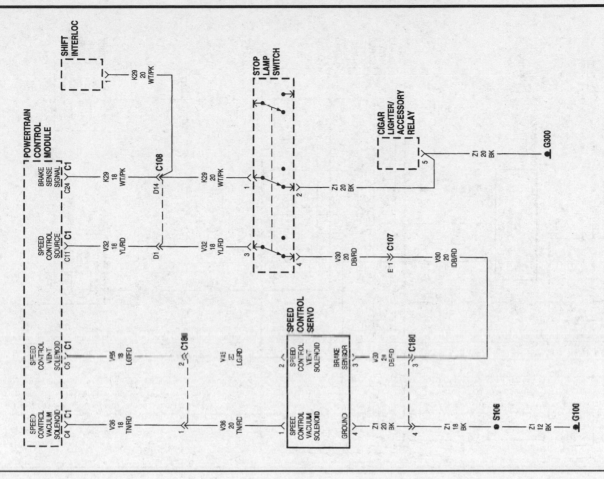

Rear lighting circuit - 1997 through 2006 models (3 of 3)

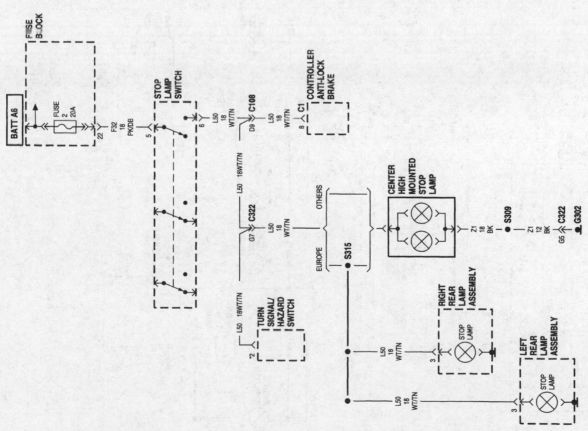

Rear lighting circuit - 1997 through 2006 models (2 of 3)

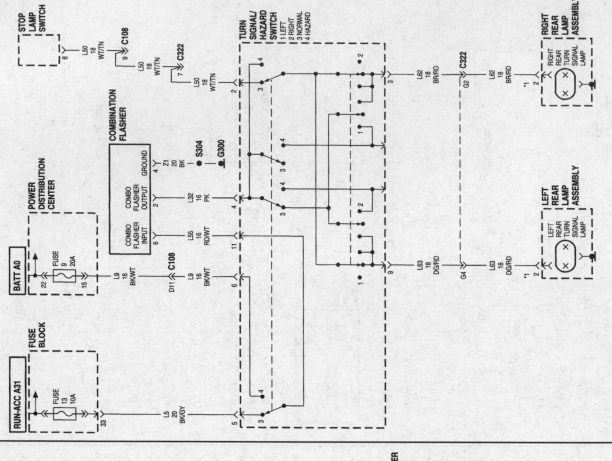

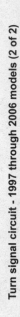

Turn signal circuit - 1997 through 2006 models (2 of 2)

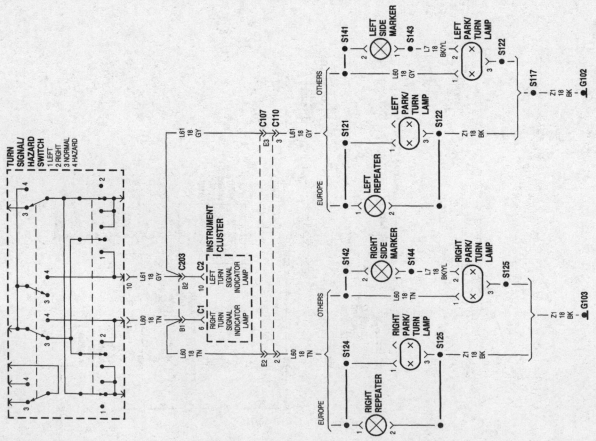

Turn signal circuit - 1997 through 2006 models (1 of 2)

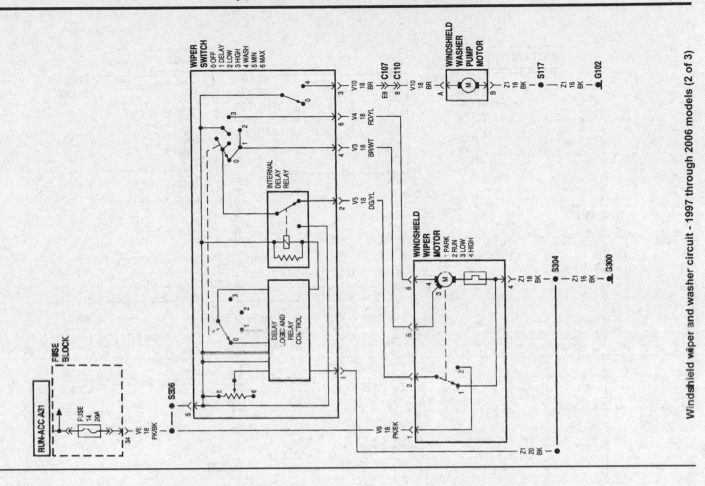

Windshield wiper and washer circuit - 1997 through 2006 models (2 of 3)

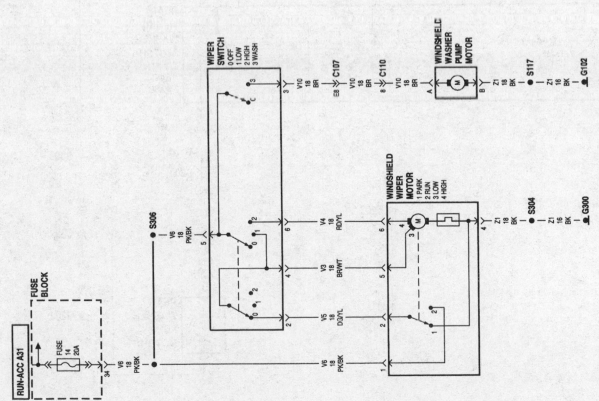

Windshield wiper and washer circuit - 1997 through 2006 models (1 of 3)

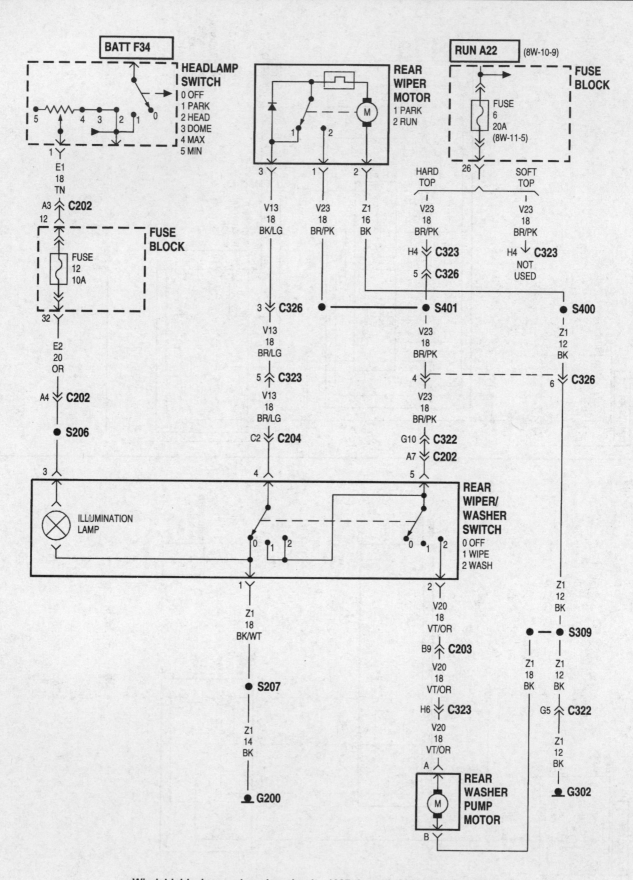

Windshield wiper and washer circuit - 1997 through 2006 models (3 of 3)

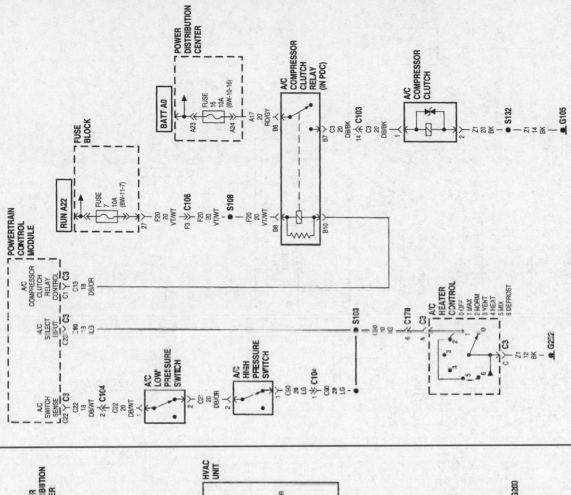

Air conditioning and heater circuit - 1997 through 2006 models (2 of 2)

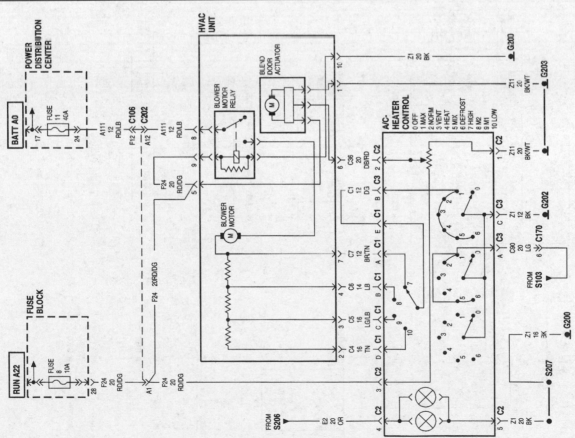

Air conditioning and heater circuit - 1997 through 2006 models (1 of 2)

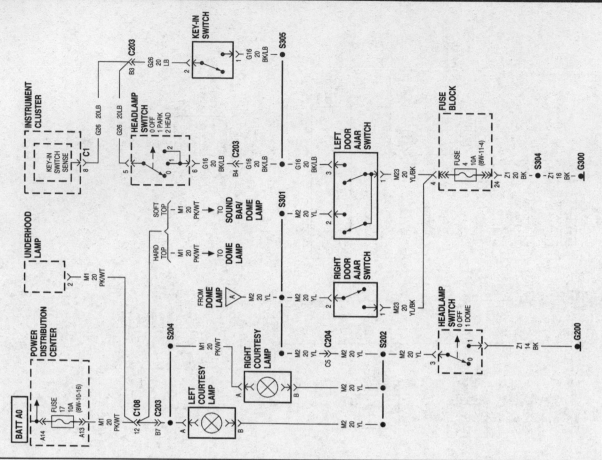

Interior lighting circuit - 1997 through 2006 models (2 of 4)

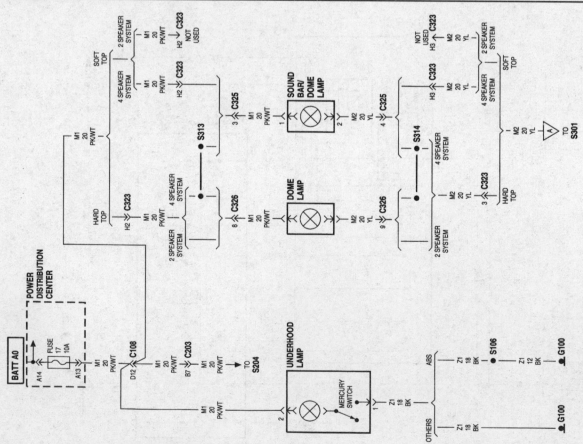

Interior lighting circuit - 1997 through 2006 models (1 of 4)

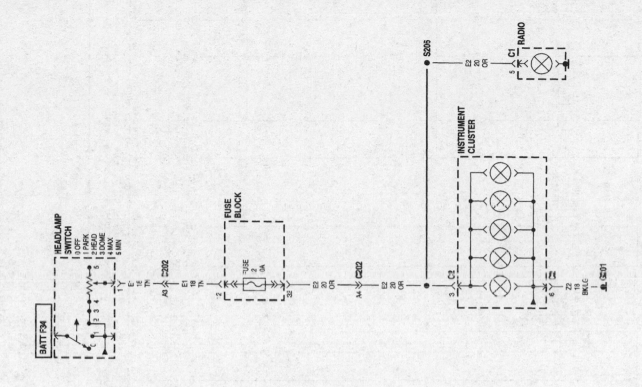

Interior lighting circuit - 1997 through 2006 models (4 of 4)

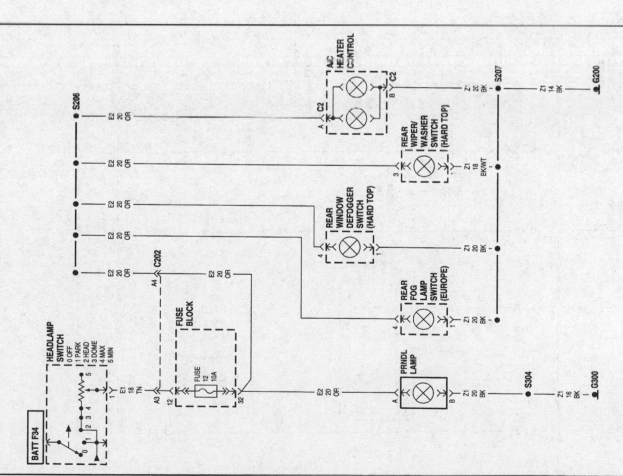

Interior lighting circuit - 1997 through 2006 models (3 of 4)

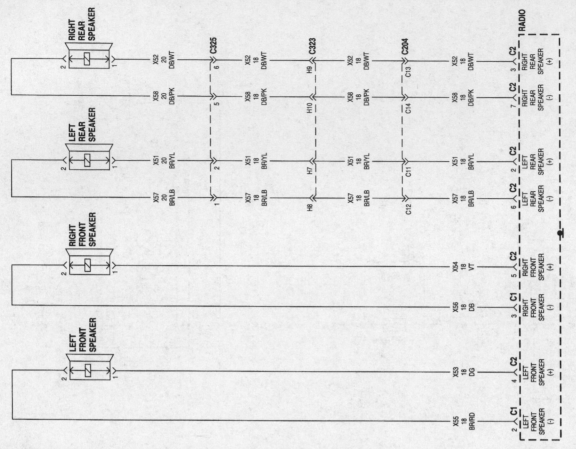

Audio system circuit - 1997 through 2006 models (2 of 2)

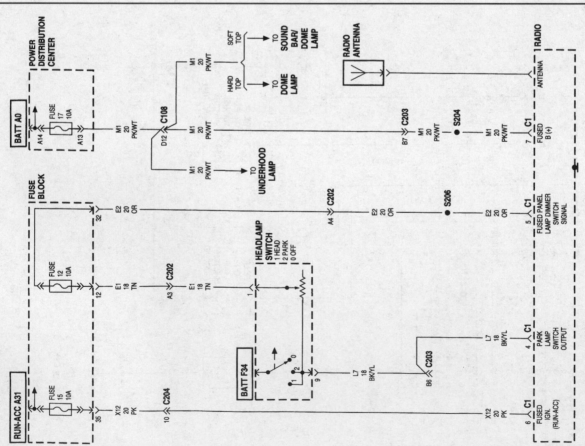

Audio system circuit - 1997 through 2006 models (1 of 2)

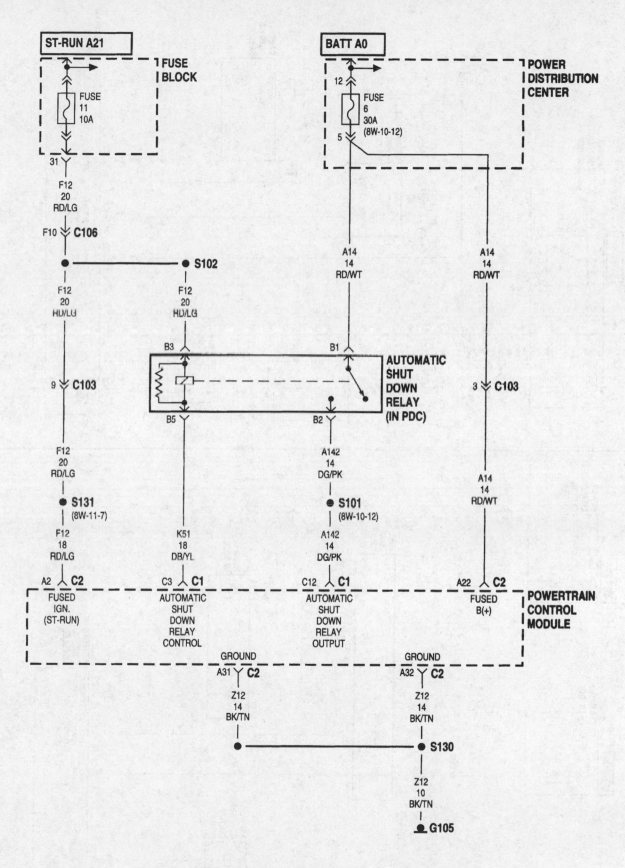

Fuel and ignition system circuit - 1997 through 2006 models (1 of 14)

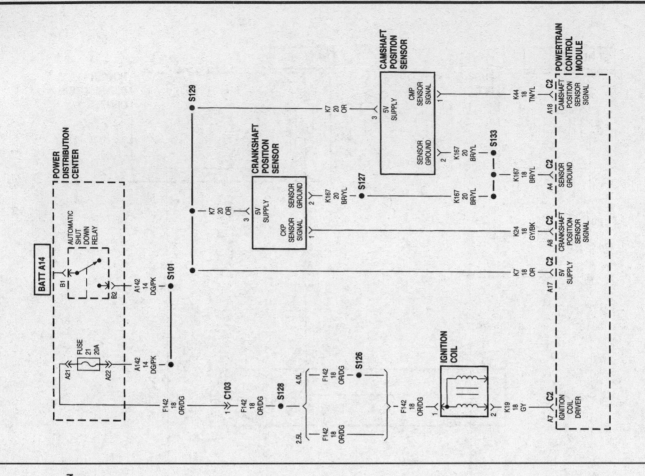

Fuel and ignition system circuit - 1997 through 2006 models (3 of 14)

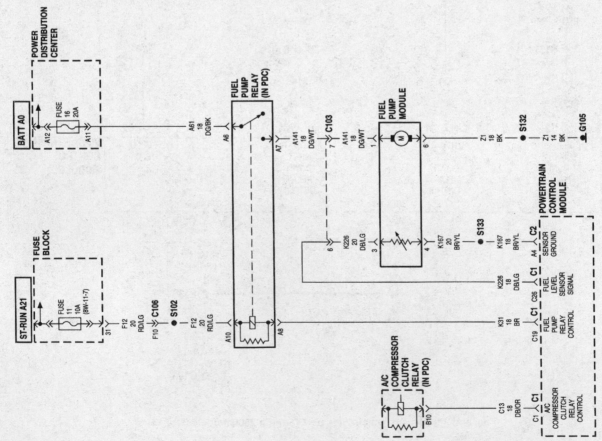

Fuel and ignition system circuit - 1997 through 2006 models (2 of 14)

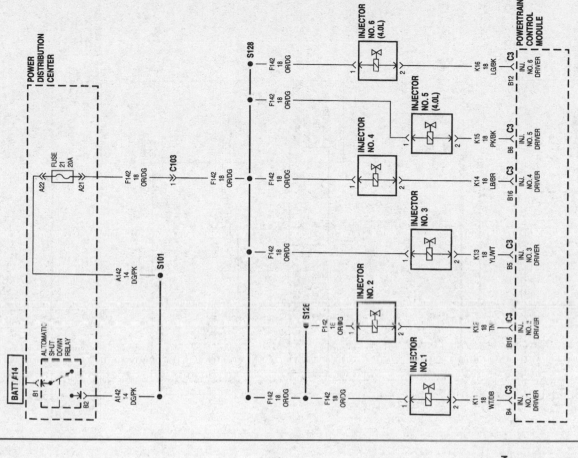

Fuel and ignition system circuit - 1997 through 2006 models (5 of 14)

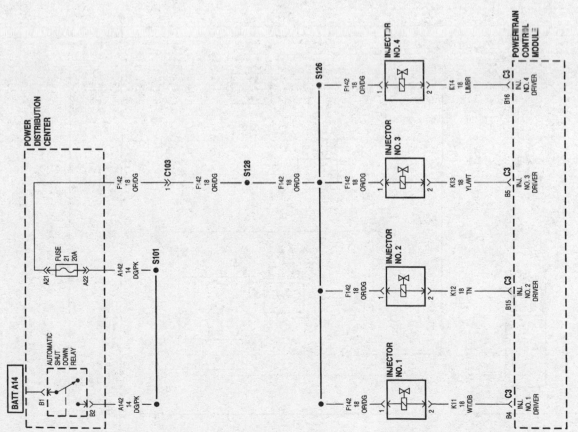

Fuel and ignition system circuit - 1997 through 2006 models (4 of 14)

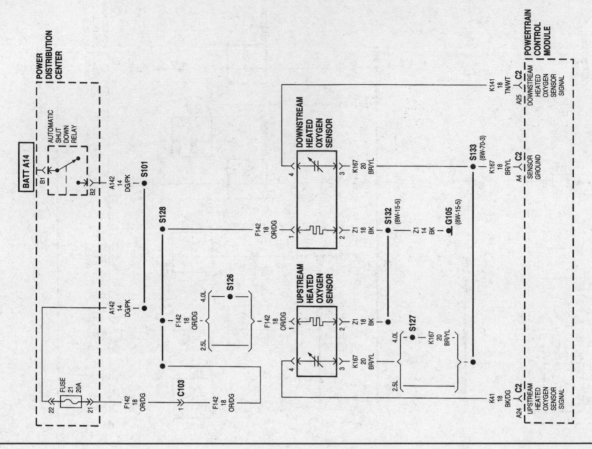

Fuel and ignition system circuit - 1997 through 2006 models (7 of 14)

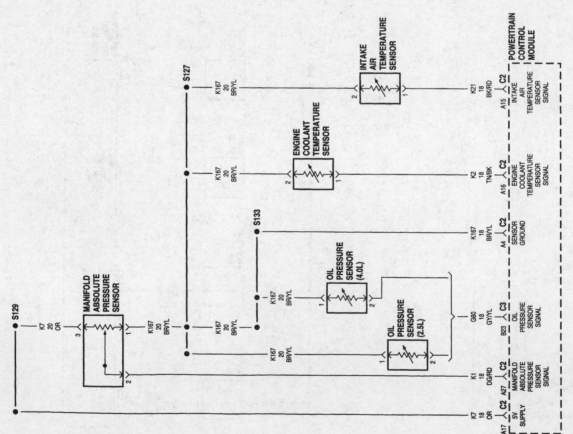

Fuel and ignition system circuit 1997 through 2006 models (6 of 14)

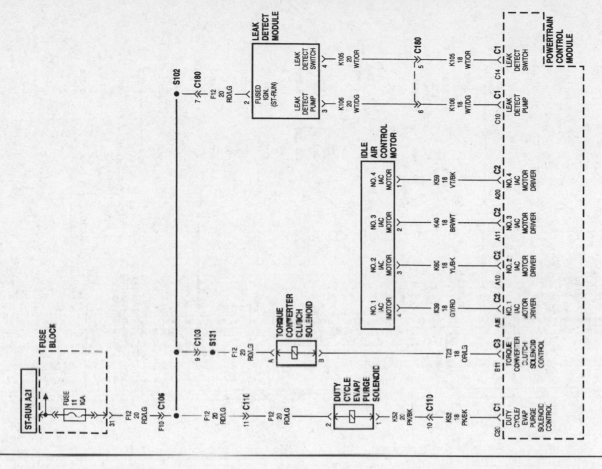

Fuel and ignition system circuit - 1997 through 2006 models (9 of 14)

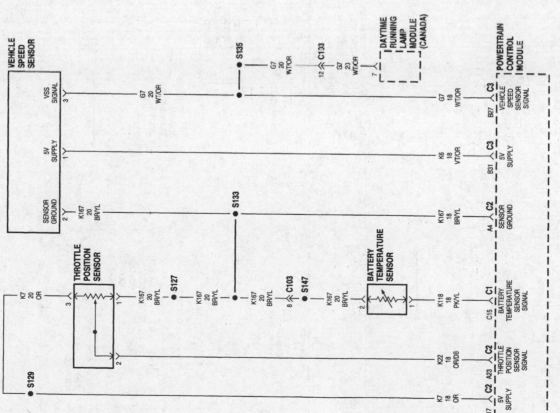

Fuel and ignition system circuit - 1997 through 2006 models (8 of 14)

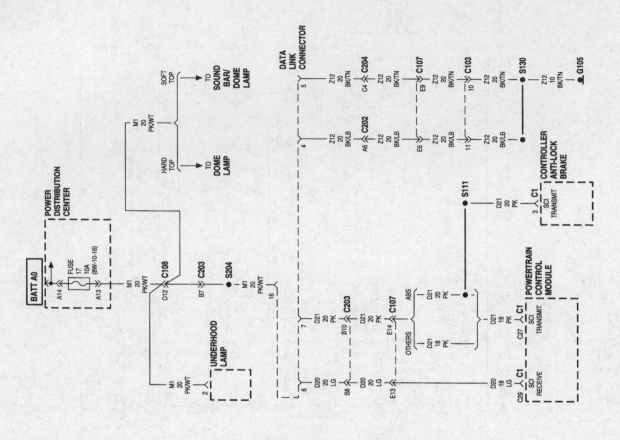

Fuel and ignition system circuit - 1997 through 2006 models (11 of 14)

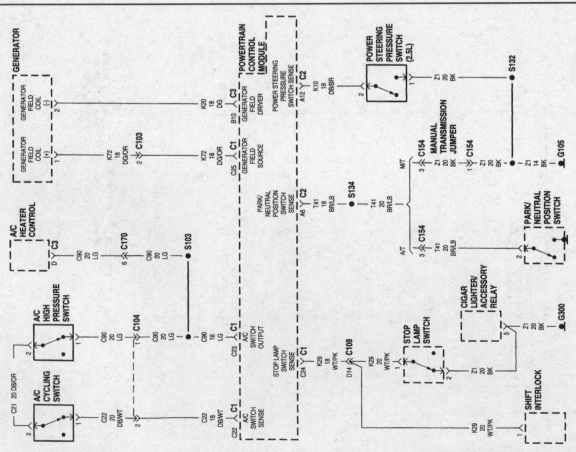

Fuel and ignition system circuit - 1997 through 2006 models (10 of 14)

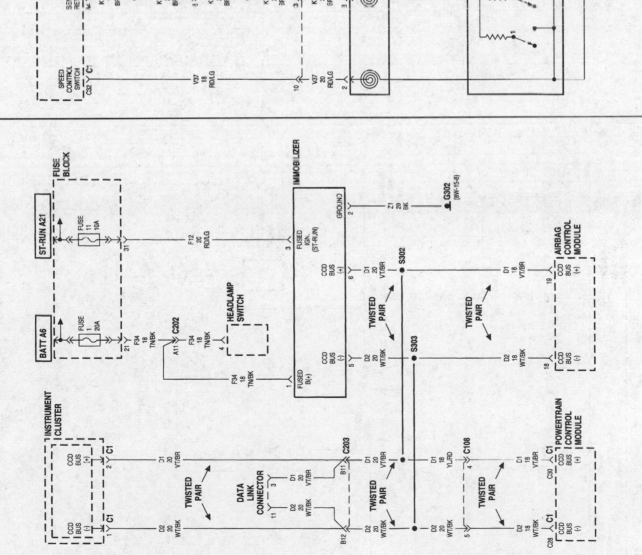

Fuel and ignition system circuit - 1997 through 2006 models (13 of 14)

Fuel and ignition system circuit - 1997 through 2006 models (12 of 14)

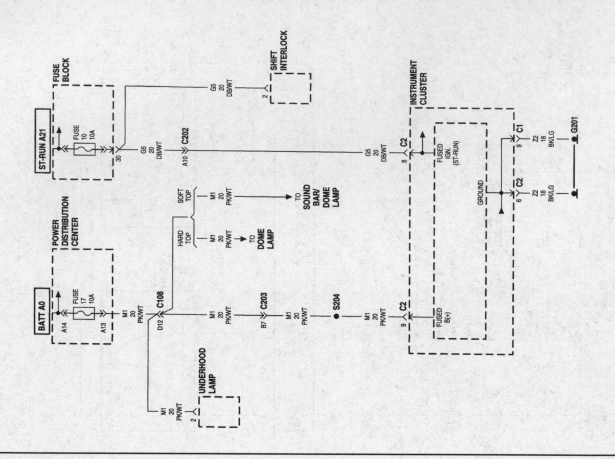

Instrument circuit - 1997 through 2006 models (1 of 8)

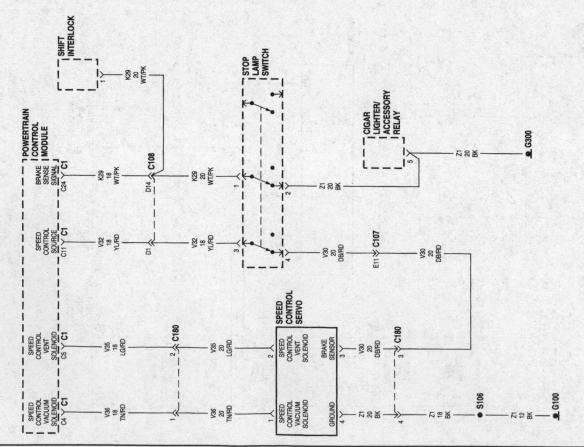

Fuel and ignition system circuit - 1997 through 2006 models (14 of 14)

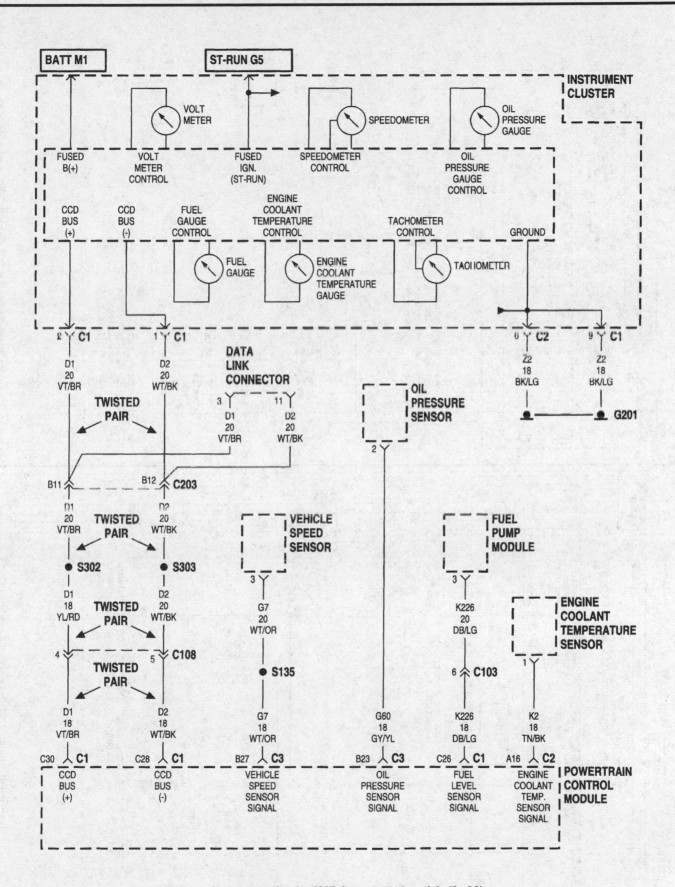

Instrument circuit - 1997 through 2006 models (2 of 8)

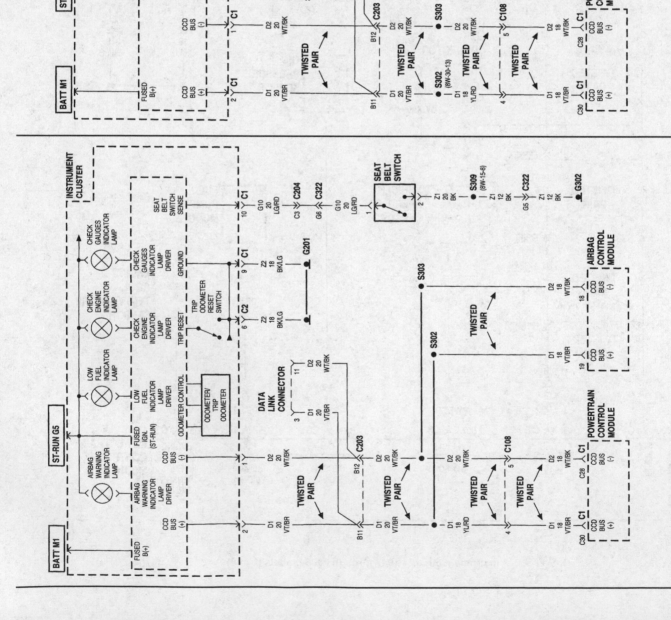

Instrument circuit - 1997 through 2006 models (4 of 8)

Instrument circuit - 1997 through 2006 models (3 of 8)

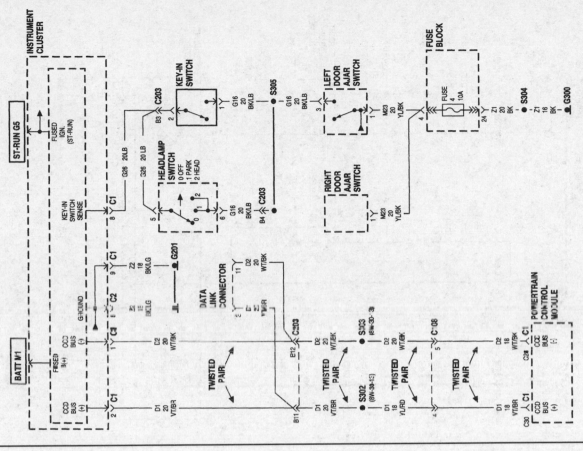

Instrument circuit - 1997 through 2006 models (6 of 8)

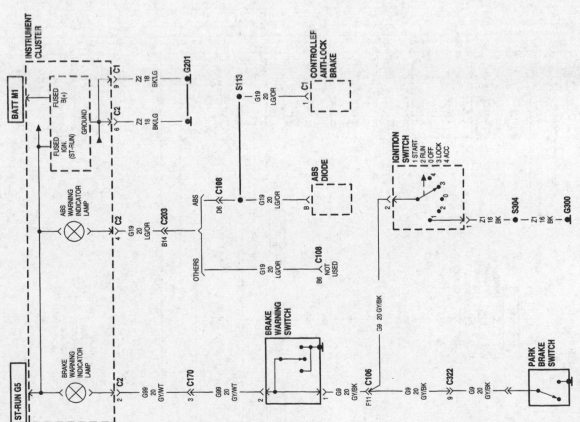

Instrument circuit - 1997 through 2006 models (5 of 8)

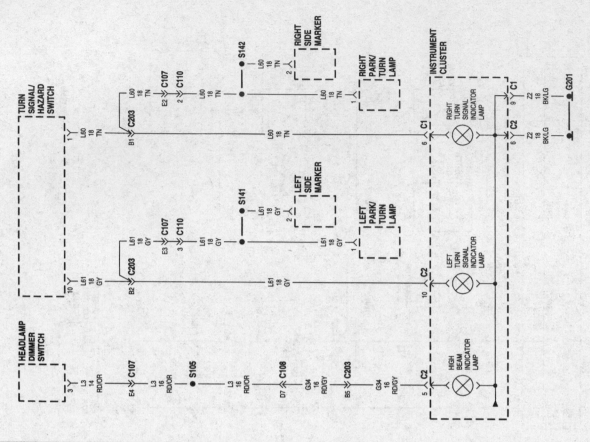

Instrument circuit - 1997 through 2006 models (8 of 8)

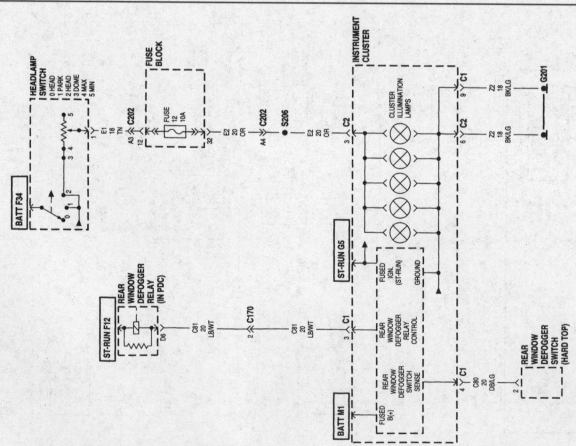

Instrument circuit - 1997 through 2006 models (7 of 8)

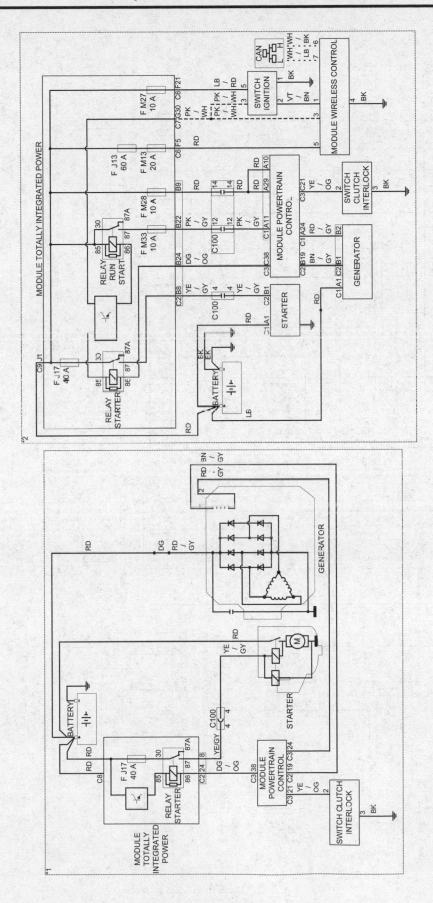

Starting and charging systems - 2007 through 2011 models

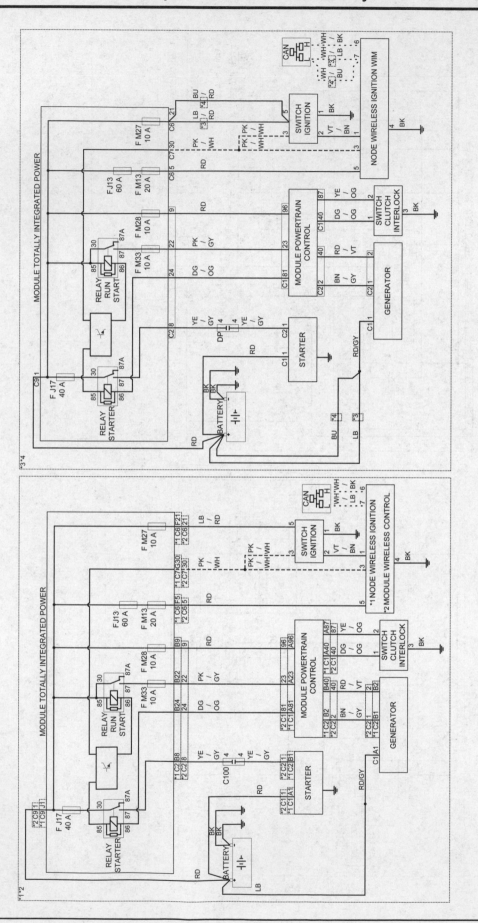

Starting and charging systems 2012 and later models

*1 For 2012
*2 For 2013
*3 From 2014 to 2016
*4 For 2017

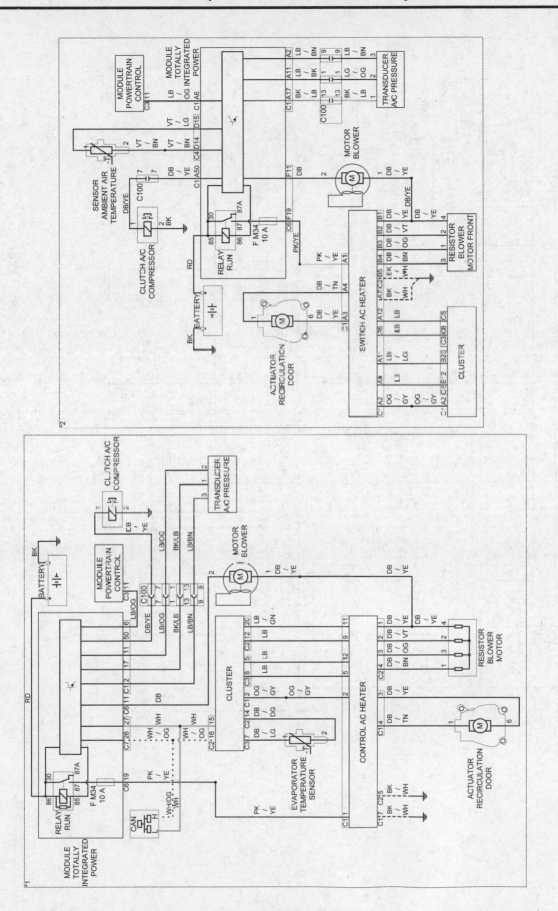

Air conditioning, heating and engine cooling systems - 2007 through 2010 models

*1 From 2007 to 2009
*2 For 2010

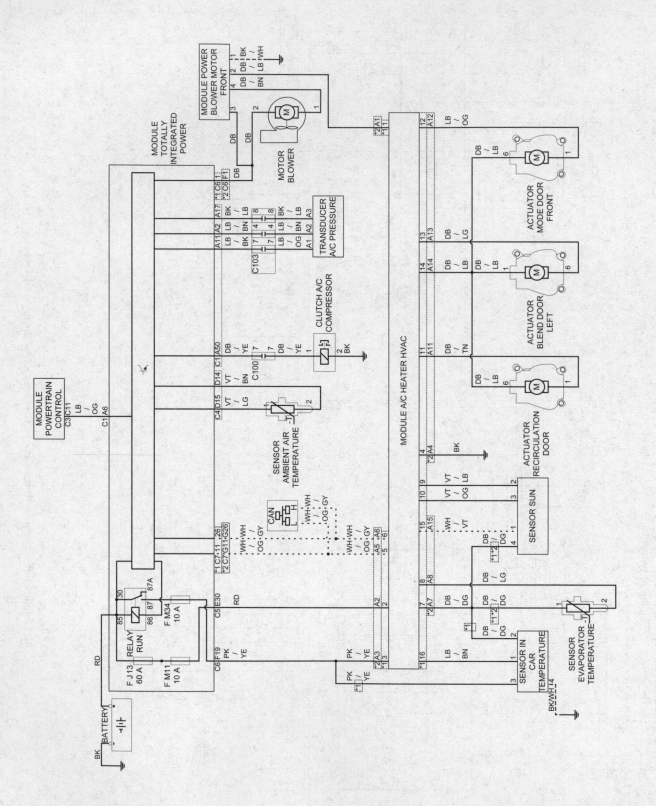

Air conditioning, heating and engine cooling systems - 2011 and 2012 models

*1 Automatic temperature control
*2 Manual temperature control

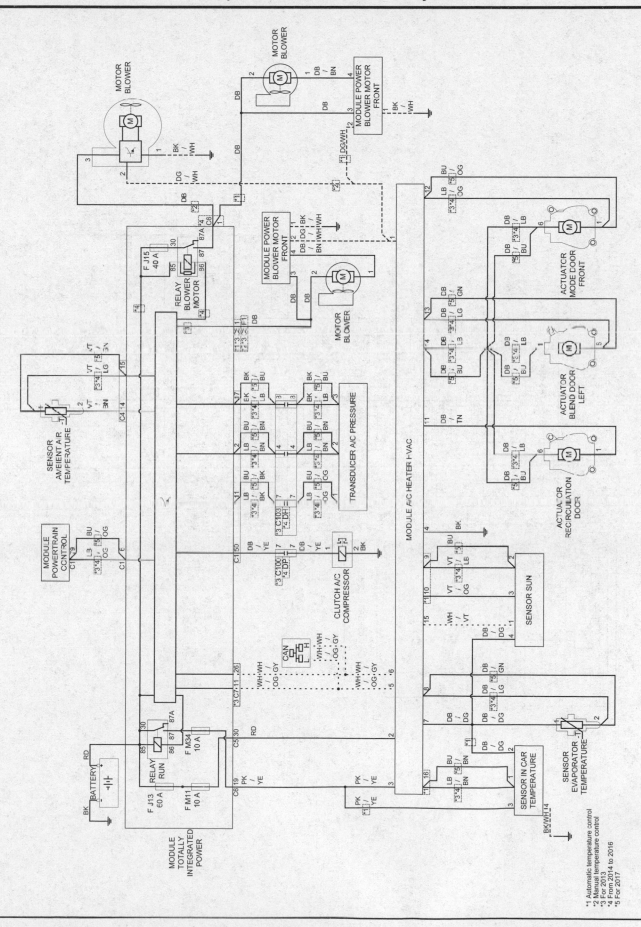

Air conditioning, heating and engine cooling systems - 2013 and later models

*1 Automatic temperature control
*2 Manual temperature control
*3 For 2013
*4 From 2014 to 2016
*5 For 2017

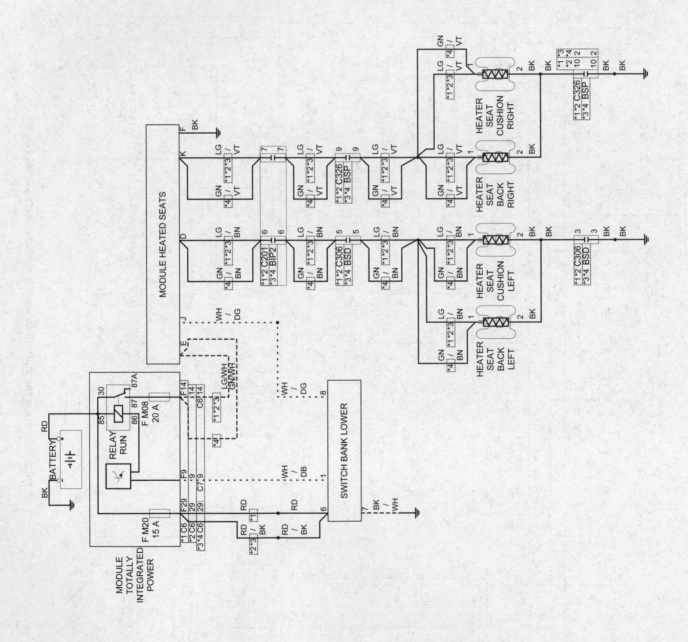

Seat heater system

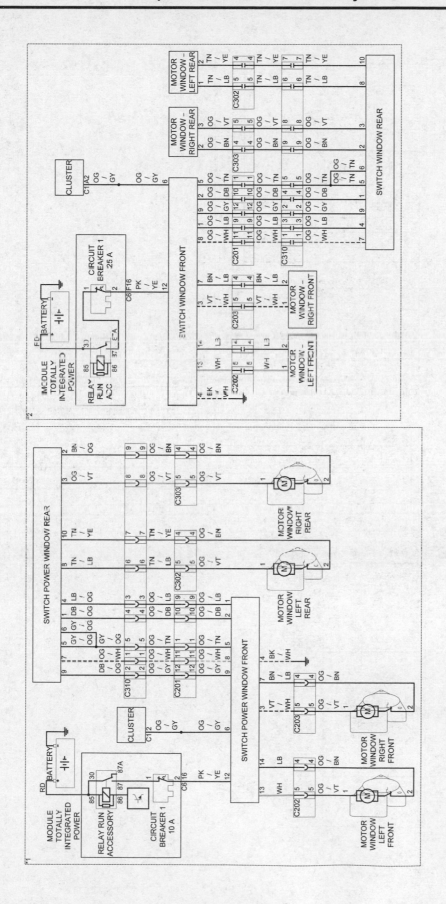

Power window system - 2007 through 2012 models

*1 From 2007 to 2009
*2 From 2010 to 2012

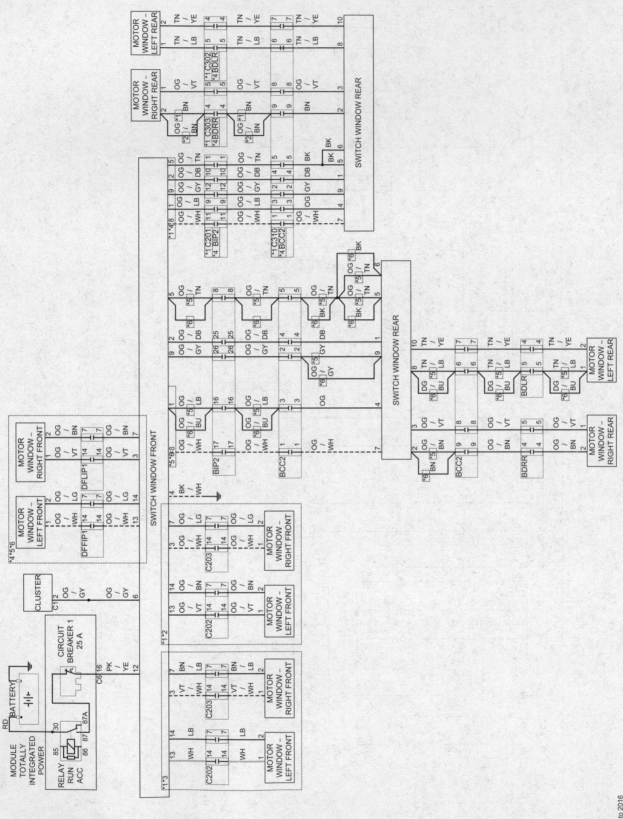

Power window system - 2013 and later models

*1 For 2013
*2 Early build
*3 Late build
*4 For 2014
*5 From 2015 to 2016
*6 For 2017

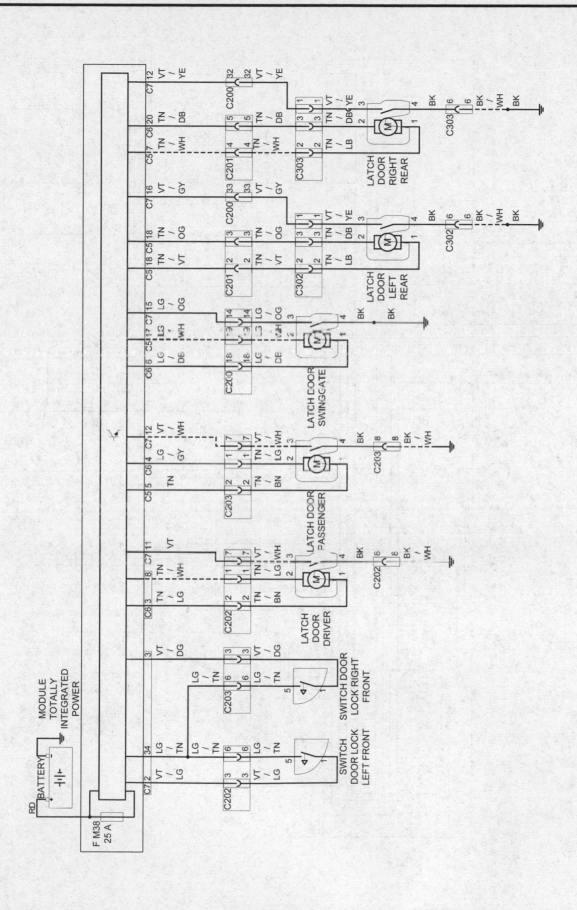

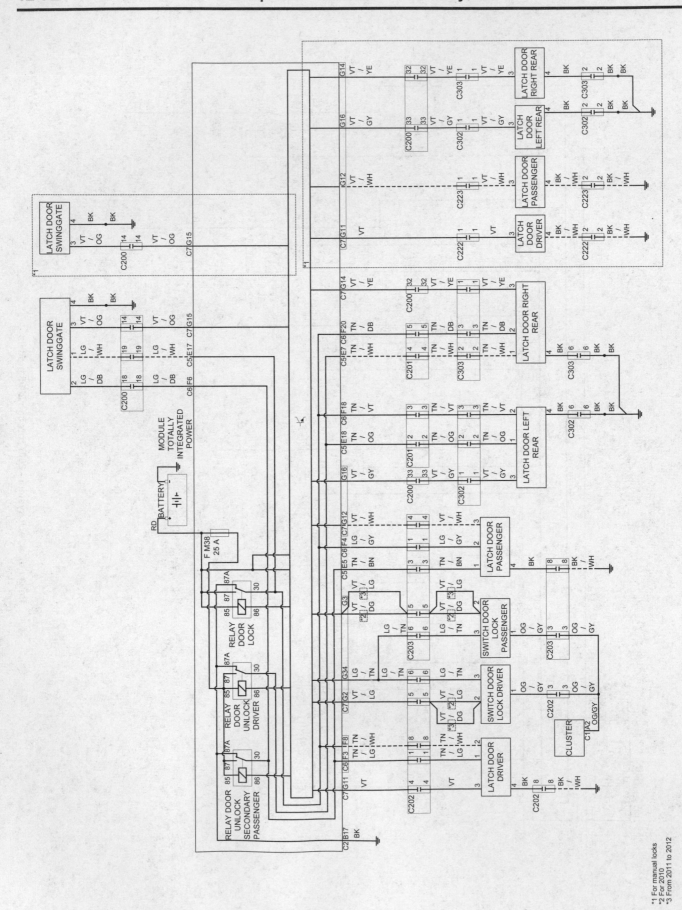

Power door lock system - 2010 through 2012 models

*1 For manual locks
*2 For 2010
*3 From 2011 to 2012

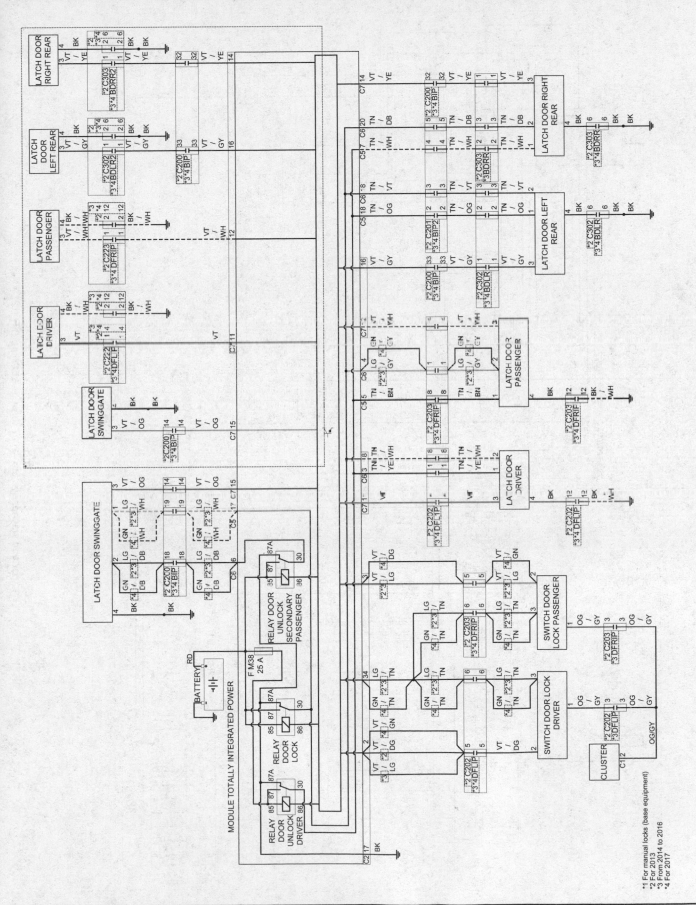

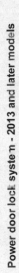

Power door lock system - 2013 and later models

*1 For manual locks (base equipment)
*2 For 2013
*3 From 2014 to 2016
*4 For 2017

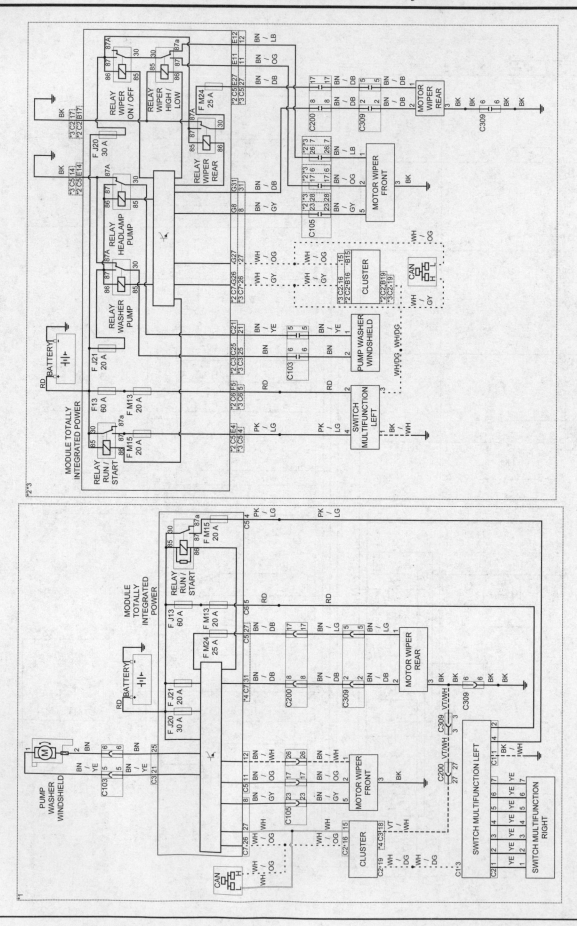

Wiper and washer system - 2007 through 2013 models

*1 From 2007 to 2009
*2 From 2010 to 2012
*3 For 2013
*4 For hard top

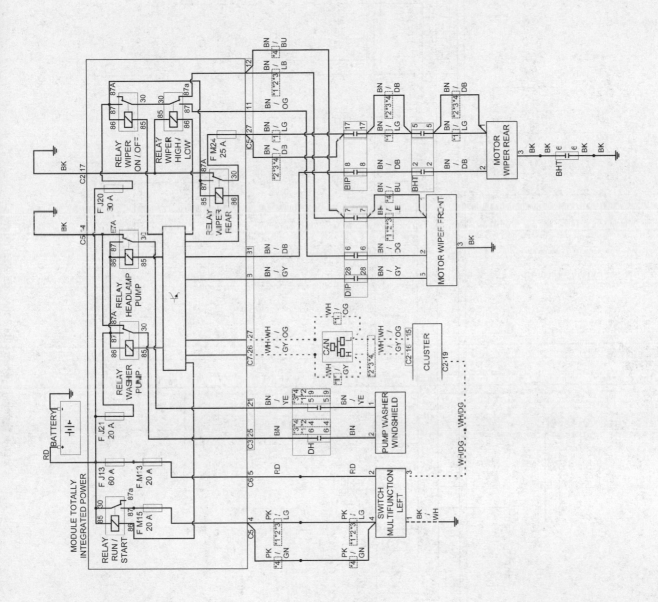

Wiper and washer system - 2014 and later models

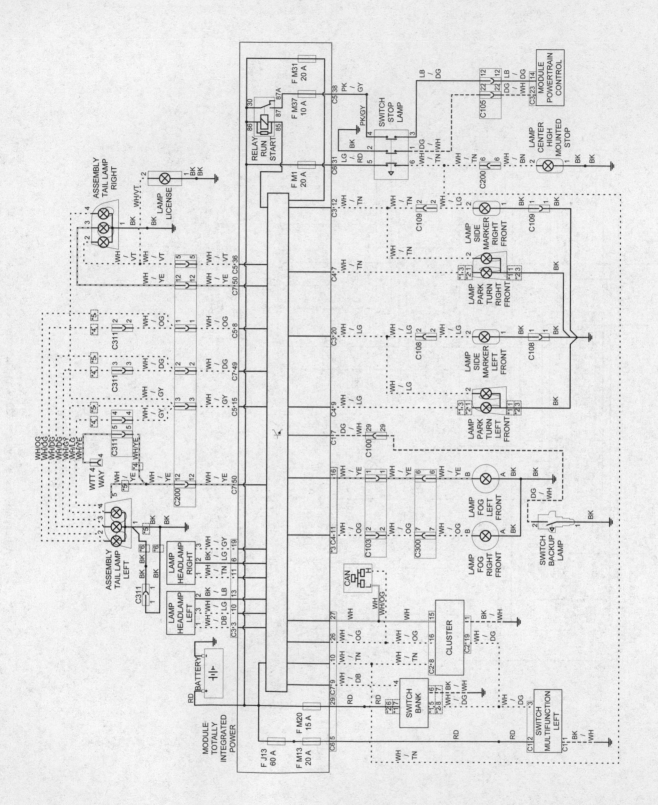

Exterior lighting system - 2007 through 2009 models

*1 Early build
*2 Late build
*3 Fog lamps
*4 Trailer tow
*5 Except trailer tow

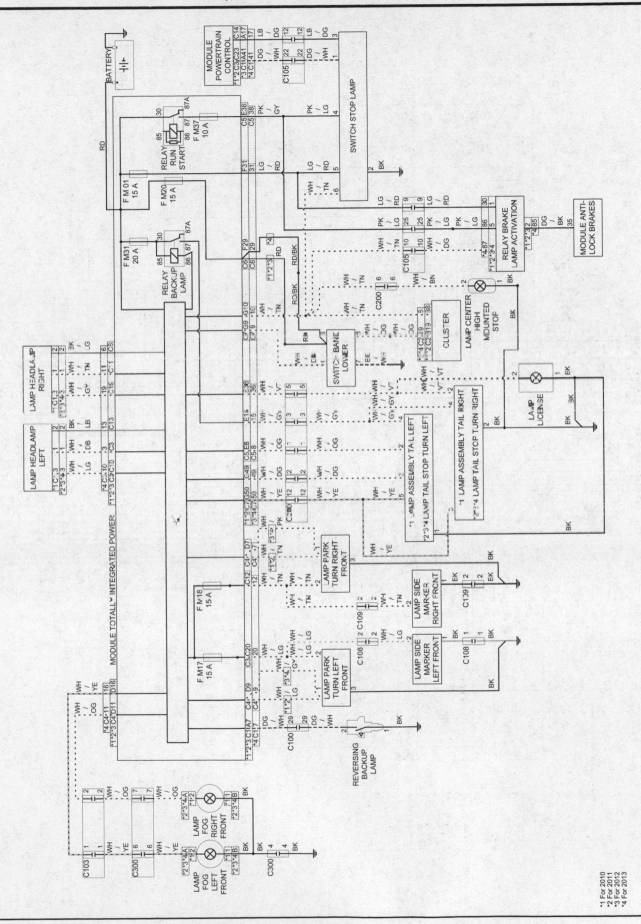

Exterior lighting system - 2010 through 2013 models

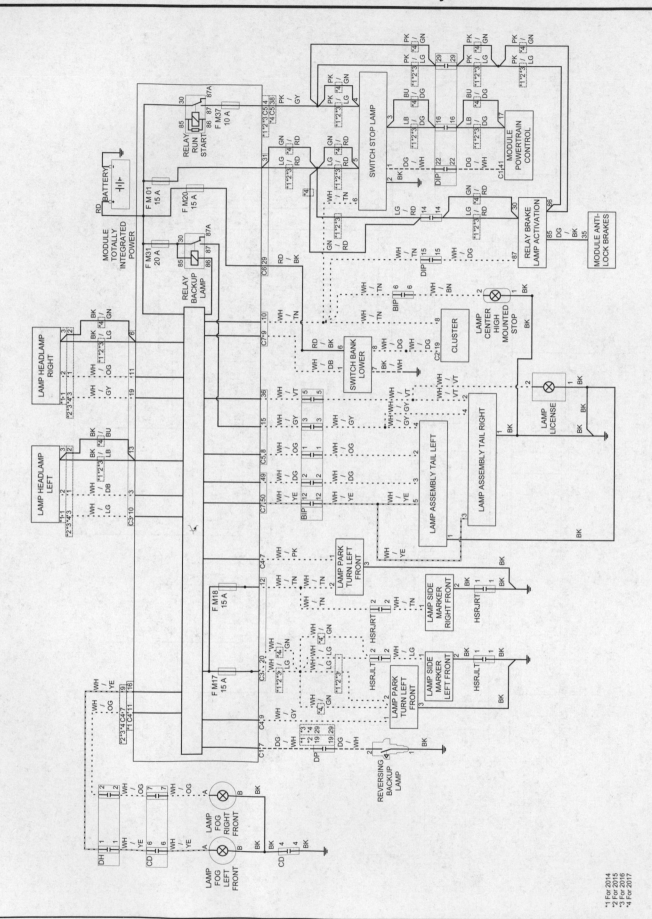

Exterior lighting system - 2014 and later models

*1 For 2014
*2 For 2015
*3 For 2016
*4 For 2017

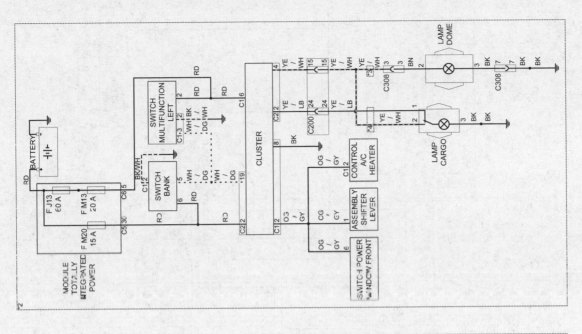

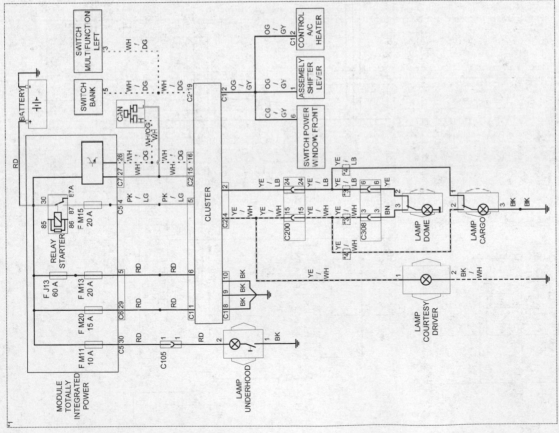

Interior lighting system - 2007 through 2009 models

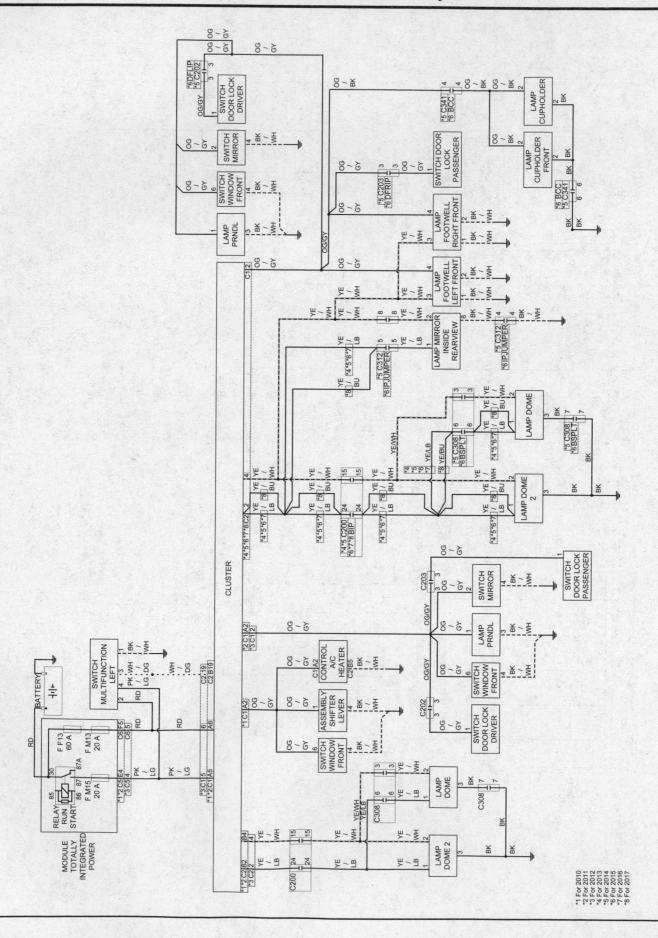

Interior lighting system - 2010 and later models

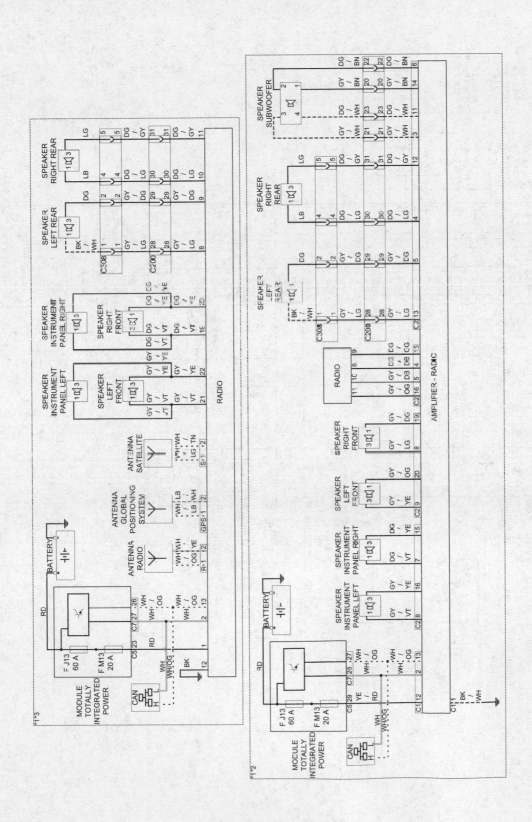

Audio system - 2007 through 2009 models

*1 From 2007 to 2009
*2 With amplifier
*3 Without amplifier

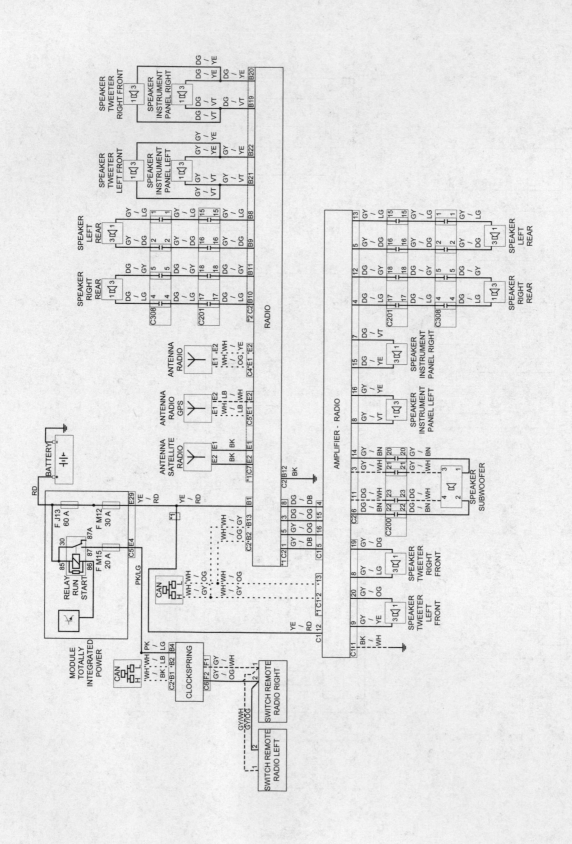

Audio system - 2010 models

*1 Premium audio
*2 Base audio

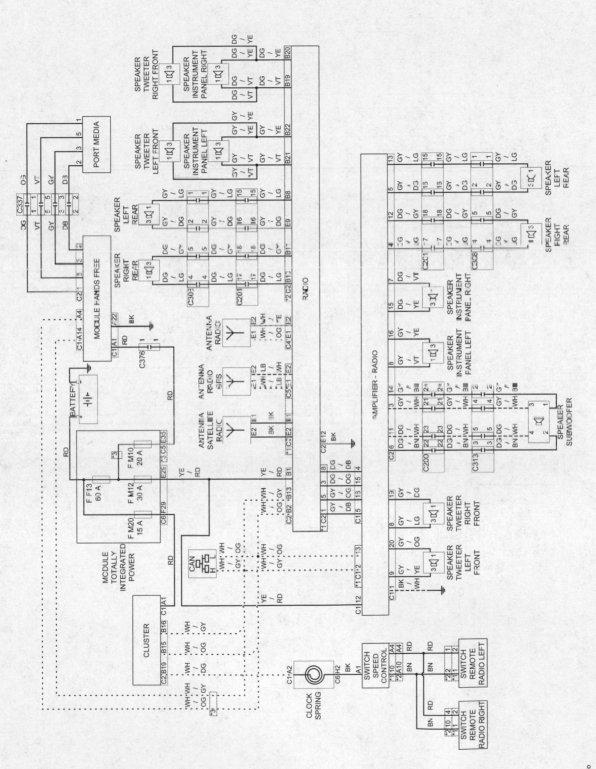

Audio system - 2011 and 2012 models

*1 Premium audio
*2 Base audio
*3 Media port

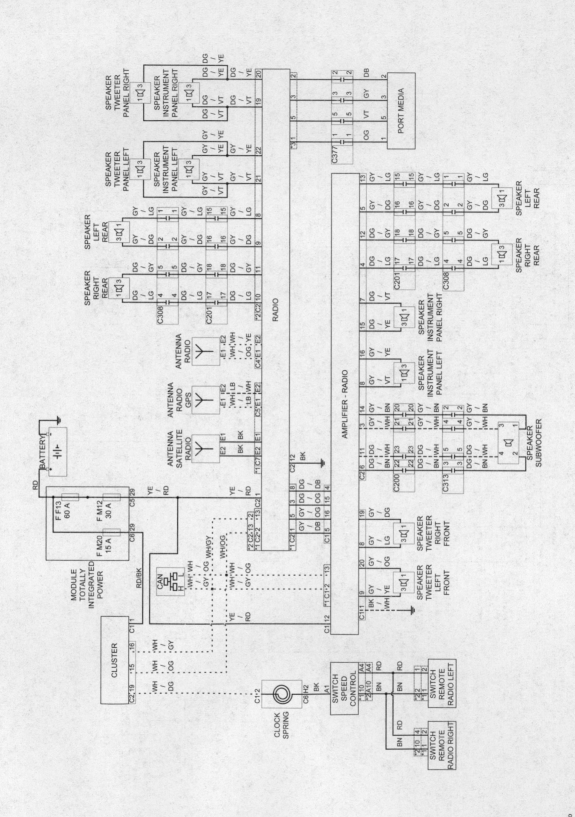

Audio system - 2013 models

*1 Premium audio
*2 Base audio
*3 Media port

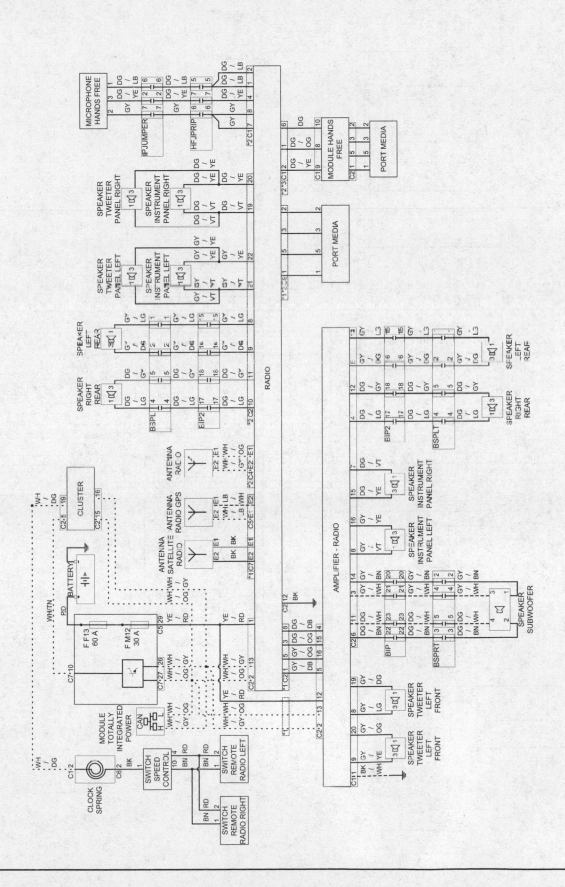

Audio system - 2014 models

*1 Premium audio
*2 Base audio
*3 Media port

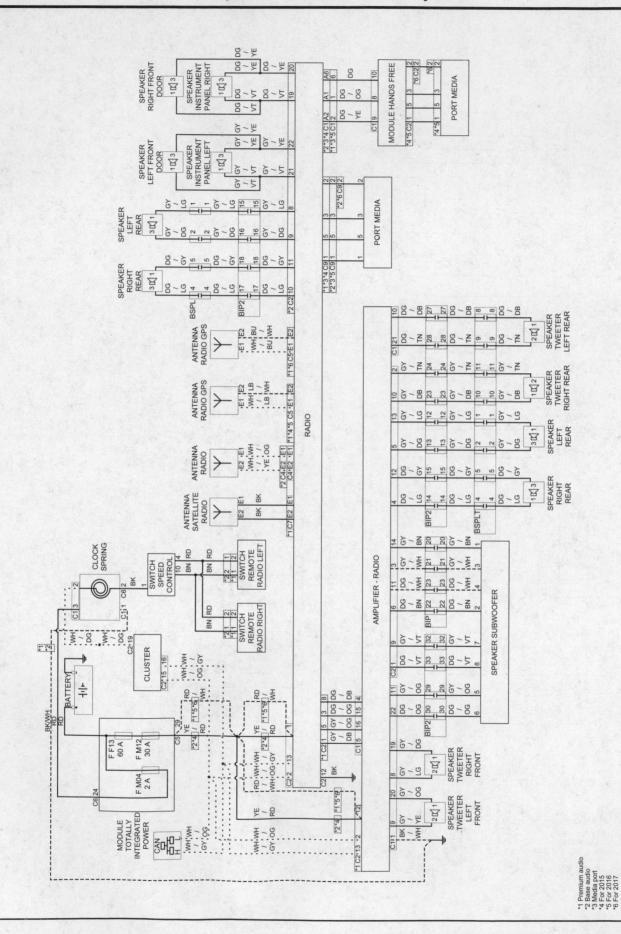

Audio system - 2015 and later models

*1 Premium audio
*2 Base audio
*3 Media port
*4 For 2015
*5 For 2016
*6 For 2017

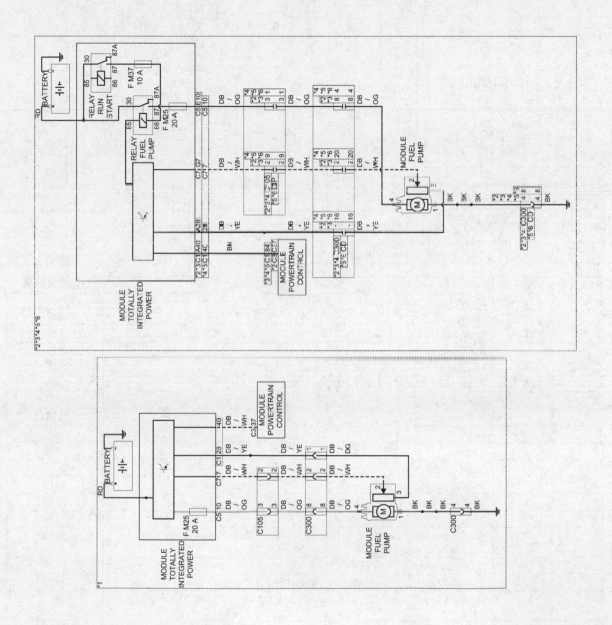

Fuel pump system - 2007 and later models

*1 From 2007 to 2009
*2 From 2010 to 2011
*3 For 2012
*4 For 2013
*5 For 2014
*6 From 2015 to 2017

TOTALLY INTEGRATED POWER MODULE (TIPM) FROM 2007 TO 2009

FUSE/RELAY	VALUE	DESCRIPTION	OEM NAME
1	20 A	Brake light switch (15 A also used)	M1
2	-	Not used	M2
3	20 A	Lock relay	M3
4	-	Not used	M4
5	-	Not used	M5
6	20 A	Relay run / accessory relay output	M6
7	-	Not used	M7
8	-	Not used	M8
9	-	Not used	M9
10	20 A	Radio	M10
11	10 A	Lamp under hood	M11
12	30 A	Radio, Amplifier radio	M12
13	20 A	Multifunction switch, Instrument cluster, Tire pressure receiver	M13
14	-	Not used	M14
15	20 A	Automatic sway bar system, Steering column control unit, Multifunction switch, Instrument cluster,	M15
16	10 A	Restraint control unit (RCM)	M16
17	15 A	Front left parking light, Marker lights, Rear left lights	M17
18	15 A	Front right parking light, Marker lights, Rear rights lights, Number plate light	M18
19	30 A	Power train control, Ignition coil, Fuel injection (25 A also used)	M19
20	15 A	Cluster, Switch bank	M20
21	20 A	Engine control unit	M21
22	-	Not used	M22
23	10 A	Horn	M23
24	25 A	Wiper rear	M24

Fuses and relays - 2007 and later models (1 of 4)

25	20 A	Fuel pump	M25
26	-	Not used	M26
27	10 A	Ignition switch	M27
28	10 A	Engine control unit	M28
29	10 A	Seat occupancy or not used	M29
30	15 A	Rear wiper system, Diagnostic connector	M30
31	20 A	Tail lights	M31
32	10 A	Occupancy sensing control unit	M32
33	20 A	Engine control unit (10 A also used)	M33
34	10 A	Compass unit, Heating, Ventilation and air conditioning (HVAC)	M34
35	-	Not used	M35
36	20 A	Power outlet console	M36
37	10 A	Automatic sway bar system, Steering column control unit, Multifunction switch, Instrument cluster	M37
38	25 A	Central locking	M38
39	-	Not used	J1
40	-	Not used	J2
41	-	Not used	J3
42	-	Not used	J4
43	-	Not used	J5
44	40 A	ABS or ESP pump	J6
45	30 A	ABS valves	J7
46	-	Not used	J8
47	-	Not used	J9
48	-	Not used	J10
49	30 A	Automatic sway bar system, ABS/ESP control unit	J11
50	-	Not used	J12
51	60 A	Ignition switch cut-off	J13
52	40 A	Rear window defogger relay output	J14
53	-	Not used	J15
54	-	Not used	J16
55	40 A	Starter circuit	J17
56	25 A	Transmission control relay output (20 A also used)	J18
57	60 A	Radiator fan motor	J19
58	30 A	Front wiper	J20
59	20 A	Front and rear windscreen washers	J21
60	-	Not used	J22
R1	-	Relay run accessory	K1
R2	-	Relay run	K2
R3	-	Relay starter motor	K3
R4	-	Relay run / accessory	K4
R5	-	Relay transmission control	K5
R6	-	Relay rear window defogger (hardtop)	K6
R7	-	Not used	K7
R8	-	Not used	R8
R9	-	Not used	K9
R10	-	Relay auto shut down	K10
R11	-	Relay radiator fan control	K11

Fuses and relays - 2007 and later models (2 of 4)

TOTALLY INTEGRATED POWER MODULE (TIPM) FROM 2010 TO 2017

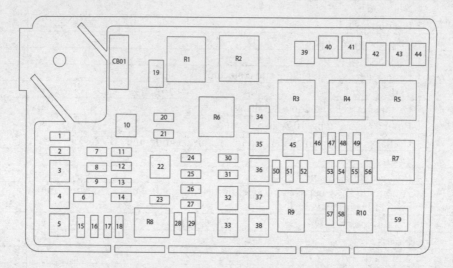

FUSE/RELAY	VALUE	DESCRIPTION	OEM NAME
CB01	25 A	Ignition Run, Accessory Control	CB01; FCB1A
1	15 A	Cabin compartment node interior light, switch bank	M20; FM20
2	10 A	Ignition switch feed, wireless module	M27; FM27
3	-	Not used	J08; FJ8
4	25 A	Driver door node	J04; FJ4
5	25 A	Passenger door node	J05; FJ5
6	20 A	Power outlet 2	M07; FM7
7	15 A	Center high-mounted stop light (CHMSL) / Switch stop lamp feed	M01; FM1
8	20 A	Relay trailer lighting (stop lamp)	M02; FM2
9	2 A	Clock spring	M04; FM4
10	-	Not used	J22; FJ22
11	10 A	Park assist, Climate control system, Headlamp wash, Compass	M34; FM34
12	20 A	Front heated seat	M8; FM8
13	20 A	Trailer tow (Export only)	M14; FM14
14	20 A	Rear heated seat - If equipped	M09; FM9
15	25 A	Power inverter - If equipped	M05; FM5
16	20 A	Power outlet 1	M06; FM6
17	10 A	Powertrain	M29; FM29
18	20 A	Power outlet	M36; FM36
19	30 A	Sway bar	J11; FJ11
20	10 A	Airbag controller	M32; FM32
21	10 A	Airbag module	M16; FM16
22	60 A	Ignition off draw (IOD) - Main	J13; FJ13
23	20 A	Ignition off draw - cabin compartment node, wireless control module, Siren, multifunction control switch	M13; FM13
24	10 A	Anti-lock brake system , electronic stability control, stop lamp switch, fuel pump relay	M37; FM37
25	15 A	Ignition off draw - vehicle entertainment system, satellite digital audio receiver (SDARS), DVD, hands-free module, radio, antenna, universal garage door open, vanity lamp	M10; FM10
26	30 A	Amplifier	M12; FM12

27	10 A	Climate control system, under hood lamp	M11; FM11
28	20 A	Fuel pump	M25; FM25
29	25 A	Rear wiper	M24; FM24
30	10 A	Heated mirrors	M35; FM35
31	15 A	Wiper motor front, diagnostic feed	M30; FM30
32	40 A	Front blower	J15; FJ15
33	-	Not used	J3; FJ3
34	40 A	Anti-lock brake system (ABS) Pump / Stability control system	J06; FJ6
35	40 A	Rear defroster	J14; FJ14
36	30 A	Transfer case module	J02; FJ2
37	60 A	Radiator fan control	J19; FJ19
38	-	Not used	J01; FJ1
39	30 A	Anti-lock brake system (ABS) Pump / Stability control system	J07; FJ7
40	30 A	Front wiper LO / HI	J20; FJ20
41	20 A	Front / rear washer	J21; FJ21
42	40 A	Flex fuel	J09; FJ9
43	40 A	Starter solenoid	J17; FJ17
44	20 A	Powertrain control module (PCM)	J18; FJ18
45	30 A	Headlamp wash relay / manifold tuning valve	J10; FJ10
46	25 A	Lock / unlock motors	M38; FM38
47	10 A	Powertrain controller	M33; FM33
48	20 A	Climate system, rear view mirror, cabin compartment node, transfer case switch, multifunction control switch, tire pressure monitor	M15; FM15
49	20 A	Front / rear axle locker relay	M03; FM3
50	15 A	Left tail / license / park lamp	M17; FM17
51	10 A	Left horn (HI / LOW)	M23; FM23
52	15 A	Right tail / park / run lamp	M18; FM18
53	10 A	Right horn (HI / LOW)	M22; FM22
54	20 A	Backup lamp	M31; FM31
55	20 A	Auto shut down (ASD 3)	M21; FM21
56	25 A	Auto shut down (ASD 1 and 2)	M19; FM19
57	10 A	Power window switch, driver window switch	M26; FM26
58	10 A	Powertrain control module	M28; FM28
59	-	Not used	J12; FJ12
R1	-	Run accessory	K1; D851
R2	-	Run	K2; D842
R3	-	Rear window defogger (EBL)	K6; D821
R4	-	Starter motor	K3; D879
R5	-	Transmission control module	K5; D833
R6	-	Run start	K4; D893
R7	-	Auto shut down	K10; D820
R8	-	HVAC rear	K9; D816
R9	-	Radiator fan control	K11; D838
R10	-	No information available or not used	-

Fuses and relays - 2007 and later models (4 of 4)

Notes

Notes

Index

Haynes Automotive Manuals

NOTE: *If you do not see a listing for your vehicle, consult your local Haynes dealer for the latest product information.*

ACURA
- 12020 **Integra** '86 thru '89 **& Legend** '86 thru '90
- 12021 **Integra** '90 thru '93 **& Legend** '91 thru '95
  Integra '94 thru '00 - see *HONDA Civic (42025)*
  MDX '01 thru '07 - see *HONDA Pilot (42037)*
- 12050 **Acura TL** all models '99 thru '08

AMC
- **Jeep CJ** - see *JEEP (50020)*
- 14020 **Mid-size models** '70 thru '83
- 14025 **(Renault) Alliance & Encore** '83 thru '87

AUDI
- 15020 **4000** all models '80 thru '87
- 15025 **5000** all models '77 thru '83
- 15026 **5000** all models '84 thru '88
  Audi A4 '96 thru '01 - see *VW Passat (96023)*
- 15030 **Audi A4** '02 thru '08

AUSTIN-HEALEY
- **Sprite** - see *MG Midget (66015)*

BMW
- 18020 **3/5 Series** '82 thru '92
- 18021 **3 Series** incl. Z3 models '92 thru '98
- 18022 **3-Series** incl. Z4 models '99 thru '05
- 18023 **3-Series** '06 thru '10
- 18025 **320i** all 4 cyl models '75 thru '83
- 18050 **1500 thru 2002** except Turbo '59 thru '77

BUICK
- 19010 **Buick Century** '97 thru '05
  Century (front-wheel drive) - see *GM (38005)*
- 19020 **Buick, Oldsmobile & Pontiac Full-size**
  (Front-wheel drive) '85 thru '05
  Buick Electra, LeSabre and Park Avenue;
  Oldsmobile Delta 88 Royale, Ninety Eight
  and Regency; **Pontiac** Bonneville
- 19025 **Buick, Oldsmobile & Pontiac Full-size**
  (Rear wheel drive) '70 thru '90
  Buick Estate, Electra, LeSabre, Limited,
  Oldsmobile Custom Cruiser, Delta 88,
  Ninety-eight, **Pontiac** Bonneville,
  Catalina, Grandville, Parisienne
- 19030 **Mid-size Regal & Century** all rear-drive
  models with V6, V8 and Turbo '74 thru '87
  Regal - see *GENERAL MOTORS (38010)*
  Riviera - see *GENERAL MOTORS (38030)*
  Roadmaster - see *CHEVROLET (24046)*
  Skyhawk - see *GENERAL MOTORS (38015)*
  Skylark - see *GM (38020, 38025)*
  Somerset - see *GENERAL MOTORS (38025)*

CADILLAC
- 21015 **CTS & CTS-V** '03 thru '12
- 21030 **Cadillac Rear Wheel Drive** '70 thru '93
  Cimarron - see *GENERAL MOTORS (38015)*
  DeVille - see *GM (38031 & 38032)*
  Eldorado - see *GM (38030 & 38031)*
  Fleetwood - see *GM (38031)*
  Seville - see *GM (38030, 38031 & 38032)*

CHEVROLET
- 10305 **Chevrolet Engine Overhaul Manual**
- 24010 **Astro & GMC Safari Mini-vans** '85 thru '05
- 24015 **Camaro V8** all models '70 thru '81
- 24016 **Camaro** all models '82 thru '92
- 24017 **Camaro & Firebird** '93 thru '02
  Cavalier - see *GENERAL MOTORS (38016)*
  Celebrity - see *GENERAL MOTORS (38005)*
- 24020 **Chevelle, Malibu & El Camino** '69 thru '87
- 24024 **Chevette & Pontiac T1000** '76 thru '87
  Citation - see *GENERAL MOTORS (38020)*
- 24027 **Colorado & GMC Canyon** '04 thru '10
- 24032 **Corsica/Beretta** all models '87 thru '96
- 24040 **Corvette** all V8 models '68 thru '82
- 24041 **Corvette** all models '84 thru '96
- 24045 **Full-size Sedans** Caprice, Impala, Biscayne,
  Bel Air & Wagons '69 thru '90
- 24046 **Impala SS & Caprice and Buick Roadmaster**
  '91 thru '96
  Impala '00 thru '05 - see *LUMINA (24048)*
- 24047 **Impala & Monte Carlo** all models '06 thru '11
  Lumina '90 thru '94 - see *GM (38010)*
- 24048 **Lumina & Monte Carlo** '95 thru '05
  Lumina APV - see *GM (38035)*
- 24050 **Luv Pick-up** all 2WD & 4WD '72 thru '82
  Malibu '97 thru '00 - see *GM (38026)*
- 24055 **Monte Carlo** all models '70 thru '88
  Monte Carlo '95 thru '01 - see *LUMINA (24048)*
- 24059 **Nova** all V8 models '69 thru '79
- 24060 **Nova and Geo Prizm** '85 thru '92
- 24064 **Pick-ups** '67 thru '87 - Chevrolet & GMC
- 24065 **Pick-ups** '88 thru '98 - Chevrolet & GMC
- 24066 **Pick-ups** '99 thru '06 - Chevrolet & GMC
- 24067 **Chevrolet Silverado & GMC Sierra** '07 thru '12
- 24070 **S-10 & S-15 Pick-ups** '82 thru '93,
  Blazer & Jimmy '83 thru '94,
- 24071 **S-10 & Sonoma Pick-ups** '94 thru '04, including **Blazer, Jimmy & Hombre**
- 24072 **Chevrolet TrailBlazer, GMC Envoy &
  Oldsmobile Bravada** '02 thru '09
- 24075 **Sprint** '85 thru '88 **& Geo Metro** '89 thru '01
- 24080 **Vans - Chevrolet & GMC** '68 thru '96
- 24081 **Chevrolet Express & GMC Savana**
  Full-size Vans '96 thru '10

CHRYSLER
- 10310 **Chrysler Engine Overhaul Manual**
- 25015 **Chrysler Cirrus, Dodge Stratus,**
  Plymouth Breeze '95 thru '00
- 25020 **Full-size Front-Wheel Drive** '88 thru '93
  K-Cars - see *DODGE Aries (30008)*
  Laser - see *DODGE Daytona (30030)*
- 25025 **Chrysler LHS, Concorde, New Yorker,**
  Dodge Intrepid, Eagle Vision, '93 thru '97
- 25026 **Chrysler LHS, Concorde, 300M,**
  Dodge Intrepid, '98 thru '04
- 25027 **Chrysler 300, Dodge Charger &**
  Magnum '05 thru '09
- 25030 **Chrysler & Plymouth Mid-size**
  front wheel drive '82 thru '95
  Rear-wheel Drive - see *Dodge (30050)*
- 25035 **PT Cruiser** all models '01 thru '10
- 25040 **Chrysler Sebring** '95 thru '06, **Dodge** Stratus
  '01 thru '06, **Dodge** Avenger '95 thru '00

DATSUN
- 28005 **200SX** all models '80 thru '83
- 28007 **B-210** all models '73 thru '78
- 28009 **210** all models '79 thru '82
- 28012 **240Z, 260Z & 280Z** Coupe '70 thru '78
- 28014 **280ZX** Coupe & 2+2 '79 thru '83
  300ZX - see *NISSAN (72010)*
- 28018 **510 & PL521 Pick-up** '68 thru '73
- 28020 **510** all models '78 thru '81
- 28022 **620 Series Pick-up** all models '73 thru '79
  720 Series Pick-up - see *NISSAN (72030)*
- 28025 **810/Maxima** all gasoline models '77 thru '84

DODGE
- **400 & 600** - see *CHRYSLER (25030)*
- 30008 **Aries & Plymouth Reliant** '81 thru '89
- 30010 **Caravan & Plymouth Voyager** '84 thru '95
- 30011 **Caravan & Plymouth Voyager** '96 thru '02
- 30012 **Challenger/Plymouth Saporro** '78 thru '83
- 30013 **Caravan, Chrysler Voyager, Town &**
  Country '03 thru '07
- 30016 **Colt & Plymouth Champ** '78 thru '87
- 30020 **Dakota Pick-ups** all models '87 thru '96
- 30021 **Durango** '98 & '99, **Dakota** '97 thru '99
- 30022 **Durango** '00 thru '03 **Dakota** '00 thru '04
- 30023 **Durango** '04 thru '09, **Dakota** '05 thru '11
- 30025 **Dart, Demon, Plymouth Barracuda,**
  Duster & Valiant 6 cyl models '67 thru '76
- 30030 **Daytona & Chrysler Laser** '84 thru '89
  Intrepid - see *CHRYSLER (25025, 25026)*
- 30034 **Neon** all models '95 thru '99
- 30035 **Omni & Plymouth Horizon** '78 thru '90
- 30036 **Dodge and Plymouth Neon** '00 thru '05
- 30040 **Pick-ups** all full-size models '74 thru '93
- 30041 **Pick-ups** all full-size models '94 thru '01
- 30042 **Pick-ups** full-size models '02 thru '08
- 30045 **Ram 50/D50 Pick-ups & Raider and**
  Plymouth Arrow Pick-ups '79 thru '93
- 30050 **Dodge/Plymouth/Chrysler RWD** '71 thru '89
- 30055 **Shadow & Plymouth Sundance** '87 thru '94
- 30060 **Spirit & Plymouth Acclaim** '89 thru '95
- 30065 **Vans - Dodge & Plymouth** '71 thru '03

EAGLE
- **Talon** - see *MITSUBISHI (68030, 68031)*
- **Vision** - see *CHRYSLER (25025)*

FIAT
- 34010 **124 Sport Coupe & Spider** '68 thru '78
- 34025 **X1/9** all models '74 thru '80

FORD
- 10320 **Ford Engine Overhaul Manual**
- 10355 **Ford Automatic Transmission Overhaul**
- 11500 **Mustang '64-1/2 thru '70 Restoration Guide**
- 36004 **Aerostar Mini-vans** all models '86 thru '97
- 36006 **Contour & Mercury Mystique** '95 thru '00
- 36008 **Courier Pick-up** all models '72 thru '82
- 36012 **Crown Victoria & Mercury Grand**
  Marquis '88 thru '10
- 36016 **Escort/Mercury Lynx** all models '81 thru '90
- 36020 **Escort/Mercury Tracer** '91 thru '02
- 36022 **Escape & Mazda Tribute** '01 thru '11
- 36024 **Explorer & Mazda Navajo** '91 thru '01
- 36025 **Explorer/Mercury Mountaineer** '02 thru '10
- 36028 **Fairmont & Mercury Zephyr** '78 thru '83
- 36030 **Festiva & Aspire** '88 thru '97
- 36032 **Fiesta** all models '77 thru '80
- 36034 **Focus** all models '00 thru '11
- 36036 **Ford & Mercury Full-size** '75 thru '87
- 36044 **Ford & Mercury Mid-size** '75 thru '86
- 36045 **Fusion & Mercury Milan** '06 thru '10
- 36048 **Mustang V8** all models '64-1/2 thru '73
- 36049 **Mustang II** 4 cyl, V6 & V8 models '74 thru '78
- 36050 **Mustang & Mercury Capri** '79 thru '93
- 36051 **Mustang** all models '94 thru '04
- 36052 **Mustang** '05 thru '10
- 36054 **Pick-ups & Bronco** '73 thru '79
- 36058 **Pick-ups & Bronco** '80 thru '96
- 36059 **F-150 & Expedition** '97 thru '09, **F-250** '97
  thru '99 **& Lincoln Navigator** '98 thru '09
- 36060 **Super Duty Pick-ups, Excursion** '99 thru '10
- 36061 **F-150** full-size '04 thru '10
- 36062 **Pinto & Mercury Bobcat** '75 thru '80
- 36066 **Probe** all models '89 thru '92
  Probe '93 thru '97 - see *MAZDA 626 (61042)*
- 36070 **Ranger/Bronco II** gasoline models '83 thru '92
- 36071 **Ranger** '93 thru '10 **& Mazda Pick-ups** '94 thru '09
- 36074 **Taurus & Mercury Sable** '86 thru '95
- 36075 **Taurus & Mercury Sable** '96 thru '05
- 36078 **Tempo & Mercury Topaz** '84 thru '94
- 36082 **Thunderbird/Mercury Cougar** '83 thru '88
- 36086 **Thunderbird/Mercury Cougar** '89 thru '97
- 36090 **Vans** all V8 Econoline models '69 thru '91
- 36094 **Vans** full size '92 thru '10
- 36097 **Windstar Mini-van** '95 thru '07

GENERAL MOTORS
- 10360 **GM Automatic Transmission Overhaul**
- 38005 **Buick Century, Chevrolet Celebrity,**
  Oldsmobile Cutlass Ciera & Pontiac 6000
  all models '82 thru '96
- 38010 **Buick Regal, Chevrolet Lumina,**
  Oldsmobile Cutlass Supreme &
  Pontiac Grand Prix (FWD) '88 thru '07
- 38015 **Buick Skyhawk, Cadillac Cimarron,**
  Chevrolet Cavalier, Oldsmobile Firenza &
  Pontiac J-2000 & Sunbird '82 thru '94
- 38016 **Chevrolet Cavalier &**
  Pontiac Sunfire '95 thru '05
- 38017 **Chevrolet Cobalt & Pontiac G5** '05 thru '11
- 38020 **Buick Skylark, Chevrolet Citation,**
  Olds Omega, Pontiac Phoenix '80 thru '85
- 38025 **Buick Skylark & Somerset,**
  Oldsmobile Achieva & Calais and
  Pontiac Grand Am all models '85 thru '98
- 38026 **Chevrolet Malibu, Olds Alero & Cutlass,**
  Pontiac Grand Am '97 thru '03
- 38027 **Chevrolet Malibu** '04 thru '10
- 38030 **Cadillac Eldorado, Seville, Oldsmobile**
  Toronado, Buick Riviera '71 thru '85
- 38031 **Cadillac Eldorado & Seville, DeVille, Fleetwood**
  & Olds Toronado, Buick Riviera '86 thru '93
- 38032 **Cadillac DeVille** '94 thru '05 **& Seville** '92 thru '04
  Cadillac DTS '06 thru '10
- 38035 **Chevrolet Lumina APV, Olds Silhouette**
  & Pontiac Trans Sport all models '90 thru '96
- 38036 **Chevrolet Venture, Olds Silhouette,**
  Pontiac Trans Sport & Montana '97 thru '05
  General Motors Full-size
  Rear-wheel Drive - see *BUICK (19025)*
- 38040 **Chevrolet Equinox** '05 thru '09 **Pontiac**
  Torrent '06 thru '09
- 38070 **Chevrolet HHR** '06 thru '11

GEO
- **Metro** - see *CHEVROLET Sprint (24075)*
  Prizm - '85 thru '92 see *CHEVY (24060)*,
  '93 thru '02 see *TOYOTA Corolla (92036)*
- 40030 **Storm** all models '90 thru '93
  Tracker - see *SUZUKI Samurai (90010)*

GMC
- **Vans & Pick-ups** - see *CHEVROLET*

HONDA
- 42010 **Accord CVCC** all models '76 thru '83
- 42011 **Accord** all models '84 thru '89
- 42012 **Accord** all models '90 thru '93
- 42013 **Accord** all models '94 thru '97
- 42014 **Accord** all models '98 thru '02
- 42015 **Accord** '03 thru '07
- 42020 **Civic 1200** all models '73 thru '79
- 42021 **Civic 1300 & 1500 CVCC** '80 thru '83
- 42022 **Civic 1500 CVCC** all models '75 thru '79

(Continued on other side)

Haynes North America, Inc., 859 Lawrence Drive, Newbury Park, CA 91320-1514 • (805) 498-6703 • http://www.haynes.com

Haynes Automotive Manuals (continued)

NOTE: If you do not see a listing for your vehicle, consult your local Haynes dealer for the latest product information.

42023 **Civic** all models '84 thru '91
42024 **Civic & del Sol** '92 thru '95
42025 **Civic** '96 thru '00, **CR-V** '97 thru '01,
Acura Integra '94 thru '00
42026 **Civic** '01 thru '10, **CR-V** '02 thru '09
42035 **Odyssey** all models '99 thru '10
Passport - *see ISUZU Rodeo (47017)*
42037 **Honda Pilot** '03 thru '07, **Acura MDX** '01 thru '07
42040 **Prelude CVCC** all models '79 thru '89

HYUNDAI
43010 **Elantra** all models '96 thru '10
43015 **Excel & Accent** all models '86 thru '09
43050 **Santa Fe** all models '01 thru '06
43055 **Sonata** all models '99 thru '08

INFINITI
G35 '03 thru '08 - *see NISSAN 350Z (72011)*

ISUZU
Hombre - *see CHEVROLET S-10 (24071)*
47017 **Rodeo, Amigo & Honda Passport** '89 thru '02
47020 **Trooper & Pick-up** '81 thru '93

JAGUAR
49010 **XJ6** all 6 cyl models '68 thru '86
49011 **XJ6** all models '88 thru '94
49015 **XJ12 & XJS** all 12 cyl models '72 thru '85

JEEP
50010 **Cherokee, Comanche & Wagoneer Limited**
all models '84 thru '01
50020 **CJ** all models '49 thru '86
50025 **Grand Cherokee** all models '93 thru '04
50026 **Grand Cherokee** '05 thru '09
50029 **Grand Wagoneer & Pick-up** '72 thru '91
Grand Wagoneer '84 thru '91, **Cherokee &
Wagoneer** '72 thru '83, **Pick-up** '72 thru '88
50030 **Wrangler** all models '87 thru '11
50035 **Liberty** '02 thru '07

KIA
54050 **Optima** '01 thru '10
54070 **Sephia** '94 thru '01, **Spectra** '00 thru '09,
Sportage '05 thru '10

LEXUS
ES 300/330 - *see TOYOTA Camry (92007) (92008)*
RX 330 - *see TOYOTA Highlander (92095)*

LINCOLN
Navigator - *see FORD Pick-up (36059)*
59010 **Rear-Wheel Drive** all models '70 thru '10

MAZDA
61010 **GLC Hatchback** (rear-wheel drive) '77 thru '83
61011 **GLC** (front-wheel drive) '81 thru '85
61012 **Mazda3** '04 thru '11
61015 **323 & Protegé** '90 thru '03
61016 **MX-5 Miata** '90 thru '09
61020 **MPV** all models '89 thru '98
Navajo - *see Ford Explorer (36024)*
61030 **Pick-ups** '72 thru '93
Pick-ups '94 thru '00 - *see Ford Ranger (36071)*
61035 **RX-7** all models '79 thru '85
61036 **RX-7** all models '86 thru '91
61040 **626** (rear-wheel drive) all models '79 thru '82
61041 **626/MX-6** (front-wheel drive) '83 thru '92
61042 **626, MX-6/Ford Probe** '93 thru '02
61043 **Mazda6** '03 thru '11

MERCEDES-BENZ
63012 **123 Series Diesel** '76 thru '85
63015 **190 Series** four-cyl gas models, '84 thru '88
63020 **230/250/280** 6 cyl sohc models '68 thru '72
63025 **280** 123 Series gasoline models '77 thru '81
63030 **350 & 450** all models '71 thru '80
63040 **C-Class:** C230/C240/C280/C320/C350 '01 thru '07

MERCURY
64200 **Villager & Nissan Quest** '93 thru '01
All other titles, see FORD Listing.

MG
66010 **MGB** Roadster & GT Coupe '62 thru '80
66015 **MG Midget, Austin Healey Sprite** '58 thru '80

MINI
67020 **Mini** '02 thru '11

MITSUBISHI
68020 **Cordia, Tredia, Galant, Precis &
Mirage** '83 thru '93
68030 **Eclipse, Eagle Talon & Ply. Laser** '90 thru '94
68031 **Eclipse** '95 thru '05, **Eagle Talon** '95 thru '98
68035 **Galant** '94 thru '10
68040 **Pick-up** '83 thru '96 & **Montero** '83 thru '93

NISSAN
72010 **300ZX** all models including Turbo '84 thru '89
72011 **350Z & Infiniti G35** all models '03 thru '08
72015 **Altima** all models '93 thru '06
72016 **Altima** '07 thru '10
72020 **Maxima** all models '85 thru '92
72021 **Maxima** all models '93 thru '04
72025 **Murano** '03 thru '10
72030 **Pick-ups** '80 thru '97 **Pathfinder** '87 thru '95
72031 **Frontier Pick-up, Xterra, Pathfinder** '96 thru '04
72032 **Frontier & Xterra** '05 thru '11
72040 **Pulsar** all models '83 thru '86
Quest - *see MERCURY Villager (64200)*
72050 **Sentra** all models '82 thru '94
72051 **Sentra & 200SX** all models '95 thru '06
72060 **Stanza** all models '82 thru '90
72070 **Titan pick-ups** '04 thru '10 **Armada** '05 thru '10

OLDSMOBILE
73015 **Cutlass** V6 & V8 gas models '74 thru '88
*For other OLDSMOBILE titles, see BUICK,
CHEVROLET or GENERAL MOTORS listing.*

PLYMOUTH
For PLYMOUTH titles, see DODGE listing.

PONTIAC
79008 **Fiero** all models '84 thru '88
79018 **Firebird** V8 models except Turbo '70 thru '81
79019 **Firebird** all models '82 thru '92
79025 **G6** all models '05 thru '09
79040 **Mid-size Rear-wheel Drive** '70 thru '87
Vibe '03 thru '11 - *see TOYOTA Matrix (92060)*
*For other PONTIAC titles, see BUICK,
CHEVROLET or GENERAL MOTORS listing.*

PORSCHE
80020 **911** except Turbo & Carrera 4 '65 thru '89
80025 **914** all 4 cyl models '69 thru '76
80030 **924** all models including Turbo '76 thru '82
80035 **944** all models including Turbo '83 thru '89

RENAULT
Alliance & Encore - *see AMC (14020)*

SAAB
84010 **900** all models including Turbo '79 thru '88

SATURN
87010 **Saturn** all S-series models '91 thru '02
87011 **Saturn Ion** '03 thru '07
87020 **Saturn** all L-series models '00 thru '04
87040 **Saturn VUE** '02 thru '07

SUBARU
89002 **1100, 1300, 1400 & 1600** '71 thru '79
89003 **1600 & 1800** 2WD & 4WD '80 thru '94
89100 **Legacy** all models '90 thru '99
89101 **Legacy & Forester** '00 thru '06

SUZUKI
90010 **Samurai/Sidekick & Geo Tracker** '86 thru '01

TOYOTA
92005 **Camry** all models '83 thru '91
92006 **Camry** all models '92 thru '96
92007 **Camry, Avalon, Solara, Lexus ES 300** '97 thru '01
92008 **Toyota Camry, Avalon and Solara and
Lexus ES 300/330** all models '02 thru '06
92009 **Camry** '07 thru '11
92015 **Celica Rear Wheel Drive** '71 thru '85
92020 **Celica Front Wheel Drive** '86 thru '99
92025 **Celica Supra** all models '79 thru '92
92030 **Corolla** all models '75 thru '79
92032 **Corolla** all rear wheel drive models '80 thru '87
92035 **Corolla** all front wheel drive models '84 thru '92
92036 **Corolla & Geo Prizm** '93 thru '02
92037 **Corolla** models '03 thru '11
92040 **Corolla Tercel** all models '80 thru '82
92045 **Corona** all models '74 thru '82
92050 **Cressida** all models '78 thru '82
92055 **Land Cruiser** FJ40, 43, 45, 55 '68 thru '82
92056 **Land Cruiser** FJ60, 62, 80, FZJ80 '80 thru '96
92060 **Matrix & Pontiac Vibe** '03 thru '11
92065 **MR2** all models '85 thru '87
92070 **Pick-up** all models '69 thru '78
92075 **Pick-up** all models '79 thru '95
92076 **Tacoma, 4Runner, & T100** '93 thru '04
92077 **Tacoma** all models '05 thru '09
92078 **Tundra** '00 thru '06 & **Sequoia** '01 thru '07
92079 **4Runner** all models '03 thru '09
92080 **Previa** all models '91 thru '95
92081 **Prius** all models '01 thru '08
92082 **RAV4** all models '96 thru '10
92085 **Tercel** all models '87 thru '94
92090 **Sienna** all models '98 thru '09
92095 **Highlander & Lexus RX-330** '99 thru '07

TRIUMPH
94007 **Spitfire** all models '62 thru '81
94010 **TR7** all models '75 thru '81

VW
96008 **Beetle & Karmann Ghia** '54 thru '79
96009 **New Beetle** '98 thru '11
96016 **Rabbit, Jetta, Scirocco & Pick-up** gas
models '75 thru '92 & **Convertible** '80 thru '92
96017 **Golf, GTI & Jetta** '93 thru '98, **Cabrio** '95 thru '02
96018 **Golf, GTI, Jetta** '99 thru '05
96019 **Jetta, Rabbit, GTI & Golf** '05 thru '11
96020 **Rabbit, Jetta & Pick-up** diesel '77 thru '84
96023 **Passat** '98 thru '05, **Audi A4** '96 thru '01
96030 **Transporter 1600** all models '68 thru '79
96035 **Transporter 1700, 1800 & 2000** '72 thru '79
96040 **Type 3 1500 & 1600** all models '63 thru '73
96045 **Vanagon** all air-cooled models '80 thru '83

VOLVO
97010 **120, 130 Series & 1800 Sports** '61 thru '73
97015 **140 Series** all models '66 thru '74
97020 **240 Series** all models '76 thru '93
97040 **740 & 760 Series** all models '82 thru '88
97050 **850 Series** all models '93 thru '97

TECHBOOK MANUALS
10205 **Automotive Computer Codes**
10206 **OBD-II & Electronic Engine Management**
10210 **Automotive Emissions Control Manual**
10215 **Fuel Injection Manual** '78 thru '85
10220 **Fuel Injection Manual** '86 thru '99
10225 **Holley Carburetor Manual**
10230 **Rochester Carburetor Manual**
10240 **Weber/Zenith/Stromberg/SU Carburetors**
10305 **Chevrolet Engine Overhaul Manual**
10310 **Chrysler Engine Overhaul Manual**
10320 **Ford Engine Overhaul Manual**
10330 **GM and Ford Diesel Engine Repair Manual**
10333 **Engine Performance Manual**
10340 **Small Engine Repair Manual,** 5 HP & Less
10341 **Small Engine Repair Manual,** 5.5 - 20 HP
10345 **Suspension, Steering & Driveline Manual**
10355 **Ford Automatic Transmission Overhaul**
10360 **GM Automatic Transmission Overhaul**
10405 **Automotive Body Repair & Painting**
10410 **Automotive Brake Manual**
10411 **Automotive Anti-lock Brake (ABS) Systems**
10415 **Automotive Detailing Manual**
10420 **Automotive Electrical Manual**
10425 **Automotive Heating & Air Conditioning**
10430 **Automotive Reference Manual & Dictionary**
10435 **Automotive Tools Manual**
10440 **Used Car Buying Guide**
10445 **Welding Manual**
10450 **ATV Basics**
10452 **Scooters 50cc to 250cc**

SPANISH MANUALS
98903 **Reparación de Carrocería & Pintura**
98904 **Manual de Carburador Modelos
Holley & Rochester**
98905 **Códigos Automotrices de la Computadora**
98906 **OBD-II & Sistemas de Control Electrónico
del Motor**
98910 **Frenos Automotriz**
98913 **Electricidad Automotriz**
98915 **Inyección de Combustible** '86 al '99
99040 **Chevrolet & GMC Camionetas** '67 al '87
99041 **Chevrolet & GMC Camionetas** '88 al '98
99042 **Chevrolet & GMC Camionetas
Cerradas** '68 al '95
99043 **Chevrolet/GMC Camionetas** '94 al '04
99048 **Chevrolet/GMC Camionetas** '99 al '06
99055 **Dodge Caravan & Plymouth Voyager** '84 al '95
99075 **Ford Camionetas y Bronco** '80 al '94
99076 **Ford F-150** '97 al '09
99077 **Ford Camionetas Cerradas** '69 al '91
99088 **Ford Modelos de Tamaño Mediano** '75 al '86
99089 **Ford Camionetas Ranger** '93 al '10
99091 **Ford Taurus & Mercury Sable** '86 al '95
99095 **GM Modelos de Tamaño Grande** '70 al '90
99100 **GM Modelos de Tamaño Mediano** '70 al '88
99106 **Jeep Cherokee, Wagoneer & Comanche**
'84 al '00
99110 **Nissan Camioneta** '80 al '96, **Pathfinder** '87 al '95
99118 **Nissan Sentra** '82 al '94
99125 **Toyota Camionetas y 4Runner** '79 al '95

Over 100 Haynes
motorcycle manuals
also available

7-12

Haynes North America, Inc., 859 Lawrence Drive, Newbury Park, CA 91320-1514 • (805) 498-6703 • http://www.haynes.com